T3-AKC-499

DISCARDED

UNIVERSITY OF WINNIPEG
LIBRARY
515 Portage Avenue
Winnipeg, Manitoba R3B 2E9

DISCARDED

EVALUATION STUDIES REVIEW ANNUAL
Volume 8

Evaluation Studies

EDITORIAL ADVISORY BOARD

Mark A. Abramson, *Office of the Assistant Secretary for Planning and Evaluation, Department of Health and Human Services*

Richard A. Berk, *Social Process Research Institute, University of California Santa Barbara*

Robert P. Boruch, *Department of Psychology, Northwestern University*

Seymour Brandwein, *Director, Office of Program Evaluation, Manpower Administration, U.S. Department of Labor*

Donald T. Campbell, *Maxwell School of Citizenship & Public Affairs, Syracuse University*

Francis G. Caro, *Institute for Social Welfare Research, Community Service Society, New York*

Thomas D. Cook, *Department of Psychology, Northwestern University*

Thomas J. Cook, *Research Triangle Institute, North Carolina*

Joseph dela Puente, *National Center for Health Service Research Hyattsville, Maryland*

Howard E. Freeman, *Institute for Social Science Research, University of California, Los Angeles*

Irwin Garfinkel, *Institute for Social Research on Poverty, University of Wisconsin, Madison*

Gene V. Glass, *Laboratory of Educational Research, University of Colorado*

Ernest R. House, *CIRCE, University of Illinois, Urnana*

Michael W. Kirst, *School of Education, Stanford University*

Henry M. Levin, *School of Education, Stanford University*

Robert A. Levine, *System Development Corporation, Santa Monica, California*

Review Annual

Richard J. Light, *Kennedy School of Government, Harvard University*
Katherine Lyall, *Director, Public Policy Program, Johns Hopkins University*
Laurence E. Lynn, Jr., *Kennedy School of Government, Harvard University*
Trudi C. Miller, *Applied Research on Public Management and Service Delivery, National Science Foundation*
David Mundell, *Education and Manpower Planning, Congressional Budget Office, Washington, D.C.*
Henry W. Riecken, *School of Medicine, University of Pennsylvania*
Peter H. Rossi, *Department of Sociology, University of Massachusetts, Amherst*
Susan E. Salasin, *National Institute of Mental Health, Rockville, Maryland*
Frank P. Sciolo, Jr., *Division of Advanced Production Research, National Science Foundation*
Lee Sechrest, *Director, Center for Research on Utilization of Scientific Knowledge, Institute for Social Research, University of Michigan*
Sylvia Sherwood, *Social Gerontological Research, Hebrew Rehabilitation Center for the Aged. Boston, Massachusetts*
Stephen M. Shortell, *Department of Health Services, School of Public Health and Community Medicine, University of Washington, Seattle*
Ernst W. Stromsdorfer, *School of Public Health, Columbia University*
Michael Timpane, *Teacher's College, Columbia University*
Carol H. Weiss, *Graduate School of Education, Harvard University*

H
I
.E77
1983

Evaluation Studies

Review Annual

Volume 8 1983

Edited by

Richard J. Light

SAGE PUBLICATIONS
Beverly Hills / London / New Delhi

Copyright © 1983 by Sage Publications, Inc.

All rights reserved. No part of this book may be reproduced or utilized in any form or by any means, electronic or mechanical, including photo-copying, recording, or by any information storage and retrieval system, without permission in writing from the publisher.

For information address:

SAGE Publications, Inc.
275 South Beverly Drive
Beverly Hills, California 90212

SAGE Publications India Pvt. Ltd. SAGE Publications Ltd
C-236 Defence Colony   28 Banner Street
New Delhi 110 024, India   London EC1Y 8QE, England

Printed in the United States of America
International Standard Book Number-8039-1987-5
International Standard Series Number 0364-7390
Library of Congress Catalog Card Number 76-15865

FIRST PRINTING

CONTENTS

About the Editor   11

Introduction
    RICHARD J. LIGHT   13

A Guide to the Collection
    RICHARD J. LIGHT   25

PART I. METHODOLOGICAL ISSUES AND PROCEDURES

1. Numbers and Narrative: Combining Their Strengths in
   Research Reviews
       RICHARD J. LIGHT and DAVID B. PILLEMER   33

2. Reviewing the Literature: A Comparison of Traditional
   Methods with Meta-Analysis
       THOMAS D. COOK and LAURA C. LEVITON   59

3. Statistical Versus Traditional Procedures for Summarizing
   Research Findings
       HARRIS M. COOPER and ROBERT ROSENTHAL   83

4. Improving the Quality of Evidence: Interconnections Among
   Primary Evaluation, Secondary Analysis, and Quantitative
   Synthesis
       DAVID S. CORDRAY and ROBERT G. ORWIN   91

5. Scientific Guidelines for Conducting Integrative
   Research Reviews
       HARRIS M. COOPER   121

6. Methods for Integrative Reviews
       GREGG B. JACKSON   133

7. Meta-Analysis: A Validity Perspective
       PAUL M. WORTMAN   157

8. On Quantitative Reviewing
       HARRIS M. COOPER and ROBERT M. ARKIN   167

9. What Differentiates Meta-Analysis from Other Forms
   of Review?
       LAURA C. LEVITON and THOMAS D. COOK   173

10. Fitting Continuous Models to Effect Size Data
        LARRY V. HEDGES   179

11. Estimation of Effect Size from a Series of
    Independent Experiments
        LARRY V. HEDGES   205

12. Alternative Strategies for Combining Data from Twin
Studies to Estimate an Intraclass Correlation: Some
Empirical Sampling Results
RICHARD J. LIGHT and PAUL V. SMITH   215

13. Comparing Effect Sizes of Independent Studies
ROBERT ROSENTHAL and DONALD B. RUBIN   235

14. A Simple, General Purpose Display of Magnitude of
Experimental Effect
ROBERT ROSENTHAL and DONALD B. RUBIN   241

15. Further Meta-Analytic Procedures for Assessing Cognitive
Gender Differences
ROBERT ROSENTHAL and DONALD B. RUBIN   245

PART II. EXAMPLES OF REVIEWS

16. Deinstitutionalization in Mental Health: A Meta-Analysis
ROGER B. STRAW   253

17. Age Differences in Subjective Well-Being: A Meta-Analysis
WILLIAM A. STOCK et al.   279

18. Utilizing Controversy as a Source of Hypotheses for
Meta-Analysis: The Case of Teacher Expectancy's Effects
on Pupil IQ
STEPHEN W. RAUDENBUSH   303

19. The Impact of Leaisure-Time Television on School Learning:
A Research Synthesis
PATRICIA A. WILLIAMS et al.   327

20. Time and Method Coaching for the SAT
SAMUEL MESSICK and ANN JUNGEBLUT   359

21. Evaluating the Effectiveness of Coaching for SAT Exams:
A Meta-Analysis
REBECCA DERSIMONIAN and NAN LAIRD   385

22. The Effects of Psychological Intervention on Recovery from
Surgery and Heart Attacks: An Analysis of the Literature
*EMILY MUMFORD, HERBERT J. SCHLESINGER,
and GENE V GLASS*   405

23. Effects of Psycho-Educational Intervention on Length of
Hospital Stay: A Meta-Analytic Review of 34 Studies
ELIZABETH C. DEVINE and THOMAS D. COOK   417

24. Meta-Analysis of Research on Class Size and Its Relationship
   to Attitudes and Instruction
      MARY LEE SMITH and GENE V GLASS   433

25. Identifying Features of Effective Open Education
      ROSE M. GIACONIA and LARRY V. HEDGES   448

26. Effects of Ability Grouping on Secondary School Students:
   A Meta-Analysis of Evaluation Findings
      CHEN-LIN KULIK and JAMES A. KULIK   473

27. Reading Instruction: A Quantitative Analysis
      SUSANNA PFLAUM et al.   487

28. Effect of Intravenous Streptokinase on Acute Myocardial
   Infarction: Pooled Results from Randomized Trials
      MEIR J. STAMPFER et al.   494

29. The Experimental Evidence for Weight-Loss Treatment of
   Essential Hypertension: A Critical Review
      MELBOURNE F. HOVELL   497

30. A Review and Critique of Controlled Studies of the Effectiveness
   of Preventive Child Health Care
      WILLIAM R. SHADISH, Jr.   507

31. Synthesis of Results in Controlled Trials of Coronary Artery
   Bypass Graft Surgery
      PAUL M. WORTMAN and WILLIAM H. YEATON   536

32. Lessons Learned from Past Block Grants: Implications for
   Congressional Oversight
      U.S. GENERAL ACCOUNTING OFFICE   552

33. The Relation of Teaching and Learning: A Review of Reviews
   of Process-Product Research
      HERSHOLT C. WAXMAN and HERBERT J. WALBERG   584

34. The Relation Between Socioeconomic Status and Academic
   Achievement
      KARL R. WHITE   602

35. A Meta-Analysis of Pretest Sensitization Effects in
   Experimental Design
      VICTOR L. WILLSON and RICHARD R. PUTNAM   623

36. Methodologically Based Discrepancies in Compensatory
   Education Evaluation
      WILLIAM M.K. TROCHIM   633

ABOUT THE EDITOR

RICHARD J. LIGHT is Professor at the Graduate School of Education and the Kennedy School of Government at Harvard University. His Ph.D. in statistics was taken at Harvard, and his work in program evaluation emphasizes methodological developments. In addition to his teaching and research, Professor Light has been director of faculty studies at the Institute of Politics, a consultant to the President's Commission on Federal Statistics, a consultant to the President's Commission on Federal Statistics, and a member of the Board of Directors of the Council on Applied Research and the Evaluation Research Society. He has recently served on National Advisory Panels for evaluation projects at the World Bank, General Accounting Office, and National Academy of Sciences. Professor Light has recently coauthored *Data for Decisions,* with D. Hoaglin, B. McPeek, F. Mosteller, and M. Stoto, a book describing how different forms of statistical evidence can be used to inform policy decisions. In his spare time, he particularly enjoys taking walks on windswept beaches with the three women in his life.

Introduction

Richard J. Light

This volume of the *Evaluation Studies Review Annual* looks at an interesting growth area in the behavioral sciences. For years, doctoral theses, journal articles, and research reports have had a standard format. First, state the problem. Second, do a literature review. Third, explain what new work is being done, and finally report the results.

It is the second step, the review, that for years got short shrift. Why? Probably for several reasons. Some scientists feel it is more exciting to develop new findings than to reexamine the old ones. Others feel that professional rewards rarely come to the fellow who "simply" pulls together what other people have done.

But I would put my chips on a different reason. I think most of us don't emphasize reviews because we simply don't know how to do them very well. Basic principles for designing a good single study are constantly being developed, debated, and refined. But what are principles for designing a good review?

Paul Smith and I took a crack at this question (Light and Smith, 1971), laying out solutions to some dilemmas that face any scientist preparing a review. This includes dealing with studies that measure outcomes differently, studies with dramatically different sample sizes, and findings that seem to conflict. In recent years, many others have put forward good ideas, and a body of techniques is beginning to crystallize. A big step forward was the work of Gene Glass and colleagues in the late 1970s (Glass 1976, 1977; Smith and Glass 1980; Glass, McGaw, and Smith 1981). Glass developed the notion of quantitative "meta-analysis" in a robust way. Also, his work was designed to help policymakers reach practical conclusions from large masses of studies. He especially popularized an outcome measure called "effect size" that enables a scientist to compare findings across many studies. The growth in methodological sophistication has stimulated a large number of reviews, especially in the last three years, using systematic methods. Indeed, two books have appeared (Glass et al., 1981; Hunter, Schmidt, and Jackson, 1982) to facilitate these efforts.

It seem constructive to stand back, then, and see what has been learned. That is the goal of this *Annual*. The material in the *Annual* is divided into two parts. The first set of essays emphasize methodology, and help us to think about how specific quantitative methods for reviewing expand or limit inferential possibilities. They offer *concrete suggestions* for carrying out reviews, and they suggest assumptions and caveats that a reviewer sometimes forgets in the excitement of discovering treatment effects or a significant relationship between variables.

The second set of papers are exemplary reviews. Some are previously unpublished. I chose them because they are convincing. Each review either puts forth an interesting finding, sheds new light on a controversy, or demonstrates a nice application of an analytic technique.

I believe that, taken together, the two parts of this collection offer some clear messages. These messages are useful to an evaluator organizing a synthesis, and also to a research manager asking whether it is worth commissioning a new study. I have pulled out six such messages.

WHAT THE COLLECTION TELLS US

(1) Most Evaluations Find Small Effects

This is not an extraordinary finding. Earlier work (Gilbert, Light, and Mosteller, 1975) reports a similar result. Its importance comes, I think, from having managers of programs understand that they shouldn't expect large, positive findings to emerge routinely from new programs. Indeed, *any* positive findings are good news. I say this not in a political sense, but rather in a statistical one. There are several reasons why, even when an innovation works, an evaluation might not notice it.

One possible explanation is low power. A sample size may not be big enough to detect a positive program effect even if it really exists. A second is errors in variables. If both a program's features and its outcomes are measured with error, then the chance of detecting small effects can drop dramatically. A third explanation for missing positive effects is that with multisite innovations, only some sites or places *really will have* the positive effects. With new programs in particular, it would be surprising if *all* sites, and all program variants, work well. Indeed, it would be extraordinary. If it is so easy to mount new programs to solve social, educational, and health problems that have persisted for so many years, we would live in an engineer's ideal world. The more likely reality is that new programs (whether CETA, Head Start, or a new hospital emergency room procedure), differ from place to place in their early format, work well in a few places, and aren't much value is others. Evaluating outcomes at a few sites may lead to just one or two showing positive findings, while other sites show nothing special.

What does "small effects" mean? It depends upon the outcome measure's form. Many of the reviews use Glass's "average effect size" as the key summary measure. For example, Devine and Cook find an average effect size of .48 in their analysis of how interventions can reduce the length of hospital stay. Wortman and Yeaton find an average effect size of approximately 10 percent in their studies of coronary artery bypass graft surgery. Williams et al. find an average effect size of -.05 for studies relating television watching to school performance.

Some years ago, Jacob Cohen suggested rough guidelines for interpreting such effect sizes. His rules of thumb were that a .2 effect size was small, a .5 was moderate, and a .8 was large. I see no reason to modify these, except to remind us all that programs having an average effect of .8 are very rare.

A different outcome measure is the simple Pearson correlation coefficient. For example, White's paper finds an average correlation of .32 between socioeconomic status and academic achievement. Stock et al. find an average correlation of .03 between age and sense of well-being. It is reasonable to wonder, what is a "large" value for a correlation coefficient?

Rosenthal and Rubin's work makes a real contribution here. They reformulate the standard correlation coefficient into a comparison between two proportions. This is easily displayed in a simple two by two contingency table. The display gives nonstatisticians (and maybe some statisticians) a much better feel for the practical meaning of an average correlation. For example, using Rosenthal and Rubin's suggestion we find that an average R^2 of .04, rarely large enough to create tremendous excitement in evaluation circles, is equivalent to a new treatment's cutting a failure rate, or death rate, or dropout rate, by one-third (say from 60 percent to 40 percent). I consider such an accomplishment worth noticing! Another example: We may ask how large an R^2 is necessary to describe a 50 percent reduction in, say, death rates. The answer is an R^2 of only .10. Such analogies are not intuitive. I know that in future research reviews, small average correlations will command new respect, at least from me.

(2) Research Design Matters

Several of the syntheses drive home a point that has been speculated about in many essays: Research design matters, and sometimes matters a lot. One example is the review by DerSimonian and Laird. They find that coaching for SAT exams can help a lot, a modest amount, or hardly at all. It depends primarily on the research design of the evaluation. Observational studies generally find that coaching helps a lot; matched designs turn up a smaller positive value; randomized designs find coaching is hardly effective. A second example is Wortman and Yeaton's review of heart bypass surgery. It appears *far* more effective than drug treatment when examined with observational designs. The difference between treatments shrinks noticeably when the comparison uses randomly assigned groups.

Should we conclude from these two examples that randomized trials always lead to less positive findings about innovations? Indeed, this idea is broadly consistent with the discussion in Hoaglin and associates (1982). They cite a research review by Chalmers (1982) of portacaval shunt surgery. It found a strong negative relationship between how well controlled evaluations were, and how well the surgery fared. Controls were adequate in seven evaluations: *None* of the seven report big enthusiasm for the surgery. For the 67 where controls were absent, 50 led to big enthusiasm. This is consistent with Hugo Muench's rule, "Results can always be improved by omitting controls" (from Bearman et al., 1974).

Yet some reviews suggest this rule is not universal. For example, in this collection, Stock and associates find no relationship between research design and outcomes in studies of age and mental well-being. Similarly, Straw finds no relationship in his review of effects of deinstitutionalization in mental health. Finally, in a thorough review done some years ago, Yin and Yates (1974) find the opposite relationship. They report that for innovations in urban government, the better controlled research designs tended to find innovations *more* effective. They suggest as an explanation that innovators who are well trained and competent enough to evaluate their effort with a strong research design are more likely than average to have also developed a thoughtful innovation, which in turn is reasonably likely to be successful.

The point here is not that any rule applies in a predictable direction. From a modest size collection of reviews, it is difficult to create a general rule about the relationship between specific research designs and positive or negative outcomes in evaluations. The point, rather, is that for many reviews, a clear relationship exists between research design and probability of a positive finding. Overall, then, this collection strengthens the hypothesis that design matters. This is a valuable principle for evaluators to remember when designing new studies. Whatever the field, some effort should be made to search for a relation between design and outcome. Finding such a relation should enrich readers' interpretations of results from any one particular study.

(3) Good Syntheses Examine Treatment Implementation and Control Group Comparability

A big contribution reviews can make is to suggest, based on an aggregation of findings, what specific features of a broad program are especially likely (or unlikely) to work. An illustration comes from Giaconia and Hedges's synthesis of open education programs. In the 1960s and early 1970s, a major movement developed to reduce rigidities in precollege education. Innovations such as multi-age grouping, open architecture, and team teaching were introduced. Any review of evaluations of such programs reporting an "on the average" finding about open education has little value to policymakers. Open education involves so many components that it is unlikely *all* of them have positive, or negative, effects. It is more likely that just a few components will matter. Identifying those few is a key contribution of a review. Giaconia and Hedges, for example, identify three features of open education that lead to clearly positive outcomes: diagnostic evaluation of children, availability of manipulative materials, and individualized instruction. Aspects of open education that generate the most publicity, such as mixed age grouping and open spaces, do not distinguish more from less effective programs.

Similar distinctions should be made among *who* is being investigated. For example, the Kulik and Kulik article reviews studies of ability grouping for high school students. Some of the studies they include examine ability grouping of particularly able students. Others focus on low achievers. Others include a broad range of achievement. Any broad conclusion about ability grouping should be tempered with careful statements about *subgroups*. Kulik and Kulik do an especially fine job dividing their analyses by type of ability grouping.

Just as the detailed nature of a *treatment* must be clear, *control groups* in comparative studies must also be carefully investigated. If a treatment's effectiveness is generally estimated by comparing it with a control group, then a reviewer must see whether control groups are comparable across studies. If not, conflicting outcomes can easily arise because controls differ.

Devine and Cook's review illustrates how to do it well. In their review of 34 interventions designed to reduce length of hospital stay, they found at least three different kinds of control groups. Some studies compared an intervention with a "usual care" group. This eliminates the possibility of a Hawthorne effect. Others used "placebo controls." Devine and Cook found that such studies reported patients in the control groups received as much attention from researchers as patients in the treatment group. Indeed, in one case, they received even more. A third group of studies included *both* of these control group types. By separating studies that use different kinds of control groups, Devine and Cook found that type of control group matters when one wants to assess the intervention. Studies using usual care for controls found a noticeably bigger treatment effect than similar efforts with placebo controls. This is strong evidence that evaluations with placebo controls underestimate treatment impact because of a Hawthorne effect.

The general point is the important one. Just because each in a group of evaluations reports is examining a certain treatment, reviewers should not casually assume that either the treatments or the controls are in fact identical across studies. Careful research reviews should specifically analyze the comparability of treatments and of controls.

(4) Publication Bias Seems to Exist

The collection of reviews demonstrates convincingly that evaluations in refereed journals report, on the average, more significant findings about a program or treatment's effectiveness than similar unpublished work. This is not an extraordinary finding. It has been speculated about for some time (Greenwald, 1975; Rosenthal, 1979). Yet the consistency with which journal reports show stronger program effects than other evaluation sources suggests that any review should involve a serious effort to track down findings from sources other than journal articles.

The approximately two dozen reviews in this collection give a clear indication of where these other, nonjournal evaluations come from. The three main sources are

(1) chapters in books often invited by an editor,
(2) research reports, produced by contract research organizations such as Abt Associates or Rand or SRI or Mathematica, or produced by government agencies such as NIE, NIH, or NICHD,

(3) doctoral and master's theses not published in the traditional sense, but listed as available on microfilm or from the author.

The reviews by Shadish, Hovell, Raudenbush, and Mumford and associates are particularly thorough in their reporting of a broad cross-section of evaluations. Examining their data sources gives a good feeling for how frequently each category of study might appear in reviews. Broadly speaking, journal articles make up at least half of the citations. Second in frequency are chapters in books, followed third by theses at universities, and finally by contract research reports.

The main argument speculating about publication bias goes as follows. Evaluations that find positive outcomes are more likely than others to be submitted to refereed journals in the first place. In addition, journal editors tend to prefer evaluations that report significant findings. Greenwald (1975) sent out questionnaires both to evaluation researchers and to journal editors. His returns gave strong confirmation to these hypotheses. This has led most observers to speculate that evaluations published in journals will have larger effect sizes and greater statistical significance than similar unpublished studies, whether they are theses or contract research reports.

Recent work, including several of the reviews in this collection, enables us to do better than speculate. Smith (1980) summarized ten reviews prepared at the University of Colorado. She found that within each of the ten, the published evaluations reported larger average program effects than the unpublished group. This finding holds up for the studies here. For example, White finds a strong relationship between effect size and where evaluations were published; Straw finds a larger effect on average for published studies; Devine and Cook find the same pattern.

These results strongly suggest two lessons important for future reviews. First, publication bias seems to be a real and relatively common occurrence. Its severity varies a lot depending upon the program being evaluated. Therefore, any review should make a serious effort to examine more than the easily available reports in published journals. In general, adding nonpublished evaluations to the review will lessen an overall assessment of a treatment's value. Second, any review that finds the opposite—that unpublished studies find *more* positive outcomes on average—should be examined particularly carefully. Readers should make a particularly strong effort to understand why this might have happened. Is there some mechanism about how evaluations get published in this particular field that might explain such an uncommon finding? If such a mechanism indeed turns up, a reviewer can then interpret findings in light of this mechanism. The main point is that such a reversal, with published studies turning out to show weaker treatment effects, should raise a red flag for reviewer and readers alike. It should stimulate all of us to ask why might this have happened.

(5) Reviews Generally Stress Main Effects a Lot; Good Ones Also Examine Interactions

This is a heartening finding. It is tempting to focus a review entirely on the bottom line question, "Does the treatment work?" Early efforts at meta-analysis sometimes tried to answer *only* this question, and ignored entirely the other more subtle one, "For whom does the treatment work best?" or, "Under what circumstance does the treatment work best?" Most of the reviews in this collection take the extra step and ask the more subtle questions. This has two virtues. First, the reviews simply demonstrate that it can be done! Second, the answers they turn up are useful. These efforts should motivate reviewers to include routinely, in future efforts, an examination of interactions in addition to main effects.

Let's look at some illustrations. Raudenbush, examining studies of how teacher expectations influence student achievement, does not even report a main effect. Rather, he argues that a main effect would be useless in aggregating across all 18 evaluations because the treatment varied in different studies. For those studies where teachers knew the children, even just a little, before an expectancy induction, the treatment effect turns up very weak—close to zero. For those studies where teachers were meeting children "blind" at the time of expectancy induction, the treatment had a modestly large and consistent effect. Raudenbush concludes that overall statements about expectancy are worth little; how the treatment is administered becomes the crucial point.

Hovell examines 21 studies of weight loss treatment for people with hypertension. He focuses in particular on 6 well-done analyses. For these, he finds that moderate weight loss (approximately 10 percent of body weight) leads to noticeable and significant declines in blood pressure. This is a valuable main effect finding. Hovell goes further to see whether there are different effects of weight loss on hypertension for extremely obese versus essentially normal weight people. He finds that even normal weight people without hypertension can lower their blood pressure by going on an extremely low calorie diet. But the amount by which their pressure is lowered is far less than for obese hypertensives. The broad conclusion is that people of any weight can reduce their blood pressure by reducing caloric intake, but that those likely to benefit most from dieting are obese hypertensives.

Williams and associates reviewed studies of children's television viewing habits and their school achievement. This topic has been debated for some years. Frequently, arguments are expressed in main effect terms: TV is either harmful to children's performance, or it is not. Williams and associates demonstrate convincingly that it is not so simple. Small amounts of viewing were *not* found to be harmful at all; indeed if anything, there is evidence that small amounts of viewing are associated with *better* school performance. Frequent viewing, however, emerges as harmful. The more frequent, the more harmful.

This review turned up another interesting finding. High IQ children seem to suffer from frequent viewing far more than low IQ children. The reviewers do not speculate why this might be, and I don't have a clear idea either. But such a finding is just the sort of stimulus that should provoke further thoughtful work.

These three examples illustrate a strategy used by most of the reviewers in this volume. A main effect is reported as the first finding. Then, special circumstances when the treatment is particularly beneficial or harmful are isolated. Finally, if a treatment has a special effect on particular kinds of people, the effect is investigated in more detail. This strategy provides useful information for both policymakers and researchers. A policymaker who must make management decisions benefits from knowing under what circumstances a program works particularly well, or particularly poorly. To say that "on the average Head Start works," when certain program features routinely don't work well at all, is not the most useful conclusion. Managers guiding evolutionary change benefit enormously from detailed information about what parts of a program work well, and what type of people benefit extra much (or are harmed extra much) from this program.

For researchers, meanwhile, knowing interesting interactions can help to guide future efforts. For one thing, identifying which program features in a large set seem to matter particularly should suggest evaluation designs for the future that formally build in the important interactions. For another, such findings help researchers to put their chips in future studies on variables with a reasonable probability of mattering. Simply eliminating some features of a program as being unlikely to matter helps to guide our allocation of scarce resources.

(6) A Few Methodological Improvements Would Help a Lot

Reviews have improved enormously in the last five years or so. Anyone doubting this assertion should simply scan a journal in evaluation or the applied social sciences from five years ago and look at a standard review. They were nearly always narrative and impressionistic. There were few efforts to systematize the analyses. Whatever one thinks of every detail in the reviews in this collection, they clearly represent a step forward. Most of them incorporate a serious effort to understand publication bias, interaction effects, and the implications of using the particular set of evaluations that are included. Especially impressive is their effort to systematically report patterns of outcomes, whether the measure they choose is average effect size, or overall significance level, or some version of vote counting. One can easily level criticisms at each review's details, but taken as a group they are impressive testimony to the improvement in review procedures being adopted by more and more evaluators. Yet evaluators can do still better, and taken as a whole this collection points to three areas where methodological improvements would help a lot.

One area is ways of applying synthesis procedures to *longitudinal data.* It is striking how every one of the exemplary reviews uses studies with either cross-sectional data or change scores between two points. Changes over time involving more than two measurements don't appear in any of the syntheses. I believe this reflects fairly the lack of existing procedures for carrying out reviews involving time series data. For example, the General Accounting Office prepared an excellent summary of CETA evaluations (GAO/IPE 82-8). But because the data sets they worked with had long-term time series information on employment and income, they were unable to use any formal quantitative synthesis procedures. Their fallback position was a heroic effort at reanalyzing the existing data sets one at a time, and then stitching the findings together using a narrative format. While this is the best approach now available, an even better approach for the future would be utilizing techniques designed for synthesizing time series. Bloom (1982) has taken a first step in this direction. More are needed.

A second area is incorporating ways of dealing with different *units of analysis*. White's review in this collection reports empirical confirmation of what statisticians have known for a long time: Summary statistics such as R^2 are heavily dependent upon the unit of analysis one chooses for any evaluation. A reviewer facing a group of studies must therefore sort out precisely what unit of analysis underlies each. Hannan (1976) and Singer (1983) develop solid statistical theory to underlie this idea. Reviewers should know that just because a dozen studies each report an R^2 between a treatment and an outcome, the R^2 values are not necessarily comparable. In general, analyses carried out at higher levels of aggregation (say, the classroom level rather than the student level) will find higher R^2s.

A third area involves dealing with outliers. Many essays have stressed the importance of including qualitative information in even the most elegant quantitative reviews (Cook and Leviton, 1980; Reichardt and Cook, 1979; Light and Pillemer, 1982). One way of doing this is to focus on extreme findings. Few of the reviews in this collection search for outliers, but the theory is well developed (Barnett and Lewis, 1978; Grubbs, 1969; Canner, Huang, and Meinert, 1981).

The main strategy is to "use the unusual as a guide to the usual, since the unusually successful (or unsuccessful) may provide a clearer picture of processes operating to a lesser extent elsewhere" (Klitgaard, 1978). Comparing clearly successful programs to clear failures may produce a list of differences in their operation, or staffing, or curriculum. These differences may simply reflect chance (Hunter, Schmidt, and Jackson, 1982), or they may explain real program differences.

Once a few explanatory candidates are isolated, a reviewer can form specific hypotheses about their relationship to program outcomes. For example, if the two most successful blood pressure reduction programs (where weight loss is the treatment) both happen to stress a diet especially low in salt, this suggests the hypothesis that a low sodium diet is more effective than an ordinary diet for reducing blood pressure. (Hovell's review discusses this possibility.)

Such hypotheses can be evaluated using information from less extreme studies. For example, if sodium intake is consistently important in its relation to blood pressure, there should be *some* evidence of this *across the entire range* of study outcomes. In fact, since public policies or regulations or legislation often are intended to influence routine rather than extraordinary cases, this step can be critical. It is also an opportunity for a reviewer to use narrative or case study information. If a particular background variable (such as a diet's sodium content) is not systematically built into an evaluation, a reviewer may have to play detective and dig out whatever information is available in bits and pieces.

A FINAL REMARK

Many scientists and program evaluators don't consider carrying out a research review to be a high priority activity. Often it is delegated to a research assistant. The high payoff activity in many people's eyes is carrying out a new evaluation, and adding another data point to what exists. Leafing through old research reports is thought to be a boring or less creative step.

I disagree. An important goal underlying scientific inquiry is the accumulation of evidence. This should be as true of program evaluation as of theoretical physics. A new finding is most valuable if there is a way of tying it to the cumulative wisdom, both theoretical and empirical, of earlier findings. Although program evaluators and applied social scientists don't do it perfectly, the collection in this *Annual* shows that big progress is being made. I hope the reviews will seem as interesting and valuable to the broad evaluation community as they are to those who work on improving the methodology of reviews.

REFERENCES

BARNETT, V. and T. LEWIS (1978) Outliers in Statistical Data. New York: John Wiley.

BEARMAN, J. E., D. B. LOEWENSON, and W. H. GULLEN (1974) "Muench's postulates, laws and corollaries." Biometrics Note 4, Bethesda, MD: Office of Biometry and Epidemiology, National Eye Institute, NIH.

BLOOM, H. (1982) "Analyzing longitudinal data sets." Cambridge, MA: Kennedy School of Government, Harvard University. (unpublished)

CANNER, P. L., Y. B. HUANG, and C. L. MEINERT (1981) "On the detection of outlier clinics in medical and surgical trials: theoretical considerations." Controlled Clinical Trials (2): 241-252.

CHALMERS, T. C. (1982) "The randomized controlled trial as a basis for therapeutic decisions," Chapter 2 in J. Lachin, N. Tygstrup, and E. Juhl (eds.) The Randomized Clinical Trial and Therapeutic Decisions. New York: Marcel Dekker.

COOK, T. D. and L. C. LEVITON (1980) "Reviewing the literature: a comparison of traditional methods with meta-analysis." Journal of Personality 48: 449-472.

GAO/IPE 82-8 (1982) "Lessons learned from past block grants: implications for congressional oversight." Washington, DC: Government Printing Office.

GILBERT, J. P., R. J. LIGHT, and F. MOSTELLER (1975) "Assessing social innovations: an empirical base for policy," in C. A. Bennett and A. A. Lumsdaine (eds.) Evaluation and Experiment. New York: Academic Press.

GLASS, G. V (1977) "Integration findings: the meta-analysis of research." Review of Research in Education 5: 351-379.

——— (1976) "Primary, secondary, and meta-analysis of research." Educational Researcher 5: 3-8.

——— B. McGAW, and M. L. SMITH (1981) Meta-Analysis of Social Research. Beverly Hills, CA: Sage.

GREENWALD, A. G. (1975) "Consequences of prejudice against the null hypothesis." Psychological Bulletin 82: 1-19.

GRUBBS, F. E. (1969) "Procedures for detecting outliers." Technometrics 11: 1-21.

HANNAN, M. (1972) Aggregation and Disaggregation in Sociology. Lexington, MA: D. C. Heath.

HOAGLIN, D., R. LIGHT, B. McPEEK, F. MOSTELLER, M. STOTO (1982) Data for Decisions. Cambridge, MA: Abt Books.

HUNTER, J. E., F. L. SCHMIDT, and G. B. JACKSON (1982) Meta-Analysis. Beverly Hills, CA: Sage.

KLITGAARD, R. (1978) "Identifying exceptional performers." Policy Analysis (Fall): 529-547.

LIGHT, R. J. and P. V. SMITH (1971) "Accumulating evidence: procedures for resolving contradictions among different studies." Harvard Educational Review 41: 429-471.

LIGHT, R. J. and D. B. PILLEMER (1982) "Numbers and narrative: combining their strengths in research reviews." Harvard Educational Review 52: 1-26.

REICHARDT, C. S. and T. D. COOK (1979) "Beyond qualitative versus quantitative methods," in T. D. Cook and C. S. Reichardt (eds.) Qualitative and Quantitative Methods in Evaluation Research. Beverly Hills, CA: Sage.

ROSENTHAL, R. (1979) "The 'file drawer problem' and tolerance for null results." Psychological Bulletin 86: 638-641.

SINGER, J. (1983) "Selection of analytic units in studies of hierarchical data." Ph.D. dissertation, Department of Statistics, Harvard University, Cambridge, MA.

SMITH, M. L. (1980) "Publication bias and meta-analysis." Evaluation in Education 4: 22-24.

——— and G. V GLASS (1980) "Meta-analysis of research on class size and its relationship to attitudes and instruction." American Educational Research Journal (17): 419-433.

YIN, R. and D. YATES (1974) Street Level Governments: Assessing Decentralization and Urban Services and Evaluation of Policy-Related Research. Santa Monica, CA: Rand Corporation.

A Guide to the Collection

Richard J. Light

The articles to follow are divided into two parts. The first is a set of discussions of what research reviews can accomplish, and how to approach them. The second part presents actual reviews that I find particularly well done and interesting.

PART I

My paper with David Pillemer presents a case for including both quantitative and qualitative information from individual studies in a review. Examples illustrate how different kinds of narrative findings can influence an evaluator's interpretation of conflicting findings. Thomas Cook and Laura Leviton present an argument that quantitative reviews are *not* particularly likely to turn up different relationships from what a traditional review would uncover. Harris Cooper and Robert Rosenthal, in contrast, emphasize the special insights that can arise when a reviewer summarizes findings across studies with a quantitative eye.

David Cordray and Robert Orwin look systematically at the assumptions underlying three different kinds of efforts: a primary evaluation, a secondary analysis, and a synthesis of many studies. Harris Cooper focuses particularly on reviews, and suggests a set of useful organizing principles. Gregg Jackson, in a widely quoted article, offers some concrete suggestions for building a group of disparate findings into a review.

Paul Wortman steps back from detailed techniques to question how numerical approaches tie into the important ideas of external, internal, and construct validity. He finds that understanding the limitations of different research designs is a crucial step that must precede any generalization. Harris Cooper and Robert Arkin participate in an ongoing colloquy of when and why quantitative methods are helpful for reviews. Laura Leviton and Thomas Cook, in the same discussion, continue to argue for using quantitative reviews cautiously. They remind us that narrative efforts are not *necessarily* weak, and that it is too tempting to park our common sense outside and rush to use an arsenal of quantitative techniques simply because they exist.

Six papers give specific methodological suggestions for dealing with groups of evaluations. Larry Hedges's two articles present statistically elegant and pathbreaking techniques for seeing whether a group of evaluations provide independent estimates for a single underlying effect size. The alternative, which Hedges argues is common, is that a group of evaluations reflect that a "family" or "cluster" of effect sizes describe the real world. Hedges develops formal methods to see which is more likely. He also offers suggestions for interpreting groups of effect sizes exhibiting more variation than ordinary sampling error.

Paul Smith and I report on the comparative behavior of three different ways of estimating an intraclass correlation across many evaluations. We find that different methods of aggregating outcomes are best depending upon what assumptions a reviewer is willing to make about outliers. Three concise articles by Robert Rosenthal and Donald Rubin give specific suggestions for how to conduct and interpret analyses of effect size. One of their most striking points is how a small to modest outcome can have large practical implications. They develop a way to display different effect sizes to clarify them for nonstatistical policymakers.

PART II

The second part of this collection gives 21 research reviews. I have selected them because I believe each is particularly well done. Some illustrate how to carry out a careful quantitative review. Others turn up interesting findings because of the authors' success in spotting ways to combine qualitative and numerical evidence. Taken as a group, I believe they weave a convincing case for how careful scientific reviews can advance knowledge both for policymakers and researchers.

Roger Straw examines the effects of deinstitutionalization in mental health. He finds strong evidence from many evaluations that most patients who are candidates for hospitalization can be treated safely and effectively in community based settings. On a related topic, William Stock, Morris Okun, Marilyn Haring, and Robert Witter find, contrary to a widely held belief, that in fact no relationship exists between age and subjective sense of well-being. In other words, young adults are not generally happier than older people.

Several other reviews turn up findings that I don't consider obvious. Stephen Raudenbush examines the teacher expectancy controversy: Do expectations influence how teachers treat children and ultimately how those children perform? He finds that some evaluations are carried out before teachers meet the children, while others involve teachers who already know their students. This turns out to be the key to understanding such studies. When teachers know children before expectations are imposed, the expectations have no effect. But when teachers arrive in class *tabula rasa,* the expectations effect can be strong. Patricia Williams and her colleagues examine the television-academic performance relationship. They find the relation to be complex. Heavy TV watching is associated with poor academic work. But small amounts of viewing go with *improved* schoolwork. Interestingly, high IQ students seem to be particularly hurt by excessive viewing.

Two pairs of reviews illustrate how they can elucidate controversies. Sam Messick and Ann Jungeblut identify an enormous number of methodological difficulties in studies of how coaching affects students SAT scores. Rebecca DerSimonian and Nan Laird follow up this point. They report a clear relation between research design and findings. Observational or poorly controlled studies show much greater coaching effects than their randomized and matched counterparts. Taken together, these reviews demonstrate convincingly that (1) coaching helps to raise SAT scores a bit, say about 10 points on average for Verbal and Quantitative, and (2) the methodology underlying any evaluation of coaching has a lot to do with a study's outcome.

Emily Mumford, Herbert Schlesinger, and Gene Glass look at effects of psychological intervention on reducing length of hospital stay after surgery. Their findings are strongly positive: the average postoperative stay of about seven days can be reduced by about two days using psychological interventions. The potential cost reductions are substantial. Elizabeth Devine and Thomas Cook build on this foundation and take the analysis even further. They examine several factors that might threaten the validity of Mumford and associates' finding. For example, they examine different kinds of control groups in different evaluations. Some controls received usual care while those in other studies got an attention placebo. They find the attention placebo has a small positive effect. Devine and Cook also investigate the possibility of publication bias. Overall, they confirm the earlier positive findings for psychological intervention, although their additional analyses reduce the expected savings from two days to about a day and a half.

Four policy questions in education have for years generated disputes. One is the importance of class size. Another is the value of open or unstructured educational settings. A third is ability grouping. A fourth is how to teach reading as effectively as possible. Research reviews in this collection offer fascinating insights on each.

Mary Lee Smith and Gene Glass report on dozens of studies of class size. Their meta-analysis finds a clear relation between class size and student performance: the smaller the class the better the performance. Smith and Glass are fully aware of many possible explanations that are other than causal. For example, maybe rich schools in rich towns have both small classes and high scoring students, and scores would be high regardless of class size. They consider such possibilities; yet they conclude clearly that very small classes are noticeably better than medium-size classes; medium-size classes are slightly better than large classes.

Rose Giaconia and Larry Hedges examine the literature on open education. They find little guidance for educators wanting both strong cognitive performance and positive nonacademic outcomes, such as good attitude and creativity. Their review establishes that commonly used descriptors of open education, such as multi-age grouping and open physical spaces, are unrelated to a school's academic success. Instead, the best potential for success lies in these programs' efforts to stimulate positive attitudes toward school.

Chen-Lin Kulik and James Kulik report that dividing children among classes according to their ability—ability grouping—can have some clear effects. Overall, aggregating across different kinds of evaluations, the Kuliks find that children in homogeneous classrooms outperform their heterogeneously assigned counterparts, although just slightly. Especially interesting is that ability grouping is particularly positive in two circumstances. One is performance of high ability students. They seem to benefit a lot from ability grouping. The other is programs where attitudes have special importance. Regardless of ability, students develop more positive attitudes toward school and academic subjects when they are ability grouped.

Susanna Pflaum, Herbert Walberg, Myra Karegianes, and Sue Rasher examine many studies of reading instruction, and discover that new or innovative methods, regardless of type, generally outperform a traditional method. They compare different traditional methods for teaching reading, and find only small differences among them. Far more important to success, they report, is the teacher organization and commitment that accompanies innovation. The Hawthorne effect is alive and well.

The next four reviews examine the effectiveness of widely used medical treatments. Meir Stampfer, Samuel Goldhaber, Salim Yusuf, Richard Peto, and Charles Hennekens report on studies of the drug streptokinase. It is a slightly controversial treatment for severe myocardial infarction, or heart attacks. They identify eight well-done evaluations of this treatment. Although findings differ across studies, their synthesis finds clear evidence that his drug reduces mortality from heart attacks. Melbourne Hovell reviews research evaluating weight loss as a treatment for essential hypertension. Research design is systematically taken into account and the result seems clear: weight loss is an effective way to lower blood pressure. This is especially true for severely overweight people with severely high blood pressure. William Shadish reviews more than three dozen evaluations of routine preventive child health care. In contrast to other reviews in the collection that argue for conclusions, Shadish points out severe methodological weaknesses in nearly all of these studies. His conclusion is that any strongly held position for or against the value of preventive care cannot be based on strong research evidence. Shadish warns us not to interpret this negatively; there are scattered encouraging findings. They simply are not solid enough to be conclusive. This is a good example of a field where a few well-designed evaluations, with reasonably high power, would win a lot for the public.

Paul Wortman and William Yeaton review studies comparing coronary bypass surgery versus drug treatment. They find a clear overall advantage of bypass surgery. Evaluations with randomization find a smaller advantage for surgery than other studies, whether mortality or survival data are used as outcomes. Since over 100,000 surgical procedures are now done annually in America, this result provides firm reassurance about its value.

The final five reviews have a slightly different emphasis. They focus on methodological issues, or ideas that are not standard operating procedure. Chapter 3 of the General Accounting Office Report GAO/IPE-82-2 is an excellent effort designed to answer a different question from all the other syntheses. Initiated to assist policymakers, the review organizers at the GAO did not ask about a program's *effects*.

Rather, they assessed the comparative *participation* of poor people in service programs using two alternative mechanisms: block grants versus categorical programs. Despite heavy political debate about which delivery method reaches more needy people, the GAO evaluation synthesis finds essentially no difference.

Hersholt Waxman and Hebert Walberg examine reviews in many fields in education. They identify definitional problems, and conclude that a lot will be gained when reviews systematize a search for similarly defined treatments, such as cognitive cues. Karl White does not examine a treatment or program. Rather, he examines a correlational question: Are social class and academic achievement related? He finds the answer is clearly yes, and along the way offers important methodological guidance. For example, he finds clear evidence of publication bias. He also confirms that the unit of analysis used in different evaluations is an important determinant of the size of a reported correlation. Victor Willson and Richard Putnam summarize evaluations that investigate whether giving people a pretest influences their performance on a posttest. They find convincing evidence that it does. An interval of less than one month between the two tests shows the strongest pretest effect. This suggests a real value of including pretest information in an analysis whenever such data are available. They should reduce the variance of prediction and lead to an expectation of higher posttest scores.

William Trochim, in the final article, looks at evaluations of compensatory education, and finds that how outcomes are measured seems to determine the chance of turning up successes. Norm referenced approaches are far more likely than regression models to turn up positive findings. Since regression is a common technique in evaluations, and so many evaluations reach disappointing conclusions, this review suggests norm-referenced models might profitably be considered more often.

I

METHODOLOGICAL ISSUES AND PROCEDURES

1

Numbers and Narrative
Combining Their Strengths in Research Reviews

Richard J. Light and David B. Pillemer

When several independent research studies examine the same program or treatment, conflicting findings often result, making it difficult to draw overall conclusions. Recent methodological work has created procedures, sometimes called meta-analysis, for combining quantitative results across studies. In this article, Richard Light and David Pillemer argue that qualitative information is equally important for explaining conflicting or puzzling outcomes. They discuss six ways in which qualitative information is essential to the process of literature review. The authors outline three broad strategies for combining different types of information in a review: quantifying descriptive reports, presenting quantitative outcomes narratively, and allying statistical and descriptive evidence while maintaining the integrity of each. They suggest that reviews organized to ally both forms of information will ultimately maximize our knowledge about the complexities of program success.

An extraordinary debate is emerging in education and related social sciences. Fundamental research paradigms are being questioned. For many years researchers in education could be divided fairly clearly into two broad camps: those who preferred qualitative case reports, and others who favored quantitative, statistically based studies. Of course there has been some overlap, but even a cursory look at any major university's course listings on research methodology turns up courses that clearly emphasize one approach or the other. These different emphases in training are then reflected directly into how researchers organize and communicate their work. Major social science journals are categorized either as "quantitative" or "qualitative," with a crossing of boundaries all too rare.

But these sharp divisions are changing. Distinguished researchers within both groups are calling upon the scientific community to dig deeper and do better. In a provocative

This work was supported by a grant from the Spencer Foundation.

Richard J. Light and David B. Pillemer, "Numbers and Narrative: Combining Their Strengths in Research Reviews," 52(1) *Harvard Educational Review* 1-26 (February 1982). Copyright © 1982 by President and Fellows of Harvard College. All rights reserved.

paper Matthew Miles (1979) describes a qualitative study of six public schools. A distinguished scholar in the field for twenty years, Miles argues that his case analysis was "intuitive, primitive, and unmanageable," leading him to conclude that "qualitative research on organizations cannot be expected to transcend storytelling" (p. 600).

Leaders of the traditionally quantitative group are also raising fundamental questions. Donald Campbell, a contributor to statistical research paradigms for decades, recently wrote: "all scientific knowing is indirect, presumptive, obliquely and incompletely corroborated at best. The language of science is subjective, provincial, approximate, and metaphoric, never the language of reality itself. The best we can hope for are well-edited approximations" (cited in Mahoney, 1976, p. 126).

The statistician John Tukey (1963) also expressed similar concerns about misplaced precision in research and policy analysis: "The most important maxim for data analysts to heed, and one which many statisticians have shunned is this: 'Far better an approximate answer to the right question, which is often vague, than an exact answer to the wrong question, which can always be made precise' "(p. 13).

Acknowledging the limitations of each approach has prompted the search for opportunities to use the best of both strategies. Rather than argue whether quantitative or qualitative research is more useful, especially in such complex situations as schools and human learning, efforts are increasingly being made to combine features of both. A major contribution here is Charles Reichardt and Thomas Cook's (1979) essay, "Beyond Qualitative *Versus* Quantitative Methods." Campbell (1975) placed this issue in a broad context: "After all, man is, in his ordinary way, a very competent knower, and qualitative commonsense knowing is not replaced by quantitative knowing. Rather, quantitative knowing has to trust and build on the qualitative, including ordinary perception. We methodologists must achieve an applied epistemology which integrates both" (p. 191).

These scientists extol the virtues of using both quantitative and qualitative information in a single study. In this article we suggest how both methods can be useful to a researcher or policy analyst who is synthesizing findings *across several studies*. For many years the "literature review" has been a routine step along the way to presenting a scientific study, or laying the groundwork for an innovation in a field such as education. Journals such as the *Psychological Bulletin* and *Review of Educational Research* report the best of these reviews. Historically these efforts to accumulate information have been unsystematic. An occasional quantitative foray involved "vote counting," a simple tally of positive, negative, or neutral findings about an innovation or treatment. But the majority of literature reviews have remained for many years narrative and subjective.

During the last decade researchers have developed procedures in an attempt to "quantify" the process of accumulating evidence. Glass (1976, 1977), Hedges and Olkin (1980), Jackson (1980), Light and Smith (1971), Pillemer and Light (1980a, 1980b), Rosenthal (1978, 1980), Smith and Glass (1977), Walberg and Haertel (1980) and others organized detailed quantitative procedures for carrying out literature reviews. Gene Glass coined the term "meta-analysis" that is now used to describe a quantitative literature review, and his tour de force (Glass, McGaw, & Smith, 1981) provides guidelines for action.

As participants in this effort to develop and use quantitative reviews, we are encouraged by the new interest in organizing information systematically. But there is a balance between the gains that accrue from quantifying program features, or outcomes, and one's ability to capture the full descriptive context of an innovation, or the setting where the innovation takes place. We believe that Campbell's suggestion about quantitative knowing building upon descriptive knowing applies to dealing with *groups* of research studies as well as each one. In this spirit we present some suggestions for approaching the task of synthesizing disparate findings from many studies. Our central theme is that by organizing the strengths and weaknesses of different kinds of studies, the most valuable syntheses will make use of both quantitative and qualitative information. We do not view these two approaches as competitors, or even as competing ideals with a trade-off. Rather, we believe that understanding program effectiveness requires examining outcomes in the context of how the program is organized, whom it serves, and where it is offered.

To this end we present our discussion in five parts. First, for readers unfamiliar with issues surrounding the aggregation of findings across many research studies, we point out some limitations of the traditional narrative literature review. Second, we summarize methods developed recently to quantify, or systematize, reviews of many studies. This leads us to discuss why information that is not easily quantifiable deserves a "say" in research synthesis. Next, we describe six ways that nonquantitative information can contribute to accumulating knowledge on a topic. We then delineate five different sources of nonquantitative information. Finally, we tie these ideas together to support the view that in many policy settings it is desirable to summarize large bodies of research by integrating qualitative and quantitative information. Examples drawn from a variety of research areas will illustrate how different types of information can be allied, leading to insights about when, where, and for whom particular programs work best.

Limitations of Narrative Reviews

Why have traditional literature reviews become a whipping post for methodologists of social science? Critics cite several weaknesses that focus upon the review's unsystematic nature.

First, the narrative review is *subjective*. Since the process has few formal rules, two well-intentioned reviewers may disagree about issues as basic as what studies to include in a review, or how to resolve conflicts between studies. The result is that rather than organizing a series of research outcomes into a set of reasonably conclusive findings, the reviews themselves are attacked for including inappropriate or poorly done studies, or for drawing conclusions subjectively. Rather than resolving conflicts among individual studies, the review may only generate new conflicts.

Second, the narrative review is *scientifically unsound*. Without formal guidelines, a reviewer may draw conclusions using methods inconsistent with good statistical practice. For example, when some studies show a positive relationship between two variables while others show no relationship or even a negative one, a common way of pulling together disparate findings is to use a "vote count." The reviewer counts the number of studies that support each side of an issue and accepts the position that receives the most "votes." This ignores sample size, effect size, and research design, and can result in serious errors (Hedges & Olkin, 1980; Light, 1979; Light & Smith, 1971).

Third, the narrative review is an *inefficient way to extract useful information*. This is especially true when the number of studies is large, perhaps fifty or more. A reviewer unarmed with formal tools to extract and summarize information must rely on extraordinary ability to mentally juggle multiple relationships among different variables.

Conflicts Between Narrative Reviews: An Example

To illustrate some of these issues, we turn to a research example: the cognitive performance of adopted children. Dozens of studies exist on this topic, and in an effort to summarize them several scholars have written narrative reviews. Our purpose here is not to resolve issues of cognitive performance. It is simply to highlight dilemmas that may arise from narrative research summaries.

For years scientists have debated the ways in which school and home environments influence children's performance, particularly their IQ test scores. In a recent review Munsinger (1974) examined a group of adoption studies and strongly concluded that environmental effects are relatively small: "Available data suggest that under existing circumstances, heredity is much more important than environment in producing individual differences in IQ" (p. 623). Kamin (1978) later reviewed the same group of studies and reached precisely the opposite conclusion. This disagreement did not change Munsinger's (1978) views.

These reviews are interesting to us here because they illustrate several of the problems listed earlier. That these two distinguished scientists interpret a set of results differently is only slightly surprising since personal belief systems can play a role in synthesizing disparate findings, especially for a topic as controversial as nature-nurture. Far more striking are their different views as to what constitutes acceptable review standards:

> The purpose of this comment, however, is to indicate that Munsinger's review of the adoption literature is in general unreliable. Though any review must be selective in its presentation and analysis of data, Munsinger's is excessively so. (Kamin, 1978, p. 194)

> Kamin accuses me of errors and selective reporting of the adoption data, but in fact Kamin's comments are quite selective and often incorrect. (Munsinger, 1978, p. 202)

Their conflicting views about evidence are particularly apparent when each comments on a study by Freeman, Holzinger, and Mitchell (1928). Kamin describes it as "large-scale and extraordinarily interesting" (p. 200), while Munsinger argues that it is "replete with methodological and statistical difficulties" (1974, p. 635).

Realizing the frustrations some readers must feel reading these conflicting reviews, Kamin (1978) concludes that "perhaps the major point to be made is that readers interested in evaluating the evidence on hereditability of IQ ought not to depend on published summaries. Those who wish to speak or to teach accurately about what is and is not known have no realistic alternative but to read this literature themselves" (p. 200). Taken literally this statement eliminates the review as a scientific or practical tool. It is simply unrealistic to expect all practitioners interested in a reading curriculum, or Head Start program, or even an issue as complicated as the environmental impact on IQ scores to read dozens of original scientific studies. Surely it is worth trying to develop systematic procedures for summarizing large numbers of studies.

The point of data synthesis is not to eliminate differences of opinion about this or any set of results. What it can offer is explicit, formal procedures for presenting and summarizing results. Two reviewers using the same synthesis procedures should develop the same statistical summary. If different techniques are used, the differences are explicit. Thus, if two reviews reach different conclusions, at least readers can see why, and then make an informed choice.

Quantitative Approaches to Data Synthesis

Mosteller and Bush (1954) were among the first statisticians to develop useful statistical synthesis procedures. Many additional methodological developments have followed in the last decade (see Glass, McGaw, & Smith, 1981; Pillemer & Light, 1980b). Some of these techniques adapt procedures used routinely for analyzing data from a single sample, and so they are accessible to a wide audience of scientists and practitioners. The emphasis in most syntheses has been to develop an "overall average conclusion" from a group of studies. This has generally been accomplished in one of two ways: conducting a combined significance test, or computing an average effect size.

Conducting a Combined Significance Test

Assume each of several independent studies compares Head Start children to a comparison group. The group differences are tested statistically in each instance. One way to reach a "grand" conclusion about Head Start is to combine the separate tests into an overall test of a common null hypothesis — generally that Head Start children are, on average, no different from non-Head Start children. Rosenthal (1978) describes several statistical techniques that accomplish this purpose.

The primary value of these combined significance tests is that the effective sample size for the grand comparison is much larger than for each individual study. The *power* of the combined test is thus much higher. Preschool innovations, for example, commonly produce short-term cognitive gains, but they tend to be modest (Gilbert, Light, & Mosteller, 1975). Evaluations with a sample of only a few children might reveal inklings of these gains, but are unlikely to produce statistically significant results. This may lead us to overlook a program that is working. When the effective sample size is increased dramatically by combining studies, the overall statistical test is far more likely to detect success.

Computing an Average Effect Size

A second way of summarizing a group of studies is to compute an effect size for each study, and then to average the results across the entire set. This technique has been pioneered by Glass (1977). A common definition for effect size is the difference between the treatment and control group means divided by the control group standard deviation. Suppose a group of high school seniors is coached before taking the SAT exam and then scores an average of 550, while a similar group without coaching averages 500. Knowing that SAT scores have a standard deviation of 100, we can then calculate the "effect size" due to coaching by taking the difference in group mean SAT scores and dividing by 100. This effect size of 0.5 indicates that the treatment and control groups' average SAT scores differed by one-half of a standard deviation. If an effect size is calculated for each of several studies, an overall average can be computed. When a combined statistical test is significant, it is useful to know whether the average effect is large enough to have practical significance.

These quantitative procedures for combining results across studies are rapidly becoming popular among researchers. In the last few years, combined significance tests and average effect sizes have been used to examine the effects of interpersonal expectancies (Rosenthal & Rubin, 1978), sex differences in decoding nonverbal information (Hall, 1978), the effectiveness of psychotherapy (Smith & Glass, 1977), and to compare Keller's system of personalized instruction to more traditional classroom teaching (Kulik, Kulik, & Cohen, 1979). In each of these examples a significant overall outcome or large average effect has been cited in support of group differences or program effectiveness (see also Walberg & Haertel, 1980).

Examining Conflicting Outcomes

When faced with dozens of studies of, say, Head Start, it is natural to hope that the findings will agree. When this happens, integrating outcomes is easy and uncontroversial. But in most real world settings, this does not occur.

We believe that, rather than viewing conflicts as a sign of trouble, these circumstances actually offer an *opportunity* to examine and explain variation in outcomes. A number of explanatory factors may underlie conflicts, such as substantive differences between treatments with the same label, or a program working well in certain settings and far less well in others. Examining these complex relationships informally is hard to do. Quantitative procedures such as searching for outliers, and regression analysis, help to structure this effort (Pillemer & Light, 1980a, 1980b).

Limitations in the Scope of Quantitative Synthesis

Quantitative synthesis procedures are being adopted rapidly in education and the social sciences. This very fact testifies to widespread dissatisfaction with traditional, informal literature summaries. Our guess is that most policymakers and social scientists have experienced the frustration of trying to integrate a vast research literature into a clear statement of what is known. Quantitative approaches appeal to this sense of futility.

Despite this appeal, debate is growing over the real value of quantitative synthesis. Some critics (for example, Eysenck, 1978; Gallo, 1978) have expressed extreme doubts. A more moderate position taken by Cook and Leviton (1980) questions whether quantitative syntheses actually turn out to be superior to traditional reviews.

We believe that arguments about the superiority of quantitative versus qualitative reviews lead nowhere. An "either-or" position is neither necessary nor productive. Quantitative synthesis offers a number of statistical tools that a reviewer can use to organize conclusions based on outcomes of many studies. Using quantitative techniques does not reduce the value of careful program descriptions, case studies, narrative reports, or expert judgment. It is the reviewer who specifies what questions are worth asking, and who must then match these questions to whatever information is most likely to provide useful answers. In the following section we attempt to reset the balance by detailing why nonquantitative information can make important contributions to organizing knowledge.

UNIVERSITY OF WINNIPEG
LIBRARY
515 Portage Avenue
Winnipeg, Manitoba R3B 2E9

Six Reasons Why Nonquantitative Information Should Have a Say

"Investigators tend to pursue only those questions which can be easily evaluated by null hypothesis testing, and they will favor those which are most likely to yield results which are statistically significant (versus epistemologically relevant). This may encourage what Mitroff and Featheringham call 'the fallacy of misplaced precision' or Type III error—having solved the wrong problem" (Mahoney, 1976, p. 102).

These comments, taken with those of Campbell and Tukey quoted earlier, reflect the belief that an overemphasis on precision in scientific research may be misguided. They remind us that quantitative precision, while often valuable, should not be pursued for its own sake. Other sources of information offer benefits as well.

Treatments May Be Individualized

Quantitative synthesis may be difficult because of treatment flexibility. Some educational and social programs are tailored idiosyncratically to the person or community receiving services (Yin & Heald, 1975). Such treatment variations do not result from haphazard implementation. Rather, there is an intentional effort to individualize.

Public Law 94-142 clearly illustrates this issue. This law, passed by Congress in the mid-seventies, requires that every child with an educational handicap receive special services. It covers many handicaps, including physical, cognitive, and emotional disabilities. The services provided are necessarily diverse and specialized. The desired outcomes vary as much as the treatments. For a child with emotional problems, the treatment might require therapeutic counseling to alleviate severe depression. For a partially deaf child, services might involve supportive aides to improve school performance. A dyslexic child might need special tutoring. A blind child would receive different services.

Quantitative synthesis across studies of children receiving different treatments aimed toward different goals is unlikely to produce useful information about overall program success. Asking the question, "Is Public Law 94-142 effective?" is rather like asking, "Is HUD effective?" It is an interesting question, but the answer will vary with the particular HUD program under discussion (rent subsidies, urban renewal, energy conservation). The same is true of education programs with clearly individualized treatments.

For these efforts, nonquantitative information becomes important in two ways. First, it is necessary to carefully document the *process* aspects of each treatment as well as the outcome. Following this, it may be possible to summarize outcomes across a group of children receiving similar services. Second, developing an *overall* estimate of program effectiveness requires us to aggregate across totally different treatment modalities. We may find that P.L. 94-142 has been highly successful in improving the school performance of deaf and dyslexic children, but much less so for blind or emotionally disturbed children. In addition, individual treatments for one subgroup of participants may be particularly expensive relative to other program components. Combining these findings into some sort of statistical average using quantitative synthesis would say little about the law's effectiveness; the differences between subject groups and their treatments might be obscured by an overall statistic. A policymaker must balance the various sources of disparate information when deciding if P.L. 94-142 is working well on the whole, or how to change it.

Critical Outcomes May Be Difficult To Measure Quantitatively

An appealing feature of quantitative synthesis is its emphasis on numerical indices. If the appropriate summary statistics are available from several research reports, synthesis can proceed smoothly. Doing this transforms complicated, unclear, or "messy" original research into precise numerical summaries.

But there is a real risk of false precision. We all know that certain outcomes are difficult to capture numerically. The context in which a program operates is sometimes far more important than any easily quantifiable feature. Even when test scores are used routinely to evaluate certain education programs, investigators may legitimately question their appropriateness under varying circumstances. One example is the perpetual debate over the interpretation of scores on standardized intelligence tests, despite their popularity in educational evaluations (Zigler & Trickett, 1978).

As Zimiles (1980) points out, this problem is particularly common in evaluations of complex programs:

> Most programs for children, especially educational programs, are aimed at producing a multiplicity of outcomes. As already noted, many of the psychological characteristics they are concerned with fostering — whether it be ego strength, or resourcefulness, or problem solving ability — are difficult or impossible to measure, especially within the time and cost constraints of an evaluation study. The usual response to this dilemma is to sift through the roster of multiple outcomes and single out for assessment, not the most important ones, but those that are capable of being measured. (p. 7)

Here an evaluator is faced with a trade-off between precision and meaning. Organizing a synthesis forces us to confront a similar dilemma. Which outcomes appearing in studies should be included in a synthesis? If we decide not to rely exclusively on quantitative measures, we must devise a method for incorporating nonquantitative evidence to strengthen our review.

Assessing Program Effects Across Multiple Levels of Impact

Quantitative synthesis procedures work best when all studies assess program effects at the same level or unit of impact. While this level is often the individual participant, programs can have an effect at other levels as well (Yin & Heald, 1975). For example, while most daycare studies focus on behaviors of participating children, the availability of substitute care also influences families and the labor market (Belsky & Steinberg, 1978).

If a program's influence is felt at several levels, an overall decision about it may force us to aggregate results across different levels as well as across outcomes measured at the same level. While synthesis at any particular level can profit from quantitative methods, aggregation across levels usually demands many qualitative decisions about trade-offs.

For example, the National Institute of Education (NIE) in the early seventies developed a new program called "Experimental Schools" (Herriot, Note 1). From more than 100 applicants, 10 rural school systems were selected to try systemic innovation. Money was offered to support these innovations for an initial trial period, with the hope that, if successful, the changes would be institutionalized. NIE also hoped that other school systems throughout the country, seeing positive results from these ten districts with "Experimental Schools" would voluntarily adopt the most successful new ideas.

Outcomes were measured at three levels: changes in students' academic performance, changes in the organization of the school system, and changes in citizens' perceptions of the schools. As one might anticipate, the results were complicated, and uniformity did not exist at any of the three levels. Yet some promising findings emerged, especially in public perceptions of what roles schools should and do play.

Now suppose a superintendent in a different school system wanted to base school reform on results from this project. If she wanted to begin by examining the available evidence, she would face a matrix of findings. For each of the three "impact levels," there is evidence from each of the ten school districts. These results could be synthesized quantitatively across any one impact level. For example, the average program effect on student test performance across the ten schools could be calculated. However, synthesis within any district would require qualitative analysis of trade offs between levels of impact. For example, judging a program's overall impact on a particular school district might require trading off a positive effect of public support, a negative impact on school organization, and no influence on student performance. This synthesis defies simple quantitative aggregation. One superintendent may have a set of weights to apply to the relative values of changes in student performance versus changes in public understanding and support for schools; another superintendent may have an entirely different set of weights. The point, in summary, is that aggregating the results of multilevel impact studies nearly always will require the introduction of nonquantitative steps.

A general framework for synthesizing results of multilevel impact programs appears in Figure 1. Note that quantitative synthesis applies across any one impact level (row), while qualitative integration of outcomes is necessary for assessing overall program impact at a particular location (column).

FIGURE 1
Framework for Aggregating Findings Across Different Levels of Impact

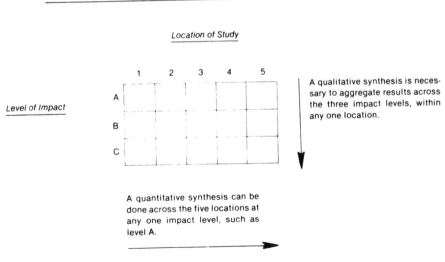

Location of Study

Level of Impact

A qualitative synthesis is necessary to aggregate results across the three impact levels, within any one location.

A quantitative synthesis can be done across the five locations at any one impact level, such as level A.

The Uncontrolled Treatment Group Versus the Treated Control Group

Salter (Note 2) points out that when several studies compare people receiving a treatment to others who are not, subtle differences between similarly labeled treatments are common. Nonquantitative information can offer valuable guidance in helping a reviewer to assess how similar the treatments really are.

Fosburg and Glantz (Note 3) provide a recent example. They reviewed a series of studies of children's nutrition programs sponsored by the U.S. Department of Agriculture. The simplest quantitative analysis would have involved computing an effect size for each study comparing the health of children who received food supplements with those who did not, and then averaging findings across the studies. But nonquantitative information included in many of the individual studies convinced them this would be fruitless. While for administrative purposes the treatment was the same in each study, information about "plate waste" — food not eaten — of the supplementary food suggested important differences among sites. In some cases the plate waste was high; other studies reported almost none. In every case, these data were informal and descriptive. But the reviewers decided they were crucial. Combining treatments having the same administrative name would in fact have amounted to combining groups receiving vastly different treatments. They were "uncontrolled."

The same dilemma arose for the control groups. All were not "pure" control groups, at least by textbook definition. Many studies reported that children at sites not receiving assistance from the Department of Agriculture were still receiving some food assistance under Title XX of the Social Security Act, which provides various forms of aid to low-income families. So, control groups in some of the studies in the review were actually quite heavily "treated," while others were in fact "pure" control groups, receiving no food assistance at all.

In this case, the qualitative descriptions of what actually happened to children in treatment and control groups in each study led the reviewers to reorganize their synthesis into subgroups. These subgroups acknowledged differences between treated versus untreated controls. A simple effect size average over all available studies would have missed this step.

Studying the "Wrong" Treatment

Occasionally when synthesizing outcomes one finds that a relationship between a program and an outcome is not as strong as was originally hoped, but that outcomes are *sometimes* successful. This may lead to a search for features of a program apart from the original treatment that might explain the success. Here, descriptive or nonquantitative data can play an important role.

A striking example comes from a recent debate in the field of criminal justice. For many years, criminal rehabilitation, especially of delinquent youths, has been a dearly sought goal of judges, educators, and social workers. Yet, despite large numbers of innovative programs implemented over the last twenty years, evaluations of program effectiveness generally offered little cause for optimism.

In 1966 Bailey reviewed 100 evaluations, concluding that "evidence supporting the efficacy of correctional treatment is slight, inconsistent, and of questionable reliability" (cited in Wilson, 1980, p. 4). In 1967 Hood reviewed a group of European studies with similarly negative findings (Hood & Sparks, 1970). But the coup de grace came from a book by Lipton, Martinson, and Wilks (1975). In their review of 231 studies, they found that, "with few and isolated exceptions, the rehabilitative efforts that have been reported so far have had no appreciable effect on recidivism" (Sechrest, White, & Brown, 1979, p. 27).

This widely circulated book threw a wet blanket over the optimism of rehabilitation researchers and practitioners. Yet a recently published study by Murray and Cox (1979) may spark new optimism. They report on 266 youths who were classified as serious delinquents. Instead of going to state reformatories, they were sent to a community-based program in Illinois called Unified Delinquency Intervention Services. While a quantitative analysis found that the rehabilitation treatment itself was not especially successful for these offenders, Murray and Cox report that another program feature, the degree of supervision of the youths, seemed to be highly related to later arrest rates. This finding was not based on an analysis formally built into the original experimental design, but rather on a qualitative observation that a treatment component not originally planned as part of the rehabilitative process seems to be crucial in determining program outcomes (rearrests). Wilson (1980) gives a good summary of this point:

> Youths left in their homes or sent to wilderness camps showed the least reduction; those placed in group homes in the community showed a greater reduction; and those put into out-of-town group homes, intensive care residential programs, or sent to regular reformatories showed the greatest reduction. If this is true, it implies that how strictly the youth were supervised, rather than what therapeutic programs were available, had the greatest effect on the recidivism rate. (p. 13)

To summarize, a quantitative analysis can systematically examine the relationship between planned program and outcome variables across many research studies. But descriptive information in one or several studies can provide clues that a different feature of the treatment, not formally built into a study's experimental design, may be more important than the original planned treatment. Murray and Cox found this, and new calls have been made for a closer look at the importance of type of supervision, rather than type of therapeutic program, in determining the success of youth delinquent rehabilitation programs.

Nonquantitative Information Can Influence Policy

A major impetus for developing quantitative synthesis methods was a wish to make research findings more useful to policymakers: "If what an integrative analysis shows cannot be stated in one uncomplicated sentence, then its message will be lost on all but a few specialists" (Glass, Note 4, p. 3). When presented with a simple numerical summary of the average effect of psychotherapy (Smith & Glass, 1977), or personalized instruction (Kulik, Kulik, & Cohen, 1979), or class size (Glass & Smith, 1978), a policymaker can evaluate program effects without wading through volumes of research reports or vague rhetoric.

The "best" format for presenting research findings remains an open and complicated question. But there are cases where qualitative findings have had a clear policy impact (Patton, 1980). One example of how qualitative information led to actual administrative changes comes from studies of the comparative effectiveness of professional versus paraprofessional "helpers." Durlak (1979) conducted a systematic review of forty-two comparative studies. He reported consistent findings across different patient populations that for certain clinical services, "paraprofessionals achieve clinical outcomes equal to or significantly better than those obtained by professionals" (p. 80).

This is not the sort of finding that many physicians expect when they review the literature on effectiveness of nurse practitioners, yet it led to a practical outcome. Lewis, Lorimer, Lindesman, Palmer, and Lewis (1974) and Merenstein, Wolfe, and Barker (1974), finding similar results, looked for qualitative information about why the nurse practitioners were so effective. A key observation was that nurses allocated their time among patients differently from physicians. The two groups also weighted the importance of various symptoms and incidents differently. The analysis of these qualitative findings resulted in physicians making adjustments in their time allocations. It is interesting to trace the sequence of events here. Because the data underlying the original comparative studies were quantitative, physicians viewed them as surprising, but took them seriously as scientific evidence. This willingness to accept surprising findings led to a qualitative search for an explanation, and ultimately to adjustments in the way some physicians allocate their time and resources.

Five Sources of Nonquantitative Evidence

In the preceding discussion, as in most discussions of nonquantitative evidence, labels like "descriptive," "qualitative," and "narrative" appear almost interchangeably. These terms all refer to information that is not precisely quantitative, but conceptual clarity about sources of nonquantitative information, and how to use them, is missing. We believe it is useful to distinguish more clearly among different types of nonquantitative evidence; a later section will suggest how each can be helpful when preparing research reviews.

Case Studies

Detailed studies of single cases are common, and techniques for analyzing such information are rapidly being developed (Herson & Barlow, 1976; Kratochwill, 1977, 1978). Observations of single individuals have contributed directly to the theories of Freud, Piaget, and Skinner — among the most influential psychologists. Dukes (1965) and Herson and Barlow (1976) present many examples of "N = 1" research in psychology. Case studies are also used in public policy analysis to examine the effects of such nonexperimental events as political decisions made by cities and towns (Yin & Heald, 1975).

The term "case study" refers to the study of a single event, or to disaggregated studies of multiple events (Kennedy, 1979). Even if a case uses a quantitative outcome, it is not possible to compute an effect size in the traditional manner. If each individual is viewed as a separate study, there is no direct measure of within group variation and no control group. However, many research syntheses could benefit from case study information.

Nonquantitative Aggregate Studies

Some research outcomes are difficult to measure objectively or numerically. A clinical psychologist may report that weight loss often improves the lives of obese people or that hypnosis is effective in helping cancer patients adjust to chemotherapy. While an implicit baseline must exist, the benefits may not have been assessed with objective tests. In fact, an investigator may feel that the psychological effects of weight loss or hypnosis cannot be assessed accurately with a simple numerical measurement. A reviewer of such studies may still want to include these nonquantitative insights (Stake, 1978).

A related situation occurs when quantitative studies do not contain sufficient information for statistical synthesis. For example, research with weak experimental designs may include a quantitative assessment. The reading performance of a group of children might be assessed with a standardized test following a special tutoring session. But without a comparison group an effect size cannot be computed. Other studies compare a treatment group to a control, but do not report sufficient information for producing a statistical summary. We recently looked carefully at a series of investigations of the effects of daycare on children's intellectual development. Of twenty-four studies comparing daycare and home-reared children, over half did not report enough information (means, standard deviations, sample sizes, or exact test statistics) to compute simple effect sizes. This leaves us with a choice: either omit these studies, or treat them in some nonquantitative manner.

Nonquantitative Information in Quantitative Studies

In preparing a research report, most authors do not simply list numerical results. The treatment and participants are carefully described, and caveats or limitations are painstakingly laid out. Often the effort put into these nonquantitative descriptions far surpasses the numerical analyses.

Quantitative reviews use only numerical information. What about all the rest of a study? Is it always appropriate or desirable to reduce a journal article to one or at most several numerical indices? Can one number accurately represent the outcomes of a research study conducted over several months or years, with attrition, changes in procedure, and a variety of unexpected or notable happenings? Most scientists would probably hesitate to ignore such information. Reviewers will often want to include information that goes beyond numerical outcomes.

Expert Judgment

Deciding to limit subjective input is itself a subjective decision. Reviewers might choose to include expert opinion at the early stages of a summary, such as in evaluating individual studies. Or they may decide to compare systematically the judgments of experts about program effectiveness. Syntheses should be able to incorporate these inputs.

Narrative Reviews of Collections of Research Studies

In arguing for quantitative synthesis procedures, researchers have focused on the negative aspects of traditional narrative reviews. While many of these points are well taken, narrative reviews are not by definition full of flaws (see Cook & Leviton, 1980). A careful narrative review, with explicit analytic procedures, can be extremely valuable for certain purposes. It may even provide useful information for reviewers doing statistical summaries.

Three Strategies for Combining Quantitative and Nonquantitative Evidence in Reviews

We have emphasized the benefits of including nonquantitative information in a review. Since both quantitative and qualitative indices often provide useful information, a review incorporating both should outperform its one-sided counterparts. The key question then becomes *how* to accomplish this integration.

Three broad strategies are useful for organizing different kinds of information in the same review: putting nonquantitative information into a quantitative format; discussing quantitative indices in narrative fashion; and using the two types of information in combination, while maintaining the integrity of each. In pursuing these strategies, all five sources of nonquantitative information become useful.

Strategy One: Quantifying Nonquantitative Information

One way to integrate qualitative and quantitative information is to translate the former into a numerical format.

Case studies and nonquantitative aggregate studies. A first strategy is to summarize each case or aggregate with a numerical index and combine them across studies. For example, outcomes of individual cases could be assigned values of + 1 (successful), 0 (neutral), or − 1 (unsuccessful), depending on a reviewer's overall evaluation of treatment success. This quantification can be done at a more detailed level by assigning numbers to several individual components of a case study and summing the ratings, or by developing weights for different indicators of success (Lazarsfeld & Robinson, 1940). This produces a single numerical index for each study, which can then be averaged or displayed in a distribution.

The "case survey" method developed by Yin and his colleagues (Yin & Heald, 1975; Yin, Bingham, & Heald, 1976) offers a more sophisticated way to quantify case studies. Each study is rated on several dimensions, such as research quality, program characteristics, and outcomes. These multiple ratings are then cumulated across studies, providing an overall numerical summary. Scorers also indicate their level of confidence for each judgment, allowing for reliability comparisons of "sure" and "unsure" ratings.

Yin and Heald (1975) used this method in reviewing 269 case studies of urban areas following decentralization of services. They found that clients' attitudes toward services improved in approximately 25 percent of the cases. This finding held whether the raters were "unsure" or "sure" of their categorization of outcomes. These summaries are not rigorously quantitative, and so they cannot be combined directly with effect sizes or significance levels calculated from quantitative studies. But they indicate roughly the overall success of urban innovations in the case study literature. That success rate can then be compared with results from quantitative reviews.

A weakness of this "numberizing" is the loss of much rich descriptive detail. Yin and Heald (1975) clearly discuss the trade-offs:

> The case survey method, in its focus on aggregating general lessons, may not give sufficient attention to the unique factors of an individual case. The trade-off here is similar to the trade-off between experimental and clinical research. Only the latter may provide a full appreciation of the individual case; the former, however, must be relied upon more heavily if the goal is to create generalizations about groups of individuals. . . . The case

survey method may be more appropriate where the primary concern is with assessment and not necessarily with the discovery of process. (p. 380)

Qualitative information in quantitative studies. Quantitative research studies usually report much information beyond statistical summaries. Most journals require careful descriptions of the treatment, information about participants and research settings, and discussions of special features. Glass, McGaw, and Smith (1981) suggest that all of this "other" information be coded when possible and brought into the formal quantitative analysis. Walberg and Haertel (1980) present many specific reviews where background features are coded and statistically related to program effectiveness.

An advantage of this approach is that it helps us identify qualitative features of studies that are formally related to the quantitative outcomes we are testing. Without statistical tools a reviewer often faces too many studies to permit an efficient search for important qualitative information. This is especially true in evaluating educational innovations, where such relationships often are modest.

On the other hand, the drawback here is the same as before. By quantifying a study's characteristics to make statistical comparisons, we lose information. Pages of text may be needed to describe a preschool curriculum adequately, yet group comparisons require a reduction into gross classifications. One criticism of meta-analysis is that grouping treatments into overly broad categories obscures important real-world differences (Presby, 1978). Similarly, it is often hard to quantify a particular study's idiosyncratic features, such as a report that testing took place on a particularly hot day, or that children in one classroom had more opportunities for informal practice than children in another class.

Expert judgment. A third way to quantify narrative information is perhaps the most controversial, yet interesting. It involves an effort to draw on the wisdom of researchers and practitioners. Some people invest years of study and thought, and acquire intimate experience with a program or curriculum. Though no individual opinion encompasses all the detailed evidence from published literature, wisdom and insight may transcend the "sterile" data of research reports. White (1977) describes this trade-off: "The aggregated knowledge collected in an enterprise such as the learning theory movement lies far beyond that possible to any individual. And yet in important regards the consensual formulations of the group are far more limited and 'stupid' than the understandings of the private individuals who participate in the group game" (p. 73).

We suggest two ways of translating expert judgment into quantitative information for use in synthesis. First, *prior* to statistical integration, a reviewer can incorporate expert evaluations of studies by weighting each study according to an expert's judgment of its overall value. Techniques already exist for weighting individual study outcomes by their sample size (Mosteller & Bush, 1954; Rosenthal, 1978) that can be adapted to experts' ratings. This procedure helps to formalize what experts do when subjectively "weighing" the results of different studies to reach an overall conclusion. If an expert believes that a study provides especially strong evidence, the results from that study will receive extra weight.

Incorporating experts' judgments could enrich a review. For example, one can compare syntheses using different experts' weightings, and then compare the various results to a simple unweighted analysis. This would explicitly mark the areas in which experts disagree. If certain studies are rated positively by some experts and negatively by others, the discrepancies should be explored. Lack of agreement may pinpoint methodological, substantive, or ideological issues that lie at the core of the controversy. When expert evaluations are consistent, we can be more confident about the innovation under investigation.

Using weights ties expert evaluations to specific research studies. Our second suggestion involves an expert's *overall* judgment about a specific issue, based on a global integration of his or her knowledge. Experts often are asked such questions as: "How big a risk does daycare pose to an infant's emotional development?" or "Is reading program A *really* better than program B?" While it is possible to give a precise numerical answer to such questions (for example, 10 percent chance of serious risk), experts may prefer to supply judgments or assessments in a more familiar verbal fashion (it is "unlikely" that emotional development will be impeded, or it is "very possible" that the new curriculum is better).

Translating these judgments into precise probability estimates requires a sophisticated conversion system. Mosteller (1976) addresses this issue by drawing on a model developed by Cliff (1959). Mosteller reports a study by Selvidge (1972) that found the median person in a sample of business students interpreted the word "possibility" to mean a 20 percent probability that an event would occur. Cliff provides numerical weightings for various adverbs, based on college students' judgments. Interestingly, the weights were surprisingly stable across different groups of respondents. Cliff proposed that an adverb (such as "very") has a multiplicative effect on the probability estimate of the adjective (such as "possible") it modifies. For example, he found the weighting or multiplicative effect of "very" to be about 1.25. So the median estimate for an event that is "very possible" would be 1.25×20, or 25 percent. As one would expect, a "very possible" event is deemed more likely to occur than an event that is simply "possible." Table 1 presents the multiplicative effect of selected adverbs on the adjective "possible."

Future work in testing and extending Cliff's model will ultimately determine its validity. It is easy to smile when looking at the results in Table 1, because many researchers in *both* groups, qualitative and quantitative, will find flaws in this system. Using a simple

TABLE 1

Multiplicative Effect of Selected Adverbs on the Subjective Probability Associated with the Adjective "Possible"

Adverb	Weight[a]	Probability Estimates for Modifications of "Possible"[b]	
Slightly	.538	Slightly possible	$.538 \times 20 = 11\%$
Somewhat	.662	Somewhat possible	$.662 \times 20 = 13\%$
Rather	.843	Rather possible	$.843 \times 20 = 17\%$
Pretty	.878	Pretty possible	$.878 \times 20 = 18\%$
Quite	1.047	Quite possible	$1.047 \times 20 = 21\%$
Decidedly	1.165	Decidedly possible	$1.165 \times 20 = 23\%$
Very	1.254	Very possible	$1.254 \times 20 = 25\%$
Unusually	1.281	Unusually possible	$1.281 \times 20 = 26\%$
Extremely	1.446	Extremely possible	$1.446 \times 20 = 29\%$

[a] Weights were obtained from Cliff's (1959) Princeton sample.
[b] The probability estimate of 20% for "possible" was obtained from Mosteller (1976).

multiplicative model to capture a complex judgment clearly provides no final answer. Yet we believe it is an intriguing beginning towards systematically using the judgments of many experts.

Strategy Two: Presenting Quantitative Studies in Narrative Fashion

A second broad strategy works to do the reverse: take quantitative evidence and present it narratively. Rather than summarizing a series of results with numerical indices, studies are discussed individually. Strengths and weaknesses are identified and weighed, and overall conclusions are offered without precise quantitative documentation.

Critics of narrative reviews have described these characteristics as drawbacks. If studies are rigorous, precision is lost when a reviewer gives an impressionistic summary. Certain purposes, however, may be served by the discursive format. For example, practitioners and policymakers who are unfamiliar with formal techniques or unwilling to rely solely on numerical indices may find narrative reviews more accessible. When writing for a broad audience, a reviewer may choose to supplement effect sizes and significance tests with discussion of specific studies.

A narrative presentation might also be appropriate for stimulating future research or encouraging program improvements. Reviews often explore such questions as: How are studies designed? What are their major strengths and weaknesses? How easy or difficult was it to implement the treatment? Are there important but "overlooked" program characteristics? Answering such questions gives newcomers to a field and nonspecialists a broad picture of "what the issues are." It gives policy makers some ideas about strengths and weaknesses of "overall" findings and how confident one can be in adopting some of the suggestions. It may offer researchers important insights, not only about how to interpret findings of existing studies, but also how to improve future efforts.

An example of using a narrative review to improve research comes from criminal justice professionals' response to Lipton, Martinson, and Wilks's (1975) review of 231 studies of rehabilitation of delinquents. Recall that their finding, mentioned earlier, was that "except for few and isolated instances, the rehabilitative efforts that have been reported so far have had no appreciable effect on recidivism" (Sechrest, White, & Brown, 1979, p. 27). This detailed summary had such profound implications for both academic researchers and corrections administrators that in 1976 the National Academy of Sciences convened a blue ribbon panel of experts. It was charged with reviewing existing evaluations "to determine whether they provide a basis for any conclusions about the effectiveness of rehabilitative techniques, clarifying the difficulties of measuring the effectiveness of treatment programs, and recommending methodological strategies for evaluating treatment programs" (Sechrest, White, & Brown, 1979, p. 4).

The panel included specialists in corrections, economists, lawyers, statisticians, psychologists, sociologists, and administrators. They represented diverse political perspectives. Using the narrative review reported by Lipton and his colleagues as a starting point, they looked carefully at existing rehabilitation research and found many weaknesses, including poor research designs, ineffective measurement of outcomes, and incompletely or poorly implemented treatments. A subsample of those studies was selected by Fienberg and Grambsch (1979) for reevaluation and reanalysis. They found that "where the original review erred, it was almost invariably by an overly lenient assessment of the methodology of a study or by a failure to maintain an appropriately critical set in evaluating statistical analyses. The net result was that Lipton et al. were, if anything, more likely to accept evidence in favor of rehabilitation than was justified" (p. 119).

Because of this National Academy review, researchers and administrators now have a context in which to place past research. Future research on delinquency rehabilitation should be strengthened by the specific suggestions of Sechrest, White, and Brown (1979, see especially chapters 3, 4, and 5). In addition, new substantive suggestions emerged from the National Academy of Sciences follow-up. For example, one recommendation is that more attention be paid to the needs of and opportunities for rehabilitative programs outside prisons. Descriptive information in evaluations often indicates that prison is an ineffective place for many interventions, such as job training and counseling. The review also found scattered evidence that timing is critical in the effectiveness of certain kinds of interventions, suggesting that research on timing might be particularly productive.

To summarize, a narrative review led to a better understanding of weaknesses in existing studies and generated specific suggestions for promising innovations in the future. The review offered a context for scattered findings, incorporating details about program implementations and study designs as well as outcomes. While a quantitative synthesis would have given more structure to the outcome summaries, the goal of research improvement was well served by the discursive format.

Strategy Three: Allying Statistical and Descriptive Evidence

Each of the above two strategies treats the synthesis process as one of *translation*. Words and numbers are different "languages." So for consistency words must be transformed into numbers or vice versa.

Both strategies have a crucial weakness. *By transforming one perspective into the other, its unique benefits are weakened.* Statistical summaries lose their precision when transformed into narratives. Similarly, case descriptions lose their richness of detail when they are summarized with a simple numerical index.

We think it worthwhile for reviewers to work hard toward building an "alliance of evidence," including both quantitative and descriptive elements in the same review, while maintaining the integrity of each. Each kind of information offers unique benefits. This view is consistent with models presented by Reichardt and Cook (1979) and others for integrating different kinds of evidence within a *single* study. Similarly, rather than choosing between numbers and narrative when combining results across several studies, we need instead to determine where each is most useful, and use them in synchrony.

But this is easier said than done. One obstacle is a polarized view of numbers and words; more of one must result in less of the other. We prefer to view them as two separate dimensions. Then we can *independently* categorize any single study along each, as in Figure 2. Cook and Leviton (1980) put it well, pointing out that the best synthesis makes the most out of both types of information:

> What we have, then, is a difference in priorities about two types of questions, each of which has value. Science needs to know its stubborn, dependable, general 'facts, and it also needs data-based, contingent puzzles that push ahead theory. Our impression is that

meta-analysts stress the former over the latter, and that many qualitative reviewers stress the latter more than the former (or at least more than meta-analysts do). Of course, neither the meta-analyst nor the qualitative reviewer *needs* to make either prioritization. Each can do both and any one reviewer can consciously use both qualitative and quantitative techniques in the same review. Indeed, s/he should. (p. 468)

FIGURE 2
Two Views of Combining Quantitative and Descriptive Information in a Research Synthesis

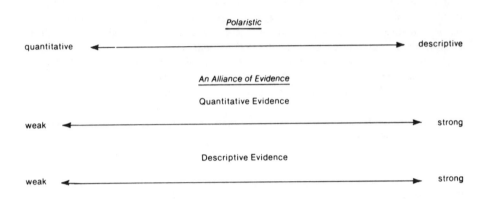

In this final section we look at three ways numerical and descriptive information interact. We believe they show how the benefits of combining quantitative and descriptive studies outweigh the simplicity afforded by an exclusive "choice" between paradigms.

Using statistics to identify relationships not apparent from visual inspection. One view of formal quantitative methods is *adversarial*. Statistical significance is a dreaded hurdle that must be cleared before a study is considered legitimate and worthy of discussion. This view is especially common among graduate students working on dissertations and researchers hoping to publish their work. Because of the relationship between statistical significance and sample size, "obviously positive" findings may be discarded because they come from studies with small samples, and therefore fail to reach an acceptable significance level.

Some recent comparisons of statistical versus visual criteria for assessing change suggest that statistics are more often ally than adversary: by relying solely on visual inspection of data summaries and subjective judgment, we are often likely to *overlook* small but reliable effects. One example is the work of Jones, Weinrott, and Vaught (1978) involving the results of operant experiments. They asked university faculty, researchers, and graduate students to visually inspect a series of graphs, and judge whether or not a reliable change had occurred. The changes also were tested statistically using standard time-series analyses. Comparison of visual and statistical procedures indicated a greater sensitivity for the latter, leading to the following conclusion: "If time-series analyses were used to supplement visual analysis . . . researchers would probably infer meaningful changes in their data more often than if visual inferences alone were used to analyze operant experiments" (p. 280).

A second example is Szucko and Kleinmuntz's (1981) comparison of clinical versus statistical procedures for detecting lies from polygraph charts. Six experienced polygraph interpreters who conducted "intuitive" evaluations were pitted against statistical procedures. The results demonstrated clear advantages of statistical detection: "Our results strongly suggest that human judges are ill-equipped to interpret polygraph protocols. . . . What we are suggesting based on our findings, therefore, is that the formula is better than the head and that lie detector tests should be interpreted actuarially rather than intuitively" (pp. 494-495). These examples are consistent with most studies comparing statistical and clinical procedures; statistics usually are more sensitive to small effects within a single study (Kratochwill, 1977; Meehl, 1965).

Can these findings be generalized to methods of combining studies as well? Apparently so. Cooper and Rosenthal (1980) asked university faculty and graduate students to summarize the results of seven investigations of sex differences in task persistence. Half the reviewers were asked to "employ whatever criteria you would use if this exercise were being undertaken for a class term paper or a manuscript for publication" (p. 445), and the other half were taught statistical combinatorial procedures. While several of the individual studies did not show significant sex differences, aggregation using statistical procedures resulted in an overall significant effect favoring females ($p = .016$).

Descriptive reviewers were significantly more likely than statistical reviewers to find little or no support for the hypothesis of a sex difference in persistence: "Traditional reviewers either neglect probabilities or combine them intuitively in an overly conservative fashion" (Cooper & Rosenthal, 1980, p. 448). However, the statistical reviewers did not unquestioningly accept the hypothesis as "proven." No one in either group concluded that there was "definite" support for the hypothesis. Furthermore, the type of reviewing procedure was not strongly related to recommendations for future research, or to judgments about the methodological adequacy of studies.

These findings suggest that statistical procedures can help a reviewer to identify relationships that may not be large enough to detect informally. Their worth should increase as the number of studies grows large, or when a program effect is small. One might wonder why a reviewer should be excited about turning up positive but small effects. We can suggest two reasons. First, limits on the degree of control that can be exerted over program participants in educational or medical innovations are likely to lead to small or incremental gains rather than "slam-bang" effects (Gilbert, Light, & Mosteller, 1975; Gilbert, McPeek, & Mosteller, 1977; Gottman & Glass, 1978). To wait for a new curriculum that doubles reading scores may often be to do nothing. Second, when a small effect is detected, it sometimes can be enhanced by program refinement. This requires a judgment about whether a modest finding is worth pursuing. Process analysis and expert judgment become particularly important here. This brings us to suggest a way to ally descriptive evidence with quantitative findings.

Using nonquantitative evidence after detecting a program effect. Statistical procedures can help both to identify small effects and to formalize the search for unusually successful or unsuccessful program outcomes, or "outliers." But such findings, standing alone, are not very informative. Suppose a reviewer looking at a dozen evaluations finds that, on the average, curriculum A slightly outperforms B, or that a review of ten studies of urban high schools shows one to be unusually effective. What should we make of these results? Formal procedures can *detect* subtle differences, but cannot *explain* them. *They offer a starting point, not a final answer.*

After an effect is identified statistically, the reviewer must try to explain why this finding exists. Is it replicable? What program characteristics are responsible? Can it be enlarged or improved. Answering these questions requires further efforts that often rely heavily on case studies and descriptive evidence. For example, McClintock, Brannon, and Maynard-Moody (1979) discuss Lazar and Darlington's (Note 5) quantitative synthesis of a group of preschool programs:

> Had each of the original investigations been a qualitative case study, then merging the data and collecting similar data at a later point in time would have been impossible. On the other hand, the absence of rich qualitative descriptions of the organizational features of the intervention programs made it difficult to explain some of the anomalies of the quantitative analyses. This suggests that research on single cases that incorporates a combination of qualitative and quantitative approaches would be optimal for secondary analysis and direct comparison with other cases. (p. 624)

Here, qualitative information was deemed necessary to explain the quantitative findings. We believe this example illustrates a more general point: qualitative case descriptions are particularly valuable in helping program managers interpret statistical findings. Most managers are conscientious and want to strengthen their program as much as possible. For them, it is especially useful to have descriptive data such as: What are the characteristics of successful implementations? How were the teachers trained? How were parents involved? What were details of the educational program? This information helps a manager to incrementally improve a program, using comparative findings from a review that give insights about *why* certain versions of a program or curriculum work better than others.

Descriptive information can help a manager make decisions at a "micro" program level, and at the same time it can provide "macro" information about program effectiveness, across hundreds of local sites. An illustration of this important function comes from federal regulations of daycare. Anticipating that the Federal Interagency Day Care Requirements would soon come up for renewal, the Department of Health, Education and Welfare in 1975 commissioned a four-year study to determine how different features of daycare centers affect participating children (Ruopp, Travers, Glantz, & Coelen, 1979). Existing studies were reviewed, and new quantitative outcome studies were conducted at fifty-seven sites. These included eight randomized trials and forty-nine "natural" experiments. The investigators expected two main policy variables to influence children: staff-to-child ratio (the higher the better) and level of staff training (the more the better). Group size, a third feature of the daycare centers, though not expected originally to be particularly important, turned out in the quantitative analysis across sites to be the most critical feature. Children in very large groups performed less well than children in smaller groups. This finding appeared in the quantitative analyses of both the randomized experiments and the "natural" studies.

To explain this unexpected result, careful process studies were done. They were qualitative and narrative in form. These analyses across many sites helped to explain why a center with four staff and thirty-two children had poorer outcomes on the average than a center with two staff and sixteen children, even though both had identical 1:8 staff-to-child ratios. Four adults in a room together spend a large fraction of their time talking to one another, rather than focusing on the children. Also, with several staff present, any one adult could assume, sometimes incorrectly, that "everyone else" is watching the children.

The quantitative analyses, together with the qualitative investigation of underlying reasons, were presented in 1979. They highlighted the unexpected importance of group size, and argued that regulators should focus on this feature of federally subsidized day-care centers as well as staff-to-child ratio and staff education. In 1980, new Federal Interagency Day Care Requirements were published. They drew heavily on both the numerical and narrative summaries, and a central feature was their limitation on group size (Boruch & Cordray, Note 6).

Using the alliance to capitalize on conflicting outcomes. We have emphasized the value of using quantitative and descriptive studies as allies rather than adversaries for data synthesis. Some years ago a review of the two different kinds of studies led to sharply contrasting findings, yet we believe this example illustrates our argument. In the 1940s a group of educators and psychologists working with mentally retarded individuals came to believe that glutamic acid would improve a person's capacity to learn, and that this would be reflected by higher IQ scores. In the late 1940s and early 1950s, a series of uncontrolled studies and case reports appeared in the medical and psychological literature, most of them finding a modest improvement in IQs of retarded people receiving the drug (Harney, 1950; Kane, 1953; Levine, 1949; Zimmerman & Burgmeister, 1950).

These findings did not go unchallenged. Skeptics pointed out many threats to the validity of the studies, and questioned how the drug worked physiologically to improve IQ. A series of controlled clinical trials were performed to examine the effects of glutamic acid more systematically (McCulloch, 1950; Quinn & Durling 1950a, 1950b; Zabrenko & Chambers, 1952). For example, McCulloch used matched experimental and control groups, with the controls receiving a placebo. Caretakers and examiners were not informed of subjects' group membership. Several of these experiments showed quickly and convincingly that glutamic acid did not outperform the placebo, though both groups showed an improvement over people receiving only the usual custodial care common in the 1940s. Astin and Ross (1960) summarized the discrepant findings between case reports and experimental studies, and concluded that the experimental evidence was far more convincing: glutamic acid is ineffective.

It is tempting to conclude from this example that the controlled, experimental, quantitative studies were "right," while the uncontrolled studies were "wrong," and that the latter served no useful scientific purpose. We come to a different conclusion: the conflicting results convey valuable information about improving the lives of retarded individuals. The controlled experiments are indeed convincing that glutamic acid does not raise IQ. But something was still working in the patients' behalf, since most of the earlier case reports documented IQ gains. Scientists were pressed to account for the improvement.

Contrasting the controlled and uncontrolled studies prompts us to examine the context in which the drug was administered. Including the uncontrolled studies in our review reveals an example of "studying the wrong treatment," discussed earlier. People receiving glutamic acid got far more environmental stimulation than was typical for people in custodial care. Increased attention and expectations also seemed to improve the performance of the "placebo group" in the experimental trials. One study (Zabrenko & Chambers, 1952) focused on the increased environmental stimulation directly and confirmed its positive impact on IQ.

This example illustrates how different forms of evidence, taken together, can lead to insights with important policy implications. The seemingly inconsistent findings end up providing information about both glutamic acid and supportive environments. Conflicts in outcomes have not hindered us. They have enriched educational practice.

The glutamic acid controversy occurred over twenty years ago, but the lesson still applies today. Different types of evidence are complementary, and single-mindedness about either quantitative or qualitative approaches to synthesis imposes unnecessary limits on what we can learn from the work of others. The pursuit of good science should transcend personal preferences for numbers or narrative.

Reference Notes

1. Herriot, R. E. *Federal initiatives and rural school improvement*. Findings from the Experimental School Program prepared for the National Institute of Education, by Abt Associates Inc., Cambridge, Mass., March 1980.
2. Salter, W. J. *Conducting social program evaluations*. Essay prepared for Bolt, Beranek, and Newman, Inc., Cambridge, Mass., August 1980.
3. Fosburg, S., & Glantz, F. *Analysis plan for the Child Care Food Program*. Submitted to the Food and Nutrition Service, U.S. Department of Agriculture, by Abt Associates Inc., Cambridge, Mass., April 1981.
4. Glass, G. V. *Bibliography of writings on the integration of research findings: The meta-analysis of research*. Unpublished manuscript, Laboratory of Educational Research, University of Colorado, 1978.
5. Lazar, I. & Darlington, R. *Lasting effects after preschool*. Final report, Department of Human Services, Cornell University, 1978.
6. Boruch, R. F., & Cordray, D. S. *An appraisal of educational program evaluations: Federal, state, and local agencies* (Report to the U.S. Department of Education, Contract 300-79-0467). Evanston, Ill.: Northwestern University, June 1980.

References

Astin, A. A., & Ross, S. Glutamic acid and human intelligence. *Psychological Bulletin*, 1960, **57**, 429-434.

Bailey, W. C. Correctional outcome: An evaluation of 100 reports. *Journal of Criminal Law, Criminology, and Police Science*, 1966, **57**, 153-160.

Belsky, J., & Steinberg, L. D. The effects of day care: A critical review. *Child Development*, 1978, **49**, 929-949.

Campbell, D. T. Degrees of freedom and the case study. *Comparative Political Studies*, 1975, **8**, 178-193.

Cliff, N. Adverbs as multipliers. *Psychological Review*, 1959, **66**, 27.

Cook, T. D., & Leviton, L. C. Reviewing the literature: A comparison of traditional methods with meta-analysis. *Journal of Personality*, 1980, **48**, 449–472.

Cooper, H. M., & Rosenthal, R. Statistical versus traditional procedures for summarizing research findings. *Psychological Bulletin*, 1980, **87**, 442–449.

Dukes, W. F. N = 1. *Psychological Bulletin*, 1965, **64**, 74–79.

Durlak, J. A. Comparative effectiveness of paraprofessional and professional helpers. *Psychological Bulletin*, 1979, **86**, 80–92.

Eysenck, H. J. An exercise in mega-silliness. *American Psychologist*, 1978, **33**, 517.

Fienberg, S., & Grambsch, P. An assessment of the accuracy of "The Effectiveness of Correctional Treatment." Appendix to L. Sechrest, S. White, & E. Brown (Eds.), *The rehabilitation of criminal offenders: Problems and prospects*. Washington, D.C.: National Academy of Sciences, 1979.

Freeman, F. N., Holzinger, K. J., & Mitchell, B. C. The influence of environment on the intelligence, school achievement, and conduct of foster children. *Twenty-Seventh Yearbook of the National Society of Education*, 1928, **27** (Pt. 1), 367–384.

Gallo, P. S., Jr. Meta-analysis — A mixed meta-phor. *American Psychologist*, 1978, **33**, 515–517.

Gilbert, J. P., Light, R. J., & Mosteller, F. Assessing social innovations: An empirical base for policy. In C. A. Bennett & A. A. Lumsdaine (Eds.), *Evaluation and experiment*. New York: Academic Press, 1975.

Gilbert, J. P., McPeek, B., & Mosteller, F. Progress in surgery and anesthesia: Benefits and risks of innovation therapy. In J. Bunker, B. Barnes, & F. Mosteller (Eds.), *Costs, risks and benefits of surgery*. New York: Oxford University Press, 1977.

Glass, G. V. Primary, secondary, and meta-analysis of research. *Educational Researcher*, 6 (9), 1976, 3–8.

Glass, G. V. Integrating findings: The meta-analysis of research. *Review of Research in Education*, 1977, **5**, 351–379.

Glass, G. V., McGaw, B., & Smith, M. L. *Meta-analysis of social research*. Beverly Hills, Calif.: Sage, 1981.

Glass, G. V., & Smith, M. L. *Meta-analysis of research on the relationship of class size and achievement*. San Francisco: Far West Laboratory for Educational Research and Development, 1978.

Gottman, J. J., & Glass, G. V. Analysis of interrupted time-series experiments. In T. R. Kratochwill (Ed.), *Single subject research*. New York: Academic Press, 1978.

Hall, J. A. Gender effects of decoding nonverbal cues. *Psychological Bulletin, 1978*, **85**, 845–857.

Harney, M. *Some psychological characteristics of retarded girls before and following treatment with glutamic acid*. Washington, D.C.: Catholic University American Press, 1950.

Hedges, L. B., & Olkin, I. Vote-counting methods in research synthesis. *Psychological Bulletin*, 1980, **88**, 359–369.

Herson, M., & Barlow, D. H. *Single-case experimental designs: Strategies for studying behavior change*. New York: Pergamon, 1976.

Hood, R., & Sparks, R. *Key issues in criminology*. New York: McGraw Hill, 1970.

Jackson, G. B. Methods for integrative reviews. *Review of Educational Research*, 1980, **50**, 438–460.

Jones, R. R., Weinrott, M. R., & Vaught, R. S. Effects of serial dependency on the agreement between visual and statistical inference. *Journal of Applied Behavior Analysis*, 1978, **11**, 277–283.

Kamin, L. J. Comment on Munsinger's review of adoption studies. *Psychological Bulletin*, 1978, **85**, 194–201.

Kane, E. D. Differential indications for the use of glutamic acid. *American Journal of Psychiatry*, 1953, **109**, 699–700.

Kennedy, M. M. Generalizing from single case studies. *Evaluation Quarterly*, 1979, **3**, 661–678.

Kratochwill, T. R. N = 1: An alternative research strategy for school psychologists. *Journal of School Psychology*, 1977, **15**, 239–249.

Kratochwill, T. R. *Single subject research*. New York: Academic Press, 1978.

Kulik, J. A., Kulik, C. C., & Cohen, P. A. A meta-analysis of outcome studies of Keller's personalized system of instruction. *American Psychologist*, 1979, **34**, 307-318.

Lazarsfeld, P., & Robinson, W. S. The quantification of case studies. *Journal of Applied Psychology*, 1940, **14**, 817-825.

Levine, E. S. Can we speed up the slow child? *Volta Review*, 1949, **51**, 269-270.

Lewis, C. E., Lorimer, A., Lindesman, C., Palmer, B. B., & Lewis, M. A. An evaluation of the impact of school nurse practitioners. *Journal of School Health*, 1974, **44**, 331-335.

Light, R. J. Capitalizing on variation: How conflicting research findings can be helpful for policy. *Educational Researcher*, 1979, **8** (8), 3-8.

Light, R. J., & Smith, P. V. Accumulating evidence: Procedures for resolving contradictions among different studies. *Harvard Educational Review*, 1971, **41**, 429-471.

Lipton, D., Martinson, R., & Wilks, J. The effectiveness of correctional treatment: A survey of treatment evaluation studies. New York: Praeger, 1975.

Mahoney, M. J. *Scientist as subject*. Cambridge, Mass.: Ballinger, 1976.

McClintock, C. C., Brannon, D., & Maynard-Moody, S. Applying the logic of sample surveys to qualitative case studies: The case cluster method. *Administrative Science Quarterly*, 1979, **24**, 612-629.

McCulloch, T. L. The effect of glutamic acid feeding on cognitive abilities of institutionalized mental defectives. *American Journal of Mental Deficiency*, 1950, **55**, 117-122.

Meehl, P. E. Seer over sign: The first good example. *Journal of Experimental Research in Personality*, 1965, **1**, 27-32.

Merenstein, J. H., Wolfe, H., & Barker, K. M. The use of nurse practitioners in a general practice. *Medical Care*, 1974, **12**, 445-452.

Miles, M. B. Qualitative data as an attractive nuisance: The problem of analysis. *Administrative Science Quarterly*, 1979, **24**, 590-601.

Mosteller, F. Swine Flu: Quantifying the "possibility." *Science*, 1976, **192**, 1286-1288.

Mosteller, F., & Bush, R. R. Selected quantitative techniques. In G. Lindzey (Ed.), *Handbook of social psychology: Theory and method* (Vol. 1). Cambridge, Mass.: Addison-Wesley, 1954.

Munsinger, H. The adopted child's IQ: A critical review. *Psychological Bulletin*, 1974, **82**, 623-659.

Munsinger, H. Reply to Kamin. *Psychological Bulletin*, 1978, **85**, 202-206.

Murray, C. A., & Cox, L. A., Jr. *Beyond probation: Juvenile corrections and the chronic delinquent*. Beverly Hills, Calif.: Sage, 1979.

Patton, M. Q. *Qualitative evaluation methods*. Beverly Hills, Calif.: Sage, 1980.

Pillemer, D. B., & Light, R. J. Benefiting from variation in study outcomes. *New Directions for Methodology of Social and Behavioral Science*, 1980, **5**, 1-12. (a)

Pillemer, D. B., & Light, R. J. Synthesizing outcomes: How to use research evidence from many studies. *Harvard Educational Review*, 1980, **50**, 176-195. (b)

Presby, S. Overly broad categories obscure important differences between therapies. *American Psychologist*, 1978, **33**, 514-515.

Quinn, K. V., & Durling, D. New experiment in glutamic acid therapy: 24 cases classified as mental deficiency, undifferentiated, treated with glutamic acid for six months. *American Journal of Mental Deficiency*, 1950, **55**, 227-234. (a)

Quinn, K. V., & Durling, D. Twelve months' study of glutamic acid therapy in different clinical types in an institution for the mentally deficient. *American Journal of Mental Deficiency*, 1950, **54**, 321-322. (b)

Reichardt, C. S., & Cook, T. D. Beyond qualitative *versus* quantitative methods. In T. D. Cook & C. S. Reichardt (Eds.), *Qualitative and quantitative methods in evaluation research*. Beverly Hills, Calif.: Sage, 1979.

Rosenthal, R. Combining results of independent studies. *Psychological Bulletin*, 1978, **85**, 185-193.

Rosenthal, R. Summarizing significance levels. *New Directions for Methodology of Social and Behavioral Science*, 1980, **5**, 33-46.

Rosenthal, R., & Rubin, D. B. Interpersonal expectancy effects: The first 345 studies. *Behavioral and Brain Sciences*, 1978, **3**, 377-415.

Ruopp, R., Travers, J., Glantz, F., & Coelen, C. *Children at the center: Report of the National Day Care Study*. Cambridge, Mass.: Abt Books, 1979.

Sechrest, L., White, S., & Brown, E. (Eds.). *The rehabilitation of criminal offenders: Problems and prospects*. Washington, D.C.: National Academy of Sciences Press, 1979.

Selvidge, J. *Assigning probabilities to rare events*. Unpublished doctoral dissertation, Harvard University, 1972.

Smith, M. L., & Glass, G. V. Meta-analysis of psychotherapy outcome studies. *American Psychologist*, 1977, **32**, 752-760.

Stake, R. E. The case study method in social inquiry. *Educational Researcher*, 1978, **7** (2), 5-8.

Szucko, J. J., & Kleinmuntz, B. Statistical versus clinical lie detection. *American Psychologist*, 1981, **36**, 488-496.

Tukey, J. W. The future of data analysis. *Annals of Mathematical Statistics*, 1963, **33**, 13-14.

Walberg, H. J., & Haertel, E. H. Research integration: The state of the art. *Evaluation in education: An international review series* (special issue), 1980, **4**, 1-142.

White, S. H. Social proof structures: The dialectic of method and theory in the work of psychology. In N. Datan & H. Reese (Eds.), *Life-span developmental psychology: Dialectical perspectives on experimental research*. New York: Academic Press, 1977.

Wilson, J. Q. "What works" revisited: New findings on criminal rehabilitation. *The Public Interest*, Fall 1980, No. 61, pp. 3-17.

Yin, R. K., & Heald, K. A. Using the case survey method to analyze policy studies. *Administrative Science Quarterly*, 1975, **20**, 371-381.

Yin, R. K., Bingham, E., & Heald, K. A. The difference that quality makes: The case of literature reviews. *Sociological Methods and Research*, 1976, **5**, 139-156.

Zabrenko, R. N., & Chambers, G. S. An evaluation of glutamic acid in mental deficiency. *American Journal of Psychiatry*, 1952, **108**, 881-887.

Zigler, E., & Trickett, P. K. IQ, social competence, and evaluation of early childhood intervention programs. *American Psychologist*, 1978, **33**, 789-798.

Zimiles, H. M. On making developmental psychology more relevant. *SCRD Newsletter*, Fall, 1980.

Zimmerman, F. T., & Burgmeister, B. B. The effect of glutamic acid on borderline and high-grade defective intelligence. *New York State Journal of Medicine*, 1950, **50**, 693-697.

2

Reviewing the Literature
A Comparison of Traditional Methods with Meta-Analysis[1]

Thomas D. Cook and Laura C. Leviton

Abstract

Meta-analysis is the name given to a set of techniques for reviewing
research in which the data from different studies are statistically combined.
Meta-analysts have criticized the more traditional qualitative methods of
review on three principal grounds: (1) that relevant information is ignored
in favor of a simplistic box count of the number of studies in which a
particular relationship is and is not statistically significant; (2) that the
sample of studies for review often contains important biases; and (3) that
box counts ignore statistical interactions. Our discussion suggests that
these criticisms are not intrinsic to qualitative reviews, but rather represent
poor practices by reviewers using traditional methods. Moreover, although
meta-analysis has some advantages, it is not without its unique limitations.
Our comparison of both methods is applied to the qualitative literature
review of Zuckerman (1979) and the meta-analysis of Arkin, Cooper, and
Kolditz (1980) which reached different conclusions about the "existence"
of self-serving attributions in studies of interpersonal influence.

Literature reviews have long played a central role in scientific
development. Science is a cumulative endeavor. In psychology,
any one study is suspect, but because of the impossibly large array
of validity threats that must be ruled out (Cook & Campbell, 1979),
and also because strong tests of a theory require that predictions
be made about multiple empirical relationships that compose a
"nomological net" (Cronbach & Meehl, 1955). One purpose of literature reviews is to establish the "facts." These are the stubborn,
dependable relationships that regularly occur despite any biases
that may be present in particular studies because of the implicit
theories behind the investigator's choice of measures, observation
schedules, and the like (Stegmuller, 1978). At present, psychologists largely depend on the qualitative literature review to establish

1. Reprint requests should be sent to the first author, Department of Psychology,
Northwestern University, Evanston, Ill. 60201. We would like to thank Drs. Albert
Erlebacher, Kenneth Howard, and Daniel Romer for their assistance and suggestions. Partial support was received from the U.S. Department of Agriculture, Contract #53-3198-9-26.

From Thomas D. Cook and Laura C. Leviton, "Reviewing the Literature: A Comparison of Traditional Methods with Meta-Analysis," 48(4) *Journal of Personality* 449-472 (December 1980).
Copyright © 1980, Duke University Press (Durham, NC). Reprinted by permission of the publisher.

"facts." Such a review requires drawing up a list of theoretically relevant studies, examining each study for "methodological adequacy," and then counting the number of adequate and relevant studies which confirm and disconfirm a particular relationship. This last step is called the "box count," and typically the box in which the highest count falls is "voted" the winner (Light & Smith, 1971).

For reasons we discuss later, some researchers have expressed dissatisfaction with qualitative reviews. Glass (1978b; Glass & Smith, 1979; Smith & Glass, 1977) and others propose a set of alternatives called "meta-analysis" which brings standard data analytic techniques to bear in reviewing research. To do this, studies relevant to a conceptual issue are collected, summary statistics from each study (e.g., means or correlations) are treated as the units of analysis, and the aggregate data are then analyzed in quantitative tests of the proposition under examination.

Meta-analysis has created recent controversy because studies undertaken with this orientation have repeatedly reached less conservative conclusions about the presence and magnitude of particular conceptual relationships than have traditional literature reviews.[2] For instance, Glass and Smith (1979) concluded that class size affects the achievement of children, while qualitative reviews were inconsistent in their conclusions (Educational Research Service, 1978; Ryan & Greenfield, 1976). Also, Smith and Glass (1977) concluded that all the types of psychotherapy they examined were effective in improving outcomes by at least one-half of a standard deviation; whereas qualitative reviews have generally disagreed both on the effectiveness of specific therapies and the effectiveness of psychotherapy overall (Bandura, 1969; Bergin, 1971; Eysenck, 1952; Luborsky, Singer, & Luborsky, 1975; Rachman, 1971). Because meta-analysis appears to be less conservative (and less "subjective") than qualitative reviews, pressure may arise in the near future to make meta-analysis obligatory for many kinds of dissertation, grant proposal, and research report, as well as for reviews in journals such as *Psychological Bulletin*.

A controversy in the *Journal of Personality* reflects the need to examine the merits of meta-analysis more closely. Using qualitative techniques, Zuckerman (1979) concluded that studies involving subjects' influence over other persons did not show self-serving

---

2. It is probably the case that qualitative reviews are more conservative in their conclusions than meta-analyses. Cooper and Rosenthal (1980) tested this hypothesis by randomly assigning graduate students and faculty members to review a set of related studies, using either a meta-analytic technique or the traditional qualitative method. Reviewers who used meta-analysis believed that there was more support for the phenomenon under study than did qualitative reviewers.

biases in attribution. But employing meta-analytic methods, Arkin, Cooper, and Kolditz (1980) concluded that such studies generally did show the bias in question. We have been asked by the editors of *Journal of Personality* to comment upon the debate between Zuckerman and Arkin, Cooper, and Kolditz by relating it to issues about meta-analysis in general. To do this, we shall describe the major meta-analytic techniques, compare them to traditional methods of review, and then use this comparison to comment upon the work of Zuckerman and of Arkin, Cooper, and Kolditz.

Some Meta-Analytic Techniques

Space does not permit us to describe either the full range of meta-evaluative techniques used by scholars (Cook & Gruder, 1978) or all the available meta-analytic techniques using data analysis. Detailed technical descriptions can be found elsewhere (Cooper, 1979; Glass, 1976, 1978b; Light & Smith, 1971). Our purpose here is to supply only enough detail for the reader to gain an idea of the purposes that each method serves.

Glass and his colleagues have developed a method of meta-analysis that relies on effect sizes as the unit of analysis. Effect sizes are computed for each study by taking the difference between the means of experimental and control groups (or some proxy for this) and dividing by the standard deviation. Glass and his colleagues then take the average of the effect sizes as their summary statistic, which is expressed in standard deviation units. By converting the findings of studies to a common metric, the estimate of average impact can be based upon a wide range of conceptually related measures and hence a larger sample of studies.

Although Glass and his colleagues use the average of effect sizes as their summary statistic, they also examine some of the methodological and substantive characteristics of studies on which the size of the effect may depend. Thus, in their meta-analysis of psychotherapy, Smith and Glass (1977) divided therapies into behavioral and nonbehavioral types and discovered that the average effect size was similar for each type. Glass and his colleagues have also employed regression analysis to make sure that effect sizes were not highly correlated with irrelevant attributes of studies. For example, the psychotherapy meta-analysis showed that an index of methodological quality accounted for only one percent of the variance in effect sizes (Glass, 1978c). This implies that, *within the limits imposed by the validity of the index*, studies of higher and lower quality reached similar conclusions about impact.

Rosenthal (1969, 1976) developed the "package" of meta-analytic techniques used by Arkin, Cooper, and Kolditz to examine self-serving biases in attribution, also used by Cooper (1979) to ascertain the conditions under which sex differences in conformity appear, and also by Rosenthal and Rubin (1978) to summarize evidence for the experimenter expectancy effect. This package consists of four elements. First, the probability values from each test of the relevant theoretical hypothesis are combined to reflect the probability, across all the studies, with which the null hypothesis can be rejected (Mosteller & Bush, 1954; Stouffer, 1949). From this same method of combining probabilities, Rosenthal and his colleagues are able to estimate the number of studies with "no effect" conclusions that would be necessary to change the obtained probability level to .05. This second element provides some assurance that, even if some studies are missed by the review, the results of the meta-analysis will not be seriously biased in favor of reaching conventional statistical significance levels.

Rosenthal's emphasis on aggregating probability values reflects his concern with testing specific theoretical hypotheses—in his case about experimenter and teacher expectancies. While combining p values is one reasonable procedure for postulating "whether an effect exists," it is not comprehensive. On the one hand, hypothesis testing does not describe the magnitude of a relationship, and on the other, it is overly dependent on sample size. For these reasons, Rosenthal now includes a third element in his package, the calculation of effect sizes, in much the same manner as Glass and his colleagues. Finally, Rosenthal and his colleagues employ a table presented by Cohen (1969) which shows the degree of overlap in the distributions of the experimental and control groups. A large average effect would indicate little overlap between the two distributions.

Light (1979; Light & Smith, 1971) has suggested a purpose for meta-analysis that is quite different from that of Rosenthal and Glass. The details of how to conduct such an analysis, and a critical examination of these details, are still lacking. While Glass and Rosenthal emphasize broad summary statements about areas of research (e.g., psychotherapy does have a beneficial effect), Light deliberately deemphasizes such statements. Instead, he advocates exploring the data from a set of similar studies to determine the populations or settings in which specific treatments do and do not have effects. To do this, he examines raw data from studies with identical measures rather than summary statistics from studies with different but conceptually related measures. Light's claim is that his procedures permit more flexibility in exploring the data, though they reduce the sample size of studies.

Because he wants to generate contingency-theoretic statements about treatments, settings, and populations, Light's approach holds potential for social psychologists who are interested in investigating the variability of findings over time and settings (Gergen, 1973), the interaction between personality traits and situations (Mischel, 1968), and the use of interactions to help specify external validity and the construct validity of manipulations, measures, and relationships (Cook & Campbell, 1979).

Criticisms of Qualitative Review Methods

Meta-analysts justify their techniques, in part, by pointing to some failings of the typical "box count" as it is employed in qualitative reviews. They make three principal criticisms about traditional review techniques. First, some information is ignored; second, the sample of studies may be biased; and third, statistical interactions may not be detected. We will now elaborate on these criticisms, citing qualitative reviews that can justly be criticized on each of these grounds. For each criticism, we then ask whether it reflects an intrinsic limitation of the qualitative review or a common poor practice that new reviews could change. Finally, we ask whether meta-analysis is itself flawless in these three regards and point to some ways in which it is not.

Information ignored by qualitative review. Light and Smith (1971) argue that the typical review ignores information about the magnitude of relationships and about their direction in favor of simple counts of the frequency with which hypotheses are and are not confirmed at conventional levels of statistical significance. Counting the incidence of significant p values is overly conservative. This is because results which are in the right direction but fail to reach statistical significance will be counted as failures to corroborate the hypothesis. Yet the statistical power of the tests in question may be so low that unrealistically large effects would have to be obtained to produce significance with the particular sample size. In psychology—with its tradition of laboratory experiments using small samples—a reliance on counts of statistical significance will predispose qualitative reviews to a modal finding of "no difference." That the power of research in social psychology is often low was illustrated by Cohen (1962) in a review of studies published in the *Journal of Abnormal and Social Psychology.*

Effect sizes and other estimates of magnitude are less dependent on sample size than are significance tests. Moreover, even if effect sizes are small and not significant for individual studies, they add information if the results are in the same direction as other studies. Indeed, Cronbach and Snow (1976) have pointed out that many unbiased studies which individually show no significant differences can lead to rejection of the null hypothesis if most of them have mean differences in the same direction. Yet in many box counts the direction of nonsignificant results is not even reported. Thus, in an analysis of a random sample of literature reviews from the behavioral sciences, Jackson (1978) found that only four of 28 reviews reporting the results of individual studies also included information about the direction of nonsignificant findings. If readers wanted to eliminate the box labeled "not statistically significant" and instead restrict the count to relationships with one sign and those with the opposite sign, they could seldom do this from the information in published reviews.

Reviews of psychotherapeutic outcomes illustrate the consequences of ignoring effect sizes and the direction of findings, since in these reviews the heavy reliance on box counts of significance tests may partly explain the discrepancy between the findings of qualitative reviewers and those of Smith and Glass (1977). For example, Bergin's (1971) influential review relied solely on statistical significance to assign studies to boxes. In some studies in Bergin's review, the sample of subjects was very small—as low as 10 and 12. While most studies had at least 30 subjects, even 30 is small when half the subjects constitute a control group. Moreover, studies of over 400 subjects appear to be weighted equally with small sample studies, and no cognizance appears to be taken of the issue of statistical power. Interestingly, magnitude estimates do appear in some reviews of psychotherapeutic outcomes, in the form of correlations (e.g., Luborsky et al., 1971). However, they are not the reviewers' primary source of information in reaching conclusions; and prior to Smith and Glass (1977) no one thought to aggregate the correlational studies because the measures were so heterogeneous (Howard, Note 1).

Is the overdependence on statistical hypothesis tests intrinsic to qualitative reviews, or does it merely reflect poor practices? The latter is the case. Some qualitative reviews make extensive use of effect sizes. For instance, Mischel (1968) used effect sizes in the form of correlations to argue for an interaction between personality traits and the situation in predicting behavior. Cartwright (1971) also used a form of magnitude estimates in showing that group decisions in the risky shift paradigm were of trivial magnitude—before he went on to show that an artifact was probably responsible for any effect there appeared to be. Qualitative reviews do use information about the direction of results (Cook et al., 1979) and sometimes differentially weight findings by sample size of the studies (Jencks et al., 1972). Criticisms of qualitative reviews based on misunderstandings of statistical significance are not criticisms of the review method. Indeed, many qualitative reviews share the same assumptions about the role of statistical significance testing that lead some meta-analysts to ignore statistical significance in favor of estimates of effect size.

If reviewers were sensitized to the problems of significance tests, these bad practices might not be so pervasive. However, a strong tendency exists in research and training in psychology, with its traditional emphasis on testing theoretical hypotheses with small samples, to accept only significant findings and not even to report, let alone discuss, the direction of nonsignificant effects or effect sizes. In this respect psychology is markedly different from economics, where statistical significance is of trivial importance and effect size is dominant; or even from education, in which recognition of the importance of effect sizes is increasing (Cronbach & Snow, 1976).

Both meta-analysis and qualitative reviews can make proper use of effect sizes and the direction of findings. For reviews with a moderate number of studies, perusal of a box count of effect sizes could well lead to the same conclusion as a meta-analytic summary. Indeed, we hope to demonstrate that this is the case for the review by Arkin, Cooper, and Kolditz. For reviews with a great many studies, we are prepared to agree that meta-analysis can be more usefully employed, for convenience and to avoid cognitive overload (Glass, 1978b).

Meta-analysis has one potential disadvantage in its reliance on effect sizes and its claim for greater precision than qualitative reviews (Arkin, Cooper, & Kolditz, 1980; Jackson, 1978). In order to take the precision of an effect size seriously, one must assume that there is equal bias across studies. That is, irrelevancies that inflate a relationship in one direction in some studies are counterbalanced by equally potent irrelevancies inflating it in the opposite direction in other studies. Alternatively, meta-analysts assume that the degree of bias can be validly estimated, and that studies can be weighted to eliminate the bias (Cooper, 1979; Mosteller & Bush, 1954). Some methods that meta-analysts use to detect bias are given in the next section. For the moment, we note that if the assumption of counterbalanced biases is wrong, a misplaced specificity will result. While qualitative reviews may be equally prone to bias, the descriptive accuracy of a point estimate in meta-analysis can have mischievous consequences because of its apparent "objectivity," "precision," and "scientism." To naive readers, these lend a social credibility that may be built on procedural invalidity.

Bias in the sample of studies. Qualitative reviews are also criticized for introducing potential biases into the sample of studies reviewed. A reviewer may introduce bias in at least three distinct

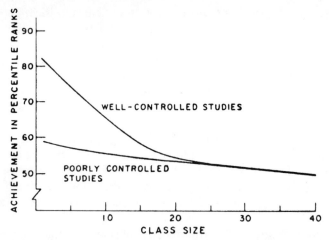

Figure 1. Effects of randomized and nonrandomized studies. Consistent regression lines for the regression of achievement (expressed in percentile ranks) onto class size for studies that were well controlled and poorly controlled in the assignment of pupils to classes.[3]

ways: the literature search may be so narrow as to omit relevant studies; some of the discovered studies may be excluded on methodological grounds; or studies may be excluded because the theoretical constructs are considered irrelevant. These three sources of bias are discussed below. Glass (1978b) notes that when studies are excluded on any grounds, it is not possible to ascertain whether the sample has become biased. His working assumption, which is shared by other meta-analysts, is that all the available published and unpublished studies of general substantive relevance should be included, and that the data should tell us whether different methods or different subsets of studies are associated with different magnitude estimates.

Meta-analysts like Rosenthal (1979) and Arkin, Cooper, and Kolditz (1980) stress the importance of a thorough literature search. Both published and unpublished studies (dissertations, for example) should be examined because editorial policies may bias published studies towards confirming replications or statistically significant studies. A recent meta-analysis by Smith (1980) supports

3. From G. V. Glass and M. L. Smith, Meta-analysis of research on class size and achievement, *Educational Evaluation and Policy Analysis,* 1979, 1, 2–16. Reprinted by permission.

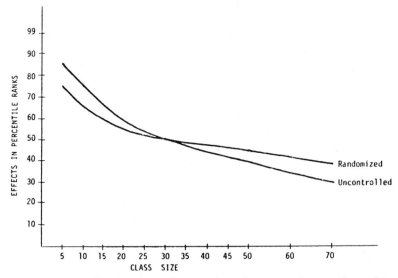

Figure 2. Effects of randomized and nonrandomized studies. Graph of the relationship of class size and effects on attitudes and instruction for studies using randomization versus uncontrolled studies (studies using matching or repeated measures produced intermediate effects and are not plotted).[4]

this contention. Published studies showed a .25 standard deviation tendency for counselors and therapists to stereotype women and view them more negatively than men, while unpublished studies showed an effect of equal magnitude for a bias against men.

Glass notes that in qualitative reviews studies are often excluded a priori for methodological reasons. This would perhaps be a reasonable procedure if all issues of methodology were resolved and no debates about methods could be heard. But such is not the case. Hence, Glass believes that if studies presumed to differ in methodological quality come to the same conclusions, then there is no point in excluding the studies of presumed lower quality. If different conclusions are reached, Glass is then prepared to give more weight to the higher quality studies. Consider Figures 1 and 2, which are taken from studies of the effects of class size on achievement (Glass & Smith, 1979) and nonachievement outcomes (Smith & Glass, 1979). Studies employing random assignment produced a pronounced effect of class size on achievement, while nonrandom

4. From Glass and Smith (1979). Reprinted by permission.

studies at best produced the effect very weakly. It seems, then, that different methods produced different conclusions, and that the results of the randomized studies should be treated as more valid. For nonachievement outcomes, on the other hand, both random and nonrandom studies showed similar effects of class size.

A bias in favor of narrowly defined constructs runs through many qualitative reviews. On the other hand, meta-analysts tend to prefer broader constructs (Arkin, Cooper, & Kolditz, 1980; Glass & Smith, 1979; Rosenthal & Rubin, 1978; Smith & Glass, 1977). Glass claims that broader constructs let the data decide whether relationships need respecifying in less global terms. Such respecification would be indicated, for example, if psychotherapy was beneficial as shown by questionnaires but not by therapists' ratings, or if "helping paradigms" resulted in attributions about performance that differed from the attributions found with other paradigms.

Letting the data specify cause and effect constructs leads to the criticism that meta-analysis aggregates "apples and oranges." In response, Glass notes that such aggregation is useful for the study of "fruit," and that it is often more useful to have knowledge about broader constructs than about subcategories. Thus he writes:

> In a field that lacks standard units of treatment and measurement, such as social psychology, all empiricism and reasoning is a problem at some level of coping with incommensurables. ... It is a common bad habit of thought in most psychological fields to press more distinctions on investigators than can be usefully made—distinctions without real or important underlying differences. (1978a, p. 395)

According to Smith and Glass (1977), the psychotherapy literature is an excellent illustration of the consequences of excluding studies from review because they do not employ preferred methods and constructs. In their own work, Smith and Glass located over 475 studies. Yet they note that qualitative reviews typically employ fewer than 100, often fewer than 40 studies; and they reach conflicting conclusions about the effectiveness of psychotherapy.

Is bias in the sample of reviewed studies intrinsic to qualitative reviews, or does the bias merely reflect poor practices? Although meta-analysis has highlighted afresh the importance of comprehensive samples, many excellent qualitative reviews have exhaustive samples. Moreover, like quantitative reviews, qualitative reviews can be self-correcting with respect to sampling bias. Thus, Jeanne Block (1976) located some studies of sex differences that Maccoby and Jacklin (1974) omitted from their mammoth review of over 1600 studies. According to Block, including these studies changed some of the original conclusions.

In addition, it is not inevitable that qualitative reviews take the narrow view and include only studies that meet restricted methodological criteria. For example, in particular substantive domains within evaluation research Boruch (1977), Campbell and Erlebacher (1970), and Director (1979), among others, have assessed the relative importance of randomized experiments compared to other alternatives. They did this by including all types of experiment and quasi-experiment in their review, examining the results for each type in a qualitative manner after having disaggregated the studies by method type, much as Glass did in his more quantitative work on class size.

Finally, qualitative reviews can take issue with the breadth or narrowness of constructs. Campbell's (1950) review of the attitude literature used qualitative methods to draw attention to the narrow use of self-report measures of attitudes, and to suggest that multiple measures of attitude were feasible and necessary if conclusions were to be drawn about a general construct, "attitude," rather than about specific constructs like "paper and pencil measures of attitude." Moreover, qualitative reviews can use broad conceptions of constructs and then "let the data decide" whether narrower definitions are necessary. For example, Block (1976) concluded from data presented by Maccoby and Jacklin (1974) that sex differences in cognitive restructuring emerged differentially for two different methods, indicating that narrower constructs were necessary for explaining the obtained data.

Sensitizing traditional reviewers to sampling bias may help them to locate studies from a wider variety of sources. Also, it may help them realize that the methodological criteria by which they evaluate a single study need not be as stringent as those they now use for including studies in a review. The major criterion for trusting the results of a single study is the appropriateness of the chosen methodology to the problem and the care with which the methods have been implemented. A review, on the other hand, can admit less successful studies provided that the assumption of zero overall bias is accepted or the set of studies can be broken down into those employing better and worse methods.

Meta-analysis has a distinct advantage over qualitative reviews when a large number of studies exist. This creates a situation of cognitive overload, particularly when many cross-tabulations are required to test for differences among methods or constructs (Cooper, 1979). The problems that arise from the multiple classification of variables is compounded when the variables under investigation have multiple levels. Consider the literature on class size. With class sizes varying from 1 to 50 it would be exceedingly difficult to make all possible comparisons of class size in a qualitative manner. For large samples, meta-analysis enhances the ease with which data can be manipulated and increases the ability to compute relationships that test whether particular irrelevancies of method or particular substantive variables influence the dependent variable in ways that aid interpretation.

If we turn now to the limitations of meta-analysis, it is worth repeating that meta-analysis cannot in and of itself detect bias that is preponderantly in one direction. The number of studies is a conceptual irrelevancy when the studies share sources of bias that predominantly operate in one direction. Indeed, the number of studies may even represent a psychological trap, for as the number of studies increases so too does the likelihood of invalid inductive leaps that create credible conclusions out of spurious findings. Campbell and Erlebacher (1970), and Director (1979) have illustrated this particular problem in their work on different substantive topics where "compensatory" treatments are assigned to persons who tend to have lower scores at the pretest when compared to no-treatment controls. This results in a constant bias to make the treatment look harmful. Wicker's (1969) review of the attitude-behavior relationship provides another example of a bias that prevailed across most of the studies in a review and produced an apparently credible consistency that in fact reflects bias. His conclusion that attitudes and behavior were only weakly related was based on the fact that in study after study their correlation seldom exceeded .30. However, errors of measurement attenuate the magnitude of relationships; and in most of the studies Wicker reviewed, reliabilities were probably closer to .5 than to 1.0. Had Wicker expressed the obtained correlations corrected for attenuation (where possible) or relative to the obtainable upper bound, his correlations would have been larger. Jack Block (1976) has made the same point about Mischel's (1968) review of the literature on consistency of individuals' behavior across situations.

An incidental negative side effect of the meta-analysts' concern with broad definitions of constructs may be a disregard for theoretical relevance and a vulnerability to misleading inductive inferences. To prevent this, meta-analysis should provide a breakdown by theoretically relevant variables. For example, if all past studies of the sleeper effect were included in a review without regard to how well the necessary conditions for a strong test of the effect were met, one would probably conclude from the many failures to obtain the effect that "it is time to lay the sleeper effect to rest" (Gillig & Greenwald, 1974). And the number of failures to obtain the effect would be psychologically impressive. Yet the very few studies that demonstrably met the theory-derived conditions for a strong test of the effect all obtained it (Cook et al., 1979), and one can surmise that these studies should be assigned greatest inferential weight because of their demonstrably higher theoretical relevance. A similar point can be made for the dissonance literature on the effects of low payments. A meta-analysis prior to 1972 would probably have concluded that the evidence for the dissonance effect was weak or inconsistent, because it seemed that for every study with posttest means in favor of the dissonance hypothesis, there was a study with means in favor of the opposite (so called, incentive) hypothesis. However, once the importance of choice and personal responsibility were fully recognized (Collins & Hoyt, 1972), the dissonance phenomenon came under theoretical control. We would consider as poor practice any literature review, qualitative or quantitative, that failed to exclude studies that were irrelevant on theoretical grounds, or that did not test for possible irrelevancies by disaggregating studies into those that provide stronger and weaker tests of theory.

We believe that meta-analysis is inappropriate for very small samples of studies if the studies are heterogeneous with respect to methods and constructs. Such heterogeneity implies that the studies are best considered as constructual replications in the broadest sense (Lykken, 1968), and with constructual replications the likelihood of method and construct factors limiting the degree of obtained correspondence is high. Yet with small samples one cannot test directly whether or not this is the case. If, on the other hand, researchers strive for "exact" replication, more confidence can be placed in small samples because the studies, while not identical, will be "somewhat" similar. Indeed, Light and Smith (1971) would often be prepared to assume that with "exact" replications one has increased the sample size of a single study. The conundrum here is that constructual replications are more valuable than exact replications, for constructual replications make heterogeneous many more of the methodological and substantive irrelevancies that can condition a particular relationship. Yet when studies are heterogeneous, we must have larger samples to be confident that the studies are representative of an underlying distribution (Gilbert, McPeek, & Mosteller, 1977). Note that, for research on novel topics where only a handful of studies exist, the sample is rarely "representative" of how later studies will be—much as the first five subjects in a study need not be "representative" of the entire sample.

The central limit theorem applies to samples of studies as to samples of subjects.

Theory building and sensitivity to interactions. Light and Smith (1971) have claimed that the traditional box count is insensitive to detecting statistical interactions. If so, this would be a serious drawback to traditional review methods, because statistical interactions play a crucial role in the testing of psychological theories. Most such theories deal with intervening variables (in the Mac-Corqudale & Meehl, 1948, sense) that will never be directly measurable, such as "anxiety," or "dissonance." Inferences about such constructs depend on postulating complex patterns of data—the "nomological net" of Cronbach and Meehl (1955)—and then seeing if obtained data patterns match the expected pattern. A further need is to rule out alternative explanations of the relationships, which is more likely if multivariate predictions are made that seem unique. Within personality and social psychology, interpretation of the forced compliance literature depends on complex interactions (Calder, Ross, & Insko, 1973; Collins & Hoyt, 1972), as does research on leadership effectiveness (Fiedler, 1964), or the interaction of situational and personological variables (Block, 1976; Mischel, 1976).

In Tukey's (1969) language, reviewers can use interactions either to confirm or explore relationships. They confirm relationships through two strategies. The first is between-studies. Reviewers search for studies that did, and studies that did not, manipulate or measure the independent variables that are crucial to the theory. The outcomes of these two sets of studies are then contrasted. The second strategy is within-studies; the reviewer conducts a standard box count or meta-analysis of outcomes in the subset of studies in which the potential interacting variables were manipulated or measured.

In the exploratory mode, reviewers examine sets of studies and try to infer any relationships that seem worth further exploration. They become detectives who use obtained data patterns as clues for generating potential explanatory concepts that specify the conditions under which a positive, null, or negative relationship holds between two variables. Light (1979) stresses such an exploratory orientation when he describes Title I evaluations in which over 50 classrooms showed achievement gains and over 50 showed losses: "In fact, do such results indicate random outcomes? I think not. Even though an 'on the average' analysis may show zero change, a study of the distribution of outcomes shows that if outcomes were random, with no underlying program effect we would expect about five significant gains and five significant losses . . ." (p. 10).

For a number of reasons, it is difficult to estimate how often qualitative reviews ignore interactions of importance. First, many reviews set out to test simple main effect propositions, and if no conclusions emerge for interactions, this may be because the interactions are considered irrelevant to the major research question. Second, in theoretical work a recognition of the need for interaction predictions often evolves slowly as the guiding theory is modified to account for past explanatory failures. When this happens, little or no information of high quality may be available from past studies about potential contingency variables. The reviewer is left with only a small sample of more recent work that can be used for sensitively testing or detecting interactions.

Qualitative reviews can detect interactions when the guiding theory is specific enough and the past studies can be organized into box counts based on whether a particular interaction did or did not occur. Collins and Hoyt (1972) did this in their "confirmatory" review of past studies of forced compliance. Qualitative reviews can also handle the exploratory mode of reviewing, and in the same way that Light (1979) suggests. The best narrative reviews identify and explain contradictory and unexpected data patterns for which no specific boxes were initially set up. Thus, Zajonc (1965) was able to develop his theory of social facilitation by bringing order into a disparate group of studies whose common features were the performance of a behavior and variation in the number of others present. He first noted an apparent contradiction, enhancement of performance in some studies but a decrement in others. He then became a detective and resolved the puzzle by illustrating that increases in performance occurred when skills were overlearned, and that decreases in performance occurred when skills were not overlearned. Extant theories of "arousal" were then used to give a theoretical explanation of the interaction that Zajonc discovered.

Glass and Rosenthal focus primarily on global summary statements rather than interactions. The interactions they do examine are based on disaggregating studies. Such disaggregation can bias the analysis towards an examination of nominal, demographic, and gross empirical characteristics such as methodological characteristics of studies, procedural details, and the sex and age of respondents. Theoretical variables are less likely to be considered. This bias is probably the result of limitations in the data base of studies for review, because potential interaction variables of theoretical interest may not be measured in every study. This does not deny the utility of interactions involving demographic variables. They often offer clues to the underlying psychological relationships that cause interactions. But they are only clues and are less direct tests of theoretical propositions than occur when a theoretical construct is directly measured.

The possibility of an inferential trap occurs when a meta-analysis across several procedural paradigms is statistically significant or reflects a large effect size, but the effect is specific to a subset of the paradigms. When this happens, some analysts tend to stress the main effect rather than the interaction that qualifies the main effect. For example, Cooper (1979) concluded that, over all paradigms, women conformed more than men. Yet a separate meta-analysis of each paradigm showed that the sex difference was confined to the set of 16 studies involving face-to-face interaction. No evidence was found with the 8 studies using fictitious group norms, and only weak trends in favor of greater female conformity were found in the 14 persuasive communication experiments. Making statements about a main effect could be interpreted to mean that greater conformity by females is transsituational, whereas it is situation-specific. Moreover, had there been fewer face-to-face studies, the obtained effect would have been smaller and perhaps not even statistically reliable. It is not comforting to think that conclusions about the generality of a main effect depend on the accidental rate at which face-to-face situations happen to have been chosen over other situations in past research. In Cooper's defense it should be noted, first, that he acknowledged the differences among procedural paradigms, and second, that Maccoby and Jacklin (1974) can be interpreted as having drawn a conclusion of no main effect across paradigms, even though they stressed the situations that predict sex-linked conformity. Our guess is that, with their stress on broad generalization, meta-analysts are even more prone than qualitative reviewers to overlook or to down play the importance of contingency-specifying interactions that in most situations have an inferential precedence over statements about main effects.

Application of These Observations to Zuckerman (1979) and Arkin, Cooper, and Kolditz (1980)

We now ask whether each of the major criticisms of qualitative reviews applies to Zuckerman's review, and whether the review of Arkin, Cooper, and Kolditz suffers from any of the disadvantages of meta-analysis. To illustrate our comparison, we refer the reader to Table 1 of Arkin, Cooper, and Kolditz (p. 438).

Zuckerman reviewed 13 studies concerning the attributions subjects made for their success or failure in influencing another person. Zuckerman divided these studies into three subcategories. The first category included five studies that used a paradigm in which the subject was a teacher and the target person a student (teacher-learner). The second category had four studies in which the subject was a therapist and the target of influence a client (client-therapist). The remaining four studies did not share a common theme or procedure (miscellaneous). These 13 studies are indicated by an asterisk in Table 1. After reviewing them, Zuckerman concluded that there was little evidence overall for a bias toward attributions that enhanced self-esteem in studies of interpersonal influence.

Arkin, Cooper, and Kolditz performed a meta-analysis of these 13 studies, together with 10 others that were not reviewed by Zuckerman. From the two articles, anonymous reviews, Zuckerman's review of Arkin et al., and Arkin's response, we gather that four of these ten studies appeared after Zuckerman's review was completed; four were potentially available but were omitted by Zuckerman; and two were omitted because—unlike Arkin, Cooper, and Kolditz—Zuckerman judged that their subject matter, helping behavior, did not fit the category of interpersonal influence situations. Overall, 23 studies were included in the meta-analysis by Arkin, Cooper, and Kolditz: 8 as teacher-student studies; 7 in the client-therapist paradigm; and 8 in the miscellaneous group. (One publication had two studies.)

Arkin, Cooper, and Kolditz performed meta-analyses, both of their own sample of 23 studies and of Zuckerman's smaller sample. Restricting ourselves for the moment to the smaller sample, Arkin, Cooper, and Kolditz agree with Zuckerman's overall conclusion: the 13 studies show little evidence for a main effect statement that attributions were self-serving. Moreover, scrutiny of Table 1 of Arkin, Cooper, and Kolditz leads us to the conclusion that any qualitative reviewer would come to the same conclusion, irrespective of whether statistical significance, the direction of findings, or effect sizes were used as the classification criterion. Arkin, Cooper, and Kolditz are correct in stating that Zuckerman ignored effect sizes and the direction of nonsignificant findings by relying on a box count of statistically significant effects. However, *in this particular instance* (though not in general) the additional information to be gained from effect sizes is somewhat marginal.

Arkin, Cooper, and Kolditz's meta-analysis of their own larger sample revealed a highly reliable main effect conclusion that attributions did show the self-serving bias. Zuckerman was, of course, not able to perform a qualitative review of this larger sample. However, when one performs a qualitative box count, one comes to the same conclusion as Arkin, Cooper, and Kolditz, although with possibly less confidence. Consider the 23 studies in their Table 1.

Eleven of these show statistically significant effects in the direction of the hypothesis, while only one would be expected by chance at the .05 level of significance. Thus, even a box count with statistical significance as the criterion shows self-serving attributions beyond a chance level in the larger set of studies. Using the direction of findings as a criterion, the same conclusion is indicated. Finally, scrutiny of the frequently large effect sizes increases our confidence in the conclusion that self-serving bias "exists" in such studies.

The above reflections suggest that Zuckerman and Arkin, Cooper, and Kolditz reached different conclusions because of differences in sampling and not because of any fundamental differences in review methods. The four studies that were reported after Zuckerman's review contribute three large and reliable findings in the positive direction and one finding reported as zero. Assuming no constant methodological bias, these buttress the conclusion that self-serving attributions were prevalent in these studies. The four studies that were available to Zuckerman, but which were overlooked, contribute two large positive findings and two findings listed as zero. Finally, the two helping studies excluded by Zuckerman add the largest and most reliable positive findings to the subcategory of miscellaneous studies that previously contained few positive findings of any reasonable magnitude. Note that the issue involved here is not meta-analysis *versus* qualitative reviews. Although meta-analysts typically prefer broader definition of constructs and larger samples, the more crucial issues concern later publication dates, more rigorous literature searches, and personal judgments about the theoretical relevance of individual studies.

In his review of the meta-analysis of Arkin, Cooper, and Kolditz, Zuckerman (Note 2) questions the relevance of including the helping studies by Stephan (1975) and Wells et al. (1977). He would probably also question the inclusion of an additional helping study by Arkin, Appelman, and Burger (1980). In addition, Zuckerman objected to the exact probability values that were reported for two studies, on the grounds that inappropriate groups were compared. These studies were Johnson, Feigenbaum, and Weiby (1964) and Schopler and Layton (1972).[5] With small samples of studies, it is difficult to resolve the issue of theoretical relevance. The typical meta-analytic strategy would be to "let the data decide." However, in this instance if one eliminated all the studies

5. Arkin, Cooper, and Kolditz appear to have complied with Zuckerman's suggested changes for three additional studies: Beckman (1970), Beckman (1973), and Mynatt and Sherman (1975), for which zero effect sizes, or simple blanks, are given.

in dispute, one would be reduced to nearly the same number of uncontested relevant studies that Zuckerman used, and the even smaller sample of contested studies would have two in which the appropriate statistics were not reported. Hence, the meta-analytic strategy of disaggregating studies is well-nigh impossible in this instance because of the small sample. It is not our task to rule on the appropriateness of the sample of Arkin, Cooper, and Kolditz. The arguments for and against including particular studies both have merit. What is needed is a greater number of studies using methods and constructs about which the contestants agree.

Although Zuckerman presented three categories of studies, he did not report conclusions for each one separately. Arkin, Cooper, and Kolditz, on the other hand, performed meta-analyses of each category, both for their own sample and for that of Zuckerman. For both samples, they concluded that the teacher-student studies showed inconsistent results, and the client-therapist studies showed reliable self-serving effects. The miscellaneous category resulted in a self-serving bias for the larger sample and in a trend in the same direction for Zuckerman's sample.

These meta-analyses of categories touch on the analysis of very small samples, Zuckerman's being five, four, and four, respectively. Consider the client-therapist studies, where by the flawed statistical significance criterion two of the studies in Zuckerman's sample suggested the effect, one showed no effects, and the fourth was statistically significant but in the opposite direction. Arkin, Cooper, and Kolditz derived an effect size of .56 for this category, favoring self-serving attributions. However, with such a small sample of heterogeneous studies the estimate of the average effect size is unstable, and it would be difficult to judge whether to treat the one contradictory study as a provisional "outlier" or as a clue indicating that an interaction theory is needed. Adding to this category the studies that Arkin, Cooper, and Kolditz found helped sway the judgment towards the first option. But it is easy to see how the results of the additional studies could have been in the opposite direction—in which case it would have been more meaningful to think in terms of interactions than of magnitude estimates for a main effect.

The treatment of interactions in these two reviews relates to their purposes. Zuckerman's major point, in the section of his review dealing with interpersonal influence studies, was not to determine whether self-serving attributions "existed," although he did conclude that evidence in favor was weak and depended on a few studies that could not be easily interpreted. Rather, Zuckerman speculated about three theoretical forces that might countervail against such attributions and prevent them from being made in the interpersonal influence situation. The clear implication is that Zuckerman would expect self-serving bias in the interpersonal influence situation at times when these countervailing forces were not operating. Arkin, Cooper, and Kolditz address a somewhat different question in their attempt to determine the "existence" of self-serving attributions, focusing on the main effect conclusion. They do consider interactions as qualifications of the main effect, and suggest that they be noted and if possible, explained. However, their own meta-analysis of interactions fails to do this. It is simply an aggregation of the heterogeneous set of interactions that past investigators happened to have reported. There is no guiding theory, and with the small sample of studies there is little hope of being able to examine *stable* interactions so as to detect data-based puzzles and begin to explain them.

As both Zuckerman and Arkin, Cooper, and Kolditz point out, the conflicting findings in the teacher-student category point to a data-based puzzle that needs resolution. Moreover, comparison of results from the interpersonal influence and other paradigms suggests that self-serving biases may be less prevalent in the interpersonal influence situation. This, too, is a possible puzzle worth speculating about. Such puzzles ultimately increase the predictive power and accuracy of theories, and are a boon to theoretical advancement. Arkin, Cooper, and Kolditz were somewhat less concerned than Zuckerman with summarizing in order to detect puzzles and speculate on novel theoretical attempts to solve the puzzles. Their principal aim was to summarize the evidence for the main effect proposition. What we have, then, is a difference in priorities about two types of questions, each of which has value. Science needs to know its stubborn, dependable, general "facts," and it also needs data-based, contingent puzzles that push ahead theory. Our impression is that meta-analysts stress the former over the latter, and that many qualitative reviewers stress the latter more than the former (or at least more than meta-analysts do). Of course, neither the meta-analyst nor the qualitative reviewer *needs* to make either prioritization. Each can do both; and any one reviewer can consciously use both qualitative and quantitative techniques in the same review. Indeed, s/he should.

Conclusions

Meta-analysis is a set of useful techniques for literature review, especially when the sample of studies for review is large. The smaller the sample, the more limitations are placed on qualitative and quantitative reviews alike. While meta-analysis requires fewer judgments from reviewers, and in this sense may be more "objective," it is still replete with judgments about the definition of the area of investigation, the relevance of methodological and substantive characteristics of studies, and the appropriate meta-analytic tools to be used. Meta-analysis is not a single technique, but rather a flexible set of techniques that can be adapted to the question at hand, provided that enough information is provided in the reports of research.

It has made a major contribution by highlighting poor practices in qualitative reviews, and should therefore serve as a stimulus to improving qualitative reviews. It may also make a contribution through establishing the "facts"—dependable, stubborn relationships between concepts. This is useful since much psychological theory has been built on relationships that are not dependable. Finally, it can offer clues to the explanation of findings, within the limits of the studies available to it. These limits may be severe if new explanatory constructs are needed for which proxies were not measured in past research.

The major limitation of meta-analysis relates to its major advantage. With large samples of studies, meta-analysis is more convenient than qualitative reviewing, and one can explore more contingency relationships. However, the larger set of studies can lead to an unwarranted psychological sense of security if there is a consistent replication of a relationship. To accept the estimate of the relationship one has also to assume that the estimate is unbiased or that subsidiary analyses have been conducted which have *validly* shown that no bias of importance resulted from the principal forces from which bias would be expected.

We have outlined several dangers inherent in poor practice of meta-analysis. Our caution is not directed at sophisticated users of the technique, to whom little of what we have said may be novel. Rather, it is directed against the potential mindless use of meta-analysis if it becomes a fad. Like all social science methods, its use involves assumptions that need to be made explicit, and if these assumptions are not clear to the user, misleading results can easily occur. Finally, if our discussion has made the best qualitative reviews seem similar to the best quantitative reviews, it is because they are similar. As we have tried to show, the weaknesses of traditional reviews are not inherent, and most of the strengths of meta-analysis can be applied to qualitative reviews to improve them.

Reference Notes

1. Howard, K. Personal communication, 1980.
2. Zuckerman, M. Personal communication, 1980.

References

Arkin, R. M., Appelman, A. J., & Burger, J. M. Social anxiety, self-presentation, and the self-serving bias in causal attribution. *Journal of Personality and Social Psychology*, 1980, in press.

Arkin, R., Cooper, H., & Kolditz, T. A statistical review of the literature concerning the self-serving bias in interpersonal influence situations. *Journal of Personality*, 1980, **48**, 435–448.

Bandura, A. *Principles of behavior modification.* New York: Holt, Rinehart & Winston, 1969.

Beckman, L. Effects of students' performance on teachers' and observers' attributions of causality. *Journal of Educational Psychology*, 1970, **61**, 76–82.

Beckman, L. Teachers' and observers' perceptions of causality for a child's performance. *Journal of Educational Psychology*, 1973, **65**, 198–204.

Bergin, A. E. The evaluation of therapeutic outcomes. In A. E. Bergin and S. L. Garfield (Eds.), *Handbook of psychotherapy and behavior change: An empirical analysis.* New York: John Wiley & Sons, 1971.

Block, J. Advancing the psychology of personality: Paradigmatic shift or improving the quality of research? In D. Endler and N. S. Magnusson (Eds.), *Interaction psychology and personality.* New York: John Wiley & Sons, 1976.

Block, J. H. Issues, problems and pitfalls in assessing sex differences: A critical review of *The psychology of sex differences. Merrill-Palmer Quarterly*, 1976, **22**, 283–308.

Boruch, R. F. On common contentions about randomized field experiments. In R. F. Boruch and H. W. Riecken (Eds.), *Experimental tests of public policy.* Boulder: Westview, 1977.

Calder, B. J., Ross, M., & Insko, C. A. Attitude attribution: Effects of incentives, choice, and consequences. *Journal of Personality and Social Psychology*, 1973, **25**, 84–99.

Campbell, D. T. The indirect assessment of social attitudes. *Psychological Bulletin*, 1950, **47**, 15–38.

Campbell, D. T., & Erlebacher, A. E. How regression artifacts in quasi-experimental evaluations can mistakenly make compensatory education look harmful. In J. Hellmuth (Ed.), *Compensatory education: A national debate*, Vol. 3, *Disadvantaged child.* New York: Brunner/Mazel, 1970.

Cartwright, D. Risk taking by individuals and groups: An assessment of research employing choice dilemmas. *Journal of Personality and Social Psychology*, 1971, **20**, 361–378.

Cohen, J. W. The statistical power of abnormal-social psychological research. *Journal of Abnormal and Social Psychology*, 1962, **65**, 145–153.

Cohen, W. *Statistical power analysis for the behavioral sciences.* New York: Academic Press, 1969.

Collins, B. E., & Hoyt, M. F. Personal responsibility-for-consequences: An integration and extension of the "forced compliance" literature. *Journal of Experimental Social Psychology*, 1972, **8**, 448–593.

Cook, T. D., & Campbell, D. T. *Quasi-experimentation: Design and analysis issues for field settings.* Chicago: Rand McNally, 1979.

Cook, T. D., & Gruder, C. L. Meta-evaluation research. *Evaluation Quarterly*, 1978, **2**, 5–51.

Cook, T. D., Gruder, C. L., Hennigan, K. M., & Flay, B. R. History of the sleeper effect: Some logical pitfalls in accepting the null hypothesis. *Psychological Bulletin*, 1979, **86**, 662–679.

Cooper, H. M. Statistically combining independent studies: A meta-analysis of sex differences in conformity research. *Journal of Personality and Social Psychology*, 1979, **37**, 131–146.

Cooper, H. M., & Rosenthal, R. Statistical versus traditional procedures for summarizing research findings. *Psychological Bulletin*, 1980, **87**, 442–449.

Cronbach, L. J., & Meehl, P. E. Construct validity in psychological tests. *Psychological Bulletin*, 1955, **52**, 281–302.

Cronbach, L. J., & Snow R. E. *Attitudes and instructional methods.* New York: Irvington Publishers, 1976.

Director, S. M. Underadjustment bias in the evaluation of manpower training. *Evaluation Quarterly,* 1979, **3**, 190–218.

Educational Research Service. *Class size: A summary of research.* Arlington, Va.: Author, 1978.

Eysenck, H. The effects of psychotherapy: An evaluation. *Journal of Consulting Psychology,* 1952, **16**, 319–324.

Fiedler, F. E. A contingency model of leadership effectiveness. In L. Berkowitz (Ed.), *Advances in experimental social psychology.* New York: Academic Press, 1964.

Gergen, K. J. Social psychology as history. *Journal of Personality and Social Psychology,* 1973, **26**, 309–320.

Gilbert, J. P., McPeek, B., & Mosteller, P. Statistics and ethics in surgery and anesthesia. *Science,* 1977, **198**, 684–689.

Gillig, P. M., & Greenwald, A. G. Is it time to lay the sleeper effect to rest? *Journal of Personality and Social Psychology,* 1974, **29**, 132–139.

Glass, G. V. Primary, secondary, and meta-analysis of research. *Educational Researcher,* 1976, **5**, 3–8.

Glass, G. V. Commentary on "Interpersonal expectancy effects: The first 345 studies" *The Brain and Behavioral Sciences,* 1978, **3**, 394–395. (a)

Glass, G. V. Integrating findings: The meta-analysis of research. *Review of Research in Education,* 1978, **5**, 351–379. (b)

Glass, G. V. Reply to Mansfield and Busse. *Educational Researcher,* 1978, **7**, 3. (c)

Glass, G. V., & Smith, M. L. Meta-analysis of research on class size and achievement. *Educational Evaluation and Policy Analysis,* 1979, **1**, 2–16.

Jackson, G. B. *Methods for reviewing and integrating research in the social sciences* (DIS 76-20398). Washington, D.C.: George Washington University, Social Research Group, May 1978 (NTIS No. PB-283 747).

Jencks, C. S., et al. *Inequality: A reassessment of the effects of family and schooling in America.* New York: Basic Books, 1972.

Johnson, T. J., Feigenbaum, R., & Weiby, M. Some determinants and consequences of the teacher's perception of causation. *Journal of Educational Psychology,* 1964, **55**, 237–246.

Light, R. J. Capitalizing on variation: How conflicting research findings can be helpful for policy. *Educational Researcher,* Oct. 1979, **8**, 3–11.

Light, R. J., & Smith, P. V. Accumulating evidence: Procedures for resolving contradictions among different research studies. *Harvard Educational Review,* 1971, **41**, 429–471.

Luborsky, L., Chandler, M., Auerbach, A. H., Cohen, J., & Bachrach, H. M. Factors influencing the outcome of psychotherapy: A review of quantitative research. *Psychological Bulletin,* 1971, **75**, 145–185.

Luborsky, L., Singer, B., & Luborsky, L. Comparative studies of psychotherapies. *Archive of General Psychiatry,* 1975, **32**, 995–1008.

Lykken, D. T. Statistical significance in psychological research. *Psychological Bulletin,* 1968, **70**, 151–159.

Maccoby, E. E., & Jacklin, C. N. *The psychology of sex differences.* Stanford, Calif.: Stanford University Press, 1974.

MacCorqudale, K., & Meehl, P. E. On a distinction between hypothetical constructs and intervening variables. *Psychological Review,* 1948, **55**, 95–107.

Mischel, W. *Personality and assessment.* New York: John Wiley, 1968.

Mischel, W. The interaction of person and situation. In D. Endler and N. S. Magnusson (Eds.), *Interaction psychology and personality.* New York: John Wiley, 1976.

Mynatt, C., & Sherman, S. J. Responsibility attribution in groups and individuals: A direct test of the diffusion of responsibility hypothesis. *Journal of Personality and Social Psychology,* 1975, **32**, 1111–1118.

Mosteller, R. L., & Bush, R. R. Selected quantitative techniques. In G. Lindzey

(Ed.), *Handbook of social psychology,* Vol. 1. Cambridge: Addison-Wesley, 1954.

Rachman, S. *The effects of psychotherapy.* Oxford: Pergamon Press, 1971.

Rosenthal, R. Interpersonal expectations: Effects of the experimenter's hypothesis. In R. Rosenthal and R. L. Rosnow (Eds.), *Artifact in behavioral research.* New York: Academic Press, 1969.

Rosenthal, R. *Experimenter effects in behavioral research,* Enlarged Edition. New York: Irvington Press, 1976.

Rosenthal, R. The "file drawer problem" and tolerance for null results. *Psychological Bulletin,* 1979, **86,** 638–641.

Rosenthal, R., & Rubin, B. D. Interpersonal expectancy effects: The first 345 studies. *The Behavioral and Brain Sciences,* 1978, **3,** 377–386.

Ryan, D. W., & Greenfield, T. B. *Clarifying the class size question: Evaluation and synthesis of studies related to the effects of class size, pupil-adult, and pupil-teacher ratios.* Toronto, Ont.: Ontario Ministry of Education, 1976.

Schopler, J., & Layton, B. Determinants of the self-attribution of having influenced another person. *Journal of Personality and Social Psychology,* 1972, **22,** 326–332.

Smith, M. L. Sex bias in counselling and psychotherapy. *Psychological Bulletin,* 1980, **87,** 392–407.

Smith, M. L., & Glass, G. V. Meta-analysis of psychotherapy outcome studies. *American Psychologist,* 1977, **32,** 752–760.

Smith, M. L., & Glass, G. V. *Class-size and its relationship to attitude and instruction.* San Francisco: Far West Laboratory, 1979.

Stegmuller, W. *The structure and dynamics of theories.* New York: Springer-Verlag, 1978.

Stephan, W. G. Actor vs. observer: Attributions to behavior with positive or negative outcomes and empathy for the other role. *Journal of Experimental Social Psychology,* 1975, **11,** 205–214.

Stouffer, S. A. *The American soldier: Vol. 1. Adjustment during army life.* Princeton: Princeton University Press, 1949.

Tukey, J. W. Analyzing data: Sanctification or detective work? *American Psychologist,* 1969, **24,** 83–91.

Wells, G. L., Petty, R. E., Harkins, S. G., Kagehiro, D., & Harvey, J. H. Anticipated discussion of interpretation eliminates actor-observer differences in the attribution of causality. *Sociometry,* 1977, **40,** 247–253.

Wicker, A. W. Attitudes versus actions: The relationship of verbal and overt behavioral responses to attitude objects. *Journal of Social Issues,* 1969, **25,** 41–78.

Zajonc, R. B. Social facilitation. *Science,* 1965, **149,** 269–274.

Zuckerman, M. Attribution of success and failure revisited, or: The motivational bias is alive and well in attribution theory. *Journal of Personality,* 1979, **47,** 245–287.

Manuscript received March 15, 1980.

3

Statistical Versus Traditional Procedures for Summarizing Research Findings

Harris M. Cooper and Robert Rosenthal

There has been increasing dissatisfaction with the procedures on which conclusions from series of related studies have customarily been based, and statistical procedures have been proposed as more appropriate alternatives. This study was designed to show whether the conclusions drawn after using traditional or statistical combining procedures differed from one another. Thirty-two graduate students and 9 faculty members were randomly assigned to use one of the two techniques to draw inferences about an identical set of related studies. It was found that users of the statistical method (a) perceived more support present in the literature and (b) estimated a larger magnitude of effect than did traditional reviewers. Conditions did not differ with regard to recommendations for future research. Although several differences were uncovered that were related to academic status (early vs. late, graduate training vs. faculty), combining procedure effects were general across academic status and reviewer gender. The desirability of adopting statistical procedures in psychology is discussed.

The vast majority of the space in psychological journals is taken up by reports of individual research projects. At the same time, however, it is probably the literature review, which involves a synthesis of individual projects, that reaches the widest audience. Certainly, at the undergraduate level and in communication with the lay public, psychological knowledge is not transmitted through primary data description but through a distillation of primary sources carried out by a literature reviewer. Because literature reviews have such great information-gatekeeping potential, it is crucial that we apply standard, replicable, and rigorous criteria to them. These criteria should be at least as demanding as those that we require for primary data handling.

Recently, the traditional method of literature review has been criticized because of a lack of just such quality control. The most glaring weakness of the traditional method seems to be its responsiveness to the biases of the particular reviewer (cf. Glass, 1976). Although subjectivity is the severest threat to the validity of traditional reviews, these reviews have also been criticized (a) because they neglect a large amount of information contained in primary research reports and (b) because they imprecisely weight their conclusions with regard to the amount of research they cover.

Statistical procedures have been suggested as an alternative to the traditional review method. These procedures (cf. Rosenthal, 1978) have a lengthy history in applied statistics, but until recently they were rarely practiced. All of the procedures, dubbed *meta-analyses* by Glass (1976), numerically combine the results of independent studies for the purpose of integrating findings. Cooper (1979) suggested a generally applicable meta-analysis package that includes (a) an unweighted combination of the independent

This research was facilitated by National Science Foundation Grant BNS78-08834 to Harris M. Cooper and by funds from the Center for Research in Social Behavior.

Requests for reprints should be sent to Harris M. Cooper, Center for Research in Social Behavior, University of Missouri, 111 East Stewart Road, Columbia, Missouri 65211.

From Harris M. Cooper and Robert Rosenthal, "Statistical Versus Traditional Procedures for Summarizing Research Findings," 87(3) *Psychological Bulletin* 442-449 (May 1980). Copyright 1980 by the American Psychological Association. Reprinted by permission of the publisher and author.

probabilities reported in the summarized experiments; (b) a weighted combined probability, with weights selected by the reviewer; (c) a fail-safe number, stating the total undiscovered null studies needed to reverse a significant overall probability (see, also, Rosenthal, 1979); and (d) two measures of the magnitude of the effect demonstrated in the literature (Cohen, 1977). The weighted and unweighted overall probabilities are meant to remove subjective error from conclusions; the fail-safe number is meant to help readers weigh conclusions relative to the number of studies summarized, and the measures of effect size are meant to capture more information from primary reports that bears on the practical significance of the effect.

Although traditional procedures are clearly open to criticism, and statistical procedures seem to address these weaknesses, the question remains as to whether the substitution of one procedure for the other would lead to changes in our perceived state of knowledge. Obviously, differences between conclusions drawn by the two procedures will depend on the particular reviewer and the research evidence involved. However, if statistical procedures replace traditional ones with some degree of generality, one should see a corresponding general alteration in the types of conclusion psychologists draw.

This article is a report of an investigation of differences in conclusions drawn as a funtion of whether statistical or traditional review procedures were used. Graduate students and faculty at a large state university were presented with identical sets of research articles and were, through random assignment, asked to use either statistical or traditional review procedures. A determination was then made of the differences between statistical and traditional review conclusions with regard to (a) perceived hypothesis support, (b) estimated relationship magnitude, and (c) recommended future research.

Hypotheses regarding the support and magnitude variables were derived from earlier case studies. Cooper (1979) found two traditional reviews in similar research areas. The same research studies surveyed in these traditional reviews were then reviewed using statistical procedures. In both cases, it was

found, the traditional reviews estimated less support in the literature (using accepted probabilistic definitions) than did the statistical procedures. Obviously, review conclusions were found to differ most dramatically when overall probabilities were nearest $p < .05$. For the present study, then, it was hypothesized that this lower estimation of support and effect by traditional reviewers would be a general observation, when the two methods were compared.

Hypotheses regarding the recommendations for future research are more speculative than are those based on the case studies. First, there are two alternative courses future research can take: replication or extension. Replication studies seek to retest an already tested hypothesis (e.g., because past research was inconclusive or methodologically unsound or because circumstances have changed). Extension research accepts a hypothesis as supported and seeks to gauge its generality or to discover its underlying causal process. If statistical reviews lead to greater perceived support for a research hypothesis, it seems only reasonable to predict that statistical reviewers will recommend less replication and more extension than will traditional reviewers.

Method

Overview of Design

Thirty-two graduate students and 9 professors were randomly assigned to either a statistical or a traditional literature review condition. All of the participants were given the same seven studies that addressed the hypothesis that females are more persistent than males. The results of the seven studies exhibited a combined probability of .025. Statistical reviewers were asked to retrieve p levels associated with each study and to generate the overall series probability. Traditional reviewers were asked to "employ whatever criteria" they would normally use. All of the participants were then asked standard sets of questions that gauged their decisions and recommendations concerning the research area.

Participants

Participants included 32 graduate students (20 males and 12 females) and 9 faculty members (7 males and 2 females) in the Department of Psychology at the University of Missouri—Columbia. Graduate students' participation was solicited through posters, class announcements, and telephone calls. A lottery was held, with $20 paid to each of half of the student participants. Faculty were chosen who were (a) unfamiliar with previous work in meta-analytics and (b) familiar enough with the first author so as not to be offended by a request for a large favor. Approximately 30% of the contacted population did not participate, either because of refusal or because of scheduling conflicts.

Participating graduate students averaged 3¼ years in graduate school. First-year graduate students were not invited to participate out of a concern that they might lack adequate exposure to statistical principles. Graduate students represented all of the areas of psychological training.

Faculty members averaged 35¼ years of age, with a median age of 35 (although two faculty members refused to answer this question). Faculty also were chosen from diverse subareas of psychology. This particular university faculty has one of the nation's highest research productivity rankings (Cox & Catt, 1977). It is safe to assume, therefore, that the research skills of participants were at least normative for the nation.

Materials

Introductory instructions. All of the participants received the same rationale and verbal instructions before viewing the written materials. These instructions contained the following information:

1. Participants were told that the purpose of the study was to examine the literature review process.

2. Participants were told that one variable that "might" be manipulated was the nature of the evidence under review. This information was conveyed solely to inhibit participants' generation of other hypotheses. Participants were also told that "different people might be asked to employ different techniques for arriving at a conclusion." This information was meant to prepare participants for the unfamiliar statistical procedures that some were asked to use.

3. Participants were told that the area of sex differences in persistence would be reviewed. They were told this area was chosen because it would likely involve language familiar to most psychologists, thus avoiding problems associated with area specialization. This rationale was meant to divert participants from hypothesizing that their own sex was a variable of interest, which, in fact, was the case. After the introductory remarks, participants were given numbered manila envelopes. They were told the envelopes contained all of the necessary materials, including the articles to be reviewed.

Cover sheet. On the materials' cover sheet, participants recorded their names, ages, sex, number of years in graduate school (students only), and areas of specialization.

Introduction sheet. The introduction sheet was identical for all of the participants. This sheet, in addition to repeating the general instructions, asked participants to make three assumptions.

Assumption 1: You are about to write a review paper, either as a term project or for journal publication, examining sex differences in persistence.

Assumption 2: You have conducted a typical literature search at the library. You have uncovered the seven articles presented as those which test the hypothesis in question.

Assumption 3: You must now read the articles and draw a conclusion about whether or not the available evidence supports the hypothesis that females are more persistent than males.

Presentation of articles. Participants then found a packet of seven articles, photocopied in their entirety and prefaced by a cover sheet. The cover sheet contained (a) the title of the pertinent article, (b) a description of the dependent variable of interest, and (c) the question, "Does this study support the conclusion that females are more persistent, or get more involved in tasks, than males?" Participants were asked to check one of two responses: does support or does not support. Participants in the statistical combining condition only were also requested to record the probability level that was associated with the dependent variable of interest.

The seven articles presented were identical for all participants and were chosen from those cited by Maccoby and Jacklin (1974) as relevant to the question of sex differences in persistence. Not all of the studies cited by Maccoby and Jacklin were presented, so the conclusion based on this subsample bears no relation to their conclusion. The articles were presented in chronological order, although the participants were free to read them in any order they desired. The seven studies and their relevant dependent variables were the following:

1. Zunich, M. Children's reactions to failure. *Journal of Genetic Psychology*, 1964, *104*, 19–24 (attempts to solve alone).

2. Wyer, R. S., Jr. Effects of task reinforcement, social reinforcement, and task difficulty on perseverance in achievement-related activity. *Journal of Personality and Social Psychology*, 1968, *8*, 269–276 (perseverence on a rope pull or puzzle).

3. Bee, H. L., Van Egeren, L. F., Streissguth, A. P., Nyman, B. A., & Leckie, M. S. Social class differences in maternal teaching strategies and speech patterns. *Developmental Psychology*, 1969, *1*, 726–734 (number of toy shifts).

4. Stouwie, R. J., Hetherington, E. M., & Parke, R. D. Some determinants of children's self-reward behavior after exposure to discrepant reward criteria. *Developmental Psychology*, 1970, *3*, 313–319 (time on an embedded figures task).

5. Pedersen, F. A., & Bell, R. Q. Sex differences in preschool children without histories of complications of pregnancy and delivery. *Developmental Psychology*, 1970, *3*, 10–15 (time spent in separate activities).

6. Friedrichs, A. G., et al. Interrelations among learning and performance tasks at the preschool level. *Developmental Psychology*, 1971, *4*, 164–172 (persistence on a pegboard).

7. Brooks, J., & Lewis, M. Attachment behavior in thirteen-month old, opposite-sex twins. *Child Development*, 1974, *45*, 243–247 (number of toy changes).

Rationale behind the choice of studies. The seven studies were chosen to reflect an evidential base that previous meta-analyses have found to be fairly representative (Cooper, 1979; Hall, 1978; Rosenthal, 1976; Rosenthal & Rubin, 1978). Of the seven studies, two found evidence that females were more persistent than males. These two studies presented probabilities of .005 and .001, respectively, one-tailed. The remaining five studies reported either (a) no statistical data or (b) no significant difference between the sexes. Using the statistical combining technique led to an overall probability of .016 or .025 (dependent on whether the reviewer recalculated the *p* levels or used those reported in the articles).

Combining condition manipulation. After reading the articles (and recording the relevant *p* values) participants in the statistical combining condition were given detailed instructions on how to apply the unweighted Stouffer method for combining results of independent studies (Rosenthal, 1978). Participants in the traditional condition were asked only to "employ whatever criteria you would use if this exercise were being undertaken for a class term paper or a manuscript for publication. Next, turn to the Review Conclusions page where your interpretation of the literature is requested."

Review conclusions sheet. The final two pages of materials were identical for all subjects. These pages asked participants to answer four sets of questions.

The first set of questions asked participants to indicate whether, "the evidence presented, in general, *supports* the conclusion that females are more persistent, or become more involved in tasks, than males." Five possible responses were provided (definitely yes, probably yes, impossible to say, probably no, or definitely no). These were scored from 1 to 5, with a higher score indicating greater perceived support. Second, participants were asked to, "on the basis of your review of the seven studies, give your best estimate of the magnitude of the relationship between gender and persistence." Six responses were provided (very large, large, moderate, small, very small, or none at all). These were scored from 0 to 5, with a higher score indicating greater perceived magnitude of effect.

The second set of questions required five responses. Five recommendations were made for future research. These recommendations were for (a) replication of previous studies because previous results are *inconclusive,* (b) replication of previous studies because previous studies were *methodologically unsound,* (c) replication of previous studies because previous studies were conducted under *different social circumstances,* (d) studies that investigate the *underlying process* that created the sex difference, and (e) studies that test the situational *generalizability* of the sex difference.

Each recommendation was rated on identical necessity scales. Participants were asked to circle a number from 0 to 10, with 0 labeled *not at all necessary* and 10 labeled *extremely necessary.*

The third set of questions simply asked, "Should research into sex differences in persistence continue at all?" Two responses were provided (should continue and should not continue) and participants checked one of these.

The fourth set of questions asked for open-ended responses. Participants were instructed to begin a paragraph with the statement, "In conclusion . . ." and summarize their impressions.

Procedure

Graduate students participated at night, in groups of from 4 to 12 persons. Each experimental condition was represented at each session, and subjects were randomly assigned to conditions (for the statistical condition, $n = 19$; for the traditional condition, $n = 22$). Introductory instructions were administered in one room, but participants were then allowed to work on the task anywhere, with the restriction that they were not to compare materials. Approximately half of the subjects were randomly assigned to each of the two experimental conditions.

Faculty were introduced to the study individually and in their own offices. Faculty took between 1 and 4 weeks to return the materials. Because faculty were recruited in a possibly biased manner (i.e., their familiarity with the first author) and because instructions were conveyed individually, faculty participants were not assigned to conditions until after all of the instructions were recited and they had agreed to participate. At this point, the experimenter flipped a coin to assign the participant to a condition, thereby preserving the internal validity of the experiment, despite the nonrandom selection of participants.

Results

Check on the Manipulations and Frequency of Differential Errors for Individual Studies

Statistics condition. Of the 19 participants in the statistical combining condition, 18 (95%) retrieved the correct *p* level that was associated with each individual study. Sixteen of the statistical reviewers (84%) combined these *p* levels correctly. Of the 3 statistical reviewers who incorrectly combined probabilities, 2 erred in a direction indicating greater support for the hypothesis than was present ($Z = 2.65$ and 2.53), and 1 erred in the opposite direction ($Z = 1.75$).

Three reviewers in the statistical condition (16%) reported that at least one of the two

Table 1
Perceived Support for the Sex Difference Hypothesis

| | Combining procedure | | | Statistical as proportion of total |
Response choice	Statistical	Traditional	Total	
Definitely no	1	3	4	.25
Probably no	5	13	18	.28
Impossible to say	8	5	13	.62
Probably yes	5	1	6	.83

Note. Cells contain the number of subjects who chose each response.

studies with significant p levels did not support the hypothesis. No nonsignificant study was reported as supportive.

Traditional condition. Eleven of the 22 reviewers in the traditional condition (50%) reported that at least one of the two studies with significant p levels did not support the hypothesis. The difference in the frequency of concluding that statistically significant studies were not supportive (16% vs. 50%) suggests that the statistical method of summarizing tends to reduce the possibility of retrieval errors, $\chi^2(1) = 6.31$, $p < .01$. No traditional reviewer reported a nonsignificant study as supporting the hypothesis.

Decisions Regarding the Research Hypothesis

Perceived support. The first question asked whether participants felt that the evidence supported a conclusion of greater female persistence. Columns 1 and 2 of Table 1 present the frequency with which each response to this question was chosen, classified by combining condition. One possible response, definitely yes, was never chosen by participants. The third column in Table 1 presents the total number of participants who chose the indicated response. The fourth column presents the proportion of total participants who gave a particular response and who were in the statistical combining condition.

Column 4 contains data that can be used to test the first hypothesis. To paraphrase Snedecor and Cochran (1967, p. 246), if the contention is that participating in the statistical procedure condition increased perceived support for the hypothesis, then the values in column 4 should increase as we move from definitely no to probably yes. A Z test for

the linear trend in the proportions shown in column 4 indicated that just such a trend existed ($Z = 2.64$, $p < .0041$, one-tailed). The data demonstrate, then, that as the response indicated more support for the hypothesis, statistical reviewers represented an increasing portion of participants who chose it. A median test, $\chi^2(1) = 6.94$, $p < .0043$, one-tailed, and a t test, $t(39) = 2.84$, $p < .0036$, one-tailed, substantiated the trend analysis.

Perceived magnitude. A similar set of analyses was conducted using the participants' estimates of the magnitude of gender differences. Table 2 presents the frequencies of response choices by experimental condition. One response, very large, was never chosen.

A Z test for the trend in proportions (exhibited in column 4) proved significant ($Z = 1.98$, $p < .024$, one-tailed). This revealed that as the response indicated a greater magnitude of gender difference, participants who chose it became more likely to be in the statistical condition. A median test, $\chi^2(1) = 3.94$, $p < .0239$, one-tailed, and a t test, $t(39) = 2.01$, $p < .0258$, one-tailed, also substantiated the trend analysis.

Other influences on decision variables. Although only one variable was manipulated by the experimenters (statistical vs. traditional procedures), there were several individual difference variables whose relation to review conclusions were of interest. Most obviously, the sex of the reviewer seemed to be a natural candidate for explaining variance in conclusions. Preliminary analyses on all of the dependent variables, however, revealed no significant main effects or interactions involving the gender of the reviewer. For this reason, gender was dropped from the analyses.

In addition, we tested the population validity (Bracht & Glass, 1968) of graduate student responses by comparing them with faculty responses. Also, students who were early in their graduate training (Years 2 and 3) were compared with those who were late (Years 4, 5, and 6) to study possible trends in attitude toward research over time. Thus, Condition (statistical vs. traditional) × Academic Status (early graduate training vs. late graduate training vs. faculty) unweighted means analyses of variance were carried out. Both decision variables produced significant early versus late graduate training comparisons. Reviewers who were early in their graduate careers perceived more support for the research hypothesis ($M = 2.87$) than reviewers who were late in training, $M = 2.04$, $F(1, 35) = 7.67$, $p < .009$. Less experienced graduate students also estimated a larger effect size ($M = 1.88$) than did more experienced graduate students, $M = 1.06$, $F(1, 35) = 5.17$, $p < .03$. Faculty did not differ from the graduate student average on either the support ($M = 2.48$) or the magnitude ($M = 1.18$) questions. Most importantly, the Combining Condition × Academic Status interactions were far from significant for both questions. This indicates that the condition effects on review decisions reported previously were generalizable over all of the three status populations, as well as over reviewer gender.

Perceived Implications for Future Research

Type of summarizing procedure was of little importance when reviewers made recommendations concerning future research. No rating of the need for future research produced a significant experimental condition main effect or interaction.

Finally, there were only five reviewers who suggested that sex differences in persistence research should not continue. This number is too small to subject to statistical analysis.

Free-Response Remarks

Most of the free-response remarks made by reviewers could be classified into four criticisms of the presented research. Most notably, reviewers took issue with the operational definitions of persistence used in the studies. First, 74% of the statistical reviewers and 68% of the traditional reviewers noted that the concepts-to-operations leap in some studies was suspect. Second, 21% of the statistical reviewers and 23% of the traditional reviewers suggested that persistence may be a task-specific phenomenon. Third, 16% of the statistical reviewers and 41% of the traditional reviewers noted that supporting studies used young children rather than adults. Finally, 26% of the statistical reviewers and 55% of the traditional reviewers bemoaned the lack of control in the studies or suggested that gender might interact with some unidentified variables. These last two criticisms produced fairly large percentage differences between combining conditions and therefore might suggest effects to be studied in future research on review procedures.

Discussion

Effects of Combining Condition

The results of this study indicate that the use of statistical procedures in the place of

Table 2
Perceived Magnitude of Sex Difference Effect

Response choice	Combining procedure			Statistical as proportion of total
	Statistical	Traditional	Total	
None at all	2	4	6	.33
Very small	6	12	18	.33
Small	6	4	10	.60
Moderate	4	2	6	.67
Large	1	0	1	1.00

Note. Cells contain the number of subjects who chose each response.

traditional ones increased (a) the perceived support for and (b) the estimated magnitude of the effect being reviewed. Specifically, it was found that 68% of the statistical reviewers were at least considering rejecting the null hypothesis, compared with only 27% of the traditional reviewers. Also, 58% of the statistical reviewers estimated at least a small degree of relationship between sex and persistence, compared with only 27% of the traditional reviewers. No reliable differences were uncovered between the combining procedures with regard to recommended future research. Although some differences in conclusions drawn were found between reviewers as a function of academic status, the previously reported conclusions were found to be general across all status groups and reviewer gender.

Appraising the Research Design

Since only one research area was involved in this study, it is important to determine whether the present findings might be an extreme example of the combining condition effect. Two aspects of the design indicate that this is not the case. First, it was reported that over 70% of all of the reviewers questioned some aspect of the way the concept of persistence was operationalized in these particular studies. Thus, although statistical reviewers observed a combined probability of $< .025$ or $< .016$, their modal response to the perceived support question was "impossible to say." Most likely, perceived conceptual problems in the literature prevented statistical reviewers from accepting the research hypothesis. In a sense, then, it is possible to conclude that perceived design and conceptual difficulties in a literature review might have mitigated the combining procedure effect. Second, the crux of the procedural difference phenomenon seems to lie in the fact that traditional reviewers either neglect probabilities or combine them intuitively in an overly conservative fashion. The series of probabilities used here was five exact null findings and two $p < .01$ supportive findings. After speaking with participants, it appeared that more disparate intuition versus lawful chance series could have been constructed. In particular, with seven studies involved, a combined

probability of $p < .01$ would likely have proved more dramatic, given psychologists' emphasis on critical levels of significance (Rosenthal & Gaito, 1963).

With these two design aspects in hand, then, it seems reasonable to conclude that the differences exhibited in this study do not represent a maximum combining procedure effect. Rather, we might expect a larger effect when there are fewer perceived conceptual difficulties and when the overall probability for the series of results is lower.

It is logically troubling that the predicted effects for future research recommendations (i.e., less replication and more extension called for when statistical procedures were applied) did not appear. Three possible reasons for this failure are (a) that a multitude of other strong influences determine our research directions, (b) that future research decisions are influenced by combining technique only when the technique effect is larger than that displayed here, and (c) that the present study may have omitted research purposes that would be influenced by combining condition.

Desirability of Adopting Statistical Procedures

Now that the effects of adopting statistical procedures for summarizing research have been estimated, we must ask if these represent a desirable outcome. Perhaps the most often mentioned criticism of statistical procedures is that they will lead reviewers to pay too little attention to methodological weaknesses in the covered studies (Rosenthal & Rubin, 1978). Most of the evidence in the present study suggests, however, that this concern is unwarranted. First, no significant difference between conditions was found on the question about the need for future research "because previous studies were methodologically unsound" (for statistical, $M = 5.38$; for traditional, $M = 5.29$). Second, the average, median, and modal response by traditional reviewers to the question about whether the evidence supported greater persistence in females was "probably no." For statistical reviewers, the average, median, and modal response was "impossible to say." If traditional reviewers found methodological problems more salient than did statistical reviewers, this would imply more conclusions on their part that particular investigations held no information, not that they held null supporting information. Given that the traditional conclusion was more definitive than the statistical one, even if greater attention is paid in traditional reviews to methods, the added precision this represents may be more than offset by a tendency for traditional reviewers to incorrectly treat methodologically flawed research as evidence against a research hypothesis.

Does the increased perception of support that is likely to accompany statistical procedures have any positive implications? To consumers of psychological research, including undergraduates and the lay public, conclusions based on meta-analyses will appear to be (and indeed they will be) more rigorous and objective. Some of the confusion and contradiction we often convey about our research may not be a function of the results we have found but of how we have chosen to synthesize them.

References

Bracht, G. H., & Glass, G. V. The external validity of experiments. *American Educational Research Journal*, 1968, *5*, 437–474.

Cohen, J. *Statistical power analysis for the behav-ioral sciences* (Rev. ed.). New York: Academic Press, 1977.

Cooper, H. M. Statistically combining independent studies: A meta-analysis of sex differences in conformity research. *Journal of Personality and Social Psychology*, 1979, *37*, 131–146.

Cox, W. M., & Catt, V. Productivity ratings of graduate programs in psychology based on publication in the journals of the American Psychological Association. *American Psychologist*, 1977, *32*, 793–813.

Glass, G. V. Primary, secondary and meta-analysis of research. *Educational Researcher*, 1976, *5*(10), 3–8.

Hall, J. A. Gender effects in decoding nonverbal cues. *Psychological Bulletin*, 1978, *85*, 845–857.

Maccoby, E. E., & Jacklin, C. N. *The psychology of sex differences*. Stanford, Calif.: Stanford University Press, 1974.

Rosenthal, R. *Experimenter effects in behavioral research* (2nd ed.). New York: Irvington, 1976.

Rosenthal, R. Combining results of independent studies. *Psychological Bulletin*, 1978, *85*, 185–193.

Rosenthal, R. The "file drawer problem" and tolerance for null results. *Psychological Bulletin*, 1979, *85*, 638–641.

Rosenthal, R., & Gaito, J. The interpretation of levels of significance by psychological researchers. *Journal of Psychology*, 1963, *55*, 33–38.

Rosenthal, R., & Rubin, B. D. Interpersonal expectancy effects: The first 345 studies. *The Behavioral and Brain Sciences*, 1978, *3*, 377–386.

Snedecor, G. W., & Cochran, W. G. *Statistical methods* (6th ed.). Ames: Iowa State University Press, 1967.

Received March 12, 1979 ∎

4

Improving the Quality of Evidence
Interconnections Among Primary Evaluation, Secondary Analysis, and Quantitative Synthesis

David S. Cordray and Robert C. Orwin

1. INTRODUCTION

An examination of recent books on evaluation reveals a number of proposals promising to enhance evaluation practices. For example, Cronbach and associates (1980) offer a path toward *reform* in evaluation, Datta and Perloff (1979) called their book *Improving Evaluations,* and Rossi, Freeman, and Wright's (1979) *Evaluation: A Systematic Approach* offers more orderly tactics for conducting evaluations. Our contribution, *Reanalyzing Program Evaluations* (Boruch, Wortman, & Cordray, 1981), proposes secondary analysis as a means of understanding and improving the quality of evaluations and their conduct. The U.S. General Accounting Office's (1982) efforts at *evaluation synthesis* take this a step further, representing an interest in accumulating evidence over multiple assessments.

As such, three levels of research are currently being used to understand the effects of planned interventions on personal and social problems. These can be labeled primary evaluation, secondary analysis (also known as secondary-evaluation, meta-evaluation, and reanalysis), and quantitative synthesis (e.g., meta-analysis, combining probabilities, and the like). While each domain has its own distinct goals and foci, little systematic attention has been devoted to how they are interrelated. Our purpose is not to introduce any new methods or tactics for evaluation; rather, we take this opportunity to examine overlap among these levels of analysis and suggest how points of convergence can be exploited to improve the utility and quality of evaluation efforts.

Overview

With three research domains there are six possible paths of influence (if we allow for bidirectional influence). We do not intend to cover all possibilities. Rather,

Authors' Note: This article was supported by NIMH 1 T32-MH17040-01 and NIMH 5 T32 MH15113-04/05. We are grateful for comments provided by L. J. Sonnefeld, Robert F. Boruch, Tom R. Tyler, Eleanor Chelimsky, and Georgine M. Pion. An earlier version of this article was presented at the American Psychological Association Annual Meetings, Washington, D.C., August 26, 1982, Richard R. Bootzin, Chair.

From David S. Cordray and Robert C. Orwin, "Improving the Quality of Evidence: Interconnections Among Primary Evaluation, Secondary Analysis, and Quantitative Synthesis," original manuscript. Copyright © 1983 by Sage Publications, Inc.

attention is directed at four areas: how quantitative synthesis can improve primary research efforts, how secondary analysis can be used to improve quantitative synthesis, how secondary analysis can improve primary research, and how quantitative synthesis will have to be altered to handle changes in primary research practices.

Section 2 focuses on expanding the utility of quantitative syntheses. To date these efforts have concentrated almost exclusively on summarizing results of studies in a particular domain (e.g., the effects of psychotherapy). This is understandable inasmuch as providing a statistically based summary of the effects over multiple assessments is the primary reason for these undertakings. However, substantial information is also obtained regarding design characteristics, types of measures, substantive factors, artifacts, and setting types that could be exploited to improve the quality of subsequent studies. We argue that systematic accumulation of information on research factors can provide an "actuarial data base" that can be useful in two ways. First, on the planning side, evidence from prior research can be used to derive estimates of the likelihood of encountering a variety of research conditions (in subsequent research). This point is illustrated using data from the Smith, Glass, and Miller (1980) meta-analysis of psychotherapy outcomes. The second way in which these actuarial data bases may be used is as a means of judging the influence of differential research quality on study outcomes. Essentially these assessments have to be viewed as merely a normative basis for judging the quality of individual studies. Such a normative framework could guide the critique phase of secondary analysis (see Boruch, Cordray, & Wortman, 1981) and evaluation synthesis (GAO, 1982). This point is illustrated using a variety of studies that appeared during the past decade.

The accuracy of the substantive findings and the value of the actuarial data stemming from quantitative syntheses depends on the quality of the evidence that is extracted from each study and the manner in which it is recorded as part of the synthesis. Here, secondary analysis may be profitably used. Two specific areas are considered in Section 3: (1) secondary analysis of primary evaluations *prior* to quantitative integration, and (2) critique and reanalysis of the quantitative syntheses. The first area is fundamental to the synthesis process, but with a few exceptions (see GAO, 1982) has been overlooked. While some reasonable arguments have been offered for ignoring secondary analysis of studies prior to statistical integration, they are not sufficiently compelling to warrant side-stepping the issue of accuracy altogether. Critique *and* reanalysis of primary studies, even if only conducted on a sample of studies (see Boruch & Cordray, 1980), is important to assure that the knowledge accumulated through statistical integration is as meaningful as possible. Further, just as primary analyses are subject to the idiosyncrasies of the research procedures that are employed, conclusions based on quantitative synthesis also rely on assumptions and the adequacy of the analysis. This section enumerates secondary analysis procedures that could be employed to verify the integrity of primary studies and quantitative syntheses.

Section 4 outlines changes in synthesis practices that should be considered. Synthesis procedures have been primarily directed at comparative studies where a probability level or a standardized metric (e.g., Cohen's d) serves as the common basis for statistical integration across studies. This approach is unnecessarily narrow. Three arguments are presented that suggest a need to expand synthesis practices: (1) comparative methods represent only one of many meaningful ways of testing the effectiveness of treatments (e.g., dose-response studies); (2) in the past five years, there has been an increased advocacy for the use of innovative methods that depart from traditional experimental/comparative procedures (see N. Smith, 1981); and (3) evaluation specialists have promoted the notion of conducting a series of small scale studies in tandem and sequentially within a single evaluation. Diversity of methods, especially nonquantitative procedures, makes traditional quantitative synthesis impossible, forcing the analyst to exclude these studies as unsuitable for synthesis. If synthesis procedures are to be useful for informing policy, attention needs to be directed at developing ways of aggregating results across studies that use nontraditional procedures. The same issue arises when multiple designs, measures, and analyses are used within a single study. Suggestions for altering synthesis practices are offered.

The last section is devoted to a brief summary of the areas where the three research domains converge. In addition, future research and development activities that will be necessary to facilitate greater correspondence among these domains are indicated. The ultimate goal is to improve the quality of evidence so that society's decision makers will be better served by the evaluation industry.

2. USING QUANTITATIVE SYNTHESIS
TO IMPROVE PRIMARY EVALUATIONS

Review of Quantitative Synthesis:
Goals and Procedures

We use the term quantitative synthesis as a general label for the practices associated with statistically based aggregation of primary research and evaluations. Although statistical procedures for combining numerical estimates of the effects of treatments are rooted in the early statistical literature (e.g., Fisher, 1938), the use of quantitative procedures to summarize and explore a body of social science literature is relatively new. Numerous terms have been given to the methods used as part of this level of analysis. These include "combining probabilities" (Cooper, 1979; Rosenthal, 1978), "validity generalization" (Hunter, Schmidt, & Jackson, 1982), "accumulating evidence" (Light & Smith, 1971), "vote-counting" (see Hedges & Olkin, 1980), and "meta-analysis" (Glass, 1976; Smith, Glass, & Miller, 1980). Walberg and Haertel (1980) provide a brief discussion of these procedures. Each topic has specific procedures that distinguish it from the others, but there remains a common theme: devising a judgment about scientific research results when multiple studies are considered. The results from hundreds of studies often need to be integrated in order to summarize the literature on a given topic. In these cases quantitative procedures can serve as an efficient mechanism for devising an overall judgment of the *prevalence* and *magnitude* of effects. They can also serve as a means of understanding differences among studies and as a means of identifying particularly potent interventions (see Pillemer & Light, 1980).

Conceptually, the quantitative synthesis process is rather simple; four steps are generally involved. First, and not unlike the more traditional literature review, the process begins with an extensive literature search covering published and unpublished (e.g., dissertations) reports pertinent to a given substantive domain. The next, and possibly most time consuming phase involves reading and recording the primary results (i.e., effect size, probability level, test statistics) along with judgments about methodological (e.g., design, attrition, reactivity of measure) and substantive (e.g., type of treatment, duration, client/subject characteristics, and the like) characteristics of each study. The third phase entails testing covariances between study characteristics and the effect size, and making preliminary decisions as to the comparability of effect sizes based on differential study characteristics. In some cases (e.g., Glass & Smith, 1979), differences in aggregate effect sizes for well controlled versus poorly controlled studies warrant reporting aggregate effects for these two groups of studies separately. The final phase simply involves providing the summary calculations and an interpretation of the results.

There are two distinctive characteristics of the quantitative synthesis process: (1) transformation of summary statistics (outcomes) from primary studies, and (2) systematic examination of study characteristics and the use of procedures to accommodate heterogeneity.

Transformations of Summary Statistics. On the outcome side the synthesis process begins with a transformation of reported statistics into a common metric that can be arithmetically manipulated. For example, the common metric in meta-analysis (Glass, 1976, 1978) is an effect size (ES) measure fashioned after Cohen's d statistic:

$$ES = \frac{M_t - M_c}{Sd_c} , \qquad [1]$$

where M_t and M_c are the means for treated and untreated groups, respectively, and Sd_c is the standard deviation for the untreated group. Across studies, then, the average ES is simply:

$$mean\ ES = \frac{\sum_{i=1}^{N} \frac{M_t - M_c}{Sd_c}}{N} \qquad [2]$$

This yields a relatively straightforward and intuitively appealing means of establishing the magnitude and direction of effects across N assessments.

Rosenthal (1978) takes a different tactic in aggregating results across multiple studies. Rather than transforming the between-group means into a common metric, as in the Glass-type meta-analysis, he relies on the early statistical literature for combining probabilities. There are a variety of methods that are applicable under certain restrictions (see Rosenthal, 1978). One common technique entails transforming the exact probability reported for a between-group difference into its corresponding Z value in a standard normal distribution. The summary calculation across studies is:

$$Z_c = \frac{\sum\limits_{i=1}^{N} Z_{p_i}}{N^{1/2}} \qquad [3]$$

The probability of Z_c is viewed as the likelihood of the combined effects of the treatment across assessments. Z_{p_i} is the normal deviate for each probability (p) in study i. N is simply the number of probability values included in the synthesis.

The primary reason for using these transformations is that measures and measurement level (e.g., dichotomous versus continuous measures) differ from one study to the next. Even when a particular measure is used consistently across studies, it is often necessary to devise a common metric prior to quantitative synthesis (see Devine & Cook's [this volume] use of a percentage difference for their synthesis of length of hospital stay). Under some conditions (i.e., comparable measures for a homogeneous cluster of studies), the procedures advocated by Light and Smith (1971) could be undertaken given the availability of microdata.

When measures differ, the interpretation of the ES can be difficult due to differential sensitivity and relevance of measures to treatment. Perhaps one of the most serious efforts at deriving uniform summary statistics prior to aggregation was carried out as part of the ESEA, Title I Evaluation and Reporting System (TIERS) by the U.S. Department of Education (see Anderson et al., 1978). In this effort, reading and mathematics achievement tests were individually normed and raw scores were transformed into normal curve equivalents (NCEs). While this was an admirable attempt, technical considerations render the selection of this transformation difficult to justify (Spencer, Note 1). At this point the most sensible step regarding choice of transformations is to carry out more than one transformation and compare the conclusions derived from each (see Devine & Cook, this volume).

Accommodating Heterogeneity. With the exception of a few knotty issues concerning the appropriateness of the transformation, the foregoing is elementary and very straightforward in the cases where research quality is consistently high across studies (e.g., in experiments where the individual estimates are unbiased).[1] Quantitative synthesis becomes more complicated when studies are heterogeneous with respect to their elegance, quality, or the type of design employed. There are at least two options to accommodate this type of heterogeneity. Studies that failed to achieve our quality standards can be *excluded* or they can be retained and *weighted* differentially in accordance with a judgment as to their elegance, quality, and so on. Rosenthal (1978) suggests that the summary calculation would assume the following form if a weighting factor were applied:

$$Z'_c = \frac{\sum_{i=1}^{N} (w_i Z_{p_i})}{\sqrt{\Sigma w_1{}^2}}, \qquad [4]$$

where the combined probability would be obtained for Z'_c rather than Z_c as in equation 3.

Another strategy for accommodating differential research quality has been used by Glass and his colleagues (e.g., Smith et al., 1980). They argue that excluding studies due to suspected flaws is inadequate as a general strategy for aggregating studies. Rather, the influence of flaws should be examined directly and accommodated in the synthesis. Statistically, this empirical assessment is carried out by examining the covariance between study characteristics and the ES measure. For example, if we are concerned about differential research quality, types of treatments, types of measures, types of subjects, subject by treatment interactions, and so on, their influence should be examined directly. A common method for examining covariance is through ordinary least squares regression:

$$\text{mean } \hat{ES} = b_0 + b_1 X_1 + \ldots + b_{k-1} X_{k-1} + b_k X_k \qquad [5]$$

where $k - 1$ factors are designated as influencing the magnitude of ES, and X_k is a dummy coded variable representing treatment types. The average ES for each comparison (e.g., Type I Therapy versus Type II Therapy) is adjusted due to covariance with factors 1 to $K - 1$. The covariance is indexed here as an unstandardized partial regression coefficient. The major advantage of the regression-based analysis is that the influence of specific variables can be examined directly. Since this is an additive model, nonlinear components (e.g., interactions) have to be modeled explicitly (see Smith et al., 1980). Given the number of potential interactions with $K > 2$ variables, some care (i.e., "theory") has to be taken in specifying the model (see Footnote 1). The weight applied to the combined probability or blocking procedures described by Rosenthal (1978) avoids these problems, provided the weight adequately characterizes the notion of research quality. Boruch and Gomez (1979) provide a statistical argument for examining the influence of degraded reliability, validity, treatment integrity, and other forms of contamination that influence estimates of power multiplicatively. This index of sensitivity could be used as a weight for differential quality (equation 4) or the components could be modeled in the regression adjustment (equation 5).

A cost of reliance on a single weight for representing quality is that neither the differential characteristics exhibited by studies nor their relative contribution to the overall weight are retrievable. As we shall see, the differential characteristics of studies can be useful for planning subsequent research. The reporting of weighted values *and* study characteristics (univariate) should be routinely conducted.

Improving Primary Analyses:
Exploiting the By-Products of Quantitative Syntheses

Many quantitative syntheses have been undertaken across a variety of substantive areas. The subsequent reports are almost exclusively devoted to the substantive topic under consideration. Most quantitative syntheses to date have paid little or no attention to the wealth of information collected about methodological characteristics of the studies. At best, the research characteristics are used in regression analyses to account for differences among treatment types. The utility of quantitative syntheses could be broadened by more considered examination of the by-products of the synthesists' efforts. This section argues that efforts to characterize the quality of prior research represent an important resource for planning subsequent research. We also show how they can be used to develop a normative frame for judging the quality of completed research/evaluations.

Planning. In well-defined research areas or settings (e.g., laboratories) the ability to plan a research project is less hampered by unknowns than is characteristic of research conducted in field settings. The field researcher is not always able to specify in advance the number of participants, whether they will remain in the project for its intended duration, which measures are most sensitive to treatment effects under field conditions, or when measurement should be undertaken. Often, the best we can do is rely on hunches or the advice of colleagues and advisory groups and devise a fall-back position in the event our guesses were wrong. Of course, postponing the assessment until pilot testing is completed remains sound advice, but it may not be feasible when program management is under pressure to install their intended services.

The methodological characteristics reported as part of quantitative syntheses may provide an empirical basis for some critical major front-end decisions. Of course, specialists in research methodology will recognize this familiar argument: the sins and exemplars of the past are illustrative and serve as a basis for improving the conduct of inquiry. Hoaglin, Light, McPeek, Mosteller, and Stoto (1982) provide numerous examples of systematic assessment concerning the adequacy of research methods used to study the effects of medical interventions. Heberlein and Baumgartner (1978), Sudman and Bradburn (1974), and Andrews (1980) have made substantial efforts to understand research factors that influence survey results. Bernstein and Freeman (1975) examined quality of research and evaluations supported by the federal government. Advice from these assessments ranges from hints as to what should be avoided to prediction equations for estimating response rates to surveys (see Heberlein & Baumgartner, 1978). Our aspirations fall somewhere between these levels of specificity.

Given the availability of computer-based literature searches, microform methods of storage, and the dramatic increase in the number of journals available for dissemination of results, it is *theoretically* possible to retrieve a substantial proportion of studies in a particular field of inquiry.[2] Systematic recording of research and treatment characteristics from this collection of studies provides a data base analogous to those used for establishing expectancies in actuarial tables. The basic notion is to establish a set of statistics that indicate the *prevalence* of specific research-related events. Just as insurance companies establish rates for premiums based on expected incidences, researchers can make their decisions about allocation of resources based on expectancies derived from previous research. The assumption here is that the sample of studies is at least representative of the variety of research conditions one would encounter in subsequent research. To make the notion of an actuarial data base concrete, it may be reasonable to illustrate how they could be developed and used.

A Short Example. For estimating numerical effects of treatment intervention, a primary concern is whether there will be sufficient statistical power to detect a treatment effect. Freiman, Chalmers, Smith, and Kuebler (1978), for example, note that this issue is overlooked in reports issued on medical interventions employing the randomized control trial. Mosteller, Gilbert, and McPeek (1980) see this as sufficiently important to warrant a recommendation that journal editors incorporate power assessments into reporting standards.

The methodological by-products of quantitative synthesis are relevant to a more systematic appraisal of power prior to mounting a new assessment. For most power analyses the issue is to determine the number of subjects necessary to achieve a specified level of power. This requires stating desired levels of Type I error, Type II error, and an estimate of the expected effect size. The effect size (ES) is determined as in equation 1 or recovered through procedures specified in Glass (1978). The difficulty usually arises in trying to obtain a sensible estimate of this noncentrality parameter (ES). If we are overly optimistic about the size of the effect, we will choose a sample size that is too small, resulting in the use of a low power test. If we err on the other side, the analysis may suggest a sample size that is prohibitively large. As an empirical means of establishing this value, it is often suggested (e.g., Cohen, 1977) that the literature be consulted. An actuarial table of noncentrality values eliminates the need for this, and will probably be more complete. Consequently, it is less likely to yield biased population estimates of the distribution's mean or variance, either of which will adversely affect the power analysis.

Table 1 shows the empirical distribution of ESs from the Smith and associates' (1980) meta-analysis of 475 psychotherapy outcome studies. Since most studies included more than one ES, the first column of Table 1 is based on 1766 effect size values. The entries in each column represent the cumulative likelihood of observing an effect size of the designated magnitude or smaller. For example, it is readily seen that across all effect sizes (see column 1), the likelihood of observing one that is ≤ 0 is .114. The likelihood of an ES *as large as 1.0* is .706. The complement of these figures is also determinable; the likelihood that an effect will exceed 2.4 is .042 (1 - .958).

TABLE 1   Cumulative Likelihood of Effect Size Values
for Six Treatment Locations

Recorded Effect Size	Overall	School	Hospital	Other Outpatient	College MH Facility	Prison/ Residential	MH Center Other Clinic
≤ .5	.020	.041		.015	.013	.062	.028
− .4	.031	.069		.015	.020	.093	.037
− .3	.040	.085		.023	.031	.103	.065
− .2	.058	.114	.015	.023	.050	.134	.074
− .1	.078	.146	.034	.030	.069	.144	.111
0	.114	.191	.059	.038	.112	.144	.166
.1	.157	.272	.093	.060	.148	.195	.222
.2	.204	.350	.118	.098	.190	.268	.250
.3	.251	.427	.172	.165	.225	.288	.296
.4	.315	.516	.240	.218	.287	.309	.388
.5	.387	.610	.348	.241	.335	.351	.472
.6	.459	.654	.466	.316	.439	.412	.528
.7	.537	.711	.559	.368	.514	.608	.546
.8	.598	.748	.642	.444	.569	.659	.556
.9	.660	.776	.686	.639	.619	.711	.638
1.0	.706	.813	.765	.752	.655	.742	.657
1.1	.747	.841	.799	.797	.692	.794	.806
1.2	.778	.866	.828	.850	.721	.804	.815
1.3	.811	.890	.882	.872	.752	.824	.852
1.4	.833	.915	.902	.880	.771	.845	.889
1.5	.857	.927	.941	.902	.801	.845	.916
1.6	.875	.935	.941	.925	.821	.897	.926
1.7	.890	.943	.951	.932	.843	.897	.935
1.8	.905	.943		.932	.855	.907	.935
1.9	.914	.943		.932	.868	.907	.944
2.0	.921	.955		.955	.876	.918	
2.1	.930				.883	.928	
2.2	.930				.892	.948	
2.3	.942				.902		
2.4	.958				.915		
2.5					.923		
2.6					.929		
2.7					.932		
2.8					.935		
2.9					.938		
3.0							
N_{ES}	1766	246	204	133	743	97	108

SOURCE: Smith, Glass, & Miller (1980).

A table of overall likelihoods is a beginning, but provides only ballpark estimates for the research planner. The precision and utility of these are increased considerably by a breakdown into subtables based on various particulars of the research situation. This way the likelihood estimates can be tailored to the research planner's individual needs. For example, columns 2-7 in Table 1 display the cumulative likelihood of observing a given ES level (or smaller) across different treatment locations. When treatment location is taken into account, likelihoods shift considerably. For example, an ES of .6 *or smaller* is more likely in school settings (.654) than it is in college mental health facilities (.439). A researcher could therefore expect to find a larger effect size in the latter than the former setting.

The advantage to an actuarial table is that individual researchers can impose their own level of risk tolerance. It seems sensible to advocate choosing two values for effect size and then determining the necessary sample size. A conservative estimate of an ES may be derived by choosing one that is associated with a small cumulative likelihood (i.e., the lower side of the distribution) *and* the median may be selected as an upper bound for the likely magnitude of the ES. If the treatment is considered to be a potent change agent, the effect size corresponding to the third quartile may be a reasonable value as an upper bound. The point here is that the decision is based on likelihoods derived from previous efforts to assess similar interventions. Of course, the accuracy of these values depends on the quality of quantitative synthesis procedures used to develop the data base, a point we will address in Section 3.

It may seem sufficient to stop here, once the value (or values) of ES to complete the power calculation have been obtained. However, the by-products can be exploited further. Specifically, the a priori power analysis determines the number of participants necessary to achieve a specified probability of detecting a true difference. This sample size value is not the most important one. Rather, we are concerned about the *achieved* sample size—the number of individuals who remain in treatment and control conditions for the intended duration of the program or assessment. The question then concerns what proportion of the sample will leave prior to posttest assessment.

Table 2 provides the cumulative probabilities of various levels of mortality for treatment and control groups for the Smith and associates (1980) data base. Since treatment settings are likely to differ in the mortality rates (i.e., many factors leading to attrition are beyond control of the researcher in field settings), Table 2 presents cumulative likelihood estimates for six different treatment locations. As with the ES distributions displayed in Table 1, mortality rates differ across treatment locations. However, the pattern of values in the upper and lower portions of Table 2 suggest that attrition/mortality is comparable for treatment and control conditions.

As a means of assuring sufficient *achieved* statistical power, the sample size calculated based on noncentrality estimates derived from Table 1 could be adjusted in accordance with expected attrition. For example, it appears that across treatments the likelihood of 20% or less mortality is in excess of .8. Increasing the initial

TABLE 2   Cumulative Likelihood of Mortality Levels
for Six Treatment Locations

Mortality Level	Treatment Locations					
Treatment Group (percentages)	School	Hospital	Other Outpatient	College MH Facility	Prison/ Residential	MH Center Other Clinic
0%	.673[1]	.631	.761	.643	.435	.704
5%	.752	.659	.804	.666	.718	.704
10%	.855	.733	.804	.764	.918	.776
15%	.869	.801	.837	.827	.929	.816
20%	.972	.824	.859	.950	.988	.857
25%	.986	.841	.935	.977	1.000	.959
30%	.986	.858	.935	.988		1.000
35%	1.000	.926	.967	.997		
40%		.932	.967	1.000		
Comparison Group (percentages)						
0%	.706	.545	.772	.733	.495	.745
5%	.743	.574	.815	.755	.871	.745
10%	.864	.625	.815	.823	.976	.775
15%	.864	.790	.859	.849	.988	.775
20%	.967	.813	.880	.950	.988	.837
25%	.972	.841	.935	.983	1.000	.918
30%	.986	.858	.935	.988		.918
35%	1.000	.858	.935	.988		1.000
40%		.864	1.000	.997		
N_{ES}	246	204	133	743	97	108
Percentage missing	13.0%	13.7%	30.8%	6.6%	12.4%	9.3%

NOTE: 1. Missing data are excluded from cumulative likelihood calculations.
SOURCE: Smith, Glass, and Miller (1980).

sample size to compensate for this expected mortality would assure that a priori estimates of Type II error are maintained throughout the course of the study.

Two caveats are in order at this point. First, none of this should be taken to imply that maintenance of sample size is sufficient to assure statistical conclusion validity (see Cook & Campbell, 1979). For any given study the causes of attrition need to be probed and their influence estimated. Jurs and Glass (1971) provide a simple analysis-of-variance-based method for diagnosing the influence of attrition (in general) and differential attrition.

The second caveat refers to the fact that the evidence provided in these tables is observational data. There are literally hundreds of combinations of factors influencing the results from comparative studies. A far more useful means of planning research would be to collect all those studies that contain conditions similar to the intended research and examine them for hints as to what should be expected. The utility of by-products of quantitative synthesis would be greatly enhanced if such tailored searching could be done. This could be accommodated if these data bases were made available as Machine Readable Data Files (MRDF).

An Extension. The preceding discussion is based on conventional notions of statistical power. Others (e.g., Boruch & Gomez, 1979; Lipsey, Note 2) have shown that power is also influenced by additional degradation of reliability and validity of the response variable due to noise in the field setting. Imperfect delivery and reception of treatment further degrade the sensitivity of the statistical test. Our review of a random sample (N = 25) of psychotherapy studies reveals that roughly 24% of the ESs could be considered diluted due to imperfect implementation of treatment (i.e., loss of integrity), reliability of outcome measures was judged to be less than .7 in 30%-40% of the ESs, and contamination of the control group occurred to a moderate extent in 29% of the ESs. Numerical estimates of these values were not always reported and had to be estimated from evidence provided in the written documents. If estimates of these additional parameters could be systematically extracted from prior research, our a priori assessments of power to detect differences would provide more informed decisions on the sensitivity of evaluation designs. If these calculations reveal substantial insensitivity we may reconsider conducting an impact assessment and avoid premature experimentation (Cook & Campbell, 1979; Riecken & Boruch, 1974).

Judgments About
the Quality of Research and Evaluation

The preceding section focuses on accumulating evidence about research factors so as to derive estimates of the likelihood of encountering specific research conditions. The fact that some studies reveal higher levels of attrition, contamination, unreliability, and the like points to the plausibility of these factors. The variation does not necessarily mean that these differential levels covary with study outcomes (i.e., threaten the validity of the overall conclusions). This can be treated as an empirical question.

Sechrest and Yeaton (1981) argue that empirical distributions such as shown in Table 1 could serve as a normative frame from which to judge the relative value of an alternative treatment modality. For example, suppose two studies are recently completed, and one produces an effect size of .5 and the other produces an effect size of .8. The cumulative likelihood graphs would reveal the relative rankings of each study. Pillemer and Light (1980) make a similar point. They argue that examining the distribution of effect sizes can be an effective means of identifying highly successful interventions. It is obvious that the same type of argument can be made for the utility of evidence for identifying the extent to which flaws (e.g., attrition) covary with study outcomes, and under what circumstances.

The Glass-type analytic strategy is well suited to examining the observed covariance to judge the general influence of research factors on summary statistics. The utility of these assessments for understanding covariance is dependent on the adequacy of the quantitative synthesis procedures. While this is not the place to articulate what constitutes "adequacy," the statistical literature on analysis of observational data specifies a myriad of factors that attenuate indices of covariance (e.g., unreliability, restriction of range) or yield spuriously high covariance. If the analysis is well executed and properly diagnosed (e.g., sensitivity analyses), however, a good bit of controversy over the presence of bias, its direction, and magnitude could be settled by these types of assessments. For example, our theory of design suggests that assignment procedures (nonrandom versus random) yield differential estimates of treatment effect, with random assignment producing an unbiased estimate. The meta-analysis of the effects of class size on achievement supports this notion (see Glass & Smith, 1979), but the lack of observed covariance between internal validity and ES in the psychotherapy meta-analysis does not (see Smith et al., 1980). The point here is that systematic assessment of the influences of methods can potentially facilitate the judgment as to how much faith (in the long run) can be placed in studies that rely on different methods.

Analogues. There are examples of research synthesis that are devoted exclusively to determining the influence of research factors on the quality of evidence. Quantitative synthesis of research factors could be patterned after these studies. For example, Sudman and Bradburn's (1974) assessment of how research and procedural factors (e.g., type of administration) influence the quality of survey responses is a classic demonstration. They transformed the results of individual studies into a response effect index and examined the influence of task, interviewer, and respondent variables on this measure of accuracy. As another example, Andrews (1980) used structural modeling to examine the quality of survey responses. His tables show clearly the direction and magnitude of influences that different characteristics (question format, item type, battery length, and so on) have on estimates of validity and reliability.

Application. These efforts are likely to be valuable tools when evaluation specialists begin using the standards and guidelines that have been developed by professional organizations (e.g., Evaluation Research Society, 1981; Joint Committee on Standards for Educational Evaluations, 1980; GAO, 1978). In the absence of a theoretical basis for judging the *relative* merits of specific procedures (i.e., accuracy of surveys based on randomized response formats versus direct questioning to solicit sensitive information), it may be difficult to know how much trust can be placed in one study relative to another which uses different procedures. Presumably, we would choose to place more confidence in the estimate derived from the procedure that usually produces a smaller relative error (from Sudman and Bradburn's analysis) and one that yields the largest reliability and validity coefficient (from Andrews's assessment). It is true that experienced researchers can make general judgments about the value of different practices with respect to the quality of evidence they provide (i.e., a randomized trial yields unbiased estimates in the long run and nonrandomized experiments are likely to be biased). This discussion argues for more fine-grain distinctions regarding the magnitude of bias. It seems that these judgments will be better informed to the extent that we systematically accumulate information as to the strength and weaknesses of our methods. Quantitative synthesis, although focused on substantive knowledge, can provide some of this evidence.

3. IMPROVING RESEARCH AND EVALUATIONS: THE ROLE OF SECONDARY ANALYSIS

Quantitative synthesis refers to the use of statistical procedures for aggregating the results of multiple studies. We have seen that the quality of the design, measures, and analyses of primary studies has been incorporated into the process most extensively by those who follow a Glass-type of synthesis strategy. Social science research methodologists have yet another set of tools that focus on the quality of evidence: secondary analysis. While secondary analysis has been acknowledged in the quantitative synthesis literature (see Glass, 1976), only passing comments have been offered as to the distinctions and similarities between those general strategies. This section makes two points: (1) routine secondary analysis, prior to quantitative synthesis, may be necessary for promoting higher quality primary studies; and (2) routine secondary analysis of quantitative syntheses may be profitable, given the type of criticism that has been leveled at early meta-analyses.

Secondary Analysis: General Goals

In its most basic form secondary analysis entails two distinct activities—critique and, when microdata or sufficient summary statistics (e.g., variance-covariance matrices) are available, reanalysis. The main issue for secondary analysis is to determine whether the conclusions offered in the original study are justified by the evidence. The products of secondary analysis include (1) simply verifying that the original analysis is accurate (see Havens, 1981); (2) reestimating the effects using statistical procedures that rely on more appropriate assumptions (e.g., Magidson, 1977); and (3) multiple competing analyses designed to bracket effects when an appropriate statistical model is unspecifiable (e.g., Wortman, Reichardt, & St. Pierre, 1978). At a minimum the secondary analyst may simply critique the evaluation, pointing out plausible flaws that limit the validity and utility of the evaluation. Boruch and associates (1981) provide an overview of secondary analysis and its historical underpinnings.

It is apparent that secondary analysis and quantitative synthesis focus on different issues and entail distinct procedures (e.g., quantitative synthesis summarizes characteristics of studies and secondary analysis entails critique and reanalysis of microdata). However, they are compatible in that the results of multiple secondary analyses could be integrated to form a single estimate using meta-analytic procedures. Cook and Gruder (1978) allude to this interface in their discussion of the varieties of meta-evaluation that may be undertaken. Light and Smith (1971) also focus on the integration of evidence across multiple studies when the micro-data are available. At these outcroppings the distinctions between meta-analysis and secondary analysis blur.

Secondary Analysis to Improve Primary Analyses

Those of us who have examined (systematically or otherwise) the quality of impact evaluations may question the extent to which quantitative synthesis is a viable option for program evaluation. Cook and Gruder (1978) review a series of assessments of prior evaluations that uniformly conclude that the quality of these efforts is certainly uneven, and in many instances so poor as to render them worthless. Our own appraisals (Boruch & Cordray, 1980; Boruch, Cordray, & Pion, 1981) have led to similar conclusions for educational evaluations.

The secondary analysis literature is quite clear that design and analysis strategies can seriously influence the magnitude and even the direction of the putative effect. For example, the original Ohio-Westinghouse assessment showed a negative effect of Head Start. On the other hand, a variety of reanalyses have since shown that the original estimate was biased due to design and analysis artifacts (see Campbell & Erlebacher, 1970; Magidson, 1977; Rindskopf, 1978, 1981). Similar artifacts have been discovered in evaluations of manpower training programs (Director, 1977) and juvenile justice evaluations (Maltz, Gordon, McDowall & McCleary, 1980). Boruch and Cordray (1980) uncovered frequent transgressions in technical common sense in unpublished local school district evaluation reports. Wolins (1962, 1981, 1982) has shown that the misapplication of statistical procedures is common in social science research.

Given these and other statistical sins, it might seem that the utility of quantitative synthesis for evaluations is seriously undercut by poor quality of primary studies. If there are substantial errors in the primary analyses, how can we rely on the aggregated results?

One solution is to reanalyze the results of primary studies prior to quantitative integration. This is a drastic solution and may be most feasible if performed on a sample of studies so that an estimate of the influence of statistical transgressions could be devised. Even in this case changes in practice regarding how we document and disseminate our data (see Linsenmeier, Wortman, & Hendricks, 1981; Robbin, 1981) and changes in professional practices (see Chalk, Frankel, & Chafer, 1980) would have to occur for this to be possible. Cordray (1982) has suggested prerelease critiques as a means of catching some obvious errors in evaluations. Multiple analyses, conducted in tandem by independent evaluators, may represent another option.

A second solution for quantitative synthesis in light of poor reporting practice, inappropriate use of statistics, and bias due to design considerations (or lack thereof) is that their covariance with the summary metric (e.g., effect size) can be examined. Cordray and Orwin (Note 3) and Orwin (1982) show that this is not done routinely and that the quality of reporting does influence the regression analysis in some cases. This brings us to our next point—the use of secondary analysis to assess the quality of quantitative synthesis.

Secondary Analysis to Improve Quantitative Synthesis

Of course if the results of quantitative synthesis efforts are to be useful in the policy arena, adequate as a means of monitoring social science progress, or helpful in improving our understanding of how to upgrade the quality of research, they must be valid representations of the phenomena under study. Judging from published commentary (see Orwin, 1982, for a review) on these procedures, a number of researchers have doubted the validity of statistical integration to date. It has been harshly criticized and even called an exercise in "mega-silliness" (Eysenck, 1978). Among the objections leveled at procedures used for quantitative integration are accusations that (1) analysts lump studies into gross categories, (2) they combine dissimilar data—mix apples and oranges, (3) the studies they work with are seriously flawed and inadequately described, and (4) they tacitly advocate low standards for judging the quality of studies. Glass and his colleagues (see Glass, 1978; Smith et al., 1980) have argued that many of their critics are misinformed as to the purposes and procedures of meta-analytic practices. They do, however, acknowledge that poor primary reporting practice can be a serious problem. Orwin (1982) demonstrates this point empirically.

Such debate is useful for articulating concerns about social science research, but whether criticism and rebuttal can settle these issues is open to question. A more positive and empirical approach to understanding the integrity of the research process is offered by secondary analysis. Until recently, secondary analysis has been focused on primary research studies. A few critics of quantitative integration have employed secondary analysis as a means of substantiating their claims (Prioleau, Murdock, & Brody, in press), and some researchers (e.g., Landman & Dawes, 1982) have supported Smith et al.'s conclusions through reanalysis. These efforts are not entirely satisfactory (see Orwin & Cordray, in press; Cordray & Bootzin, in press), however. In the remainder of this section, issues that seem ripe for critique and reanalysis are enumerated. Two general issues are pursued—characterizing quality of research and comprehensiveness of the analysis.

Characterizing Quality of Primary Evaluations and Research. Those who have discussed research integration remain rather vague as to how differential research quality can or should be accommodated. Rosenthal (1978), in describing procedures for combining probabilities, devotes one line to the use of a process that is a variation on Stouffer's weighting procedure (see equation 4). Rosenthal also proposes the use of blocking procedures as a means of taking differential quality into account. Glass is more explicit, but his recommendations on *what* factors should be considered have to be gleaned from *how* he and his colleagues have treated the topic in practice. Further, even if one looks at the procedures employed by the same meta-analyst (or group of meta-analysts) across different substantive domains, there is considerable variation in what factors are included and how the data are analyzed. For a relatively new field, this heterogeneity is healthy and necessary, but only when coupled with systematic assessment. We have found little effort devoted to testing competing procedures or the adequacy of selected procedures.

As to specific practices, the quality of primary research has been characterized with varying levels of conscientiousness in recent efforts to integrate research. In their psychotherapy meta-analysis, Smith, Glass, and Miller (1980) considered multiple facets of what constitutes quality, that is, client and therapist assignment, mortality, reactivity, type of measures, degree of experimental blinding, experimenter allegiance, and others. On the other hand, Johnson, Maruyama, Johnson, and Nelson (1981) seem to undervalue the complexity of research quality, preferring to use as an index the quality of the journal in which the report appeared. While such a simplistic index may serve as a *proxy* for research quality, it is at best a pale reflection of the construct, given that numerous other factors influence where and if a study is published. At worst, it is worthless or misleading; recent work has produced both theory (Rosenthal, 1978) and data (Smith, 1980) that challenge the traditional view that published work is methodologically superior to unpublished. In another recent meta-analysis, Posavac (1980) considered internal validity and reactivity, but did not report how they influence effect-size estimates.

Comprehensiveness of Analytical Procedures. This category entails many aspects of the data analysis process. The scope of this article does not permit a detailed elaboration of all the issues. Rather, we focus on a particular method for establishing the validity of an analysis, namely, the use of competing analyses. By competing analyses we mean the use of two or more analytic procedures applied to the same data for the explicit purpose of assessing the robustness of the findings. These procedures may include (1) alternative indices for characterizing research quality; (2) use of qualitative procedures (e.g., categorical and quantitative scales for depicting design quality); (3) use of validation procedures (e.g., sample splitting); (4) replication of findings across multiple outcomes (e.g., effect size *and* probability level); and (5) data checking procedures (e.g., determining whether values that have to be inferred from reports yield different effect-size distributions than actual values).

With a few exceptions (e.g. Glass & Smith, 1979; Smith et al., 1980) little attention has been devoted to establishing the adequacy of statistical aggregation using these or other types of procedures. Further, procedures used by one meta-analyst (e.g., Glass) have sometimes simply been copied by others as if they were well-established conventions. Johnson et al. (1981) make explicit their assumptions about the linearity of effect size with research quality indices, but there is no evidence offered as to the validity of such an assumption. Rather than simply stating the assumption, the procedures suggested above would argue for an examination of whether the relationship is linear or nonlinear. Such methods are not often used, even though professional societies advocate making these assessments (see Evaluation Research Society, 1980; Joint Committee on Educational Evaluation, 1980).

4. THE INFLUENCE OF DIVERSITY OF RESEARCH METHODS
ON THE QUANTITATIVE SYNTHESIS PROCESS

Despite the fact that quantitative syntheses may contain hundreds of studies, an examination of the bibliography for a given synthesis may reveal two types of omissions: (1) comparative studies that were simply overlooked, and (2) studies relying on methods deemed unsuitable for quantitative synthesis as it is currently undertaken. The first category of omissions is important, but it merely reflects an inadequacy of the search strategy. The second type of omission represents a more fundamental issue. This issue concerns the adaptibility of the synthesis process to changes in method of inquiry. The past five years have witnessed extensive growth in alternative methods for assessing aspects of programs or their overall effects. The long-term survival of quantitative synthesis as a research enterprise will require changes in practice that accommodate diversity of methods.

We have seen two types of diversity—(1) an expansion of the types of activities that are considered as legitimate evaluation tools, and (2) an increase in the number of methods employed in a particular evaluation. The latter represents a better understanding of what is meant by comprehensive evaluation, whereas the former refers to an increased diversification of our evaluation portfolio.

Glass (1980) identifies numerous models of evaluation, and the list of procedures used within distinct models has grown exponentially. In broadening our methodological portfolio, considerable attention has been devoted to innovative approaches to evaluation (see N. Smith, 1981). The preference for new methods is clearly visible in reactions to our recommendations for use of high quality designs (relative to statistical standards) in educational evaluations (see Boruch & Cordray, 1980, 1981; House, 1981; Bunda, 1981; Kennedy, 1981; Cronbach, 1982). Although there is no clear consensus as to what constitutes the most appropriate model for evaluation, one statement that would not engender excessive debate is that we cannot rely on the one-shot, prepost, stand-alone evaluation study to provide unambiguous and comprehensive evidence on the effects of an educational or social program. Cronbach and associates (1980) offer a strong argument for this type of statement, citing political, methodological, ethical, practical, and logical reasons. On the political side, with many constituencies associated with programs and evaluations, it is unlikely that all relevant questions will be answered within a given study (comparative or otherwise). On the methodological side, countless critiques of prior evaluation studies show that methodological deficiencies exist in a substantial proportion. On the practical side, when money is limited, cheaper methods may be more feasible—though not necessarily as accurate as higher quality designs. Often, good ethical arguments can be made against withholding a treatment. Further, even when studies are methodologically sound, inductive inference is logically restricted. All of this has contributed to the need for developing and utilizing methods in addition to classical experimental procedures. The general consensus is that we should only resort to the use of high quality designs when there is an interest in estimating impact and when there are sufficient resources to do the job well. This decision is not divorced from considerations about program maturity, ethics, and timeliness.

Implications. Currently, quantitative synthesis is applied to comparative studies. The foregoing suggests that many other types of assessment strategies will be undertaken beyond the comparative study. If these replace the more traditional methods for estimating numerical effects of programs, the pool of studies eligible to be quantitatively synthesized will diminish and, more importantly, efforts to estimate impact that are not based on experimental/comparative models will be ignored. Thus, it is reasonable to begin devoting attention to how nontraditional procedures should be synthesized.

The Institute of Program Evaluation at the General Accounting Office has begun thinking about ways to synthesize diverse sources of data. Hoaglin and associates (1982) have also tackled this problem and provide general guidelines for judging the quality of various evaluation strategies. How these pieces of evidence should be weighted remain as the major obstacle to synthesis.

The application of alternative methods that do not rely on the use of control groups for testing the effects of interventions is not new. Campbell (1975) has argued that case studies can be used for hypothesis testing when theory is well specified. Dose-response studies, treatment component studies, and within-subject control studies have been extensively used to understand the psychotherapy process. These studies are not usually considered in quantitative synthesis procedures. Hunter, Schmidt, and Jackson (1982) provide a means of broadening the evidential base for quantitative synthesis. Their reiteration of the simple statistical relation between the point biserial correlation and the d statistic broadens the options of what types of studies can be transformed into a common metric and integrated. For those who believe that broadening the options for synthesis in this way (i.e., integrating studies that are more diverse than is already the case) simply adds to the confusion, it should be remembered that covariance between *type* of study and effect sizes (or summary statistics) can be examined. If this assessment reveals substantial differences, the conclusions can be reported separately. The only key issue is that the differences between types of studies is well represented by the synthesis process. This should include (1) careful consideration of the quality of the research procedures used in each study, (2) careful examination of the adequacy of operational realizations of treatment conditions, (3) considered selection of relevant measures, and (4) consideration of differences (across studies) in context, clients, and researcher characteristics.

The increased complexity of individual studies reveals much the same type of problem for the synthesis process. Our examination of the psychotherapy meta-analysis suggests that considerable information is ignored when ESs are extracted from individual studies. Redundant measures are excluded, as are certain types of control groups and side studies. The standards and guidelines issued by various professional organizations all recommend that cross-validation efforts be undertaken as part of the evaluation. It would therefore seem counterproductive to ignore these at the synthesis stage.

Others have attempted to synthesize studies that use special control groups (e.g., placebo manipulations) in an effort to test the construct validity of interventions. For example, Prioleau et al. (in press) averaged all measures reported in a given study *as if* each were equally relevant and sensitive to the treatment versus placebo distinction (see Cordray & Bootzin, in press). Given the types of measures reported for each study, this is a questionable practice. Devine and Cook (this volume) are more sensitive to the judgmental nature of this type of assessment and use a series of breakdowns to show the effects of treatments beyond placebo conditions.

Another level of complexity is introduced by efforts to move beyond reliance on the use of single designs. For example, Lipsey, Cordray, and Berger (1981) adopt a strategy of multiple lines of evidence to evaluate the effects of a juvenile justice program. Here, numerous designs were used in tandem and sequentially to estimate effects and cross-validate the conclusions from other analyses. This evaluation included the use of short interrupted time series data to characterize community level impact and a series of quasi-experiments to estimate individual level impact of treatment services. Implementation of the program was also assessed and side studies were conducted to establish the relevance and sensitivity of methods and measures. The basic rationale for this strategy was the open recognition that although each line of evidence would be flawed in some regard, the convergence among sources of evidence would yield a more valid interpretation. This is the type of evaluation procedure that Cronbach and associates (1980) advocate, as do Cook and Campbell (1979). It is not clear how quantitative synthesis can be applied to this type of study, given practices employed to date. Two levels of analysis seem necessary. First, the covariance of design characteristics with outcomes needs to be examined for each outcome (ES). The second level is more judgmental and requires a synthesis of the pattern of data. This could be accomplished through the specification of a *range* of observed effects that attempt to bracket the true effects of the treatment and an overall judgment of the quality of the *study*.

The quantitative synthesis process cannot rely on the application of statistical procedures to yield meaningful results—these procedures are simply tools that aid human judgment. We suspect that in the future the quantitative synthesis process will evolve toward a better balance between extracting statistics and judgment. The judgment might be characterized by recording a second number or code for the meaning (as judged by the synthesist) of the statistic or study characteristic. For example, the type of placebo manipulation should be recorded along with a second rating that indicates the judged adequacy of the manipulation as a means of controlling expectancies. These judgmental ratings can be used as classification variables to provide a more fine-grained analysis.

5. INTEGRATION AND RECOMMENDATIONS

Efforts to understand the influence of planned personal and social interventions have been carried out at three levels of research: primary evaluation/research, secondary analysis, and quantitative synthesis. Each level has been pursued with little attention devoted to their interdependencies. As a preliminary step toward correcting this state of affairs, areas of convergence between levels of analysis and departures—areas of neglect—were described.

Summary

A minor reorientation in the quantitative synthesis process can facilitate better planning of primary studies. Specifically, accumulated evidence on research factors (e.g., effect sizes, mortality, reliability, integrity of treatments, contamination of comparisons, and the like) from prior research efforts can serve as a normative, that is, actuarial, data base for deriving a sense of the conditions that are likely to be encountered in subsequent research. Taking advantage of prior research experience should facilitate quality of research in two ways: (1) it allows researchers to capitalize on successful practices (e.g., methods to reduce attrition); and (2) it avoids *blind guesses* as to the likelihood of encountering specific conditions.

Evidence about the prevalence or likelihood of research conditions can also be used, as has been demonstrated in some quantitative syntheses (e.g., Smith et al., 1980; Sudman & Bradburn, 1974), to guide judgments on the relative merits of differential research designs and procedures. Research methodologists often argue that a particular design is flawed (biased) due to an artifact that can be viewed as a plausible rival explanation. Often, this is demonstrated mathematically (e.g., Campbell & Boruch, 1975) or empirically (e.g., Magidson, 1977). In other cases the plausibility of a rival explanation is based on logical reasoning that merely establishes the *possibility* of its influence. Campbell (1969) has argued that a more empirical approach to understanding the degree of plausibility of rival explanations is warranted. To this end some research has been initiated to understand the effects of specific threats to valid inference (see Rosenthal & Rubin, 1978). If artifacts and research procedures are well represented in quantitative syntheses, these efforts can be utilized as another means of examining the influence of research flaws. The adequacy of this type of empirical assessment rests on the quality of research practices underlying the synthesis process.

We also argued that secondary analysis can be exploited as a means of understanding the strengths and limits of the synthesis process in two ways. First, routine secondary analysis of primary studies can potentially offset the problems associated with poor reporting practices, inappropriate use of statistical procedures, and other flaws. The benefit of secondary analysis applied at this level is the improvement of primary studies, and this in turn should lead to more meaningful quantitative syntheses. The second contribution of secondary analysis is in assuring the quality of quantitative syntheses. Specifically, arguments about the meaningfulness and integrity of quantitative syntheses can be potentially settled through routine critique and reanalysis. The statistical and judgmental issues for this level of assessment are not unlike those that must be addressed in primary and secondary studies. Analytic procedures can be questioned, as can selection procedures, exclusion rules, and the adequacy of operationalizations of important constructs (e.g., quality of the primary research).

In the absence of empirical evidence, critical commentary often remains at the level of conjecture or debate. Although specification of assumptions and efforts to test the viability of these assumptions (e.g., sensitivity analysis) is a necessary part of the research process, a particular research effort (at any level of analysis) will never satisfy all the potential concerns. Critique and reanalysis may help to clarify the strengths and weaknesses of quantitative synthesis procedures more readily than vigorous debate or argument. Improvement of synthesis procedures will advance more rapidly to the extent that weaknesses are identified and empirically demonstrated. Competing analyses, using different transformations of study outcomes, multiple operationalizations of important constructs, and alternative statistical models represent important methods/procedures for establishing integrity of research evidence.

Quantitative synthesis has focused primarily on the integration of simple aspects of comparative studies. Primary evaluation and research methods are increasingly becoming more complex *or* they rely on simple, cheap, methods focused on providing understandable and useful evidence. The current synthesis procedures are poorly suited for both varieties of studies. Evaluation synthesis, as proposed by GAO, seems to be a move towards resolving some of these problems. The efforts of Hoaglin and associates (1981) are directed at the quality of research across a variety of methodologies and Hunter et al. (1982) provide a conceptual foundation for synthesis of a broader range of studies.

Tactics and Conditions for Increasing Correspondence

The first step toward promoting greater correspondence among levels of research is perhaps a simple description of areas of overlap and neglect. This has been the aim of this article. Having identified some of these issues, it seems sensible to isolate changes in research practice that may facilitate further development.

A central concept embedded in much of the preceding discussion is the notion of access to microdata. This is particularly relevant to secondary analysis of primary evaluations and quantitative synthesis. Data transfer is not simply a technical process. Restrictions on access are motivated by legal and professional concerns, and a balance has to be achieved to protect the interests of all parties. Even if access issues are resolved, successful reanalysis can only be meaningfully carried out if the microdata (and procedures that produced them) are well documented. Further, the utility of quantitative synthesis efforts as a means of planning subsequent research depends on these efforts being accessible. It is unlikely that information can be developed in reports that will satisfy the needs of the majority of researchers. Smith and Glass made their data file available upon our request, but the process is time consuming and likely to be a burden to the original investigators. Finally, synthesis of evidence (at any level of analysis) requires numerous judgments. Some of these judgments rely on the application of statistical criterion and others are more subjective. All of these decisions/judgments need to be well documented.

Access. Boruch and Cordray (1982) identified five mechanisms for facilitating access to microdata. These include the legal system, international standards, granting agencies, editorial policy, and professional organizations. For example, the Freedom of Information Act serves as a means of obtaining access to federally sponsored data collections efforts. The Bellagio Principles, while having no legal standing, specify general concerns and issues on disclosure of government-sponsored collection. These were developed by an international group of scholars representing Western and European countries. In an effort to promote access to research data, the National Science Foundation and National Institute of Justice make submission of a well-documented machine-readable data file a condition of the grant award. Other federal agencies in this country maintain a more informal posture toward data access (see Boruch et al., 1981).

Access to nongovernment research data is not subject to the same conditions. Efforts to promote a spirit of disclosure and access have been undertaken in other ways. Rather than relying on policy or law, some professional societies have adopted standards and guidelines for professional conduct that encourage open access to microdata (see Chalk et al., 1980). Although the guidelines are sufficiently vague, allowing a researcher to easily deny access for a variety of seemingly legitimate reasons, other tactics are more direct. For example, as editor of the *Journal of Personality and Social Psychology,* Greenwald (1976) requested authors of articles published in that journal to maintain their data for a period of five years in a form that would facilitate secondary analysis by interested researchers. Other editorial decisions have facilitated access. For example, the *Yale Law Journal* maintains copies of data and detailed calculations used in the Bowers and Pierce (1975) reanalysis of Isaac Erhlich's research on capital punishment. Although many of these professional practices are unique, their existence reflects, at least to some, a need for open disclosure of the evidence underlying the social science knowledge base.

These issues apply to all levels of research we have considered. Some would undoubtedly argue that access to all data is unwarranted for practical and scientific reasons. On the scientific side, the editorial process is supposed to ensure that conclusions are justified, given the evidence that is presented. We have reviewed evidence in Section 3 that suggest this process is not always successful—some studies are flawed despite the editorial review process. As a partial solution to this problem, a few editors have initiated policies whereby more extensive data summaries are submitted and reviewers are given an opportunity to examine the analysis prior to rendering a judgment on a study's acceptability for publication.

On the practical side, the volume of research that is produced each year precludes examination of all microdata. This is a sensible concern. On the other hand, however, the quality of the analysis reported in a primary study is a fundamental issue for quantitative synthesis. The use of statistical adjustment for differential research quality (equation 4) is only a partial solution to this problem. A more direct test of the adequacy of current synthesis practices may be to aggregate a sample of studies that have been reanalyzed and contrast the results with a synthesis of the evidence as it was reported (prior to reanalysis). The policies of a specific journal may facilitate this test.

The Need for Additional Methodological Detail. Characterizing the quality of primary research is hampered by omissions regarding methodological procedures. Even well-known procedures (e.g., random assignment) can assume a variety of forms (see Mosteller et al., 1980). Providing a detailed account of subject selection, assignment, measurement, attrition, statistical analyses, and the like are the primary focus of recent standards and guidelines issued by the Evaluation Research Society and others. All of this detail is unlikely to be included in published reports. Limited journal space is likely to be devoted to reporting substantive findings and conclusions. Given an interest in accumulating knowledge through statistical procedures, more space is needed for methodological detail.

Some journals have made creative attempts to promote reanalysis and synthesis. For example, *Analytic Chemistry,* published by the American Chemical Association, makes some data and information on methodological details available to interested readers through supplementary subscription. This material is stored on microfiche, avoiding the excessive costs of publishing raw data.

Dissemination. Using prior quantitative syntheses for purposes beyond the substantive conclusions about the cumulative effects of a set of interventions requires either making the additional evidence available in a prespecified form (see Tables 1-2), providing access to the microdata, or making it available through a centralized location where individuals could request specific breakdowns or configurations of studies.

As for mechanisms, archives maintained at the University of Michigan, at NORC, and the National Archives are likely points for dissemination. Other more radical options exist, however. For example, according to Boruch (1982), the American Society for Metals (AMS) and the National Bureau of Standards (NBS) have jointly sponsored the Alloy Phase Diagram Project, which is devoted to acquiring, evaluating, and disseminating data on structural properties of alloys. The data from various research efforts are submitted to the project staff, added to the data bank, and made available to other users (see National Bureau of Standards, 1980). With enough interest in accumulation of social science evidence, a system of this sort may be devised. The President's Commission on Federal Statistics (1981) has described alterations in the federal statistical system that facilitates coordinating data collection efforts. The system could be adapted to serve as an input and dissemination mechanism, similar to the AMS/NBS efforts.

Adapting to Fiscal Constraint

The social science research community has recently suffered a drastic reduction in available research funds. The reasons for this go beyond the scope of this discussion, but Chelimsky (1983) has some interesting speculations. Response to this era of scarcity has taken a number of forms. Less expensive methods are being developed, advocated, or used, some federal requirements for evaluation have been abolished, evaluation has been relocated to nonfederal levels of jurisdiction, and the like.

Reanalysis of previously collected data represents an additional adaptive response to a constrained fiscal environment. Here, prior data can be pressed into service to answer new questions, test new hypotheses, and to understand the strength and limitations of designs, measures, and analytic strategies. Quantitative synthesis is another adaptive device. Both of these areas can be exploited to make better decisions about how to allocate scarce resources through systematic documentation of successful practice and through identifying factors to be avoided. Facilitating the use of these efforts to carefully target resources for future social experiments and to assure that high quality tests of new interventions are undertaken is a primary rationale for examining the points of overlap and neglect among these levels of research. Accumulating knowledge on research practice now, while we are waiting for the next Experimenting Society, will hopefully give the social science research industry a head start.

NOTES

1. The quantitative synthesis process is made more complicated by any difference across studies. We have chosen to focus on the influence of design characteristics because they are more tractable due to the presence of statistical theory. Given the non-experimental character of the data within a quantitative synthesis all comparisons across clusters of studies will be subject to competing interpretations.

2. Eleanor Chelimsky has argued that supplemental methods of identifying literature studies are often necessary. Her colleagues, for example, have used professionals in a given field as a means of identifying omissions (i.e., those studies that remained unpublished or were otherwise missed due to misclassification, obtuse titles, or simply overlooked).

REFERENCE NOTES

1. Spencer, B. D. On interpreting test scores as social indicators: Statistical considerations. School of Education, Northwestern University, Evanston, IL. Manuscript under review, 1982.

2. Lipsey, M. W. A scheme for assessing measurement sensitivity in program evaluation and other applied research. Psychology Department, Claremont Graduate School, Claremont, California. Manuscript under review, 1982.

3. Cordray, D. S., & Orwin, R. G. Technical evidence necessary for quantitative integration of research and evaluation. Paper presented at IASSIST-IFDO Conference, Grenoble, France, September 18, 1981.

REFERENCES

ANDERSON, J. K. et al. The U.S. Office of Education models to evaluate ESEA Title I: Experiences after one year of use. Washington, DC: U.S. Office of Education, 1978.

ANDREWS, F. Measuring the quality of measurement: Estimates from structural modeling techniques. Invited address, American Psychological Association, September 4, 1980.

BERNSTEIN, I. N., & FREEMAN, H. E. Academic and entrepreneurial research. New York: Russell Sage, 1974.

BORUCH, R. F. Definitions, products and distinctions in data sharing. In R. F. Boruch et al., Access to research data. Report to the Subcommittee on Data Sharing, Committee on National Statistics, National Research Council, 1982.

BORUCH, R. F., & CORDRAY, D. S. Professional codes and guidelines in data sharing. In R. F. Boruch et al., Access to research data. Report to the Subcommittee on Data Sharing, Committee on National Statistics, National Research Council, 1982.

BORUCH, R. F., & CORDRAY, D. S. (Eds.). An appraisal of educational program evaluations: Federal, state, and local agencies. Washington, DC: U.S. Department of Education, 1980.

BORUCH, R. F., & CORDRAY, D. S. Reactions to criticism of the Holtzman Report. Educational Researcher, 1981, 10, 10-12.

BORUCH, R. F., & GOMEZ, H. Sensitivity, bias and theory in impact evaluations. Professional Psychology, 1977 (November), 411-434.

BORUCH, R. F., CORDRAY, D. S., & PION, G. M. How well are educational evaluations carried out? In L. Datta (Ed.), Local, state, and federal evaluation. Beverly Hills, CA: Sage, 1981, 13-40.

BORUCH, R. F., CORDRAY, D. S., & WORTMAN, P. M. Secondary analysis: Why, when and how. In R. F. Boruch, P. M. Wortman & D. S. Cordray (Eds.), Reanalyzing program evaluations. San Francisco: Jossey-Bass, 1981.

BORUCH, R. F., WORTMAN, P. M., CORDRAY, D. S. and Associates. Reanalyzing program evaluations: Policies and practices for secondary analysis of social and educational programs. San Francisco: Jossey-Bass, 1981.

BOWERS, W., & PIERCE, G. The illusion of deterrence in Isaac Ehrlich's research on capital punishment. Yale Law Journal, 1975, 85, 187-208.

BUNDA, M. A. Some comments on the recommendations in the Holtzman Project. Educational Researcher, 1981, 10 (April), 14.

CAMPBELL, D. T. "Degrees of freedom" and the case study. Comparative Political Studies, 1975, 178-193.

CAMPBELL, D. T. Prospective: Artifact and control. In R. Rosenthal and R. L. Rosnow (Eds.), Artifacts in behavioral research. New York: Appleton-Century-Crofts, 1969.

CAMPBELL, D. T., & BORUCH, R. F. Making the case for randomized assignment to treatment by considering the alternatives: Six ways in which quasi-experimental evaluations in compensatory education tend to underestimate effects. In C. A. Bennett and A. A. Lumsdaine (Eds.), Evaluation and the experiment: Some critical issues in assessing social programs. New York: Academic Press, 1975.

CAMPBELL, D. T., & ERLEBACHER, A. How regression artifacts in quasi-experimental evaluations can mistakenly make compensatory education look harmful. In J. Hellmuth (Ed.), Compensatory education: A national debate. New York: Brunner/Mazel, 1970.

CHALK, R., FRANKEL, M. S., & CHAFER, S. B. AAAS Professional Ethics Project: Professional ethics activities in scientific and engineering societies. Washington, DC: American Association for the Advancement of Science, 1980.

CHELIMSKY, E. Improving the cost effectiveness of evaluation. In M. C. Alkin (Ed.), The costs of evaluation. Beverly Hills, CA: Sage, 1983.

COHEN, J. Statistical power analysis for the behavioral sciences (Rev. ed.). New York: Academic Press, 1977.

COOK, T. D., & CAMPBELL, D. T. Quasi-experimentation: Design and analysis issues for field settings. Chicago: Rand McNally, 1979.

COOK, T. D., & GRUDER, C. Metaevaluation research. Evaluation Quarterly, 1978, 2, 5-51.

COOPER, H. M. Statistically combining independent studies: A meta-analysis of sex differences in conformity research. Journal of Personality and Social Psychology, 1979, 37, 131-146.

CORDRAY, D. S. The Evaluation Research Society Standards: An assessment of their utility. New Directions in Program Evaluation, 1982, 15, 67-81.

CORDRAY, D. S., & BOOTZIN, R. R. Placebo controls: Test of theory or effectiveness? Brain and Behavioral Sciences, in press.

CRONBACH, L. J. Designing evaluations for educational and social programs. San Francisco: Jossey-Bass, 1982.

CRONBACH, L. J. and Associates. Toward reform of program evaluation. San Francisco: Jossey-Bass, 1980.

DATTA, L., & PERLOFF, R. (Eds.). Improving evaluations. Beverly Hills, CA: Sage, 1979.

DEVINE, E. C., & COOK, T. D. Effects of psycho-educational interventions on length of post-surgical hospital stay: A meta-analytic review of 34 studies. (This volume.)

DIRECTOR, S. M. Underadjustment bias in evaluation of manpower training. Evaluation Quarterly, 1979, 3, 190-218.

Evaluation Research Society. Standards for program evaluation. Potomac, MD: Evaluation Research Society, 1981.

EYSENCK, H. J. An exercise in mega-silliness. American Psychologist, 1978, 33, 517.

FISHER, R. A. Statistical methods for research workers (7th ed.). London: Oliver & Boyd, 1938.

FREIMAN, J. A., CHALMERS, T. C., SMITH, H., Jr., & KUEBLER, R. F. The importance of beta, the Type II error and sample size in the design and interpretation of the Randomized Control Trial. New England Journal of Medicine, 1978, 299, 690-694.

GLASS, G. V. Evaluation research. Annual Review of Psychology, 1980.

GLASS, G. V. Integrating findings: The meta-analysis of research. In L. Shulman (Ed.), Review of research in education (Vol 5). 1978.

GLASS, G. V. Primary, secondary and meta-analysis of research. Educational Researcher, 1976, 3-8.

GLASS, G. V & SMITH, M. L. Class-size and its relationship to attitudes and instruction. Unpublished paper, Laboratory of Educational Research, University of Colorado, Boulder, July 1979.

GREENWALD, A. An editorial. Journal of Personality and Social Psychology, 1976, 33, 1-7.

HAVENS, H. S. U.S. General Accounting Office: The role of reanalysis in an oversight agency. In R. F. Boruch, P. M. Wortman, & D. S. Cordray (Eds.), Reanalyzing program evaluations. San Francisco: Jossey-Bass, 1981.

HEBERLEIN, T. A., & BAUMGARTNER, R. Factors affecting response rates to mailed questionnaires: A quantitative analysis of the published literature. American Sociological Review, 1978, 43(4), 447-462.

HEDGES, L. V., & OLKIN, I. Vote-counting methods in research synthesis. Psychological Bulletin, 1980, 88, 359-369.

HOAGLIN, D. C., LIGHT, R. J., McPEEK, B., MOSTELLER, F., & STOTO, M. A. Data for decisions: Information strategies for policy makers. Cambridge, MA: Abt Books, 1982.

HOUSE, E. Critique of the Northwestern Report. ERS Newsletter, 1981, 5(2), 8.

HUNTER, J. E., SCHMIDT, F. L., & JACKSON, G. B. Meta-analysis: Cumulating research findings across studies. Beverly Hills, CA: Sage, 1982.

JOHNSON, D. W., MARUYAMA, R. J., JOHNSON, R. T., & NELSON, D. Effects of cooperative, competitive, and individualistic goal structures on achievement: A meta-analysis. Psychological Bulletin, 1981, 89, 47-62.

Joint Committee on Standards for Educational Evaluation. Standards for evaluation of educational programs, products, and materials. New York: McGraw-Hill, 1980.

JURS, S. G., & GLASS, G. V. The effects of experimental mortality on internal and external validity of the randomized comparative experiment. Journal of Experimental Education, 1971, 40, 52-66.

KENNEDY, M. Assumptions and estimates of evaluation utility. Educational Researcher, 1981, 10(10), 6-9.

LANDMAN, J. T., & DAWES, R. M. Psychotherapy outcome: Smith and Glass's conclusions stand up under scrutiny. American Psychologist, 1982, 37, 504-576.

LIGHT, R. J., & SMITH, P. V. Accumulating evidence: Procedures for resolving contradictions among different research studies. Harvard Educational Review, 1971, 41, 429-471.

LINSENMEIER, J., WORTMAN, P. M., & HENDRICKS, M. Need for better documentation: Problems in a reanalysis of teacher bias. In R. F. Boruch, P. M. Wortman, & D. S. Cordray (Eds.), Reanalyzing program evaluations. San Francisco: Jossey-Bass, 1981.

LIPSEY, M. W., CORDRAY, D. S., & BERGER, D. E. Evaluation of a juvenile diversion program: Using multiple lines of evidence. Evaluation Review, 1981, 5, 283-306.

MAGIDSON, J. Toward a causal model approach for adjusting for pre-existing differences in the non-equivalent control group situation. Evaluation Quarterly, 1977, 2, 511-520.

MALTZ, M. D., GORDON, A. C., McDOWALL, D., & McCLEARY, R. An artifact in pre-post designs: How it can mistakenly make delinquency programs look effective. Evaluation Review, 1980, 4, 216-225.

MOSTELLER, F., GILBERT, J. P., & McPEEK, B. Reporting standards and research strategies for controlled trials: Agenda for the editor. Controlled Clinical Trials, 1980, 1, 37-58.

National Bureau of Standards, Alloy Data Center. ASM/NBS Alloy phase diagram program. Washington, DC: National Bureau of Standards, 1980.

ORWIN, R. G. The influence of reporting quality in primary studies on meta-analytic outcomes: A conceptual critique and reanalysis. Unpublished doctoral dissertation, Department of Psychology, Northwestern University, August 1982.

ORWIN, R. G., & CORDRAY, D. S. Smith and Glass's psychotherapy conclusions need further probing: A comment on Landman and Dawes' reanalysis. American Psychologist, in press.

PILLEMER, D. B., & LIGHT, R. J. Synthesizing outcomes: How to use research evidence from many studies. Harvard Educational Review, 1980, 50(2), 176-195.

POSAVAC, E. J. Evaluations of patient education programs: A meta-analysis. Evaluation & the Health Professions, 1980, 3, 46-62.

PRIOLEAU, L., MURDOCK, M., & BRODY, N. An analysis of psychotherapy vs. placebo studies. Brain and Behavioral Sciences, in press.

President's Reorganization Project. Federal statistical system: Access and dissemination. In R. F. Boruch, P. M. Wortman, D. S. Cordray, & Associates, Reanalyzing program evaluations. San Francisco: Jossey-Bass, 1981.

RIECKEN, H. W., & BORUCH, R. F. (Eds.). Social experimentation: A method for planning and evaluating social intervention. New York: Academic Press, 1974.

RINDSKOPF, D. M. Structural equation models in analysis of non-experimental data. In R. F. Boruch, P. M. Wortman, & D. S. Cordray (Eds.), Reanalyzing program evaluations. San Francisco: Jossey-Bass, 1981.

RINDSKOPF, D. Secondary analysis: Using multiple analysis approaches with Head Start and Title I data. New directions for program evaluation, 1978, 4, 75-88.

ROBBIN, A. Technical guidelines for documenting machine-readable files. In R. F. Boruch, P. M. Wortman, & D. S. Cordray (Eds.), Reanalyzing program evaluations. San Francisco: Jossey-Bass, 1981.

ROSENTHAL, R. Combining results of independent studies. Psychological Bulletin, 1978, 85, 185-193.

ROSENTHAL, R., & RUBIN, D. B. Interpersonal expectancy effects: The first 345 studies. Brain and Behavioral Sciences, 1978, 3, 377-415.

ROSSI, P., FREEMAN, H., & WRIGHT, S. Evaluation: A systematic approach. Beverly Hills, CA: Sage, 1979.

SECHREST, L., & YEATON, W. Empirical basis for estimating effect size. In R. F. Boruch, P. M. Wortman, & D. S. Cordray (Eds.), Reanalyzing program evaluations. San Francisco, CA: Jossey-Bass, 1981.

SMITH, M. L. Sex bias in counseling: A meta-analysis. American Psychologist, 1980.

SMITH, M. A., GLASS, G. V, & MILLER, T. I. The benefits of psychotherapy. Baltimore, MD: Johns Hopkins University Press, 1980.

SMITH, N. L. (Ed.) New techniques for evaluation (Vol 2). Beverly Hills, CA: Sage, 1981.

SUDMAN, S., & BRADBURN, N. M. Response effects in surveys: A review and synthesis. Chicago: Aldine, 1974.

U.S. General Accounting Office. Exposure draft: The evaluation synthesis method. Washington, DC: U.S. General Accounting Office, March 10, 1982.

U.S. General Accounting Office. Assessing social program impact evaluations: A checklist approach. Washington, DC: U.S. General Accounting Office, October 1978.

WALBERG, H. J., & HAERTEL, E. H. (Guest Editors) Research integration: The state of the art. Special Issue of Evaluation in Education, 1980, 4, 1-42.

WOLINS, L. Research mistakes in the social and behavioral sciences. Ames: Iowa State University Press, 1982.

WOLINS, L. Reanalyzing studies of race differences in intelligence: Scale dependent mistakes. In R. F. Boruch, P. M. Wortman, & D. S. Cordray (Eds.), Reanalyzing program evaluations. San Francisco: Jossey-Bass, 1981.

WOLINS, L. Responsibility for raw data. American Psychologist, 1962, 17, 657-658.

WORTMAN, P. M., REICHARDT, C. S., & ST. PIERRE, R. G. The first year of the Educational Voucher Demonstration: A secondary analysis of the student achievement test scores. Evaluation Quarterly, 1978, 2, 193-214.

5

Scientific Guidelines for Conducting Integrative Reserach Reviews

Harris M. Cooper

The inferences made in integrative research reviews are as central to the validity of behavioral science knowledge as those made in primary research. Therefore, research reviewers must pay the same attention to rigorous methodology that is required of primary researchers. This article conceptualizes the research review as a scientific inquiry involving five stages that parallel those of primary research. The functions, sources of variance, and potential threats to validity associated with each stage are described.

The behavioral sciences recently underwent a sharp increase in manpower and research (Garvey & Griffith, 1971). To accommodate this expansion, outlets for research reports became plentiful and their accessibility was facilitated by the computerized literature search. The scholarly activity affected most by the research explosion was the integrative research review, or the synthesis of separate empirical findings into a coherent whole. As the empirical base expanded, the reviewer's task became more complex while simultaneously taking on added status. Today most researchers find they cannot keep abreast of primary data reports except within a few specializations. Researchers rely heavily on integrative research reviews to define the state of knowledge.

Because of the changes in reviewing, researchers can no longer take the conclusions of reviews at face value. They must recognize that the integration of separate research projects involves scientific inferences as central to the validity of knowledge as the inferences made in primary data interpretation. While substantial attention has been paid to validity issues in primary research (Bracht & Glass, 1968; Campbell, 1969; Campbell & Stanley, 1966), behavioral scientists have no systematic guidelines for evaluating the validity of review outcomes.

This article conceptualizes the integrative review as a research process containing five stages: (1) problem formulation; (2) data collection; (3) evaluation of data points; (4) data analysis and interpretation; and (5) presentation of results. Each stage serves

This paper was written with the support of the National Science Foundation's Division of Social and Developmental Psychology (BNS78-08834).

There were numerous people involved in the preparation of the manuscript. Bert Boyce, chairman of UMC's Information Science Department, gave the author a crash course in research on information systems and users. Several members of UMC's Psychology Department, Mel Marx, John Mueller, and Rich Petty, made comments on an earlier draft. Cheri Christensen pilot tested a literature search while the article was written. Gail Hinkel straightened out my English and Janice Sato and Pat Shanks decoded my hieroglyphics.

From Harris M. Cooper, "Scientific Guidelines for Conducting Integrative Research Reviews," 52(2) *Review of Educational Research* 291-302 (Summer 1982). Copyright © 1982. American Educational Research Association, Washington, D.C. Reprinted by permission.

121

a function similar to the one it serves in primary research. Differences in review methodologies, like differences in primary research methodologies, create variation in conclusions. Most important, methodological choices at each review stage may engender threats to the validity of the review's conclusions (see Table I).

A Definition of Research Review

According to Jackson (1980):

> Some [reviewers] are primarily interested in sizing up new substantive and/or methodological developments in a given field. Some are primarily interested in verifying existing theories or developing new ones. Some are interested in synthesizing knowledge from different lines of research, and still others are primarily interested in *inferring generalizations about substantive issues from a set of studies directly bearing on those issues.* (p. 438, italics added)

The fourth kind of review, which will be called integrative, is this paper's primary focus. The goal of an integrative review is to summarize the accumulated state of knowledge concerning the relation(s) of interest and to highlight important issues that research has left unresolved (Taveggia, 1974). From the reader's viewpoint, an integrative research review is intended to (a) replace papers that have fallen behind the research front (Price, 1965), and (b) direct future research so that it yields a maximum amount of new information.

The Problem Formulation Stage

The variables involved in a behavioral science inquiry are defined in two ways. First, the variables are given conceptual definitions. Conceptual definitions differ in abstractness: If the meaning of one concept is included in the meaning of another, the more general concept is considered more abstract (Reynolds, 1971). Second, variables are operationally defined. An operational definition relates an abstract concept to observable events. Both primary researchers and research reviewers must define concepts and specify the operations included in the definitions.

Primary researchers have little choice but to operationalize their concepts before the inquiry begins. In contrast, the research reviewer can evaluate the concept relevance of different operations as they are encountered in the search for relevant studies. Of course, most reviewers begin with some a priori specification of operations. It is not unusual, however, for a reviewer to come across concept-relevant operations during the search that were not initially considered for inclusions.

A more significant distinction between primary research and reviewing is that primary research typically involves only one or two operational definitions. Research review can, and usually does, involve many different operations defining the same concept.

How Operational Diversity Affects Review Outcomes

Operational diversity affects review outcomes in two ways. First, the operational definitions chosen by research reviewers can vary. Two reviewers using an identical label for a concept may employ different operational definitions or levels of abstraction. Each definition may contain some operations excluded by the other, or one reviewer's definition may completely contain the other.

TABLE I

TABLE I

The Integrative Review Conceptualized as a Research Project

Stage Characteristics	Stage of Research				
	Problem Formulation	Data Collection	Data Evaluation	Analysis and Interpretation	Public Presentation
Research Question Asked	What evidence should be included in the review?	What procedures should be used to find relevant evidence?	What retrieved evidence should be included in the review?	What procedures should be used to make inferences about the literature as a whole?	What information should be included in the review report?
Primary Function in Review	Constructing definitions that distinguish relevant from irrelevant studies.	Determining which sources of potentially relevant studies to examine.	Applying criteria to separate "valid" from "invalid" studies.	Synthesizing valid retrieved studies.	Applying editorial criteria to separate important from unimportant information.
Procedural Differences That Create Variation in Review Conclusions	1. Differences in included operational definitions. 2. Differences in operational detail.	Differences in the research contained in sources of information.	1. Differences in quality criteria. 2. Differences in the influence of nonquality criteria.	Differences in rules of inference.	Differences in guidelines for editorial judgment.
Sources of Potential Invalidity in Review Conclusions	1. Narrow concepts might make review conclusions less definitive and robust. 2. Superficial operational detail might obscure interacting variables.	1. Accessed studies might be qualitatively different from the target population of studies. 2. People sampled in accessible studies might be different from target population of people.	1. Nonquality factors might cause improper weighting of study information. 2. Omissions in study reports might make conclusions unreliable.	1. Rules for distinguishing patterns from noise might be inappropriate. 2. Review-based evidence might be used to infer causality.	1. Omission of review procedures might make conclusions irreproducible. 2. Omission of review findings and study procedures might make conclusions obsolete.

Second, diversity among studies related to the same concept means reviewers can vary in their treatment of operations *after* the data archives have been searched. One reviewer may decide to meticulously identify the operational distinctions among studies while another ignores the finer points. The first reviewer might recognize that the outcome of reviewed studies is mediated by a methodological variation that the second reviewer did not examine. Therefore, two reviewers employing identical conceptual definitions and reviewing the same set of studies may still reach different conclusions.

Threats to validity. Reviewers who focus on a limited set of operational definitions typically do so to ensure consensus about the meaning of a concept. However, multiple realizations of concepts are desirable in behavioral research; if multiple operations produce similar results they rule out rival conceptualizations of the findings (Campbell & Fiske, 1959; Webb, Campbell, Schwartz, & Sechrest, 1973). Also, very narrow definitions provide little information about whether a finding applies across various situations. Thus, reviewers who employ broad conceptual definitions (or who believe many operations are concept-relevant) can *potentially* reach more definitive and robust conclusions than reviewers using narrow definitions.

The second threat to validity is associated with how study operations are treated in the review. Lack of attention to study details might mask important distinctions in results. As Presby (1978) notes: "Differences [in studies] are cancelled in the use of very broad categories, which leads to the erroneous conclusion that research results indicate negligible differences in outcomes..." (p. 514). Reviewers who examine more operational details probably will produce more valid review conclusions. These reviewers present more information about the contextual variations that do and do not influence the review conclusion.

Protecting validity. Reviewers should protect their conclusions from threats to validity. Archive searches should begin with the broadest possible conceptual definition in mind. The reviewer should begin with a few central operations but remain open to the possibility that other relevant operations will be discovered during the search. To complement conceptual broadness, reviewers should be exhaustive in their attention to distinctions in study procedures. Any suspicion that differences in study results are associated with procedural distinctions should receive attention.

Reviewers should also allow the users of their work to assess the degree to which these validity threats are present. As completely as possible, reviewers should (a) describe all the operational variations that were considered concept-relevant, and (b) report all variations in study methods that were related to study outcomes.

The Data Collection Stage

The major decision during data collection involves choosing the population of elements that will be the referent for the inquiry. The *target population* includes those elements the inquirer hopes to represent in the study. The *accessible population* includes those elements the inquirer is pragmatically able to obtain (Bracht & Glass, 1968). Both primary research and research review involve specifying target and accessible populations and considering how they might differ from one another.

Identifying populations for research reviews is complicated by the fact that reviews involve two targets. First, the reviewer wants the findings to pertain to *all previous research* on the problem. Reviewers exert some control over whether this goal is achieved through their choice of which and how many data archives to search.

Second, the reviewer hopes that the retrieved studies will allow generalization to the *unit of analysis that interests the topic area.* Here, the reviewer is constrained by the types of units sampled by primary researchers.

Techniques for Information Retrieval

There are at least five techniques a reviewer can use to retrieve information on a research problem: (1) the "invisible college" approach; (2) the ancestry approach; (3) the descendency approach; (4) the use of abstracting services; and (5) the on-line computer search. The invisible college is the most informal approach. Crane (1969) notes that "scientists working on similar problems are usually aware of each other and in some cases attempt to systematize their contacts by exchanging reprints with one another" (p. 335). The ancestry approach retrieves information by "tracking" citations from one study to another. Most reviewers are aware of several studies bearing on their problem, and these studies provide bibliographies which cite earlier, related research. The descendency approach, or the *Science* or *Social Science Citation Indexes,* is employed to retrieve studies that cite papers central to a topic and then screen these for topic relevance. To use abstracting services, the reviewer selects a set of keywords or phrases and compares them with the indicators used to index studies. In the on-line computer search, the computer exhaustively scans abstracting services and citation indexes at phenomenal speed. A problem with using the computer is that it eliminates "browsing," or following up promising leads that arise during a manual search.

How Information Retrieval Techniques Affect Review Outcomes

Every past study does not have an equal chance of being retrieved by the reviewer. It is likely that studies contained in all the above sources are different from studies that never become public information. For instance, Greenwald (1975) found that about half of researchers who produced a rejection of the null hypothesis would submit a report for publication, while only 6 percent who failed to reject the null hypothesis would attempt to publish. McNemar (1960) speculates that findings that contradict conventional wisdom are relatively less likely to be visible to other researchers.

Studies that are not available in the retrieval system do not create variability in review conclusions because they are absent from all reviews. However, discrepancies between review conclusions are created by differences in the sources reviewers use to retrieve information. Two reviewers using different techniques to locate studies may end up with different evidence and reach different conclusions. Regrettably, little is known about how information sources differ. This problem is complicated by the fact that the effect of information source probably varies from one topic area to another. Some generic differences, however, may be offered, based on commonly held beliefs.

The studies available through invisible colleges are probably (a) more homogeneous in operations, and (b) less carefully scrutinized for methodological flaws than all relevant studies available to a reviewer. Invisible college studies are also probably more uniformly supportive of the findings of central researchers than evidence found through more diverse sources. A similar homogeneity of findings and methods might be anticipated for studies located through citation indexes. However, because citation indexes primarily contain studies that have been scrutinized by editors or dissertation advisors, fewer methodologically flawed studies should be included than in informal communications. Searching bibliographies is likely to overrepresent published research, particularly research within a circumscribed communication network (Xhignesse & Osgood, 1967).

Finally, abstracting services and computer searches probably contain the studies most closely approximating all publicly available research. These sources have the least restrictive requirements for a study to gain entry into the system. Their limitation is that there is typically a long lag between when a study is completed and when it will appear in the abstracts. Clearly, a reviewer who is well connected to an active invisible college is more likely to retrieve current research than a reviewer who must rely solely on the abstracting services.

Threats to validity. It is necessary to examine the adequacy of a reviewer's archive search with respect to two targets. The review must be evaluated by (a) how the retrieved studies might differ from all studies, and (b) how the units contained in retrieved studies might differ from all units of interest.

The first threat to validity associated with the data-gathering phase of reviewing, then, is that the studies in the review might not include, and probably will not include, all studies pertinent to the topic of interest. The second threat to validity is that the units in retrieved studies might not represent all units in the target population. The reviewer cannot be faulted for the existence of this threat *if* retrieval procedures were exhaustive.

Protecting validity. Reviewers should access as many information sources as possible to ensure that as many studies as possible are located. The biases contained in one source can be partially obviated through the use of another source. In their manuscripts, reviewers should be explicit about how studies were gathered, including information on sources, years, and keywords covered in the search. Reviewers should present other indices of potential retrieval bias if they are available. For instance, Rosenthal and Rubin (1978) distinguished journal research from dissertations in an attempt to determine if the evidence from the two sources differed. Cooper, Burger, and Good (1981) reviewed only journal studies but speculated that there was little bias because the report titles rarely mentioned the hypothesis of interest.

The research reviewer should also describe the sample characteristics of individuals used in the separate studies. Missing samples and overrepresented samples should be discussed with reference to their potential impact on the findings.

The Evaluation of Data Stage

After data are collected, critical judgments are made about the quality of individual data points. Each data point is examined in light of surrounding evidence to determine if it is contaminated by too many factors irrelevant to the problem of interest. These procedures are performed whether the data pertain to the units of interest or to the results of studies.

How Evaluative Criteria Create Variance in Reviews

Review outcomes can differ because reviewers differ over how reliable they think the results of individual studies are. This variance in conclusions is created by a divergence in reviewers' criteria for evaluating the quality of research. A demonstration of differences in qualitative judgments was carried out by Gottfredson (1978).

He studied editors and authors in nine psychological journals and suggested that interjudge agreement was relatively modest. Gottfredson reported intraclass coefficients ranging from .16 to .49 on nine subscales of an evaluative device.

Variance in review conclusions also occurs because reviewers differ in the degree to which factors other than research quality affect their evaluative decisions. One extraneous factor is the reviewer's prior expectations concerning the review outcome. Lord, Ross, and Lepper (1979), for instance, found that readers rated proattitudinal studies as better conducted than counterattitudinal studies. More strikingly, the study evaluators showed polarization in attitudes even though they all read the same two research abstracts.

Threats to validity. The use of any evaluative criteria other than substantive methodological discriminations is a threat to the validity of a research review. As Mahoney (1977) states, "To the extent that researchers display [confirmatory] bias, our adequate understanding of the processes and parameters of human adaptation may be seriously jeopardized" (p. 162).

A second threat to validity during data evaluation is wholly beyond the control of the reviewer. This threat involves the potential for unreliable outcomes due to incomplete reporting by primary researchers. Many research reports omit discussion of some hypotheses that were tested. Other reports give only incomplete information on the tests that were mentioned. If a reviewer must estimate or omit what happened in these studies, wider confidence intervals must be placed around review conclusions.

Protecting validity. It is difficult to suggest the kinds of substantive criteria reviewers should use for judgments about methodology. The topic is far too complex and opinions are too varied for brief treatment. Some suggestions can be made, however, about how criteria should be applied. For instance, reviewers should develop evaluative criteria before the literature is searched. Criteria for excluding studies should be stated as objectively as possible. More than one evaluator should be employed, and interevaluator agreement should be quantified and reported. The persons applying the criteria should be blind to the author, outlet, and results of the study.

The Analysis and Interpretation Stage

During analysis and interpretation, the separate data points are synthesized into a unified statement about the research problem.

Until recently, there has been little similarity in how analysis and interpretation was carried out by primary researchers and integrative research reviewers. Primary behavioral researchers have been obligated to present summary statistics and to substantiate the existence of any aggregate relations with probability tests. While statistical aids to interpretation have been criticized (Bakan, 1966; Cornfield & Tukey, 1956; Lykken, 1968), most primary researchers feel uncomfortable about synthesizing data without some assistance (or credibility) supplied by statistical procedures.

Integrative reviewers have not been obligated to apply *any* standard analysis and interpretation techniques in their synthesis process. Most frequently, reviewers interpret data using inexplicit rules of inference. This potential for subjectivity has led some critics to voice considerable skepticism about the outcome of many reviews.

Gene Glass (1976) writes: "A common method for integrating several studies with inconsistent findings is to carp on the design or analysis deficiencies of all but a few studies—those remaining frequently being one's own work or that of one's students or friends—and then advance the one or two acceptable studies as the truth of the matter" (p. 4).

The Quantitative Literature Review

The information explosion in the behavioral sciences has focused considerable attention on the lack of standardization in how reviewers arrive at general conclusions. For some topic areas, a separate verbal description of all relevant studies will now be impossible. Focusing on one or two studies chosen from dozens or hundreds will fail to accurately portray the accumulated state of knowledge (Cooper, 1979). The present day reviewer also faces problems when attempting to relate variance in the results of studies with variance in procedures. The reviewer will find a distribution of results for studies sharing a particular procedural characteristic and an overlap in the distributions of results involving different procedures.

Quantitative reviewing techniques have been suggested as a remedy to this problem (Glass, McGaw, & Smith, 1981; Rosenthal, 1980). As Glass (1977) notes, "The accumulated findings of... studies should be regarded as complex data points, no more comprehensible without statistical analysis than hundreds of data points in a single study..." (p. 352). The application of quantitative inference procedures to reviewing seems to be a crucial response to the expanding literature (Cooper, 1981; Cooper & Arkin, 1981). The value of quantitative reviewing, however, has been questioned along lines similar to those used to criticize primary data analysis (Barber, 1978; Eysenck, 1978). The question is still open, and both sides will probably revise their positions before the debate is over.

How Interpretation Techniques Affect Review Outcomes

Review conclusions can differ because reviewers employ different interpretation techniques. A systematic relation that cannot be distinguished from noise under one set of rules might be identifiable under another set. While the relative validity of different inference strategies is difficult to assess, Cooper and Rosenthal (1980) did demonstrate some of the objective differences between quantitative and nonquantitative procedures for research review. They asked graduate students and faculty to summarize seven research articles on a simple hypothesis. All reviewers evaluated the same set of studies, but half used quantitative procedures and half used whatever criteria appealed to them. Quantitative reviewers reported more support for the hypothesis and a larger relationship between variables than did traditional reviewers. Quantitative reviewers also tended to view future replicative research as less necessary than traditional reviewers, although this finding did not reach statistical significance.

Threats to validity. The first threat to validity accompanying analysis and interpretation is that the rules of inference a reviewer employs may be inappropriate. In nonquantitative reviews, it is difficult to gauge the appropriateness of inference rules because they are not often made public. For quantitative reviews, the suppositions underlying statistical tests are generally known and some statistical biases in reviews can be removed. Regardless of the strategy used for analysis and interpretation, the possibility always exists that the reviewer has used an invalid rule for inferring a characteristic of the target population.

The second threat to validity is the misinterpretation of review-based evidence as supporting statements about causality. To be more specific, research reviews contain two different sources of evidence about relations. The first, study-based evidence, comes from single studies testing whether the relation of interest is or is not present. Research reviews also contain review-based evidence. As mentioned earlier, reviewers try to associate differences in study results with differences in study instruments, participants, and/or testing conditions (Light, 1979). Review-based evidence is unique to examinations of accumulated results.

Study-based evidence is capable of establishing causal precedence among variables while review-based evidence is always purely associational. The problem with review-based evidence is not causal direction because it would be unreasonable to argue that a study's outcome caused the investigator's choice of variables. However, another ingredient of causality, nonspuriousness, is problematic. A plethora of other procedural characteristics are potentially confounded with the original researcher's choice of variables. These third variables cannot be eliminated as an explanation for review-based findings because the reviewer did not randomly assign procedures to experiments.

Protecting validity. Recommendations about what interpretative assumptions are appropriate for a reviewer to make will depend on the purposes and the peculiarities of a problem area. This is as true of quantitative procedures as of nonquantitative procedures. However, reviewers should open their rules of inference to public inspection by stating them explicitly. If there is any evidence bearing on the validity of the rules, it should be presented.

Also, reviewers should be careful to distinguish study- from review-based inferences. The potentially more equivocal nature of review-based inferences means that if this type of evidence indicates that a relation exists, the reviewer should call for the relation to be tested within a single study.

The Public Presentation Stage

The translation of an inquirer's notes, printouts, and remembrances into a public document is a task with profound implications for the accumulation of knowledge. The importance of the public presentation of results is readily acknowledged, but suggestions about how dissemination is best carried out are limited. Apparently the scientific community gives considerable latitude to an inquirer concerning what information about a study to make public and how the information should be presented (Ziman, 1969). Both primary researchers and literature reviewers are confronted by these editorial judgments.

The literature reviewer's dilemma may be similar in kind to that of the primary researcher, but the dilemma is more dramatic in degree. Reviewers have no formal guidelines describing how to structure the final report. At best, the reviewer follows informal guidelines provided by research reviews on the same or related topics. In most cases, the reviewer chooses a format convenient for the particular review problem.

How Editorial Judgments Create Variance in Reviews

The variation that differences in editorial judgments create is not found in the magnitude or direction of conclusions, but in the particular design aspects and results that are included in the report. One reviewer might believe that a methodological characteristic or result of the review would only clutter the manuscript. A second reviewer might think that same information would be of interest to some readers and decide that the clutter is worthwhile.

Threats to validity. The two threats to validity accompanying report writing relate to the different target populations of the review. First, the omission of details about how the review was conducted is a potential threat to validity. As with primary research, an incomplete report reduces the replicability of the review conclusion. A review's external validity is threatened to the extent that a complete knowledge of review procedures is not approximated in the report.

The second validity threat in report writing involves the omission of evidence about units and relations that other inquirers find important. Matheson, Bruce, and Beauchamp (1978) observe that "as research on a specific behavior progresses, more details concerning the experimental conditions are found to be relevant" (p. 265). A review will quickly become obsolete if it does not address the variables and relations that are (or will be) important to an area.

Protecting validity. This article contains many suggestions that might guide research review writing. If they are followed, reviewers will probably find themselves using the presentation format (Introduction/Methods/Results/Discussion) already familiar to behavioral scientists. However, reviewers will never be able to perfectly predict which omitted characteristic or result will eventually render their conclusions invalid or obsolete.

Some Post Hoc Issues

First, the five stages of reviewing contain 10 threats to validity. It is likely that other validity threats were overlooked in this treatment. Campbell and Stanley's (1966) list of validity threats to primary research was expanded by Campbell (1969), Bracht and Glass (1968), and Glass, Wilson, and Gottman (1975). It is expected that other threats to the validity of the integrative review will be uncovered.

Second, several of the threats to validity are shared by both primary research and literature review. This suggests that *any* threat associated with a particular research design will be applicable to the results of an integrative review in which the design is predominant.

Third, the standardization and exhaustiveness of the procedures presented here will reduce the variability in review conclusions most when applied to problem areas containing many studies. Of course, this does not mean that reviewers of highly specialized literatures or recent trends can ignore rigorous procedures. In addition, the accumulation of evidence will forever increase the irrelevance of this distinction.

Finally, it will be considerably more costly to undertake reviews using the guidelines set forth in this article. Also, reviewers cannot expect perfectly valid conclusions. The guidelines, then, must be viewed as optimal criteria which rarely will be achieved. This is the same spirit with which behavioral scientists presently undertake primary research.

Conclusion

This article began with the supposition that integrative research reviewing was a data-gathering exercise that needed to be evaluated against scientific criteria. It was proposed that because of the growth in empirical research, the conclusions of research reviews in the behavioral sciences would become less and less trustworthy unless something is done to standardize the process and make it more rigorous. Hopefully, the conceptualization has convinced readers that it is possible and desirable to require reviews to be more scientific. Because of the increasing role that reviews play in our definition of knowledge, it seems that these adjustments in procedures are inevitable if behavioral scientists hope to retain their claim to objectivity.

References

Bakan, D. The test of significance in psychological research. *Psychological Bulletin*, 1966, *66*, 423–437.

Barber, T. Expecting expectancy effects: Biased data analyses and failure to exclude alternative interpretations in experimenter expectancy research. *The Behavioral and Brain Sciences*, 1978, *3*, 388–390.

Bracht, G., & Glass, G. The external validity of experiments. *American Educational Research Journal*, 1968, *5*, 437–474.

Campbell, D. Reforms as experiments. *American Psychologist*, 1969, *24*, 409–429.

Campbell, D., & Fiske, D. Convergent and discriminant validation by the multitrait-multimethod matrix. *Psychological Bulletin*, 1959, *56*, 81–104.

Campbell, D., & Stanley, J. *Experimental and quasi-experimental designs for research.* Chicago: Rand McNally, 1966.

Cooper, H. Statistically combining independent studies: A meta-analysis of sex differences in conformity research. *Journal of Personality and Social Psychology*, 1979, *37*, 131–146.

Cooper, H. M. On the significance of effects and the effects of significance. *Journal of Personality and Social Psychology*, 1981, *41*, 1013–1018.

Cooper, H., & Arkin, R. On quantitative reviewing. *Journal of Personality*, 1981, *49*, 225–230.

Cooper, H., Burger, J., & Good, T. Gender differences in the academic locus of control beliefs of young children. *Journal of Personality and Social Psychology*, 1981, *40*, 562–572.

Cooper, H., & Rosenthal, R. Statistical versus traditional procedures for summarizing research findings. *Psychological Bulletin*, 1980, *87*, 442–449.

Cornfield, J., & Tukey, J. Average values of mean squares in factorials. *The Annals of Mathematic Statistics*, 1956, *27*, 907–949.

Crane, D. Social structure in a group of scientists: A test of the "invisible college" hypothesis. *American Sociological Review*, 1969, *34*, 335–352.

Eysenck, H. An exercise in mega-silliness. *American Psychologist*, 1978, *33*, 517.

Garvey, W., & Griffith, B. Scientific communication: Its role in the conduct of research and creation of knowledge. *American Psychologist*, 1971, *26*, 349–361.

Glass, G. Primary, secondary, and meta-analysis of research. *Educational Researcher*, 1976, *5*(9), 3–8.

Glass, G. Integrating findings: The meta-analysis of research. *Review of research in education* (Vol. 5). Itasca, Ill.: F. E. Peacock, 1977.

Glass, G., McGaw, B., & Smith, M. *Meta-analysis in social research.* Beverly Hills: Sage, 1981.

Glass, G., Wilson, V., & Gottman, J. *Design and analysis of time-series experiments.* Boulder, Colo.: Colorado Associated University Press, 1975.

Gottfredson, S. Evaluating psychological research reports. *American Psychologist*, 1978, *33*, 920–934.

Greenwald, A. Consequences of prejudices against the null hypothesis. *Psychological Bulletin*, 1975, *82*, 1–20.

Jackson, G. Methods for integrative reviews. *Review of Educational Research*, 1980, *50*, 438–460.

Light, R. Capitalizing on variation: How conflicting research findings can be helpful for policy. *Educational Researcher*, 1979, *8*(9), 7–11.

Lord, C., Ross, L., & Lepper, M. Biased assimilation and attitude polarization: The effects of prior theories on subsequently considered evidence. *Journal of Personality and Social Psychology*, 1979, *37*, 2098–2109.

Lykken, D. Statistical significance in psychological research. *Psychological Bulletin*, 1968, *70*, 151–159.

Mahoney, M. Publication prejudices: An experimental study of confirmatory bias in the peer review system. *Cognitive Therapy and Research*, 1977, *1*, 161–175.

Matheson, D., Bruce, R., & Beauchamp, K. *Experimental psychology* (3rd ed.). New York: Holt, Rinehart & Winston, 1978.

McNemar, Q. At random: Sense and nonsense. *American Psychologist*, 60, *15*, 295–300.

Presby, S. Overly broad categories obscure important differences between therapies. *American Psychologist*, 1978, *33*, 514–515.

Price, D. Networks of scientific papers. *Science*, 1965, *149*, 510–515.

Reynolds, P. *A primer in theory construction*. Indianapolis: Bobbs-Merrill, 1971.

Rosenthal, R. Summarizing significance levels. *New Directions for Methodology of Social and Behavioral Science*, 1980, *5*, 33–46.

Rosenthal, R., & Rubin, D. Interpersonal expectancy effects: The first 345 studies. *The Behavioral and Brain Sciences*, 1978, *3*, 377–415.

Taveggia, T. Resolving research controversy through empirical cumulation. *Sociological Methods and Research*, 1974, *2*, 395–407.

Webb, E., Campbell, D., Schwartz, R., & Sechrest, L. *Unobtrusive measures: Nonreactive research in the social sciences.* Chicago: Rand McNally, 1973.

Xhignesse, L., & Osgood, C. Bibliographical citation characteristics of the psychological journal network in 1950 and 1960. *American Psychologist*, 1967, *22*, 779–791.

Ziman, J. Information, communication, knowledge. *Nature*, 1969, *224*, 318–324.

AUTHOR

HARRIS M. COOPER, Associate Professor of Psychology and Research Associate, Center for Research in Social Behavior, 111 East Stewart Rd., Columbia, MO 65211. *Specializations:* Research methodology; social psychology of education.

6

Methods for Integrative Reviews

Gregg B. Jackson

This study examined methods for reviews of research that focus on inferring generalizations about substantive issues from a set of studies directly bearing on those issues. The purposes were to: (1) develop a conceptualization of the various methodological tasks of integrative reviews and of the alternative approaches to each task, (2) estimate the frequency with which current reviews published in high quality social science journals use each of the alternative approaches, (3) evaluate critically the strengths and weaknesses of the alternative approaches, and (4) suggest some ways in which more powerful and valid integrative reviews might be done. The primary source of data was a content analysis of two samples of such reviews.

Reviews of research are a fundamental activity in the behavioral sciences; they usually precede any major new research study and also are done as independent scholarly works. The focuses and purposes of such reviews vary substantially. Some investigators are primarily interested in sizing up new substantive and/or methodological developments in a given field. Some are primarily interested in verifying existing theories or developing new ones. Some are interested in synthesizing knowledge from different lines or fields of research, and still others are primarily interested in inferring generalizations about substantive issues from a set of studies directly bearing on those issues.

This paper is addressed only to reviews with the last purpose. They are referred to as "integrative reviews." Parts of the paper are probably applicable to other reviews, but no attempt has been made to discuss all types.

Given the importance and widespread conduct of integrative reviews, one might expect a fairly well-developed literature on methods, techniques, and procedures for conducting such reviews, but this is not the case. An earlier examination by this author of a convenience sample of 39 books on general methodology in sociological, psychological, and educational research revealed very little explanation of matters other than the use of card catalogs, indexes to periodicals, and note taking. Only four of these books discussed how to define or sample the universe of sources to be

The research reported herein was supported by Grant No. DIS 76-20398 from the National Science Foundation to the Social Research Group of the George Washington University. A more detailed discussion of the work is provided in the final project report (Jackson, 1978), which is available through the National Technical Information Service (PB 283747/AS). All opinions, findings, conclusions, and recommendations expressed herein are those of the author and do not necessarily reflect the views of the National Science Foundation. Many persons have provided assistance with this research, especially Jomills Braddock, Ira Cisin, and Judith Miller.

From Gregg B. Jackson, "Methods for Integrative Reviews," 50(3) *Review of Educational Research* 438-460 (Fall 1980). Copyright © 1980. American Educational Research Association, Washington, D.C. Reprinted by permission.

reviewed, three discussed criteria by which to judge the adequacy of each study, and only two discussed how to synthesize validly the results of different studies. None of the discussions exceeded two pages in length.

Similarly, a preliminary examination of journal article titles in *Sociological Abstracts* (from January 1973 through October 1975), *Psychological Abstracts* (from January 1973 through December 1975), and *Current Index to Journals in Education* (from January 1973 through June 1975) revealed a dearth of work on integrative review methods. Entries under the following subject headings were examined: literature reviews, methods, methodology, research methods, and research reviews. Only five of the titles from approximately 2,050 entries appeared directly relevant. Upon examination, one of the sources proved to be inappropriate and another could not be located. The remaining three are discussed briefly later in this section.

Additional evidence that there are few explicated methods, techniques, and procedures for integrative reviews is that few published integrative reviews adequately describe the methods used. A preliminary examination of 87 review articles in the 1974 and 1975 volumes of *American Sociological Review, Sociological Quarterly, Social Problems, Psychological Bulletin,* and *Review of Educational Research* found only 12 articles that provided some statement on the methods used.

Doing a good integrative review is never easy. It might seem that if all or almost all of the studies on the topic yielded similar results, the work would be easy, but this is incorrect because a careful reviewer is still obliged to determine whether all the studies have biases in the same direction that caused similar but invalid results. In the more prevalent case where the studies on the topic have different and apparently contradictory results, the work is obviously difficult. A good review of such research should explore the reasons for the differences in the results and determine what the body of research, taken as a whole, reveals and does not reveal about the topic.

The most valuable previous writings on integrative review methods have been done during the last decade. Feldman (1971) wrote that there is "little formal or systematic analysis of either the methodology or the importance of . . . reviewing and integrating . . . the 'literature'" (p. 86). He suggests that "half-hearted commitment in this area might account in part for the relatively unimpressive degree of cumulative knowledge in many fields of the behavioral sciences" (p. 86). Feldman mentioned the problem of not being able to know the parameters of the universe of relevant studies. He suggested the utility of examining the distributions of results in more than one manner and indicated that inconsistent results can sometimes be explained by differences in subjects, treatments, settings, and the quality of the research methods. He warned that reviews should avoid hypercriticalness as well as hypocriticalness and indicated that a good review of research "shows how much is known in an area, [and] also shows how little is known" (p. 100).

Light and Smith's excellent article (1971) discussed the present lack of systematic efforts to accumulate information from a set of disparate studies. Light and Smith used a four-category typology to characterize most present integrative reviews. The first category comprises those reviews that merely *list* any factor that has shown an effect on a given dependent variable in at least one study. A second category comprises reviews that *exclude* all studies except those supporting one given point of view. The third category is for those reviews that in one way or another *average* the relevant statistics across a complete set of studies. The fourth category is comprised of *vote taking*. This entails counting the positive significant results, the nonsignificant results, and the negative significant results; if a plurality of studies have one of these findings, then that finding is declared the truth. Light and Smith pointed out the weaknesses and resulting consequences of these procedures and proposed as ·a superior alternative a paradigm for secondary analysis of data from various studies having a common focus. The paradigm suggests that the data be analyzed within strata that take into account different characteristics of subjects, treatments, contextual variables, and effects of interaction among these. Ironically Light and Smith failed to point out that such a paradigm could also be useful for integrating results of different studies when secondary data analysis is not feasible. (Time constraints, promises about the confidentiality of data, lost data sets, and other factors can sometimes preclude secondary data analysis.)

During the last 3 years at least four investigators have begun work on improved methods for integrating results across studies. All began their work independently and without knowledge of the others' work, but luckily most of their efforts have been complementary rather than duplicative. In his 1976 AERA presidential address, Gene Glass stated the need for "a rigorous alternative to the casual, narrative discussions of research studies which typify our attempts to make sense of the rapidly expanding research literature," and proposed an approach that he calls meta-analysis; that approach is discussed later in this article. Rosenthal (1978) recently published a paper on aggregating results of independent studies by combining their probability values; his approach assumes that the studies are essentially replicates of each other, an assumption that is not necessary for Glass' approach. Schmidt, Hunter, and their colleagues (1973, 1976, 1978) have analyzed variations in the observed criterion validity of some personnel tests over repeated validation studies and demonstrated that the variation is substantially due to statistical artifacts rather than to situation-specific validity as had formerly been thought; their analysis is applicable whenever there are several independent studies using the same or similar measures, particularly when the studies have relatively small sample sizes. This writer (1978) has recently conducted an empirical investigation of the methodological approaches used in published review articles and queried journal editors and federal research agencies on the standards they use to judge integrative reviews. Some of the results of that work are discussed in this article.

The lack of explicit methods for doing integrative reviews is a serious problem for at least four reasons. First, the lack of explicit methods appears to be largely the result of social scientists failing to give much thought to such methods; thus it probably means that they are not using methods as powerful as could be developed for accumulating social science evidence. Second, it makes it difficult to have standards for judging the quality of integrative reviews. Third, it makes it difficult to train graduate students to do competent research reviews. Fourth, the lack of review methods hinders the accumulation of valid knowledge from previous research. Despite the lack of explicit methodology for doing integrative reviews, each review is the result of implicit methods, consciously or unconsciously selected by the reviewer.

This study primarily focused on the methods currently being used for integrative reviews of empirical research in educational research, psychology, and sociology. The study had four objectives:

(1) to develop a conceptualization of the various methodological tasks of integrative reviews and of the alternative approaches to each task;

(2) to estimate the frequency with which current reviews published in high-quality social science journals used each of the alternative approaches;

(3) to evaluate critically the strengths and weaknesses of the alternative approaches; and

(4) to suggest some ways in which more powerful and valid integrative reviews might be done.

Data Collection

The study investigated several sources of information on the methods used for integrative reviews. The first was a purposive sample of 16 integrative review articles that were suggested by various people as being methodologically exemplary. The second was a random sample of 36 review articles from prestigious social science periodicals; not all the sampled reviews were primarily directed towards inferring generalizations about substantive issues from a set of studies directly bearing on those issues, but all used at least part of the review for this purpose. Three articles were sampled from each of the 1975 and 1976 volumes of *Psychological Bulletin, Annual Review of Psychology, Review of Educational Research,* and *Annual Review of Sociology;* three articles were sampled from each of the 1974 and 1975 volumes of *Review of Research in Education;* one article was sampled from each of the 1975 and 1976 volumes of *American Sociological Review, Sociological Quarterly,* and *Social Problems;* thus there were 12 articles from psychology, 12 from educational research, and 12 from sociology. The third source was published rejoinders to the 36 randomly sampled articles; the fourth was Glass' papers on or using meta-analysis (1976, 1977; Smith & Glass, 1977) and personal communications with him (1977b, 1977d). Another source was responses to queries sent to editors of prestigious social science periodicals that frequently publish integrative reviews (*Psychological Bulletin, Annual Review of Psychology, Annual Review of Sociology, Review of Research in Education,* and *Review of Educational Research*). Responses to queries sent to officials of 10 national organizations thought to have major responsibilities for reviewing and synthesizing research in the social, biological, or physical sciences were the sixth and final source of information used.

This article focuses primarily on the results from the coding and analysis of the 36 randomly sampled articles and on a brief critique of Glass' proposed meta-analysis. The purposive sample of allegedly methodologically exemplary review articles was examined primarily to aid in conceptualizing the nature of review methodology and to suggest desirable approaches for various methodological tasks of a review. The other sources of information did not prove to be very enlightening.

It appears useful to conceptualize the methodology of integrative reviews as involving six basic tasks: (1) selecting the questions or hypotheses for the review, (2) sampling the research studies that are to be reviewed, (3) representing the characteristics of the studies and their findings, (4) analyzing the findings, (5) interpreting the results, and (6) reporting the review.

These tasks are analogous to those performed during primary research (research that involves collecting original data on individual subjects or cases). Indeed, this conceptualization was based on the presumption that reviewers and primary researchers share a common goal and encounter similar difficulties. The common goal is to make accurate generalizations about phenomena from limited information.

Since the methodology of primary research was used to conceptualize the methodology of integrative reviews, the standards for competent primary research were thought to be the appropriate evaluative criteria for judging the alternative methodological approaches that were investigated in this study. The problem, of course, was to determine those standards. Though the methodology of primary research is more highly developed than the methodology of integrative reviews, it has many aspects about which there is much disagreement among social scientists. There is much agreement, however, on certain topics. Sampling theory, as discussed for instance by Kish (1965), is widely thought to provide the best guidelines for samples when the purpose is to generalize from a relatively small sample to a much larger population. There is much agreement (and some disagreement) on the appropriateness of alternating descriptive and inferential statistics that are described, for example, by Bradley (1968), Hays (1963), and Kerlinger and Pedhazur (1973). Also there is substantial agreement on some of the major threats to the internal and external validity of any study, as discussed, for instance, by Campbell and Stanley (1963) and Bracht and Glass (1968).

An instrument was developed to code several aspects of, and approaches to, each of these tasks. The final version of the coding instrument had 66 items. It was used to code the 36 randomly sampled articles. Each article was coded independently by two coders. Intercoder agreement ranged from a low of 44.0 percent to a high of 100.0 percent for the various items, with an overall average of 78.6 percent. All discrepant codings were carefully resolved by the coders, with referral back to the coded article. The resolved coding was used as data for the analyses reported below. The articles were coded in a random order. The stability over time of the resolved coding was tested using a split-half procedure. Sixty-five items were individually tested for differences at the 0.10 level. Only five of the hypotheses were rejected, but this is well within the range of expected false rejections.

Results and Discussion

Task 1: Selecting the Questions or Hypotheses

This task was reconceptualized after coding the 36 randomly sampled review articles. Consequently, data were not coded for several important aspects of it.

Sometimes reviewers start with one or more very broad questions about a body of research, such as asking what the available research indicates about the relationship of X to other factors. Sometimes the initial questions may be more narrow, such as asking what increases Y. Occasionally the questions are quite specific, such as asking whether X_1 or X_2 increases Y.

The first two kinds of questions require a search for tentative answers and then verification of those tentative answers. The last kind of question is adequate for beginning the verification or hypothesis-testing stage.

Skill in asking good questions is probably as important to the progress of science as skill in finding tentative answers or verifying those answers. Zetterberg's work (1965; p. 68–100) on propositional statements outlines alternative forms of relationships among variables. Questions for reviews can reflect any of these forms.

There are two distinct levels at which questions can be asked in a review. One level concerns only the phenomenon itself. For example, does X causally influence Y, or does X causally influence Y when Z_1 prevails but not when Z_2 prevails? The second level considers what variations in the methods of studies $S_1, S_2, \ldots S_n$ might account for variations in the results. If the findings of the studies appear consistent, the second level of question is superfluous. But if the findings of the studies display apparent inconsistencies, this level is essential for a productive investigation. Without it one may conclude that available research on the question is inconclusive when that is not true.

There are at least four important sources that ought to be consulted when developing questions, searching for tentative answers, or formulating hypotheses for a review. The time at which these sources ought to be consulted may vary with many circumstances, but it would seem that almost all reviewers can benefit from consulting them.

One source is available theory that bears on the topic. Just as theory can be useful in formulating questions or hypotheses for investigation in primary research, it can be helpful in formulating questions or hypotheses for a review. Theory can suggest potentially important relationships for investigation. It also can provide a framework for a series of questions.

The discerning examination of prior research on a topic is well known to be useful for preparing and interpreting subsequent research on the topic. Similarly, the discerning examination of prior reviews on a topic can be useful when conducting subsequent reviews on that topic.

Seventy-five percent of the 36 randomly sampled integrative review articles cited previous reviews on the topic or on similar topics. But only 2 of these 27 provided any critique of the previous reviews.

The uncritical acceptance and use of previous reviews is as undesirable as the uncritical acceptance and use of any other research. One of the widely recognized responsibilities of a researcher is to examine critically all evidence used in his or her research. Important decisions about the focus, methods, and interpretations of a review are probably sometimes heavily influenced (consciously or unconsciously) by examinations of previous reviews on the topic or similar topics. There is nothing incorrect or undesirable about this if the reviewer uses scholarly judgment in evaluating the strengths and weaknesses of the previous work.

A good example of critically examining previous reviews on the topic is provided by Lambert (1976). He examined a number of previous reviews on his topic, sought reasons for their discrepant conclusions, and then used that information to improve his own review.

A third important source to consult when developing the questions or hypotheses for a review is the primary research that is expected to be reviewed. It is inadvisable to finalize the questions or hypotheses before examining the research studies that are expected to be used in the review. The examination may indicate that the initial questions or hypotheses are broader or narrower than is desirable. It may reveal that few studies directly bear on the selected questions or hypotheses, but that much more or better research is available on others of equal importance; or it may suggest that additional questions must be asked in order to interpret the answers to the initially selected ones.

One's intuition, insight, and ingenuity is a fourth source that ought to be consulted before finalizing the questions or hypotheses for a review. The most common challenge of integrative reviews of modern social science is finding order in apparent chaos. Intuition, insight, and ingenuity can help by suggesting new questions or hypotheses. These resources have so often proved important in virtually all fields of scientific endeavor that they shouldn't be overlooked when doing reviews. It should be remembered, however, that intuition and insight are grossly inadequate means of verifying tentative answers.

Task 2: Sampling

The results of any integrative review will be affected by the population of primary studies upon which the review is focused and by the manner in which the actually reviewed studies are selected from that population.

Only one of the 36 randomly selected review articles reported the indexes (such as *Psychological Abstracts* of *Dissertation Abstracts*) or information retrieval systems used to locate primary or secondary studies for possible inclusion in the review. Only 3 of the 36 review articles reported the bibliographies of previous reviews that were searched to locate appropriate sources for the review.

It seems reasonable to assume that these results mainly reflect the failure of reviewers to report how they searched for sources, rather than a failure to use the indicated means for the search. It is almost inconceivable that most reviewers do not use indexes or bibliographies. The failure of almost all integrative review articles to give information indicating the thoroughness of the search for appropriate primary sources does, however, suggest that neither the reviewers nor their editors attach a great deal of importance to such thoroughness.

It is desirable that a reviewer locate as many of the existing studies on the topic as possible. There is no way of ascertaining whether a set of *located* studies is representative of the full set of *existing* studies on the topic. Consequently, the best protection against an unrepresentative set is to locate as many of the existing studies as possible. Cost-benefit considerations will, however, often suggest a search that is somewhat short of being thorough. In such cases, it is particularly important for the investigator to report the search strategy so that others can judge its adequacy. Reports of this information also allow subsequent reviewers to expand upon previous searches without needless and expensive duplication.

An attempt was made to assess whether the studies *cited* in the integrative reviews were representative of the full set of existing studies on the topic. Such an assessment is not really of the methodology used in the reviews, but rather of the product of the search and citation process used by the reviewer.

The representativeness of the cited studies was judged by three rather crude indicators. All the randomly sampled integrative reviews were judged by at least one of three criteria to have a representative selection of citations. Five were also judged by at least one of the criteria to have an unrepresentative selection of citations. Given the limitations of the indicators, however, it seems wise to withhold inferences about this matter.

Data were collected on the extent to which the reviewer analyzed or discussed the full set of *located* studies on the topic. One of the 36 randomly sampled reviews analyzed or discussed the full set of located studies; 6 of the reviews clearly did not; and for the 29 other reviews, the information given in the published article was insufficient for making a judgment on this matter.

Data were not collected on how reviewers selected studies for analysis or discussion from the located studies. The coders' impressions from reading the reviews are that subsets were usually purposive samples of "methodologically adequate studies" or of "representative" studies. For instance, Glass (1976a) analyzed only those studies that had a control group. Sechrest (1976) indicated "No pretense of breadth or depth of coverage is made here. The materials cited were chosen because they fit a topic or illustrate a point to be made" (p. 9). Demerath and Roof (1976) indicated "It is manifestly impossible to summarize the entire recent literature. Instead, we have highlighted empirical studies that mark significant conceptual and/or methodological advances" (pp. 19–20).

If one wishes to analyze representative studies, there seems to be good reason for selecting the studies at random from the set(s) to be represented. Such selection does not assure a representative sample, but neither does any other approach, and random samples have the advantage of allowing an estimate of the probability of drawing a significantly unrepresentative sample.

Many reviewers wish to eliminate from their analyses those studies with results that have been seriously biased by methodological inadequacies. This seems reasonable and desirable, but it faces several difficulties. First, almost all research studies have at least a few methodological inadequacies. Second, methodological inadequacies do not always cause biased findings (as is discussed in more detail later in this paper). Third, it sometimes is difficult to determine reliably when methodological inadequacies have caused biased findings and when they haven't.

Some reviewers are inclined to use the simple strategy of eliminating all the studies with methodological flaws. They often end up with only one or two studies. When there is good reason to think all the eliminated studies have substantially biased results this strategy seems justified, but that seldom is the case.

Generally it is desirable to include in the analyses all studies for which there is not good evidence of biased findings. Replication is widely considered one of the most powerful tools for validating findings. If there is a consistent pattern in the findings of numerous studies on a topic, that pattern is more likely to be valid than a pattern exhibited by one or two allegedly unflawed studies.

When including studies with methodological inadequacies, it is important to analyze whether the different inadequacies are correlated with the studies' findings. When such correlations occur, they must be taken into account when making inferences about the phenomena being investigated. This is discussed further in respect to Task 4.

Task 3: Representing Characteristics of the Primary Studies

The representation of the characteristics of the primary studies is, in effect, the data collection of integrative reviews. The manner in which this is done can substantially affect the results and interpretation of the review.

Eight of the 36 reviews did not report the findings of most of the reviewed studies and did not indicate how many or what percentage of the studies had each type of finding or result. Only 18 of the 36 represented any of the findings of the primary or secondary research with an indication of the direction and magnitude of the result, and few did this for each analyzed finding. Only four of the reviews made any clear distinctions among significant positive findings, nonsignificant positive findings, nonsignificant negative findings, and significant negative findings.

It was fairly common for the reviewer to report the findings of individual studies in a manner such that it was impossible to judge how the reviewer had represented most of the findings when analyzing them. The impression of this writer is that such ambiguities were present in about 80 percent of the review articles. For instance, it was common to find reports that "Johnson found a relation between X and Y, but Alexander and Henderson did not." It was often impossible to know whether reported relations were statistically significant or included those that were "substantially" different from zero but not statistically significant. It also was common for findings of primary studies to be reported as statistically significant with no explicit indication of their direction.

Every reviewer has to represent the findings of the primary studies in some manner. Of the alternatives, magnitude measures with a directional sign are clearly the preferred way of representing the findings of the primary studies. To analyze these it is necessary to reduce them to a common metric, a chore that is not always easy but one on which some developmental work is currently being done (Glass, 1977a, 1977c). The next best alternative is representing the findings as significant (+), nonsignificant (+), zero, nonsignificant (−), and significant (−). This alternative may be best if magnitude measures, or the data needed to calculate them, are not reported in most of the primary studies, but it is quite inferior to the first approach. This is discussed further in the next subsection. The worst of the alternatives is representing findings as a significant difference in one given direction or not so. This alternative should usually be avoided, for it produces ambiguous data unless most of the primary studies being reviewed used one-tailed tests of their hypotheses. For instance, if 9 out of 23 findings are significantly positive, is this good evidence of a positive relation for the studied phenomena? It largely depends on how many of the remaining 14 studies had significantly negative findings.

No data were collected on how the reviewer represented the independent variables of the primary studies. A preliminary examination had shown that review articles hardly ever indicate this. The representation of the independent variables of primary studies can have a major impact on the results of a review.

Only 1 of the 36 randomly sampled review articles indicated that the reviewer, when encountering reports of primary and secondary studies that did not have all the information needed for the analyses, sought to get the information from other sources. It is just about inconceivable that 35 of the 36 reviewers did not encounter problems with missing information. What cannot be determined from this study is whether the failure of review articles to report efforts to obtain such information reflects an omission in the reports or a failure to seek the information. This writer suspects that it is some of each, but predominantly the latter.

In primary research today it is quite common for the investigators to make rather extensive efforts to minimize missing data and to report those efforts briefly. It would appear that similar efforts and reporting procedures are equally desirable for reviewers.

Task 4: Analyzing the Primary Studies

Analysis is the process by which the reviewer makes inferences from the primary studies. It includes judgments about the implications of identified methodological strengths or weaknesses in the primary studies, estimates of population parameters of the studied phenomena, and assessments of how varying characteristics of subjects, content, and treatments or suspected causal variables may affect the phenomena.

The analytic task of a review is seldom simple. Usually the findings of the examined studies vary moderately. Sometimes they vary so much as to appear contradictory.

Even in the rare case when the findings of the different studies are quite similar, a careful reviewer has some work. He or she should examine whether all of the findings are invalid. Congruent but invalid findings can occur if one or more methodological flaws are common to all the studies or if all the findings have about the same net bias (caused, however, by different methodological flaws in different studies). The latter is not particularly likely, but it is possible.

When the findings of the reviewed studies vary moderately or substantially, there can be at least three causes. The variations may be due to sampling error, differences in the methodological adequacy of the studies, or differences in the phenomena that were studied.

Sampling theory indicates that when there is a set of studies from a given population, the findings will vary some. About one-half of the study findings will be greater than the population parameter and about one-half will be less than the population parameter. In addition, in a large set of studies, if each study's findings are tested for statistical significance at the .05 level with the null hypothesis being the true population parameter, as many as 2.5 percent will have findings statistically significantly greater than the population parameter, and as many as 2.5 percent will have findings statistically significantly less than the population parameter. This sampling error has to be taken into account when judging whether or not variations in the findings should be considered congruent.

In the random sample of 36 examined reviews there were *at least* 18 that did not provide adequate information for judging whether or not the reviewer had interpreted variations in the findings of the primary studies in light of expected sampling error. In addition, there were several reviews where the authors clearly failed to take sampling errors into account when drawing inferences from a set of primary studies. For instance, Barnes and Clawson (1975) reported "The efficacy of advanced organizers has not been established. Of the 32 studies reviewed, 12 reported that advance organizers facilitate learning and 20 reported that they did not" (p. 651). An examination of their evidence, however, indicates that the 12 studies yielded statistically significant positive findings and that the other 20 may have yielded nonsignificant (+) findings, zero difference, nonsignificant (−) findings, and perhaps significant (−) findings. Barnes and Clawson did not report how many of the 20 studies yielded each type of finding. If the population value was zero, and all 32 studies tested their hypotheses at the .05 level, only about one of the studies would be expected to have statistically significant (+) findings, rather than the 12 that actually did. Unless several of the 20 studies had statistically significant (−) findings, Barnes and Clawson's data strongly suggest that advanced organizers have at least a small positive effect on learning. If there are considerably more than the expected number of both significant (+) and significant (−) findings, it is possible that the population has a bimodal distribution or that the examined studies are of two or more populations, despite appearances to the contrary.

Another example of reviewers failing to take sampling errors into account when making inferences from a set of studies is the review by Schultz and Sherman (1976). Twenty-two of the 62 studies cited in this review had significant (+) findings; no information is provided on the number of significant (−) findings. Schultz and Sherman wrote:

> The many nonsupportive studies, the qualification to some of the supportive studies, and in particular, the consistent failure to replicate interactions between social class and reinforcers lead us to several conclusions. 1) Social class differences in reinforcer preferences can *not* be assumed. (p. 39)

If the population value were zero, 62 studies tested at the 0.05 level would be expected to yield not more than two significant (+) findings rather than the 22 that did occur. There is, however, a factor suggested by Schultz and Sherman that does complicate the interpretation. They claim that methodologically superior replicates of earlier studies that had found significant (+) findings often failed to yield such findings. This does raise a legitimate concern, but there are some questions as to its implications. First, Schultz and Sherman indicated that only three of the 22 studies with significant (+) findings were unsuccessfully replicated (by a total of 9 studies). Second, Schultz and Sherman did not indicate whether these failures to replicate yielded nonsignificant (+) findings, nonsignificant (−) findings, or significant (−) findings, and such information is important in interpreting the findings. Third, investigators who conduct a replication may be predisposed to disprove the original study, and these predispositions may create some biases in their investigations despite some real methodological improvements.

Care has to be exercised when analyzing the distribution of findings among the four categories of statistically significant (+), nonsignificant (+), nonsignificant (−), and significant (−). One complication is that the above discussion has to be modified unless the null hypotheses tested in each primary study were ones of "no difference" or "no relationships." Null hypotheses usually are stated as such, but occasionally they are not. A second complication is that the above discussion presumes that all the tests of hypotheses were two-tailed tests. A third complication is that the above discussion presumes that all the primary studies tested their hypotheses at the same level of Type I errors. A fourth complication is that the above indicated analysis does not provide information on the magnitude of the differences or relationships. If the sample sizes of many of the primary studies are quite large (say, greater than 500), the method could lead to the conclusion that there is a difference even if the population parameter is only trivially greater or less than zero. This conclusion would not be incorrect, but it would be unimportant.

It is also possible to analyze the distribution of findings among the two categories of positive and negative. This can be done by using the binomial distribution or an approximation of it. This method is subject to all the above-mentioned complications except the third one. It can yield trivial conclusions either if many of the N's of the primary studies are quite large or if a quite large number of findings are analyzed.

Twenty-six of the 36 reviewers described what were considered to be the major methodological difficulties or shortcomings of the primary research that was reviewed. Some of the other 10 reviewers may have examined these difficulties or shortcomings but failed to report on them.

If more than a small portion of the reviewed studies have serious methodological weakness, these limitations can sometimes lead to invalid inferences unless their effects are considered before drawing inferences about the topic. No data were collected on how identified weaknesses in the methods of the primary studies were taken into account when making inferences from those studies. The impression of this writer is that the most common approach was to indicate that inferences about the topic were unreliable if many weaknesses were found. The second most common approach appeared to be to discard the methodologically "inadequate" studies and base the inferences on the remaining ones. A third approach was to identify weaknesses in the research that supported one point of view, thus discrediting the evidence for that point of view, without applying the same standards of methodological adequacy to research that supported another point of view.

All three strategies raise the question of what constitutes a serious threat to the validity of a given study and what does not, but there is no simple answer. It should be noted, however, that the actual threat to the internal and external validity of a study is not determined exclusively by the design of the study. Campbell and Stanley's (1973) important and widely read monograph on experimental and quasi-experimental designs shows which threats are controlled by various different designs; but the monograph does not indicate which threats are likely to be trivial in a given study or which threats can be reasonably controlled by other means. For instance, instrument decay may be a serious threat to internal validity when using a rater's judgment of people's emotional health, but is unlikely to be a serious threat when measuring children's heights using the kind of device that is common in physicians' offices. Similarly, obtrusive measures of a variable pose a more serious threat of testing effects than do unobtrusive measures. Also, studies where the data are collected over a brief period of time are less likely to have their validity threatened by history and maturation than are studies where the data collection extends over a longer period of time.

It is the impression of this writer than some reviewers will label as methodologically inadequate any studies not having experimental or strong quasi-experimental designs. Sometimes this is appropriate, but the above discussion ought to indicate that it is not always appropriate.

A third reason for varying findings among a set of studies on a given topic is that the phenomena investigated in the studies varied. The variables may have been measured by instruments that appeared to tap the same constructs but did not. Supposedly similar levels of variables may have differed because the instruments used had dissimilar metrics despite tapping the same constructs. In addition, contextual variables that were unmeasured in some or all of the studies may have varied among the studies. Under any of these circumstances it is possible for all findings in an apparently incongruent set to be valid. For instance, X_1 may increase Y_1 but not affect Y'_2; X_1 may increase Y_1 but X'_2 may not increase Y_1; a given level of X_1 may increase Y_1 but another level of X_1 may have no effect on Y_1; or X_1 may increase Y_1 when Z_1 is at a given level, but X_1 may not affect Y_1 when Z_1 is at some other level.

When the findings of the reviewed studies vary, statistical analyses can be used to explore which differing aspects of the studies may have contributed to differences in the findings. For instance, in a set of 20 studies, there may be (1) 15 that had adequate controls for instrument decay and five that did not; (2) 11 that used measurements that may have had obtrusive effects and 9 that did not; (3) 7 that used only male college freshmen as the participants, 5 that used both male and female college freshmen, and eight that used a random sample of adults aged 20–25 in a middle-sized industrial town; and (4) 6 that used a recall measure of the criterion and 14 that used a multiple-choice measure of the criterion. The findings of each study need to be expressed in terms of a common magnitude measure (how this can be done is discussed later); statistical procedures can be used to explore the extent to which the differences above *may* have effected variations in the findings. Given the small number of studies in this example, univariate tests would need to be used. If the results were not statistically significant when tested at a modest probability level, such as .10, we would be able to conclude that there is little reason to think that any of these characteristics seriously affected the findings. If one or more of the statistical tests yielded significant results, however, then we would conclude that some of the characteristics *may* have affected the results.

For instance, in this example we might find that the studies using recall measures of the criterion had an average effect for a given treatment of +2.6 and that the studies using a multiple-choice measure of the criterion had an average effect for the same treatment of −0.3. If this difference was statistically significant, we could conclude, with a given probability of error, that the difference in the type of criterion measure or something correlated with the type of criterion measure did cause some difference in the findings.

None of the 36 randomly sampled reviews did such an analysis in a multivariate manner, where two or more of the varying characteristics of the primary and secondary studies were simultaneously tested for relationships with the varying results. Two of the 36 reviews did univariate analyses, examining the relationship of a single characteristic of the studies to the varying results. Another 5 of the 36 reviews made such analyses in a systematic discursive manner, whereby they discussed how one or more characteristics of the primary and secondary studies were related to differences in the findings across the full set of analyzed studies. A total of only 7 out of the 36 articles reported analyses by any of the above three means.

The impression of this writer is that most of the reviews did suggest some explanation for the observed differences in the findings, and many offered some evidence for the explanation, but the evidence was usually less systematic than that coded as "systematic discursive." Reviews were not coded as using systematic discursive analyses unless they discussed how a characteristic of the study related to differences in the findings across *all or most studies* in the analyzed set. Most reviewers failed to be so thorough. Instead, they would do something like point out that the study having the highest Y also had a higher X than the study that had the lowest Y, while not mentioning the relation between X and Y in the other studies on the topic.

It is not at all clear why systematic analyses of the correlates of varying findings are not done more often in integrative reviews. Clearly, it is not because reviews fail to encounter discrepant findings; 32 of the 36 sampled reviews examined primary studies with at least some discrepancies in the findings. Perhaps it is because the reviewers find so many differences among studies that they despair of being able to find systematic relations, or perhaps it is because the reviewers simply have not thought to do such analyses.

Whatever the reasons, the effect of this omission is obvious and serious. Without such analyses reviewers will sometimes incorrectly infer that the findings of a reviewed set of studies are contradictory and that the available evidence is inconclusive. It seems almost certain that some of the confusion that surrounds many topics in the social sciences is a result of reviewers' frequent failure to search systematically for explanations of the varying results. Multicolinearity or weak correlations will sometimes preclude explanations of the variations, but the search ought to be conducted despite such possibilities.

A multivariate approach to the search is usually preferred, since there are often several possible explanations for the observed differences and one or more may simultaneously be partly correct. If the number of cases is not adequate for such analyses, a series of univariate analyses is the next best option. Systematic discursive analyses cannot be as precise as statistical analyses and should therefore generally be avoided when testing hypotheses. They can be used, however, in generating hypotheses that are then tested by more precise means.

Data were collected on the types of characteristics of the primary studies that were analyzed for possible relations to the variations in the study findings. Since only 7 of the 36 randomly sampled reviews did such analyses, the numbers are small. Three of the seven investigated the relation of varying subject characteristics to the variations in the findings, 5 investigated the relation of varying treatment or suspected causal variables, one investigated the relation of varying contextual variables or scope conditions, two investigated the relations of varying criterion variables, and two investigated the relation of varying research design or statistical analyses to the variations in the findings.

Since no category of characteristics is inherently more important to investigate, the reviewer should investigate all characteristics of the primary studies that are thought to be related to the variations in the findings. If the number of tests is large, the probability of a few Type I errors will become great and no heavy reliance should be placed on a single statistically significant relation.

Glass' Meta-analysis

Glass' meta-analytic approach involves transforming the findings of individual studies to some common metric, coding various characteristics of the studies, and then using conventional statistical procedures to determine whether there is an overall effect, subsample effects, and relations among characteristics of the studies and the findings. The original data for each unit of analysis in a study are *not* used. Rather, the unit of analysis is the study, and summary data from each study are analyzed. For instance, if there is a set of experimental studies that investigate the impact of X on Y, for *each* study one might code the average age and social-economic status of subjects, the duration of treatment (X), the setting in which the treatment was applied, an estimate of the reactivity or "fakeability" of the outcome measure used, an estimate of the internal validity of the research design, and the date when the study was conducted. Then these variables would be used in a univariate or multivariate manner to predict a standardized measure of the findings. Glass (1977c, p. 39) suggests that when most of the studies are experiments with a control group, the standardized measure of the findings should be a standard score difference measure calculated by the mean difference of the experimental and control groups divided by the within-group standard deviation of the control group. He suggests that if most of the studies are correlational and use different measures of association, the standardized measure should be a product-moment correlation; he provides formulas for estimating product-moment correlations from various other measures of association such as the point-biserial correlation, Spearman's rank-order correlation, and Mann-Whitney U, as well as t and F (Glass, 1977a, pp. 4–10).

The meta-analytic approach has a number of strengths. First, it is a systematic, clearly articulated, and replicable approach to integrating findings from a set of studies. Second, it can be used with information from both the best and the less-than-best studies on a topic, but with controls for possible biases caused by various flaws in the available studies. Third, it can provide estimates of the population parameters. Fourth, when using multivariate statistical procedures, it provides a method for simultaneously investigating the relationships among studies' methods, population of subjects, scope conditions, duration of treatments, and findings. No approach used to date for integrative reviews has been capable of doing this.

Glass, in several of his publications, has indicated some difficulties and unresolved questions about the application of his approach. He has pointed out that (1) it is sometimes difficult to get a standardized measure of the finding from a study because of insufficient data, (2) variance stabilization transformations may be desirable for measures of the finding where distribution of the criterion variable is attenuated, (3) the normal distribution assumption when transforming dichotomous data via probit transformations needs to be examined, (4) there is a problem of how to analyze findings that are nested within variables analyzed in a study, (5) findings perhaps should be weighted by their sample size, and (6) there are problems of analyzing aggregate data (the study as the unit of analysis) when trying to make inferences about unaggregated phenomena.

There are some other limitations and problems in the application of this approach that have not yet been discussed in published form and that are mentioned below. It should be noted that *most* of these difficulties are common to all analytic approaches to integrative reviews. Nevertheless they are important to keep in mind when doing or interpreting meta-analyses.

One limitation of the meta-analytic approach is that it can assess only relatively direct evidence on a given topic. Sometimes a topic of importance has not been directly investigated but there are studies with indirect evidence that can be reviewed and woven together. For instance, if the topic is "Will substance X reduce chronic depression in adults?" there may not have been any studies on that question, but there may have been studies of the effects of X on depression in baboons and studies of the similarity of effects of other chemicals on depression in baboons and humans. The meta-analytic approach can be used for evaluating the results within each set of studies, but it cannot weave together the evidence across sets of studies on related topics.

A second limitation of the meta-analytic approach is that it cannot be used to infer which characteristics of studies on a given topic *caused* the differing results. Statistical analyses can provide good evidence of causal relations only when the data are from experiments or strong quasi-experiments, or when there is a clear temporal ordering of the independent variables—which is not the case when analyzing characteristics of completed studies. The characteristics of reviewed primary studies are not systematically manipulated in an experiment or quasi-experiment, even when all the studies used experimental designs to investigate the given topic.

The third limitation of meta-analysis is applicable when the set of primary studies is a sample from a larger population and when multivariate statistics are used to analyze the findings. Under such circumstances, there must be a substantial number of primary studies on the topic, but there are no clearly documented standards for sample sizes when doing multiple regression. Kerlinger and Pedhazur (1973, p. 282) suggest at least 30 cases for each predictor. Other well-respected statisticians think these suggestions are excessive (Coleman, 1975; Glass, 1977b). It should be noted, however, that the number of cases may well be greater than the number of studies, because Glass suggested using an "effect" as the unit of analysis in meta-analysis and each study may have more than one effect. An effect is defined as any analysis *within* a study of a given treatment and outcome at a given time of measurement.

A fourth problem when doing meta-analyses is deciding whether or not a set of studies on a topic ought to be considered a universe or a sample. This has a bearing both on whether tests of statistical significance are appropriate and on the number of cases needed to use various statistical tools appropriately. Some sets are obviously samples, such as when a random sample of articles is drawn from a specified sampling frame or when a convenience sample is assembled (the latter does not meet the assumptions of inferential statistics). When the set is a result of a thorough search, the matter is not so clear. First, it is quite likely that even a thorough search will miss some, if not many, of the unpublished studies. Second, even if the search was successful in locating virtually all of the completed studies on the topic, these studies might be considered only a sample of the phenomena being studied or a sample of all possible studies on the topic. Glass initially suggested that the located studies be considered a population (1976b), but he subsequently has treated them as samples (1977a, 1977c). This writer's tentative opinion is that the set of studies should usually be considered a sample because the analysis of an integrative review is usually intended to make inferences about the phenomena investigated in the individual studies rather than about studies on the phenomena.

A fifth problem when doing meta-analysis is the lack of common metrics for the measures used and reported in the various primary studies on the topic. There are at least three aspects of this problem. First, different constructs are sometimes studied under a single topic. For instance, the outcomes of various studies on the effects of psychotherapy include emotional health, happiness, social relations, and others. Second, for any given construct there are alternative measures, the metrics of which may not be equivalent. For instance, what is described as upper-middle SES on one measure may be described as middle SES on a second measure. Third, the statistics used to measure a relationship between two or more variables can vary in different studies. Studies may use r_p, t, ρ, τ, or others.

Glass has suggested the first aspect of the problem is often not serious and can be ignored (1977d). He argues that all the various outcomes mentioned above in the example of psychotherapy are aspects of mental health and can be lumped together for a general investigation of the effects of psychotherapy. When the effects are thought to perhaps vary among different outcome constructs, Glass suggests including data that indicate major distinctions among the constructs and using them as a predictor in multiple regression analyses or as a stratifying factor for nested analyses. Though Glass directs his suggestion to variations in the construct of the criterion, it is equally appropriate for variations in the construct of predictors.

The second aspect of the problem is one that past reviewers have often complained about. When different studies use different measures of the same construct, and when the measures have not been validated, there is a serious question about the equivalence of the values generated by the different measures. For some characteristics such as age and sex, there is seldom any problem, but for others such as self-image and social support, there often will be a problem for which there is no simple solution. It should be noted that it is incorrect to rationalize that variations existing in the metric of some variable will only serve to reduce the strength of the relationship between that variable and some second variable and therefore can be ignored if strong relationships are found. This will be true if the variations in the metric are not correlated with the second variable, but generally there is no assurance that this will be the case.

Glass and his students have already completed some work that reduces the third aspect of the problem. They have assembled equivalency functions for some statistics and developed others (White, 1976; Glass, 1977a). Some of these functions are mathematical identities, but others are approximations. To date that work has not indicated the conditions under which the approximations become poor ones. This is a fertile subject for future research.

It should be noted that Glass' proposal of analyzing standardized effect measures obscures the absolute magnitude of the effects. It is possible for the average standardized effect for one subset of studies to be twice that of another subset of studies whereas the absolute magnitude of the difference is trivial for all practical purposes.

A sixth problem faced in meta-analysis is achieving valid and reliable coding of the characteristics of the primary studies to be analyzed. When the set of reviewed studies is relatively small, the coding is likely to be done by a single investigator; but coding, say, 40 studies may require as many as 60–80 hours, and this work may be stretched over a 4- to 6-week period, thus raising serious threats to coding stability. When large numbers of studies are being reviewed, a number of coders may be used, which raises the additional problem of intercoder reliability. Memory failures, boredom, and migraine headaches can undermine sustained coding reliability. When the coding is done over a lengthy period of time, intercoder reliability should be assessed more than once; reliability over time should also be assessed, and periodic retraining may be needed.

A seventh problem faced in meta-analysis is how to control for the effects of poor research design among the reviewed studies. Glass provocatively argued that it is wasteful to discard poorly designed studies from the analysis because "a study with a half-dozen design or analysis flaws may be valid . . . [and] it is an empirical question whether relatively poorly designed studies give results significantly at variance with those of the best designed studies" (p. 4). Glass suggests testing whether methodological characteristics such as the reactivity of the outcome measure and the internal validity of the design are related to the distribution of findings. He does not specify how this should be done other than by examining the covariation between the design characteristics and the findings. This analysis, however, is not as straightforward as it may appear.

The results of the analysis may be misleading if there is not at least a modest number of studies with good overall design. Since there usually is no reason to think that the relationship between the quality of design and the findings is linear or monotonic, there is no basis for extrapolating from the relation that holds for studies of poor and mediocre design to the studies with good design. In integrative reviews of some topics, there may be very few, if any, primary studies with good control of the threats to internal and external validity, and thus in these cases the possible effects of less-than-good design cannot be assessed.

If there is a modest number of well-designed primary studies, but a much larger number of studies with poor or mediocre design, regression slopes computed for the full sample of cases can still provide misleading results. This is because regression lines are fitted so as to minimize the squared deviations of the bivariate or multivariate points, and relatively little weight would be given to the small number of points from the well-designed studies.

Earlier, it was indicated that the congruence of findings does not assure their validity, and the lack of congruence is not proof of invalidity. When there is strong congruence in the findings and no good evidence of a strong common threat to the validity of all or almost all of the studies, there is suggestive, but not conclusive, evidence that any methodological weakness that existed in *some* of the studies did not have a substantial effect on the findings of those studies. In the more common situation, where there are apparent incongruencies in the findings, it is important to have at least a modest number of studies in a sample that are of good overall design if one is to empirically assess whether the methodological weaknesses that vary over the studies may have affected the findings.

What constitutes sufficient overall internal and external validity for these purposes cannot be simply explicated. It probably depends on a number of factors and needs further thought. It is important, however, to remember that threats of validity can be controlled by means other than design, and that some of the threats are likely to be trivial in any given study. This was discussed earlier in this paper.

Glass (1977b) has suggested that if the quality of a study is found to be related to the findings, a greater stake "should be put in the better designed study." This might be done by (1) some sort of weighting, (2) nesting analyses within subsets of the good- and poor-quality studies with more reliance put on the results of the former, or (3) by disregarding the poor-quality studies.

This discussion has very briefly outlined the major advantages of the use of meta-analysis for integrative reviews and has presented, in considerably more detail, some difficulties with the approach. The disproportionate attention given to the difficulties should not mislead the reader into thinking that meta-analysis has more disadvantages than advantages, or more disadvantages than other analytical approaches, when doing integrative reviews. In the opinion of this writer, the approach is methodologically sounder than most currently used approaches. Though it does have some serious difficulties, most of these difficulties are common to the other approaches. Also, the other approaches have additional difficulties or limitations that are not true of meta-analysis.

In short, the meta-analytic approach is an important contribution to social science methodology. It is not a panacea, but it will often prove to be quite valuable when applied and interpreted with care.

In general, it appears that current integrative reviews often fail to proceed beyond the stage of grounded hypothesis development. The reviewers carefully examine the available primary research, discover some apparent pattern or lack of pattern, and then report it. Seldom do the reviewers systematically and rigorously determine the extent to which the primary research coincides with the perceived pattern. Rigorous hypotheses testing is as desirable in reviews as it is in primary research, and, as was discussed above, there are better methods for doing it than are currently being applied in most reviews.

Task 5: Interpreting the Results

Seven of the 36 randomly selected reviews induced and reported new theory, confirmed old theory, or disproved old theory; 6 of the 36 induced and stated recommendations for policy or practice, and 4 of those 6 discussed conditions that might affect the impact of the policies or practices; 28 of the 36 suggested desirable focuses or methods for future primary or secondary studies on the topic; and only 3 of the 36 suggested desirable focuses or methods for future *reviews* on the topic or related topics.

There are other types of conclusions that the review articles may have stated that were not coded, but it is surprising that only one-third made conclusions about theory, policy, or practice. It may be that most integrative reviews are oriented toward making suggestions for improving the primary research, or it may be that most start with the aim of making suggestions for theory, policy, or practice, but subsequently decide to withhold inferences because they judge the available evidence to be inconclusive. The latter reason seems unlikely since 32 of the 36 studied reviews reported one or more inferences about the topic.

This writer has no strong suspicions as to why most review articles do not make suggestions for future reviews. Perhaps it is because reviewers do not think carefully about the methods of doing a review; perhaps it is because after completing the often herculean task of doing a review, the reviewers would not want to wish the task on anyone else; or perhaps it is for some other reason. Regardless, it is quite apparent that the resulting omission is unnecessary and harmful to the progress of science. As with primary research, it is virtually impossible to do a major review carefully without encountering some ideas for improved methods and some additional questions that need to be answered but that the given review cannot answer. These ideas and questions may be a valuable contribution to other investigators and ought to be reported, even if they can be used only after the accumulation of further primary research.

Task 6: Reporting the Review

A widely held precept in all the sciences is that reports of research ought to include enough information about the study that the reader can critically examine the evidence. This precept probably also should apply to integrative reviews, since such reviews are a form of research. As a minimum, it is widely held that the report ought to describe the sampling, measurement, analyses, and findings. Where unusual procedures have been used, it is expected that they will be described in some detail.

The previously discussed results indicate that many of the 36 review articles failed to report important methodological aspects of the review, particularly with respect to sampling and representing characteristics of the primary studies. Only 1 of the 36 articles reported the indexes and information retrieval systems used to search for primary studies on the topic. Only 3 of the 36 reported the bibliographies used as a means of locating studies. Only 7 indicated whether or not they analyzed the full set of located studies on the topic, instead of some subset. Only one-half of the 36 reported the direction and magnitude of the findings of *any* of the reviewed primary studies, and few did this for *each* finding. In addition, very few review articles systematically reported characteristics of the primary research that may have affected the findings.

Taken together, these results indicate that integrative review articles commonly fail to report their studies in the detail that is fairly common for primary research articles. A number of important functions are served by reporting various aspects of the review.

There are two reasons for carefully reporting the literature-search process in an integrative review article. First, it helps the reader to judge the comprehensiveness and representativeness of the sources that are the subject of the review. Just as the sample in a primary study can critically influence the findings of the study, the selection of the primary and secondary studies that are included in a review can seriously affect the results of the review. The bibliography of a review article indicates what individual studies were included in the review, but it does not indicate what broad classes of possibly relevant studies were excluded. A person with a thorough knowledge of the research on the topic will be able to infer such omissions by carefully examining the bibliography, but persons with less-thorough knowledge of the topic will not be able to do so. Second, briefly detailing the literature-search process in a review article allows future reviewers of the topic to easily extend the review without duplicating it. If it is known that most of the articles included in the review are those listed under certain descriptors of certain years of certain indexes, or are found in the bibliographies of specified sources, it is very easy for a subsequent reviewer to broaden or deepen the search for relevant sources without duplicating the earlier work.

If some located primary studies were excluded from the analysis, those studies ought to be identified and the rationale for their exclusion should be reported. The selection of studies to be analyzed in a review can seriously affect the inferences drawn during the review. Consequently the details of that selection should be reported so that they can be critically examined by the readers.

One-half of the 36 reviews often reported findings of the primary studies by stating a generalization followed by the citation of some studies that support the generalization. Such reporting can be very misleading. Unless used in conjunction with reporting the findings of each study, this practice also precludes the reader from critically examining the inferences of the reviewer without consulting the original reports of each study. For instance, Dusek (1975) reported "there is considerable evidence that during classroom interactions teachers treat groups of students differently (e.g., Davidson, 1972; Good & Brophy, 1970; Schwebel & Cherlin, 1972)" (p. 662). Hoffman (1972) reported "Several investigators report that while dependency in boys is discouraged by parents, teachers, peers, and the mass media, it is more acceptable in girls (Kagan & Moss, 1962; Kagan, 1964; Sears, Rau, & Alpert, 1965)" (p. 144). Both of these statements give an implication of consensus among the available research evidence, but neither of the statements would be *incorrect* even if the majority of the located evidence contradicted their points. Jacoby (1976) made a similar type of statement, reporting "Not surprisingly studies which utilized price as the only independent variable (261, 262, 316, 452) generally found a significant main effect" (p. 336). Though "generally" in this statement provides an explicit warning that the evidence was not entirely consistent, it still does not indicate what percentage of the studies supported the finding, nor does it indicate the magnitude of the findings. Some reviewers stated juxtaposed generalizations such as "Several studies found that X causes Y (Ace, 1967; Bace, 1953; Cace, 1969; Dace, 1970), but a few did not (Eace, 1968; Face, 1970)." This type of presentation is less ambiguous than the above examples, but it still obscures the magnitude and statistical significance of the findings.

When the number of reviewed studies is less than about 40, it is usually easy to present a single-page table indicating a number of characteristics of the primary studies including their findings, stated in either standardized or unstandardized form, or both, with the direction and statistical significance indicated. Such information would allow any reader to reanalyze the studies and second-guess the reviewer's inferences. Such opportunity is always a little threatening, but one of the oldest conventions of the scientific community is making one's methods and evidence easily available for the scrutiny of other researchers. When the number of primary studies is quite large, it is not practical to include all the data in the published report, but it should be available on request.

Characteristics of the Primary Research

A number of characteristics of the primary research that might have affected the methodological approaches used in each review are coded. These characteristics are (1) whether the primary research was psychological, sociological, or educational; (2) whether the topic of the review was about a condition, association, or causal relation; (3) the types of construct investigated in the primary research; (4) the predominant research orientation of the primary research; (5) the percentage of primary studies that investigated at least one statistical interaction effect; and (6) a crude estimate of when research was first done on the given topic.

The analyses failed to discover reliable evidence of a relationship between any of the examined characteristics of the reviewed research and any of the examined approaches to the methodological tasks of an integrative review. This, of course, should not be interpreted as indicating that there are no such relationships, but only that given the small sample size and the skewed distributions of some of the variables of interest, no reliable inferences could be made.

Other Sources of Information on Integrative Review Methods

Only 5 published rejoinders to the 36 randomly sampled reviews could be located. The analysis of these rejoinders was not terribly enlightening and is not discussed in this paper.

The editors of five prestigious social science journals that frequently publish integrative reviews were asked about the evaluation criteria and standards that they use to decide whether or not to publish submitted integrative reviews. One editor provided printed guidelines that he provides to prospective reviewers and to his editorial assistants, one editor failed to reply to repeated follow-ups, and three editors said essentially that they rely on the professional judgments of their editorial assistants or of the authors of invited reviews.

The officials of 10 organizations thought to have major responsibilities for integrative reviews in the social, biological, and physical sciences were asked about (1) the formal or informal guidelines or standards used by their offices to facilitate high-quality reviews of sets of empirical-research studies, (2) the evaluative criteria used to judge the quality of such reviews, and (3) examples of such reviews that they consider to be of unusually high quality. There were basically three types of responses. A couple of the responders reported some guidelines or evaluative standards, but they generally were not very specific. Some of the respondents indicated that they rely almost exclusively on the judgments of the scientists doing their reviews. Two of the respondents thought that integrative reviews were not often done in their disciplines (mathematics and physics, and space sciences), though subsequently it was discovered by this author that *Reviews of Modern Physics* frequently publishes such reviews.

Conclusion

It appears that relatively little thought has been given to the methods for doing integrative reviews. Such reviews are critical to science and social policy making and yet most are done far less rigorously than is currently possible. It seems likely that some of the confusion that surrounds many topics in the social sciences is partly a result of nonrigorous reviews of research on the topic.

This paper, the meta-analytic approach of Glass, and the work of Schmidt and Hunter provide several ideas for improving the prevailing methods for reviews. None of the ideas should at this stage be considered definitive. Rather, there is need for scientists who do integrative reviews or use them to consider the merits of the ideas, to think more about the problems to which they are directed, to try new approaches that appear promising, and to evaluate the effectiveness of those approaches.

Postscript. Over the 2 years since this paper was submitted to *RER* for publication, much work has been done on developing and applying new methods for integrative reviews. Three particularly interesting papers are those of Light (1979), Rosenthal and Rubin (1978), and Schmidt, Hunter, Pearlman, and Shane (1979).

References

Barnes, B. R., & Clawson, E. V. Do advance organizers facilitate learning? Recommendations for further research based on an analysis of 32 studies. *Review of Educational Research,* 1975, *45,* 637–659.

Bracht, G. H., & Glass, G. V The external validity of experiments. *American Educational Research Journal,* 1968, *5,* 437–469.

Bradley, J. V. *Distribution-free statistical tests.* Englewood Cliffs, N.J.: Prentice-Hall, 1968.

Campbell, D. T., & Stanley, J. C. *Experimental and quasi-experimental designs for research.* Chicago: Rand McNally, 1963.

Coleman, J. S. Recent trends in school integration. *Educational Researcher,* 1975, *4*(7), 3–12.

Demerath III, N. J., & Roof, W. C. Relition—recent strands in research. *Annual Review of Sociology,* 1976, *2,* 19–33.

Dusek, J. B. Do teachers bias children's learning? *Review of Educational Research,* 1975, *45*(4), 661–684.

Feldman, K. A. Using the work of others; some observation on reviewing and integrating. *Sociology of Education,* 1971, *44,* 86–102.

Glass, G. V *Primary, secondary, and meta-analysis of research.* Presidential address to the Annual Meeting of the American Educational Research Association, San Francisco, April 21, 1976. (a)

Glass, G. V Primary, secondary, and meta-analysis of research. *Educational Researcher,* 1976, *5,* 3–8. (b)

Glass, G. V, Coulter, D., Hartley, S., Hearold, S., Kahl, S., Kalk, J., & Sherretz, L. *Teacher 'indirectness' and pupil achievement: An integration of findings.* Unpublished manuscript, University of Colorado, 1977. (a)

Glass, G. V Personal communication, October, 1977. (b)

Glass, G. V Integrating findings: The meta-analysis of research. *Review of Research in Education* vol. 5. 1977. (c)

Glass, G. V Personal communication, November, 1977. (d)

Hays, W. L. *Statistics.* New York: Holt, Rinehart & Winston, 1963.

Hoffman, L. W. Early childhood experiences and women's achievement motives. *Journal of Social Issues*, 1972, *28*(2), 129–155.

Jackson, G. B. *Methods for reviewing and integrating research in the social sciences.* Final report to the National Science Foundation 1978. (NTIS No. PB28374-7/AS)

Jacoby, J. Consumer psychology: An octennium. *Annual Review of Psychology*, 1976, *27*, 331–358.

Kerlinger, F. N., & Pedhazur, E. J. *Multiple regression in behavioral research.* New York: Holt, Rinehart, & Winston, 1973.

Kish, L. *Survey sampling.* New York: John Wiley. 1965.

Lambert, M. J. Spontaneous remission in adult neurotic disorders: A revision and summary. *Psychological Bulletin*, 1976, *83*(1), 107–119.

Light, R. J., & Smith, P. V. Accumulating evidence: Procedures for resolving contradictions among different research studies. *Harvard Educational Review*, 1971, *41*, 429–471.

Light, R. J. Capitalizing on variation: How conflicting research findings can be helpful for policy. *Educational Researcher*, 1979, *8*(9), 7–14.

Platt, J. R. Strong inference. *Science*, 1964, *146*, 347–353.

Rosenthal, R. Combining results of independent studies. *Psychological Bulletin*, 1978, *85*, 185–193.

Rosenthal, R. & Rubin, D. B. Interpersonal expectancy effects: The first 345 studies. *The Behavioral and Brain Sciences*, 1978, *3*, 377–415.

Schmidt, F. L., Berner, J. G., & Hunter, J. E. Racial differences in validity of employment tests: Reality or illusion? *Journal of Applied Psychology*, 1973, *58*, 5–9.

Schmidt, F. L., Hunter, J. E., & Urry, V. W. Statistical power in criterion-related validation studies. *Journal of Applied Psychology*, 1976, *61*, 473–485.

Schmidt, F. L., & Hunter, J. E. Development of a general solution to the problem of validity generalization. *Journal of Applied Psychology*, 1977, *62*, 529–540.

Schmidt, F. L., Hunter, J. E., Pearlman, K., & Shane, G. S. Further tests of the Schmidt-Hunter bayesian validity generalization procedure. *Personnel Psychology*, 1979, *32*, 257–276.

Schultz, C. B., & Sherman, R. H. Social class, development, and differences in reinforcer effectiveness. *Review of Educational Research*, 1976, *46*, 25–59.

Sechrest, L. Personality. *Annual Review of Psychology*, 1976, *27*, 1–27.

Smith, M. L., & Glass, G. V Meta analysis of psychotherapy outcome studies. *American Psychologist*, 1977, *32*, 752–760.

White, K. R. The relationships between socioeconomic status and academic achievement. (Doctoral dissertation, University of Colorado, 1976). *Dissertation Abstracts International*, 1977, *38*, 5067A-5068-A. (University Microfilms No. 77-3250.)

Zetterberg, H. L. *On theory and verification in sociology* (3rd ed.). New York: Bedminister Press, 1965.

AUTHOR

GREGG B. JACKSON Project Director, Washington Center for the Study of Services, 1518 K St. N.W., Washington, D.C. 20005. *Specialization:* Research methods, evaluation, interaction analysis, teacher effectiveness, and minority pupil education.

7

Meta-Analysis
A Validity Perspective

Paul. M. Wortman

The past few years have been seen the development, application, and widespread adoption of a new statistical technique for aggregating the results from many research studies. This method has been called "meta-analysis" or the "analysis of analyses" by its originator (Glass, 1976). Although other similar statistical procedures have been developed and applied (Rosenthal, 1978; Cooper, 1979), the term and method promulgated by Glass and his associates have been by far the most utilized. In fact, the rapidity of its diffusion is somewhat of a methodological phenomenon in its own right. In their recent book discussing the meta-analysis procedure, Glass et al. (1981) cite over 40 different applications in nearly as many areas of research in the five-year period since its introduction. Many of these applications have been in psychology and the trend is growing, as indicated by the recent spate of articles in *Psychological Bulletin* (see Burger, 1981; Johnson et al., 1981; Strube and Garcia, 1981), the major review journal for the discipline. While the majority of these examples involve the synthesis of basic research, the method is applicable, relevant, and useful in applied areas as well (e.g., Smith and Glass, 1977). In particular, there are many evaluative areas with sufficient studies to warrant meta-analysis.

In its simplest form, meta-analysis involves the computation of the average effect size (ES or, more recently, Δ in the Glass et al. notation) for a group of studies. The effect size measure used by Glass is the standard score obtained by subtracting the mean of the control group from that of the treatment group (i.e., T – C) and dividing this difference by the standard deviation of the control group (SD_C). An effect size can be calculated for each relevant outcome or dependent variable in a study. In such situations the unit of analysis becomes the effect size rather than the study (see below). The effect sizes are then summed and divided (by the total number of effects) to obtain a single quantitative number, the average effect size. Then, assuming that the results are normally distributed, a Z-table can be consulted to determine the percentile rank of the average person, as indicated by the average

From Paul M. Wortman, "Meta-Analysis: A Validity Perspective," *Annual Review of Psychology*, Volume 34, 1983, 223-260. Copyright © 1983 by Annual Reviews, Inc. Reprinted by permission.

effect size, in the treated group. A positive effect size would usually indicate a beneficial treatment, while a negative value would indicate that the treatment was ineffective or even harmful.

Social scientists are used to dealing with small effects, and Cohen (1962) has even gone so far as to provide rules of thumb for categorizing effects as small, medium, or large depending on their absolute value. Nevertheless, Glass et al. (1981) exhort their readers to cease from such labeling, claiming that there is "no wisdom whatsoever" in this practice. Sechrest and Yeaton (1981) agree that it is inappropriate to use absolute values to interpret an effect size. They note that small effects may be "deceptively worthwhile," while effects that seem large may be considered "trivial." Sechrest and Yeaton discuss two ways of classifying an effect-size estimate, which they call "judgmental" and "normative" approaches.

The judgmental approach involves an assessment by a relevant individual such as a policymaker or expert. Sechrest and Yeaton feel that experts are especially suited to make such judgments since experts probably share a common "experiential background," and, therefore, a similar, implicit metric. They briefly discuss two small studies where they found that experts were able to predict the size of effects found in experimental treatments. It is also likely that such experts share a common scientific body of knowledge. For that reason groups of experts might produce even better estimates than individuals given the available pooled knowledge and experience. On a more informal basis, such consensus activities are currently being conducted by the National Institutes of Health to assess the scientific evidence bearing on new medical technologies (Wortman et al., 1982).

The second, or normative procedure for interpreting the magnitude of an effect involves the use of comparative rather than absolute standards. This approach would compare an effect with the prevailing norm derived from previous studies. Thus, if a new effect is larger than any previously found, it would be judged as (comparatively) a significant finding. Sechrest and Yeaton feel this is a more common occurrence. Such a use of effect sizes has been recommended by Posavac (1980) in a meta-analysis of patient education programs.

Glass (1977) has advocated meta-analysis as a replacement for the traditional way of summarizing the research literature—the review article. The method apparently delivers an objective result borne of a straightforward statistical procedure. Moreover, the resulting effect-size estimate has both direction and magnitude—an improvement over the subjective judgments that make up most literature reviews. In synthesizing the literature the reviewer is asked to perform an almost impossible cognitive task: combining the results from dozens of studies using different research designs and outcome measures that may vary in both quality and appropriateness. It is not surprising that such reviews typically call for more definitive research or rely on the small minority of studies that are scientifically relatively spotless. Statistical methods for research synthesis, such as Glass's meta-analysis, avoid cognitive overload and much of the subjective bias it entails. It thus allows a single, objective summary finding to emerge that may not have been apparent in the single study or review.

A dramatic example of the potential benefits of such data-integration methods is provided by a recent article in the medical literature (Baum et al., 1981). These authors performed a formal synthesis of all RCTs using no-treatment controls to assess the effectiveness of antibiotics as a prophylactic in colorectal surgery. Effectiveness was determined by examining both abdominal wound infection and mortality rates. They located 26 studies published between 1965 and 1980, and in 22 of them found that antibiotics produced a lower rate of infection. The temporal pattern of the effect sizes was displayed graphically. Overall, the infection rate was reduced by about 20% for those patients treated prophylactically with antibiotics. The mortality rate also indicated a consistent benefit for those treated by antibiotics, with the average rate about 6% lower, or about 60% fewer deaths than in the control group.

The investigators did not directly calculate a standardized effect size. Instead, they report only the 95% confidence intervals for mean differences, also using another interesting graph to reveal the temporal pattern of the cumulative findings. In both cases this interval does not contain zero, thus indicating a statistically significant effect for antibiotics. In fact, the 95% confidence interval for infection rates excluded zero by 1969 (after only five studies). Glass et al. (1981) recommend using a probit transformation to obtain an effect-size estimate for such data. The differences noted above correspond to effect sizes of approximately .6 and .4 standard deviation units for infection and mortality rates, respectively.

Baum and associates (1981) demonstrate a major advantage of research synthesis by showing that the cumulative findings from these research studies yielded a statistically reliable positive effect for antibiotic prophylaxis as early as 1975. At that time, only nine of twelve studies indicated a lower postoperative-infection rate, in which only three had statistically significant results. Moreover, the synthesis provides enough cases for the analysis of mortality data—something that was not possible for any single study because there were too few outcomes. Finally, the authors claim that the results of these studies indicate that the continued use of no-treatment control groups is inappropriate. They recommend instead that future studies employ a "previously proved standard of comparison" even though they realize that this leads to a "scientific dilemma," since it will be much more difficult to demonstrate additional gains in effectiveness for new treatments. For example, using one of the effective drugs as a control in a new RCT would require over 1000 patients to demonstrate a reduction in infection by another 50%. Thus it would be prohibitively expensive to demonstrate similar gains in mortality.

VALIDITY

Although they were developed to assess the quality of individual studies, the validity categories discussed above are relevant to the discussion that has surrounded the introduction and application of meta-analysis. They provide a useful approach to organizing these comments and examining the limitations of the method. In this section the four types of validity developed by Campbell and his associates (Campbell and Stanley, 1966; Cook and Campbell, 1979) will be applied to a critical examination of meta-analysis.

External Validity

One of the major objections to meta-analysis is that it mixes "apples and oranges" (Gallo, 1978; Presby, 1978). For example, these critics of Smith and Glass's (1977) meta-analysis of psychotherapy have claimed that it is inappropriate to cluster or stratify different kinds of therapy into a single category. This is listed as "Criticism #1" by Glass et al. (1981) in their discussion of the meta-analysis method. They are not persuaded by this criticism and even find it inconsistent. They claim that subjects within a study are as different as those between studies.

Elashoff (1978), in commenting on whether to aggregate the results of several studies, addresses this external validity issue. Specifically, she recommends against synthesis when the results are not "homogeneous across different patient populations." She cites as examples the differential effects of steroid therapy for alcoholic hepatitis found in males and females, and the improved efficacy of cimetidine in treating duodenal ulcer as a function of duration of therapy.

There are statistical procedures for determining the homogeneity of the results (Gilbert et al., 1977; Hunter et al., 1982). Elashoff applied the procedure recommended by Gilbert and associates to the two reviews noted above (i.e., steroid therapy for alcoholic hepatitis and cimetidine for duodenal ulcer) and found it appropriate to combine the results of the cimetidine studies, but not those from the steroid therapy studies. For the latter, the standard deviation for the percentage differences in mortality was 27, of which only 7 percentage points could be expected from sampling variation alone.

Hunter et al. (1982) have addressed the issue from another perspective. These investigators ask whether the variability in the effect sizes can be accounted for by sampling alone. If not, other variables need to be entered into the analysis. In other words, apples and oranges may be included in the latter situation by appropriate blocking or stratifying variables that separate the fruits of one's analysis. These techniques thus reduce the debate over external validity to a statistical test of the homogeneity of variance. Baum et al. (1981) used this procedure before pooling the results of the studies on antibiotic prophylaxis in colon surgery.

Construct Validity

The apples and oranges problem is to a large extent an issue in construct validity. The determination of the study's scope is probably the first question asked. This is a critical issue, for it sets the boundary on what studies should or should not be included in the meta-analysis. As Glass et al. (1981) acknowledge, the solution "depends entirely on the exact form of the question being addressed." If studies are testing the same hypothesis, then aggregation would be appropriate. However, critics contend that the operationalization of the theoretical construct (i.e., the independent variable) presents the problem. Thus, for example, should behavior modification be treated as equivalent to rational-emotive therapy (Presby, 1978)? Again, the answer appears to follow from the question posed, as Glass et al. contend. If a policy decision to reimburse clinical psychologists for psychotherapy is being considered, then a general question concerning the effectiveness of all therapies seems appropriate. Similarly, the Baum et al. (1981) study did not ask which specific antibiotic was most effective in preventing adverse consequences of colorectal surgery. If one finds heterogeneous results using the above methods, it may be that too broad a theoretical construct (or construct of causes) is being investigated. Fortunately, this is an empirical question that can be easily addressed.

Where there is faulty operationalization it may be necessary to exclude studies. For example, DeSilva et al. (1981) found it appropriate to aggregate only six of 15 RCTs in determining the effectiveness of lignocaine (or lidocaine) in preventing irregular heartbeats in patients who had suffered a heart attack. The excluded studies used "subtherapeutic concentrations of lignocaine," either an improper initial dose or an incorrect injection. These are both violations of construct validity.

A related construct validity issue concerns the appropriateness of the measures (or dependent variables) employed in the various studies. Berk and Chalmers (1981) attempted to integrate the research literature dealing with the cost-effectiveness of ambulatory care. They found that only 4 of 78 studies used an appropriate measure of costs. In such situations studies may have to be excluded, even if the ability to conduct the meta-analysis is jeopardized. There is considerable room for judgment here and the research investigator should explicitly state the construct being investigated and the studies actually excluded on these grounds.

In evaluation research standardized measures are typically employed. Then the decision to include these studies involves the quality of the measures and their similarity. Although standardized achievement tests have been shown to vary in the skills they assess (Porter et al., 1978), most researchers would agree that such tests are similar enough to be used to integrate study findings. In evaluation research the debate is more often on the comprehensiveness or fairness of these measures in assessing the variety of programmatic objectives (House, 1980; House et al., 1978).

Internal Validity

The role of internal validity considerations in the proper conduct of meta-analysis has, as might be expected, figured prominently in the discussion of this new method. What is unexpected is the heated nature of the debate and the accompanying level of invective. Such words and phrases as "simplistic," "tendentious diatribes," "astute dismantling of [author's name] myth," and "abandonment of scholarship" have littered the verbal landscape of the exchanges between Glass and his critics. The reader may wonder what provoked such emotional reactions and whether the criticisms are, in fact, legitimate.

The major controversy concerns whether design quality (i.e., internal validity) affects the results (Mansfield and Busse, 1977; Eysenck, 1978; Jackson, 1980;

Marshall, 1980). Critics such as Mansfield and Busse (1977) maintain that studies with more threats to internal validity (i.e., "poorly designed") are more likely to report large effects than those with few plausible threats to internal validity (i.e., "well designed"). Instead, they recommend a triage strategy: throw out those studies with significant methodological problems and divide the remainder into well-designed and less well-designed categories. Separate meta-analysis can then be performed to see if there is convergence in the results. If there is not, then the results from the well-designed group are more credible. There is considerable empirical evidence to support the contention that design quality is inversely related to effect size in other areas such as health (e.g., Gilbert et al., 1977; Wortman, 1981) and even Glass's own work (Glass and Smith, 1979) in education has shown that quality can affect the results.

For his part, Glass (1977, 1978) and his associates (Glass and Smith, 1978; Glass et al., 1981) have steadfastly maintained that "it's bad advice to eliminate virtually any studies on strictly methodological grounds." They contend that the effect of design quality can be detected a posteriori without excluding any studies that may, in the final analysis, have comparable effects to those deemed better. Glass consistently cites the results of his meta-analysis of psychotherapy (Smith and Glass, 1977) where design quality had "virtually no correlation with study findings." If this is not the case, as in the Glass and Smith (1979) study, then "the sensible course was elected" and the results of the well-controlled studies were emphasized. They attribute the need to control for design quality to the small effects found in that meta-analysis. Glass et al. (1981) acknowledge that research quality is a "central concern in meta-analysis" but maintain that it is an "empirical matter." They offer as additional evidence the results of twelve other meta-analyses where there is little variation in results attributable to internal validity. They conclude that this should be "an effective antidote to rampant a priorism" that seeks to exclude studies from the meta-analysis.

A number of points can be made in rebuttal, however. First, the majority of the studies in the Smith and Glass (1977) meta-analysis of psychotherapy—65% according to a recent reanalysis (Landman and Dawes, 1982)—were well controlled. In fact, the quality of the studies, as a whole, was quite high. Thus the correlation between quality and effect size would be expected to be low since the range (of internal validity) was restricted. Second, Glass et al. (1981) categorized studies as high, medium, or low in internal validity. They do not define the coding procedure, but it is apparently somewhat subjective. Recently, there have been some published reports on procedures for grading and coding study quality (Mosteller et al., 1980; Chalmers et al., 1981). These methods require attention to a large variety of methodological detail (i.e., over thirty study characteristics in the Chalmers et al. system) that is not captured in the broad categories used by Glass et al. Moreover, ratio scales can be constructed to assess internal validity from the Chalmers et al. system; these are likely to be more sensitive than the nominal scales used by Glass and his associates. Finally, the Chalmers et al. procedure incorporates most of the threats to validity described by Cook and Campbell (1979), along with other design features, and allows direct comparisons with other research syntheses (e.g., Baum et al., 1981).

Finally, many studies may have to be excluded from the meta-analysis because they lack the appropriate statistical information to calculate an effect size. Despite the ingenious, and even heroic, methods that Glass (1977) and his collaborators (Glass et al., 1981) have developed for salvaging this information, it may not be possible to obtain an estimate of the effect size. These studies are often the worst ones from a methodological standpoint and thus would not be available for the correlational analyses performed by Glass et al. (1981). In work examining the school desegregation literature (Wortman et al., 1982), 79% of the studies had to be excluded largely for this reason.

From the perspective of internal validity, there do appear to be a number of (what one critic has called) "logical considerations" that must be handled a priori. The type of control group used—whether no treatment, placebo, or existing standard—is just as essential to the estimate of effect size as the type of treatments were from an external validity perspective. The estimate of effect size is likely to decrease as one moves from a no-treatment control group to one composed of the existing standard. This was one of the major criticisms cited by Landman and Dawes (1982) for their reanalysis of the Smith and Glass (1977) meta-analysis of psychotherapy. Landman and Dawes, therefore, confined their secondary analysis to RCTs having no-treatment controls. They also performed a separate analysis for those studies including placebo controls. Their results are in substantial agreement with those of Smith and Glass. This is not surprising given the high quality of the studies in the original analyses, but it does avoid the methodological controversy noted above. Moreover, the type of control group does affect the results. Landman and Dawes report an effect size reduced by nearly one-third when a placebo control is employed.

The type of design can also affect the results of a meta-analysis. One of the major threats to the internal validity of nonrandomized studies is differential selection. If subjects systematically differ along a crucial dimension of concern to the study's hypothesis, then the results will be biased. Moreover, the effect-size estimate used by Glass implicitly assumes a randomized study. For quasi-experiments, a second term in the equation is needed to remove the preexisting difference or initial effect size due to improper selection. (This term would have an expected value of zero for RCTs.) Since most evaluation studies are quasi-experiments, it is important to remove the pretest differences between the treatment and control groups. Fred Bryant's paper illustrates this point. When such a pretest-adjusted meta-analysis was conducted for the predominantly quasi-experimental literature dealing with the effects of school desegregation on minority achievement, statistically significant differences were found. The paper by Bill Yeaton will illustrate the magnitude of the difference between quasi- and true-experiments in evaluating a medical technology. In both cases the bias introduced by threats to internal validity is shown to be both substantial and systematic.

Glass (1978) has even gone so far as to lament that the weaker pretest-posttest quasi-experimental design studies were not included in the meta-analysis of psychotherapy. In addition to the selection problems noted above, the results would also be confounded by maturation and statistical regression. All of these threats to internal validity would probably increase the estimate of effect size. As a consequence, studies using such designs should probably be excluded from the meta-analysis. Without other evidence, it would be impossible to correct for the bias introduced by those validity problems.

In conclusion, differences in the type of control group and design can affect the result of a meta-analysis. As Jackson (1980) has noted, it is likely that there will be "incongruencies in the findings," and then some well-designed studies to determine whether internal validity is a source of the variation will be needed. A simple solution is to perform separate analyses on the relevant categories (i.e., no-treatment and placebo control, randomized or quasi-experiment). One cannot assume that these threats will be either self-cancelling, small, or sparse. In particular, adjustments to eliminate preexisting group differences should be considered in meta-analysis of quasi-experiments. Alternatively, where there are sufficient studies one can confine the analysis to RCTs with no-treatment control groups as was done by Baum et al. (1981).

Statistical Conclusion Validity

The final validity issue concerns the appropriateness of the statistical methods employed. A number of related concerns, such as testing for homogeneity and adjusting for pretest differences in quasi-experiments, have already been noted. The most consistent statistical comment has focused on the practice of combining multiple results from a single study. Landman and Dawes (1982) noted five different kinds of nonindependence of measures (e.g., multiple measures from the same subject, at multiple points in time, and so on). Glass et al. (1981) consider this technical criticism to be the most cogent. Their stated position is that

> The simple (but risky) solution is to regard each finding as independent of the others. The assumption is untrue, but practical [1981: 200].

Landman and Dawes (1982) followed the practice employed by other investigators and used the study as the unit of analysis by pooling the multiple effect size estimates in each report to produce an average effect size. Glass et al. (1981) claim this is a "facile solution," which is "likely to obscure many important questions" that could be answered by the multiple measures. They recommend more esoteric procedures such as Tukey's jackknife method to handle interdependent data. However, most meta-analysts, including Smith and Glass (1977), have taken the simple path. Landman and Dawes found that there was "no consistent impact" on the results when the study was the unit of analysis. Such a cautious approach, however, seems reasonable given the uncertainty in resolving this issue. An analogy from analysis of variance methodology may be appropriate here: test for main effects before looking for simple effects and interactions.

SUMMARY

There is no doubt that formal methods for synthesizing research results from many studies represent a significant methodological innovation. The meta-analysis procedure, in particular, is illustrative of these statistical methods, their utility, and limitations. These techniques can often burn through the haze of uncertainty that surrounds any one study and clearly reveal effects only dimly perceived before. On the other hand, the allure of such apparently simple statistical magic can blind the potential user to the limitations of these methods.

For all its computational simplicity, such methods are usually quite laborious. They require a scouring of the literature for all potential studies. This is followed by a sequence of judgmental steps that are all open to various threats to validity. These involve the selection of studies addressing the topic or hypothesis and using comparable measures (i.e., construct validity), the use of stratifying or moderating variables (i.e., external validity), the exclusion of studies with weak designs or inappropriate control groups (i.e., internal validity), and the appropriate unit of analysis (i.e., statistical conclusion validity). As with any new innovation, there is a period of development and adjustment. Meta-analysis, and other similar research synthesis methods, are clearly in this early stage of trial-and-error learning despite their widespread diffusion. The validity concepts developed for assessing the quality of individual evaluative studies provide a useful framework for examining these data-aggregation approaches. There are, however, other limitations involving coding of the studies, the type of inferences that can be made, and problems in using regression analyses (see Jackson, 1980, for a discussion). It is important that the methodological consumer of these new evaluation techniques be aware of their potential problems as well as their strengths.

REFERENCES

BAUM, M. L., D. S. ANISH, T. C. CHALMERS, H. S. SACKS, H. SMITH, and R. M. FAGERSTROM, (1981) "A survey of clinical trials of antibiotic prophylaxis in colon surgery: evidence against further use of no-treatment controls." New England J. of Medicine 305: 795-799.

BERK, A. A., and T. C. CHALMERS, (1981) "Cost and efficacy of the substitution of ambulatory for inpatient care." New England J. of Medicine 304: 393-397.

BURGER, J. M. (1981) "Motivational biases in the attribution of responsibility for an accident: a meta-analysis of the defensive-attribution hypothesis." Psych. Bull. 90: 496-512.

CAMPBELL, D. T., and J. C. STANLEY, (1966) Experimental and Quasi-Experimental Designs for Research. Chicago: Rand McNally.

CHALMERS, T. C., H. SMITH, B. BLACKBURN, B. SILVERMAN, B. SCHROEDER, D. REITMAN, and A. AMBROZ (1981) "A method for assessing the quality of a randomized control trial." Controlled Clinical Trials 2: 31-49.

COHEN, J. (1962) "The statistical power of abnormal-social psychological research: a review." J. of Abnormal Social Psychology 65: 145-153.

COOK, T. D., and D. T. CAMPBELL (1979) Quasi-Experimentation: Design and Analysis Issues for Field Settings. Chicago: Rand McNally.

COOPER, H. M. (1979) "Statistically combining independent studies: a meta-analysis of sex differences in conformity research." J. of Personality and Social Psychology 37: 131-146.

DeSILVA, R. A., C. H. HENNEKENS, B. LOWN, and W. CASSCELLS, (1981) "Lignocaine prophylaxis in acute myocardial infarction: an evaluation of randomized trials." Lancet 2: 855-858.

ELASHOFF, J. D. (1978) "Combining results of clinical trials." Gastroenterology 75: 1170-1172.

EYSENCK, H. J. (1978) "An exercise in mega-silliness." Amer. Psychologist 33: 517.

GALLO, P. S., Jr. (1978) "Meta-analysis—a mixed meta-phor?" Amer. Psychologist 33: 515-517.

GILBERT, J. P., B. McPEEK, and F. MOSTELLER (1977) "Progress in surgery and anesthesia: benefits and risks of innovative therapy," pp. 124-169 in J. P. Bunker, B. A. Barnes, and F. Mosteller (eds.) Costs, Risks, and Benefits of Surgery. New York: Oxford Univ. Press.

GLASS, G. V (1978) "Reply to Mansfield and Busse." Educ. Research 7:3.

——— (1977) "Integrating findings: the meta-analysis of research," pp. 351-379 in L. S. Shulman (ed.) Review of Research in Education, Vol. 5. Itasca, IL: Peacock.

——— (1976) "Primary, secondary, and meta-analysis of research." Educ. Research 5: 3-8.

——— and B. McGAW, M. L. SMITH (1981) Meta-analysis in Social Research. Beverly Hills, CA: Sage.

——— and M. L. SMITH (1979) "Meta-analysis of research on class size and achievement." Education Evaluation Policy Analysis 1: 2-16.

——— (1978) "Reply to Eysenck." Amer. Psychologist 33: 517.

HOUSE, E. R. (1980) Evaluating with Validity. Beverly Hills, CA: Sage.

——— and G. V GLASS, L. D. McLEAN, and D. F. WALKER (1978) "No simple answer: critique of the Follow Through evaluation." Harvard Educ. Rev. 48: 128-160.

HUNTER, J. E., F. L. SCHMIDT, and G. JACKSON (1982) Meta-Analysis: Cumulating Research Findings Across Studies. Beverly Hills, CA: Sage.

JACKSON, G. B. (1980) Methods for Integrative Reviews. Rev. of Educ. Research 50: 438-60.

JOHNSON, D. W., G. MARUYAMA, R. JOHNSON, D. NELSON, and L. SKON (1981) "Effects of cooperative, competitive, and individualistic goal structures on achievement: a meta-analysis." Psych. Bull. 80: 47-62.

LANDMAN, J. T., and R. M. DAWES (1982) "Psychotherapy outcome: conclusions stand up under scrutiny." Amer. Psychologist 37: 504-516.

MANSFIELD, R. S., and T. V. BUSSE (1979) "Meta-analysis of research: a rejoinder to Glass." Educ. Research 6: 3.

MARSHALL, E. (1980) "Psychotherapy works, but for whom?" Science 207: 506-508.

MOSTELLER, F., J. P. GILBERT, and B. McPEEK (1980) "Reporting standards and research strategies for controlled trials." Controlled Clinical Trials 1: 37-58.

PORTER, A. C., W. H. SCHMIDT, R. E. FLODEN, and D. J. FREEMAN (1978) "Practical significance in program evaluation." Amer. Education Research J. 15: 529-539.

POSAVAC, E. J. (1980) "Evaluations of patient education programs: a meta-analysis." Evaluation and the Health Professions 3: 47-62.

PRESBY, S. (1978) "Overly broad categories obscure important differences between therapies." Amer. Psychologist 33: 514-515.

ROSENTHAL, R. (1978) "Combining results of independent studies." Psych. Bull. 85: 185-193.

SECHREST, L., and H. YEATON (1981) "Assessing the effectiveness of social programs: methodological and conceptual issues." New Directions in Program Evaluation 9: 41-56.

SMITH, M. L., and G. V GLASS (1977) "Meta-analysis of psychotherapy outcome studies." Amer. Psychologist 32: 752-760.

STRUBE, M. J., and J. E. GARCIA (1981) "A meta-analytic investigation of Fiedler's model of leadership effectiveness." Psych. Bull. 90: 307-321.

WORTMAN, P. M. (1981) "Randomized clinical trials," pp. 41-60 in P. M. Wortman (ed.) Methods for Evaluating Health Services. Beverly Hills, CA: Sage.

——— and A. VINOKUR, L. SECHREST and associates (1982) Evaluation of the NIH Consensus Development Process—Phase I: Final Report. Ann Arbor, MI: Institute for Social Research.

8

On Quantitative Reviewing

Harris M. Cooper and Robert M. Arkin

Abstract

Cook and Leviton (1980) recently discussed the merits and disadvantages of quantitative literature reviewing. They apparently view the method with favor, but they also noted that several shortcomings may result from the method itself. It is argued that these particular deficiencies are unrelated to the method, and instead are attributable to poor reviewer practices. These issues are examined in an effort to avert any undue hesitancy on the part of future reviewers to quantify their efforts.

Whenever a novel method first appears in the literature, it is essential that its merits and shortcomings be thoroughly discussed. In response to recent reviews of a particular literature—one using quantitative procedures (Arkin, Cooper, & Kolditz, 1980) and one using solely a qualitative approach (Zuckerman, 1979)—Cook and Leviton (1980) presented their reactions regarding the use of quantitative procedures for literature reviewing. Cook and Leviton are apparently supportive of the use of quantitative techniques. However, they also cite several obstacles which they feel might hinder the application of such procedures. Many of the obstacles they cite are important, but they should not be taken to mean that quantitative reviewing should not be adopted. In fact, as Cooper (Note 1) demonstrates, several of Cook and Leviton's obstacles are unrelated to the analysis and interpretation stage of reviewing. In order to minimize any unnecessary hesitancy to implement quantitative procedures, it seems important to note where such hindrances may be overcome by skilled reviewers and an informed readership.

Definitions of Quantitative Techniques and Meta-Analyses

Cook and Leviton operate within a limited definition of meta-analysis. They define a meta-analysis as a review in which "sum-

1. This paper was written while the first author was supported by grant #BNS78-08834 from the National Science Foundation. Correspondence and reprint requests may be sent to Harris M. Cooper, Department of Psychology, University of Missouri–Columbia, Columbia, Missouri 65211.

From Harris M. Cooper and Robert M. Arkin, "On Quantitative Reviewing," 49(2) *Journal of Personality* 225-230 (June 1981). Copyright©1981, Duke University Press (Durham, NC). Reprinted by permission of the publisher.

mary statistics from each study (e.g., means or correlations) are treated as the units of analysis, and the aggregate data are then analyzed in quantitative tests of the proposition under examination" (p. 450). This definition excludes from meta-analyses reviews that report quantitative information from individual reports but do not synthesize it in any formal way ("Some qualitative reviews make extensive use of effect sizes"; Cook and Leviton, 1980, p. 454). This definition separates the issue of whether or not quantification of reviews is advisable from that of whether or not meta-analyses should be employed. The distinction between quantitative reviews that do and do not present summary statistics usurps from meta-analysts what is probably their primary claim: Increased quantification will generally improve the precision of literature reviews (cf. Cooper, 1979).

The definition may be unwarranted for another reason. Apparently, a distinction is made between reviews that do and do not aggregate studies. Meta-analysts ordinarily both quantify *and* aggregate. This may create the impression that problems in aggregation (i.e., claiming that two studies actually test the same hypothesis) are more relevant for quantitative than qualitative reviewers. In fact, aggregation occurs in *all* literature reviews, whether or not quantitative procedures are used (cf. Cooper, Note 1). Qualitative reviewers also must, through some unspecified process, draw conclusions concerning generality across studies. A reviewer's decisions about aggregation are not logically related to decisions about whether or not to quantify the intended synthesis. Cook and Leviton's discussion of problems in choosing to aggregate, while valid, are issues for literature reviewers in general and should not be confounded with quantification issues. Study aggregations can be defined either broadly or narrowly, but the issue of quantifying the review still remains.

We would like to suggest that literature reviews be conceived as forming a continuum. The continuum ranges from purely qualitative to exhaustively quantitative. It has been the position of meta-analysts (cf. Cooper, 1979; Glass, 1978; Rosenthal & Rubin, 1978), reviewers leaning toward the quantitative end of the continuum, that the more thoroughly a literature's underlying evidential base is described the "better" the review will be.

Quantification and Mystification

Quantification, of course, can have its drawbacks. Cook and Leviton correctly state that ". . . meta-analysis can have mischievous consequences because of its apparent 'objectivity,' 'precision,' and 'scientism.' To naive readers, these lend a social credibility that may be built on procedural invalidity" (p. 455).

This statement requires two qualifications to assure that it is not misleading. First, the meta-analytic method is not in and of itself mischievous. It can only become so in the hands of a particular reviewer, as a result of either intention or ignorance. Second, the statement is true of *any* innovative methodology, be it meta-analysis, time series analysis, cross-lagged panel correlation, or even the *t* test, when it was first employed. As an alert to review readers, Cook and Leviton's "scientism" caution was appropriate and well meant. However, we hope that it does not also serve to dissuade researchers from adopting meta-analytics. Serious researchers should not let a potential claim of "scientism" deter them from employing a new method, if they feel the method is appropriate to the task. Science always involves skepticism on the part of the research audience as well as objectivity on the part of the research-er. Our goal as scientists should be to dispel our naiveté, and not to reject a new method merely because it is unfamiliar.

Effect Size Estimates in Meta-Analysis

Cook and Leviton's discussion of effect size (ES) estimates in meta-analyses contains an assumption about the purpose of the reviewer which should be made explicit. The assumption is that the reviewer wishes the estimate to relate to the entire body of research (including studies that were not retrieved) and to potential studies not yet conducted. In fact, it is not necessary to assume anything about meta-analytic ES estimates other than that they are descriptive of the particular literature search. As such, the ESs are legitimate descriptive statistics. If an unbiased inference is to be made from the ES estimate, it is that *other literature reviews* using similar retrieval procedures should expect to uncover similar ESs. Researchers who want to use meta-analytic ESs in power analysis or policy makers needing to estimate the likely impact of programs need to adjust ES estimates dependent upon whatever sources of bias (with whatever impact) they feel may have been present in the particular literature search. Cook and Leviton are correct to point out how tenuous this latter inferential leap can be. We must also remember, however, that meta-analyses' ESs perform more admirably when put to less ambitious tasks.

The Width of Conceptual Definitions

We do not share Cook and Leviton's perception that "a bias in favor of narrowly defined constructs runs through many qualitative reviews . . ." while ". . . meta-analysts tend to prefer broader constructs" (p. 458). Instead, we would suggest that for practical reasons, qualitative reviews ordinarily employ *only* narrow constructs while meta-analyses can (and have) been both broad *and* narrow in conceptual scope. It is the enhanced ability of quantitative reviews to handle larger numbers of studies that makes possible truly broad conceptual definitions. Previous meta-analyses have taken advantage of this potential, but we don't feel they have unwittingly neglected narrow conceptual definitions in doing so. For instance, Cook and Leviton point out that Arkin, Cooper, and Kolditz (1980) performed a disaggregated meta-analysis, while Zuckerman (1979) performed no comparable disaggregation in his qualitative review. In addition, Rosenthal and Rubin (1978) examined expectation effects in different research paradigms, and Smith and Glass (1977) examined different forms of psychotherapy. A true instance of method-generated nearsightedness on the part of meta-analysts will be difficult to find.

Main Effects Versus Interactions

Cook and Leviton suggest that the use of meta-analytics leads reviewers to ignore interactions and concentrate instead on main effects. They write, "Our guess is that, with their stress on broad generalization, meta-analysts are even more prone than qualitative reviewers to overlook or to down play the importance of contingency-specifying interactions . . ." (p. 464). This conclusion may be premature for several reasons. First, if an interest in main effects does presently predominate in the meta-analytic literature, it is probably the main effect interest that led to the use of the method and not vice versa. Typically, reviewers interested in main effects will find many more tests of their hypothesis than reviewers interested in a particular interaction. Accordingly, main effect reviewers have often confronted the problem of what to do when large numbers of potential tests of a hypothesis are uncovered. It seems likely that the problems created by large literatures have drawn reviewers to meta-analytics and not the reverse. Future reviewers who wish to give inferential preference to interactions should not fear that the adoption of quantitative procedures will somehow change their perspective; there is nothing inherent in quantitative reviewing that leads one to believe more weight should be given to main effects than to interactions. Meta-analytics can be just as successfully applied to accumulated tests of interactions as main effects. In addition, we suspect that, with time, tests of particular interactions will accumulate and reviewers will begin to test interactions through meta-analysis techniques. The present paucity of converging interaction tests may lead reviewers to ignore needed qualifications to main effects, but this is a shortcoming of the particular literature reviewed and not a characteristic of the reviewing approach. Moreover, the common practice of disaggregating studies according to various potentially interactive factors reflects a sensitivity among meta-analysts to the issue of interactive variables.

This is not to say that there are no problems associated with studying interactions in research reviews. The major problem reviewers face involves the difficulty in assessing the strength of manipulations in various studies. It is often the case that interactions are obtained only when the appropriate levels of the variables involved are implemented. This fact, coupled with the lack of information about treatment strength present in the typical primary research report, will make the interpretation of variability in interaction effect sizes somewhat more difficult than studying main effects.

Conclusion

It was the purpose of this comment to alert readers to some important issues raised by Cook and Leviton's (1980) commentary. In our view, a careful examination of many of their concerns reveals them to be either (a) unrelated to quantitative reviewing or (b) caused by reviewer practices and not the method itself. A careful use of quantitative reviewing techniques in conjunction with qualitative analyses will improve upon current practices.

Reference Note

1. Cooper, H. The literature review: Elevating its status to scientific inquiry (Technical Report No. 238). Columbia, Mo.: University of Missouri–Columbia, Center for Research in Social Behavior, December, 1980.

References

Arkin, R., Cooper, H., & Kolditz, T. A statistical review of the literature concerning the self-serving bias in interpersonal influence situations. *Journal of Personality,* 1980, **48**, 435–448.
Cook, T., & Leviton, L. Reviewing the literature: A comparison of traditional methods with meta-analysis. *Journal of Personality,* 1980, **48**, 449–471.
Cooper, H. Statistically combining independent studies: A meta-analysis of sex differences in conformity research. *Journal of Personality and Social Psychology,* 1979, **37**, 131–146.
Glass, G. Integrated findings: The meta-analysis of research. *Review of Educational Research,* 1978, **5**, 351–379.

Rosenthal, R., & Rubin, B. Interpersonal expectancy effects: The first 345 studies. *The Brain and Behavioral Sciences,* 1978, **3**, 377–386.

Smith, M. L., & Glass, G. V. Meta-analysis of psychotherapy outcome studies. *American Psychologist,* 1977, **32**, 752–760.

Zuckerman, M. Attribution of success and failure revisited, or: The motivational bias is alive and well in attribution theory. *Journal of Personality,* 1979, **47**, 245–287.

Manuscript received September 3, 1980; revised January 12, 1981.

9

What Differentiates Meta-Analysis from Other Forms of Review?

Laura C. Leviton and Thomas D. Cook

Abstract

An issue of friendly disagreement between Cooper and Arkin (1981) and Cook and Leviton (1980) involves the definition of meta-analysis. Cooper and Arkin favor a definition stressing the degree of quantification in review studies, while we claim that studies labeled as "meta-analysis" are differentiated from other reviews in terms of the aggregation of effect sizes or probability values across studies for the purpose of reaching numerical estimates of the average magnitude of a relationship (as preferred by Glass) or the probability of reaching the average probability by chance (as originally preferred by Rosenthal). This definitional issue is important because the major objection to past meta-analytic studies raised by Cook and Leviton involved the possibility that meta-analysis might be used uncritically by some persons to derive "bottom line" estimates that are biased because confounds biasing the estimate in one direction are more prevalent than confounds biasing it in the opposite direction. Defining *meta-analysis* as more quantification takes much of the steam out of our critique, but it also reduces the saliency of what has been unique about past efforts labeled as meta-analysis—the generation of a single numerical estimate of a relationship derived from a set of many related studies.

The reader who follows the friendly debate we are having with Cooper and Arkin (1981) should not lose sight of one crucial fact: that everyone in the debate is an advocate of meta-analytic techniques to help summarize the literature on a particular topic. While we are more cautious in our advocacy than they, we would be saddened if our work discouraged use of the method. Indeed, our aim in writing Cook and Leviton (1980) was to foster the *self-critical* use of meta-analysis! We are not going to respond to the points made by Cooper and Arkin, because we agree with many of them. Instead, we prefer to discuss two issues raised in their paper: the manner in which we distinguish meta-analysis from traditional re-

1. This research was funded in part by a contract from the U.S. Department of Agriculture, #53-3198-9-26. Requests for reprints should be sent to Thomas D. Cook, Department of Psychology, Northwestern University, Evanston, Illinois 60201.

From Laura C. Leviton and Thomas D. Cook, "What Differentiates Meta-Analysis from Other Forms of Review?" 49(2) *Journal of Personality,* 231-236 (June 1981). Copyright © 1980, Duke University Press (Durham, NC). Reprinted by permission.

views, and the contexts in which meta-analysis may be a superior technique of reviewing.

The definitional issue. Cooper and Arkin object to the definition of meta-analysis that is implicit in the description of meta-analysis we offered—viz., "studies relevant to a conceptual issue are collected, summary statistics from each study (e.g., means or correlations) are treated as the units of analysis, and the aggregate[2] data are then analyzed in quantitative tests of the proposition under examination." Cooper and Arkin believe that this definition is overly narrow and advocate a definition that includes the reporting of quantified information from the collected studies, whether summary statistics are calculated or not. Cooper and Arkin describe a continuum with "purely" qualitative reviews at one endpoint and "exhaustively" quantitative approaches at the other. Meta-analyses are presumably the more heavily quantified reviews in this continuum.

The definition of meta-analysis as "quantitative" literature reviews ignores a central conclusion of our paper (Cook & Leviton, 1980): that all literature reviews share both qualitative judgments and quantitative techniques. Meta-analysis is rife with qualitative judgments—about the population of studies that are relevant, the breadth of the constructs to be investigated, the criteria by which studies are to be grouped into those of high and low methodological quality, etc. To ignore the qualitative judgments inherent in meta-analysis is to invite abuse of the method by having it be seen as an infallible "objective" test that needs only to be pulled off the shelf and some data plugged into it. Just as quantitative research presupposes qualitative judgments, so qualitative research is impossible without quantitative estimates. At the most primitive these are "less than, more than" types of statements, as when box counts take place in traditional reviews. If Cooper and Arkin (1981) are proposing a quantitative-qualitative distinction as a heuristic device, we approve, but we would never want to make the distinction without adding the restriction that each is unrealizable in practice.

When meta-analysis is understood as some (unspecified) high degree of quantification, the best of past review practices would indeed seem like "meta-analysis," so defined. We agree with Cooper and Arkin on the disadvantages of using statistical significance criteria for categorizing studies as "obtaining" an effect or

---

2. Cooper and Arkin misunderstood our use of the word "aggregate." We were making the mundane point that the data of meta-analysis as practiced by Glass and Rosenthal are aggregates from individual scores, such as means or correlations.

not. We agree with them, and with many others who made the same point prior to the advent of meta-analysis (e.g., Cohen, 1962, 1969; Tversky & Kahneman, 1971; Elashoff & Snow, 1971) that magnitude estimates provide better summaries of the results of single studies. On the basis of these past discussions, we argued that many of the critiques of traditional review practices were aimed at poor practices by reviewers in the past rather than at intrinsic limitations to reviewing that pertained prior to the arrival of meta-analysis. After all, some earlier reviews had consistently used effect size estimates (e.g., Elashoff & Snow, 1971), though they never computed average effect sizes and have never been claimed as forerunners of meta-analysis. Nonetheless, the point is that we would have no disagreement with Cooper and Arkin if meta-analysis were understood as a "high" degree of quantification, for then the best of traditional review methods using effect sizes could be relabeled as "meta-analyses."

However, the unique feature of meta-analysis seems to us to be the statistical aggregation of findings *across* studies in order to arrive at a numerical estimate of the average size of an effect. We do not mean to suggest, as Cooper and Arkin are concerned that we might, that only meta-analyses aggregate studies. All literature reviews group studies and consider them together. But only meta-analysis treats a group of studies as a data set from which to derive a "bottom line," a numerical estimate of the strength of an association. Cooper and Arkin will search in vain for a literature review labeled meta-analysis that does not result in such a numerical estimate. Indeed, all the position papers and technical descriptions of meta-analysis of which we are aware emphasize methods for statistically combining the results of studies as average effect sizes or average probabilities (Glass, 1976, 1978; Cooper, 1979; Light & Smith, 1971; Rosenthal, 1978).

Defining meta-analysis in terms of statistical aggregation, rather than quantification per se, avoids confusion. If quantification were the defining feature of meta-analysis, then the work of, say, Luborsky et al. (1971) would count as an instance, because these authors reported both correlations (a form of effect size) and statistical significance in their review. Yet Smith and Glass (1977) performed their meta-analysis of psychotherapy outcome studies in part because reviews such as Luborsky's had not statistically combined the results of studies. We wonder how Cooper and Arkin would classify Rosenthal's (1969) early work in which he averaged probabilities across studies in order to reach quantitative summary statements about average *p* values? If one locates Rosenthal's early review on a continuum of quantification, many box counts are more likely to be labeled "meta-analysis" because they report more quantified information than only the p values that Rosenthal then emphasized. The discriminandum of meta-analysis seems to us to be the average effect sizes and average probability values rather than a little more quantification.

Contexts for the use of meta-analysis. It remains to assess the contexts in which meta-analysis is desirable. We take issue with the assertion of Cooper and Arkin (1981) that increased quantification will *necessarily* improve the inferences made in literature reviews. The debate over qualitative versus quantitative reviewing is in many ways similar to the more general debate about qualitative versus quantitative methods (Reichardt & Cook, 1979). Just as in the latter debate, we see no logical reason for claiming that quantitative methods are better than qualitative ones, though they often will be. It is the context and purpose that determines the appropriateness of methods.

In Cook and Leviton (1980) we noted that the primary advantage of meta-analysis is convenience, especially when the number of studies under review is large. In this context, the traditional reviewer is potentially vulnerable to missing some ways of disaggregating the studies that may prove to be important. We also noted that meta-analysis can improve traditional reviewing practices. We are persuaded that the *only* way to do box counts properly is to report the direction of effects or, in many cases, effect sizes. Prior to the emergence of meta-analysis, reviews of significance tests were the primary source of information for making inferences about the presence of an effect. Although correlations, "variance accounted for," and other analogues of effect sizes were reported in some reviews, they were not reported systematically, they were not the primary source of evidence, and they were usually not made comparable to each other in the same way that effect sizes are now routinely made comparable.

We can think of some contexts in which the contribution of meta-analysis may be small, or even potentially misleading. For example, we would argue that a single falsification of a hypothesis in a study involving a demonstrably strong test of assumptions does more to enhance the quality of a review than would a box count or meta-analysis of 30 confirmations through weaker tests. Also, reviews in the exploratory mode may not require box counts or meta-analyses, especially if only one or two studies have certain characteristics on which it comes to appear that the direction of a particular causal relationship depends. Finally, when most of the reviewed studies share a common bias, neither meta-analysis nor a box count is appropriate, and other forms of reviewing are necessary such as a critical appraisal of methodology. As Cook and Gruder (1978) point out, meta-analysis is only one of many models for reviewing literature and evaluating completed studies and, like all methods, its limitations are of uncritical practice rather than of intrinsic error. In the hands of careful users sensitive to assumptions, we welcome the method; in the hands of uncritical users swayed by its simplicity, promise, and promotion, we fear the possibility of inadvertently mischievous consequences.

But enough of this. We are fans of meta-analysis. We see many advantages of the method, for convenience, for enhancing statistical power, and for demonstrating the stability of many psychological relationships (Epstein, 1980). We remain cautious about potential abuses of the method. But these can be anticipated and controlled, and we have tried here to do our little bit to foster the self-critical use of meta-analytic methods, however one defines them.

References

Cohen, J. W. The statistical power of abnormal-social psychological research. *Journal of Abnormal and Social Psychology*, 1962, **65**, 145–153.

Cohen, J. W. *Statistical power analysis for the behavioral sciences.* New York: Academic Press, 1969.

Cook, T. D., & Gruder, C. L. Metaevaluation research. *Evaluation Quarterly*, 1978, **2**, 5–51.

Cook, T. D., & Leviton, L. C. Reviewing the literature: A comparison of traditional methods with meta-analysis. *Journal of Personality*, 1980, **48**, 449–472.

Cooper, H. M. Statistically combining independent studies: A meta-analysis of sex differences in conformity research. *Journal of Personality and Social Psychology*, 1979, **37**, 131–146.

Cooper, H. M., & Arkin, R. On quantitative reviewing. *Journal of Personality*, 1981, **49**, 225–230.

Elashoff, J. D., & Snow, R. E. *Pygmalion reconsidered.* Worthington, Ohio: Charles A. Jones Publishing Co., 1971.

Epstein, S. The stability of behavior: II. Implications for psychological research. *American Psychologist*, 1980, **35**, 790–806.

Glass, G. V. Primary, secondary and meta-analysis of research. *Educational Researcher*, 1976, **5**, 3–8.

Glass, G. V. Integrating findings: The meta-analysis of research. *Review of Research in Education*, 1978, **5**, 351–379.

Light, R. J., & Smith, P. V. Accumulating evidence: Procedures for resolving contradictions among different research studies. *Harvard Educational Review*, 1971, **41**, 429–471.

Luborsky, L., Chandler, M., Auerbach, A. H., Cohen, J., & Bachrach, H. M. Factors influencing the outcome of psychotherapy: A review of quantitative research. *Psychological Bulletin*, 1971, **75**, 145–185.

Reichardt, C. S., & Cook, T. D. Beyond qualitative versus quantitative methods. In T. D. Cook and C. S. Reichardt (Eds.), *Qualitative and quantitative methods in evaluation research.* Beverly Hills: Sage Publications, 1979.

Rosenthal, R. Interpersonal expectations: Effects of the experimenter's hypothesis. In R. Rosenthal and R. L. Rosnow (Eds.), *Artifact in behavioral research.* New York: Academic Press, 1969.

Rosenthal, R. Combining results of independent studies. *Psychological Bulletin,* 1978, **85**, 185–193.

Smith, M. L., & Glass, G. V. Meta-analysis of psychotherapy outcome studies. *American Psychologist,* 1977, **32**, 752–760.

Tversky, A., & Kahneman, D. Belief in the law of small numbers. *Psychological Bulletin,* 1971, **76**, 105–110.

Manuscript received November 7, 1980.

10

Fitting Continuous Models to Effect Size Data

Larry V. Hedges

Key words: *Meta-analysis, research synthesis, effect size, regression analysis, model specification, specification error*

ABSTRACT. Quantitative methods for research synthesis usually involve calculation of an estimate of effect size for each of a series of studies. Statistical analyses in research synthesis attempt to relate explanatory variables to the effect sizes obtained from the series of studies. Some problems with ad hoc methods, such as ordinary least squares regression analysis using estimates of effect size, are described. Maximum likelihood estimation of the parameters in linear models for effect sizes is discussed and the asymptotic distribution of the estimators is obtained. An alternative estimator is derived which is computationally simpler, but has the same asymptotic distribution as the maximum likelihood estimator. A natural test for model specification is also given. The small sample accuracy of the asymptotic distribution theory derived in this paper is investigated via a simulation study.

There recently has been a great deal of interest in methods for the quantitative synthesis of research. Glass (1976) was among the first to propose the synthesis of research results by extracting a quantitative estimate of effect size (a standardized mean difference) from each study. These estimates of effect size then become the data for statistical analyses designed to assess the overall effect size across studies. One obvious question is whether the overall magnitude of the effect is nonzero. For this purpose Glass suggested averaging effect sizes. Hedges (1981, 1982a) has provided some statistical theory for averages and weighted averages of effect size estimators.

Estimation of the average effect size was soon supplemented by efforts to assess the relationship between characteristics of studies and their effect sizes. Glass (1978) recommended the general strategy of coding the characteristics of studies as a vector of predictor variables and then regressing the effect size estimates on the predictors to determine the relationship between characteristics of studies and effect size. For example, Smith and Glass (1977) used ordinary linear regression to determine the relationship between several coded characteristics of studies (e.g., type of therapy, duration of treatment, internal validity of the study) and the effect size in their meta-analysis of psychotherapy outcome studies. The same method has been used in many research syntheses, including the meta-analyses of the effects of class size (Glass & Smith, 1979; Smith & Glass, 1980) and a series of meta-analyses conducted by Walberg and his associates (e.g., Uguroglu & Walberg, 1979).

From Larry V. Hedges, "Fitting Continuous Models to Effect Size Data," 7(4) *Journal of Educational Statistics* 245-270 (Winter 1982). Copyright © 1982 American Educational Research Association, Washington, DC. Reprinted by permission of the publisher.

Although the regression method advocated by Glass is appealing, there are at least two problems with the method. First, the assumptions of regression analysis are not met since the variances of the individual effect size estimates are proportional to $1/n$, where n is the sample size of the study. Thus, when the studies to be integrated have different sample sizes, the individual "error" variances may be dramatically different. Second, even if the regression coefficients are properly estimated, Glass's method gives no indication of the goodness of fit of the regression model. That is, there is no indication that the model is correctly specified.

The Importance of Model Specification

There has been a considerable amount of criticism of meta-analysis as a research synthesis technique. Some critics have argued that meta-analysis may lead to oversimplified conclusions about the effect of a treatment because it condenses the results of a series of studies into a few parameter estimates. For example, Presby (1978) argued that even when studies are grouped according to variations in the treatment, reviewers might reasonably disagree on the appropriate groupings. Grouping studies into overly broad categories and calculating a mean effect size for each category might serve to wash out real variations among treatments within the categories. Thus it would appear that variations in treatment were unrelated to effect size because the mean effect sizes for the categories did not differ. An obvious extension of this argument is that reviewers might reasonably disagree on explanatory variables that could be related to effect sizes. Hence, failure to find variables that are systematically related to effect size does not imply that the effect sizes are consistent across studies. It may only imply that the reviewer has examined the wrong explanatory variables.

A related criticism is that the studies in a collection may give fundamentally different answers (e.g., have different population effect sizes) perhaps because of the artifacts of a multitude of design flaws (e.g., see Eysenck, 1978). Any analysis of the effect sizes is therefore an analysis of estimates that are influenced by a variety of factors other than the true magnitude of the effect of the treatment. Thus, meta-analyses may be another case of "garbage in— garbage out." The argument underlying this criticism is that flaws in studies may influence effect sizes.

The statistical methods presented in this paper can be used to examine the validity of the criticisms mentioned previously. The tests of model specification provide a mechanism for testing whether variations in the results are explained by the data analysis model. In this simplest case the reviewer summarizes the results of a series of studies by the average effect size estimate. Is this an oversimplification of the results of the studies? The test of homogeneity of effect size (Hedges, 1982a) provides a method of empirically testing whether the variation in effect size estimates is greater than would be expected by chance alone. If the hypothesis of homogeneity is not rejected, the reviewer is in a strong position vis-à-vis the argument that studies exhibit real variability, which is obscured by coarse grouping. If the model of a single population effect size fits the data adequately, then a desire for parsimony suggests this model should be considered seriously.

Failure to reject the homogeneity of effect sizes from a series of studies does not necessarily disarm the criticism that the results of the studies are artifacts of design flaws. For example, if all studies in a series share the same flaw, consistent results across the series of studies may be an artifact of just that flaw. That is, the design flaw in all the studies may act to make the effect sizes of the studies consistent and consistently wrong as an estimate of the treatment effect. On the other hand, the studies may not all have the same flaws. If a variety of different studies, with different design flaws all yield consistent results it may be implausible to explain the consistency of the results of those studies as the result of different artifacts all yielding the same bias. Thus, the reviewer who finds consistency in research results and who knows the limitations of the individual studies is in a strong position against the "garbage in—garbage out" argument. It should be emphasized that careful examination of the individual research studies and some scrutiny of the attendant design problems are essential. Without such analysis of the studies, a single source of bias is a very real and plausible rival explanation for empirical consistency of research results.

When a reviewer explains the effect sizes from a series of studies via a model involving explanatory variables (e.g., the effect size varies according to grade level), tests of model specification play a role analogous to that of the test of homogeneity. Some tests of the specification of categorical models were given by Hedges (1982b). It is difficult to argue that additional variables are needed to explain the variation in effect sizes if the specification test suggests that additional variables are not needed.

Evidence that the model is correctly specified does not necessarily mean that the artifacts of design flaws may be ignored. If all studies share a common design flaw, then the results of all the studies may be biased to an unknown extent. If design flaws are correlated with explanatory variables, then the effects of those flaws are confounded with the effects of the explanatory variables. It may be difficult or impossible to determine the real source of the effect. However, if design flaws are uncorrelated with explanatory variables and if simple models appear to be correctly specified, then it seems implausible that inferences drawn about the effect sizes are artifacts of biases due to those flaws.

Outline

This paper presents alternative methods for fitting models to effect size data when those models include continuous or discrete independent variables. These methods provide consistent, asymptotically efficient estimates of the parameters of the model, and also permit large sample tests of significance. In addition, the methods can provide an explicit test of the specification of the model. Thus, it is possible to test whether or not a model adequately explains the observed variability in effect size estimates.

The first section is an exposition of the structural model and the notation used in this paper. The next section is a development of the theory for maximum likelihood estimation of the model parameters. An alternative method for estimating model parameters is then presented. The alternative estimator is shown to have the same asymptotic distribution as the maximum likelihood estimator, while being much easier to compute. Some simulation studies on the small sample behavior of the alternative estimator are presented in the next section. The last section provides an example of the application of methods presented in this paper.

Notation and Model

Suppose that the data arise from a series of k independent, two-group experiments and let Y_{ij}^E and Y_{ij}^C be the jth experimental (E) and control (C) group scores in the ith experiment. Assume that Y_{ij}^E and Y_{ij}^C are independently normally distributed within groups of the ith experiment; that is,

$$Y_{ij}^E \sim \mathfrak{N}\left(\mu_i^E, \sigma_i^2\right), \qquad j = 1,\ldots,n_i^E, i = 1,\ldots,k,$$

and

$$Y_{ij}^C \sim \mathfrak{N}\left(\mu_i^C, \sigma_i^2\right), \qquad j = 1,\ldots,n_i^C, i = 1,\ldots,k.$$

The effect size for the ith experiment is the parameter

$$\delta_i = \frac{\mu_i^E - \mu_i^C}{\sigma_i}, \tag{1}$$

where σ_i is assumed to be positive. The effect size is the population value of the treatment effect (mean difference) if the dependent variables are scaled to have unit variance within groups. Note that the effect size is invariant under linear transformations of the observations.

In this paper, the standardized mean difference δ_i for the ith experiment depends on a vector of p fixed concomitant variables $(x_{i1}, x_{i2},\ldots,x_{ip})$, where $p \leqslant k$. The vectors $(x_{i1},\ldots,x_{ip})'$, $i = 1,\ldots,k$, are denoted $\mathbf{x}_i$ and the matrix

$$\mathbf{X} = \begin{pmatrix} \mathbf{x}_1' \\ \vdots \\ \mathbf{x}_k' \end{pmatrix} = \begin{pmatrix} x_{11} & \cdots & x_{1p} \\ \vdots & & \vdots \\ x_{k1} & \cdots & x_{kp} \end{pmatrix},$$

is assumed to have rank p. The assumption that $\mathbf{X}$ has rank p simply assures that none of the column vectors of $\mathbf{X}$ is linearly redundant. The vector $(\beta_1,\ldots,\beta_p)'$ of regression coefficients is denoted β. Thus, the standardized mean difference for the ith experiment is $\delta_i = \mathbf{x}_i \boldsymbol{\beta} = x_{i1}\beta_1 + \cdots + x_{ip}\beta_p$. Denoting the vector of effect sizes by $\boldsymbol{\delta}$, i.e., $\boldsymbol{\delta}' = (\delta_1, \ldots, \delta_k)$, we can write the model for the effect sizes as

$$\boldsymbol{\delta} = \mathbf{X}\boldsymbol{\beta}.$$

A compact representation of the structural model for the observations in the ith experiment depends explicitly on $\mathbf{x}_i$; $\boldsymbol{\beta}$; the within-group standard deviation, σ_i; a location (scale mean) parameter, γ_i; and a residual term, ε. The complete structural model for the observations is

$$
\begin{aligned}
Y_{ij}^E &= \mathbf{x}_i'\boldsymbol{\beta}\sigma_i + \gamma_i\sigma_i + \varepsilon_{ij}^E, \qquad j = 1,\ldots,n_i^E, i = 1,\ldots,k, \\
Y_{ij}^C &= \gamma_i\sigma_i + \varepsilon_{ij}^C, \qquad j = 1,\ldots,n_i^C, i = 1,\ldots,k,
\end{aligned}
\tag{2}
$$

where ε_{ij}^E and ε_{ij}^C are independently distributed as $\mathfrak{N}(0, \sigma_i^2)$.

Estimators of Effect Size

Define the estimator g_i of δ_i via

$$g_i = \frac{\overline{Y}_i^E - \overline{Y}_i^C}{S_i}, \qquad i = 1,\ldots,k, \tag{3}$$

where $\overline{Y}_i^E$ and $\overline{Y}_i^C$ are the experimental and control group sample means and S_i is the pooled, within-group sample standard deviation. Define the vector $\mathbf{g}$ by $\mathbf{g}' = (g_1, \ldots, g_k)$, and let

$$
\begin{aligned}
N &= \sum_{i=1}^{k} \left(n_i^E + n_i^C \right), \\
\pi_i^E &= n_i^E/N, \qquad \pi_i^C = n_i^C/N.
\end{aligned}
\tag{4}
$$

Hedges (1981) has shown that if π_i^E and π_i^C, $i = 1,\ldots,k$ remain fixed as $N \to \infty$, the vector $\mathbf{g}$ has an asymptotic multivariate normal distribution given by

$$\sqrt{N}\,(\mathbf{g} - \boldsymbol{\delta}) \sim \mathfrak{N}[0, \mathbf{V}(\boldsymbol{\delta})], \tag{5}$$

where $\mathbf{V}(\boldsymbol{\delta}) = \mathrm{diag}[v_1(\delta_1), \ldots, v_k(\delta_k)]$, $v_i(\delta_i)$ is the asymptotic sampling variance of g_i given by

$$v_i(\delta) = \frac{\pi_i^E + \pi_i^C}{\pi_i^E \pi_i^C} + \frac{\delta^2}{2\left(\pi_i^E + \pi_i^C\right)}, \tag{6}$$

and we write $\mathbf{V}(\boldsymbol{\delta})$ to indicate that the covariance matrix $\mathbf{V}(\boldsymbol{\delta})$ depends on $\boldsymbol{\delta}$.

The Effects of Measurement Error

If the dependent variable is subject to measurement error, this error of measurement attenuates the population effect size, δ. Let ρ_i denote the reliability of the response measure in the ith experiment, and let δ_i be the effect size. Let δ_i' be the effect size in the ith experiment if the measurements were error free. Hedges (1981) showed that

$$\delta_i = \sqrt{\rho_i}\, \delta_i'.$$

Because $\rho \le 1.0$, this implies that measurement error attenuates effect size. Since g_i estimates δ_i, it follows that $g_i/\sqrt{\rho_i}$ is an estimator of δ_i', the disattenuated effect size. It also follows that the variance of $g_i/\sqrt{\rho_i}$ is $1/\rho_i$ times the variance of g_i. If the reliability ρ_i is known, the methods used in this paper can be corrected for measurement error by substituting $g_i/\sqrt{\rho_i}$ for g_i and $v_i(\delta_i)/\rho_i$ for $v_i(\delta_i)$ wherever either occurs in expressions for estimators or test statistics.

Maximum Likelihood Estimation of β

One approach to estimation of β is the method of maximum likelihood. Maximum likelihood estimation has the advantages that the estimates depend on the data through sufficient statistics, are consistent, and are asymptotically efficient. Below, the likelihood equations for estimation of β are developed, and it is shown that these equations cannot be solved in closed form. Following that, the asymptotic distribution of the maximum likelihood estimator of β is obtained.

The Likelihood Equations

The log likelihood for the ith experiment under model (2) is

$$L_i = \frac{n_i^E + n_i^C}{2} \log(2\pi) - \left(n_i^E + n_i^C\right)\log \sigma_i$$

$$- \frac{1}{2\sigma_i^2}\left[\sum_{j=1}^{n_i^E}\left(Y_{ij}^E - \sigma_i x_i' \beta - \sigma_i \gamma_i\right)^2 + \sum_{j=1}^{n_i^C}\left(Y_{ij}^C - \sigma_i \gamma_i\right)^2\right].$$

Setting the derivatives of $L = \sum_{i=1}^{k} L_i$ equal to zero yields a system of $2k + p$ likelihood equations

$$\frac{\partial L}{\partial \gamma_i} = \frac{n_i^E \bar{Y}_i^E + n_i^C \bar{Y}_i^C}{\sigma_i} - n_i^E x_i' \beta - \left(n_i^E + n_i^C\right)\gamma_i = 0, \qquad i = 1,\ldots,k, \text{(7a)}$$

$$\frac{\partial L}{\partial \sigma_i} = -\frac{n_i^E + n_i^C}{\sigma_i} + \frac{1}{\sigma_i^3}\left[\sum_{j=1}^{n_i^E}\left(Y_{ij}^E\right)^2 + \sum_{j=1}^{n_i^C}\left(Y_{ij}^C\right)^2 - n_i^E \sigma_i \bar{Y}_i^E x_i' \beta \right.$$

$$\left. - \left(n_i^E \bar{Y}_i^E + n_i^C \bar{Y}_i^C\right)\sigma_i \gamma_i\right] = 0, \qquad i = 1,\ldots,k, \quad \text{(7b)}$$

$$\frac{\partial L}{\partial \beta_s} = \sum_{i=1}^{k} n_i^E x_{is}\left[\frac{\bar{Y}_i^E}{\sigma_i} - x_i' \beta - \gamma_i\right] = 0, \qquad s = 1,\ldots,p. \quad \text{(7c)}$$

Equations 7 are easily solved for γ_i in terms of σ_i, $x_i'\beta$, and sample data, $i = 1,\ldots,k$. These solutions are then inserted into (7b) and the resulting equations are quadratic in σ_i. The quadratic equations are then solved by the quadratic formula for σ_i in terms of $x_i'\beta$ and sample data. The correct sign is chosen by observing that one choice of sign yields only negative values for σ_i and that $\sigma_i > 0$, $i = 1,\ldots,k$, by hypothesis. Substitution of the resulting expressions for σ_i into (7c) yields a system of p equations, which apparently cannot be reduced further. The equation is

$$\sum_{i=1}^{k} \tilde{n}_i x_{is}\left[(Z_i - 2)\mathbf{x}'_i\boldsymbol{\beta} \pm \sqrt{(\mathbf{x}'_i\boldsymbol{\beta}Z_i)^2 + 4Z_i\left(n_i^E + n_i^C\right)/\tilde{n}_i}\,\right] = 0,$$

$$s = 1,\ldots,p, \quad (8)$$

where $\tilde{n}_i = n_i^E n_i^C/(n_i^E + n_i^C)$, $Z_i = \tilde{n}_i g_i^2/(\tilde{n}_i g_i^2 + n_i^E + n_i^C - 2)$, and the sign of the ith term is determined by the sign of g_i. Although, Equations (8) cannot be solved algebraically, it is not difficult to obtain the solutions numerically.

The Asymptotic Distribution of the Maximum Likelihood Estimator

Although the likelihood Equations 7a, 7b, and 7c do not lead to closed-form expressions for the maximum likelihood estimator of $\boldsymbol{\beta}$, the inverse of the asymptotic covariance matrix of the maximum likelihood estimator $\hat{\boldsymbol{\beta}}_M$ of $\boldsymbol{\beta}$ can be obtained as minus the expectation of the matrix of second-order partial derivatives of the log likelihood function. This gives the asymptotic distribution stated below and derived in the appendix.

Theorem 1. If $\hat{\boldsymbol{\beta}}_M$ is the solution of (8) (i.e., the maximum likelihood estimator of $\boldsymbol{\beta}$ under model 2), if N, π_i^E, and π_i^C are defined as in (4) and if the π_i^E, π_i^C, $i = 1,\ldots,k$ remain fixed as $N \to \infty$, then the asymptotic distribution of $\hat{\boldsymbol{\beta}}_M$ is given by

$$\sqrt{N}\left(\hat{\boldsymbol{\beta}}_M - \boldsymbol{\beta}\right) \sim \mathcal{N}(\mathbf{0}, \boldsymbol{\Sigma}), \quad (9)$$

where $\boldsymbol{\Sigma}^{-1} = (\sigma^{st})$, and

$$\sigma^{st} = \sum_{i=1}^{k} x_{is} x_{it} \frac{2\left(\pi_i^E + \pi_i^C\right)\pi_i^E\pi_i^C}{2\left(\pi_i^E + \pi_i^C\right)^2 + \pi_i^E\pi_i^C(\mathbf{x}'_i\boldsymbol{\beta})^2}, \quad s, t = 1,\ldots,p. \quad (10)$$

Note that σ^{st} is the same as a weighted sum of inverses of variances of g_i; that is

$$\sigma^{st} = \sum_{i=1}^{k} \frac{x_{is} x_{it}}{v_i(\delta_i)}, \quad (11)$$

where $v_i(\delta_i)$ is given by (6). When $p = 1$, and $x_{i1} = 1$, $i = 1,\ldots,k$ the asymptotic distribution (9) is identical to the asymptotic distribution of the maximum likelihood estimator of a common effect size from a series of k experiments given by Hedges (1982a).

An Alternative Estimator of $\boldsymbol{\beta}$

A model for the estimator g could be rewritten using g, X, $\boldsymbol{\beta}$, and a residual vector $\boldsymbol{\eta}$ as

$$\mathbf{g} = \mathbf{X}\boldsymbol{\beta} + \boldsymbol{\eta},$$

where η has the same asymptotic distribution as $(g - \delta)$; that is,

$$\sqrt{N}\,\eta \sim \mathcal{N}[0, V(\delta)],$$

where $V(\delta) = \text{diag}[v_1(\delta_1),\ldots,v_k(\delta_k)]$ and $v_i(\delta_i)$ is given by (6). If the values of $v_i(\delta_i)$ were known, we could use generalized least squares to obtain an estimator of β. Unfortunately $V(\delta)$ depends on δ, which is unknown. However, it is still possible to obtain estimates of β by using an estimated covariance matrix. The following theorem states that the resulting estimator can be easily computed and has the same asymptotic distribution as the maximum likelihood estimator of β. Therefore, the alternative estimator is consistent and asymptotically efficient. This alternative estimator is also much easier to compute than is the maximum likelihood estimator.

Theorem 2. Define the matrix $V(g)$ in the same way as $V(\delta)$ except that the elements of vector g are used in place of the elements of δ; that is,

$$V(g) = \text{diag}[v_1(g_1),\ldots,v_k(g_k)],$$

where $v_i(g)$ is given by (6). Define N, π_i^E, and π_i^C as in (4). An estimator $\hat{\beta}_A$ of β under model (2) is given by

$$\hat{\beta}_A = [X'V^{-1}(g)X]^{-1}X'V^{-1}(g)g. \tag{12}$$

If the π_i^E, π_i^C, $i = 1,\ldots,k$ remain fixed as $N \to \infty$, then $\hat{\beta}_A$ has an asymptotic distribution given by

$$\sqrt{N}\left(\hat{\beta}_A - \beta\right) \sim \mathcal{N}(0, \Sigma),$$

where $\Sigma^{-1} = (\sigma^{st})$, $s, t = 1,\ldots,p$ and σ^{st} is given in (11). That is, $\hat{\beta}_A$ has the same asymptotic distribution as $\hat{\beta}_M$.

Proof. Define $K(g) = [X'V^{-1}(g)X]^{-1}X'V^{-1}(g)$. Then $\hat{\beta}_A = K(g)g$. Since $g \to \delta$ in probability as $N \to \infty$, $K(g) \to K(\delta)$ in probability as $N \to \infty$. This implies that $K(g)[\sqrt{N}(g - \delta)]$ has the same asymptotic distribution as $K(\delta)[\sqrt{N}(g - \delta)]$. Note that the limiting distribution of $K(\delta)[\sqrt{N}(g - \delta)]$ can be obtained directly using Cramér's (1946) delta method.

The estimate $\hat{\beta}_A$ is defined as $[X'V^{-1}(g)X]^{-1}X'V^{-1}(g)g = K(g)g$, and $K(g)\delta = K(g)X\beta = [X'V^{-1}(g)X]^{-1}X'V^{-1}(g)(X\beta) = \beta$. Therefore,

$$K(g)\left[\sqrt{N}(g - \delta)\right] = \sqrt{N}\left(\hat{\beta}_A - \beta\right),$$

and the asymptotic distribution of $\sqrt{N}(\hat{\beta}_A - \beta)$ is the same as that of $K(\delta)[\sqrt{N}(g - \delta)]$; that is,

$$\sqrt{N}\left[K(\delta)g - K(\delta)\delta\right] \sim \mathcal{N}\left\{0, \left[X'V^{-1}(\delta)X\right]^{-1}\right\}.$$

Evaluation of the inverse of the matrix $X'V^{-1}(\delta)X = \Sigma^{-1} = (\sigma^{st})$ leads to the expression for σ^{st} given in (11). ||

The estimator of β and the distribution theory given in Theorem 2 depend on the model for effect sizes, (1). In particular, these results depend on the fact that the predictor variables are "fixed." In some cases, such as when a mean achievement test score is used as a predictor, the predictors may be random variables. As in the usual case of multiple linear regression, we may use the approach of performing the analysis conditionally. That is, we perform the analysis using the assumption that $\mathbf{X}$ is a fixed matrix and interpret it as conditional on the particular value of $\mathbf{X}$ used.

Confidence Intervals for Components of β

The asymptotic distribution of $\hat{\beta}_A$ can be used to provide large sample confidence intervals for β. The large sample normal approximation to the distribution of $\hat{\beta}_A$ is given by

$$\hat{\beta}_A \sim \mathfrak{N}\left\{\beta, \left[\mathbf{X}'\mathbf{V}^{-1}(\delta)\mathbf{X}\right]^{-1}/N\right\}.$$

By substituting the consistent estimator $\mathbf{g}$ for δ in the expression for the covariance matrix we obtain the approximation

$$\hat{\beta}_A \sim \mathfrak{N}\left\{\beta, \left[\mathbf{X}'\mathbf{V}^{-1}(\mathbf{g})\mathbf{X}\right]^{-1}/N\right\},$$

which can be used to obtain large sample confidence intervals for components of β, That is, if $[\mathbf{X}'\mathbf{V}^{-1}(\mathbf{g})\mathbf{X}]^{-1} = (s_{uv})$ and $\hat{\beta}_A = (\hat{\beta}_1,\dots,\hat{\beta}_p)$ then a $100(1-\alpha)$ percent confidence interval for β_u is given by

$$\hat{\beta}_u - z_{\alpha/2}\sqrt{s_{uu}/N} \leqslant \beta_u \leqslant \hat{\beta}_u + z_{\alpha/2}\sqrt{s_{uu}/N},$$

where $z_{\alpha/2}$ is the 100α percent critical value of the standard normal distribution. The usual theory for the normal distribution can be used, for example, if one-tailed or simultaneous confidence intervals are desired.

Sometimes it is useful to test the hypothesis that $\beta = 0$; that is, that all the components of β are simultaneously zero. The following theorem provides the method for conducting this test.

Theorem 3. Define N, π_i^E, π_i^C, $\mathbf{V}(\mathbf{g})$, β, and $\hat{\beta}_A$ as in Theorem 2. If the π_i^E, π_i^C, $i = 1,\dots,k$ remain fixed as $N \to \infty$, then the hypothesis that $\beta = 0$ can be tested using the statistic

$$H_1 = \hat{\beta}_A'\mathbf{X}'\mathbf{V}^{-1}(\mathbf{g})\mathbf{g}.$$

If $\beta = 0$, H_1 has an asymptotic chi-square distribution given by

$$NH_1 \sim \chi_p^2.$$

Proof. Define the $(k \times k)$ matrix $\mathbf{A}(\mathbf{g})$ by

$$\mathbf{A}(\mathbf{g}) = \mathbf{V}^{-1}(\mathbf{g})\mathbf{X}\left[\mathbf{X}'\mathbf{V}^{-1}(\mathbf{g})\mathbf{X}\right]^{-1}\mathbf{X}'\mathbf{V}^{-1}(\mathbf{g}).$$

Therefore,

$$NH_1 = N\mathbf{g}'\mathbf{A}(\mathbf{g})\mathbf{g}. \tag{13}$$

When $\beta = 0$, $\delta = \mathbf{X}\beta = 0$, which implies that NH_1 is a quadratic form in $\sqrt{N}\,(\mathbf{g} - \delta)$; that is,

$$NH_1 = \sqrt{N}\,(\mathbf{g} - \delta)'\mathbf{A}(\mathbf{g})\sqrt{N}\,(\mathbf{g} - \delta).$$

Since $\mathbf{A}(\mathbf{g})$ is a continuous function of $\mathbf{g}$ it follows that

$$\sqrt{N}\,(\mathbf{g} - \delta)'\mathbf{A}(\mathbf{g})\sqrt{N}\,(\mathbf{g} - \delta) - \sqrt{N}\,(\mathbf{g} - \delta)'\mathbf{A}(\delta)\sqrt{N}\,(\mathbf{g} - \delta)$$

tends to zero in probability as $N \to \infty$, and therefore NH_1 has the same limiting distribution as

$$\sqrt{N}\,(\mathbf{g} - \delta)'\mathbf{A}(\delta)\sqrt{N}\,(\mathbf{g} - \delta). \tag{14}$$

Because (14) is a quadratic form in $\sqrt{N}\,(\mathbf{g} - \delta)$, it follows from the asymptotic normality of $\sqrt{N}\,(\mathbf{g} - \delta)$ that (14) has the same asymptotic distribution as a quadratic form in normal variates with the distribution given in (5). Standard results in generalized least squares theory therefore give the limiting distribution of (14) as χ_p^2. ||

The test that $\beta = 0$ at the significance level, α, therefore consists of comparing the obtained value of NH_1 to the $100(1 - \alpha)$ percent critical value of the chi-square distribution with p degrees of freedom. If the value of NH_1 exceeds the critical value, the hypothesis that $\beta = 0$ is rejected. Note that the statistic NH_1 is analogous to the weighted sum of squares due to the regression in weighted least squares. Therefore the test that $\beta = 0$ corresponds to a test that the weighted sum of squares due to the regression is greater than would be expected if $\beta = 0$.

Testing Model Specification

At the beginning of this article we argued that tests of model specification are an important step in the analysis of effect size data. The test of model specification is a way of determining whether the observed effect size estimates are reasonably consistent with the model used in the data analysis. If the number k of effect size estimates exceeds the number of predictors p, then a natural test of model specification is given by the next theorem.

Theorem 4. Define N, π_i^E, π_i^C, $\mathbf{X}$, β and $\hat{\beta}_A$ as in Theorem 2. If $k > p$, then a natural test of model specification uses the statistic

$$H_2 = \mathbf{g}'\mathbf{V}^{-1}(\mathbf{g})\mathbf{g} - H_1 = \mathbf{g}'\mathbf{V}^{-1}(\mathbf{g})\mathbf{g} - \hat{\beta}_A\mathbf{X}'\mathbf{V}^{-1}(\mathbf{g})\mathbf{g}.$$

If π_i^E, π_i^C, $i = 1,\ldots,k$, remain fixed as $N \to \infty$, and the model $\delta = \mathbf{X}\beta$ is correctly specified, then the asymptotic distribution of H_2 is given by

$$NH_2 \sim \chi_{k-p}^2.$$

Proof. The derivation of the asymptotic distribution of NH_2 when $k > p$ and $\delta = \mathbf{X}\beta$ is similar to the derivation of the distribution of NH_1. Define the

$(k \times k)$ matrix $\mathbf{B}(\mathbf{g})$ by

$$\mathbf{B}(\mathbf{g}) = \mathbf{V}^{-1}(\mathbf{g}) - \mathbf{V}^{-1}(\mathbf{g})\mathbf{X}\left[\mathbf{X}'\mathbf{V}^{-1}(\mathbf{g})\mathbf{X}\right]^{-1}\mathbf{X}'\mathbf{V}^{-1}(\mathbf{g}).$$

Then

$$NH_2 = N\mathbf{g}'\mathbf{B}(\mathbf{g})\mathbf{g}. \tag{15}$$

It is easy to see that $\boldsymbol{\delta}'\mathbf{B}(\mathbf{g})\mathbf{g} = \mathbf{g}'\mathbf{B}(\mathbf{g})\boldsymbol{\delta} = \boldsymbol{\delta}'\mathbf{B}(\mathbf{g})\boldsymbol{\delta} = 0$. Hence,

$$NH_2 = N(\mathbf{g} - \boldsymbol{\delta})'\mathbf{B}(\mathbf{g})(\mathbf{g} - \boldsymbol{\delta}).$$

Because the elements of $\mathbf{B}(\mathbf{g})$ are continuous functions of $\mathbf{g}$, it follows that

$$\sqrt{N}\,(\mathbf{g} - \boldsymbol{\delta})'\mathbf{B}(\mathbf{g})\sqrt{N}\,(\mathbf{g} - \boldsymbol{\delta}) - \sqrt{N}\,(\mathbf{g} - \boldsymbol{\delta})'\mathbf{B}(\boldsymbol{\delta})\sqrt{N}\,(\mathbf{g} - \boldsymbol{\delta})$$

tends to zero in probability as $N \to \infty$. Therefore NH_2 has the same limiting distribution as

$$\sqrt{N}\,(\mathbf{g} - \boldsymbol{\delta})'\mathbf{B}(\boldsymbol{\delta})\sqrt{N}\,(\mathbf{g} - \boldsymbol{\delta}). \tag{16}$$

Because (16) is a quadratic form in $\sqrt{N}\,(\mathbf{g} - \boldsymbol{\delta})$, it follows from the asymptotic normality of $\sqrt{N}\,(\mathbf{g} - \boldsymbol{\delta})$ that (16) has the same asymptotic distribution as a quadratic form in normal variates with the distribution given in (5). Standard results from generalized least squares theory therefore give the limiting distribution of (16) as χ^2_{k-p}. $||$

The test for model specification at a significance level, α, therefore consists of comparing the obtained value of NH_2 with the $100(1 - \alpha)$ percent critical value of a chi-square distribution with $(k - p)$ degrees of freedom. If the obtained value of NH_2 exceeds the critical value, then model specification is rejected. Note that NH_2 is analogous to the weighted residual sum of squares. Thus, the test for model specification is a test for greater residual variation than would be expected if $\boldsymbol{\delta} = \mathbf{X}\boldsymbol{\beta}$.

The test for model specification will often be used to demonstrate that the data (sample effect sizes) are reasonably consistent with the model used in data analysis. It is therefore important to have some understanding of the factors affecting the power of the test for model specification. Two factors that influence the power of the test are the number, k, of studies and the sample sizes, $(n_i^E$ and $n_i^C)$, of those studies. The latter factor is often the most significant because the specification test statistic NH_2 can be loosely described as a sum of squares of standardized residuals. The residual for the ith study is "standardized" by the square root of the sampling variance of the ith effect size estimate. When $n_i^E = n_i^C = n_i$, this sampling variance is approximately $2/n_i$. Therefore, if the sample size, n_i, in each group is large, even a small deviation from the model may result in a large contribution to the test statistic. Similarly, if the within-group sample sizes, n_i, are small, even reasonably large deviations from the model may not yield a large "standardized residual" contribution to the test statistic. These arguments can be formalized into a rigorous development of power functions under so called local alternative hypotheses, but the formal arguments will not be given in this paper.

It is not necessarily true that large numbers of studies (large values of k) lead to rejection of model specification. The author has seen relatively simple models that fit well with over 100 studies, and many examples of well-specified models for 40–80 effect sizes. If a particular model does not fit well, then diagnostic procedures are called for. Examination of residuals is often helpful. Such examination may reveal patterns that suggest variables that should be added to the model. Alternatively, some studies may consistently yield effect size estimates that deviate greatly from the prediction of the model and therefore merit closer examination.

Computing Estimates and Test Statistics

The estimates and test statistics presented in this section can be easily calculated using any computer program package that manipulates matrices (such as SAS Proc Matrix). A simpler alternative to the computation of estimates and test statistics is the use of a computer program (such as SAS Proc GLM) that can perform weighted least squares analyses.

Weighted least squares involves estimation of linear model parameters by minimizing a weighted sum of squares of differences between observations and estimates. Given a design matrix $\mathbf{X}$, a vector of observations $\mathbf{Y}$, and a diagonal weight matrix $\mathbf{W}$, the weighted least squares estimate of β in the model $\mathbf{Y} = \mathbf{X}\beta$ is

$$\hat{\beta}_W = (\mathbf{X}'\mathbf{W}\mathbf{X})^{-1}\mathbf{X}'\mathbf{W}\mathbf{Y}.$$

Note that the form of this estimator is the same as that of $\hat{\beta}_A$. Thus $\hat{\beta}_A$ is a special case of $\hat{\beta}_W$ where the weight matrix $\mathbf{W}$ is given by $\mathbf{V}^{-1}(\mathbf{g})$.

It is usually more convenient to use a slightly different weight matrix, however. The matrix $\mathbf{V}(\mathbf{g})$ depends on the ratios $\pi_i^E = n_i^E/N$ and $\pi_i^C = n_i^C/N$, $i = 1,\ldots,k$. These ratios are useful in stating asymptotic distributions but are not necessary for calculating $\hat{\beta}_A$ or any of the test statistics given in this section. It is usually easiest to use the weight matrix $N\mathbf{V}^{-1}(\mathbf{g})$, which can be calculated directly from $\mathbf{g}$ and the sample sizes n_i^E, n_i^C, $i = 1,\ldots,k$. Because $\mathbf{V}(\mathbf{g})N$ is a diagonal matrix, the diagonal elements of $N\mathbf{V}^{-1}(\mathbf{g})$ are merely the reciprocals of the diagonal elements of $N\mathbf{V}(\mathbf{g})$. That is, the ith diagonal element of $\mathbf{V}^{-1}(\mathbf{g})/N$ is

$$w_i = \left(\frac{v_i(g_i)}{N}\right)^{-1} = \frac{2(n_i^E + n_i^C)n_i^E n_i^C}{2(n_i^E + n_i^C)^2 + n_i^E n_i^C g_i^2}, \qquad i = 1,\ldots,k,$$

and the weight matrix is $\mathbf{W} = \mathrm{diag}(w_1,\ldots,w_k)$.

The estimator $\hat{\beta}_A$ is the weighted least squares estimator of β using design matrix $\mathbf{X}$, data vector $\mathbf{g}$, and the weights $w_1,\ldots,w_k$ given above. The large sample covariance matrix of $\hat{\beta}_A$ was previously given as $[\mathbf{X}'\mathbf{V}^{-1}(\mathbf{g})\mathbf{X}]^{-1}/N$ (note the final N). This large sample covariance matrix is given by the weighted sum of squares and cross-products matrix $(\mathbf{X}'\mathbf{W}\mathbf{X})^{-1}$ in the weighted least squares.

If the computer program fits a "no-intercept" model, the test statistic NH_1 for testing that $\beta = 0$ is given by the weighted sum of squares due to the regression in the weighted least squares. A similar statistic for testing that all components of β except the intercept are simultaneously zero is given if the weighted least squares program fits an intercept. In the latter case, the weighted sum of squares about the regression has a chi-square distribution on $k - p - 1$ degrees of freedom when $\delta = \mathbf{X}\beta$. The test statistic NH_2 for testing model specification will always be the value of the weighted sum of squares about the regression line (the error sum of squares). Thus, all the statistics described in this section may be obtained from a single run of a standard packaged computer program.

The Accuracy of the Asymptotic Theory in Finite Samples

The methods described in this paper depend on the asymptotic distributions of $\hat{\beta}_A$, H_1, and H_2. Although large sample approximations are often reasonably accurate in small samples, each approximation must be evaluated separately. Arguments based on moments (see, e.g., Johnson & Welch, 1939) suggest that the distribution of g tends to normality fairly rapidly as n increases (for fixed δ). Simulation studies of the distribution of g (Hedges, 1982a) confirm that the large sample approximation to the distribution of g is very accurate when $\delta < 1.5$ and $n^E + n^C \geqslant 20$. Therefore the asymptotic distribution theory for $\hat{\beta}_A$, H_1, and H_2 might be expected to be reasonably accurate for sample sizes and values of δ in the same ranges. Simulation studies of the distribution of $\hat{\beta}_A$ and H_2 in some special cases (Hedges, 1982a) suggest that the general theory presented in this paper may be useful for the range of sample sizes and effect sizes usually encountered in syntheses of educational research. Yet some might urge caution in the use of large sample theory in particular cases without extensive evidence of the accuracy of that theory in small samples.

Simulation studies provide one method of studying the small-sample accuracy of large-sample distribution theory. No simulation or group of simulations could examine all aspects of the general linear model. Thus, only an illustrative simulation was conducted to show the performance of the methods presented in this paper. We make no claim that this is an exhaustive Monte-Carlo study. However the results of the simulation do confirm expectations that the large sample approximations perform adequately in the situations that were examined.

The simulation described in this section is based on normal and chi-squared random numbers generated by the International Mathematical and Statistical Libraries (1977) library subroutines GGNML and GGCHS. The range of δ (effect size) values was between -1.25 and 1.25. These effect sizes were chosen because virtually all meta-analyses have found effect sizes in this range. For each "study," the experimental and control group sample sizes were set equal;

that is, $n_i^E = n_i^C = n_i$. The g_i values were generated based on the identity

$$g_i = Z/\sqrt{S/m},$$

where Z is a normal with mean $\delta = \beta_1 x_1 + \beta_2 x_2$ and variance $2/n_i$, and S is a chi-square random variable with $m = 2n_i - 2$ degrees of freedom.

Two different design matrices were used for $k = 6$ studies in each case. In the first design matrix $(\mathbf{X})$ the predictors have correlation $r = .1$ and in the second design matrix $(\tilde{\mathbf{X}})$ the predictors have correlation $r = .5$. The design matrices are

$$\mathbf{X} = \begin{bmatrix} 2.000 & 0.500 \\ 0.500 & -1.000 \\ 0.000 & -2.150 \\ 0.000 & 2.150 \\ -0.500 & 1.000 \\ -2.000 & -0.500 \end{bmatrix}, \quad \tilde{\mathbf{X}} = \begin{bmatrix} 2.000 & 0.500 \\ 0.500 & 0.500 \\ 0.000 & -0.985 \\ 0.000 & 0.985 \\ -0.500 & -0.500 \\ -2.000 & -0.500 \end{bmatrix},$$

and the regression coefficients chosen are

$$\beta = \begin{pmatrix} 0.00 \\ 0.00 \end{pmatrix}, \quad \beta = \begin{pmatrix} 0.20 \\ 0.20 \end{pmatrix}, \quad \beta = \begin{pmatrix} 0.20 \\ 0.50 \end{pmatrix}, \quad \text{and} \quad \beta = \begin{pmatrix} 0.50 \\ 0.50 \end{pmatrix}.$$

For each design matrix and each β, six sets of sample sizes were studied. The sample sizes were $n_i^E = n_i^C = 10, 20,$ or 50 in each study. In three configurations, the sample sizes of all six studies were equal. The other three sample size configurations involved one-half the studies with one sample size and the other half with a different sample size. All the reported data are based on 2,000 replications for each design matrix, β, and sample size configuration.

The results of the empirical sampling investigation of the distribution of $\hat{\beta}_A$ are given in Table I. Means and variances of the estimates as well as the empirical proportions of (nonsimultaneous) confidence intervals that included β_1 or β_2 are reported. These results suggest that the bias of $\hat{\beta}_A$ is small and that confidence intervals based on Theorem 2 are reasonably accurate, even for sample sizes as small as $n_i^E = n_i^C = 10$.

The results of the empirical sampling study of the distribution of the statistic H_1 are presented in Table II. The mean and variance of NH_1 are tabled along with the empirical proportions of NH_1 values that exceed the (asymptotic) critical values for various significance levels. Note that the empirical distribution of NH_1 is evaluated only under the null hypothesis that $\beta = \mathbf{0}$. The results of this simulation suggest that critical values based on the large sample distribution of NH_1 are reasonably accurate, even for sample sizes as small as $n_i^E = n_i^C = 10$.

The results of the empirical sampling study of the distribution of the specification statistic H_2 are presented in Table III. The means and variances of NH_2 are tabled along with the empirical proportions of NH_2 values that

TABLE I
The Small Sample Behavior of Confidence Intervals for β
Based on the Asymptotic Distribution

$r(x_1,x_2)$[a]	$n\,1-3$	$n\,4-6$[b]	$\hat\beta$	Mean of $\hat\beta$	Variance of $\hat\beta$	Proportion of Confidence Intervals Including Beta — Nominal Significance Level of Interval					
						.60	.70	.80	.90	.95	.99
$\beta_1 = 0.0,\ \beta_2 = 0.0$											
0.10	10	10	B1	−0.004	0.026	0.595	0.692	0.794	0.896	0.943	0.989
			B2	−0.002	0.017	0.634	0.723	0.809	0.908	0.951	0.994
0.10	20	20	B1	−0.001	0.012	0.622	0.717	0.815	0.918	0.955	0.991
			B2	−0.003	0.009	0.603	0.706	0.796	0.894	0.955	0.990
0.10	50	50	B1	−0.000	0.005	0.595	0.704	0.803	0.901	0.956	0.994
			B2	0.002	0.003	0.615	0.709	0.809	0.913	0.957	0.992
0.10	10	20	B1	0.002	0.016	0.615	0.716	0.808	0.894	0.946	0.990
			B2	−0.003	0.011	0.606	0.710	0.804	0.909	0.950	0.995
0.10	10	50	B1	−0.000	0.008	0.612	0.700	0.814	0.901	0.953	0.989
			B2	0.002	0.006	0.609	0.707	0.809	0.908	0.956	0.990
0.10	20	50	B1	0.002	0.007	0.615	0.712	0.797	0.904	0.954	0.991
			B2	0.002	0.005	0.589	0.692	0.800	0.895	0.949	0.989
0.50	10	10	B1	0.001	0.033	0.604	0.696	0.811	0.906	0.942	0.988
			B2	−0.008	0.093	0.605	0.698	0.793	0.910	0.955	0.990
0.50	20	20	B1	−0.001	0.017	0.592	0.686	0.794	0.900	0.943	0.991
			B2	0.005	0.047	0.615	0.697	0.799	0.896	0.947	0.989
0.50	50	50	B1	0.000	0.006	0.595	0.695	0.792	0.899	0.949	0.989
			B2	0.001	0.019	0.598	0.703	0.796	0.890	0.949	0.988
0.50	10	20	B1	−0.001	0.021	0.600	0.703	0.804	0.903	0.956	0.990
			B2	0.001	0.061	0.597	0.696	0.804	0.904	0.949	0.992
0.50	10	50	B1	−0.003	0.010	0.622	0.727	0.817	0.913	0.959	0.992
			B2	0.003	0.032	0.593	0.697	0.789	0.893	0.945	0.986
0.50	20	50	B1	−0.005	0.009	0.589	0.703	0.805	0.912	0.952	0.991
			B2	−0.002	0.026	0.604	0.702	0.801	0.903	0.954	0.994

(Continued on next page)

TABLE I (continued)

$r(x_1, x_2)^a$	Sample Sizes $n1-3$	$n4-6^b$	Mean of $\hat{\beta}$	Variance of $\hat{\beta}$	.60	.70	.80	.90	.95	.99

Column group "Proportion of Confidence Intervals Including Beta — Nominal Significance Level of Interval" spans columns .60–.99.

$\beta_1 = .2,\ \beta_2 = .2$

$r(x_1,x_2)^a$	$n1-3$	$n4-6^b$	Mean of $\hat{\beta}$	Variance of $\hat{\beta}$	.60	.70	.80	.90	.95	.99
0.10	10	10 B1	0.205	0.026	0.591	0.688	0.796	0.894	0.950	0.991
		B2	0.198	0.019	0.602	0.703	0.804	0.894	0.946	0.989
0.10	20	20 B1	0.200	0.013	0.605	0.695	0.798	0.897	0.950	0.989
		B2	0.202	0.009	0.597	0.702	0.790	0.900	0.950	0.988
0.10	50	50 B1	0.200	0.005	0.604	0.696	0.795	0.899	0.949	0.990
		B2	0.200	0.003	0.604	0.706	0.815	0.904	0.949	0.989
0.10	10	20 B1	0.203	0.016	0.609	0.708	0.800	0.915	0.957	0.988
		B2	0.201	0.012	0.610	0.712	0.806	0.899	0.953	0.989
0.10	10	50 B1	0.204	0.009	0.586	0.691	0.790	0.890	0.941	0.987
		B2	0.200	0.006	0.616	0.715	0.809	0.906	0.954	0.991
0.10	20	50 B1	0.200	0.007	0.617	0.714	0.810	0.905	0.950	0.990
		B2	0.203	0.005	0.585	0.696	0.802	0.902	0.950	0.993
0.50	10	10 B1	0.195	0.033	0.615	0.708	0.803	0.908	0.953	0.987
		B2	0.213	0.094	0.602	0.707	0.804	0.901	0.949	0.990
0.50	20	20 B1	0.199	0.017	0.582	0.691	0.788	0.887	0.943	0.990
		B2	0.208	0.046	0.593	0.688	0.794	0.901	0.950	0.993
0.50	50	50 B1	0.206	0.007	0.581	0.683	0.798	0.900	0.946	0.989
		B2	0.192	0.018	0.580	0.697	0.794	0.899	0.957	0.995
0.50	10	20 B1	0.202	0.023	0.600	0.682	0.789	0.890	0.946	0.989
		B2	0.209	0.064	0.581	0.678	0.794	0.891	0.951	0.992
0.50	10	50 B1	0.202	0.011	0.581	0.687	0.800	0.900	0.949	0.988
		B2	0.210	0.031	0.609	0.705	0.806	0.896	0.949	0.988
0.50	20	50 B1	0.204	0.009	0.592	0.699	0.802	0.906	0.959	0.992
		B2	0.200	0.027	0.594	0.696	0.792	0.901	0.950	0.989

$\beta_1 = .2, \beta_2 = .5$

0.10	10	10	B1	0.206	0.028	0.586	0.693	0.796	0.885	0.940	0.987
			B2	0.502	0.020	0.616	0.712	0.806	0.905	0.951	0.989
0.10	20	20	B1	0.204	0.013	0.604	0.696	0.794	0.893	0.947	0.991
			B2	0.502	0.010	0.601	0.705	0.805	0.890	0.940	0.988
0.10	50	50	B1	0.199	0.005	0.588	0.688	0.790	0.897	0.950	0.985
			B2	0.502	0.004	0.603	0.695	0.793	0.896	0.945	0.989
0.10	10	20	B1	0.202	0.017	0.589	0.696	0.792	0.893	0.949	0.990
			B2	0.502	0.014	0.571	0.675	0.783	0.892	0.945	0.986
0.10	10	50	B1	0.199	0.008	0.580	0.683	0.800	0.907	0.953	0.992
			B2	0.502	0.007	0.597	0.697	0.799	0.899	0.949	0.989
0.10	20	50	B1	0.204	0.008	0.583	0.677	0.780	0.890	0.947	0.987
			B2	0.501	0.006	0.597	0.689	0.793	0.907	0.955	0.989
0.50	10	10	B1	0.197	0.034	0.613	0.711	0.801	0.897	0.950	0.991
			B2	0.495	0.095	0.619	0.715	0.809	0.903	0.957	0.989
0.50	20	20	B1	0.201	0.017	0.592	0.688	0.795	0.899	0.949	0.988
			B2	0.502	0.047	0.610	0.711	0.807	0.904	0.951	0.988
0.50	50	50	B1	0.202	0.006	0.614	0.721	0.821	0.904	0.953	0.989
			B2	0.500	0.019	0.613	0.696	0.795	0.902	0.947	0.993
0.50	10	20	B1	0.202	0.021	0.606	0.707	0.809	0.913	0.958	0.994
			B2	0.501	0.061	0.617	0.708	0.814	0.901	0.953	0.990
0.50	10	50	B1	0.200	0.011	0.599	0.698	0.796	0.900	0.946	0.990
			B2	0.503	0.030	0.606	0.701	0.808	0.908	0.960	0.991
0.50	20	50	B1	0.202	0.010	0.604	0.696	0.799	0.902	0.950	0.989
			B2	0.498	0.027	0.599	0.704	0.809	0.904	0.951	0.988

(Continued on next page)

TABLE I (continued)

	Sample Sizes			Mean of $\hat{\beta}$	Variance of $\hat{\beta}$	Proportion of Confidence Intervals Including Beta					
						Nominal Significance Level of Interval					
$r(x_1, x_2)^{[a]}$	$n1-3$	$n4-6^{[b]}$				.60	.70	.80	.90	.95	.99
$\beta_1 = .5,\ \beta_2 = .5$											
0.10	10	10	B1	0.509	0.031	0.584	0.686	0.784	0.893	0.948	0.991
			B2	0.502	0.019	0.615	0.710	0.807	0.906	0.961	0.990
0.10	20	20	B1	0.506	0.015	0.594	0.696	0.798	0.897	0.952	0.988
			B2	0.502	0.010	0.603	0.699	0.804	0.899	0.949	0.987
0.10	50	50	B1	0.501	0.005	0.614	0.717	0.814	0.910	0.959	0.991
			B2	0.502	0.004	0.593	0.695	0.792	0.882	0.943	0.994
0.10	10	20	B1	0.506	0.021	0.590	0.688	0.789	0.890	0.945	0.985
			B2	0.504	0.014	0.601	0.699	0.797	0.892	0.944	0.987
0.10	10	50	B1	0.503	0.010	0.577	0.689	0.795	0.909	0.950	0.991
			B2	0.501	0.006	0.610	0.715	0.820	0.910	0.953	0.989
0.10	20	50	B1	0.504	0.008	0.604	0.702	0.798	0.903	0.951	0.993
			B2	0.502	0.006	0.594	0.691	0.794	0.900	0.947	0.986
0.50	10	10	B1	0.499	0.039	0.608	0.708	0.801	0.895	0.945	0.987
			B2	0.502	0.108	0.573	0.688	0.786	0.889	0.935	0.986
0.50	20	20	B1	0.506	0.019	0.598	0.694	0.801	0.901	0.951	0.991
			B2	0.495	0.049	0.584	0.692	0.789	0.896	0.945	0.990
0.50	50	50	B1	0.500	0.007	0.598	0.704	0.807	0.903	0.953	0.994
			B2	0.497	0.018	0.607	0.706	0.803	0.909	0.953	0.993
0.50	10	20	B1	0.496	0.025	0.586	0.683	0.788	0.894	0.946	0.992
			B2	0.503	0.064	0.598	0.704	0.796	0.900	0.951	0.989
0.50	10	50	B1	0.499	0.013	0.594	0.692	0.788	0.892	0.948	0.987
			B2	0.499	0.030	0.620	0.705	0.796	0.903	0.958	0.992
0.50	20	50	B1	0.507	0.011	0.606	0.701	0.797	0.896	0.945	0.989
			B2	0.489	0.027	0.599	0.698	0.795	0.897	0.949	0.989

Note. For each sample size configuration, β, and correlation between predictors, 2,000 replications were generated.

[a] $r(x_1, x_2)$ is the correlation between the predictors x_1 and x_2.

[b] In each case $k = 6$ studies, three studies have sample sizes $n_i^E = n_i^C = n1 - 3$, and three studies have sample sizes $n_i^E = n_i^C = n4 - 6$.

TABLE II

The Small Sample Behavior of the Test Statistic H_1

Sample Sizes			Mean of NH_1	Variance of NH_1	Proportion of Test Statistics Exceeding Critical Chi-Squares Nominal Significance Level of Chi-Square					
$r(x_1, x_2)$[a]	$n1-3$	$n4-6$[b]			.40	.30	.20	.10	.05	.01
0.10	10	10	1.957	3.887	0.396	0.301	0.198	0.096	0.045	0.010
0.10	20	20	1.950	4.007	0.391	0.287	0.184	0.095	0.045	0.011
0.10	50	50	1.921	3.684	0.393	0.291	0.187	0.090	0.047	0.008
0.10	10	20	1.942	3.734	0.381	0.294	0.198	0.099	0.046	0.008
0.10	10	50	1.945	3.878	0.393	0.298	0.188	0.092	0.046	0.009
0.10	20	50	1.982	3.840	0.395	0.298	0.201	0.098	0.051	0.009
0.50	10	10	1.958	3.823	0.391	0.291	0.190	0.092	0.046	0.011
0.50	20	20	2.034	4.476	0.399	0.299	0.206	0.107	0.055	0.012
0.50	50	50	2.031	4.336	0.405	0.316	0.209	0.102	0.051	0.013
0.50	10	20	1.972	3.710	0.397	0.300	0.194	0.092	0.045	0.009
0.50	10	50	1.953	3.861	0.387	0.283	0.201	0.102	0.043	0.010
0.50	20	50	1.964	3.744	0.406	0.305	0.191	0.092	0.040	0.006

Note. For each sample size configuration and correlation between predictors, $\beta = 0$, and 2,000 replications were generated.

[a] $r(x_1, x_2)$ is the correlation between predictors x_1 and x_2.

[b] In each case $k = 6$ studies, three studies have sample size $n_i^E = n_i^C = n1 - 3$, and three studies have sample size $n_i^E = n_i^C = n4 - 6$.

TABLE III
The Small Sample Behavior of the Model Specification Test Statistic H_2

$r(x_1, x_2)^a$	Sample Sizes $n1 - 3$	$n4 - 6^b$	Mean of NH_2	Variance of NH_2	Proportion of Test Statistics Exceeding Critical Chi-Squares Nominal Significance Level of Chi-Square					
					.40	.30	.20	.10	.05	.01
$\beta_1 = 0.0, \beta_2 = 0$										
0.10	10	10	4.180	9.172	0.425	0.323	0.230	0.106	0.058	0.018
0.10	20	20	3.964	8.306	0.392	0.293	0.194	0.107	0.055	0.007
0.10	50	50	3.935	8.114	0.373	0.286	0.197	0.101	0.045	0.010
0.10	20	10	4.102	8.374	0.416	0.327	0.224	0.116	0.057	0.009
0.10	50	10	4.009	8.239	0.400	0.308	0.203	0.102	0.051	0.010
0.10	50	20	4.043	8.179	0.410	0.310	0.206	0.103	0.055	0.010
0.50	10	10	4.153	8.596	0.432	0.316	0.215	0.108	0.063	0.013
0.50	20	20	4.085	7.604	0.417	0.308	0.206	0.102	0.048	0.008
0.50	50	50	3.984	7.753	0.394	0.300	0.198	0.108	0.043	0.008
0.50	20	10	4.250	8.758	0.437	0.333	0.229	0.118	0.060	0.015
0.50	50	10	4.151	8.462	0.420	0.324	0.219	0.108	0.057	0.011
0.50	50	20	4.122	8.395	0.409	0.320	0.221	0.109	0.056	0.011
$\beta_1 = .2, \beta_2 = .2$										
0.10	10	10	4.256	8.579	0.430	0.343	0.231	0.116	0.056	0.014
0.10	20	20	4.214	8.767	0.438	0.331	0.231	0.119	0.055	0.010
0.10	50	50	4.077	8.405	0.402	0.311	0.217	0.114	0.054	0.009
0.10	20	10	4.078	8.192	0.408	0.302	0.210	0.103	0.052	0.011
0.10	50	10	4.037	8.065	0.410	0.308	0.203	0.108	0.055	0.010
0.10	50	20	4.014	7.678	0.407	0.310	0.201	0.093	0.046	0.007

0.50	10	10	4.267	8.993	0.439	0.330	0.235	0.117	0.056	0.014
0.50	20	20	4.079	8.052	0.416	0.321	0.200	0.108	0.049	0.009
0.50	50	50	4.034	8.537	0.393	0.300	0.204	0.112	0.055	0.012
0.50	10	20	4.155	8.473	0.423	0.324	0.219	0.110	0.051	0.013
0.50	10	50	4.020	7.956	0.408	0.309	0.201	0.099	0.054	0.010
0.50	20	50	4.013	7.949	0.398	0.304	0.195	0.094	0.048	0.012

$\beta_1 = .2, \beta_2 = .5$

0.10	10	10	4.279	9.016	0.439	0.339	0.242	0.124	0.062	0.014
0.10	20	20	4.141	8.487	0.422	0.320	0.218	0.115	0.059	0.011
0.10	50	50	4.014	7.505	0.412	0.295	0.196	0.094	0.042	0.010
0.10	10	20	4.114	8.858	0.405	0.305	0.212	0.112	0.061	0.013
0.10	10	50	4.273	9.292	0.424	0.337	0.235	0.124	0.070	0.014
0.10	20	50	4.004	7.696	0.408	0.313	0.210	0.106	0.047	0.008

0.50	10	10	4.226	8.486	0.430	0.321	0.224	0.124	0.060	0.012
0.50	20	20	4.098	8.223	0.423	0.315	0.215	0.111	0.054	0.008
0.50	50	50	4.025	8.264	0.404	0.296	0.214	0.102	0.049	0.009
0.50	10	20	4.169	8.353	0.411	0.319	0.226	0.118	0.058	0.010
0.50	10	50	4.225	9.001	0.424	0.337	0.230	0.119	0.059	0.009
0.50	20	50	4.110	7.931	0.415	0.318	0.214	0.109	0.056	0.010

(Continued on next page)

TABLE III (continued)

$r(x_1, x_2)^a$	Sample Sizes		Mean of NH_2	Variance of NH_2	Proportion of Test Statistics Exceeding Critical Chi-Squares Nominal Significance Level of Chi-Square					
	$N1-3$	$N4-6^b$			.40	.30	.20	.10	.05	.01
$\beta_2 = .5, \beta_2 = .5$										
0.10	10	10	4.219	8.495	0.434	0.337	0.229	0.111	0.061	0.011
0.10	20	20	4.042	7.898	0.413	0.305	0.200	0.104	0.050	0.009
0.10	50	50	4.046	8.569	0.397	0.310	0.209	0.100	0.058	0.011
0.10	10	20	4.080	8.331	0.418	0.320	0.203	0.106	0.051	0.010
0.10	10	50	4.228	8.526	0.439	0.331	0.228	0.114	0.056	0.006
0.10	20	50	4.146	8.839	0.423	0.320	0.214	0.113	0.059	0.013
0.50	10	10	4.131	8.404	0.422	0.310	0.211	0.109	0.057	0.011
0.50	20	20	4.096	8.293	0.410	0.309	0.202	0.104	0.055	0.011
0.50	50	50	4.035	8.161	0.406	0.302	0.204	0.105	0.052	0.011
0.50	10	20	4.046	8.404	0.406	0.305	0.211	0.108	0.054	0.012
0.50	10	50	4.114	8.744	0.410	0.305	0.216	0.113	0.063	0.013
0.50	20	50	4.069	8.381	0.401	0.307	0.206	0.104	0.055	0.012

Note. For each sample size configuration, β, and correlation between predictors, 2,000 replications were generated.

[a] $r(x_1, x_2)$ is the correlation between predictors x_1 and x_2.

[b] In each case $k = 6$ studies, three studies have sample size $n_i^E = n_i^C = n1 - 3$, and three studies have sample size $n_i^E = n_i^C = n4 - 6$.

exceed the (asymptotic) critical values for various significance levels. The results of this simulation suggest that critical values based on the large sample distribution of NH_2 are reasonably accurate when the sample sizes exceed $n_i^E = n_i^C = 10$. These critical values seem to be somewhat more accurate when the sample sizes are at least $n_i^E = n_i^C = 20$.

Example

In this section, the methods described in this paper are applied to some effect size data collected by Hedges, Giaconia, and Gage (1981). Table IV presents some data from randomized experiments that examined the effect of open classroom and traditional classroom teaching on student attitudes toward school. The grade level was believed to influence effect size. In addition, some of the studies used systematic observations to determine that the nominally open classrooms were actually using open teaching practices. It was thought that these studies would have a more consistent treatment and therefore might yield systematically different effects. Therefore the data was analyzed using a linear model that included a grand mean (β_1), an effect for observations (β_2), and an effect for grade level (β_3). The design matrix is

$$\mathbf{X} = \begin{bmatrix} 1 & 1 & 0 \\ 1 & 1 & 0 \\ 1 & 0 & 1 \\ 1 & 0 & 1 \\ 1 & 0 & 1 \\ 1 & 0 & 0 \\ 1 & 0 & 0 \end{bmatrix}$$

and the value of the test statistic for model misspecification is $NH_2 = 7.13$. Comparing this value to the 95 percent critical value of the chi-square

TABLE IV

Data from Randomized Experiments that Examined the Effect of Open and Traditional Education on Attitudes Toward School

Study	n_i^E	n_i^C	Observations Used	Grade Level	g_i	$v_i(g_i)$
1	40	40	Yes	Higher	.649	.0526
2	90	90	Yes	Higher	−.043	.0222
3	79	49	No	Lower	.503	.0341
4	84	45	No	Lower	.458	.0349
5	78	55	No	Lower	.577	.0322
6	38	110	No	Higher	.588	.0367
7	38	93	No	Higher	.392	.0377

Note. These data are from Hedges, Giaconia, and Gage (1981).

distribution with four degrees of freedom (9.49), we see that we cannot reject model specification at the $\alpha = .05$ level. The parameter estimate $\hat{\beta}_A$ is

$$\hat{\beta}_A = \begin{pmatrix} .491 \\ -.329 \\ .023 \end{pmatrix}.$$

The estimated covariance matrix $\hat{\Sigma}/N = [\mathbf{X'V}^{-1}(\mathbf{g})\mathbf{X}]^{-1}/N$ of $\hat{\beta}_A$ is

$$(10^2)\hat{\Sigma}/N = \begin{pmatrix} 1.86 & -1.86 & -1.86 \\ -1.86 & 3.42 & 1.86 \\ -1.86 & 1.86 & 2.98 \end{pmatrix}.$$

Simultaneous 95 percent confidence intervals for β_1, β_2, and β_3, based on the Bonferroni inequality are

$$.200 \leqslant \beta_1 \leqslant .782,$$
$$-.715 \leqslant \beta_2 \leqslant .070,$$
$$-.345 \leqslant \beta_3 \leqslant .390.$$

Therefore only the grand mean, β_1, appears to be different from zero in this example.

Appendix: Derivation of the Asymptotic Variance of the MLE

The inverse of the covariance matrix of the maximum likelihood estimator of β is obtained from the expectation of the matrix of second-order, partial derivatives of the likelihood function. If the vector of parameters is ordered as in the vector $\theta = (\sigma_1, \dots, \sigma_k, \gamma_1, \dots, \gamma_k, \beta_1, \dots, \beta_p)$, the matrix $\Psi = -E(\partial^2 L/\partial\theta_i\, \partial\theta_j)/N$ may be partitioned into relatively simple submatrices. A well-known identity for the inverse of a partitioned matrix is then used to obtain an expression for the last p rows and columns of Ψ^{-1}.

The expectations of the second-order, partial derivatives of the likelihood function are

$$E\left[\frac{\partial^2 L}{\partial\gamma_i^2}\right] = -N\left(\pi_i^E + \pi_i^C\right), \qquad i = 1, \dots, k, \tag{1a}$$

$$E\left[\frac{\partial^2 L}{\partial\sigma_i^2}\right] = -N\left[\frac{2\left(\pi_i^E + \pi_i^C\right) + \pi_i^E(x_i'\beta + \gamma_i)^2 + \pi_i^C\gamma_i^2}{\sigma_i^2}\right], \qquad i = 1, \dots, k, \tag{1b}$$

$$E\left[\frac{\partial^2 L}{\partial\gamma_i\, \partial\sigma_i}\right] = N\left[\frac{\pi_i^E x_i'\beta + \left(\pi_i^E + \pi_i^C\right)\gamma_i}{\sigma_i}\right], \qquad i = 1, \dots, k, \tag{1c}$$

$$E\left[\frac{\partial^2 L}{\partial\gamma_i\, \partial\sigma_j}\right] = E\left[\frac{\partial^2 L}{\partial\gamma_i\, \partial\gamma_j}\right] = E\left[\frac{\partial^2 L}{\partial\sigma_i\, \partial\sigma_j}\right] = 0, \qquad i \neq j;\ i, j = 1, \dots, k, \tag{1d}$$

$$E\left[\frac{\partial^2 L}{\partial \beta_s \, \partial \beta_t}\right] = -N \sum_{i=1}^{k} x_{is} x_{it} \pi_i^E, \qquad s,t = 1,\ldots,p, \qquad (1e)$$

$$E\left[\frac{\partial^2 L}{\partial \sigma_i \, \partial \beta_s}\right] = -N \frac{\pi_i^E x_{is}(\mathbf{x}_i'\boldsymbol{\beta} + \gamma_i)}{\sigma_i}, \qquad i = 1,\ldots,k; \, s = 1,\ldots,p, \quad (1f)$$

$$E\left[\frac{\partial^2 L}{\partial \beta_s \, \partial \gamma_i}\right] = -N \pi_i^E x_{is} \gamma_i, \qquad i = 1,\ldots,k; \, s = 1,\ldots,p. \qquad (1g)$$

With the parameters ordered according to $\boldsymbol{\theta} = (\sigma_1,\ldots,\sigma_k, \gamma_1,\ldots,\gamma_k, \beta_1,\ldots,\beta_p)$, the matrix $\boldsymbol{\Psi} = -E[\partial^2 L/\partial \theta_i \, \partial \theta_j]/N$ can be partitioned into

$$-\left(\begin{array}{cc|c} \mathbf{D}_1 & \mathbf{D}_2 & \\ & & \mathbf{B} \\ \mathbf{D}_2 & \mathbf{D}_3 & \\ \hline & \mathbf{B}' & \mathbf{C} \end{array}\right),$$

where $\mathbf{D}_1$, $\mathbf{D}_2$ and $\mathbf{D}_3$ are $k \times k$ diagonal matrices and $\mathbf{B}$ is a $2k \times p$ matrix. The last p rows and columns of $\boldsymbol{\Psi}^{-1}$ are given by H^{-1} where

$$\mathbf{H} = \mathbf{C} - \mathbf{B}'\mathbf{A}\mathbf{B}, \qquad (2)$$

and

$$\mathbf{A} = \begin{pmatrix} \mathbf{D}_1 & \mathbf{D}_2 \\ \mathbf{D}_2 & \mathbf{D}_3 \end{pmatrix}^{-1} = \begin{pmatrix} \mathbf{A}_1 & \mathbf{A}_2 \\ \mathbf{A}_2 & \mathbf{A}_3 \end{pmatrix}.$$

Note that the matrix $\mathbf{B}$ can be written as

$$\mathbf{B} = \begin{pmatrix} \mathbf{D}_u \\ \mathbf{D}_v \end{pmatrix}\mathbf{X}, \qquad (3)$$

where $\mathbf{D}_u = \mathrm{diag}(u_1,\ldots,u_k)$, $\mathbf{D}_v = \mathrm{diag}(v_1,\ldots,v_k)$,

$$u_i = \frac{\pi_i^E(\mathbf{x}_i'\boldsymbol{\beta} + \gamma_i)^2 + \pi_i^C \gamma_i^2}{\sigma_i}, \qquad i = 1,\ldots,k,$$

and

$$v_i = \frac{\pi_i^E \mathbf{x}_i'\boldsymbol{\beta} + \left(\pi_i^E + \pi_i^C\right)\gamma_i}{\sigma_i}, \qquad i = 1,\ldots,k.$$

Substitution of (3) into (2) gives

$$\mathbf{H} = \mathbf{C} - \mathbf{X}'(\mathbf{D}_u'\mathbf{A}_1\mathbf{D}_u + \mathbf{D}_v'\mathbf{A}_3\mathbf{D}_v + \mathbf{D}_u'\mathbf{A}_2\mathbf{D}_v + \mathbf{D}_v'\mathbf{A}_2\mathbf{D}_u)\mathbf{X}. \qquad (4)$$

The expressions (1a) to (1g) are inserted into (4), which after simplification yields (10) in the text. ‖

Acknowledgement

This research was supported by the Spencer Foundation. I thank Betsy Jane Becker for helpful comments and for programming the simulation study reported in this paper. I also thank an Associate Editor and an anonymous reviewer for valuable suggestions.

References

Cramér, H. *Mathematical methods of statistics*. Princeton, N.J.: Princeton University Press, 1946.

Eysenk, H. J. An exercise in mega-silliness. *American Psychologist*, 1978, *33*, 517.

Glass, G. V Primary, secondary, and meta-analysis of research. *Educational Researcher*, 1976, *5*, 3–8.

Glass, G. V Integrating findings: The meta-analysis of research. In L. S. Shulman (Ed.), *Review of research in education* (Vol. 5). Itasca, Ill.: F. E. Peacock, 1978.

Glass, G. V, & Smith, M. L. Meta-analysis of the relationship between class size and achievement. *Educational Evaluation and Policy Analysis*, 1979, *1*, 2–16.

Hedges, L. V. Distribution theory for Glass's estimator of effect size and related estimators. *Journal of Educational Statistics*, 1981, *6*, 107–128.

Hedges, L. V. Estimating effect size from a series of independent experiments. *Psychological Bulletin*, 1982, *92*, 490–499. (a)

Hedges, L. V. Fitting categorical models to effect sizes from a series of experiments. *Journal of Educational Statistics*, 1982, 7, 119–137. (b)

Hedges, L. V., Giaconia, R. M., & Gage, N. L. *The empirical evidence on the effectiveness of open education*. (Final Report of the Stanford Research Synthesis Project, volume 2.) Stanford, Calif.: Stanford University, 1981.

International Mathematical and Statistical Libraries, Inc. *IMSL Library* 1. (7th ed.). Houston, Tex.: Author, 1977.

Johnson, N. L., & Welch, B. L. Applications of the noncentral *t*-distribution. *Biometrika*, 1939, *31*, 362–389.

Presby, S. Overly broad categories obscure important differences. *American Psychologist*, 1978, *33*, 514–515.

Smith, M. L., & Glass, G. V Meta-analysis of psychotherapy outcome studies. *American Psychologist*, 1977, *32*, 752–760.

Smith, M. L., & Glass, G. V Meta-analysis of class size and its relationship to attitudes and instruction. *American Educational Research Journal*, 1980, *17*, 419–433.

Uguroglu, M. E., & Walberg, H. J. Motivation and achievement: A quantitative synthesis. *American Educational Research Journal*, 1979, *16*, 375–390.

Author

HEDGES, LARRY V. Assistant Professor, Department of Education, The University of Chicago, 5835 Kimbark Avenue, Chicago, Illinois 60637. *Specialization*: Statistical methods.

11

Estimation of Effect Size from a Series of Independent Experiments

Larry V. Hedges

Recent interest in methods for the quantitative synthesis of research has produced many quantitative syntheses but little statistical theory for the methods used in these syntheses. The present article extends statistical theory for procedures based on Glass's estimator of effect size. An unbiased estimator of effect size is given. A weighted estimator of effect size based on data from several experiments is defined and shown to be optimal (asymptotically efficient). An approximate (large-sample) test for homogeneity of effect size across experiments is also given. The results of an empirical sampling study are used to show that the large-sample distributions of the weighted estimator and the homogeneity statistic are quite accurate when the experimental and control group sample sizes exceed 10 and the effect sizes are smaller than about 1.5.

A number of authors have recently shown an interest in empirical methods of combining the results of a series of independent studies. Glass (1976) was among the first authors to call for the use of quantitative procedures in research integration as a supplement to the discursive review. Examples of the use of these techniques include a review of psychotherapy outcome studies (Smith & Glass, 1977), a review of interpersonal expectancy effects in psychological research (Rosenthal & Rubin, 1978), a review of the effects of teaching methods (Kulik, Kulik, & Cohen, 1979), and a review of the effects of class size on academic achievement (Glass & Smith, 1979).

Despite the extensive application of the techniques suggested by Glass, there has been relatively little attention to some fundamental statistical issues in the use of quantitative methods for research synthesis. Investigators have not always clearly distinguished sample *estimates* of effect size from the population parameter they wish to estimate. There has also been little discussion

of whether it is reasonable to think that population effect sizes are constant across a series of studies. Given a series of effect size estimates from *k* studies, most investigators calculate the average of these effect size estimates and refer to the average value as *the* effect size. Representation of the results of a collection of studies by a single estimate of effect magnitude can be misleading if the underlying (population) effect sizes are not identical in all of the studies. For example, suppose a treatment produces large positive (population) effects in one-half of a collection of studies and large negative (population) effects in the other half. Then representation of the overall effect of the treatment as zero is misleading because all of the studies actually have underlying effects that are different from zero.

When a series of studies seems to have a common population effect size, there is the question of the best procedure for estimating that common effect size. All investigators seem to start by obtaining an effect size estimate for each study using Glass's estimator of effect size. Some investigators have advocated the use of a combined estimator weighted by sample size. Other investigators combine estimates from individual studies without weighting. Neither choice seems to have been supported by formal statistical reasoning.

There has not been a great deal of literature on statistical aspects of research syn-

This research was supported by the Spencer Foundation.

I thank Betsy Jane Becker for her helpful comments and for programming the simulation study reported in the article.

Requests for reprints should be sent to Larry V. Hedges, Department of Education, University of Chicago, 5835 S. Kimbark Avenue, Chicago, Illinois 60637.

From Larry V. Hedges, "Estimation of Effect Size from a Series of Independent Experiments," 92 (2) *Psychological Bulletin* 490-499 (September 1982). Copyright 1983 by the American Psychological Association. Reprinted by permission of the publisher and author.

thesis using estimates of effect size. Glass (1976, 1978) proposed estimation of effect size but presented no sampling theory for his procedures. Hedges (1981) obtained the distribution of Glass's estimator of effect size and used that distribution to show that Glass's estimator is biased. Hedges also obtained an unbiased estimator of effect size that has smaller variance than Glass's estimator.

The present article extends Hedges' results by considering the statistical problem of estimating effect size from a series of experiments. A model for the results of a series of experiments is given, and some estimators of effect size for a single experiment are discussed. A large-sample test for the equality of k effect sizes is also given. This approximate test can be used as an indication of whether it is reasonable to pool the effect size estimates from a series of studies. A procedure for pooling estimates is given, and this procedure is shown to yield a pooled estimator with the same asymptotic distribution as the maximum likelihood estimator of effect size. Hence, the pooled estimator is asymptotically efficient. The validity of the large sample results is investigated with an empirical sampling study. Finally, the methods presented in this article are applied to some data from educational psychology.

Assumptions and Model

Earlier treatments of effect size have not adequately emphasized the assumptions underlying effect size estimation and testing. Cohen (1977) proposed the measure d of effect size in connection with the t test for the difference between means. Glass (1976) proposed the quantitative synthesis of the results of a collection of experimental/control group studies by estimating d for each study and then combining the estimates across studies. The statistical analyses in such studies typically involve the use of a t or F test to test for differences between the groups. If the assumptions for the validity of the t test are met, it is possible to derive the properties of estimators of d exactly. We start by stating these assumptions explicitly.

Suppose that the data arise from a series

of k independent studies, where each study compares an experimental group (E) with a control group (C). Let $Y_{ij}{}^E$ and $Y_{ij}{}^C$ be the jth scores on the ith experiment from the experimental and control groups, respectively. Assume that for fixed i, $Y_{ij}{}^E$ and $Y_{ij}{}^C$ are normally distributed with means $\mu_i{}^E$ and $\mu_i{}^C$ and common variance $\sigma_i{}^2$, that is,

$$Y_{ij}{}^E \sim \mathcal{N}(\mu_i{}^E, \sigma_i{}^2),$$

$$j = 1, \ldots, n_i{}^E, \quad i = 1, \ldots, k,$$

and

$$Y_{ij}{}^C \sim \mathcal{N}(\mu_i{}^C, \sigma_i{}^2),$$

$$j = 1, \ldots, n_i{}^C, \quad i = 1, \ldots, k.$$

In this notation, the *effect size* for the ith study (δ_i) is defined as

$$\delta_i = \frac{\mu_i{}^E - \mu_i{}^C}{\sigma_i}, \tag{1}$$

where we use the Greek letter δ (instead of d) to denote that this effect size is a *population* parameter.

Note that the effect size δ is invariant under linear transformation of the observations. The values of the population means and the standard deviations change under linear transformations, but the effect size remains the same. This implies that if the same population of test scores is represented on two tests that are linearly equatable, the effect sizes will be identical. The virtue of effect sizes is that they are comparable even though they may be derived from different but linearly equatable measures.

Conversely, if two measures are not linearly equatable, then the same population of test scores would in general yield different effect sizes when represented on the two measures. In particular, if two tests do not measure the same construct, there is little reason to believe that effect sizes based on those two tests would be the same. The implication is that even if a treatment produces a uniform effect size on measures on one construct (such as mathematics achievement), there is little reason to expect that effect size to be the same as the effect size for studies that measure the influence of the same treatment on another construct (such as attitude).

Estimating Effect Size

The definition of effect size given in (1) above defines a population parameter δ_i in terms of other population parameters μ_i^E, μ_i^C, and σ_i. We will seldom, if ever, know the exact values of μ_i^E, μ_i^C, and σ_i; thus, we will have to *estimate* δ_i. Glass (1976) proposed a statistic g_i' to estimate δ_i by essentially replacing μ_i^E, μ_i^C, and σ_i in the definition of δ_i by their sample analogues. Specifically, Glass proposed the estimator g_i' of δ_i, where g_i' is defined by

$$g_i' = \frac{\bar{Y}_i^E - \bar{Y}_i^C}{S_i^C}, \quad i = 1, \ldots, k, \quad (2)$$

where $\bar{Y}_i^E$ and $\bar{Y}_i^C$ are the experimental and control group sample means for the ith study and S_i^C is the control group sample standard deviation. Hedges (1981) showed that under the assumptions of the previous section, the estimator (2) is biased and that a less biased estimator results when S_i^C is replaced with the usual pooled within-groups standard deviation. We denote this estimator by g_i, that is,

$$g_i = \frac{\bar{Y}_i^E - \bar{Y}_i^C}{S_i}, \quad i = 1, \ldots, k, \quad (3)$$

where S_i^2 is the pooled estimate of the variance

$$S_i^2 = \frac{(n_i^E - 1)(S_i^E)^2 + (n_i^C - 1)(S_i^C)^2}{n_i^E + n_i^C - 2}.$$

We emphasize that g_i is a *sample statistic* and therefore has a sampling distribution of its own. Our assumptions imply that g_i is distributed as $(1/\sqrt{\tilde{n}_i})$ times a noncentral t random variable with $n_i^E + n_i^C - 2$ df and noncentrality parameter $\sqrt{\tilde{n}_i}\delta_i$, where $\tilde{n}_i = n_i^E n_i^C/(n_i^E + n_i^C)$. This distribution leads immediately to exact expressions for the bias and variance of g_i, which are given in Hedges (1981). One should also note that g_i is an inference-sufficient statistic for δ_i.

An Unbiased Estimator of Effect Size

A simple unbiased estimator of δ was obtained by Hedges (1981) based on the assumptions of the previous section. The unbiased estimator g_i^U is given by

$$g_i^U = c(m)g_i, \quad (4)$$

where $m = n_i^E + n_i^C - 2$, $c(m)$ is given exactly by

$$c(m) = \frac{\Gamma(m/2)}{\sqrt{m/2}\,\Gamma[(m-1)/2]}, \quad (5)$$

$\Gamma(x)$ is the gamma function defined, for example, in Mood, Graybill, and Boes (1974), and $c(m)$ is given approximately by

$$c(m) \approx 1 - \frac{3}{4m-1}$$

It is clear that as m becomes large, g_i^U tends to g_i, so g_i is almost unbiased in large samples. Because $c(m) < 1$, the variance of the unbiased estimator g_i^U is always smaller than the variance of g_i. Hence, g_i^U has uniformly smaller mean squared error than does g_i. The exact variance of g_i^U is

$$\frac{[c(n_i^E + n_i^C - 2)]^2[n_i^E + n_i^C - 2][1 + \tilde{n}_i\delta^2]}{(n_i^E + n_i^C - 4)\tilde{n}_i}$$
$$- \delta^2, \quad (6)$$

where $\tilde{n}_i = n_i^E n_i^C/(n_i^E + n_i^C)$ and $c(m)$ is given by (5).

Asymptotic Distribution of the Unbiased Estimator

In small samples, the estimator g_i^U of effect size has a sampling distribution that is a constant times the noncentral t distribution. When the samples sizes in the experimental and control groups are large, however, the asymptotic distribution of g_i^U provides a satisfactory approximation to the exact distribution of g_i^U. The large-sample approximation is given by

$$g_i^U \sim \mathcal{N}[\delta_i, \sigma_i^2(\delta_i)], \quad (7)$$

where

$$\sigma_i^2(\delta_i) = \frac{n_i^E + n_i^C}{n_i^E n_i^C} + \frac{\delta_i^2}{2(n_i^E + n_i^C)}, \quad (8)$$

and we use the expression $\sigma_i^2(\delta_i)$ to indicate that the variance of g_i^U depends on the true effect size δ_i. This large-sample approximation is used by substituting an estimator of the effect size for δ_i in (8). In the case of a single effect size, we substitute g_i^U for δ_i in (8) to obtain an expression for the variance of g_i^U.

Testing Homogeneity of Effect Size

Before pooling estimates of effect size from a series of k studies, it is important to ask whether the studies can reasonably be described as sharing a common effect size. A statistical test for the homogeneity of effect size is formally a test of the hypothesis

$$H_0: \delta_i = \delta, \quad i = 1, \ldots, k$$

versus the alternative that at least one δ_i differs from the rest.

A large-sample (approximate) test for the equality of k effect sizes uses the test statistic

$$H = \sum_{i=1}^{k} \frac{(g_i^U - g.)^2}{\sigma_i^2(g_i^U)}, \qquad (9)$$

where $g.$ is the weighted estimator of effect size given below in (13).

The test statistic H is the sum of squares of the g_i^U about the weighted mean $g.$, where the ith square is weighted by the reciprocal of the estimated variance of g_i^U. The defining formula (9) is helpful in illustrating the intuitive nature of the statistic H, but a computational formula is more useful for actual calculation of H. The computational formula is

$$H = \sum_{i=1}^{k} \frac{(g_i^U)^2}{\sigma_i^2(g_i^U)} - \frac{\left(\sum_{i=1}^{k} \frac{g_i^U}{\sigma_i^2(g_i^U)} \right)^2}{\sum_{i=1}^{k} \frac{1}{\sigma_i^2(g_i^U)}}, \quad (10)$$

where $\sigma_i^2(\delta_i)$ is given by (8). A similar test is given by Rosenthal and Rubin (1982).

When each study has a large sample size, the asymptotic distribution of H can be used as the basis for an approximate test of the homogeneity of the δ_i. (See the Appendix.) If all the k studies have the same population effect size (i.e., if H_0 is true), then the test statistic H has an asymptotic chi-square distribution given by

$$H \sim \chi_{k-1}^2.$$

Therefore, if the obtained value of H exceeds the $100(1 - \alpha)\,\%$ critical value of the chi-square distribution with $(k - 1)\,df$, we reject the hypothesis that the δ_i are equal. If we reject this null hypothesis we may decide not to pool all of the estimates of δ because they are not estimating the same parameter.

When the sample sizes are *very* large, however, it is probably worthwhile to consider the actual variation in the values of g_i^U because rather small differences may lead to large values of the test statistic. If the g_i^U values do not differ much in an absolute sense, the investigator may elect to pool the estimates even though there is reason to believe that the underlying parameters are not identical.

Estimation of Effect Size From a Series of Homogeneous Studies

If a series of k independent studies share a common effect size δ, it is natural to estimate δ by pooling estimates from each of the studies. If the sample sizes of the studies differ, then the estimates from some (the larger) studies will be more precise than the estimates from other (smaller) studies. In this case, it is reasonable to give more weight to the more precise estimates when pooling. This leads to weighted estimators of the form

$$\sum_{i=1}^{k} w_i g_i^U, \qquad (11)$$

where $w_i > 0$, $i = 1, \ldots, k$, and $\sum_{i=1}^{k} w_i = 1$. It is easy to show that the weights that minimize the variance of (11) are given by

$$w_i = \frac{1/v_i}{\sum_{j=1}^{k} 1/v_j}, \quad i = 1, \ldots, k, \quad (12)$$

where v_i is the variance of g_i^U given in (6). The practical problem in calculating the most precise weighted estimate is that the ith weight depends on the variance of g_i^U, which in turn depends on δ.

One approach to the problem of weighting is to use weights that are based on some approximation to the v_i that does not depend on δ. This procedure results in a pooled estimator that is unbiased, but it will usually be less precise than if the optimal weights are used. For example, weights could be derived by assuming that

$$v_i = [c(n_i^E + n_i^C - 2)]^2(n_i^E + n_i^C - 2)/$$
$$\tilde{n}_i(n_i^E + n_i^C - 4).$$

The weights thus derived are only optimal if $\delta = 0$. If δ is near zero these weights will be close to optimal because v_i depends on δ^2, which will be small. If a nonzero a priori estimate of δ is available, then weights could be estimated by inserting that value of δ in expression (6) for the variance of g_i^U and using the formula (12) for w_i. In general, the result will be an unbiased pooled estimator of δ that is slightly less precise than the most precise weighted estimator.

Estimating Weights

Another approach to obtaining a weighted estimator of δ is to estimate δ and use the sample estimate of δ to estimate the weights for each study. Define the weighted estimator $g.$ by

$$g. = \frac{\sum_{i=1}^{k} \frac{g_i^U}{\sigma_i^2(g_i^U)}}{\sum_{i=1}^{k} \frac{1}{\sigma_i^2(g_i^U)}}, \qquad (13)$$

where $\sigma_i^2(\delta_i)$ is given by (8). The estimator $g.$ is therefore obtained by calculating the weights using g_i^U for δ_i in (8). Although the g_i^U are unbiased, $g.$ is not. The bias of $g.$ is small in large samples and tends to zero as the sample sizes tend to infinity.

This estimator could be modified by replacing g_i^U by $g.$ in the expression for $\sigma_i^2(g_i^U)$ and iterating. That is, calculate the estimator $g.^{(1)}$ defined by

$$g.^{(1)} = \frac{\sum_{i=1}^{k} \frac{g_i^U}{\sigma_i^2(g.)}}{\sum_{i=1}^{k} \frac{1}{\sigma_i^2(g.)}}, \qquad (14)$$

where $\sigma_i^2(\delta_i)$ is given by (8). The iterated estimator $g.^{(1)}$ will tend to be less biased than $g.$. If the effect size is homogeneous across experiments, the iteration process usually will not change the estimate very much.

The asymptotic distribution of $g.$ is easily obtained and can be used to obtain large sample confidence intervals for δ based on $g.$. The definition of "large sample" in this case is that the sample sizes n_i^E and n_i^C, $i = 1, \ldots, k$ are tending to infinity at the same rate. (See the Appendix.) The large sample approximation is

$$g. \sim \mathcal{N}[\delta, \sigma.^2(\delta)], \qquad (15)$$

where

$$\sigma.^2(\delta) = \frac{1}{\sum_{i=1}^{k} \frac{1}{\sigma_i^2(\delta)}}, \qquad (16)$$

and $\sigma_i^2(\delta)$ is given by (8). We use this large-sample approximation by substituting the (consistent) estimator $g.$ for δ in (15). A $100(1 - \alpha)\%$ asymptotic confidence interval for δ is therefore

$$g. - z_{\alpha/2}\sigma.(g.) \le \delta \le g. + z_{\alpha/2}\sigma.(g.),$$

where $z_{\alpha/2}$ is obtained from a table of the standard normal distribution. Similarly, an asymptotic test of the hypothesis that $\delta = 0$ uses the test statistic

$$z(g.) = \frac{g.}{\sigma.(g.)}.$$

If the obtained value of $z(g.)$ is larger in absolute value than the $100(1 - \alpha/2)\%$ critical value of the standard normal distribution, we reject the hypothesis that $\delta = 0$ at the $100\alpha\%$ significance level.

The formal asymptotic distribution of the iterated estimator $g.^{(1)}$ is the same as that of $g.$. We use the large-sample approximation to the distribution of $g.^{(1)}$ by substituting $g.^{(1)}$ for δ in (16). Therefore, confidence intervals and significance tests for δ based on $g.^{(1)}$ are calculated in the same way as for $g.$. The only difference when using $g.^{(1)}$ is that $g.$ is replaced by $g.^{(1)}$ wherever the former occurs.

Efficiency of the Weighted Estimator

The weighted estimators discussed in previous sections were derived by finding the expression for weights that minimize the variance of the resulting weighted estimator. One might ask whether the best (most precise) weighted estimator is the most precise in some larger class of estimators of effect size, including those that are *not* weighted linear combinations of the g_i. The answer to this question is that $g.$ is asymptotically efficient in the sense that the asymptotic variance of $g.$ is the theoretical minimum (Cramér-Rao bound). Thus, no other consistent estimator has smaller asymptotic variance. This result implies that g has the same asymptotic distribution as the maximum-likelihood estimator of δ based on k experiments.

Accuracy of the Large-Sample Approximation

The statistical procedures described in this article depend on large-sample approximations to the distributions of g_i^{U}, g, and H. Although large-sample approximations are sometimes reasonably accurate in small samples, the uncritical use of large-sample

statistical theory is unjustified. The asymptotic theory used in this article is correct for any fixed δ, but we would expect this asymptotic theory to be most accurate in small samples when δ is small. In order to evaluate the accuracy of the large-sample approximations used here, a simulation study was conducted. All the simulations described in this section are based on standard normal deviates and chi-squared random numbers generated by the International Mathematical and Statistical Libraries (1977) subroutines GGNML and GGCHS. In each simulation four representative effect sizes were used: $\delta = .25$, $\delta = .50$, $\delta = 1.00$, and $\delta = 1.50$.

Table 1

Small-Sample Accuracy of Confidence Intervals for δ Based on the Normal Approximation to the Distribution of g^{U}

Sample size $n = n^{E} = n^{C}$	Mean of g^{U}	Variance of g^{U}	Proportion of confidence intervals containing δ with nominal significance level					
			.60	.70	.80	.90	.95	.99
$\delta = .25$								
10	.252	.20631	.621	.714	.813	.910	.955	.991
20	.255	.10291	.604	.704	.806	.903	.951	.990
30	.246	.06730	.608	.708	.809	.908	.954	.989
40	.248	.05138	.601	.703	.800	.900	.950	.991
50	.250	.03946	.612	.709	.809	.904	.952	.991
100	.251	.02028	.600	.705	.808	.903	.949	.990
$\delta = .50$								
10	.504	.21386	.620	.714	.807	.906	.954	.990
20	.497	.10452	.609	.709	.807	.904	.955	.990
30	.500	.06977	.603	.699	.800	.903	.952	.990
40	.499	.05225	.599	.700	.803	.903	.952	.991
50	.496	.04194	.597	.696	.799	.904	.953	.990
100	.498	.02052	.606	.698	.799	.906	.954	.989
$\delta = 1.00$								
10	.993	.24119	.602	.703	.801	.901	.952	.992
20	.993	.11202	.609	.707	.808	.907	.955	.992
30	.993	.07754	.594	.697	.799	.897	.952	.991
40	.995	.05683	.607	.709	.805	.901	.953	.992
50	.996	.04604	.603	.706	.806	.900	.951	.989
100	1.000	.02252	.607	.702	.805	.905	.953	.990
$\delta = 1.50$								
10	1.498	.28182	.599	.696	.797	.901	.953	.990
20	1.501	.13707	.601	.697	.797	.898	.950	.989
30	1.505	.09090	.600	.699	.797	.899	.950	.991
40	1.502	.06884	.594	.693	.796	.899	.949	.990
50	1.500	.05572	.593	.691	.794	.897	.949	.991
100	1.500	.02606	.603	.705	.810	.906	.955	.990

Note. Data for $n = 100$ are based on 4,000 replications. All other figures are based on 10,000 replications.

These effect sizes were chosen because virtually all meta-analyses have found effect sizes in this range. One should be cautious, however, about extrapolating the results of this (or any) simulation beyond the actual range of parameters studied. In each simulation, the experimental and control group sample sizes were set equal, that is, $n_i^E = n_i^C$. The g_i values were generated based on the identity

$$g = X/\sqrt{S/m},$$

where X is a normal with mean δ and variance $2/n$ and S is a chi-square random variable with $m = 2n - 2$ df. The g values were then transformed into g^U values using (4).

The large-sample normal approximation (7) underlies the other large-sample approximations used in this article. The accuracy of this approximation was studied by generating g_i^U values and using the approximation (7) to construct confidence intervals. The empirical accuracy of those confidence intervals is reported in Table 1. It is clear that the large-sample approximation (7) is quite accurate for sample sizes as small as $n^E = n^C = 10$. It also appears that the accuracy of the approximation is satisfactory throughout the range of effect sizes studied.

The distributions of the weighted estimators g given in (13) and $g^{(1)}$ given in (14) were also investigated. The cases $k =$

Table 2

Small-Sample Accuracy of Confidence Intervals for δ Based on the Normal Approximation to the Distribution of g and $g^{(1)}$

	Summary of empirical proportions of confidence intervals containing δ for nominal significance level α								
	$1 - \alpha = .90$[a]			$1 - \alpha = .95$[b]			$1 - \alpha = .99$[c]		
δ	Minimum	Median	Maximum	Minimum	Median	Maximum	Minimum	Median	Maximum
			Estimator g $k = 2$						
.25	.898	.908	.920	.944	.953	.964	.989	.990	.994
.50	.891	.903	.919	.943	.954	.962	.988	.990	.995
1.00	.891	.904	.914	.946	.954	.960	.988	.991	.995
1.50	.890	.903	.917	.945	.950	.959	.988	.991	.992
			Estimator g $k = 5$						
.25	.894	.906	.922	.946	.954	.964	.987	.991	.993
.50	.894	.903	.915	.938	.950	.961	.986	.9895	.993
1.00	.883	.895	.917	.937	.947	.957	.987	.989	.994
1.50	.886	.900	.906	.941	.948	.952	.984	.991	.993
			Estimator $g^{(1)}$ $k = 2$						
.25	.893	.904	.912	.942	.951	.957	.988	.990	.992
.50	.888	.902	.912	.943	.952	.960	.987	.990	.995
1.00	.891	.901	.913	.939	.951	.957	.987	.990	.995
1.50	.884	.898	.904	.942	.947	.954	.986	.990	.993
			Estimator $g^{(1)}$ $k = 5$						
.25	.894	.902	.911	.940	.950	.959	.984	.990	.993
.50	.889	.899	.908	.936	.946	.958	.985	.988	.993
1.00	.881	.896	.911	.938	.946	.957	.985	.989	.993
1.50	.878	.896	.903	.938	.948	.959	.980	.990	.992

Note. Sample sizes for each estimate were $n_i^E = n_i^C = 10, 20, 30, 40,$ or 50. For $k = 2$, 15 combinations of sample sizes were used. For $k = 5$, 20 configurations of sample sizes were used. For each configuration of sample sizes, 2,000 replications were generated.
[a] The standard error of each estimated proportion is approximately .0067.
[b] The standard error of each estimated proportion is approximately .0049.
[c] The standard error of each estimated proportion is approximately .0022.

Table 3
Small-Sample Behavior of the Homogeneity Test Statistic H

	Summary of empirical proportions of text statistics exceeding the nominal significance level α								
	$\alpha = .10$[a]			$\alpha = .05$[b]			$\alpha = .01$[c]		
δ	Minimum	Median	Maximum	Minimum	Median	Maximum	Minimum	Median	Maximum
				$k = 2$					
.25	.082	.096	.110	.040	.048	.056	.005	.009	.012
.50	.083	.092	.114	.041	.047	.058	.007	.011	.014
1.00	.090	.098	.106	.041	.048	.056	.002	.009	.013
1.50	.093	.099	.109	.043	.049	.056	.006	.010	.016
				$k = 5$					
.25	.079	.094	.107	.035	.044	.056	.004	.008	.012
.50	.088	.096	.108	.040	.048	.057	.005	.009	.012
1.00	.083	.090	.098	.037	.046	.051	.005	.008	.014
1.50	.089	.105	.112	.041	.052	.057	.007	.010	.017

Note. Sample sizes for each estimate were $n_i^E = n_i^C = 10, 20, 30, 40,$ or 50. For $k = 2$, 15 combinations of sample sizes were used. For $k = 5$, 20 configurations of sample sizes were used. For each configuration of sample sizes, 2,000 replications were generated.
[a] The standard error of each estimated proportion is approximately .0067.
[b] The standard error of each estimated proportion is approximately .0049.
[c] The standard error of each estimated proportion is approximately .0022.

2 and $k = 5$ (two or five independent studies) were studied extensively.

For $k = 2$, all 15 possible combinations of the five sample sizes ($n_i^E = n_i^C = 10, 20, 30, 40,$ and 50) were studied. For $k = 5$, 20 different configurations of the sample sizes were studied. The most extreme configurations were $n_i^E = n_i^C = 10$ for all five estimators and $n_i^E = n_i^C = 50$ for all five estimators. A total of 2,000 replications of each sample size configuration were generated for each population effect size. The large-sample approximation was used to calculate confidence intervals for δ. Means and variances of the estimates as well as the empirical proportion of confidence intervals that contained δ were calculated for each sample size configuration for each effect size.[1] The results of these simulations suggest that the large-sample approximation to the distribution of the estimators is reasonably accurate for the range of δ examined, even when all the studies have a sample size of 10 per group. The accuracy of the approximation tends to improve as the sample sizes increase. As expected, the estimator g. has a slight negative bias, tending to underesti-

mate δ. The simulation verifies that the iterated estimator $g.^{(1)}$ is less biased than $g.$, although neither estimator is markedly superior to the other. A summary of the empirical proportions of confidence intervals that contained δ is given in Table 2.

The accuracy of the chi-square test for homogeneity of effect size was also studied. The distribution of the statistic H was studied for $k = 2$ and $k = 5$ for the same combinations of sample sizes as were used in the study of $g.$ and $g.^{(1)}$. The large sample approximation to the distribution was also fairly accurate even when $n^E = n^C = 10$. The actual significance values of H have a slight tendency to be lower than the nominal significance levels. Thus, the test for homogeneity may be slightly conservative. The large sample distribution of H is also more accurate as δ and the sample sizes increase. Table 3 is a summary of the results on the empirical distribution of H.

---

[1] A complete report of the results of the simulation study is available from the author.

Table 4
Data for the Example: The Effects of Open (O) Versus Traditional (T) Teaching on Student Curiosity

Study	n O	T	g_i^U	$\sigma_i^2(g_i^U)$	$\sigma^2(g)$	$\hat{w}_i^a$	$\hat{w}_i^b$
1	16	11	.459	.1573	.1537	.081	.082
2	30	30	.181	.0672	.0668	.190	.188
3	30	30	.521	.0689	.0668	.185	.188
4	44	40	.097	.0478	.0478	.267	.263
5	37	55	.425	.0462	.0453	.276	.279

[a] Weight based on estimating δ by g_i^U.
[b] Weight based on estimating δ by g.

Example

The techniques described here were applied to some studies in research on teaching by Hedges, Giaconia, and Gage (Note 1). Some data from five studies that examined the effects of open versus traditional teaching on student curiosity are given in Table 4. Sample sizes, the effect size estimate, and weights are given for each study. The homogeneity statistic H has the value $H = 9.02$. Comparing this value with the 95% critical value (9.49) of the chi-square distribution with 4 df, we see that we cannot reject homogeneity of effect sizes for these five studies.

The weighted estimates of δ are $g = .119$ and $g^{(1)} = .118$. A 95% confidence interval for δ based on g is

$$-.103 \leq \delta \leq .339$$

and a 95% confidence interval based on $g^{(1)}$ is

$$-.102 \leq \delta \leq .338.$$

Because these confidence intervals contain zero, we cannot reject the hypothesis that $\delta = 0$ at the $\alpha = .05$ level. This example illustrates that g and $g^{(1)}$ are usually quite similar as are confidence intervals derived from the two estimators.

Reference Note

1. Hedges, L. V., Giaconia, R. M., & Gage, N. L. *The empirical evidence on the effects of open education* (Final report of the Stanford Research Synthesis Project, Vol. 2). Stanford, Calif.: Stanford University, School of Education, 1981.

References

Cohen, J. *Statistical power analysis for the behavioral sciences* (Rev. ed.). New York: Academic Press, 1977.
Glass, G. V. Primary, secondary, and meta-analysis of research. *Educational Researcher*, 1976, *5*, 3-8.
Glass, G. V. Integrating findings: The meta-analysis of research. In L. S. Schulman (Ed.), *Review of research in education* (Vol. 5). Itasca, Ill.: Peacock, 1978.
Glass, G. V., & Smith, M. L. Meta-analysis of the relationship between class-size and achievement. *Educational Evaluation and Policy Analysis*, 1979, *1*, 2-16.
Hedges, L. V. Distribution theory for Glass's estimator of effect size and related estimators. *Journal of Educational Statistics*, 1981, *6*, 107-128.
International Mathematical and Statistical Libraries, Inc. *IMSL Library 1* (7th ed.). Houston, Tex.: Author, 1977.
Kulik, J. A., Kulik, C. C., & Cohen, P. A. A meta-analysis of outcome studies of Keller's personalized system of instruction. *American Psychologist*, 1979, *34*, 307-318.
Mood, A. M., Graybill, F. A., & Boes, D. C. *Introduction to the theory of statistics* (3rd ed.). New York: McGraw-Hill, 1974.
Rao, C. R. *Linear statistical inference and its applications.* New York: Wiley, 1973.
Rosenthal, R., & Rubin, D. B. Interpersonal expectancy effects: The first 345 studies. *Behavioral and Brain Sciences*, 1978, *3*, 377-415.
Rosenthal, R., & Rubin, D. B. Comparing effect sizes of independent studies. *Psychological Bulletin*, 1982, *92*, 500-504.
Smith, M. L., & Glass, G. V. Meta-analysis of psychotherapy outcome studies. *American Psychologist*, 1977, *32*, 752-760.

Appendix

Formal Statement of Results Used in This Paper

The distribution of H and g can be obtained as direct consequences of a theorem on the large-sample distribution of weighted estimators (see, e.g., Rao, 1973, pp. 389–390). A formal statement of the theorem requires a regularity condition that the n_i^E and n_i^C, $i = 1, \ldots, k$ tend to infinity at the same rate. The actual results used in this article follow.

Result 1

If H_0 is true, $N = \sum\limits_{i=1}^{k} (n_i^E + n_i^C)$, $\pi_i^E = n_i^E/N$, $\pi_i^C = n_i^C/N$, $i = 1, \ldots, k$, and π_i^E, π_i^C remain fixed as $N \to \infty$, then the asymptotic distribution of H given in (9) is χ^2_{k-1}.

Result 2

If $N = \sum\limits_{i=1}^{k} (n_i^E + n_i^C)$, $\pi_i^E = n_i^E/N$, $\pi_i^C = n_i^C/N$, $i = 1, \ldots, k$, and π_i^E, π_i^C remain fixed as $N \to \infty$, then the asymptotic distribution of g defined in (13) is given by

$$\sqrt{N}(g. - \bar{\delta}.) \sim \mathcal{N}(0, \bar{\sigma}.^2),$$

where

$$\bar{\sigma}.^{-2} = \sum_{i=1}^{k} \frac{1}{\bar{\sigma}_i^2(\delta_i)},$$

$$\bar{\sigma}_i^2(\delta_i) = \frac{\pi_i^E + \pi_i^C}{\pi_i^E \pi_i^C} + \frac{\delta_i^2}{2(\pi_i^E + \pi_i^C)},$$

$$\bar{\delta}. = \frac{\sum\limits_{i=1}^{k} \dfrac{\delta_i}{\bar{\sigma}_i^2(\delta_i)}}{\sum\limits_{i=1}^{k} \dfrac{1}{\bar{\sigma}_i^2(\delta_i)}}$$

A straightforward calculation shows that $\bar{\sigma}.^2$ is the minimum asymptotic variance. Write the observations of the ith study in terms of δ, a location (scale mean) parameter γ_i, and a residual ϵ, that is,

$$Y_{ij}^E = \delta\sigma_i + \gamma_i + \epsilon_{ij}^E,$$

$$j = 1, \ldots, n_i^E, \; i = 1, \ldots, k,$$

$$Y_{ij}^C = \gamma_i + \epsilon_{ij}^C, \; j = 1, \ldots, n_i^C, \; i = 1, \ldots, k,$$

where ϵ_{ij}^E and ϵ_{ij}^C are distributed independently as $\mathcal{N}(0, \sigma_i^2)$. The second derivatives of the likelihood yield a $(2k + 1) \times (2k + 1)$ matrix. The expectation of this matrix can be inverted using standard formulas for inversion of a patterned matrix. After simplification, the entry corresponding to the minimum asymptotic variance of a consistent estimator of δ is $\bar{\sigma}.^2$. Because this is also the asymptotic variance of the maximum-likelihood estimator, we deduce that g. has the same asymptotic distribution as the maximum-likelihood estimator.

12

Alternative Strategies for Combining Data from Twin Studies to Estimate an Intraclass Correlation
Some Empirical Sampling Results

Richard J. Light and Paul V. Smith

Sometimes in medical or genetic research, data are particularly precious. When data are rare, and important inferences will be made, we often need to pool the results from several studies. An example is the estimation of heritability of human intelligence from pairs of children. From studies of monozygotic (MZ) twins reared apart, geneticists have used the components of variance model of Eisenhart (1947) to estimate genetic aspects of human intelligence. In these efforts the intraclass correlation coefficient (Fisher, 1925) has generally been used to provide an estimate of the proportion of phenotypic variance in a population attributable to heredity.

In a much-quoted review of such studies, Erlenmeyer-Kimling and Jarvik (1963) summarized results from data that had been collected from various twin and sibling studies over the previous 40 years. For MZ twins reared apart, data were difficult to obtain. Only four studies exist, with a total of 122 twin pairs. Erlenmeyer-Kimling and Jarvik reported the median of the four intraclass correlations. The median has been similarly used for other pair studies, such as unrelated foster children reared together (only five such studies are known). Yet these medians comprise an integral part of estimation procedures for much subsequent research. For example, Nichols (1965), Jensen (1968, 1969), and Light and Smith (1969) use these data to fit additive models that essentially specify human intelligence as a function of a genetic component, an environmental component, and their interaction.

This work raises a question that goes far beyond these specific examples of measuring human intelligence. There are many continuous metric traits whose heritabilities are important, yet cases are infrequent. Suppose we wish therefore to combine several studies, taken at different times and locales, to develop an overall estimate of an intraclass correlation. Then we may ask what estimating procedures are most efficient for this purpose. Eaves (1969) develops sampling designs for an

From Richard J. Light and Paul V. Smith, "Alternative Strategies for Combining Data from Twin Studies to Estimate an Intraclass Correlation: Some Empirical Sampling Results," original manuscript. Copyright © 1983 by Sage Publications, Inc.

efficient selection of new samples. However, since Fisher (1925), there has been no investigation of the available pooling procedures for existing studies. In this article we report results of an empirical sampling investigation of combining twin studies, and offer researchers some operational guidelines. To do this, we compare three procedures for estimating an overall intraclass correlation:

(1) For each study, compute the intraclass correlation. Take the median of the set.
(2) For each study, compute the intraclass correlation, and apply Fisher's z-transformation. Take the mean of the transform.
(3) Compute a single intraclass correlation from the pooled raw data.

Note that the third procedure requires an investigator to have all of the original data from each study, the second requires him to know only the intraclass correlations and number of twins from each study, the first simply requires knowledge of the intraclass correlations from each study.

A BRIEF SUMMARY OF THEORETICAL RESULTS

The theoretical development of the intraclass correlation has been laid out by Pearson (1901), Harris (1913), and most extensively by Fisher (1925). We give here selected results for classes of size two (pairs) and for large populations. Extensions to classes of larger size and to finite populations are available in Fisher and in Haggard (1958), and to variable-sized classes in Kendall and Stuart (1967).

Assume n pairs of responses, each response denoted by X_{ij}, i = 1, . . . , n, and j = 1,2 within each pair. Then denoting the sample mean by mean X, the intraclass correlation is:

$$R = \sum_{i=1}^{n} (X_{i_1} - \text{mean } X) (X_{i_2} - \text{mean } X)/ns^2 \qquad [1]$$

where $s^2 = \dfrac{1}{2n} \sum_{i=1}^{n} \sum_{j=1}^{2} (X_{ij} - \text{mean } X)^2$

For samples of n pairs, a large sample approximation is available for the sampling variance of R. Letting ρ be the population intraclass correlation:

$$\text{Var}(R) = [(1 - \rho)(1 + \rho)]^2/n \qquad [2]$$

This approximation is poor as the population ρ approaches either +1 or -1. Further, the true value of ρ is seldom known in advance. Fisher introduced a transformation of R that has a sampling variance independent of population parameters.

$$z = \frac{1}{2} \left[\log(1 + R) - \log(1 - R) \right]$$ [3]

and its inverse:

$$R = (e^{2z} - 1)/(e^{2z} + 1)$$ [4]

Fisher established that R is a negatively biased estimate of ρ. If the z-transform of ρ is ζ, then the bias of an estimate of ζ is independent of all population parameters, and can be corrected by adding $C(n)$:

$$C(n) = \frac{1}{2} \ell n \left(\frac{n}{n-1} \right)$$ [5]

The z-transform has sampling variance:

$$Var(z) = \frac{1}{n - 1.5} .$$ [6]

PROCEDURES FOR COMBINING STUDIES

We consider briefly the rationale for using each of three procedures to combine twin studies.

Median Intraclass Correlation

In general the median is inefficient. For any normally distributed variable the median has an asymptotic efficiency relative to the mean of only 63.7% (Kendall and Stuart, 1967: 237). However, since the median is relatively unaffected by the behavior of values at the extreme ranges of a sample, it is sometimes used with the hope that it offers enough protection against bias due to outliers to offset its relative inefficiency. We denote the z transform of this estimate by z_m.

Mean Z

Fisher has suggested that to estimate ρ from m studies, where z_i is the z transform of the intraclass correlation R_i from the ith study, compute:

$$z_u = \frac{1}{m} \sum_{i=1}^{m} z_i$$ [7]

and then use equation 4 to transform z_u to an estimate of ρ. For varying numbers of pairs per study, n_i, make the weighted estimate:

$$z_w = \frac{1}{\sum\limits_{i=1}^{m} w_i} \sum_i w_i z_i \qquad [8]$$

where $w_i = n_i - 1.5$. If all studies are of the same size and from the same population, then z_u will have the same bias as a single study of n pairs. Its efficiency relative to a single estimate with $N = mn$ pairs approaches 100% as the number of studies increases.

Pooling the Raw Data

When raw scores from all pairs in all studies are available, a single intraclass correlation can be computed from the pooled data. Note that if the phenotypic scores are scaled differently from study to study, or if the studies cannot be viewed as different samples from a common population, then the pooled estimate should not be used. We denote the z transform of this pooled estimate by z_p.

CRITERIA FOR COMPARING ESTIMATION PROCEDURES

We use three criteria to judge a procedure. First, a procedure is preferred if it yields a less biased statistic. Let the bias of an estimate from method k, in z units, be $b_k = E(z_k) - \zeta$. z_k is the estimate from the kth procedure (that is, z_m, z_u, z_w, or z_p). Second, of two procedures leading to equally biased estimates, the one with the smallest sampling variance is preferred.

Suppose $Var(z_k)$ is the sampling variance of k. The we define the *effective sample size* for method k as:

$$v_k = \frac{1}{Var(z_k)} + 1.5 \qquad [9]$$

We define the absolute efficiency of method k as $100v_k/N$. We define the relative efficiency of method k with respect to another method of combining studies ℓ as $100v_k/v_\ell$. Finally, the two criteria above can be combined into the rule that the procedure yielding an estimate of ζ with minimum root-mean-square error is preferred.

THE NATURE OF THE COMPUTER SIMULATIONS

The simulation program was written in FORTRAN IV and run on an IBM 360/65 computer. Because of the length of the calculations, only single precision floating point arithmetic was employed. Where random numbers were required, we used versions of the uniform and normal random number generators from the IBM Scientific Subroutine Package.

Without going into the details of the computer program, we outline the steps in the simulation procedure. We are simulating a research setting in which there are m studies with n pairs of scores in each study, all drawn from a population with an intraclass correlation of ρ. Let X_{i1} and X_{i2} be the two scores for the ith pair in a study. For each pair, we draw three independent $N(0,1)$ random numbers, y_1, y_2, y_3. Then,

$$X_{il} = \sqrt{\rho}\, y_1 + \sqrt{1 - \rho}\, y_2$$

$$X_{i2} = \sqrt{\rho}\, y_1 + \sqrt{1 - \rho}\, y_3.$$

This process is repeated for all n pairs in each study. For each study, we then compute the simple intraclass correlation from its data, and then retain that value as well as the raw data. When all m studies are completed, we compute the z transforms for the median estimate z_m, the mean z estimate z_u, and the pooled estimate z_p. Finally, the entire procedure is repeated 200 times. For each of the three statistics, the means z_k and unbiased variances s_{zk}^2 of the 200 estimates are computed. We estimate the bias b_k as mean $z_k - \zeta$. We estimate the absolute efficiency of the kth procedure as $100v_k/nm$, where $v_k = (1/s_{zk}^2) + 1.5$. The computer program also allows modifications, which will be mentioned shortly.

SIMULATION RESULTS

We will discuss three cases. First, we consider studies of equal size n drawn from the same population with parameter ρ. Second, we let the study sizes, n_i, i = 1, ..., ½ m, vary. Third, we return to equal n, but permit a probability ϕ that any study will come from an outlying population with parameter ρ'.

For all cases we chose $\rho = .8$, which is in the range of the usual estimates of highly heritable traits in MZ twin studies. All our results are given in z units, rather than R units. Thus they are not a function of ρ. Readers who have an application in mind should translate our results into an expected confidence interval about their estimated ρ before deciding upon a method to combine studies.

Case 1: Equal Size Studies; No Outliers

Bias

We wish to compare the three combining procedures under various combinations of n and m. In Table 1 the columns represent m = 3, 5, 7, 9, 15, and 25. On the rows, n = 5, 10, 15, 20, 25, and 50 pairs per study. For example, the cell in the upper left gives the case of three studies, each with five pairs of subjects. Vacant cells were not simulated because of limitations on computer time. Each cell of Table 1 gives the residual bias for each of the three methods:

$$B_k = b_k + C(t) \qquad [10]$$

where $C(t)$ is Fisher's correction for bias from (5), and $t = n$ for B_m and B_u while t $= N = nm$ for B_p.

Several conclusions emerge from Table 1. The pooled estimate has consistently small bias. For $N \leqslant 30$ or $n < 10$, the pooling procedure yields substantially less bias than the other two. Elsewhere all residual biases are small, nearly always less than .02.

Efficiency

Table 2 gives the efficiencies of the three procedures. The format for Table 2 parallels that for Table 1. For the pooled estimate, we give the absolute efficiency. For the median and mean z estimates, we give the relative efficiency with respect to the pooled procedure. The random nature of the simulation process endows some sets of twins with more and others with less than the theoretically expected amount

TABLE 1   Residual Bias after Fisher's Correction in Units of z[a]

		m = 3	m = 5	m = 7	m = 9	m = 15	m = 25
n = 5	B_m	−.0429	−.0433	−.0081	−.0201	−.0037	−.0173
	B_n	−.0289	−.0397	−.0021	−.0343	−.0165	−.0240
	B_p	−.0140	−.0157	.0169	−.0070	.0076	−.0008
n = 10	B_m	−.0339	.0061	.0029	.0111	−.0090	.0015
	B_n	−.0287	.0063	−.0035	.0081	−.0077	−.0015
	B_p	−.0187	.0075	.0064	.0100	−.0038	.0012
n = 15	B_m	−.0033	−.0047	−.0102	−.0047	−.0002	
	B_n	−.0072	−.0037	−.0053	−.0032	−.0048	
	B_p	−.0068	−.0090	−.0063	−.0003	−.0025	
n = 20	B_m	.0057	.0080	−.0233	.0054		
	B_n	.0066	.0081	−.0142	.0019		
	B_p	.0081	.0077	−.0108	.0038		
n = 25	B_m	−.0179	.0068	.0051	.0038		
	B_n	−.0120	.0131	.0027	.0038		
	B_p	−.0127	.0030	.0024	.0039		
n = 50	B_m	−.0011	−.0015				
	B_n	−.0036	.0000				
	B_p	−.0034	−.0008				

NOTE: a. For combinations of fixed study size n and number of studies m.

of variation. The absolute efficiency of the pooled estimate has an expected value of 100%. Observed departures from this expected value are due solely to the simulation variance. By taking relative efficiencies most of the effects of such fluctuations are cancelled out.

Table 2 shows several effect. For m = 3, the median's efficiency exceeds the 63.7% expected from asymptotic normal theory, averaging in the mid-seventies. For m ≥ 5, n = 5, the median's efficiency is lower than expected, averaging in the mid-fifties. Elsewhere, the median has approximately its expected efficiency. The mean z procedure is always more efficient than the median, and its efficiency increases with larger n.

From the results in Tables 1 and 2 we offer the following conclusions. Pooling is always the best procedure. The mean z approach is always preferable to taking a median. When raw data cannot be found, thus eliminating the pooled estimate, the mean z approach can be used with no great cost in efficiency for n ≥ 15, and no great cost in bias for n > 5, N > 30.

We have presented the results only for m odd, with the median defined as the mid-value. For m even, several of the middle studies may be combined by taking

TABLE 2   Absolute Efficiencies of z_p, and Relative Efficiencies of z_m and z_n with Respect to z_p,[a]

		m = 3	m = 5	m = 7	m = 9	m = 15	m = 25
	z_m	71.0	58.4	57.1	56.3	52.5	56.0
n = 5	z_n	79.9	73.4	67.2	66.9	72.3	73.4
	z_p	101.4	98.4	97.1	98.6	108.1	87.6
	z_m	69.3	64.7	62.5	73.3	54.2	61.2
n = 10	z_n	92.4	90.7	84.9	90.2	82.8	81.6
	z_p	96.5	96.3	122.0	101.8	95.6	100.6
	z_m	74.7	70.3	65.4	61.6	63.3	
n = 15	z_n	93.0	91.8	92.2	90.0	95.8	
	z_p	118.4	103.3	104.2	109.3	103.2	
	z_m	82.2	74.1	69.2	69.4		
n = 20	z_n	101.8	94.4	93.5	92.7		
	z_p	88.1	107.5	117.2	111.0		
	z_m	75.7	69.0	72.3	63.3		
n = 25	z_n	96.0	98.7	97.6	97.2		
	z_p	105.7	108.9	87.1	96.6		
	z_m	73.1	58.2				
n = 50	z_n	98.1	94.6				
	z_p	117.7	97.3				

NOTE: a. For combinations of fixed study size n and number of studies m.

their mean z, or pooling, in order to estimate the median. In this case the median estimate will become more efficient, falling between the median and mean z results in Table 2. For example, when four studies are combined and the median is estimated from the mean z of the two middle studies, the median can be viewed as a Winsorized mean, and should have an efficiency relative to the mean z estimate of less than 100%, but more than 63.7%. As m increases beyond about six, however, the gain in efficiency of the median due to mid-study pooling will become very slight.

Case 2: Varying Size Studies, No Outliers

Even when the available studies are known to come from the same population, n_i usually varies. For this case we must adjust our pooling procedures, and specify the distributions from which the study sizes are drawn.

Theory and Notation

The median estimate and the pooled estimate need not be redefined. The mean z estimate now exists in a weighted and an unweighted version. Define the *weighted* mean z estimate z_w as in equation 8. In this case the z from each study is weighted by the inverse of its variance. Assume the bias correction $C(n_i)$ is exact. Then the bias of z_w would be:

$$b_w = -\frac{1}{2N - 3m} \sum_{i=1}^{m} w_i \, \ell n(n_i/[n_i - 1]) \qquad [11]$$

The unweighted mean z estimate z_u, from equation 7, would have bias:

$$b_u = -\frac{1}{2m} \sum_{i=1}^{m} \ell n(n_i/[n_i - 1]) \qquad [12]$$

For either measure, an approximate correction based on the average sample size mean n is:

$$C'(\text{mean } n) = \frac{1}{2} \ell n(\bar{n}/[\bar{n} - 1]) \qquad [13]$$

Distributions of Study Sizes

We examined three distributions for n_i: the normal, uniform, and falling ramp. All three are continuous distributions, the uniform and ramp with integer endpoints, and the normal with an integer mean. The necessarily integer n_is were secured from the uniform and ramp by truncation, and from the normal by rounding. The uniform and the normal were chosen because they are frequently encountered. The ramp reflects the rarity of suitable data for pair studies, where the availability of a sample is inversely proportional to the desired size.

The means and variances of the uniform and ramp distributions, with endpoints on integers a and b, and range $b - a = r$, are:

	continuous		truncated integer	
	n	σ_n^2	mean n	σ_n^2
Uniform	$a + \dfrac{r}{2}$	$\dfrac{r^2}{12}$	$a + \dfrac{(r-1)}{2}$	$\dfrac{(r^2-1)}{12}$
Ramp	$a + \dfrac{r}{3}$	$\dfrac{r^2}{18}$	$a + \dfrac{(2r-1)(r-1)}{6r}$	$\dfrac{(2r^2+1)(r^2-1)}{36r^2}$

The derivations of truncated integer statistics appear in the Appendix at the end of this article.

For the truncated integer distributions, not all means and variances are possible.

We therefore selected combinations of means and variances which led to close matches among the distributions. We used distributions with $n \cong 20$, 30, and 50, and $\sigma_n^2 \cong 6.7$, 14.2, 26.9, and 40.5. The effects of the three distributions, their mean n, and σ_n^2, were then examined for sets of seven studies.

Simulation Results, Bias

Table 3 gives the residual bias B_k from equation 10, after the approximate correction C'. The four values of σ_n^2 head the columns, with the three distributions given for each variance. The four B_k's appear on the rows, for each of the three values of mean n. The primary conclusion from Table 3 is that regardless of mean n, σ_n^2, or distribution of n_i, all biases are extremely small, never exceeding .02. The approximate correction in equation 13 is thus effective for mean $n \geqslant 20$.

Simulation Results, Efficiency

Table 4 has the same format as Table 3. The relative efficiencies are shown for z_m, z_w, and z_u. The absolute efficiencies are given for z_p, as before. Examination of Table 4 shows z_m to have an average efficiency of about 65% everywhere; z_w has a relative efficiency in the ninetieth percentile throughout the table, increasing slightly for larger mean n. Except for mean $n = 20$, $\sigma_n^2 \geqslant 26.9$, where z_u has much lower efficiency, z_u is nearly identical to z_w. The weighted procedure is the minimum variance estimator. The unweighted alternative departs further from this minimum as σ_n^2/mean n increases. Therefore, the drop in the relative efficiency of z_u with respect to z_w is greatest when mean n is small and σ_n^2 is large.

Combining Tables 3 and 4 leads to several conclusions. In general, the statistics z_w, z_u, and z_p have similar biases and efficiencies. The exception is when studies are small but highly variable in size. Here, z_w and z_p are preferred to z_u. Everywhere, z_m is consistently the least efficient estimate. Finally, the most important conclusion is that the distribution of n_i has no substantial effect on z_m, z_w, and z_p.

Case 3: Protection Against Outliers

An important concern when combining several studies is to avoid including data from a population other than the one intended. A median estimate is often used to give some protection against the inclusion of extreme valued outliers. Our concern in comparing the three procedures now focuses upon how the presence of outliers affects their relative performance.

To investigate outliers, the computer program was changed slightly. We returned to equal n's. Instead of drawing all studies from the same population with $\rho = .8$, a deviant value for an outlier was specified, say ρ', together with its probability, say ϕ. The program then carried out its previous routine, except that each study now had probability $(1 - \phi)$ of coming from a population with parameter ρ, and probability ϕ of coming from a population with parameter ρ'. For the simulation we chose values of $\rho' = .20$ and $.60$, and $\phi = .3$ and $1/m$.

Comparative Bias

Tables 5a and 5b give the data on residual bias, after correction, in units of z. In 5a, m = 5, 7, 9, 15 for n = 5. This sets forth the effects of the number of studies. In 5b, m = 5, while n = 5, 10, 50. This shows the effects of different size studies. In both tables the rows give the four combinations of ϕ and ρ'.

The major conclusion from both tables is that the residual bias of all three methods of combining studies is appallingly bad. The *best* performance in both tables, the behavior of the pooled estimate when there is 1 chance in 15 that any one of 15 studies to be combined, is from a deviant population with $\rho' = .6$, is $-.03$. As a heritability estimate, this would correspond to an error of more than 1% of the variance when $\rho = .8$. Errors of as high as 10% of the variance are common.

Of the three procedures, the median is generally the least biased. Of the other two, the mean z is less biased than the pooled estimate, except when n = 5 and $\rho' = .6$. This suggests the unexpected conclusion that the mean z procedure provides some protection against outlier bias for moderate and large n.

An important result appears in Table 5b. As the size of the studies increases, the bias of z_m decreases substantially, the bias of z_u decreases slowly, while the bias of z_p remains constant. Thus, for large studies the *median estimate* offers the best protection against outlier bias.

Comparative Efficiencies

Tables 6a and 6b have the same format as 5a and 5b, but give the absolute efficiencies for z_m, z_u, and z_p. It is clear that the efficiencies of all three procedures

TABLE 3   Residual Bias in Units of z[a]

		Variance of n = 6.7 Uniform Normal Ramp			Variance of n = 14.2 Uniform Normal Ramp			Variance of n = 26.9 Uniform Normal Ramp			Variance of n = 40.5 Uniform Normal Ramp		
		Uniform	Normal	Ramp	Uniform	Normal	Ramp	Uniform	Normal	Ramp	Uniform	Normal	Ramp
mean n = 20	B_m	-.0061	-.0004	-.0031	-.0085	.0103	.0054	-.0097	.0040	.0088	-.0009	.0062	-.0147
	B_w	.0014	-.0072	-.0049	-.0056	-.0013	.0008	-.0055	.0058	.0102	.0038	.0108	-.0074
	B_u	.0010	-.0084	-.0055	-.0089	-.0008	.0003	-.0062	.0037	.0087	.0004	.0007	-.0112
	B_p	.0019	-.0043	-.0032	-.0070	-.0011	.0038	-.0058	.0082	.0095	.0038	.0114	-.0069
mean n = 30	B_m	-.0020	.0075	-.0121	.0045	-.0068	.0001	-.0015	.0152	.0061	-.0037	-.0008	.0000
	B_w	.0032	.0012	-.0122	-.0003	-.0017	.0035	-.0002	.0102	.0016	.0011	-.0014	-.0011
	B_u	.0030	.0019	-.0122	-.0001	-.0020	.0029	-.0013	.0114	.0016	.0000	-.0037	-.0001
	B_p	.0033	.0034	-.0097	.0013	-.0018	.0028	-.0017	.0107	.0006	.0013	-.0006	-.0018
mean n = 50	B_m	.0036	-.0035	.0040	-.0047	.0030	-.0039	.0043	-.0061	-.0116	-.0102	-.0056	.0019
	B_w	.0002	-.0039	.0032	-.0050	.0029	-.0022	.0042	-.0051	-.0114	-.0048	-.0011	-.0023
	B_u	.0001	-.0040	.0033	-.0050	.0027	-.0019	.0040	-.0052	-.0118	-.0049	-.0010	-.0023
	B_p	-.0001	-.0037	.0034	-.0061	.0032	-.0024	.0053	-.0049	-.0110	-.0056	-.0013	-.0025

NOTE: a.   After the approximate Fisher's correction, C'; for z_m, z_w, z_u, and z_p.

225

TABLE 4 Relative Efficiency of z_m, z_w, and z_u, and Absolute Efficiency of z_p^a

	Variance of n = 6.7 Uniform Normal Ramp			Variance of n = 14.2 Uniform Normal Ramp			Variance of n = 26.9 Uniform Normal Ramp			Variance of n = 40.5 Uniform Normal Ramp		
mean n = 20												
z_m	67.3	65.7	71.7	59.2	69.0	61.3	58.8	60.0	54.5	67.5	72.1	68.1
z_w	92.5	94.4	98.3	94.9	96.6	92.2	94.0	84.4	94.6	95.1	97.3	93.9
z_u	90.3	93.5	971.1	94.9	95.6	88.0	85.1	83.2	86.5	87.7	79.4	86.4
z_p	98.6	97.1	93.6	99.6	103.1	104.4	95.4	107.3	96.4	90.5	103.5	99.8
mean n = 30												
z_m	64.6	66.2	71.3	62.	59.1	63.6	65.2	63.0	65.5	62.3	68.9	69.4
z_w	100.2	96.8	101.7	93.8	91.7	97.3	92.8	97.3	97.1	97.8	94.7	97.1
z_u	99.4	97.7	102.1	90.3	89.8	96.4	91.1	93.9	95.2	91.3	93.3	93.6
z_p	87.8	100.7	88.3	115.1	115.1	112.2	109.1	105.4	114.0	116.3	106.4	104.2
mean n = 50												
z_m	70.4	68.6	67.6	71.0	79.0	81.7	72.0	69.5	70.2	61.6	65.7	64.6
z_w	97.5	98.9	96.9	100.2	99.3	97.2	95.8	94.9	100.1	98.4	100.1	98.5
z_u	97.9	100.2	96.8	97.7	98.3	96.7	95.6	94.1	98.7	100.1	98.5	99.1
z_p	111.5	96.8	93.8	126.5	122.3	77.4	111.8	100.0	109.5	93.6	96.5	115.4

NOTE: In sets of seven studies, when the study sizes n are drawn from integer uniform, normal, and ramp distributions with the means and variances included.

TABLE 5a   Residual Bias in z After Fisher's Correction for z_m, z_n, and z_p[a]

		m = 5 n = 5	m = 7 n = 5	m = 9 n = 5	m = 15 n = 5
$\phi = 1/m$					
$\rho' = .6$	B_m	-.0923	-.0853	-.0528	-.0454
	B_n	-.1008	-.0975	-.0703	-.0592
	B_p	-.1047	-.0859	-.0576	-.0323
$\rho' = .2$	B_m	-.1705	-.0912	-.0894	-.0421
	B_n	-.2134	-.1234	-.1282	-.0604
	B_p	-.2417	-.1640	-.1378	-.0758
$\phi = .3$					
$\rho' = .6$	B_m	-.1642	-.1395	-.1562	-.1198
	B_n	-.1598	-.1578	-.1556	-.1464
	B_p	-.1355	-.1564	-.1458	-.1465
$\rho' = .2$	B_m	-.2960	-.2769	-.2248	-.2323
	B_n	-.3134	-.3039	-.2674	-.2851
	B_p	-.3624	-.3606	-.3374	-.3472

NOTE: a. Where there is a probability ϕ of a study from a population with a parameter ρ (all other studies from a population $\rho = .8$), and there are m studies of size n.

have been adversely affected by the presence of outliers. For example, we see from Table 6b that when n = 10, $\phi = .3$, and $\rho' = .2$, the median estimate is no better than a single study with one-fifth the number of cases.

Table 6a shows no important effects of different m's on the absolute efficiencies. However, the procedures behave differently depending upon the magnitude of $(\rho - \rho')$. For small $(\rho - \rho')$, z_p is clearly most efficient. However, for large $(\rho - \rho')$, z_u and z_p have similar efficiencies.

The effects in Table 6b are even more striking. As n increases, the absolute efficiencies drop precipitously. However, when n = 50, for all values of ρ' and ϕ the mean z procedure is the most efficient. Generalizing, in the presence of outliers it appears that z_u is more efficient than z_p for large n.

Comparative RMSEs

Tables 7a and 7b give root mean square errors in units of z. The format is similar to the previous tables. The most striking observation is the large size of all the RMSEs, even for studies as large as n = 50. This implies that confidence limits set up to estimate ρ will be very wide. Throughout Table 7a, which has n = 5, z_p is substantially the best procedure. However, from Table 7b we see that as n increases, z_m and z_u become superior to z_p. The general conclusion from these tables is that

TABLE 5b   Residual Bias in z After Fisher's Correction for z_m, z_n, and z_p^a

		m = 5 n = 5	m = 5 n = 10	m = 5 n = 50
$\phi = .2$				
$\rho' = .6$	B_m	−.0923	−.0883	−.0469
	B_n	−.1008	−.0939	−.0696
	B_p	−.1047	−.1076	−.0866
$\rho' = .2$	B_m	−.1705	−.1415	−.0971
	B_n	−.2134	−.1967	−.1992
	B_p	−.2417	−.2451	−.2627
$\phi = .3$				
$\rho' = .6$	B_m	−.1642	−.0788	−.0968
	B_n	−.1598	−.0883	−.1197
	B_p	−.1355	−.1078	−.1396
$\rho' = .2$	B_m	−.2960	−.2202	−.1867
	B_n	−.3141	−.2875	−.2600
	B_p	−.3624	−.3604	−.3409

NOTE: a. When there is probability ϕ of a study from a population with parameter ρ' (all other studies from a population with $\rho = .8$), and there are m studies of size n.

when studies are large, and an outlier may be present, the mean z procedure is usually best; the pooled estimate is *least* desirable.

Discussion

There is one section of Table 7b that indicates that taking the median is preferable to other procedures. This occurs when $\rho' = .2$ and $\phi = .2$. This is the case where we would expect one substantial outlier among a set of large studies. But this is also when traditional tests for outliers (Grubbs, 1969) would also be most effective in detecting the deviant study. It is at the other extreme, $(\rho - \rho')$ small, ϕ large and n small, that the exposure to risk is greatest because standard outlier tests are ineffective. We therefore conclude the discussion of outliers with two points. First, the pooled estimate is best when the exposure to risk is greatest. Second, the presence of an undetected outlier sharply reduces the efficiency of all three procedures.

SUMMARY OF FINDINGS

No Outliers Suspected

(1) When no outliers are suspected, pooling the raw data always provides the best estimate.

TABLE 6a   Absolute Efficiency of z_m, z_n, and z_p[a]

		$m = 5$ $n = 5$	$m = 7$ $n = 5$	$m = 9$ $n = 5$	$m = 15$ $n = 5$
$\phi = 1/m$					
$\rho' = .6$	z z_m	52.9	56.9	51.2	53.5
	z_n	72.6	77.3	68.0	68.5
	z_p	93.9	95.2	84.0	98.3
$\rho' = .2$	z_m	42.8	46.5	52.4	57.3
	z_n	58.3	73.0	60.5	73.1
	z_p	58.7	72.2	54.6	68.9
$\phi = .3$					
$\rho' = .6$	z_m	47.4	47.0	50.1	43.3
	z_n	65.4	64.6	66.3	57.3
	z_p	75.9	75.0	78.5	79.9
$\rho' = .2$	z_m	33.5	29.3	31.9	32.6
	z_n	52.2	45.7	50.2	45.6
	z_p	49.8	44.4	50.9	43.5

NOTE: a. Where there is a probability ϕ of a study from a population with a parameter ρ' (all other studies from a population $\rho = .8$), and there are m studies of size n.

TABLE 6b   Absolute Efficiency of z_m, z_n, and z_p^a

		$m = 5$ $n = 5$	$m = 5$ $n = 10$	$m = 5$ $n = 50$
$\phi = .2$				
$\rho' = .6$	z_m	52.9	49.1	32.7
	z_n	72.6	67.9	50.4
	z_p	93.9	71.3	42.5
$\rho' = .2$	z_m	42.8	37.1	10.1
	z_n	58.3	45.9	12.4
	z_p	58.7	32.4	8.8
$\phi = .3$				
$\rho' = .6$	z_m	47.4	51.2	24.1
	z_n	65.4	70.9	37.5
	z_p	75.9	71.3	34.4
$\rho' = .2$	z_m	33.5	20.8	5.0
	z_n	52.2	32.0	10.5
	z_p	49.8	27.8	8.3

NOTE: a. When there is probability ϕ of a study from a population with parameter ρ' (all other studies from a population with $\rho = .8$), and there are m studies of size n.

TABLE 7a   Root Mean Square Error of z_m, z_n, and z_p^a

		$m = 5$ $n = 5$	$m = 7$ $n = 5$	$m = 9$ $n = 5$	$m = 15$ $n = 5$
$\phi = 1/m$					
$\rho' = .6$	z_m	.356	.305	.271	.224
	z_n	.324	.287	.259	.222
	z_p	.247	.203	.179	.124
$\rho' = .2$	z_m	.433	.329	.292	.218
	z_n	.426	.311	.310	.220
	z_p	.380	.271	.256	.163
$\phi = .3$					
$\rho' = .6$	z_m	.415	.360	.345	.293
	z_n	.375	.346	.326	.301
	z_p	.285	.263	.232	.201
$\rho' = .2$	z_m	.558	.515	.437	.402
	z_n	.517	.491	.437	.433
	z_p	.487	.460	.410	.397

NOTE: a. When there is probability ϕ of a study from a population with parameter ρ' (all other studies from a population with $\rho = .8$), and there are m studies of size n.

TABLE 7b   Root Mean Square Error of z_m, z_n, and z_p^a

		$m = 5$ $n = 5$	$m = 5$ $n = 10$	$m = 5$ $n = 50$
$\phi = .2$				
$\rho' = .6$	z_m	.356	.251	.125
	z_n	.324	.228	.120
	z_p	.247	.207	.132
$\rho' = .2$	z_m	.433	.310	.231
	z_n	.426	.329	.279
	z_p	.380	.365	.344
$\phi = .3$				
$\rho' = .6$	z_m	.415	.242	.168
	z_n	.375	.222	.166
	z_p	.285	.207	.178
$\rho' = .2$	z_m	.558	.432	.358
	z_n	.517	.429	.336
	z_p	.487	.466	.412

NOTE: a. When there is probability ϕ of a study from a population with parameter ρ' (all other studies from a population with $\rho = .8$), and there are m studies of size n.

(2) When the total number of pairs in all studies to be combined exceeds 30, the mean z estimate can be substituted for the pooled estimate with little loss in efficiency.

(3) The use of the median offers no advantage in either efficiency or protection against bias.

(4) Regardless of the range of study sizes, the approximate correction for bias C' works well.

(5) When study sizes vary, the unweighted mean z estimate can be substituted for the weighted version if the average size exceeds 30, or if the variance in sizes is small.

Outliers Suspected

(1) Regardless of the nature of the suspected outlier, when studies are small ($n < 10$) the pooled estimate should be used.

(2) For larger study sizes, the mean z is best, except when there is a small probability of a large outlier.

(3) When there is a small probability of a large outlier (among large studies), the median offers the best protection.

(4) But in general, the presence of outliers greatly reduces the efficiency of all methods of combining studies.

APPENDIX

The mean and variance of the discrete uniform distribution are known (Beyer, 1968: 19). Although simple, the discrete ramp statistics are not available. We derive these statistics first for the continuous case, and then for the integer case.

Let a, b be the integer endpoints of the falling ramp, with range $r = b - a$. Translate a to the origin (for convenience) and the density is as shown in Figure A1. The ordinate at point x equals $h(1 - \frac{x}{r})$. But since $\frac{1}{2}hr = \int_0^r f(x)dx = 1$, then $h = \frac{2}{R}$, and

$$f(x) = \frac{2(r - x)}{r^2} \qquad [A1]$$

Integrating with respect to x' gives the cumulative distribution,

$$F(x) = \int_0^x \frac{2(r - x')}{r^2} dx' = \frac{x(2r - x)}{r^2} \qquad [A2]$$

For the mean in the continuous case:

$$E(x) = \int_0^r x'f(x')dx' = \int_0^r x' \frac{2(r - x')}{r^2} dx' = \frac{r}{3} \qquad [A3]$$

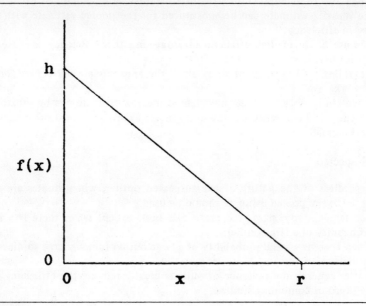

Figure A1

For the variance in the continuous case:

$$\text{Var}(x) = \int_0^r f(x')\, (x' - E(x))^2 \, dx' = \int_0^r \frac{2(r - x')}{r^2} \, (x'^2 - \frac{2}{3}rx' + \frac{r^2}{9})dx'$$

$$= \frac{r^2}{18} \tag{A4}$$

For the integer case, let $i = 1, 2, \ldots, r$, and define the probability mass function:

$$C(i) = P(x: i - 1 \leqslant x \leqslant i) = F(i) - F(i - 1) \tag{A5}$$

Then, by equation A2,

$$C(i) = \frac{i(2r - i)}{r^2} - \frac{(i - 1)(2r - i + 1)}{r^2} = \frac{2(r - i) + 1}{r^2} \tag{A6}$$

Since the values of the variable are secured by truncation from the continuous ramp, the value $v(i)$ in the interval $(i - 1)$ to i, equals $i - 1$. (We are using the fact that the original endpoints a, b were integers.) Writing x^* for the truncated integer ramp random variable, we find the mean:

$$E(x^*) = \sum_{i = 1}^r v(i)C(i) = \sum_{i = 1}^r (i - 1) \frac{(2(r - i) + 1)}{r^2}$$

$$= \frac{(2r - 1)(r - 1)}{6r} = \frac{r}{3} + \frac{1}{6r} - \frac{1}{2} \tag{A7}$$

For the variance:

$$Var(x^*) = \sum_{i=1}^{r} v(i)^2 C(i) - [E(x^*)]^2 = \sum_{i=1}^{r} (i-1)^2 \frac{(2(r-i)+1)}{r^2} - [E(x^*)]^2$$

$$= \frac{(2r^2+1)(r^2-1)}{36r^2} = \frac{r^2}{18} - \frac{1}{36r^2} - \frac{1}{36}.$$
                                                                    [A8]

The original coordinates are restored by adding "a" to $E(x)$ and $E(x^*)$.

REFERENCES

BEYER, W. H. (1968) Handbook of Tables for Probability and Statistics. Cleveland: Chemical Rubber.

EAVES, L. J. (1969) "The genetic analysis of continuous variation: a comparison of experimental designs applicable to human data. British J. of Mathematical and Statistical Psychology 22: 131-147.

EISENHART, C. (1947) "The assumptions underlying the analysis of variance." Biometrics, 3: 1.

ERLENMEYER-KIMLING, L. and L. F. JARVIK (1963) Genetics and intelligence: a review. Science 142: 1477-1479.

FISHER, R. A. (1925) Statistical Methods for Research Workers. Edinburgh: Oliver & Boyd.

GRUBBS, F. E. (1969) "Procedures for detecting outlying observations in samples." Technometrics 11, 1: 1-21.

HAGGARD, E. A. (1958) Intraclass Correlations and the Analysis of Variance. New York: Dryden.

HARRIS, J. A. (1913) "On the calculating of intraclass and interclass coefficients of correlation from class moments when the number of possible combinations is large." Biometrika 9: 446-472.

JENSEN, A. R. (1969) How much can we boost IQ and scholastic achievement? Harvard Education Rev. 39, 1: 1-123.

——— (1968) "Social class, race, and genetics: implications for education." Amer. Education Research J. 5: 1-42.

KENDALL, M. G. and A. STUART (1967) The Advanced Theory of Statistics, Vol. 1. London: Griffin.

LIGHT, R. J. and P. SMITH (1969) "Social allocation models of intelligence." Harvard Education Rev. 39, 3: 484-510.

NICHOLS, R. C. (1965) "The inheritance of general and specific ability." National Merit Scholarship Corporation Research Reports 1: 1-9.

PEARSON, K. et al. (1901) "Mathematical contributions to the theory of evolution. IX: On the principle of homotyposis and its relation to heredity, to variability of the individual, and to that of race. Part I: Homotyposis in the vegetable kingdom." Philosophical Transactions of the Royal Society, Series A, 197: 285-379.

13

Comparing Effect Sizes of Independent Studies

Robert Rosenthal and Donald B. Rubin

This article presents a general set of procedures for comparing the effect sizes of two or more independent studies. The procedures include a method for calculating the approximate significance level for the heterogeneity of effect sizes of studies and a method for calculating the approximate significance level of a contrast among the effect sizes. Although the focus is on effect size as measured by the standardized difference between the means (d) defined as $(M_1 - M_2)/S$, the procedures can be applied to any measure of effect size having an estimated variance. This extension is illustrated with effect size measured by the difference between proportions.

In a previous article (Rosenthal & Rubin, 1979) we presented methods for comparing two or more statistical significance (p) levels based on independent studies. These methods were not designed to compare the magnitudes of experimental effects. Nevertheless, because of the relationship between significance levels and effect sizes when the sample sizes of the experiments are kept constant, the comparison of ps across experiments can in many cases be thought of as rough comparisons of effect sizes across experiments.

The purpose of this article is to present procedures for directly comparing, by approximate significance levels, the effect sizes from two or more independent studies when (a) the effect sizes are measured by the standardized difference between the means (d) defined as $(M_1 - M_2)/S$ (Cohen, 1977; Glass, 1980), (b) a set of obtained effect sizes is to be compared with a particular set of predicted effect sizes (i.e., when a contrast is to be computed among the obtained effect sizes), and (c) effect sizes are being measured by some measure other than d. Related work includes Hsu (1980), which presents

Preparation of this article was supported in part by the National Science Foundation. The order of authors was determined alphabetically.

Requests for reprints should be sent to Robert Rosenthal, Department of Psychology and Social Relations, Harvard University, 33 Kirkland Street, Cambridge, Massachusetts 02138.

a formula for comparing the effect sizes of two studies measured by d, a formula that is appropriate only when d is small and sample sizes are large; Hedges (1981), which displays the distribution of d under normality; and Hedges (1982), which extends Hedges's earlier work and presents supporting simulation results.

Comparing Many Studies

For Result 1 we suppose that there are K experiments and so let the index j run from 1 to K.

Result 1

Let the d_j be the effect sizes d, and let

$$\frac{1}{w_j} = \left(1 + \frac{t_j^2}{2v_j}\right)\bigg/ f_j$$

be the estimated variance of d_j, where $f_j = n_{1j} n_{2j}/(n_{1j} + n_{2j})$, that is, half the harmonic mean of the two sample sizes in the two conditions in the jth experiment; $v_j = (n_{1j} + n_{2j} - 2)$, that is, the df in the jth study; and t_j is the t statistic testing the hypothesis of no effect in the jth study. Then for modestly large sample sizes,

$$\sum_{j=1}^{K} w_j [d_j - (\sum_{j=1}^{K} w_j d_j)/\sum_{j=1}^{K} w_j]^2$$

$$= \sum_{j=1}^{K} w_j (d_j - \bar{d})^2$$

From Robert Rosenthal and Donald B. Rubin, "Comparing Effect Sizes of Independent Studies," 92 (2) *Psychological Bulletin* 500-504 (September 1982). Copyright 1982 by the American Psychological Association. Reprinted by permission of the publisher and author.

is approximately distributed as χ^2 with $K - 1$ df, where

$$\bar{d} = \sum_{j=1}^{K} w_j d_j / \sum_{j=1}^{K} w_j \text{ is the weighted mean } d.$$

Hedges (1982) presents the same χ^2 test statistic, which is a generalization of one presented in Snedecor and Cochran (1980, p. 187). Under normality, analytic results presented in our Appendix and simulation results presented by Hedges suggest that this approximation will be adequate in most practical applications. The results in our Appendix, however, suggest that the approximation will be less accurate when sample sizes are small and t statistics are large.

Example 1

Table 1 shows the results of four studies of the effects of teachers' expectations on pupils' gains in intellectual performance (Rosenthal & Rubin, 1978, p. 383). Our question is whether the four effect sizes, d, differ significantly from one another. The weighted mean

$$\bar{d} = \sum_{j=1}^{K} w_j d_j / \sum_{j=1}^{K} w_j$$

$$= [.93(3.85) + 1.64(2.34) + 2.90(.47)$$

$$+ 2.26(1.48)]/7.73 = 1.57.$$

Then, using Result 1 we have

$$.93(3.85 - 1.57)^2 + 1.64(2.34 - 1.57)^2$$

$$+ 2.90(.47 - 1.57)^2 + 2.26(1.48 - 1.57)^2$$

$$= 9.33,$$

which is referred to the distribution of χ^2 with $K - 1 = 3$ df. For the four ds of Table 1, we found p to be .025. We conclude that the four effect sizes of Table 1 are unlikely to have been drawn by random sampling from a single population with a mean estimated by our mean d of 1.57 (i.e., the four obtained ds differ from one another more than we expect from sampling error). Note the similarity of that conclusion to that from the test of significance levels for the same data presented in Rosenthal and Rubin (1979), that is, $p = .015$. This result supports the contention that in some circumstances

Table 1
Example of Comparing Four Effect Sizes

Grade level in study[a]	t	$\dfrac{M_1 - M_2}{S}$	f[b]	w[c]	Linear λ
2	6.67	3.85	3	.93	3
3	4.06	2.34	3	1.64	1
4	.82	.47	3	2.90	-1
5	2.57	1.48	3	2.26	-3

[a] $n_1 = n_2 = 6$ for all studies.
[b] $f = n_1 n_2 / (n_1 + n_2)$.
[c] $w = f \Big/ \left[1 + \dfrac{t^2}{2(n_1 + n_2 - 2)} \right]$

with similar sizes of studies, comparisons of p values can be considered to be rough comparisons of effect sizes.

Contrasts in the Studies

Although we now know how to answer the broad question of the significance of the differences among a collection of ds, we may often be able to ask a more focused and more useful question. For the four studies of Table 1, for example, we are far more interested in whether larger effect sizes are found at lower grade levels. Result 2 handles such questions.

Result 2

Suppose $\sum_{j=1}^{K} \lambda_j d_j = 0$, where $\sum_{j=1}^{K} \lambda_j = 0$. Then, for modestly large sample sizes,

$$\sum_{j=1}^{K} \lambda_j d_j / [\sum_{j=1}^{K} \lambda_j^2 / w_j]^{1/2}$$

is approximately distributed as a standard normal deviate. (See the Appendix for discussion of this approximation.)

Example 2

The column labeled Linear λ of Table 1 gives the weights of a linear contrast to address the question of whether larger effect sizes (ds) are found more often at lower grade levels. The analysis shows a clear linear trend for younger children to show larger

Table 2
Example of Comparing a Set of Differences Between Proportions

Study	$N = (n_1 + n_2)$	$d' = p_1 - p_2$	$\dfrac{1}{w'} = \text{Var}(p_1 - p_2)^a$	w'	Linear λ
1	30	.70	.017	58.8	3
2	45	.45	.018	56.4	1
3	20	.10	.050	20.2	−1
4	25	−.15	.039	25.6	−3

^{a} Estimated by $[p_1(1 - p_1)/n_1] + [p_2(1 - p_2)/n_2]$; to obtain an expression that depends only on total sample size N and effect size d', we approximated this expression by $(1 - d'^2)/N$, which holds exactly when p_1 and p_2 are the same amount above and below .5 and $n_1 = n_2$.

effects of teacher expectations:

$$[(3)3.85 + (1)2.34$$

$$+ (-1).47 + (-3)1.48] \Bigg/$$

$$\left(\frac{3^2}{.93} + \frac{1^2}{1.64} + \frac{-1^2}{2.90} + \frac{-3^2}{2.26} \right)^{1/2}$$

$$= 2.35 = Z, \quad p = .0094 \text{ (one-tailed)}.$$

Again notice the rough similarity of conclusion to that resulting from the test of p values for the same data presented in Rosenthal and Rubin (1979), that is, $p = .006$.

We now know that the four effect sizes (ds) of Table 1 differ among themselves, $\chi^2(3) = 9.33$, $p = .025$, and that there is a linear trend for the ds to be related to grade level, $Z = 2.35$, $p = .0094$. Because the 3 df χ^2 of 9.33 is the sum of (a) the 1 df χ^2 of 5.52 corresponding to the linear trend and (b) an independent 2 df χ^2 corresponding to deviations from the linear trend, the difference $(9.33 - 5.52) = 3.81$ is distributed as χ^2 with 2 df. This value of χ^2 indicates no strongly significant departure from linearity ($p = .149$); studying the source of this curvature is beyond the scope of this article because of the nonorthogonality arising from the unequal w_j.

Other Measures of Effect Size

When measures of effect size other than d are employed, we use the same formulas modified so that $1/w_j$ is replaced by the variance of the effect size. For example, suppose the effect size is the difference between two proportions $p_{1j} - p_{2j}$. Then the variance of this difference is estimated by $[p_{1j}(1 - p_{1j})/$

$n_{1j}] + [p_{2j}(1 - p_{2j})/n_{2j}]$ as long as n_{ij} is not too small and p_{ij} is not too close to zero or one. A conservative procedure when n_{1j} is small is to replace $p_{ij}(1 - p_{ij})$ by .25, its maximal value.

Table 2 presents an example that uses the differences between proportions as estimated effect sizes. We call the difference between two proportions d' to distinguish it from d, the standardized differences between means of Table 1. Then the weighted mean difference between proportions d' is given by

$$\bar{d}' = \sum_{j=1}^{K} w'_j d'_j \bigg/ \sum_{j=1}^{K} w'_j ,$$

where w'_j is the reciprocal of the variance of d'_j. For the data of Table 2 our weighted mean d' is

$$[58.8(.70) + 56.4(.45)$$

$$+ 20.2(.10) + 25.6(-.15)]/$$

$$(58.8 + 56.4 + 20.2 + 25.6) = .40.$$

Then, using Result 1 we have

$$58.8(.70 - .40)^2 + 56.4(.45 - .40)^2$$

$$+ 20.2(.10 - .40)^2 + 25.6(-.15 - .40)^2$$

$$= 15.00,$$

which is referred to the distribution of χ^2 with $K - 1 = 3$ df. For the four differences between proportions of Table 2, we found p to be .0018. We conclude that the four differences between proportions of Table 2 are unlikely to have been drawn by random sampling from a single population with a mean estimated by our mean d' of .40.

The four studies of Table 2 have been shown to be significantly heterogeneous, but we can often do much better than asking so unfocused a question as to whether there are some differences among a set of effect sizes. Suppose, for example, that Studies 1–4 differed among themselves in the age level of the subjects of the experiments, with subjects increasing in age linearly from Studies 1 to 4. We might then want to ask whether the effect size decreases linearly with the age of subjects. We use Result 2 to address this question:

$$[(3).70 + (1).45 + (-1).10 + (-3)-.15] \Big/$$

$$\left[\frac{3^2}{58.8} + \frac{1^2}{56.4} + \frac{-1^2}{20.2} + \frac{-3^2}{25.6} \right]^{1/2}$$

$$= 3.83 = Z, \quad p = .000063 \text{ (one-tailed)}.$$

As we showed in Example 2, we can test for curvilinearity in the relationship between age and effect size by subtracting the $\chi^2(1) = Z^2$ for linear trend ($3.83^2 = 14.67$) from the overall $\chi^2(3)$ of 15.00. The remainder (.033) is distributed as χ^2 with 2 df. In this case, then, χ^2 is so small ($p = .85$) that we have no reason to suspect curvilinearity.

Conclusion

In this article we have shown the general principle of how to calculate the approximate significance of the heterogeneity of effect sizes for two or more independent studies for any type of effect size assuming estimates of its variance are available. In addition, we hope to have encouraged the use of more focused questions in making comparisons among a set of effect sizes by showing how to calculate the significance of contrasts.

References

Cohen, J. *Statistical power analysis for the behavioral sciences.* (Rev. ed.) New York: Academic Press, 1977.

Glass, G. V. Summarizing effect sizes. In R. Rosenthal (Ed.), *New directions for methodology of social and behavioral science: Quantitative assessment of research domains.* San Francisco, Calif.: Jossey-Bass, 1980.

Hedges, L. V. Distribution theory for Glass's estimator of effect size and related estimators. *Journal of Educational Statistics,* 1981, *6,* 107–128.

Hedges, L. V. Estimation of effect size from a series of independent experiments. *Psychological Bulletin,* 1982, *92,* 490–499.

Hsu, L. M. Tests of differences in *p* levels as tests of differences in effect sizes. *Psychological Bulletin,* 1980, *88,* 705–708.

Johnson, N. L., & Kotz, S. *Discrete distributions.* Boston: Houghton-Mifflin, 1969.

Johnson, N. L., & Kotz, S. *Continuous univariate distributions in statistics* (Vol. 2). Boston: Houghton-Mifflin, 1970.

Rosenthal, R., & Rubin, D. B. Interpersonal expectancy effects: The first 345 studies. *Behavioral and Brain Sciences,* 1978, *3,* 377–386.

Rosenthal, R., & Rubin, D. B. Comparing significance levels of independent studies. *Psychological Bulletin,* 1979, *86,* 1165–1168.

Snedecor, G. W., & Cochran, W. G. *Statistical methods* (7th ed.). Ames, Iowa: Iowa State University Press, 1980.

(Appendix follows on next page)

Appendix: Technical Comments

For normal data, the effect size estimate d_j may be written as $t_j/\sqrt{f_j}$, where t_j is the associated t statistic; t_j has a noncentral t distribution with $v_j = n_{1j} + n_{2j} - 2\ df$ and noncentrality parameter $T_j = \Delta_j\sqrt{f_j}$, where $\Delta_j = (\mu_{1j} - \mu_{2j})/\sigma_j$ is the population parameter being estimated by d_j; T_j is the population quantity being estimated by t_j. Consider fixed T_j and fixed n_{1j}/n_{2j}, and let v_j go to infinity; that is, consider a sequence of bigger and bigger experiments with constant ratio of numbers of experimental to control units where the power is effectively remaining constant. These asymptotics are relevant to practice because small studies are usually conducted when relatively big effect sizes are of concern, whereas large studies are usually conducted to detect smaller effect sizes. As $v_j \to \infty$, the distribution of $t_j \to N(T_j, 1)$, so the results in this article hold in the limit. To study how well the results might hold in practice, we consider large but not infinite v_j.

Expressions in Johnson and Kotz (1970, p. 204) show that, for large v_j, the expected value of t_j is $\left(1 + \dfrac{3}{4v_j}\right)T_j$, the variance of t_j is $1 + T_j^2/(2v_j)$, and the skewness-moment ratio of t_j is $T_j(3 - T_j^2/v_j)/v_j$. Hence, for large v_j

$$E(d_j) = \left(1 + \frac{3}{4v_j}\right)T_j\bigg/\sqrt{f_j}$$

$$V(d_j) = \left(1 + \frac{T_j^2}{2v_j}\right)\bigg/f_j$$

$$S(d_j) = \frac{T_j}{v_j\sqrt{f_j}}\left(3 - \frac{T_j^2}{v_j}\right).$$

Because $E(d_j) = [1 + 3/(4v_j)]\Delta_j$, as long as each v_j is larger than, say, 10, the bias of d_j for estimating Δ_j is of little consequence, being less than 8%; furthermore, if all studies have approximately the same v_j, the bias of d_j is of little consequence for comparing two studies or comparing many by χ^2 because the bias will be the same for all studies under the hypothesis of constant effect size. Hence, d_j is effectively unbiased for Δ_j.

With the observed value of t_j substituted for T_j, $V(d_j)$ is the expression used for the variance of d_j in our results. Hsu's (1980) expression for the variance of d_j (i.e., $1/f_j$) should be used only when the squared t statistic, t_j^2, is substantially less than $2v_j$ (e.g., $t_j^2 < v_j/5$); in large studies this will usually hold because very large t statistics for comparisons of primary interest are unusual.

The quantity $S(d_j)$ will usually be near zero even with moderate sample sizes unless the t statistics are extremely large relative to the sample sizes. Consider Table 1, which presents four very small studies with two extremely significant results; the four values of $S(d_j)$ with the values of t_j substituted for T_j are $-.56$, $.32$, $.13$, and $.35$. To judge how skewed these distributions are, consider the binomial distribution, which has skewness-moment ratio $(1 - 2p)[Np(1 - p)]^{-1/2}$ (Johnson & Kotz, 1969, p. 52). A skewness of $-.56$ corresponds roughly to $p = .8$ and $N = 7$, so using the normal approximation in the worst case of the extreme data of Table 1 appears to be about as bad as using the normal approximation for the mean of a binomial distribution when there are five or six successes out of seven trials. The skewness for the two highly significant studies in Table 1 correspond roughly to binomial skewness with four successes out of six trials.

A full study of the consequences of using the approximation

$$d_j \sim N\left[\Delta_j, \left(1 + \frac{T_j^2}{2v_j}\right)\bigg/f_j\right]$$

is beyond the scope of this article and of Hedges (1982) as well because it would investigate sensitivity to nonnormality as well as behavior in small samples. Of course, there are many useful test statistics, like the ones presented here, which can be shown to perform well in large and moderate normal samples, even though their behavior in small or nonnormal samples is not fully understood.

14

A Simple, General Purpose Display of Magnitude of Experimental Effect

Robert Rosenthal and Donald B. Rubin

We introduce the binomial effect size display (BESD), which is useful because it is (a) easily understood by researchers, students, and lay persons; (b) widely applicable; and (c) conveniently computed. The BESD displays the change in success rate (e.g., survival rate, improvement rate, etc.) attributable to a new treatment procedure. For example, an r of .32, the average size of the effect of psychotherapy, is said to account for "only 10% of the variance"; however, the BESD shows that this proportion of variance accounted for is equivalent to increasing the success rate from 34% to 66%, which would mean, for example, reducing an illness rate or a death rate from 66% to 34%.

Traditionally, behavioral researchers have concentrated on reporting significance levels of experimental effects. Recent years, however, have shown a welcome increase in emphasis on reporting the magnitude of experimental effects obtained (Cohen, 1977; Fleiss, 1969; Friedman, 1968, Glass, Note 1, Hays, 1973; Rosenthal, 1978; Rosenthal & Rubin, 1978; Smith & Glass, 1977).

Despite the growing awareness of the importance of estimating sizes of effects along with estimating the more conventional levels of significance, there is a problem in interpreting various effect size estimators such as the Pearson r. For example, we found experienced behavioral researchers and experienced statisticians quite surprised when we showed them that the Pearson r of .32 associated with a coefficient of determination (r^2) of only .10 was the correlational equivalent of increasing a success rate from 34% to 66% by means of an experimental treatment procedure; for example, these values could mean that a death rate under the control condition is 66% but is only 34% under the experimental condition. We believe (Rosenthal & Rubin, 1979) that there

may be a widespread tendency to underestimate the importance of the effects of behavioral (and biomedical) interventions (Mayo, 1978; Rimland, 1979) simply because they are often associated with what are thought to be low values of r^2.

The purpose of the present article is to introduce an intuitively appealing general purpose effect size display whose interpretation is perfectly transparent: the binomial effect size display (BESD). In no sense do we claim to have resolved the differences and controversies surrounding the use of various effect size estimators (e.g., Appelbaum & Cramer, 1974). Our display is useful because it is (a) easily understood by researchers, students, and lay persons; (b) applicable in a wide variety of contexts; and (c) conveniently computed.

The question addressed by BESD is What is the effect on the success rate (e.g., survival rate, cure rate, improvement rate, selection rate, etc.) of the institution of a certain treatment procedure? It displays the change in success rate (e.g., survival rate, cure rate, improvement rate, selection rate, etc.) attributable to a certain treatment procedure. An example shows the appeal of our procedure.

In their meta-analysis of psychotherapy outcome studies, Smith and Glass (1977) summarized the results of some 400 studies. An eminent critic stated that the results of their analysis sounded the "death knell" for psychotherapy because of the modest size of

Order of authors was determined alphabetically. Preparation of this paper was supported in part by the National Science Foundation.

Requests for reprints should be sent to Robert Rosenthal, Department of Psychology and Social Relations, Harvard University, William James Hall, 33 Kirkland Street, Cambridge, Massachusetts 02138.

From Robert Rosenthal and Donald B. Rubin, "A Simple, General Purpose Display of Magnitude of Experimental Effect," 74(2) *Journal of Educational Psychology* 166-169 (April 1982). Copyright © 1982 by the American Psychological Association. Reprinted by permission of the publisher and authors.

Table 1
The Binomial Effect Size Display: An Example "Accounting for Only 10% of the Variance"

Condition	Treatment outcome		
	Alive	Dead	Σ
Treatment	66	34	100
Control	34	66	100
Σ	100	100	200

the effect (Rimland, 1979). This modest effect size was calculated to be equivalent to an r of .32 accounting for "only 10% of the variance" (p. 192).

Table 1 is the BESD corresponding to an r of .32 or an r^2 of .10. The table shows clearly that it is absurd to label as "modest indeed" (Rimland, 1979, p. 192) an effect size equivalent to increasing the success rate from 34% to 66% (e.g., reducing a death rate from 66% to 34%).[1]

Table 2 shows systematically the increase in success rates associated with various values of r^2 and r. Even so small an r as .20, accounting for only 4% of the variance, is associated with an increase in success rate from 40% to 60%, such as a reduction in death rate from 60% to 40%. The last column of Table 2 shows that the difference in success rates is identical to r. Consequently the experimental success rate in the BESD is computed as $.50 + r/2$, whereas the control group success rate is computed as $.50 - r/2$. Cohen (1965) and Friedman (1968) have

Table 2
Binomial Effect Size Displays Corresponding to Various Values of r^2 and r

r^2	r	Success rate increased		Difference in success rates
		From	To	
.01	.10	.45	.55	.10
.04	.20	.40	.60	.20
.09	.30	.35	.65	.30
.16	.40	.30	.70	.40
.25	.50	.25	.75	.50
.36	.60	.20	.80	.60
.49	.70	.15	.85	.70
.64	.80	.10	.90	.80
.81	.90	.05	.95	.90
1.00	1.00	.00	1.00	1.00

Table 3
Computation of r From Common Test Statistics

Test statistic	r^a given by
t	$\sqrt{\dfrac{t^2}{t^2 + df}}$
F^b	$\sqrt{\dfrac{F}{F + df \text{ (error)}}}$
$\chi^{2,c}$	$\sqrt{\dfrac{\chi^2}{N}}$

[a] The sign of r should be positive if the experimental group is superior to the control group and negative if the control group is superior to the experimental group.
[b] Used only when df for numerator = 1 as in the comparison of two group means or any other contrast.
[c] Used only when df for χ^2 = 1.

useful discussions of computing the r associated with a variety of test statistics, and Table 3 gives the three most frequently used equivalences.

We propose that the reporting of effect sizes can be made more intuitive and more informative by using the BESD. It is our belief that the use of the BESD to display the increase in success rate due to treatment will more clearly convey the real world importance of treatment effects than do the commonly used descriptions of effect size based on the proportion of variance accounted for. The BESD is most appropriate when the variances within the two conditions are similar, as they are assumed to be whenever we compute the usual t test.

It might appear that the BESD can be

[1] To show how r and r^2 are obtained from Table 1 we note that from Table 3 we have

$$r = \sqrt{\frac{\chi^2(1)}{N}}$$

and

$$\chi^2(1) = \frac{(AD - BC)^2 N}{(A + B)(C + D)(A + C)(B + D)}$$
$$= \frac{(66^2 - 34^2)^2\, 200}{(100)(100)(100)(100)}$$
$$= 20.48$$

so

$$r = \sqrt{\frac{20.48}{200}} = .32$$

and $r^2 = .10$.

Table 4

Effects on Correlation Coefficients of Dichotomizing Normally or t(3) Distributed Variables

Continuous	Dichotomized	
ρ	ϕ^a	ϕ^b
.05	.04	.06
.10	.08	.13
.15	.12	.19
.20	.16	.25
.25	.20	.31
.30	.25	.38
.35	.29	.44
.40	.34	.50
.45	.39	.55
.50	.44	.61
.55	.49	.66
.60	.55	.72
.65	.61	.76
.70	.67	.81
.75	.74	.86
.80	.82	.90
.85	.89	.93
.90	.96	.96
.95	.998	.99

[a] Assumes scores to be normally distributed within treatment conditions.
[b] Assumes scores to be t distributed ($df = 3$) within treatment conditions.

employed only when the outcome variable is dichotomous and the mean outcome in one group is the same amount above .5 as the mean outcome in the other group is below .5. Actually, the BESD is often a realistic representation of the size of treatment effect when the variances of the outcome variable are approximately the same in the two approximately equal sized groups, as is commonly the case in educational and psychological studies. The following technical discussion supports this position.

Suppose Y is an outcome variable with the same variance in two treatment groups, which are assumed to be of equal size. If Y is binomial, with the same variance in each treatment group, then in one group the mean is p and in the other group the mean is $(1 - p)$, just as we have assumed in the BESD. Also, suppose that Y is either (a) symmetrically distributed in each group (e.g., normally distributed), or (b) asymmetrically distributed with opposite shape in the groups (e.g., binomial with mean p in one group and mean $1 - p$ in the other group).

Let Y^* be the dichotomized version of Y defined by: $Y^* = 1$ if $Y >$ median (Y) and $Y^* = -1$ if $Y <$ median (Y). If effects are summarized on the basis of Y^*, the BESD is the correct summary, since Y^* is dichotomous with means in the treatment groups equally above and below .5. How different can the correlation, ρ, between treatment and Y be from the correlation, ϕ, between treatment and Y^*? We can show[2] that $\phi = 1 - 2T$, where T is a function of $\rho/\sqrt{1 - \rho^2}$. For example, if Y is normally distributed, T is the one-tailed p value associated with $\rho/\sqrt{1 - \rho^2}$; if Y follows the t distribution with df degrees of freedom, T is the one-sided p value associated with

$$\frac{\rho}{\sqrt{1 - \rho^2}} \Big/ \sqrt{\frac{df}{df - 2}}.$$

Table 4 shows the agreement between ρ and ϕ for these two distributions. Usually, as this table suggests, ρ and ϕ are quite similar; thus having a value of ρ and displaying it as a BESD is often negligibly different from dichotomizing Y, calculating ϕ, and then displaying ϕ as a BESD. In some cases, it might be desirable to adjust the value of the correlation to be used to form the BESD. For example, given the correlation $\rho = .55$, if the raw data are normal, use $\phi = .49$ for the BESD, whereas if the raw data are quite long-tailed, use $\phi = .66$ for the BESD.

---

[2] In order to relate ϕ and ρ, we establish the following notation. Let $X = -1, +1$ indicate group membership, and let $E(Y|X) = X\mu, \mu > 0$, and $Var(Y|X) = 1$. Then $E(X) = 0$, $Var(X) = 1$, $E(Y) = 0$, $Var(Y) = 1 + \mu^2$, $Var(Y^*) = 1$, $Corr(X,Y) = \rho = \mu/\sqrt{1 + \mu^2}$ or $\mu = \rho/\sqrt{1 - \rho^2}$. Also, $Corr(X,Y^*) = \phi = 1 - 2T$, where T is the area from 0 to ∞ under the $X = -1$ group's Y distribution, or equivalently, the area from $-\infty$ to 0 under the $X = +1$ group's distribution, or equivalently, the area from μ to ∞ under the $X = -1$ group's distribution translated to have mean zero. Thus, we can express ϕ as a function of ρ by $\phi = 1 - 2T$, where T is the area from $\rho/\sqrt{1 - \rho^2}$ to ∞ under the $X = -1$ group's distribution translated to have mean zero (and by assumption, scaled to have variance 1).

Reference Note

1. Glass, G. V. *Primary, secondary, and meta-analysis of research.* Paper presented at the meeting of the American Educational Research Association, San Francisco, April 1976.

References

Appelbaum, M. I., & Cramer, E. M.   The only game in town.   *Contemporary Psychology*, 1974, *19*, 406–407.

Cohen, J.   Some statistical issues in psychological research.   In B. B. Wolman (Ed.), *Handbook of clinical psychology*.   New York: McGraw-Hill, 1965.

Cohen, J.   *Statistical power analysis for the behavioral sciences* (Rev. ed.).   New York: Academic Press, 1977.

Fleiss, J. L.   Estimating the magnitude of experimental effects.   *Psychological Bulletin*, 1969, *72*, 273–276.

Friedman, H.   Magnitude of experimental effect and a table for its rapid estimation.   *Psychological Bulletin*, 1968, *70*, 245–251.

Hays, W. L.   *Statistics for the social sciences*. (2nd ed.).   New York: Holt, Rinehart & Winston, 1973.

Mayo, R. J.   Statistical considerations in analyzing the results of a collection of experiments.   *The Behavioral and Brain Sciences*, 1978, *3*, 400–401.

Rimland, B.   Death knell for psychotherapy?   *American Psychologist*, 1979, *34*, 192.

Rosenthal, R.   Combining results of independent studies.   *Psychological Bulletin*, 1978, *85*, 185–193.

Rosenthal, R., & Rubin, D. B.   Interpersonal expectancy effects: The first 345 studies.   *The Behavioral and Brain Sciences*, 1978, *3*, 377–386.

Rosenthal, R., & Rubin, D. B.   A note on percent variance explained as a measure of the importance of effects.   *Journal of Applied Social Psychology*, 1979, *9*, 395–396.

Smith, M. L., & Glass, G. V.   Meta-analysis of psychotherapy outcome studies.   *American Psychologist*, 1977, *32*, 752–760.

15

Further Meta-Analytic Procedures for Assessing Cognitive Gender Differences

Robert Rosenthal and Donald B. Rubin

We describe procedures for (a) assessing the heterogeneity of a set of effect sizes derived from a meta-analysis, (b) testing for trends by means of contrasts among the effect sizes obtained, and (c) evaluating the practical importance of the average effect size obtained. On the basis of applying these procedures to data presented in Hyde (1981) on cognitive gender differences, we conclude the following: (a) that for all four areas of congitive skill investigated, effect sizes for gender differences differed significantly across studies (at least at $p < .001$); (b) that studies of gender differences conducted more recently show a substantial gain in cognitive performance by females relative to males (unweighted mean r across four cognitive areas = .40); (c) that studies of gender differences show male versus female effect sizes of practical importance equivalent to outcome rates of 60% versus 40%.

In an interesting and important recent article, Hyde (1981) reported the results of a meta-analysis of studies of gender differences in cognitive abilities. The general purpose of the present note is to extend Hyde's analyses by the application of procedures with general utility in meta-analyses. More specifically we address the following three questions: (a) Are the results of studies of gender differences homogeneous within each type of cognitive ability or do these results show significant heterogeneity? (b) Are the results of studies of gender differences stable over time or do more recent studies show significantly larger or smaller gender differences than do older studies? (c) Are the magnitudes of the obtained gender differences of any practical importance?

In her meta-analyses, Hyde employed both ω^2 and d as her effect size estimates. In our analyses we employed only d for the following two reasons: (a) d is by nature a directional estimate, whereas ω^2 is nondi-

rectional, and (b) d was more accurately estimated than ω^2 (two vs. one significant digit). Every study reporting both a d and the size of the sample (N) was included. The definition of d employed by Hyde was $(M_1 - M_2)/\overline{SD}$; that is, the difference between the mean scores of females and males divided by the mean of the standard deviations of the female and male samples. Since separate sample sizes for females and males were not reported, we assumed sample sizes to be equal.

It should be noted that, of all the studies summarized by Hyde, only one half (51%) yielded a reported value of d. Following the valuable suggestion of one of our reviewers, we were able to check for one type of possible bias in the availability of d. If there were no "significance level" bias, we might expect to find the same percentage (51%) of ds available for studies showing a significant gender difference and for those not showing a significant gender difference. We found, however, that of the 45 studies showing significant effects, 60% permitted a report of d, whereas of the 33 studies not showing significant effects, only 39% permitted a report of d. Since studies showing significant effects tend to yield larger ds than studies not showing significant effects (Rosenthal & Rubin, 1978; 1979), it is likely that the studies summarized quantitatively tend to

Preparation of this article was supported in part by the National Science Foundation. The order of authors was determined alphabetically.

Requests for reprints should be sent to Robert Rosenthal, Department of Psychology and Social Relations, Harvard University, 33 Kirkland Street, Cambridge, Massachusetts 02138.

From Robert Rosenthal and Donald B. Rubin, "Further Meta-Analytic Procedures for Assessing Cognitive Gender Differences," 74 (5) *Journal of Educational Psychology* 708-712 (October 1982). Copyright 1982 by the American Psychological Association. Reprinted by permission of the publister and authors.

Table 1

Summary of Statistics Employed in Meta-Analysis of Gender Differences in Cognitive Abilities

Statistic	Type of ability			
	Verbal	Quantitative	Visual-spatial	Field articulation
1. Number of studies	12	7	7[a]	14
2. Total number of persons	62,083	55,931	11,015	911
3. Weighted mean d ($\bar{d}$)	.30	-.35	-.50	-.51
4. Z for mean d[b]	36.54	-40.65	-25.81	-7.45
5. p for Z for mean $d <$	.001	.001	.001	.001
6. χ^2 for heterogeneity of ds	769	333	111	34.9
7. df for χ^2 above	11	6	6	13
8. p for χ^2 above $<$	.001	.001	.001	.001
9. Z for linear contrast	2.79	0.80	1.88	3.38
10. p for Z above (one-tailed)	.0026	.21[c]	.030	.00037
11. r between recency and d	.29	.21[c,d]	.46	.60
12. r corresponding to mean d	.15	-.17	-.24	-.25

[a] An 8th d was available, but because the N for that d was not available it was not included in our analysis.
[b] Computed as $\bar{d}\sqrt{\Sigma w}$.
[c] This is not a typographical error but is simply a coincidence.
[d] Although this r does not differ significantly from zero, it also does not differ significantly from the other three correlations or from their mean (all Zs < 1).

overestimate gender differences. Offsetting biases may, of course, also be operating if there were studies with large gender differences that were not reported, for example, because of fear that the results would be used to maintain traditional sex typing.

Before beginning our analyses, we want to endorse strongly Hyde's own emphasis on effect-size estimation and reporting as well as her recommendation that effect sizes be supplied with all significant results in reports of research. Indeed, we feel that any time the results of a significance test are reported, significant or not, an effect size should also be reported. If it could be arranged logistically, we would prefer basic summary data being made a part of the original article—as is now strongly encouraged for all articles involving the analysis of real data published in the *Journal of the American Statistical Association* of which one of us (D. B. R.) is currently the Coordinating and Applications Editor.

Testing for Heterogeneity of Gender Differences

Our first question asked whether the magnitudes of gender differences differed significantly from study to study for each type of cognitive ability. We have given the

details elsewhere (Rosenthal & Rubin, 1982b); here we give only the basic χ^2 test for the heterogeneity of a set of effect sizes

$$\chi^2(K - 1) = \Sigma[w(d - \bar{d})^2]$$

where K is the number of effect sizes to be assessed for heterogeneity, w is the reciprocal of the estimated variance of d in each of the K studies, d is the estimated effect size in each of the K studies, and $\bar{d}$ is the mean d weighted by w. Details on the estimation of w are in the reference just above, but when sample sizes are nearly equal and not smaller than, say, 10 it can be estimated by

$$w = \frac{2N}{8 + d^2},$$

where N is the total sample size in the study.

The first row of Table 1 shows the number of studies available for analysis and the second row shows the total number of persons upon which these studies were based. The third row gives the weighted mean ds for all four areas of cognitive skill. A positive d means that females performed better than males, whereas a negative d means that males performed better than females. For the area of verbal ability, females performed better than males; for the areas of quantitative, visual–spatial, and field articulation, males performed better than females. The fourth row gives the Z testing the significance of the difference of each mean d from zero, and the fifth row gives the p values associated with each of the obtained Z. Actually, all four p values are very much smaller than the ps of .001 shown.

The sixth row of Table 1 shows the χ^2 test of heterogeneity of ds for each of the four types of ability. The seventh row gives the df on which each of the χ^2s is based, and the eighth row gives the p values associated with each of the obtained χ^2s. All four of the p values are less than .001; for the areas of verbal ability, quantitative, and visual–spatial, the actual p values are very much smaller than .001. Thus, for all four areas of cognitive functioning, the effect sizes differed significantly among themselves.

The computation of these χ^2s is illustrated

in Table 2 for one of the four types of ability—visual–spatial ability. For each of the seven studies for which both d and N were available, Table 2 provides the two quantities from each study required to obtain the weighted mean $\bar{d}$—d and w, the latter being the reciprocal of the estimated variance of d. The computation of d is shown near the bottom of Table 2, followed by the computation of χ^2 for heterogeneity, which requires for its ingredients, d, w, and $\bar{d}$.

Testing for Stability of Gender Differences

Although it was useful to learn that the ds differed significantly from each other, more focused questions can be addressed. One specific question is whether gender differences were found to be stable over time or

Table 2
Illustration of Meta-Analytic Procedures: Gender Differences in Visual-Spatial Ability

Study	Date	N	d^a	w^b	λ^c
1	1975	105	.04	26	4.3
2	1975	102	.48	25	4.3
3	1961	128	.60	31	−9.7
4	1967	6,167	.41	1,510	−3.7
5	1972	2,925	.83	673	1.3
6	1967	355	.52	86	−3.7
7	1978	1,233	.25	306	7.2^d
Σ	13,795	11,015	3.13	2,657	
Unweighted M	1970.7	1573.6	.45	379.6	

Weighted mean $\bar{d}$:

$$\bar{d} = \frac{\Sigma(wd)}{\Sigma w} = \frac{26(.04) + 25(.48) + 31(.60) + 1,510(.41) + 673(.83) + 86(.52) + 306(.25)}{2,657}$$

$$= \frac{1,330.55}{2,657} = .50.$$

χ^2 *for heterogeneity of ds:*

$$\chi^2(K-1) = \Sigma[w(d - \bar{d})^2] = 26(.04 - .50)^2 + 25(.48 - .50)^2 + 31(.60 - .50)^2 + 1510(.41 - .50)^2$$
$$+ 673(.83 - .50)^2 + 86(.52 - .50)^2 + 306(.25 - .50)^2$$
$$= 110.502, \text{ rounded to } 111.$$

Z *for linear contrast (ds predicted from date of study):*

$$Z = \frac{\Sigma(\lambda d)}{[\Sigma(\lambda^2/w)]^{1/2}} = \frac{\begin{array}{c}(4.3)(.04) + (4.3)(.48) + (-9.7)(.60) + (-3.7)(.41) + (1.3)(.83) + \\ (-3.7)(.52) + (7.2)(.25)\end{array}}{\begin{array}{c}[(4.3)^2/(26) + (4.3)^2/(25) + (-9.7)^2/(31) + (-3.7)^2/(1510) + (1.3)^2/(673) \\ (-3.7)^2/(86) + (7.2)^2/(306)]^{1/2}\end{array}}$$

$$= \frac{4.15}{[4.83]^{1/2}} = 1.88.$$

[a] In this table a positive d means that males performed better than females.   [b] Estimated for $2N/(8 + d^2)$ and presented to nearest integer.   [c] Defined as publication date minus mean year of publication.   [d] Rounded down to keep $\Sigma\lambda = 0$.

whether they were found to be changing over time. If they are found to be changing over even the short span of 20 or so years covered by Hyde's meta-analyses, one should be reluctant to make strong biogenic interpretations on the basis of this evidence.

To test whether effect sizes have been changing linearly over the years, we compute a linear contrast. We give the details elsewhere (Rosenthal & Rubin, 1982b), but essentially we compute the test statistic Z from the following:

$$Z = \frac{\Sigma(\lambda d)}{[\Sigma(\lambda^2/w)]^{1/2}} ,$$

where λ is the contrast weight for each study and d and w are as defined earlier. Contrast weights were defined as the year of publication minus the mean year of publication.

The computation of these Z tests of linear contrasts is illustrated in Table 2 for visual–spatial ability. The last column of that table provides the weights or λs that, along with d and w, are required to compute Z. In this case, the predicted values of the contrast could be conveniently obtained as residuals from the mean year of publication. (It should be noted that the sum of the λs must equal zero.) The Table 2 note shows each step of the computation of Z.

Row 9 of Table 1 shows the Zs obtained, Row 10 shows the p levels associated with each Z; Row 11 shows the correlation (r) between the recency of the study (year of publication) and degree of female superiority (d). These results are quite striking. In all four areas of cognitive skills, including the three areas showing male superiority, as years went by, females gained in cognitive skill relative to males. The mean r, weighted by df, was .43 (unweighted mean $r = .40$)—quite a large effect (Cohen, 1977).

Of course we cannot say whether this marked linear trend for females to gain relative to males in cognitive skills is due to changes in the relative ability of females and males or to changes in the nature of the studies conducted over the years; for example, differential gender selection for college over the years (since disproportionately many of these studies employed college samples), or to changes in both. But we can say that whatever the reason, in these studies

Table 3
Binomial Effect Size Display for Gender Differences

Gender and Σ	Relative performance		
	Above *Mdn*	Below *Mdn*	Σ
Females	60	40	100
Males	40	60	100
Σ	100	100	200

females appear to be gaining in cognitive skill relative to males rather faster than the gene can travel!

Practical Importance of Gender Differences

Although we agree in a general way with much of Hyde's work, we are less inclined to minimize the importance of the gender differences obtained in her meta-analysis. For example we do not agree that "gender is a poor predictor of one's performance on ability tests in any of these areas" (Hyde, 1981, p. 897). To show why we disagree, we employ the Binomial Effect Size Display (BESD), a general purpose effect-size display that shows clearly the practical importance of an effect size (Rosenthal & Rubin, 1982a). The BESD is particularly easy to calculate from the effect size r, so we have shown the r that corresponds to each mean d for gender difference in the bottom row of Table 1. The mean of the absolute values of the four rs shown was .20, either weighted by df or unweighted. Table 3 shows the BESD for this correlation as though females performed better. (If males performed better we would only have to interchange the rows.) The BESD shows that a correlation of only .20 accounting for only 4% of the variance is associated with the difference between 60% and 40% of a group's performing above average. Such a difference must be seen as nontrivial. For example, if obtaining a particular job required scoring above the median on a test that correlated .20 with being female, then for every 100 females and 100 males that applied, 60 of the women but only 40 of the men would be job-eligible. Put into a different context to show the generality of the BESD, if we had a new biomedical treatment whose use correlated

.20 with survival, that treatment would be associated with a reduction in death rate of from 60% to 40%!

Conclusion

On the basis of these analyses we conclude the following: (a) that for all four areas of cognitive skill investigated, effect sizes for gender differences differed significantly from study to study (at least at $p < .001$); (b) that studies of gender differences conducted more recently show a substantial gain in cognitive performance by females relative to males (unweighted mean $r = .40$); (c) that studies of gender differences show female versus male effect sizes of practical importance equivalent to outcome rates of 60% versus 40%.

References

Cohen, J. *Statistical power analysis for the behavioral sciences* (Rev. ed.). New York: Academic Press, 1977.

Hyde, J. S. How large are cognitive gender differences? A meta-analysis using ω^2 and d. *American Psychologist*, 1981, *36*, 892–901.

Rosenthal, R., & Rubin, D. B. Interpersonal expectancy effects: The first 345 studies. *The Behavioral and Brain Sciences*, 1978, *3*, 377–386.

Rosenthal, R., & Rubin, D. B. Comparing significance levels of independent studies. *Psychological Bulletin*, 1979, *86*, 1165–1168.

Rosenthal, R., & Rubin, D. B. A simple, general purpose display of magnitude of experimental effect. *Journal of Educational Psychology*, 1982, *74*, 166–169.   (a)

Rosenthal, R., & Rubin, D. B. Comparing effect sizes of independent studies. *Psychological Bulletin*, *92*, 1982, 500–504.   (b)

II

EXAMPLES OF REVIEWS

16

Deinstitutionalization in Mental Health
A Meta-Analysis

Roger B. Straw

HISTORY

It has been well-documented (see Bloom, 1977; Ewalt, 1979) that the origins of federal interest in deinstitutionalization were coincidental with a growing recognition that a significant portion of the American population suffered from mental health problems. The principal impetus for this development was the incidence of mental health problems in both recruits and combat soldiers during World War II. In 1946 Congress passed the National Mental Health Act (PL79-487), which created the National Institute of Mental Health (NIMH) and gave it the broad mission of not only understanding all aspects of mental health, but also promoting it by supporting training programs for professionals and by assisting states in improving their mental health programs. In its early years NIMH focused primarily on traditional academic concerns of training, research, and treatment.

In the middle to late 1950s three developments took place that changed the course of mental health policy much more strongly toward community care and away from state-run institutions. First, the introduction of the major tranquilizers and new treatment philosophies, among other factors, resulted in the beginning of a continuing decline in state hospital populations. Second, Congress gave NIMH money to support improvements in state mental hospital treatment programs with the goal of returning even more patients to productive life. Finally, a joint project between the federal government (Mental Health Study Act PL84-182) and private and professional organizations was conducted to reassess the entire mental health system of the United States (Joint Commission on Mental Illness and Health, 1961).

This paper is based on the author's dissertation (Northwestern University, 1982), which can be obtained from University Microfilms, Inc., Ann Arbor, MI (ADG82-26026). Some material had to be removed to shorten the manuscript; this included a review and critique of meta-analysis, a functional analysis of deinstitutionalization, and some detail from the methods, results and discussion. The dissertation was supported, in part, by National Science Foundation grant DAR-7820374. Correspondence should be addressed to Roger Straw, Section on Medical Psychology, Bowman Gray School·of Medicine, Winston-Salem, NC 27103.

From Roger B. Straw, "Deinstitutionalization in Mental Health," original manuscript. Copyright © 1983 by Sage Publications, Inc.

Within two years after the joint commission issued its final report, Congress, under strong pressure from President Kennedy, created the legal apparatus for the public mental health system as it exists today. The cornerstone of this system was the Community Mental Health Center, which was to provide comprehensive services to a local community in the prevention and treatment of mental illness. No stronger renunciation of the traditional institution-oriented mental health system could have been envisioned. The emphasis on community care carried with it the presumption that deinstitutionalization would follow and be effective.

Few important changes have occurred in this fundamental system since 1963. The number of operational CMHCs is now approximately 600, providing an estimated 29% of the total outpatient care (Kiesler, 1980). However, another source (Edelman, 1978) estimated that CMHC programs received only 4.2% of the total money expended for mental health care. During the same period, *resident populations* in mental hospitals declined, although the *number* of inpatient episodes have increased, both in absolute terms (34% over 18 years) and relative to the U.S. population (Kiesler, 1980). Kiesler also notes that over 70% of the mental health dollar is still spent on inpatient care in nursing homes and public and private hospitals.

POLICY OR PROGRAM?

A careful reading of the preceding section suggests that a paradox exists between the historical intent of the mental health legislation and the data on the types of care presently being given to patients. Most psychiatric treatment, both in terms of episodes and cost, occurs in institutional settings. In one of the few nongovernmental discussions of national mental health policy, Kiesler (1980) suggests that the discrepancy between the intent of the law and the actual care provided results from a confusion of the de jure and de facto mental health policies.

With respect to the de jure mental health system, Kiesler argues that "no planned, intentional national mental health policy really exists. National policy is an ad hoc aggregate of uncoordinated laws, historical accidents, and normative practices that almost defies discussion" (Kiesler, 1980, p. 1067). Later, however, he states that "the two major thrusts of de jure national policy in mental health are outpatient services through the community mental health centers and deinstitutionalization" (p. 1073). Significant progress has been made in the availability of outpatient care and in the *long-term* populations of mental institutions.

> *Nonetheless, for a variety of reasons, the national de facto mental health policy is institutionalization.* This is true partly because of inability of the mental health field to abandon the medical model, partly a function of the lack of control over alternative forms of institutionalization, partly due to the structural press of legislation that allows one to pay for mental health services often only if hospitalization is required; partly because of the control of mental health policy by medicine and by health policy, and partly due to a

lack of involvement of psychologists and behavioral scientists in questions of mental health policy, that would make these issues more empirical than philosophical [Kiesler, 1980, pp. 1073-1074, original emphasis].

Although it is clear that—as a psychologist interested in mental health—Kiesler has certain biases, he does make two important, empirically valid points. First, the medical community controls both the important policy-making positions and the major sources of psychiatric treatment. Doctors serve as the chief administrators of NIMH and other relevant health policy agencies. By definition, hospitals and mental institutions are controlled by doctors. Community mental health centers average four psychiatrists. Only 12% of the centers are not directly related in some way to a hospital of some type (Edelman, 1978).

Second and more importantly, public (Medicaid) and private payments (e.g., insurance plans) for mental health services are structured in such a way that institutionalization is virtually required to obtain reimbursement. Medicaid alone paid out $4 billion in 1977 for mental health services; 50% of that total was spent on nursing home care (Kiesler, 1980).

If the preceding characterization leads the reader to the conclusion that the mental health system is splintered, confusing, and hard to define, I have accomplished one goal. Mental health policy is, truly, whatever happens in the name of mental health. The other primary goal was to establish the fact that there is no single deinstitutionalization program that could be evaluated at a national level. Instead, the question to be asked concerns whether or not there are any types of treatment approaches that are demonstrably effective and show promise of being applicable to other settings and/or populations.

A broad definition of deinstitutionalization will be used to include the widest possible range of treatment approaches in the following meta-analytic evaluation of the relative effectiveness of deinstitutionalization. The effectiveness of individual programs and/or treatment approaches can be assessed relative to a standard (accepted treatment) and also relative to each other. Finally, going beyond the initial question of whether or not effective programs exist, a number of important policy questions concerning cost, exportability, and generalizability exist (see Kiesler, 1980). Fragmentary evidence in a subsample of studies is available on some of these issues; other questions will require qualitative judgments and some will have to be left unanswered. As Kiesler (1980) notes, scientific (i.e., academic) involvement in issues of mental health policy has been virtually nonexistent.

METHODS

Population Definition

A study was considered relevant if it met three criteria. First, the subjects (patients) had to be identified as suffering from mental illnesses that had either required hospitalization in the immediate past or presently warranted institutionalization. The purpose of this restriction was to include only studies of patients to whom the policy of deinstitutionalization is targeted and to exclude many of the studies of psychotherapy outcome that Smith, Glass, and Miller (1980) had already analyzed. However, a small overlap does naturally exist because psychotherapy and psychotropic drugs are used extensively in both populations.

The second major criteria was that one group of patients had to have been exposed to a treatment program that took place, at least in part, outside of an inpatient setting. The important point here is not the form of treatment, but the setting in which it took place. In many cases the components or elements of treatment given to patients are identical; only the custodial arrangements differ. This focus reflects the belief of many that institutions are, by their very nature, negative influences on patients, their immediate social network, and the society in general.

Finally, each study included had to contain an explicit comparison between a group of patients given an innovative treatment and another group exposed to the traditional or normal system of mental health care. The explicit comparison is required in order to calculate a meaningful effect size.

Search Procedures

Computerized Searches

Several computerized databases, which might contain citations to the desired literature, were searched with the aid of librarians experienced in their use. *Psychological Abstracts, National Institute of Mental Health* database, and *MED-LARS* (Index Medicus) were all searched in their entirety. In addition, a specialized *Databank of Program Evaluations* (DOPE) was contacted for assistance because empirical evaluations of health and mental health programs are specially targeted by this database. Unfortunately, the program was in the process of phasing down and writing final reports and was not able to supply a requested search.

Bibliographic Followup

The meta-analyst must also rely on two time-honored methods of locating relevant literature: reference lists and review articles. Both were fully pursued in the course of locating studies for this meta-analysis. The use of review articles proved relatively disappointing except for locating drug studies using outpatients (Davis, Schaffer, Killian, Kinard, & Chan, 1981). The two most recent reviews (Braun, Kochansky, Shapiro, Greenberg, Gudeman, Johnson, & Shore, 1981; Mosher & Keith, 1981) of community programs, such as those to be analyzed later, have relatively short reference lists compared to the total number of studies located for this meta-analysis. Mosher and Keith (1981) have 20 of the 85 references included in this meta-analysis (24%). Braun et al. (1981), looking only at alternatives to inpatient care, discussed 21 of 39 studies included in the meta-analysis (54%). In both cases the references include mostly well-known, often-cited studies. The studies not included tend to be from foreign publications, less prestigous journals and/or books; these represent certain of the types of references termed "fugitive" by Glass and others.

The identification of studies by reference lists was somewhat more useful, but not altogether rewarding. Many authors did only cursory literature reviews; in these cases the studies cited were usually the ones that almost everybody cited. One of the more useful aspects of checking reference lists was the repeated confirmation, over a number of studies, of no new citations.

Scanning of Journals

The final search procedure used to locate studies consisted of scanning back issues of selected journals. The initial set (*Archives of General Psychiatry, Hospital and Community Psychiatry,* and *Community Mental Health Journal*) was chosen on an impressionistic basis. Later, a running tally of citation locations was used to determine which additional journals to search. Journals with more than three studies were examined in their entirety. The only additional journal to meet that criteria was the *American Journal of Psychiatry.*

Working Model of Treatments and Outcomes

One of the most persistent criticisms of meta-analysis is that combining different studies results in comparing apples with oranges. While Glass's (1978) answer is glib, it is nonetheless elegant in the abstract:

> This mindless criticism is surely spoken thousands of times each day in one context or another and is all too seldom rebutted. Of course, they are comparing apples and oranges; such comparisons are the only endeavor befitting competent scholarship. Comparing apples and apples is a technical triviality. One compares apples and oranges in the study of fruit [p. 395].

To be concrete, the important issue in integrating findings is not whether two measures or two treatments are operationally the same; such a constraint is overly strict. It is at the more general level of constructs that the integration and summarization of studies is directed. What follows is one conceptual model of deinstitutionalization. With meta-analysis other researchers can generate their own conceptual models and test them using the same data.

In terms of deinstitutionalization the studies can first be separated into two groups on the basis of whether the patients are being returned to the community from an institution (i.e., alternatives to traditional aftercare), or are being kept in the community instead of going to an institution (i.e., alternatives to hospitalization). Within these two groups, treatment can be characterized first as to whether or not it has a component that fulfills one of the functional attributes of deinstitutionalization: custody/asylum, treatment, rehabilitation. Second, within each functional category the type of service can be described and categorized. For example, custodial types of living arrangements for patients include families, halfway houses, and the like.

The classification of outcomes is a more complex process and certainly one about which knowledgeable researchers will disagree. The functional aspects of desinstitutionalization suggest some reasonable basic categories. The treatment function suggests a class of measures related to *psychiatric symptomatology*. Rehabilitation outcomes could include measures of *personal, vocational, and social skills*. The underlying philosophy of deinstitutionalization suggests that measures of *community tenure* (or recidivism), *productivity* (i.e., employment), and *cost* are also important classes of outcome. However, some outcome measures, including *global adjustment ratings,* are hard to classify and will often contain elements of both treatment and rehabilitation. In initial analyses these types of measures will be kept as a separate class, although it is anticipated that they will react to treatment in ways similar to measures of symptomatology.

Coding of Studies

The data for a meta-analysis must be systematically gleaned from the original research reports. This entails the development and testing of a coding form with which to standardize the information taken from primary studies. The development of the coding form for the deinstitutionalization meta-analysis proceeded in three stages: initial development, testing and refinement, and reliability assessment.

The initial development took two approaches to generating general categories of information, and the specific questions and codes within general categories. First, other meta-analyses were scanned for useful variables. Second, the model described earlier guided the development of specific treatment and outcome variables. The general categories of information are: (1) study characteristics; (2) descriptors of subject population; (3) parameters of the innovative treatment; (4) parameters of the comparison treatment; (5) design characteristics; and (6) for each outcome, measurement characteristics and effect sizes. These categories are present, to some extent at least, in most meta-analyses. The principal differences among meta-analyses tend to be in the depth with which each is explored. A special effort was made in this meta-analysis to address methodological and measurement issues that might affect the magnitude of effect.

After an initial set of coding questions was developed, it was pilot-tested on several studies to be included in the meta-analysis. Two raters (the author and a Ph.D. clinical psychologist) coded three studies independently and then compared results. Areas of disagreement were noted and questions rephrased or codes added to clarify any misunderstandings. Some new questions were added to account for data considered important but not coded elsewhere. For example, a question on the original form asked for the average number of years of prior hospitalization. It became apparent that a second question addressing the average number of prior hospitalizations was necessary to adequately capture the notion of chronicity. The following are a selected set of variables and coding conventions:

Major Diagnosis. The majority of studies in deinstitutionalization deal with severely ill individuals. For this reason the categories could reasonably be limited to schizophrenic, mixed psychotic, and mixed psychotic and other diagnoses.

TABLE 1   Treatment Characteristics Coded in Meta-Analysis

Characteristic	Innovation	Standard
Presence of custody	Yes	Yes
Type of custody	Yes	Yes
Presence of treatment	Yes	Yes
Type of treatment	Yes	Yes
Presence of rehabilitation	Yes	Yes
Type of rehabilitation	Yes	Yes
Presence of medication	Yes	Yes
Treatment modality	Yes	Yes
Treatment course	Yes	Yes
Treatment duration	Yes	Yes
Training of therapist	Yes	Yes
Experience of therapist	Yes	Yes
Allegiance of author to innovation	Comparative	
Strength of treatment	Comparative	
Integrity of treatment	Yes	No

Type of Episode. This variable was developed to attempt to capture a sense of the chronicity of the mental problems in the sample. It ranged from a code of 1 for all subjects with a first episode of mental illness, to 5 for subjects who were characterized as chronic mental patients.

Treatment Characteristics. Table 1 presents some of the characteristics of treatments coded for both the innovation and the comparison group. In each case the presence or absence of a treatment component intended to fulfill one of the functions of an institution was coded, along with the type of component if one was present. For example, home care by foster families was coded as a custody function.

Internal Validity. The overall design of the evaluation, including mortality, was rated on a seven-point scale. Some types of designs do not appear and so have no codes (e.g., regression discontinuity). Randomized studies were divided, at this phase, into studies with low mortality (less than 15%), studies with more than 15% mortality, and studies with evidence of failed randomization. Prospectively matched groups, cohorts, and convenience (retrospective) samples with or without matching were the remaining categories.

Outcome Category. This is a first pass at making fruit out of apples and oranges, to use Glass's metaphor. For example, there are any number of scales designed to assess signs and symptoms of mental illness, including the Brief Psychiatric Rating Scale, the Psychiatric Status Schedule, and many others. All of these are lumped into a category called symptomatology. Other categories include global adjustment, percentage rehospitalized, and vocational outcomes.

Reactivity Rating. This variable is intended to represent the best judgment of the coder about the corruptibility of a particular outcome. For example, ratings of symptomatology by a blind assessment team should be less reactive than similar ratings by nonblind assessors. The reactivity of hospitalization data is hard to assess because potential biases would not be evident in the administrative records that are the only source of information. Reactivity is coded on a scale from 1 to 5, with 1 meaning that it was very plausible that the results on that outcome measure would favor the innovative treatment.

Blinding. This coding variable is used to represent the degree of knowledge for treatment status that the assessor (rater) had for that particular measure. In many cases it was not even clear who the rater was. In this case the variable was coded as unclear but not blind. No measure was coded as blind unless it was explicitly stated to be the case.

Time of Measurement. There are two common ways of timing measurement waves in this type of study. The first approach is to time waves from the pretest or beginning of treatment. The definition of posttest as being that measure taken at the end of treatment might therefore be after 10 weeks in one study and 50 weeks in another. The second approach is to time waves from the end of treatment. The meaning of a one-year followup under the two systems might be quite different. Each effect-size estimate is therefore characterized both in terms of the approach used and the number of weeks "post" at which it was made.

Effect-Size Estimates. Given the means and standard deviations, the estimation of effect sizes is straightforward (Cohen, 1977). Without them, fallback options must be exercised. Two approaches were used most frequently in this study. If a t

and degrees of freedom (sample sizes) are given, mean ES = t $\sqrt{\dfrac{1}{N_1} + \dfrac{1}{N_2}}$. If there

is a significant difference and sample size is known, the t for the appropriate probability level and degrees of freedom is substituted. If a result was not significant, and no additional information was available, mean ES = 0. Each of these procedures results in a conservative bias on average effect sizes.

Differences between proportions were converted to effect sizes using the arcsine transformation proposed by Cohen (1977). A simple difference measure $(P_1 - P_2)$ is not an appropriate effect-size index because the power to detect differences depends on where along the scale from 0 to 1 the difference is measured. The arcsine transformation of the proportion ($\phi = 2$ arcsine $\sqrt{\text{Proportion}}$) results in equal differences between ϕ being equally detectable. The effect-size estimate for a difference between proportions is, therefore, h = $\phi_1 - \phi_2$. Cohen (1977) provides tables for converting P to ϕ and for estimating power from h and sample size.

Reliability of Coding

An approximately 10% random sample (10 studies) was coded by two raters, the author and a Ph.D. clinical psychologist with experience in community mental health settings. The percentage agreement across all studies and coding variables was 77% of 450 ratings. An additional 7% were within one scale unit of agreement.

This approach to estimating reliability, however, is inappropriate to the intended use of the coded information. If the characteristics were to be used as a profile to describe types of evaluations, there would be some justification for that approach. The intended use of coded data is, however, as independent variables in cross-tabulations and other analyses for explaining variations in effect sizes. As such, the within-variable reliability or interrater agreement is the more important measure. Overall agreement as a measure may well mask a few highly unreliable individual categories.

In this study 39 of the 45 categories had better than 80% agreement (within one category) after the coding form had been refined to a final set. Treatment modality and average treatment duration for both innovation and comparison groups were problematic because of the individualized nature of treatment packages in this literature, and often insufficient information. Many disagreements in similar coding variables resulted from the two raters responding to different bits of contradictory information in the reports. For example, a study might report that services X, Y, and Z were available, and later state that very few people received Z. Should Z be coded as present or absent? Is a treatment package implemented poorly if Z is to be given as needed, but rarely given? Variables with low levels of agreement were double coded for all studies, and disagreements resolved through discussion.

RESULTS

Introduction

The presentation of the results will be divided into two broad categories: (1) community-based alternatives to hospitalization compared to inpatient care (30 studies = 31 comparisons); (0) and (2) special outpatient programs compared to traditional aftercare services (49 studies, 68 comparisons). All *studies* within each area are independent in the sense of having different patient populations. Most, but not all, of the *comparisons* are independent. The dependence of comparisons is caused by having several different treatment groups compared to one or more control group(s). In no case is the same treatment group represented more than once in a particular group of studies.

To help the reader follow the presentation of the results, a few comments may be helpful. First, with one exception, whenever N is presented it refers to the *number of effect size estimates*. The only exception is that whenever the number of comparisons or studies is involved, that fact will be explicitly stated. Several types of dependence are introduced in an analysis based on effect sizes and have been discussed in other sources. The disaggregation of results by program and type of outcome removes most, but not all, of the dependence. Second, whenever the impact of a program on an outcome is discussed, the quantity presented will be a simple arithmetic average of the N individual effect sizes. The standard deviation and standard error (when presented) are based on the same N individual effect sizes. These statements refer to both the text and the tables.

Alternatives to Hospitalization

Description of Sample

The search procedures located 30 studies of alternatives to hospitalization, yielding 31 comparisons. The lack of multiple comparisons within a study probably reflects the high cost of developing and implementing a systematic treatment program as well as the demands of conducting an evaluation. With respect to study characteristics, almost 80% of the studies reporting their source of funding were demonstration projects of the U.S. government (NIMH, VA, and so on). In 58% of the studies a physician was the primary author or investigator; most of the rest (26%) were done by Ph.D. psychologists or sociologists. The results of the studies were reported mostly in the early 1970s (50% between 1971 and 1976), and almost all were in journal (84%) or book form (13%).

In terms of subject characteristics, schizophrenia in its various forms was the most often reported diagnosis, but only 23% of the studies restricted their samples to schizophrenics. Most often all diagnoses except organic brain syndromes were included (61%). Screening, which occurred in 80% of the studies, was more often on clinical grounds (i.e., how sick the person was) than diagnostic criteria. The samples of subjects across studies were on the average 34 years-old and were 50% male. Chronicity, as described by study authors, ranged from all acute first admissions to all chronic state hospital patients.

Information on prior years of hospitalization, socioeconomic status, homogeneity, and selection ratios were missing for many of the studies. On the basis of the available data, the samples tended to be fairly acute (one year or less of prior psychiatric hospitalization), lower class, and relatively homogeneous in terms of education, socioeconomic status, and the like. Most eligible patients participated (80-100%), but substantial numbers of patients were selected out as ineligible (50-70%). An educated guess would suggest that the selection ratio would be higher if additional data were available.

In terms of the treatment components described earlier, only one study had no type of custody arrangement and only six provided no formal psychiatric treatment. On the other hand, most (77%) had no planned rehabilitation function. Only three comparisons involved studies in which medication was explicitly not given (one placebo group and two drugless treatment groups). The majority of the studies used multiple treatment modalities (69%); however, a substantial minority (19%) employed individual treatment only (usually medication checks). In the studies reporting treatment duration (67%), the average length of treatment was 18 weeks (median 12 weeks). Most of the treatment was administered by doctors or teams headed by doctors. Their experience in working with this population was only reported 50% of the time and then only globally. The reports revealed an overwhelming endorsement of the innovations by their authors.

The comparison group was always an inpatient (hospitalized) sample treated with drugs and standard inpatient therapy (multimodal, milieu, and the like). Again, little or no formal rehabilitation was reported. Treatment duration tended to be slightly shorter than for the innovative treatments (mean, 13 weeks; median, 10 weeks). In terms of my ratings of treatment strength, the standard treatments were most often judged to be equivalent to (43%) or stronger than (43%) the innovations. Finally, no information on which to judge implementation is given in 71% of the studies, and the rest have insufficient information to make reasonable judgments. However, by reputation, most were considered to be above-average inpatient programs.

After all of the studies were read and coded, they were then classified into four basic types on the basis of treatment descriptions: day or partial hospitals (10), halfway houses (14), home or foster home care (13), and outpatient treatment (4). For the sake of definition, day hospitals typically control 8 to 12 hours of the patient's day, and send them home at night. The treatments given are often very similar to those available to the inpatient group. Halfway houses are 24-hour residences for small groups of patients who have considerable freedom to structure their own time. Treatment is often limited to a milieu approach, with some patients receiving outpatient psychiatric therapy. Studies in the home treatment group utilize the patient's family or surrogate family to provide custody functions. Treatment, in a formal sense, may or may not be part of the program. Outpatient studies were limited to those in which no formal custody function was employed. Because of the small number of studies involved and the strong relationship between the type of custody function and rational category, the statistical grouping methods were not considered appropriate for this set of studies.

There were very few systematic differences among the sets of studies in this case. Studies of day hospitals are somewhat older than the other studies and they spread out over more years. The home care studies were done more often by researchers with Ph.D. degrees than the other groups, where physicians were more prevalent. There are also some variations across programs in age and percentage male. None of these variations appear to be very important in determining outcomes. However, the variation among the types of programs in the duration of treatment is an important factor to consider. Day hospitals average less than eight weeks of treatment, while the other types of programs average between five and six months. It is also the only group of studies where the comparison group received a longer course of treatment than did the innovative treatment group (fifteen weeks).

A total of 183 effect sizes were retrievable from the 31 comparisons. There were, therefore, an average of 5.9 effect sizes reported per study, with a range from 1 to 24. The distribution was strongly skewed toward fewer effect sizes per study, with 60% having 5 or less. Approximately one-third of the effect sizes were estimated by each of three methods: Proportions (e.g., percentage rehospitalized), and other methods (mainly no significant differences, mean ES = 0.00). Using proportions produced higher effect-size estimates (mean ES = .28) than did either actual data sources (mean ES = .14) or other estimation methods (mean ES = .00). The reason is probably related more to the nature of the outcomes reported as proportions (percentage rehospitalized, percentage employed) than to the calculation of effect size. The issues involved in using rehospitalization as an outcome measure will be considered in the discussion.

Program-Related Effects

As a group, the alternatives to hospitalization have only a very small advantage in comparison to inpatient treatment. Across all outcomes, the average effect size is

TABLE 2   Average Effect Size as a Function of Type of Outcome:
Alternatives to Hospitalization

Outcome type	N_{ES}	mean ES	s.d.	s.e.[1]
Percentage rehospitalized	35	.30	.41	.07
Days in hospital	7	.39	.28	.11
Global adjustment	26	.16	.23	.05
Symptomatology	49	−.02	.32	.05
Vocational outcomes	19	.35	.32	07
Social and family outcomes	24	.04	.20	.04

1. s.e. = s.d. $\overline{ES^1 \sqrt{N_{ES}}}$ (Glass, 1980).

only .14 standard deviations ($s^2 = .12$). In terms of a percentage overlap between the two groups (see Cohen, 1977), only about 10% of the two groups are *not* overlapped. However, when outcomes are broken down by type (see Table 2), it is clear that the alternative programs differentially affect the various outcomes. There are no differences between the alternative programs and inpatient treatments in terms of symptomatology and social/family adjustment, and only a small difference favoring the innovative treatments in global adjustment. Percentage rehospitalized, days in hospital, and vocational outcomes show considerably larger effect sizes favoring the alternative programs, although still small by Cohen's (1977) standards. Most of the larger effect-size estimates are based on proportions. In that context an effect size of 0.30 represents a difference in proportions ($P_1 - P_2$) from .08 to .15. This is equivalent to a maximum phi coefficient (fourfold correlation) of 0.19.

In terms of raw percentage rehospitalized (see Figure 1), the inpatient groups show a slow but steady increase in cumulative percentage over time. The treatment groups initially have better results, but as active treatment becomes more remote, they come much closer to the comparison groups. The relative stability over time of the percentage rehospitalized in the comparison groups suggests the relative homogeneity of the various inpatient results. Alternatively, the variability in the results of the innovative treatments may well be the result of differential effectiveness among the various types of innovative programs, the types of patients treated, the times of measurement, and innumerable other factors. The following examination of these factors is severely restricted by the small number of data points.

When outcomes are broken down by the type of program (home care, partial hospitalization, and the like), outpatient programs have the largest impact; it is, however, not large in any absolute sense. Table 3 breaks these differences down further by the types of outcome examined. The pattern of results is very similar to that for the sample as a whole. Percentage rehospitalized and vocational outcomes tend to show the largest effect sizes, with the other outcome measures showing very small or no effects.

Thus far, the results suggest that the types of treatments studied, in their average form, are not particularly effective relative to the standard of hospitalization.

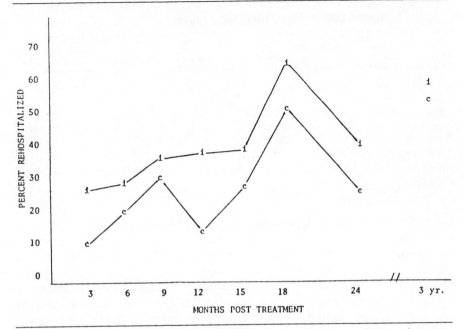

Figure 1: Changes in percentage rehospitalized as a function of time for community (C) and inpatient (I) groups.

Partial (day) hospital and outpatient programs do, however, seem to have some small advantage over the other types with respect to the ultimate objectives of rehospitalization and employment. Equally important is the finding that none of the programs is *less* effective than inpatient treatment. Finally, all but one of those reporting data on cost (N = 7) were less expensive over the initial treatment episode.

The Effects of Other Factors

Two approaches were taken to identify variables that might be related to the magnitude of observed effects. For quantitative variables (e.g., treatment duration), the correlation between effect size and the variable was calculated (see Table 4). The reader is, however, reminded that not all of the effect sizes are independent, and therefore the correlations should be interpreted cautiously. For qualitative variables (e.g., form of publication, diagnosis), average effect size within levels of the variable was examined. Again, the problem of dependence must be recognized as having a potential impact on these results. In the following presentation, variables that were found to be related to effect size will be discussed. In addition, other variables, such as internal validity and strength of treatment, will be presented because of their theoretical interest in the evaluation of social programs.

Of the study characteristics coded, only one was related to effect size. Journal articles (mean ES = 0.17; N = 144) reported slightly higher effect sizes than books

TABLE 3   Average Effect Size as a Function of Program Type and Outcome:
Alternatives to Hospitalization

| Outcome | Home | Program Type | | Outpatient |
		Halfway	Partial	
Percentage rehospitalized	.21 (18)[1]	.20 (4)	.35 (10)	.83 ((3)
Days in hospital				.39 (7)
Global adjustment	.15 (17)	0 (1)	.29 ((5)	.02 (3)
Symptomatology	−.06 (23)	−.03 (6)	−.03 (14)	.03 (10)
Vocational outcomes	.12 (5)	.14 (3)	.57 (1)	.50 (10)
Social and family outcomes	0 (9)	.16 (4)	.02 (10)	0 (1)

1. $\dfrac{\text{mean}}{\text{ES}}$ (N_{ES})

(mean ES = −.03; N = 31). This result might be indicative of a bias toward more positive findings in peer-reviewed publications. Publication date, which was different across the types of programs, was not related to the magnitude of effect. In terms of subject variables, studies in which subjects were screened had higher effect estimates (mean ES = .15, N = 144) than those with unscreened subjects (mean ES = .00, N = 24). In addition, programs given to either all acute or all chronic patients tended to be more effective. It should, however, be noted that only a few programs treated all acute patients or all chronic patients.

Two treatment variables were related to effect size. The duration of treatment was positively related to effect size (r = .28, N = 122). Longer treatments tended to produce larger effects. The subjective rating of the strength of the innovative treatment relative to traditional inpatient treatment was also related to effect size (r = .31, N = 165), with stronger program producing generally larger results. A breakdown of the types of programs by duration of treatment (median split) and strength of treatment (weaker versus equivalent or stronger) suggested that the outpatient programs may have had larger effects because they were both stronger and longer. All of the day hospital programs were short, but at least equivalent in strength to inpatient programs. Almost all of the home care and half-way house programs were rated as weak. Thus at least some of the difference among the various types of programs could be explained by variations in strength and/or duration of treatment.

However, it must be recognized that ratings of the strength of treatment were made by the coders on the basis of the descriptions of the treatments contained in the primary report. The ratings are, therefore, subject to a number of limitations, including the coder's personal beliefs and experiences with psychiatric treatments, and the amount of detail included in the original reports. Interpretations of the relationship of this variable and its outcomes should take this into consideration. However, because the direction of the findings in this case follow reasonable expectation, these limitations are less problematic.

Finally, the evaluation research literature has shown that a variety of methodological and measurement variables can and do influence the results of an individual

TABLE 4   Correlation of Effect Size with Selected Variables:
Alternatives to Hospitalization

Variable	Correlation	N_{ES}
Publication date	.02	176
Years prior hospitalization	.18	68
Mean age	.15	136
Percent male	−.06	134
Presence of screening	.15	168
Type of episode	.24*	114
Socioeconomic status	.18	65
Homogeneity of subjects	.24*	131
Duration of treatment	.28*	122
Allegiance to innovation	−.34*	175
Strength of treatment	.31*	165
Internal validity	.07	175

*$p < .05$

evaluation. The direction of over-all bias is often unpredictable, and its magnitude usually incalculable. There is, at this time, no clear understanding of the degree to which the same factors will bias the results of multiple evaluations summarized within a meta-analytic approach. Thus, the best advice is to examine critically the full range of potential biases, and to begin with the assumption that the direction of bias in a group of studies will mimic that expected in an individual study.

For example, one might suspect that evaluations with random assignment and low attrition might provide systematically different estimates than evaluations of lower quality (i.e., quasi-experiments). In this set of evaluations, however, such a prediction is not supported. Studies employing random assignment (mean ES = 0.14; N = 135) had virtually the same effect size as all other studies (e.g., retrospective, matched groups, and the like) combined (mean ES = 0.11; N = 40). Internal validity, rated by the coders on a seven-point scale, did not correlate with effect size (r = 0.07; N = 175). In addition, the degree of maintenance of randomization (in terms of attrition) did not affect the average effect size (poor: mean ES = 0.16; N = 3; better: mean ES = 0.14; N = 47; best: mean ES = 0.15; N = 85).

Two measurement variables were also related to the magnitude of effect size. The first was the degree of blinding of the person(s) doing the measurements. When the degree of blinding was explicitly reported (assessor did treatment, assessor knew group membership but did not do treatment, and blind), the average effect size within each category was 0. However, in ambiguous situations in which the blinding of the assessor was not reported (i.e., probably not blind), the average effect size was 0.26 (N = 70). Part of the reason for the higher average effect size in ambiguous situations is the fact that most of the rehospitalization data fall into the ambiguous category. This fact suggests that the findings discussed in the preceding paragraph are closely related to the data on blinding.

Reactivity, the second variable, is a global rating by the coder of the plausibility that the outcome measure could be biased toward demonstrating a treatment effect. As with ratings of the strength of treatment, it is an impressionistic rating and is subject to the same constraints. With the exception of measures rated as very low in reactivity, there is a very strong relationship between reactivity and average effect size. Measures rated high in reactivity tended to have higher average effect sizes.

Alternatives to Traditional Aftercare Services

The final aspect of deinstitutionalization to be explored concerns alternatives to the traditional system of community care for the mentally ill who have been released from hospitals (termed "aftercare"). Before evaluating the effectiveness of alternative programs, two related questions must be examined. First, a definition and description of typical aftercare services must be given. Second, because medication checks represent the primary mode of treatment in traditional aftercare, the effectiveness of psychotropic medication in preventing rehospitalization will be examined as one baseline against which to measure the effectiveness of alternative programs.

Description of Traditional Aftercare Services

The first issue to be addressed concerns what the traditional system of care for this population is. Typically, a patient who has been confined to a mental hospital is, upon release, referred to a local community agency for follow-up care. That agency may or may not be aware of the referral. The percentage of patients who actually appear for follow-up visits is fairly low. In a study of 129 consecutively released patients in West Virginia (Byers & Cohen, 1979), 39% never even contacted the community agency. In a similar study (Stickney, Hall, & Gardener, 1980), only 22% made contact. Clearly, substantial numbers of formerly hospitalized patients receive either no additional services or unplanned services after release.

Those who do choose to obtain additional help may receive a variety of different services, but the majority are seen individually as outpatients for brief supportive therapy and medication adjustment. Byers & Cohen (1979) report that 90% of the patients who receive any services saw mental health aides or nonmedical interns. The median number of visits per month was one, with an average duration of 30 to 45 minutes. In another study (Meltzoff & Blumenthal, 1966), patients averaged 2.3 visits per month, and 94% had been prescribed medication.

The normal aftercare services control group might, therefore, be described as having 50% or more of their members receiving no services whatsoever, and the rest having only infrequent support and/or medication checks. In this context consideration must be given not only to the functions of custody, treatment, and rehabilitation in an innovative treatment, but also to the possibility that either a greater number of patients are taking their medication or are being more compliant as a result of the increased level of attention involved in an experimental program.

Effectiveness of Maintenance Medication

The effectiveness of psychotropic drugs in the treatment of mental illness on an outpatient basis has been evaluated in a number of double-blind placebo trials. In fact, all 10 of the studies located (13 comparisons) used the double-blind procedure with random assignment to groups. Almost all of the studies were published prior to 1975, although two comparisons were completed in 1977. The subjects tend to be relatively young (mean age = 27), seriously ill chronic mental patients. The treatment received in addition to medication was usually limited to brief, supportive contact. In essence, this approach is the same as that described for traditional aftercare services.

Only two types of outcome were measured: percentage hospitalized and symptomatology (mostly percentage relapsed). The average effect size across both outcomes was 0.34 (N = 56). The effect on rehospitalization was, however, considerably smaller (mean ES = .21; N = 41) than on symptomatology (mean ES = .80; N = 13). The reason for this difference is that many of the studies used the return of psychotic symptoms as the endpoint, and introduced drugs to "failed" placebo patients without hospitalizing them. In normal settings, patients with florid symptoms might well be rehospitalized without any additional attempt at intervention. This same argument can be applied to comparisons of innovative programs with conventional community treatments; subjects in experimental programs are much more likely to be treated before, rather than after, hospitalization.

However, the influence of this factor on effect size is in opposite directions for the two groups of comparisons. For drug studies it will tend to decrease the average effect size for hospitalization by decreasing the proportion of control subjects hospitalized. For innovative treatments it will increase the average effect size by decreasing the proportion of treatment subjects hospitalized.

None of these studies investigated compliance with the prescribed medication regimen beyond occasional and infrequent pill counts or urine tests. Neither of these monitoring approaches yields reliable or valid information about routine compliance behavior. Pills need only be dumped to assure that the count is accurate. Urine tests are only sensitive to behavior immediately prior to the visit. Nonetheless, what data were collected indicated fairly high compliance.

A second group of seven studies does, however, address the compliance question in at least a peripheral way. In these studies, oral psychotropic medications were compared to injectable medications in double-blind trials using outpatients. Compliance with injectable medication is assured as long as injections are given; compliance with oral medication can vary. Across all outcomes, there was no difference between medication given orally or by injection (mean ES = -.02; N = 16). The only notable difference between the two modes of medication was in the occurrence of side effects. It is possible that higher levels of medication are associated with the "forced" compliance and thus account for the increased incidence of side effects. It has been my experience that some patients will self-regulate their own medication to avoid the unpleasant side effects associated with psychotropic medication.

In summary, medication has a fairly large positive effect on symptomatology (mean ES = .80). The effect on rehospitalization is considerably smaller, but is probably underestimated by the way the studies were conducted. It would certainly have been much greater if all relapses had been hospitalized. Compliance, on the other hand, does not seem to be a major factor in determining outcome, at least with the limited information available. It would, however, be a mistake to disregard the potential impact that the increased attention and contact associated with innovative programs could have on the compliance of patients with a medication regimen. In interpreting the presumed effects of these innovative programs, the drug-placebo effect can be used as a sort of baseline against which to judge the relative strength of elements of treatment beyond a possible medication-attention difference.

Innovative Alternatives

Descriptive Data. The 44 comparisons of innovative programs with traditional community services (or drug only groups) were divided into five different groups on the basis of the types of treatment component offered. Three groups have some relatively minor treatment intervention added to the traditional drug-oriented aftercare model: (1) individual psychotherapy and drugs compared to drugs only, (2) group psychotherapy and drugs compared to drugs only, and (3) volunteer contact and drugs compared to drugs only. The fourth group of studies compared day hospitals to traditional treatment. Day hospitals are programs in which patients spend as many as 12 hours per day participating in structured activities in a protective environment. In some ways day hospital treatment programs are similar to inpatient programs without any sleeping arrangements. Their potential strength comes from the many hours of daily contact that patients have with a therapeutic environment. The fifth and final group of studies includes special programs in which most, if not all, of the functions of an institution are addressed. In particular, most (86%) have an explicit, articulated rehabilitation component; 57% also have some form of custody function. Well-known examples of special programs include Fairweather's Lodge (Fairweather, Sanders, Maynard, & Cressler, 1969) and Hill House (Wolkon, Karmen, & Tanaka, 1971).

The five groups of studies are very similar to each other in terms of study, subject, and methodological variables with a few xceptions. Nonmedical investigators predominate in all groups except group therapies with medication. Special programs appear in somewhat older studies and are more often published in books. This is probably a reflection of their more comprehensive character; the greater number of measurements per study is also indicative of their thoroughness. All of the groups are characterized by a large amount of missing data across many of the coded variables. The use of randomization is, however, impressively high (60-85%) for an area that has been characterized as lacking adequate methodological sophistication.

Substantive Results. Table 5 contains the average effect sizes for the major categories of outcome for each of the five types of programs described earlier. In

TABLE 5   Average Effect Size as a Function of Program Type and Outcome:
Alternatives to Traditional Aftercare

| Outcome | Program Type | | | | |
	Drug Plus versus Drug	Drug + Group versus Drug	Volunteer	Partial (Day) Hospital	Special Programs
Percentage rehospitalized	.34 (21)[1]	.32 (9)	.42 (5)	.32 (14)	.31 (17)
Days in hospital/community	–	–	–	–	1.67 (7)
Symptomatology	.28 (14)	0 (8)	–	.26 (4)	0 (2)
Global adjustment	.04 (5)	–	–	0 (1)	–
Social and family outcomes	0 (1)	–	–	.37 (1)	–
Vocational outcomes	–	–.04 (1)	–	.39 (1)	.97 (11)
Total	.28 (41)	.16 (81)	.42 (5)	.30 (21)	.53 (53)

1. $\dfrac{\text{mean}}{\text{ES } (N_{ES})}$

terms of overall effect size, special programs (mean ES = 0.53, N_{ES} = 53) had a relatively large advantage over the other types of programs where average effect sizes ranged from 0.16 (N = 18) to 0.42 (N_{ES} = 5). To provide a frame of reference, an effect size of 0.50 (one-half standard deviation) would correspond to an approximately 25% difference in rehospitalization between innovation and standard treatment. A difference of this magnitude would probably be considered an accomplishment by mental health professionals.

However, as an examination of the individual outcomes indicates, each of the types of programs have roughly the same effect on rehospitalization, with effect sizes ranging from 0.3 to 0.4. Remembering that the average effect of medication (versus placebo) is 0.21, the additional reduction in hospitalization brought about by these innovative programs is not at all impressive. Simple programs designed to maintain drug compliance would probably be just as effective for *this particular* outcome.

On the other hand, there is some evidence that other categories of outcomes are differentially affected by specific programs. For example, special programs with an explicit rehabilitation focus did have a substantial effect on vocational outcomes (mean ES = .97; N = 11). Unfortunately, almost none of the other types of studies measured this type of outcome. However, an average effect size of almost 1.0 is well above the level of almost all of the other average effect sizes in this literature. Day hospitals and good outpatient programs (drugs plus some intervention) had a small effect on symptomatology, while the others had no effect.

Taken as a group, the results of these studies suggest a rather gloomy picture about our present ability to affect significantly the problems of this population. Only special programs that meet the custodial, treatment, and rehabilitation needs of the population seem to have much effect, and then only over relatively limited time spans. This conclusion is supported not only by the similarity in rehospitalization rates, but also by the observation that the large advantage in vocational

TABLE 6   Correlations of Effect Size with Selected Variables:
Alternatives to Traditional Aftercare

Variable	Correlation	N_{ES}
Publication date	−.03	219
Years prior hospitalization	−.17	99
Average age	.13	166
Percent male	.01	137
Presence of screening	.03	174
Type of episode	−.01	188
Socioeconomic status	−.37*	99
Homogeneity of subjects	−.03	149
Duration of treatment	.18*	166
Allegiance to innovation	−.18*	216
Strength of treatment	.21*	216
Internal validity	.05	218

*$p < .05$

outcome in the special programs group diminishes over time, with outcomes measured before the end of treatment being greater (mean ES = 1.06) than those measured later (mean ES = 0.58). None of the other outcomes show the same time dependency.

The Effects of Other Factors. Table 6 presents the correlations of various study, subject, and other variables with effect size across all program types. The same cautions presented earlier about dependence in this type of analysis hold here as well. While there are several significant correlations, only socioeconomic status seems large enough to be of any interest. The subject samples were split approximately equally between the lowest category (N = 45) and the next higher category (N = 45), with a few in the middle category of the five possible (N = 9). A much higher average effect size was found in the lowest category (mean ES = .63) than the next higher (mean ES = .22), with virtually no effect in the middle category (mean ES = .04).

The remaining statistically significant correlations very closely replicate the results found in the preceding section. Longer periods of treatment produce relatively greater effects. Studies in which the investigator favors the innovation tend to show more positive findings than studies with more neutral investigators. In fact, for this group of studies, in the one comparison in which the investigator slightly favored the standard, it outperformed the innovation (mean ES = −.22, N = 3). Finally, the rated strength of treatment was again positively correlated with effect size. The strongest treatment produced the largest effect sizes (mean ES = 0.50, N = 93), with treatments having the smallest average effect size rated as equivalent (mean ES = 0.13, N = 32).

As with the set of studies discussed in the preceding section, internal validity was not linearly related to effect size (r = 0.05, N = 218). In fact, the average effect sizes across the different types of designs is not at all what might have been predicted. The average effect size for each type of design is very similar. The only difference occurs within the subgroups of randomized designs. Despite the fact that one might predict higher effects in the more poorly maintained studies, substantially larger effects were found in the best (from a design point of view) studies.

In this group of studies, as with the last, the importance of experimental design (i.e., random assignment) is again overshadowed by the quality of the measurement strategies. Reactivity, a global rating of the potential for bias on a particular outcome measure, was negatively correlated with effect size ($r = -0.40$; $N = 218$). Measures rated as high in reactivity had greater effect sizes (mean ES = 0.96; $N = 25$) than those rated as moderately reactive or less (mean ES = 0.25, $N = 192$). The blinding of the assessors was also important, with blind assessors having generally smaller effect size estimates (mean ES = 0.27, $N = 50$) than nonblind assessors (mean ES = 0.39, $N = 152$). Finally, as in the last set of studies, effect size was unrelated to sample size. The average power across all outcomes is relatively low, averaging 0.44. It exceeds 0.50 (statistically significant) only for rehospitalization and vocational outcomes.

DISCUSSION

As discussed earlier, deinstitutionalization is a very complex issue involving much more than a simple, relatively homogeneous approach to a circumscribed problem. While this is not unusual within the sphere of social policy issues, it does require researcher-evaluators to define and limit their boundaries. Deinstitutionalization describes a social philosophy that holds that institutions are inherently dysfunctional places and *almost any alternative* is preferable. It has been applied to mental, penal, and other institutions and their associated aftercare components (parole, medication, maintenance, and the like).

The present study has been limited to an examination of deinstitutionalization in the mental health area. Part of the reason for this is substantive; community mental health is an area I am familiar with, and in which I feel psychologists can and should begin to make greater contributions (see also Kiesler, 1980). In addition, there are some subtle, and some not-so-subtle differences among the various areas. For example, prisons serve a punishment function that not only is absent in the mental health system, but also makes decreases in the use of prisons unlikely from a political standpoint.

Highlights of the Results

(1) The evaluations of alternatives to hospitalization demonstrate quite convincingly that most, if not all, patients who might be hospitalized can be treated in the community. On the other hand, the evidence available does not allow us to conclude confidently that the innovations are superior on any outcome. The cost of these programs does appear to be lower, but the lack of consideration of indirect costs (e.g., housing and food) and the small scale of their implementation makes generalization to a national program of similar alternatives suspect.

(2) Traditional aftercare services for formerly hospitalized mental patients consist of relatively infrequent, short duration visits to a mental health worker for support and medication checks. Many do not even receive this minimal level of care. However, the drug studies reviewed clearly show that medication is a very effective treatment when the drugs are taken as prescribed.

(3) Although the meta-analysis of evaluations of alternatives to traditional aftercare services showed that some innovations were somewhat more effective than others, the overall impression is that none of them are much more effective than medication and support administered well, as in the drug versus placebo studies.

(4) Across all subgroups of studies and with the preceding conclusions in mind, innovations with an explicit rehabilitation function produced more impressive vocational outcomes. In addition, the strength of the innovation relative to the standard, and the duration of the innovative treatment were both positively related to outcomes favoring the innovative treatments. These three factors, along with adequate medication, may be the most important elements in successful interventions for this group of patients. They certainly deserve more attention in future evaluations. Unfortunately, only the effect of medication has been systematically investigated in past evaluations.

(5) Studies that were high in internal validity (i.e., used random assignment) did not produce systematically different outcomes than did studies using quasi-experimental designs. However, we must recognize that random assignment has been found to be important in other meta-analyses. The point being made is that we should not make a priori exclusions of potentially valid and important studies simply because they do not conform to our own subjective standards. Meta-analysis allows us to quantitatively examine the effects of variations in quality. On the other hand, in designing an individual evaluation, random assignment and blind assessment remain the best choices for obtaining unbiased estimates of treatment effects.

(6) For both the alternatives to hospitalization and the alternatives to traditional aftercare services, three methodological factors were identified that need to be considered further before we can confidently discuss the policy implications of this meta-analysis:

(a) The tone of the research reports (termed allegiance in the results) in general strongly favored the innovation. The stronger the allegiance was, the higher the average effect size was.

(b) The blinding of the assessors was also related to effect size. The effect sizes were greater for measures where the blinding of the assessors was ambiguous than for measures where the status of the assessors was explicitly stated. This finding is also related to the type of outcome measure. Rehospitalization outcomes were almost always coded as ambiguous on the blinding variable.

(c) Reactivity, a global rating of the plausibility that a measure could be biased toward the innovation (coded prior to calculating effect sizes), was also related to effect size. Measures rated as more reactive showed effects more favorable to the innovation.

Potential Bias Due to Methodological Factors

Throughout the results and into the discussion reference has been made to the possibility that a systematic bias is present in these studies of deinstitutionalization. The data on rehospitalization has been pointed out as particularly suspect, but other outcomes could also be affected. The argument for a positive bias, based on three factors, is intended only to establish the plausibility that the bias exists—not to prove that the bias explains all of the findings. First, the generally inadequate measurement strategies and the demonstrated dependence of effect size on certain measurement variables provides the empirical basis for a presumption of biased treatment effect estimates. Second, the finding that the author's allegiance both strongly favors the innovation and is positively related to effect size, combined with the general understanding that demonstration projects have enthusiastic, dedicated, and well-trained staffs who are committed to the success of their programs, would suggest that the bias favors the innovative program. Finally, the fact that the assessment of outcomes is either done by individuals associated with the innovative programs (even if they do not actively provide the treatment), or by separate groups of assessors who are also associated with the treatment programs they are evaluating provides further support for the possibility that the bias favors the innovation.

Beyond the empirical evidence contained in the meta-analysis, an argument can be made that different clinicians have different standards of what to consider deviant behavior and when to hospitalize any particular patient. In discussing the possibility of a bias in rehospitalization outcomes, I suggest that personnel in community-based agencies will be less prone to hospitalize patients than are either hospital-based personnel or general community physicians. Data reported by Sheridan and Teplin (1981) support this assertion. In their study, acutely disturbed patients were brought by police to either a state hospital or a community mental health center for consultation. Although the study has many methodological flaws, statistical analysis showed that the two groups were very comparable on all available pretest measures. Significantly fewer patients in the community mental health center sample (56% of 293) than in the state hospital sample (79% of 128) were subsequently hospitalized. If we assume that it is more likely that patients in alternative, community-based programs will be considered for readmission by clinicians associated with those programs, the plausibility of a bias favoring the innovative programs on hospitalization measures seems very high.

Extending the argument for a positive bias to other outcomes such as symptomatology and adjustment requires demonstrating that the finding in the results chapter that outcomes in terms of symptomatology and adjustment average zero (mean ES = 0.00) is probably not an accurate estimate of the actual, measured impact of the innovative programs. The authors of the evaluation reports often stated that there were nonsignificant trends favoring the innovations on measures of adjustment and symptomatology. However, these favorable results could often not be coded because the reports did not contain the necessary information to estimate effect sizes.

Comparison to Other Substantive Reviews

How do the conclusions of this meta-analysis compare to other reviews of the same literature? As a point of departure it should be noted that comprehensive reviews of the deinstitutionalization literature have only recently focused on the *effectiveness* of innovative programs rather than issues of access, availability, and cost. Effectiveness has usually been assumed because of the demonstration that patients could be treated successfully in the community. Four major reviews have appeared in the last year (Mosher & Keith, 1981; Davis et al., 1981; Braun et al., 1981; Kiesler, 1982). Mosher and Keith (1981) has the least overlap with the meta-analysis in that their focus is on psychosocial treatments for schizophrenia, regardless of setting. The Davis et al. (1981) review deals only with drug therapy in schizophrenia. Both Braun et al. (1981) and Kiesler (1982) are based on exactly the same population of studies as the portion of the meta-analysis dealing with alternatives to hospitalization.

The conclusions of these reviews are remarkably similar to those based on the meta-analysis. For example, Mosher and Keith (1981) detail the flaws of research on psychosocial research as (1) testing weak treatments; (2) inadequately reporting treatment, therapist, and patient characteristics; and (3) using inadequate or mis-guided measurement designs. Similar shortcomings were noted by Braun et al. (1981). The substantive conclusions of the two reviews are also very similar to the findings of the meta-analysis. Braun et al. (1981) conclude, "With these qualifications, experimental alternatives to hospital care of patients have led to psychiatric outcomes not different from and occasionally superior to those of patients in control groups" (p. 736). Mosher and Keith (1981), in summarizing their findings, "conclude that the most effective types of psychosocial treatments for schizophrenia are those that provide the most comprehensive, corrective, and sustaining social support systems" (p. 154).

One important difference between the traditional reviews of deinstitution-alization and the preceding meta-analysis, beyond the obvious difference in method of cumulation, is in the comprehensiveness of the sample of studies reviewed. For example, Mosher and Keith's (1981) review of psychosocial treatment for schizophrenia should contain almost all of the studies used in the meta-analysis. However, only 23 non-inpatient studies are cited; almost three times as many studies are included in the meta-analysis. In the area of psychotherapy Mosher and Keith cited 10 studies, while the meta-analysis located a total of 28 comparisons.

In a more direct comparison Braun et al. (1981) reviewed exactly the same literature on alternatives to hospitalization as the meta-analysis included. They described their search procedure as follows:

> We performed an extensive search of published works, including a Medical Literature Analysis and Retrieval System (MEDLARS) search of the medical literature (1966-1978), and consulted previous reviews published by Bach-rach, Test and Stein, and the Group for the Advancement of Psychiatry. In 1977, we contacted the departments of mental health in the 50 states; as well

as officials at NIMH and the President's Commission on Mental Health, for information on unpublished and ongoing studies [p. 739].

They review 11 studies on alternatives to hospitalization. This is only 35% of the studies of alternatives included in the meta-analysis. Similarly, Kiesler (1982) reviewed 10 randomized studies of alternatives to hospitalization; 20 randomized studies were used in the meta-analysis.

Only one major discrepancy in terms of results exists between the traditional literature reviews and the meta-analysis. Despite recognizing flaws in the measurement strategies, none of the traditional reviews suggest that an argument could be made for a systematic bias favoring the innovations. In fact, Kiesler (1982) suggests that the bias might be in the opposite direction. His argument is based on the observation that, in a few studies, the inpatient treatment staff did not believe that the innovation could be successful. However, Dr. Kiesler's analysis does not recognize that inpatient staffs rarely deliver the innovations and never are the sole source of information on outcomes for either the comparison group or the innovative treatment group.

However, it should be noted that neither the comprehensiveness of the sample nor the discovery of a possible systematic bias are directly attributable to the method of review. For example, there are many exhaustive narrative literature reviews (see Maccoby & Jacklin, 1974, on sex differences), just as there are less comprehensive meta-analyses. Reviewers' persistence rather than the review method will determine the adequacy of their sample. In the case of the deinstitutionalization meta-analysis both the almost complete overlap with other recent reviews, and the substantially greater numbers of studies found, increases my confidence that the sample of studies is at least the most comprehensive presently available. The knowledge that Braun et al.'s survey of government officials and other experts did not generate any additional studies suggests that the sample may well be close to exhaustive. I do feel that the emphasis on systematic searches, the concern with comprehensiveness, the systematic coding of information, and the quantification of outcomes makes it more likely that meta-analyses will be more comprehensive and sensitive to potential biases.

REFERENCES

BLOOM, B. L. Community mental health: A general introduction. Monterey, CA: Brooks/Cole, 1977.

BRAUN, P., KOCHANSKY, G., SHAPIRO, R., GREENBERG, S., GUDEMAN, J. E., JOHNSON, S., & SHORE, M. F. Overview: Deinstitutionalization of psychiatric patients, a critical review of outcome studies. American Journal of Psychiatry, 1981, 138, 736-749.

BYERS, E. S., & COHEN, S. H. Predicting patient outcome: The contribution of prehospital, inhospital, and posthospital factors. Hospital and Community Psychiatry, 1979, 30, 327-331.

COHEN, J. Statistical power analysis for the behavioral sciences (Rev. ed.). New York: Academic Press, 1977.

DAVIS, J. M., SCHAFFER, C. B., KILLIAN, G. A., KINARD, C., & CHAN, C. Important issues in drug treatment of schizophrenia. In National Institute of Mental Health, Special Report: Schizophrenia, 1980 (DHHS #ADM 81-1064). Rockville, MD: Department of Health and Human Services, 1981.

EDELMAN, P. B. (Coordinator). Report of the Task Panel on Community Mental Health Centers Assessment. President's Commission on Mental Health (Vol. 2) (#040-000-00391-6). Washington, DC: Government Printing Office, 1978.

EWALT, J. R. The mental health movement, 1949-1979. Milbank Memorial Fund Quarterly, 1979, 57(4), 507-515.

FAIRWEATHER, G. W., SANDERS, D. H., MAYNARD, H., & CRESSLER, D. L. Community life for the mentally ill: An alternative to institutional care. Chicago: Aldine, 1969.

GLASS, G. V. Commentary on "Interpersonal expectancy effects: The first 345 studies." Behavioral and Brain Sciences, 1978, 3, 394-395.

Joint Commission on Mental Illness and Health. Action for Mental Health. New York: Basic Books, 1961.

KIESLER, C. A. Mental health policy as a field of inquiry for psychology. American Psychologist, 1980, 35(12), 1066-1080.

KIESLER, C. A. Mental hospitals and alternative care: Noninstitutionalization as potential public policy. American Psychologist, 1982, 37, 349-360.

MACCOBY, E. E., & JACKLIN, C. N. The psychology of sex differences. Stanford, CA: Stanford University Press, 1974.

MELTZOFF, J., & BLUMENTHAL, R. L. The day treatment center: Principles, application and evaluation. Springfield, IL: Charles C Thomas, 1966.

MOSHER, L. R., & KEITH, S. J. Psychosocial treatment: Individual, group, family and community support approaches. In National Institute of Mental Health. Special Report: Schizophrenia, 1980 (DHHS #ADM 81-1064). Rockville, MD: Department of Health and Human Services, 1981.

SHERIDAN, E. P., & TEPLIN, L. A. Recidivism in difficult patients: Differences between community mental health center and state hospital admissions. American Journal of Psychiatry, 1981, 138, 688-690.

SMITH, M. L., GLASS, G. V, & MILLER, T. I. The benefits of psychotherapy. Baltimore: Johns Hopkins University Press, 1980.

STICKNEY, S. K., HALL, R.C.W., & GARDNER, E. R. The effect of referral procedures on aftercare compliance. Hospital and Community Psychiatry, 1980, 31, 567-569.

WOLKON, G. H., KARMEN, M., & TANAKA, H. T. Evaluation of a social habilitation program for recently released psychiatric patients. Community Mental Health Journal, 1971, 7(4), 312-322.

17

Age Differences in Subjective Well-Being
A Meta-Analysis

William A. Stock, Morris A. Okun,
Marilyn J. Haring, and Robert A. Witter

Are there age differences in subjective well-being? Attempts to address this question empirically have contributed to making subjective well-being the most extensively investigated topic within social gerontology (Maddox & Wiley, 1976). Interest in adult age differences in subjective well-being (SWB) has been kindled by several factors, including (1) the aging of the U.S. populace, (2) the concern about the aged as a social problem, and (3) the growing emphasis on adaptation across the adult life span (George, 1980, 1981; Maddox & Wiley, 1976).

Previous Research Syntheses

Initial literature reviews, though not solely focused on the age/SWB relationship, concluded that young adults are happier than older adults (Riley & Foner, 1968; Wilson, 1967). Adams (1971) and Kozma and Stones (1978) in subsequent reviews concluded that there was no consistent relationship between age and SWB. In another review Larson (1978) went a step further and provided quantitative estimates of the magnitude of the age/SWB relationship. He estimated that age uniquely accounted for between 0 to 1% of the variance in SWB. More recently, Witt, Lowe, Peek, and Curry (1980) and Herzog and Rodgers (1981) employed replicated secondary data analysis to examine the age/SWB relationship. Based on data from 17 national polls taken between 1948 and 1977, Witt et al. (1980) found that the mean correlation between age and happiness was −.03. Using seven large-scale social surveys, Herzog and Rodgers (1981) regressed happiness and life satisfaction ratings on age. The mean standardized bivariate regression coefficients were −.02 and .04 for happiness and life satisfaction, respectively. Thus, previous attempts at research synthesis have resulted in discrepant conclusions. This article

Work on this article was supported by funds from the College of Education and Provost's office, Arizona State University. Individuals interested in obtaining a copy of the list of sources from which effect sizes were extracted should write to William A. Stock, Department of Educational Psychology, Arizona State University, Tempe, AZ 85287.

From William A. Stock et al., "Age Differences in Subjective Well-Being: A Meta-Analysis," original manuscript. Copyright © 1983 by Sage Publications, Inc.

reports on a meta-analysis (Glass, 1976, 1977) of the relationship between SWB and age among U.S. adults.

Definition of Subjective Well-Being

Following Larson (1978), we have used SWB as an umbrella construct. SWB refers to the self-perceived, general, affective experience of individuals in terms of a positive-negative continuum. The conceptualization and operationalization of SWB in terms of more specific indicators, such as happiness, life satisfaction, and morale, has been inadequate (George & Bearon, 1980; Sauer & Warland, 1982).

Some researchers (e.g., Andrews & Withey, 1976; Campbell, Converse, & Rodgers, 1976) have attempted to define global measures of SWB as a composite of measures of well-being within specific domains, such as work, marital relations, community relations, and personal health. In addition, there has been some research (Andrews & Withey, 1976; Bradburn, 1969) indicating that SWB is related to mental well-being and general adjustment. In the present study we operationalized SWB as any global measure of happiness, life satisfaction, or morale. In addition, global measures of quality of life and well-being are included. Measures of SWB in specific domains of life or measures of mental health and adjustment were excluded.

DEFINITION OF AGE

Though the vast majority of studies measured age chronologically, a few studies employed subjective age measures. Typically, subjective age was measured by asking respondents which age group they identified with (age identification) or, more rarely, how old they felt (perceived age). In the present study we included both chronological and subjective measures of age.

This meta-analysis was limited to *cross-sectional* estimates of the age/SWB relationship. *Longitudinal* estimates were not included because the number of data points was insufficient. In cross-sectional estimates individuals of varying ages are compared at the same point in time. Consequently, they differ not only in their ages, but also in their birth years (i.e., cohorts). Therefore, in cross-sectional estimates it is not possible to disentangle variance associated with age from variance associated with cohort (see Mason, Mason, Winsborough, & Poole, 1973; Schaie, 1965). Strictly speaking, the effect sizes extracted from sources in the present study were estimates of age *differences* as opposed to age *changes* in SWB.

Research Questions

This study used meta-analysis techniques suggested by Glass, McGaw, and Smith (1981) and by Hedges and Olkin (in press) to address the following questions:

(1a)   What is the empirical frequency distribution of zero-order effect sizes between age and measures of SWB? What is the central tendency and variability of this distribution?

(1b) What is the empirical distribution of first order effect sizes between age and SWB? What is the central tendency and variability of this distribution?

(2a) What study and sample characteristics are statistically significantly related to zero-order estimates?

(2b) What study and sample characteristics are statistically significantly related to first-order estimates?

(2c) Are first order estimates statistically significantly related to the type of control variable?

The tests of hypotheses implied by research questions 2a and 2b are typical of past meta-analyses. These relate the magnitude of the effect size to a variety of study and sample characteristics, some of which will be more interesting to researchers examining the age/SWB relationship, while others will be more interesting to methodologists. The results of all tests will be presented, but the discussion will focus on the characteristics we believe have most interest. In addition to the research questions specified above, we examined the magnitude of the zero- and first-order effect sizes within certain homogeneous groupings, including effect sizes from male and female samples, from younger and older samples, and from racially homogeneous samples.

METHOD

This study was conducted as part of a larger meta-analysis of SWB (Stock, Okun, Haring, Miller, Kinney, & Ceurvorst, 1982); with the focus here on the relationship of age and SWB. The project consisted of four major phases: (1) identification and collection of the potential data base, (2) selection and coding of the data base, (3) extraction of data points for computer analysis, and (4) statistical analyses.

Literature Search for Data Base

The potential data base was the extant empirical literature on SWB in adulthood through 1979 (restricted to studies conducted on U.S. adults). The empirical literature was defined as including all articles, books, technical reports, dissertations, theses, and any other accessible papers. A bibliography compiled by Linda K. George (Note 1) and the reference lists of the reviews by Adams (1971) and Larson (1978) provided the initial point of search. References in these sources were obtained, as were references in their reference lists (the process of obtaining references of references continued to the point of virtually no return on effort). At a point where more than 100 separate sources had been collected, the reference lists of these sources were inspected for publication outlets, providing a list of 32 separate journals. These journals were reviewed manually from the date of first publication through 1979. Any article containing any of the following keywords in the title was automatically included in the data base: (life) satisfaction, (avowed) happiness, morale, quality of life, and (subjective) well-being. In addition, *Psychological Abstracts, Dissertation Abstracts, Dissertation Abstracts International,*

Social Science Citation Index, and *Master's Abstracts* all were searched manually using the same keywords.

Next, computerized searches were conducted of the *Educational Resources Information Center, National Technical Information System, Psychological Abstracts, Sociological Abstracts, Social Science Citation Index,* and *National Institute of Mental Health* data bases. At this point an advertisement was placed in the *APA Monitor* of the American Psychological Association soliciting contributions to the data base. An attempt was made to secure all identified sources. As a final step a complete bibliography of identified sources was compiled and sent for review to 10 persons considered experts on the topic of SWB. The reviewers' efforts resulted in the addition of about 30 additional sources to the data base. During the coding process described below a few additional sources were added to the data base, culminating in a bibliography of 556 sources.

Selection and Coding of Data Base

After the final data base was selected, information was extracted from each research study according to procedures outlined in an 80-page codebook (Stock, Okun, Haring, Kinney, & Miller, Note 2), which was written to facilitate the identification and calculation of effect sizes, and to standardize the procedures for recording sample and study characteristics. The codebook was essential because of the complexity of the overall project. The complexity of the overall project stemmed from several sources. First, the project was designed to synthesize empirical research that examined relationships between SWB and 11 frequently cited correlates (activity, age, education, health, income, marital status, occupation, race, SES composite, sex, and work status). Second, the operational definition of SWB encompassed five related constructs (life satisfaction, happiness, morale, quality of life, and well-being). Third, effect sizes were initially defined as any zero-order or multiple correlation (including those calculable from other summary statistics in the source), and all reported higher order partial correlations with any measure of SWB as the criterion variable. In addition, where reported statistics in the original source permitted, selected first-order partial correlations were computed and coded. These included all first-order partial correlations between any measure of SWB and any measure of the 11 correlates listed above, with any of the 11 correlates as a control variable.

The process of coding involved a careful reading of the prospective source in order to decide whether it should be coded. In some cases this decision was easy to make, such as when the source only contained non-U.S. subjects, or did not contain an effect size involving SWB (nor data to estimate one). In other cases the decision was less clear cut, such as when the origin of the subjects was not specified or when an estimate had to be made from summary statistics. Whether ultimately accepted or rejected, each source had basic information regarding year of publication, date of coding, type of source (dissertation, journal, or book), and coder recorded. If a source was rejected, the reason for rejection was also recorded. Once a decision to accept a source was made, the procedures outlined in the codebook were followed.

The coding process extended over a nine-month period. There were four coders; three coded two-sevenths of the sources each, and one coded one-seventh of the sources. The sources were alphabetized and cyclically assigned to each coder. Two coders proceeded through the list in alphabetical order, and two proceeded in reverse alphabetical order.

A reliability study of coding processes was completed prior to actual coding and has been reported elsewhere by Stock et al. (1982). Three questions were addressed in this reliability study; namely, to what extent do independent coders agree on (1) which sources to integrate; (2) characteristics of study, sample, and estimates of effects; and (3) calculations pertaining to the extraction of these characteristics and estimates? Using a random sample of 30 sources from the data base, they found high intercoder reliability on all but two decisions. These were decisions about the total number of subsamples to be coded from a source and decisions about an overall rating of study quality. After analyzing all sources of disagreement, making modifications in the codebook, and adopting a nine-item rating index of study quality (Kohr & Suydam, 1970), all coders were given additional training in the coding process using the revised materials. The coders then independently coded an additional 15 sources. Reliability results on all coding processes were considered high enough to proceed.

Extraction of Data Points

The literature on SWB contains several different types of data from which estimates of effect size (correlations, partial correlations, higher order partial correlations, and multiple correlations) can be formed. Some data, such as some zero- and first-order partial correlations, could be coded directly onto the coding forms. Other data, such as frequency counts, were converted to a codable statistic; e.g., a phi correlation coefficient or Cramer's index. Nine different types of bivariate relationship were extracted from the Pearson product-moment correlation coefficients, Spearman rank order correlation coefficients, point-biserial and biserial correlation coefficients, phi correlation coefficients, tetrachoric correlation coefficients, Cramer's index for general contingency tables, correlation ratio (eta and epsilon) from analysis of variance tables, and eta derived from automatic interaction detection analysis. For first-order partial relationships four different types of effect size were recorded: standardized regression coefficients, first-order semi-partial correlation coefficients, first-order partial correlation coefficients, and first-order estimates derived from the square root of differences in R^2s. Standardized mean differences, derived from experimental studies, were excluded since less than 10 studies used experimental designs, and these usually dealt with the effects of a specific treatment on the magnitude of SWB. Thus, the experimental studies were not commensurate, in terms of potential correlates, with the rest of the research literature.

The coding of the independent variables followed procedures of other meta-analysts (Glass et al., 1981) and included study and sample characteristics. For this study, these characteristics have been listed in the first column of Tables 1 and 2.

It should be noted that effect size, rather than source, was the unit of observation in our analyses. There were not a sufficient number of studies reporting data on Hispanics, Native American, and Asian racial/ethnic minorities to justify analysis. Thus the percentage Caucasian also served as an index of the percentage Black in the sample. When a source reported sufficient data to obtain effect sizes on significant subsamples, these effect sizes were coded and the sample characteristics associated with the subsamples were also coded. For first-order effect sizes the type of control variable became an additional study characteristic coded.

Entry of Data Points for Statistical Analyses

The most effective way to enter the data for statistical analyses was to consider an individual effect size, rather than the source, as the fundamental unit of analysis. To help facilitate data entry an 11-page data entry dictionary was written and used to transcribe data from the working coding forms to data entry forms. Two coders were responsible for transcription, the third was responsible for checking the transcriptions of the first two, while the fourth coder entered the data into the computer. After all data was entered on the computer, the first three coders manually checked listings of the data against the computer coding forms. Finally, a preliminary statistical analysis using SAS PROC UNIVARIATE was run on all variables to scan for out-of-bound or illogical values, and all identified errors were corrected.

Overview of Data Analysis Procedures

The sets of zero- and first-order effects were analyzed separately. Prior to analyses, all effect sizes were transformed to Fisher's z according to the formula

$$z = 1/2 \, \ln[(1 + r)/(1 - r)]$$

where r = the effect size, a procedure recommended by Hedges and Olkin (in press). This transformation produces a normalized distribution with variance independent on the effect size parameter being estimated, a characteristic that allows the application of inferential procedures they developed for synthesizing research results. Two types of statistical analyses were undertaken to address the research questions: (1) a stem and leaf plot of the original effect sizes, along with measures of central tendency and variability; and (2) univariate analyses relating effect sizes to each study and sample characteristic. The analyses of effect sizes grouped by various homogeneous groupings (e.g., gender) were also accomplished using the univariate analysis procedures.

The univariate analyses were done using weighted regression procedures developed by Hedges and Olkin. Hedges and Olkin showed that under assumptions of (1) multivariate normal distribution of the effect size estimates, and (2) a linear regression model relating population effect size parameters, θ, to predictors; i.e.,

$$\theta = XB$$

where X is a design matrix and B is a vector of predictor parameters, that two chi-square statistics may be obtained by maximum likelihood (or generalized least squares) estimation. The first statistic provides a test of the nullity of the B, and the second provides a test of the goodness of fit of the model.

The first statistic is given by

$$q = n\, TB'U^{-1}B$$

where n is total sample size, T is the vector of effect size estimates, B the vector of estimates of model parameters, and U the covariance matrix of these estimates, and has a chi-square distribution with p degrees of freedom (the predictor degrees of freedom).

The second statistic is given by

$$Q = n[T'S^{-1}T - B'U^{-1}B]$$

where S^{-1} is a diagonal matrix of weights, and has a chi-square distribution with k - p degrees of freedom (the error degrees of freedom).

Using PROC GLM from the SAS statistical computing package, both of these statistics were computed using the weighted general linear model option, with the vector of sample sizes corresponding to the vector of effect sizes serving as the weight vector required by the program. In the output from GLM the first statistic, q, is given by the sums of square for the model, and the second statistic, Q, is given by the sums of squares error. The degrees of freedom corresponding to these sums of squares are correct.

The relation of these two statistics to each other is straightforward. The q statistic is a test of the predictive effectiveness of the chosen predictor. Thus, q is comparable to an F statistic in regression. When the value of q is statistically significant, one concludes that the predictor is significantly related to variation in effect sizes. This is analogous to the conclusion drawn from an F test in a regression setting with one predictor. While a predictor may account for a significant amount of variation in effect sizes, as indicated by the significant q, it is also possible that the model is actually a poor one. In ordinary regression it is possible for a test of goodness of fit to be conducted, which requires a partition of the error variance into goodness of fit and pure error components, but this procedure requires the identification of replicate data points and is hardly ever encountered in behavioral research. Using the procedure outlined by Hedges and Olkin (in press), the Q statistic provides a straightforward test of the adequacy of the model implied by the predictors being fit. In evaluating predictors using the two chi-square statistics then, one would search for significant q's and nonsignificant Qs, which would indicate the presence of predictors that accounted for a significant amount of variation in effect sizes (significant q) and fit the data well (nonsignificant Q). Given such a set of findings, the model is said to adequately specify the data.

These procedures have several desirable characteristics that make them preferable to ordinary least squares analyses. First, in estimating the effects of a particular characteristic on the effect-size parameter, the sample sizes corresponding to the effect-size estimates are taken into account. This is desirable because effect-size estimates derived from large samples are more stable than those derived from smaller samples, and the analytic procedure should be sensitive to this stability. Further, with large samples the procedures, which allow the specification and testing of any estimable linear model, including tests of hypotheses, are known to be efficient, consistent, and unbiased. In addition, the sampling distributions of the model parameters are known and estimation of simultaneous confidence intervals on these parameters is possible. Finally, the procedures provide a test of significance on the model parameters, that is q, and a test of model specification, that is Q.

There is one final note on the presentation of results. While the inferential analyses were all performed using Fisher's z transformation of the effect size, the descriptive statistics accompanying the presentation of these analyses were returned to the original metric for the purposes of presentation and discussion. We did this to reduce the burden on the reader, who we felt would be familiar with the meaning of r, but not z. For each type of analysis the results for the zero-order effect sizes have been presented first, followed by the results of the first-order effect sizes.

RESULTS

Descriptive Analyses

The empirical frequency distributions for the zero- and first-order effects were displayed in stem-and-leaf format (Tukey, 1977) in Figures 1 and 2. The first digit in the vertical column along the left margin is the stem, and all the numbers on the same line to the right of a stem are called leaves, with the combination of one stem and one leaf indicating the value of one estimate to two decimal places of accuracy (decimal points have been omitted). For example, in Figure 1 the leaves 5, 5, 5 to the right of the stem 2 represent three zero-order effect sizes, i.e., correlations of .25. Also displayed in Figures 1 and 2 are the summary statistics for these distributions.

The mean, median, and mode effect sizes for the zero-order correlations were .03, .07, and .10, respectively, while the range extended from the smallest estimate of -.65 to the largest of .61. Also, indicated are the first quartile, -.07; the third quartile, .14; and the standard deviation, .18. Using the jackknife technique (see Mosteller & Tukey, 1977), the 95% confidence interval about the overall mean of zero-order effect sizes, based upon 221 estimates from 119 different sources, extended from .01 to .06. The order of the measures of central tendency indicate some negative skew to the distribution. A Komologorov-Smirnov goodness-of-fit test had a p < .01; sufficiently small to conclude the distribution was nonnormal. There were 34 effect sizes between .08 and .10. The second largest clump consisted of 15 effect sizes between -.02 and .00. Approximately 41% of all zero-order effect sizes were below .01.

```
 6  1
 5  8
 4  5
 4  2
 3  68
 3  00012
 2  555666779
 2  000112223344
 1  5555566667777889999
 1  0000000000000001112222222233333334444
 0  5555556666677777888888888999999999999
 0  122223344
-0  444333322211100000000000
-0  99998887777777766665
-1  4443332221111111000
-1  986666665
-2  32
-2  877665
-3  43
-3  97
-4  33
-4  7
-5  2
-5  5
-6  5
```

Mean   = .03

Median = .07

Mode   = .10[f]

Q_3 = .14

Q_1 = -.07

SD   = .18

Range   = 1.26

95 percent jackknife confidence interval .01 - .06

Figure 1: Stem-and-leaf distribution of zero-order effect-size estimates with indices of central tendency and variability in the key.

```
 4   4
 3   9
 3   22
 2   9
 2   1223
 1   666777889
 1   000001222222222233333333444
 0   667779999999
 0   111344
-0   44444443322222222100000
-0   99999988888888777777777766666666665555555
-0   44433332222211111000000000
-1   9999
-2   44320
-2   9855
-3   865
-4
-4
-5   53
```

Mean	=	-.02
Median	=	-.04
Mode	=	-.07
Q_3	=	.10
Q_1	=	-.10
SD	=	.15
Range	=	.99

95 percent jackknife confidence interval   -.07   -   .02

Figure 2:   Stem-and-leaf distribution of first-order effect-size estimates with indices of central tendency and variability in the key.

The mean, median, and mode effect sizes for the first-order correlations were -.02, -.04, and -.07, respectively, while the range extended from -.55 to .44. Also indicated are the first quartile, -.10; the third quartile, .10; and the standard deviation, .15. The 95% jackknife confidence interval around the overall mean of first-order effect sizes, based on 168 estimates from 28 different sources, extended from -.07 to .02. Compared to the zero-order correlations this confidence interval is wider, and contains the value .00. A close examination of Figure 2 reveals bimodality about the points $r = -.07$ to $r = -.05$ and $r = .12$ to $r = .14$. A Komologorov-Smirnov test of goodness-of-fit confirmed nonnormality ($p < .01$). Approximately 64% of all first-order effect sizes were below .01. Relative to the zero-order data base (M = 1.86), the number of effect sizes per contributing source is much greater in the first-order data base (M = 6.00).

Univariate Inferential Analyses

Tables 1 and 2 contain results of the univariate analyses of study and sample characteristics for zero- and first-order estimates. For each characteristic two inferential statistics are reported: (1) q, the chi-square statistic associated with the test of nullity on the predictor parameters (B = 0); and (2) Q, the chi-square statistic associated with the test of model specification. Degrees of freedom are listed below each statistic. In addition to the chi-square statistics, the means, standard deviations, and number of effect sizes are given for each level of each categorical source or sample characteristic. For the characteristics with continuous properties, the correlation between values of the characteristic and the effect size is given.

There are a number of overall impressions that follow from an examination of these tables. First, using the q statistics to evaluate the statistical significance of the different independent variables almost always leads to rejection of the null hypothesis. An examination of the cell means for each categorical effect and the correlation for each continuous effect indicates q statistics are very sensitive to small differences. Second, the Q statistics, which provide a test of goodness of fit for the model associated with the particular predictor, are all very large relative to their respective degrees of freedom, indicating a poor fit for every one of these univariate models. The fact that no univariate model adequately accounts for the variability in the effect sizes suggests that multiple predictor models should be explored.

Due to the large number of indicators, we decided to focus our discussion on selected variables, including source of publication, theoretical framework, composite quality rating of the source, SWB keyword area, reliability of SWB scale, and sample characteristics (percentages institutionalized, Caucasian, and male, and an estimate of the midpoint of the age of the sample).

Effect size covaried with publication outlet of the source. For both zero- and first-order correlations, effect sizes reported in "other" publication outlets had the lowest mean. Therefore, reviewers ignoring other publication outlets may be introducing a serious bias into their reviews of the age/SWB relationship.

Within social gerontology much research on SWB was spawned by the debate between disengagement and activity theory. Surprisingly, although neither theory makes specific predictions concerning the age/SWB relationship, effect sizes derived from activity theory are lower than effect sizes derived from studies using disengagement theory or another/no theoretical framework. Perhaps researchers testing activity theory systematically differ on methodological variables, relative to other SWB researchers; which, in turn, effect the age/SWB relationship.

A composite index of the quality of the study was found to be significantly related to effect sizes in the weighted regression analyses. Effect sizes derived from sources with higher quality ratings tended to be smaller than those derived from sources with lower quality ratings. This finding has been reported in other meta-analyses as well (Light, Note 3).

TABLE 1   Zero-Order Effects: Univariate Inferential Analyses (q and Q) and Associated Descriptive Statistics for All Independent Variables

Study Characteristics	Mean[a]	SD[a]	N[b]	r[a]	q df	Q[c] df
Year of Publication			221	−.08	35.84+ 1	2486.04 211
Source of Publication			221		440.84+ 3	2081.04 209
Journals	.05	.19	77			
Books	.04	.18	19			
Dissertations	.03	.20	92			
Other	.00	.17	33			
Type of Sampling			221		11.19+ 2	2510.69 210
Random	.03	.13	114			
Judgment	.03	.24	97			
Not Specified	.06	.17	10			
Scope of Sampling			216		29.86+ 2	2422.03 205
National/Regional	.03	.14	60			
Within State	.03	.21	153			
Not Specified	.16	.05	3			
Region of Sample			158		173.67+ 4	825.76 146
Northeast	.01	.30	34			
Northcentral	.08	.18	50			
South	−.01	.17	43			
West	.06	.16	29			
Not Specified	.23	.04	2			
Total Sample Size			221	−.04	4.77* 1	2517.11 211
Longtitudinal Sample			221		7.84+ 1	2514.03 211
Yes	.12	.13	6			
No	.03	.19	215			
Theoretical Framework			221		224.40+ 2	2388.07 210
Activity	−.13	.21	14			
Disengagement	.03	.06	4			
None/Other	.04	.19	203			
Composite Quality Rating			221	−.08	133.81+ 1	2388.07 211
Multiple SWB Measures			221		1.49 1	2520.39 211
Yes	.04	.13	44			
No	.03	.20	177			
SWB Keyword			211		80.04+ 4	2441.83 208
Life Satisfaction	.03	.22	118			
Morale	.04	.15	57			
Well-Being	.01	.16	8			
Quality of Life	.03	.16	6			
Happiness	.04	.12	32			

TABLE 1   Continued

Study Characteristics	Mean[a]	SD[a]	N[b]	r[a]	q / df	Q[c] / df
SWB Measure			220		511.43+	1978.34
LSR	−.07	.01	4		13	198
LSI	−.04	.31	2			
LSIA	−.02	.29	43			
LSIB	.02	.16	6		(values reflected)	
LSIZ	−.07	.24	6			
ABS Total Score	−.06	.15	2			
PAS subscore	−.11	.00	2			
NAS subscore	−.05	.03	2			
Cavan	.15	.16	13			
PGCMS	.00	.13	31			
Cantril Ladder	.01	.14	16			
Single Item Scale	.05	.13	50			
Multiple Item Scale (Other)	.14	.14	37			
Kutner Morale Scale	−.03	.19	6			
Number of SWB Items in scale			204	.06[d]	65.54+ 1	2287.93 194
Report of Reliability in source			221		115.49+ 2	2406.39 210
No	.03	.19	162			
From another source	.19	.19	13			
New	−.01	.18	46			
Reliability Value Reported			58	.18[d]	5.21* 1	342.84 51
Type of Effect Size			221		265.64+ 5	2256.24 207
Pearson	−.02	.20	119			
Spearman	.12		1			
Point Biserial	−.08	.34	3			
Phi	.09	.14	32			
Cramer's Index	.07	.15	42			
Eta	.15	.16	24			
Number of Effect Sizes in Source			221	−.05	2.13 1	2519.75 211
Estimate from Sample or Subsample			221		37.64+ 1	2484.24 211
Sample	.04	.16	143			
Subsample	.01	.24	78			
Type of Age Measure			221		46.70+ 1	2475.18 211
Chronological	.03	.19	210			
Subjective	.05	.23	11			

TABLE 1   Continued

Characteristics	Mean[a]	SD[a]	N[b]	r[a]	$\dfrac{q}{df}$	$\dfrac{Q^c}{df}$
Percentage of Sample Institutionalized			195	.06[d]	.24 1	2380.77 188
Percentage of Sample Caucasian			112	−.00[d]	23.37+ 1	1171.73 106
Percentage of Sample Male			177	−.01[d]	63.94+ 1	2052.82 172
Age Midpoint of the Sample			174	−.12	184.19+ 1	1910.04 166

a. Reported in the metric r.
b. Number of effect sizes for the analysis.
c. All Q statistics significant at $p < .01$.
d. In the weighted regression analysis, the sign of the regression weight changed.
* $p < .05$
+ $p < .01$

TABLE 2   First-Order Effects: Univariate Inferential Analyses (q and Q) and Associated Descriptive Statistics for All Independent Variables

Study Characteristics	Mean[a]	SD[a]	N[b]	r[a]	$\dfrac{q}{df}$	$\dfrac{Q^c}{df}$
Year of Publication			168	.10[d]	.04 1	1270.15 157
Source of Publication			168		319.41+ 2	950.78 156
Journals	.06	.08	31			
Dissertations	−.03	.18	101			
Other	−.06	.10	36			
Type of Sampling			168		133.23+ 1	1136.97 157
Random	−.04	.12	115			
Judgment	.02	.20	53			
Scope of Sampling			167		74.09+ 1	1128.12 156
National/Regional	−.05	.14	53			
Within State	−.01	.16	114			
Region of Sample			114		58.50 3	239.73 102
Northeast	.07	.18	33			
Northcentral	.07	.18	12			
South	−.01	.15	40			
West	.05	.10	27			
Not Specified	.06	.14	2			
Total Sample Size			168	−.21+	405.89+ 1	864.31 157

TABLE 2   Continued

Study Characteristics	$Mean^a$	SD^a	N^b	r^a	q df	Q^c df
Longitudinal Sample			168			1270.19
Yes	.06	.14	2		not	158
No	−.02	.16	166		estimated	
Theoretical Framework			168		556.08+	714.11
Activity	−.12	.22	30		1	157
None/Other	.00	.13	138			
Composite Quality			168	−.32+	561.69+	708.51
Rating					1	157
Multiple SWB Measures			168		1.92	1268.27
Yes	−.02	.11	53		1	157
No	−.02	.17	115			
SWB Keyword			168		371.11+	899.09
Life Satisfaction	−.02	.18	68		4	154
Morale	−.01	.13	55			
Well-Being	−.08	.03	25			
Quality of Life	.15	.02	4			
Happiness	−.00	.21	16			
SWB Measure			168		410.49+	859.72
LSIA	−.07	.30	13		8	150
LSIZ	−.08	.11	10			
ABS Total Score	.13		1			
PAS Subscore	−.09	.02	12			
NAS Subscore	−.07	.04	12		(values reflected)	
PGCMS	−.02	.13	49			
Cantril Ladder	.02	.16	32			
Single Item Scale	−.03	.17	26			
Multiple Item Scale						
(other)	.10	.04	13			
Number of SWB			159	$.02^d$	2.60	1243.93
Items in Scale					1	150
Report of Reliability						
in Source			168		29.66+	1240.54
No	−.02	.14	119		1	157
New	−.03	.18	49			
Reliability Value			49	.64+	94.58+	88.46
Reported					1	39
Control Variable			168		175.32+	1094.88
Activity	−.09	.18	24		10	148
Age	.39		1			
Education	.00	.14	23			
Health	−.03	.18	32			
Income	−.02	.13	26			
Marital Status	−.02	.12	21			
Occupational Status	−.06	.12	8			

(continued)

TABLE 2   Continued

Study Characteristics	Mean[a]	SD[a]	N[b]	r[a]	q / df	Q[c] / df
Race	.10	.07	8			
SES Composite	−.02	.11	6			
Gender	.02	.10	11			
Work Situation	.02	.21	8			
Number of Effect Sizes in Source			168	−.09[d]	9.95+ / 1	1260.24 / 157
Estimate from Sample or Subsample			168		.26 / 1	1269.93 / 157
Sample	−.00	.14	95			
Subsample	−.04	.17	73			
Type of Age Measure			167		67.97+ / 1	1202.19 / 156
Chronological	−.02	.15	166			
Subjective	.39		1			

Sample Characteristics	Mean[a]	SD[a]	N[b]	r[a]	q / df	Q[c] / df
Percentage of Sample Institutionalized			162	.31+	132.31+ / 1	906.34 / 151
Percentage of Sample Caucasian			112	.04	2.05 / 1	487.70 / 110
Percentage of Sample Male			155	−.12[d]	201.55+ / 1	1066.14 / 153
Age Midpoint of the sample			133	−.26+	326.56+ / 1	666.34 / 130

a. Reported in the metric r.
b. Number of effect sizes for the analysis.
c. All Q statistics significant at $p < .01$.
d. In the weighted regression analysis, the sign of the regression weight changed.
+ $p < .01$

SWB keyword area was significantly related to zero- and first-order effect size magnitude in the weighted regression analyses. Previously, Campbell, Converse, and Rodgers (1976) had indicated that happiness decreases and life satisfaction increases with age. However, our results for zero- and first-order effects alike indicate that the means for the happiness and life satisfaction keyword areas were of comparable magnitude.

The relationship between the value of the reported reliability and the magnitude of the estimate varied greatly in zero- and first-order correlations. For zero-order correlations the regression weight was negative; for first-order correlations it was positive. Moreover, although Q was still significant at the .01 level, the p value for the first-order effect sizes was much larger than the p value for any other zero- or first-order uni-parameter model.

All of the characteristics of the sample were significantly related to effect-size magnitude in the weighted regression analyses (except percentage institutionalized for zero-order correlations and percentage Caucasian for first-order correlations). The results for percentage male were comparable (in the same direction) for both zero- and first-order effect sizes. In each case higher effect sizes were associated with a higher percentage of males in the weighted regression analyses. For age midpoint the results were also comparable (in the same direction) for zero- and first-order correlations alike. As the age midpoint of the sample increased, the effect size decreased. Another way of examining the effects of these samples is to group and analyze effect sizes by homogeneous categories. We now turn to the results of these analyses. They were restricted to homogeneous categories that included a minimum of 10 correlations per cell.

Specifically, we investigated effect-size magnitude differences between samples that were (1) all Caucasian or all Black, (2) all male or all female, and (3) younger versus older. In addition, we examined the crossing of gender and age for zero-order correlations. All other analyses were not conducted because cells were either empty or too small. For first-order correlations these analyses were modified by introducing the type of control variable as a predictor prior to assessing the effects of the characteristic being analyzed. This modification was introduced to control for differences due to type of covariate present in the original effect size.

In examining Black and Caucasian differences, samples were categorized into one or the other set if 100% of the sample (from which the effect size was derived) was from that racial group. For zero- and first-order correlations, there was no difference in the age/SWB relationship between the Black and the Caucasian set. For the zero-order effects this result is unexpected in light of the significant covariation between percentage Caucasian and the correlations in the weighted regression analysis (see Table 1).

When the effect sizes were separated into sets according to gender there was a significant difference between the sets, with the correlations being higher in the male as compared to the female set. These results were consistent with the univariate analyses showing that percentage male was directly related to zero- and first-order effect sizes.

Samples were categorized into younger and older sets by including samples with a midpoint less than 65 in the younger group and those with a midpoint greater than 65 in the older group. These results parallel those reported from the univariate analyses. For zero-order and first-order correlations, the mean effect size was higher in the younger than in the older group.

When zero-order estimates were categorized by both age and gender, significant main effects were again present. However, these main effects need to be qualified in light of the significant age by gender interaction effect. Specifically, the mean correlation for older women ($r = -.13$) was substantially lower than the mean correlations for younger men ($r = .06$), younger women ($r = .07$) and older men ($r = .08$). For all homogeneous analyses the models were inadequately specified.

With the first-order correlations it was possible to determine whether type of control variable was statistically significantly related to mean differences in effect-size magnitude. As can be seen in Table 2, type of control measure was related to effect size. When activity is the control variable, the mean effect size dropped to -.09 (N = 24), indicating that the age/SWB relationship is actually slightly stronger when activity is controlled. In contrast, when race is the control variable, the mean estimate rose to .10 (N = 8). Last, since there was only one estimate of the age/SWB relationship controlling on age, nothing can really be said about this effect.

DISCUSSION

Previous reviews (e.g., Adams, 1971; Kozma & Stones, 1978; Larson, 1978; Wilson, 1967) including an examination of the age/SWB relationship have a number of problems common to traditional (literary) literature reviews (Glass, 1977). Reviewers (1) were selective in the choice and number of research studies reviewed, (2) lacked information on potential moderating variables, and (3) did not examine the magnitude of effect size with respect to changes in study and sample characteristics. These limitations have been redressed in the present meta-analysis.

First, an effort was made to retrieve all accessible sources with age/SWB data and to include data points extracted from them in the analyses. Thus, we have included many studies omitted from previous reviews, thereby addressing typical criticisms of reviewer selection bias and insufficient representation of the research data base. Where Larson (1978) reviewed 11 studies that contained age/SWB data, in the present study 119 separate sources were used.

Self-imposed constraints on our data base included restricting the research to U.S. adults, to sources published before 1980, and to sources defining SWB by one of the five keyword topics. While these constraints may also have inherent biases, it is important to note the distinction. Biases in traditional reviews are neither observable nor readily remedied, whereas biases in the present study are both observable and readily remedied. Extension and/or replication of our procedures with research using non-U.S. populations, with studies from 1980 to the present, and with other definitions of SWB would all form companion works to the present one. Descriptive and inferential work presented in this study can be readily integrated with new information. In fact, one major benefit of our work is the creation of a computer data base containing all of the information upon which the present meta-analysis was conducted.

Second, this study presents the most comprehensive quantitative examination of the magnitudes of the age/SWB relationship. The most notable contribution of the descriptive statistics is the estimates from the first-order distribution. The estimates of the magnitude of semi-partial correlation between age and SWB controlling for a number of important correlates of SWB are a unique contribution. Although Herzog and Rodgers (1981) and Witt et al. (1980) investigated the relationship between age and SWB controlling on a number of relevant covariates in replicated secondary data analyses, their analyses were restricted to one-item happiness and life satisfaction measures.

Finally, the examination of effect-size magnitude changes relative to specific changes in study and sample characteristics provides clues about the effects of these characteristics. Taken as a whole the univariate analyses indicated significant variation in effect-size magnitude is accounted for by most study and sample characteristics. These analyses also indicate that no single characteristic adequately specifies the variation in effect-size magnitude. Inspection of the cell means in Tables 1 and 2 led us to conclude that many of the characteristics are accounting for small but statistically significant differences in effect size. We attribute this sensitivity to the analytical procedures of Hedges and Olkin (in press). In such circumstances investigators must make their own decisions about which differences are practically important. In the remainder of this discussion we review the basic findings, develop our implications, and note limitations.

Zero- and First-Order Estimates

The distribution of zero-order effect sizes indicates a minimal, though statistically significant, positive relation between age and SWB. The mean of this distribution appears to be just above .00 and the 95% confidence interval extends from .01 to .06. The mean of the distribution of first-order effect sizes is slightly lower than .00, while the 95% confidence band extends from −.07 to .02. Thus, when single control variables are introduced, the relationship between age and SWB remains weak and becomes negative and statistically nonsignificant. Although there is some variation in the mean first-order effect size by type of control variable, the amount of variance in SWB explained by age (except in the single instance where age was also the control variable) never rises above 1%. The introduction of multiple covariates appears to only slightly increase the amount of variance in SWB uniquely accounted for by age (Herzog & Rodgers, 1981; Witt et al., 1980). These results provide support for Larson's (1978) contention that age uniquely accounts for between 0% and 1% of the variance in SWB.

The distributions of zero-order and first-order effect sizes are not normal. There are a number of dependencies that causes clumping of data points. Investigators conduct multiple studies. As individuals they have preferences and limitations affecting the design of their research, thereby inducing subtle dependencies. Related to this phenomenon each study, particularly in the first-order data base, usually provides more than one estimate based upon the same sample. Glass et al. (1981) have estimated that the intraclass correlation between effect sizes from the same source is as high as .6, suggesting that clumping of data points is an enduring problem in meta-analysis. Secondary analysis of national probability samples also contributes to the clumping phenomenon. Another contribution to the nonnormality of the first-order correlations is the mixing of effect sizes with different control variables. Since the univariate analysis by type of control indicated a significant difference, the unconditional distribution of effect sizes was certainly affected.

Implications for Research

Quality of Studies. Our results suggest that researchers provided inadequate documentation of study and sample characteristics. One need only note that there were 389 zero- and first-order estimates, and that analyses by source and sample characteristics were often conducted using far smaller sets of data points (for lack of documentation in the original report). Also, reports often contained insufficient summary statistics for secondary and meta-analyses. For example, the absence of full correlation tables hindered our attempts to extract partial correlation information. Concerned about space, journal editors may discourage or demand the deletion of such tables. However, according to Seltzer (1975), these practices have contributed to making psychogerontology noncumulative.

Special Populations. The univariate analyses of sample characteristics and the subgroup analyses on homogeneous samples point out the need for investigators to do analyses on significant subsamples contained in their data bases. For example, the difference in the mean zero-order effect size between older women and young women, young men, and older men deserves further exploration. It is also clear that the relationship between age and SWB has only been minimally studied in certain minority groups, such as Hispanics or Native Americans.

Nonlinear Trends. As indicated in Table 1, the majority of our zero-order effect sizes were based on indices of association that are sensitive only to linear relationships. As mentioned earlier, cross-sectional estimates reflect both age-related and cohort-related variance. Quite possibly, in cross-sectional estimates, cohort effects contribute both to the amount of linearly and nonlinearly related variance in SWB accounted for by age (Rodgers, 1982). For example, inspection of the graph of the age/life satisfaction relationship provided by Campbell et al. (1976, p. 152) reveals considerable departure from linearity, with life satisfaction scores being lowest for the cohorts who were 30 and 50 years-old. The correlation between age and SWB will also be affected by the age range and distribution of the sample. Cross-sectional estimates should be based on representative samples spanning the entire adult age range, and assumptions of linearity should be checked.

The Measurement of SWB. There is considerable controversy over whether SWB is unidimensional or multidimensional (Campbell et al. 1976; Costa & McCrae, 1980; George, 1979; Larson, 1978). Campbell et al. (1976) distinguished between happiness, a temporally constrained affective construct; and life satisfaction, a cognitive/evaluative construct temporally focused on one's past life. They reported that happiness decreases and life satisfaction increases with age. Our results do not support their conclusion. We found minimal differences between scales classified as operationalizing life satisfaction and happiness in terms of mean zero-order and mean first-order effect sizes.

We believe that the issue of the dimensionality of SWB must first be resolved before further substantive progress can be made. The next crucial step involves constructing a structure of SWB model (see Okun, Stock, & Covey, in press) and validating it. Then, existing SWB scales could be modified or new scales developed within the framework of a validated model.

Theory-Based Research. Studies of age differences in SWB have often been atheoretical. As suggested by Maddox and Eisdorfer (1962), attention should be shifted from age as an independent variable to age-related factors that may impact on SWB. In this regard the life events theoretical approach might be useful

(Chiriboga & Cutler, 1980). Hultsch and Plemons (1979) have identified major life events (e.g., retirement) that are age-linked. In addition, there may be differences in the frequency with which certain mundane life events (hassles and uplifts) are experienced. Zautra and his associates (Goodstein, Zautra, & Goodhart, 1982; Reich & Zautra, 1981; Zautra & Reich, 1980, 1981) have been demonstrating a relationship between the experience of positive life events and perceptions of control of events and SWB. It will be interesting to see how well number of positive *and* origin age-related major and mundane life events predict positive affect (Kanner, Coyne, Schaefer, & Lazarus, 1981).

Limitations of the Meta-Analysis

No investigation is without its limitations. We have noted the self-imposed limitations with regard to restrictions to studies published prior to 1980, using U.S. adults, and employing indices of happiness, life satisfaction, morale, quality of life, and well-being. The remaining limitations have to do with the meta-analytic process itself.

First, the estimates and characteristics used in the meta-analytic process are only as good as the primary research base provide. Therefore, we could not correct the previously mentioned deficiencies that existed in the primary research on the age/SWB relationship. In addition, we felt particularly limited by the handful of *longitudinal* estimates of the effects of age on SWB. Although longitudinal estimates confound ontogentic change with time of measurement effects (see Schaie, 1965), they are generally preferable to cross-sectional estimates. We hope that the increased availability of longitudinal data bases will lead secondary data analysts to provide more longitudinal estimates of the age/SWB relationship (Kozma & Stones, 1978). If this were done, an update of the present meta-analysis could compare the magnitude of cross-sectional and longitudinal effect size estimates of the relationship between age and SWB.

Second, the meta-analysis is limited by the characteristics chosen for analysis. Other investigators might have chosen characteristics that would have covaried more strongly with the age/SWB effect size. For example, the standard deviation of the SWB measure might well be an efficient predictor of effect-size magnitude.

Third, the meta-analysis process requires a continuous effort to maintain coding efficiency and consistency. This is particularly true when the research base is as large as that for SWB. During the course of the entire project we were often engaged in checking and rechecking the computation of estimates, the coding of ancillary information, and the transcription of data. While we are very confident that the vast majority of information extracted has been done with a very high degree of reliability, one can always question the process. This is particularly true for characteristics such as study quality, which involved nine separate judgments on the part of the coder.

Fourth, while substantial strides have been made in the establishment of rigorous theory for the process of meta-analysis (e.g., the work of Hedges and his associates), there are still pressing needs in the development of analytical tools. Foremost is the need for accessible analytical tools that address the complicated issue of dependencies among estimates. We believe that the weighted regression procedures we used provide a more accurate assessment of effects than have previous procedures, but they are not optimal for dealing with dependencies among estimates (Hedges, Note 4).

Finally, being a quantitative synthesis of extant literature, meta-analysis does not necessarily create new and qualitatively different perspectives. That is, it does not necessarily follow that a meta-analysis will provide a new theoretical perspective from which research will follow. Indeed, the ideas that we discussed for future directions came from two sources. First, the meta-analysis has provided us with an overview of the research base, and the relation of effect-size magnitude to study and sample characteristics. This view has led us to the belief that some changes are necessary in conduct of future research. These changes have been mentioned in the appropriate places above, and they are primarily technical in nature. Second, the reading and discussion of the literature guided our thinking about the direction subsequent research should take.

REFERENCE NOTES

1. George, L. K. Bibliography of research on life satisfaction. Working paper, 1979.
2. Stock, W. A., Okun, M. A., Haring, M. J., Kinney, C., & Miller, W. Codebook for deriving and coding data points in meta-analysis: The sample case of subjective well-being. Limited circulation manuscript, 1979.
3. Light, R. Discussant's remarks. In M. A. Okun (Chair), *Research synthesis of the health-life satisfaction relationship.* Symposium presented at the meeting of the Gerontological Society of America, Boston, November 1982.
4. Hedges, L. V. Personal communication. September, 1982.

REFERENCES

ADAMS, D. L. Correlates of satisfaction among the elderly. Gerontologist, 1971, 11, 64-68.
ANDREWS, F. M. & WITHEY, S. B. Social indicators of well-being. New York: Plenum, 1976.
BRADBURN, N. M. The structure of psychological well-being. Chicago: Aldine, 1969.
CAMPBELL, A., CONVERSE, P. E., & RODGERS, W. L. The quality of American Life. New York: Russell Sage, 1976.
CHIRIBOGA, P. A., & CUTLER, L. Stress and adaptation: Life span perspectives. In L. W. Poon (Ed.), Aging in the 1980s. Washington, DC: American Psychological Association, 1980.
COSTA, P. T., & McCRAE, R. R. Still stable after all these years: Personality as a key to some issues in adulthood and old age. In P. B. Baltes and O. G. Brim (Eds.), Life-span development and behavior (Vol. 3) New York: Academic Press, 1980.
GEORGE, L. K. The happiness syndrome: Methodological and substantive issues in the study of social-psychological well-being in adulthood. Gerontologist, 1979, 19, 210-216.
GEORGE, L. K. Role transitions in later life. Monterey, CA: Brooks/Cole, 1980.
GEORGE, L. K. Subjective well-being: Conceptual and methodological issues. In C. Eisdorfer (Ed.), Annual review of gerontology and geriatrics (Vol. 2) New York: Springer, 1981.

GEORGE, L. K., & BEARON, L. B. The meaning and measurement of quality of life in older persons. New York: Human Sciences, 1980.

GLASS, G. V. Primary, secondary, and meta-analysis of research. Educational Researcher, 1976, 5, 3-8.

GLASS, G. V. Integrating findings: the meta-analysis of research. In L. Schulman (Ed.), Review of research in education (Vol. 5) Itasca, IL: Peacock, 1977.

GLASS, G. V, McGAW, B., & SMITH, M. L. Meta-analysis in social research. Beverly Hills, CA: Sage, 1981.

GOODSTEIN, J., ZAUTRA, A., & GOODHART, D. A test of the utility of social indicators for behavioral health service planning. Social Indicators Research, 1982, 10, 273-295.

HEDGES, L. V., & OLKIN, I. Regression models in research synthesis. American Statistician. (in press)

HERZOG, A. R., & RODGERS, W. L. Age and satisfaction: Data from several large surveys. Research on Aging, 1981, 3, 142-165.

HULTSCH, D. F., & PLEMONS, J. K. Life events and life span development. In P. B. Baltes and O.G. Brim (Eds.), Life span development and behavior (Vol. 2) New York: Academic Press, 1979.

KANNER, A. D., COYNE, J. C., SCHAEFER, C., & LAZARUS, R. S. Comparison of two modes of stress management: Daily hassles and uplifts versus major life events. Journal of Behavioral Medicine, 1981, 4, 1-39.

KOHR, R. L., & SUYDAM, M. N. An instrument for evaluating survey research. Journal of Educational Research, 1970, 64, 78-85.

KOZMA, A., & STONES, M. J. Some research issues and findings in the assessment of well-being in the elderly. Canadian Psychological Review, 1978, 19, 241-249.

LARSON, R. Thirty years of research on the subjective well-being of older Americans. Journal of Gerontology, 1978, 33, 109-125.

MADDOX, G., & EISDORFER, C. Some correlates of activity and morale among the aged. Social Forces, 1962, 4, 254-260.

MADDOX, G. L., & WILEY, J. Scope, concepts, and methods in the study of aging. In R. Binstock and E. Shahas (Eds.), Handbook of aging and the social sciences. New York: Van Nostrand Reinhold, 1976.

MASON, K. O., MASON, W. M., WINSBOROUGH, H. H., & POOLE, W. K. Some methodological issues in cohort analysis of archival data. American Sociological Review, 1973, 38, 242-258.

MOSTELLER, F., & TUKEY, J. W. Data analysis and regression: A second course in statistics. Reading, MA: Addison-Wesley, 1977.

OKUN, M. A., STOCK, W. A., & COVEY, R. Assessing the effects of older adult education on subjective well-being. Educational Gerontology. (in press)

REICH, J. W., & ZAUTRA, A. Life events and personal causation: Some relationships with distress and satisfaction. Journal of Personality and Social Psychology, 1981, 41, 1002-1012.

RILEY, M. W., & FONER, A. Aging and society: An inventory of research findings (Vol. 1) New York: Russell Sage, 1968.

RODGERS, W. Trends in reported happiness within demographically defined subgroups, 1957-78. Social Forces, 1982, 60, 826-842.

SAUER, W. J., & WARLAND, R. Morale and life satisfaction. In D. J. Mangen and W. A. Peterson (Eds.), Clinical and social psychology (Vol. 1). Minneapolis: University of Minnesota, 1982.

SCHAIE, K. W. A general model for the study of developmental problems. Psychological Bulletin, 1975, 64, 92-107.

SELTZER, M. M. The quality of research is strained. Gerontologist, 1975, 15, 503-507.

STOCK, W. A., OKUN, M. A., HARING, M. J., MILLER, W., KINNEY, C., & CEURVORST, R. W. Rigor in data synthesis: A case study of reliability in meta-analysis. Educational Researcher, 1982, 11, 10-14, 20.

TUKEY, J. W. Exploratory data analysis. Reading, MA: Addison-Wesley, 1977.

WILSON, W. Correlates of avowed happiness. Psychological Bulletin, 1967, 67, 294-306.

WITT, D. D., LOWE, G. D., PEEK, C. W., & CURRY, E. W. The changing association between age and happiness: Emerging trend or methodological artifact? Social Forces, 1980, 58, 1302-1307.

ZAUTRA, A., & REICH, J. W. Positive life events and reports of well-being: Some useful distinctions. American Journal of Community Psychology, 1980, 8, 657-670.

ZAUTRA, A., & REICH, J. W. Positive events and quality of life. Evaluation and Program Planning, 1981, 4, 355-361.

18

Utilizing Controversy as a Source of Hypotheses for Meta-Analysis
The Case of Teacher Expectancy's Effects on Pupil IQ

Stephen W. Raudenbush

This chapter examines how recent qualitative and quantitative innovations in meta-analysis (Pillemer and Light, 1980; Rosenthall and Rubin, 1982) were used to account for variability in outcomes of experiments assessing the effect of teacher expectancy on pupil IQ (Raudenbush, 1982).

More generally, this inquiry employed the strategy of using controversy over the causes of outcomes of early experiments as a source of hypotheses to account for variability in the outcomes of later experiments (Pillemer and Light, 1980). In using this strategy a systematic review of the introductions and discussion sections of research reports becomes just as vital to meta-analytic success as a close examination of the statistical tables is. The collective thinking of many investigators shapes the questions the meta-analysis asks and the interpretation of its answers' meaning. In turn the meta-analytic evidence supplies an empirical constraint on the speculation offered so freely in the final pages of research reports. Some speculations bear fruit, others lead to dead ends. Indeed, the greatest promise of meta-analysis may be to bring some order to what otherwise often seems a chaotic, individualistic social science research enterprise. Without meta-analysis, for every research finding there are several speculations about its cause and significance, but limited avenues for assessing their merits.

A second general strategy applied here is to locate the research question in its social and ideological context. Especially in the case of the Pygmalion controversy, these contextual issues seemed to have motivated much of the research and continue to influence our interpretation of the practical significance of the findings.

THE PYGMALION CONTROVERSY:
ITS SOCIAL AND IDEOLOGICAL CONTEXT

When Robert Rosenthal and Lenore Jacobson published *Pygmalion in the Classroom* (1968), they could hardly have anticipated the whirlwind of controversy

From Stephen W. Raudenbush, "Utilizing Controversy as a Source of Hypotheses for Meta-Analysis: The Case of Teacher Expectancy's Effects on Pupil IQ," original manuscript. Copyright © 1983 by Sage Publications, Inc.

that would quickly surround them. Nor could they have predicted the extraordinary research effort subsequently launched to test the validity of their findings. Fourteen years and hundreds of studies later, researchers continue to dispute the adequacy of the evidence supporting their central contention: that children's rates of intellectual growth depend in part upon the rates at which their teachers expect them to grow.

Though researchers have been characteristically unable to resolve the debate over teacher expectancy effects, Rosenthal and Jacobson's conceptualization and vocabulary have enjoyed widespread dissemination as a focus for further research and a guide to educational reform:

- While studing the Pygmalion effect the researchers artificially induced changes in teacher expectations in order to assess their effects experimentally; other investigators (Leacock, 1969; Miller, McLaughlin, & Chomsby, 1969; Palardy, 1969; Rist, 1970; Mazer, 1971; Yee, 1968; Seaver, 1971; Kleinfield, 1972; Brophy & Good, 1974) have sought to discover the bases on which teachers naturally derive their expectations for children's intellectual growth.

- Other researchers have asked how their expectations, once formed, influence the ways teachers interact with children in the classroom, both verbally (Good, 1970; Brophy & Good, 1970, 1974; Mendoza, Good, & Brophy, 1972) and nonverbally (Rowe, 1969; Chaiken, Seigler, & Derlaga, 1974).

- Research on the formation and communication of expectancies has provided the basis for new strategies in teacher education (Brophy & Good, 1971) and in inservice teacher training (Terry, 1977; Greenfield, Banuazizi, & Gagnon, 1979; Kerman, 1979).

- The teacher expectancy hypothesis has influenced school effectiveness research. Edmonds (1980) cited "implied expectations derived from teacher behavior in the classroom" as one of the five institutional characteristics related to school effectiveness, while Rutter, Maughm, Mortimore, & Dusten (1979) identified teacher expectations as a constituent of "school ethos" related to the outcomes of schooling in inner city London schools.

- Evaluators of two large-scale educational innovations, the Career Intern Program (Gibboney & Langsdorf, 1977) and the Street Academies (Young, 1982) have found the level of teacher expectations an important determinant of program success.

- Black plaintiffs in California entered the Pygmalion findings as evidence in their successful suit to ban the use of IQ tests in the assignment of black children to "educable mentally retarded" classes when such assignment led to the racial imbalance of those classes (Jensen, 1980). Pygmalion also provided the basis for the banning of IQ tests in one city's schools (Elashoff & Snow, 1971, p. 9).

The irony of Rosenthal's and Jacobson's work is that, despite its rather powerful impact on later research and practice, the truth of its central proposition remains contested or flatly denied. For instance, Jensen (1980) wrote:

> Just as Ovid's myth of Pygmalion's creation of the beautiful Galatea endures because of its wish-fulfilling appeal to human emotions, so too does the myth of the expectancy effect on IQ persist for much the same reason, despite a dozen attempts to replicate the expectancy effect, all without success [p. 608].

To Miller (1980), the alleged failure of attempts at replicating Pygmalion exemplifies how "hard data" stubbornly resist liberal academics' attempts to "wish away social deviance, mental handicaps, and the lower half of the normal distribution curve of ability" (p. 79). "Ultimately," he wrote:

> Many of those still convinced that the expectations thesis is correct turned to ethnography, abandoning a scientific process that kept providing "no difference" results. Since the labelling theory had to be true, science must be wrong [p. 75].

These recent examples suggest that the bitterness surrounding the Pygmalion controversy, and its ideological undertones, have not entirely subsided over the past 14 years. The more extreme disputants operate as if they live in different worlds. In one world the self-fulfilling prophecy is a major discovery, crucial to understanding classroom life, school effectiveness, and innovative programming. In another world the self-fulfilling prophecy in education is an illusion, a liberal dream that failed when tested by careful research, and meanwhile lives on only in the imaginations of idealists misled by "academic myth-makers" (Miller, 1980). Let us briefly trace the origin and development of this enduring disagreement.

Controversy Over the Original Study

The first stage in the controversy focused on the Pygmalion study itself. In that now famous experiment all of the predominantly poor children in the so-called Oak Hill elementary school were administered a test pretentiously labeled the "Harvard Test of Inflected Acquisition." After explaining that this newly designed instrument had identified those children most likely to show dramatic intellectual growth during the coming year, the experimenters gave the names of these "late bloomers" to the teachers. In truth, the test was a traditional IQ test and the bloomers were a randomly selected 20% of the student population. After retesting the children eight months later, the investigators announced that those predicted to bloom had in fact gained significantly more in total IQ (nearly four points) and reasoning IQ (seven points) than the control group children. Further, at the end of the study the teachers rated the experimental children as intellectually more curious, happier, better adjusted, and less in need of approval than their control group peers.

Provocatively, for experimental boys the "Mexicanness" of their facial features, as rated by independent judges, correlated positively with the size of their IQ gains. The authors speculated that without any experimental intervention, the teachers may have had "the lowest expectations of all for these boys," who, therefore, may have had the most to gain from enhanced expectancies.

The ideological climate in 1968 was ripe with potential both for eager, non-critical acceptance and for unusually harsh criticism of the study and its findings. Researchers, educators, and political activists were already engaged in a heated debate over the causes of poor children's depressed school achievement. In the context of this explosive debate relevant social scientific findings took on an added public significance.

The Pygmalion experiment became a centerpiece in the attack on the thesis that poor children's home backgrounds were to blame for their school problems (Moynihan et al., 1965; Coleman et al., 1966; Hess, Shipman, Brophy, & Bear, 1968). Rosenthal and Jacobson did not invent the idea that teacher expectations cause disadvantaged children's depressed school achievement, of course (see Clark, 1963). Rather, the crucial ingredient they added was an apparently scientific basis for the assertion.

In his widely read *Blaming the Victim,* William Ryan (1971) wrote:

> It remained for Robert Rosenthal to demonstrate once and for all that teachers' expectations do in fact have a dramatic effect in the classroom and test performances of school children. . . . It takes no great leap of logic to conclude further that the pervasively low teacher expectations found in slum and ghetto schools must be a major cause of the poor achievement in those schools. . . . We are dealing, it would seem, not so much with culturally deprived children, but with culturally depriving schools. . . . To continue to define the difficulty as inherent in the raw material—the children—is plainly to blame the victim and to acquiesce in the continuation of educational inequality in America [Ryan, 1972, pp. 61-62].

Ryan's emphasis on Pygmalion's scientific character echoed the earlier review, published in the New York Review of Books, by Herbert Kohl (1971):

> The implications of these results will upset many school people yet these are hard facts. Can failure in ghetto schools be attributed to teacher expectations, and not to the students' environment or ability? . . . [These results] condemn the tracking system prevalent in elementary and secondary schools throughout the country [p. 84].

If its apparent scientific credibility was its most appealing feature to its admirers, Pygmalion's seeming scientific *incredibility* served as a starting point in its critics' search for flaws. Thus, Nate Gage (1971) wrote:

How plausible are statements about intentional changes in human intelligence? Half a century of research has shown that such changes are hard to make. . . . I had this kind of feeling for the plausibilities when I encountered the work of Robert Rosenthal and Lenore Jacobson. . . . It seemed implausible to me that IQ, which had proven so refractory, would yield to the admittedly weak treatment administered to the teachers in their experiment.

Bitterly condemning Pygmalion's influence on the educational policy debate, Thorndike (1968), Jensen (1969), and Elashoff and Snow (1971) claimed that because of its alleged methodological flaws the study provided no basis for the widely heralded findings. A classical methodological battle ensued (see Rosenthal & Rubin, 1971; Rosenthal, 1974, for replies).

Replication Efforts

Eventually debate over the original study subsided and the disputants focused instead on replication attempts. Baker and Crist (1971) reviewed 25 early studies and found that 11 of the 14 studies using teacher-pupil interaction as the outcome had found significant effects of expectancy. Of the 12 studies employing pupil achievement as the outcome, half reported significant effects. However, none of the nine studies utilizing IQ as an outcome showed overall significant effects. The authors concluded that expectancy probably does not affect pupil IQ, a finding "supported by a background of decades of research suggesting the stability of human intelligence and its resistance to alterations by environmental manipulation" (p. 61).

Rosenthal (1974) reviewed 185 studies of the effects of interpersonal expectancy conducted in laboratories, and 57 others conducted in classrooms, offices, and factories. Since nearly a third of the studies reported significant findings in the predicted direction with very few in the opposite direction, the author concluded that interpersonal expectancy effects are a widely generalized phenomenon. However, his review mentioned no study other than Pygmalion reporting significant IQ effects.

More recently, Rosenthal and Rubin's (1978) review of 345 studies further substantiates the expectancy effect in a wide variety of settings including classrooms, but leaves clouded the specific question of expectancy's IQ effects. Smith (1980) found an average effect size of .38 standard deviation for 78 estimates of expectancy's effects on achievement and an average effect size of only .16 for 22 estimates of expectancy's IQ effects.[1] She concluded that teacher expectancy had minimal effect on pupil ability.

Expectancy Effects and IQ

A cause of the explosiveness of the Pygmalion controversy and a continuing source of its confusion is the intersection between the teacher expectancy hypothesis and the IQ debate. To those who have read the vigorous methodological criticisms of Pygmalion and reports of early replication failures using IQ as the outcome, teacher expectancy may appear a dead issue. Others, familiar only with the original study or later reviews of studies that mainly use *non-IQ* outcomes, may assume that expectancy's *IQ* effects have been fully validated.

It may appear then that the confusion can be solved simply by declaring that teacher expectancies have effects, but not on IQ. However, there were compelling methodological and substantive reasons to look more deeply into experiments hypothesizing such effects.

The Baker and Crist (1971) review, while seeming to provide strong evidence undermining hypothesized effects of expectancy on IQ, actually exemplifies a common but weak strategy for synthesizing study findings, a strategy that has been termed "taking a vote" (Light & Smith, 1971). According to Light and Smith, vote taking works as follows:

> Three possible outcomes are defined. The relationship between the independent and the dependent variable is either significantly positive, significantly negative, or there is no significant relationship in either direction. . . . If a plurality of studies falls into the other two, the modal category is declared the winner [p. 433].

As Light and Smith explain, the most obvious weakness in this approach is a loss of statistical power. For instance, several studies pooled together can produce a highly significant effect even if none of them separately achieves statistical significance.

An alternative to vote taking is meta-analysis (Glass, 1977). In meta-analysis individual studies conducting tests of the same hypothesis become cases in a "study of all the studies." This method enables the investigator both to conduct a combined test of the null hypothesis by using the statistical results from a set of studies, and to estimate the average effect of a treatment across all available studies. Smith (1980) conducted such a meta-analysis, mentioned earlier, for expectancy's IQ effects. However, the computation of an average effect size or of a combined significance test overlooks a major source of the continuing controversy. When studies have reported significant expectancy effects, critics have offered rival explanations for those effects (Thorndike, 1968; Jensen, 1980). On the other hand, when studies have reported null effects, critics have constructed explanations--other than the failure of the expectancy hypothesis--for those findings. To test these rival explanations requires that we attempt to account for *variability* in findings. Do the variables postulated to explain past study outcomes predict later findings? This question determined the logic of the present meta-analysis.

In summary, Pygmalion's relevance to the ideological warfare of the late 1960s stimulated intense controversy over the expectancy hypothesis. One major source of confusion in the ensuing debate was a common failure to disentangle expectancy's effects on non-IQ outcomes from those on IQ. While it has become increasingly difficult to deny expectancy's effects on teacher-pupil interaction, student attitudes, and achievement, the question of expectancy's IQ effects is far from settled. To assess the IQ effects required employing the methods of meta-analysis. Moreover, the logic of inquiry suggested a subtle adjustment in meta-analysis strategy. Instead of computing an average effect, this strategy called for the utilization of the various explanations postulated to account for experimental findings. The goal was then to use controversy over the studies as a source of independent variables in an attempt to account for variability in experimental outcomes.

METHOD

Generation of Hypotheses

A careful reading of the original Pygmalion study (Rosenthal & Jacobson, 1968); of the original study's main critics (Thorndike, 1968; Jensen 1969; Elashoff & Snow, 1971); of early replication failures cited by Baker and Crist (1971); and of critics of those early failures to replicate (Rosenthal & Rubin, 1971; Carter, 1970; Brophy & Good, 1974) generated hypotheses for the synthesis.

Three hypotheses emerged from the original study. First, the authors speculated that younger children were more susceptible to the influence of expectancy than older children, as indicated by a correlation of −.86 between grade level and mean expectancy advantage. Second, since the more Mexican-looking experimental boys tended to gain more in IQ than other experimental boys, the authors suggested that disadvantaged children may have "the most to gain by the introduction of a more favorable expectation into the mind of the teacher" (p. 83). Third, since the experiment revealed no significant effect after four months, but did reveal an effect after eight months, the authors speculated that a minimal "incubation period" may be necessary to produce IQ changes.

From criticisms of Pygmalion emerged hypotheses (1) that statistical methods may influence results (Jensen, 1969; Elashoff & Snow, 1971); (2) that group-administered tests for young children lead to uncontrolled and invalid measurement, suggesting that the reported gains were not valid IQ gains (Thorndike, 1968); (3) that the findings may have resulted by selective test coaching of experimental children (Thorndike, 1968; Pellegrini & Hicks, 1972).

From early failures to replicate Pygmalion's findings emerged the hypothesis that the timing of expectancy induction may influence its outcome: If researchers provide teachers with expectancy inducing information *after* the teachers know the students well, the information may be unpersuasive, leading to null effects (Carter, 1971; Rosenthal & Rubin, 1971; Brophy & Good, 1974; Jose & Cody, 1971).

From among all the hypotheses generated by various commentators, major hypotheses were identified for emphasis in analysis and presentation. First, the questions of whether a treatment was implemented seemed to be one to be considered prior to all other questions, and the timing of expectancy induction seemed crucial to implementation. Second, of the hypotheses concerning study methods, validity of measurement seemed critical. Any generalizations emerging from the meta-analysis would be invalid if measurement were invalid. Third, among subject background characteristics, child age seemed both crucial and also most amenable to analysis since studies frequently reported comparisons by grade. Major hypotheses and their rationale are discussed below, though all hypotheses were tested.

Timing of Expectancy Induction

Experiments assessing teacher expectancy effects actually involve two conceptually distinct phases. In the first phase researchers provide teachers with biased test scores or other information designed to elevate the teachers' expectancies for specific children who had actually been assigned at random to the experimental group. This is the expectancy induction phase.

The second phase of these experiments tests the expectancy hypothesis: Do teachers' expectations, once altered by the expectancy induction, influence their behavior and subsequent pupil response? Clearly, if the induction fails there can be no treatment effect, not because of any failure in the theory, but simply because no treatment was implemented. Careful reading of several early studies reviewed by Baker and Crist (1971) suggests that if one wishes to account for variability in experimental findings, one must attempt to account for the variability in the success of expectancy induction. Further, evidence suggests that the timing of expectancy induction may prove crucial to its success.

Five studies mentioned by Baker and Crist as using IQ as an outcome also measured the influence of the induced expectancies on teacher behavior. Close examination of three of these studies (Anderson & Rosenthal, 1968; Flowers, 1966; Kester, 1969) reveals the following pattern: (1) in each case expectancy induction occurred *before* teachers had had extensive contact with their pupils; (2) in each case teachers significantly differentiated their behavior toward experimental and control children; (3) in each case there was some evidence of IQ change.[2]

In contrast, in the two remaining studies (Claiborn, 1969; Jose & Cody, 1971): (1) expectancy induction occurred during the spring of the school year, after months of teacher-student contact; (2) experimenters reported no teacher behavior effects; and (3) there was no evidence of IQ change. Further, Jose and Cody (1971) provided evidence that the teachers in their study had rejected the expectancy-inducing information. At the completion of that experiment a survey revealed that

61% of the teachers "had not expected the children to show improvement as a result of the test information." Further,

> Others stated that they knew the children and their backgrounds and knew what the children could be expected to do. . . . The modification of expectancy *may have been too weak to overcome prior teacher expectancy based on other knowledge of the child* [p.47, emphasis added].

The notion that the timing of the expectancy induction influences its subsequent effects, while based on evidence from only five studies, is also consistent with cognitive dissonance theory (Festinger, 1957). Researchers have found that when persons are involuntarily exposed to new information, they tend to tune out, misperceive, invalidate, or forget information discrepant with ingrained beliefs or established patterns of behavior (Hastdorf & Cantril, 1954; Wallen, 1942; Ewing, 1942; Brock & Balloun, 1967; Kleinhesselink & Edwards, 1975).

Fleming and Anttonen (1971) employed the language of dissonance theory explicitly in interpreting their results. They attempted to induce changes in teacher expectancies in the fall, though apparently after at least two weeks of teacher-student contact. The experimenters reported IQ scores inflated by 16 points for the experimental children and retested them again in the spring. The two groups' gains were nearly identical. Asked to assess the accuracy of the scores reported to them, teachers rated the experimental group's scores as significantly less accurate than the control group's. The authors concluded:

> The external imposition of an expectancy which creates dissonance for a teacher when she is confronted with discrepant behavior in the real world of children and tests appears not to reflect itself in improved pupil performance. . . . The present study . . . suggests that teachers *assess children, reject discrepant information,* and operate on the basis of previously developed attitudes toward and knowledge about the children and tests [p. 251, my emphasis].

A major hypothesis of this inquiry, then, emerging from an examination of early replication attempts and consistent with dissonance theory, was that how well teachers know their pupils, as indicated by the amount of time spent with them in the classroom prior to expectancy induction, influences their susceptibility to persuasion by researcher-provided information about the children's intellectual potential. This hypothesis could not be tested directly since few experiments attempt to measure changes in teachers beliefs or behavior. However, if the hypothesized expectancy effects on IQ are real, then the hypothesis concerning the timing of the expectancy induction leads to the prediction that the size of the expectancy effects will correlate negatively with the number of weeks of teacher-student contact predating expectancy induction.

Uncontrolled Measurement and Tester Bias

Critics of the original Pygmalion study emphasized allegedly poor measurement of IQ as a source of skepticism about its findings (Thorndike, 1968; Jensen, 1969; Elashoff & Snow, 1971). The statistically significant effects of teacher expectancy on pupil IQ depended on the rather dramatic gains reported for the experimental children in grades one and two. As Thorndike (1968) noted, very young children's scores on a paper and pencil test are especially sensitive to their willingness to try the test items. Perhaps as a result, the younger children's scores were both unexpectedly low and highly variable at the pretest. Thorndike suggested that the experimental treatment may have influenced children's motivation and that the group-testing may have rendered the test scores unusually sensitive to such motivational effects.

Further, since in Pygmalion the teachers administered the post-tests, Thorndike (1968) suggested that the reported IQ effects may have been caused by test coaching at the posttest. Pellegrini and Hicks (1972) designed their study specifically to test the hypothesis that expectancy effects operate through test coaching. Since expectancy effects were found when testers were aware of the researcher-provided designations of children's intellectual potential, but were not found when the testers were blind to those designations, the authors concluded that the expectancy effects both in their study and in the original study had probably resulted from the test coaching of the experimental children.

The hypothesis that expectancy effects are made possible only by uncontrolled measurement or test coaching was tested by data provided by replication attempts that varied in the conditions of their test administration.

Ages and Background of Subjects

The original Pygmalion suggested for further research study of treatment-by-subject interactions. Therefore, the present inquiry sought to discover relationships between treatment effect and the age, race, socioeconomic background, and sex of the subjects whenever possible.

Sample of Studies

Literature reviews (Baker & Crist, 1971; Rosenthal, 1974; Brophy & Good, 1974; Jensen, 1980) and an ERIC search produced 18 experimental studies of teacher expectancy where IQ or aptitude served as an outcome and children in grades 1 through 7 as subjects. Though Raudenbush (1980) employed studies (n = 18) as the unit of analysis, this reanalysis employs grade-level effect (n = 33) as the sampling unit. The grade-level data enabled clearer demonstration of recent meta-analytic methods. From these, all studies employing IQ as an outcome and normal children in grades one through seven as subjects were included in the sample for the synthesis (n = 18).[3]

Analytic Procedure

Statistical methods for assessing variations among findings responded to two different kinds of questions. First, do subgroups of studies differ significantly *from each other* in their findings? To answer this question, Rosenthal and Rubin's (1982a) statistical test of the significance of a contrast among study effect sizes was computed. Second, if it is found that two or more subgroups do differ significantly in their reported effects, do the combined results within any subgroup of studies indicate an experimental effect significantly *greater than zero?* To answer this type of question, two tests were employed: Mosteller and Bush's (1954) method for adding z's, and Fisher's (1938) method for adding logs (see Rosenthal 1978, for details). Both tests were used because Rosenthal (1978) has reported that there is no uniformly best test and that the weaknesses of the two methods are to some degree offsetting.

There were two main outcome variables for the meta-analysis:

(1) The effect size denoted by the symbol d, which is the treatment effect in IQ points divided by the control group's standard deviation at the posttest. Note that in studies where the experimental children gain more in IQ than the control children, d is positive. But when controls gain more than experimentals, d is negative. (Effect sizes were based on total IQ scores and not on subtest scores.)

(2) The one-tail p value reported by each study. When experimentals gain more than controls, p is less than .5. When controls gain more than experimentals, p is greater than .5.

RESULTS

All Effects Combined

The 33 effects sizes of the 18 studies, in standard deviation units, ranged from −.26 to .71 (m = .08, sd = .25); 6 of the effects achieved statistical significance, 4 at the 5% and 2 at the 1% level of significance. Of the remaining nonsignificant effects, in 15 cases the experimental children scored higher than the control children, while in 12 cases the control children scored higher. No effect, however, was both negative and statistically significant.

Timing of Expectancy Induction

The earlier analysis (Raudenbush, 1982) showed the importance of prior contact in predicting outcomes when studies served as the sampling unit. Prior contact accounted for more than half the variation in study effect sizes. When grade level effects served as the sampling units, the relationship between prior contact and effect size was more modest, r = –.39. However, a scatter plot showed an extreme curvilinear relationship. Since the correlation coefficient is a measure of the strength of *linear* association, it underestimates relationships that are actually curvilinear. One common way to facilitate study of curvilinear relationships is to transform the units in which the two variables are measured, that is to linearize the relationship. After employing a suitable transformation (Kirk, 1979),[3] a second plot and a recomputed correlation coefficient, r = –.49, showed a stronger negative association between weeks of prior contact and effect sizes. Thus the grade level suggests a smaller effect of prior contact than the study level data had suggested, though the effect is still substantial.

To further explore the relationship between the timing of expectancy induction and experimental effects, the effects were dichotomized into high (more than one week) and low (one week or less) categories of prior teacher-student contact. The two categories were found significantly different in their effect sizes, z = 2.82, one-tail p = .002. Further, each of the five combined significance tests showed an expectancy effect significantly greater than zero for low contact studies; no method revealed a significant effect, in either direction, for the high contact studies (Table 1).

The hypothesis that the duration of treatment influences results (Rosenthal & Jacobson, 1968) was more difficult to test. Low contact effects varied little in the duration of their treatments, which typically spanned the school year. However, high contact effects did vary in their durations of treatment and for them, duration was not associated with effect size. Thus while duration may or may not influence outcomes of low contact studies, a long-term treatment seems hardly capable of surmounting the effects of prior teacher-student acquaintance.

Uncontrolled Measurement and Tester Bias

To test the hypothesis that expectancy effects on IQ are made possible only by uncontrolled measurement, effects were broken down according to whether tests were individually or group administered (Table 2). Though only three effects used individual tests, their results bore a strong resemblance to results of effects based on using group tests when only considering the low contact effects.

To test the hypothesis that expectancy's IQ effects are made possible only by test coaching (Thorndike, 1968; Pellegrini & Hicks, 1972), effects employing testers aware of the researcher-provided designations of children's intellectual potential were compared to effects employing testers blind to those designations. The results indicated no main effect of tester awareness, z = –.694, and no significant inter-action between prior contact and awareness, z = .338. Among the low contact effects both aware and blind conditions produced significantly positive effects of expectancy (Table 3.) These results suggest that the effect of prior teacher-student contact works independently of tester awareness of designations about children's intellectual potential.

TABLE 1. Results of Five Statistical Tests of the Effect of Expectancy on IQ,
Computed Separately for Effects Low and High in Teacher-Student
Contact Prior to Expectancy Induction

| | Prior Contact | | | |
| | Low (Two Weeks or Less) | | High (More Than Two Weeks) | |
	Test Statistic	P	Test Statistic	P
Fisher (1938)[a]	x^2 (22) = 59.96	<.001	x^2 (44) = 39.52	n.s.
Edgington (1972)[b]	$\sum_{1=1}^{N} P_i$ = 2.91	<.003	$\sum_{i=1}^{N} P_i$ = 11.61	n.s.
Winer (1971)[c]	Z = 4.20	<.001	Z = −.21	n.s.
Mosteller and Bush (1954)[d]	Z = 3.99	<.001	Z = −.29	n.s.
Mosteller and Bush (1954)[e] (weighted by degrees of freedom)	Z = 3.51	<.001	Z = −.185	n.s.

a. $x^2 (2N) = -2 \sum_{i=0}^{N} \ln p_i$

where p_i = one-tail probability observed for study i (i = 1, 2, . . . N)

b. $P_T = \sum_{i=0}^{M} \binom{N}{i} \frac{(S-i)^N}{N!} (-1)^i$

where P_T = combined one-tail probability across all studies

S = sum of individual probabilities (one-tail)
M = largest integer smaller than S
N = number of studies

c. $Z = \sum_{i=1}^{N} T_i / [\sum_{i=1}^{N} f_i / (f_i - 2)]^{1/2}$

where T_i = value of a t-test for study i (i = 1, 2, . . . N)
f_i = degrees of freedom associated with T
Z is a standard normal deviate

d. $Z = \sum_{i=1}^{N} Z_i / N^{1/2}$

where Z_i = z value associated with observed one-tail p for study i (i = 1, 2, . . . N)
Z, N defined as above

e. $Z = \sum_{i=1}^{N} f_i Z_i / (\sum f_i^2)^{1/2}$

where Z, f_i, Z_i and N are defined as above.

TABLE 2   Mean Effect Sizes and Results of Two Significance Tests for Experiments Depending on Type of IQ Test (Individual versus Group) and Extent of Teacher-Student Contact (High or Low) Prior to Expectancy Induction

	N	mean d	Mosteller and Bush (1954) (unweighted)		Fisher (1938)	
			z	p less than	X^2 (2N)	p less than
Low Contact						
Individual tests	2	.37	3.01	.01	18.18	.01
Group tests	9	.24	2.99	.01	38.79	.001
High Contact						
Individual tests	1	.16	.67	n.s.	2.77	n.s.
Group tests	21	−.07	−1.46	n.s.	36.75	n.s.

Other direct or indirect measures of study quality—sophistication of statistical tests used, source of study (doctoral dissertation or journal), year of publication, and a composite measure of methodological quality (based on percentages of attrition, testing procedures, and statistical methods) were also employed as independent variables in the analysis. In each case, once prior teacher-student contact was accounted for, other information provided no help in understanding outcomes.

The Influence of Children's Age

Mean effect sizes, broken down by three grade levels and two levels of prior conact, are shown in Table 4.

The analysis with respect to grade level effects revealed the following findings (Raudenbush, 1982):

(1) The data were first analyzed after excluding grade seven comparisons from the analysis. The main effect of prior contact was significant, z = 1.87, one-tail p = .31. The main effect of grade was nonsignificant, z = 1.26. The interaction of prior contact and grade was significant, z = 1.85, one-tail p = .32.

(2) Considering all three grade levels, there was again a significant effect of prior contact, z = 2.24, one-tail p = .013. The apparent, though unanticipated, quadratic trend across grade levels within low contact (Table 4) was suggestive, though nonsignificant, z = 1.62.

(3) Expectancy effects were significantly greater than zero only for low contact studies at grades one, two, seven (Table 4).

TABLE 3   Effect of Test Administrator (Aware versus Blind) and
Prior Contact (High or Low) on Experimental Outcomes

(A) *Contrasts:* Do subgroups of studies differ significantly from each other?

Main effect of prior contact	$z = .82, p = .002$
Main effect of test administrator	$z = -.694$, n.s.
Interaction	$z = .338$, n.s.

NOTE: Contrasts among effect sizes were computed as follows (Rosenthal and Rubin 1982, p. 501):

$$Z = \sum_{j=1}^{k} \lambda_i \, d_i \, / \, [\, \Sigma \, \lambda_1^2 \, / \, w_i \,]^{1/2}$$

where λ_i: are contrast coefficients for studies (i = 1, 2, ... N)

d_i = effect size for study i

$w_i = n_1 n_2/(n_1+n_2)/[1+t_i^2/ 2(n_1+n_2 - 2)]$

t_i = t-test for study i

(B) For each subgroup does the mean effect differ significantly from zero?

	N	mean d	Mosteller and Bush (1954) (unweighted) Z	p less than	Fisher (1938) X^2 (2N)	p less than
Low Contact						
Aware	7	.23	3.39	.001	28.41	.02
Blind	4	.30	2.44	.01	28.55	.001
High Contact						
Aware	10	-.14	-1.02	n.s.	16.28	n.s.
Blind	12	.01	.53	n.s.	23.24	n.s.

Effects of Race, SES, and Socioeconomic Backgrounds of Subjects

The data reported in the 18 studies provided only a limited basis for testing the hypothesis that subject background variables moderate expectancy effects; 5 studies reported experimental versus control comparisons for minority children; 3 studies reported such comparisons for majority children. For SES the numbers were only slightly higher. After breaking these comparisons down by amount of prior teacher-student contact (high versus low), the cell sizes were too small to estimate differential effects for subgroups. However, the results (Table 5) did suggest that no

TABLE 4   Mean Effect Sizes and Results of Two Significance Tests Depending on Grade Level of Subjects and Prior Contact

	N	mean d	Mosteller and Bush (1954) (unweighted)		Fisher (1938)	
			z	p less than	X^2 (2N)	p less than
Low Contact (two weeks or less)						
Grades 1-2	7	.31	3.20	.001	38.07	.001
Grades 3-6	9	.04	.87	n.s.	22.39	n.s.
Grade 7	3	.23	2.40	.01	16.36	.02
High Contact (more than two weeks)						
Grades 1-2	8	−.09	−1.18	n.s.	19.66	n.s.
Grades 3-6	6	.03	.55	n.s.	13.07	n.s.

TABLE 5   Mean Effect Sizes and Results of Two Significance Tests Depending on Race, Socioeconomic Status and Sex of Students and Prior Contact

	N	mean d	Mosteller and Bush (1954) (unweighted)		Fisher (1938)	
			z	p less than	X^2 (2N)	p less than
Race						
Low Contact						
Minority	4	.23	1.99	.05	17.69	.025
Majority	1	.30	1.72	.05	6.29	.05
High Contact						
Minority	1	.17	1.28	n.s.	4.60	n.s.
Majority	3	−.02	−.87	n.s.	3.74	n.s.
SES						
Low Contact						
Low SES	7	.12	2.17	.015	27.28	.025
Middle SES	2	.30	2.59	.005	15.42	.005
High Contact						
Low SES	1	.22	1.25	n.s.	4.49	n.s.
Middle SES	3	−.03	−.69	n.s.	4.00	n.s.
Sex						
Low Contact						
Boys	5	.26	2.82	.005	26.64	.005
Girls	5	.14	1.90	.05	18.43	.05
High Contact						
Boys	3	.12	.69	n.s.	6.74	n.s.
Girls	3	−.05	−.77	n.s.	2.76	n.s.

subgroup of children, be it minority or white, middle or low SES, was invulnerable to the effects of expectancy in low contact studies.

To assess the effect of sex differences on effect sizes, the data are slightly better. For eight studies reporting experimental effects by pupil sex, there was no significant effect of contact, $z = 1.35$; no main effect of sex, $z = .780$; and no significant interaction, $z = .285$. Taken separately, however, low contact studies revealed expectancy effects significantly greater than 0 for both boys and girls (Table 5).

DISCUSSION

The major goal of this inquiry was to utilize controversy over reported findings as a source of hypotheses to account for variability in study outcomes. Two of the first reported failures to replicate the study (Claiborn, 1969; Jose & Cody, 1971) inspired the criticism that expectancy induction may have occurred too late in the school year to alter teacher opinions (Carter, 1971; Rosenthal & Rubin, 1971; Brophy & Good, 1974). These critics suspected that it may be difficult to persuade teachers to alter their expectations for children whom they already know well. Study level analysis strongly supported this assertion (Raudenbush, 1982). Grade level data led to a smaller but still substantial estimate of this effect.

Practical Significance of the Expectancy Effect

Probably the single most startling and important result of this synthesis is the consistency of the treatment effect, given little or no prior teacher-student contact. Indeed, without the stability of these effects, we could not have discovered the importance of prior teacher-student contact. The effect's robustness across methods of test administration strongly undermines the thesis that reported expectancy effects on IQ are made possible only by invalid measurement. But how large is the effect?

The practical significance of the effect is open to a variety of interpretations. Table 6 shows four measures of effect size for studies depending on the number of weeks of prior contact. The traditional measures r and r^2 are well known. Cohen's (1977) U_3 indicates the percentage of the experimental group expected to outgain the lowest half of the control group.

Expectancy Induction and Dissonance

An unanticipated result of the reanalysis was how little prior contact is apparently required before the teachers become invulnerable to influence by biased, external information. If the expectancy induction occurs more than one week into the school year it is apparently too late to be persuasive. Discussion about this result with friends who teach has led to two speculations about its cause.

First, many teachers view the first week or two of school as a time of dissonance. Both the teacher and the students are uncertain and perhaps apprehensive about what the future year will bring and what their mutual expectations are.

TABLE 6.   Four Measures of Effect Size for 18 Experiments Depending on Grade Level of Child (for Low Contact Studies Only)

Weeks of Prior Contact	Number of Studies	mean d[a]	r	r^2	U_3 (Cohen, 1977)
1, 2	7	.31	.15	.02	.62
3-6	9	.04	.02	.00	.51
7	3	.23	.11	.01	.59

NOTE: Assumes equal group sizes and equal within-group variances. Under these conditions, $r^2 = d^2 \,/\, (d^2 + 4)$.

a. The r's, r^2's, and U_3 shown above are those associated with the mean d shown in this column.

A major goal of many teachers during this time is to organize the daily routine of the class, to clarify expectations and limits. Often the creation of ability groups serves to structure classroom life and reduce such dissonance. Perhaps external information received *after* these routines have been established—information that implies a renegotiation of group assignments and expectations—rearouses intolerable dissonance and is likely to be rejected.

Second, Fleming and Antonnen's (1971) result suggests that teachers are keen judges of children's academic standing. Carew and Lightfoot (1979) and Kellaghan, Madaus, and Arasian (1982) suggest that teachers often reject test information if they have personal knowledge contradictory to it. Perhaps test information is persuasive only in the absence of such personal knowledge.

The Effects of Grade Level

The tendency, first reported in Pygmalion, for relatively strong expectancy effects to appear in the first and second grades, only to disappear in grades three through six, is supported by this synthesis. The speculation that this disappearance reflects children's decreasing vulnerability to the effects of adult influence, however, is flatly contradicted by the reappearance of the effect at grade seven. This reappearance also contradicts the speculation that expectancy's reported IQ effects signify changes in young children's motivation in test taking and not their aptitude (Thorndike, 1968).

Why then do expectancy effects decrease during elementary years? One plausible alternative explanation is consistent with dissonance theory. The grade seven studies (Kester, 1969; Carter, 1971; Flowers, 1966) were among those taking care to prevent prior teacher knowledge of students from diluting the impact of the expectancy-inducing information. Further, their ability to do so may have been enhanced by the fact that the junior high school teachers in these studies had little or no contact with the children's previous teachers in elementary school.

Shortcomings in the reporting of the data prevented the synthesis from testing Rosenthal and Jacobson's speculation that subgroups of children for whom teachers naturally hold the lowest expectations stand to gain most from elevated expectancies. The evidence does suggest, however, that neither boys nor girls, minority nor majority, middle nor low SES children, are immune to the effects of favorable expectations.

Implications for Further Research

Questions for future research derive from the need to replicate findings presented here and to expand the attempt to account for the variability in expectancy effects. Do the results presented here hold up for non-IQ outcomes? Meta-analytic techniques used here may prove more powerful in accounting for variability in non-IQ outcomes, since studies employing such outcomes are more numerous, adding degrees of freedom needed for a more powerful multivariate model to account for variability in experimental effects. The question of the timing of expectancy induction and variability in effects across grade levels should especially be investigated. Hypotheses concerning differential effects for children of varied backgrounds may be more successfully addressed when the outcome variable is not restricted to IQ.

Methodological Lessons

A major advantage of meta-analysis is that it increases the information-value of each study synthesized by providing a vehicle for systematic secondary analysis. However, most meta-analyses use only a small fraction of the information contained in each study: a probability value or an effect-size estimate. One purpose of the synthesis reported here was to utilize more fully the information contained in each study and in commentaries on the studies. Specifically, the synthesis sought to draw on the speculative thinking of researchers and other critics as a source of hypotheses to account for variability in study findings. Consistent with this reasoning is the notion that controversy offers a special opportunity for learning. First controversy may, as in the Pygmalion case, inspire intense research activity, producing a large body of research for meta-analysis. Second, ideological controversy requires the disputants to specify the empirical propositions undergirding their arguments. Such specification may lead to new, potentially productive, research questions and hypotheses for future meta-analysis.

NOTES

1. Smith's (1980) meta-analysis consisted of 47 studies reporting 147 comparisons between experimental and control children. There were 22 comparisons or "effects" where IQ served as the outcome.

2. Anderson and Rosenthal (1969) led counselors at a summer camp for retarded children to believe that certain children would become more self-reliant. At the end of the summer the high expectancy children did score significantly higher on a self-help measure than their control peers. The counselors, however, had left these experimental children alone significantly more than control children, whom they may have viewed as needier. By the end of the summer,

perhaps as an unintended consequence of such benign neglect, the experimental children showed a statistically significant and marked *decline* in reasoning IQ compared to the control children.

In a study actually predating Pygmalion (Flowers, 1966), investigators arbitrarily assigned one of two similarly tested groups of junior high school students to a moderately higher level section for a year, a procedure implemented in two different schools. In one school the experimental children gained 5.1 IQ points more on the average than control children, $t(36) = 1.526$, $p < .08$. At the other school, the experimental and control children remained nearly even.

Kester reported no group means, but stated flatly that an analysis of variance of gain scores had revealed "no effect" for IQ. Fortunately, however, he generously included his complete data set in the appendix of his dissertation. This author reanalyzed the data, first using an analysis of gain scores as Kester had done, and then using the more powerful analysis of covariance with the pretest as a covariate. The more powerful analysis of covariance revealed a modest-sized but statistically significant effect of expectancy, $t = 1.65$ (one-tail $p < .05$).

3. The reciprocal transformation (Kirk, 1979, p. 66) was employed here, after first adding a constant since both variables had values at or near 0:

$$x_{new} = -1/(2 + x_{old})$$

REFERENCES

ANDERSON, D. F., & ROSENTHAL, R. Some effects of interpersonal expectancy and social interaction on institutionalized retarded children. Proceedings of the Seventy-Sixth Annual Convention of the American Psychological Association, 1968, 478-479.

BAKER, P. J., & CRIST, J. L. Teacher expectancies: A review of the literature. In R. E. Snow & J. D. Elashoff (Eds.), Pygmalion reconsidered. Worthington, OH: Charles A. Jones, 1971.

BROCK, T. C., & BALLOUN, J. L. Behavioral receptivity to dissonant information. Journal of Personality and Social Psychology, 1967, 6, 413-428.

BROPHY, J. E., & GOOD, T. L. Teacher's communication of differential expectancies for children's classroom performance. Journal of Educational Psychology, 1970, 61(5), 365-374.

BROPHY, J. E., & GOOD, T. L. Looking in classrooms. New York: Harper & Row, 1971.

BROPHY, J. E., & GOOD, T. L. Teacher-student relationships: Causes and consequences. New York: Holt, Rinehart & Winston, 1974.

CAREW, J. V., & LIGHTFOOT, S. L. Beyond Bias. Cambridge, MA: Harvard University Press, 1979.

CARTER, D. L. The effect of teacher expectations on the self-esteem and academic performance of seventh-grade students. (Doctoral dissertation, University of Tennessee, 1970). Dissertation Abstracts International, 1971, 31, 4539-A. (University Microfilms No. 7107612)

CHAIKEN, A., SEIGLER, E., & DERLAGA, V. Nonverbal mediators of teacher expectancy effects. Journal of Personality and Social Psychology, 1974, 30(1), 144-149.

CLAIBORN, W. Expectancy effects in the classroom: A failure to replicate. Journal of Educational Psychology, 1969, 60, 377-383.

CLARK, K. B. Educational stimulation of racially disadvantaged children. In E. H. Passow (Ed.) Education in Depressed Areas. New York: Teachers College, Columbia University, 1963.

COHEN, J. Statistical Power Analysis for the Social Sciences, (Rev. ed.). New York: Academic Press, 1977.

COLEMAN, J. S. et al. Equality of Educational Opportunity. Washington, DC: U.S. Department of Health, Education and Welfare, Office of Education, 1966.

EDGINGTON, E. S. An additive model for combining probability values from independent experiments. Journal of Psychology, 1972, 80, 351-363.

EDMONDS, R. Speech given to the Conference on Urban Schools. Sponsored by the Council for Basic Education, Wasington, DC, 1980.

ELASHOFF, J., & SNOW, R. Pygmalion Reconsidered. Worthington, OH: Charles A. Jones, 1971.

EWING, T. A. A study of certain factors involved in changes of opinion. Journal of Social Psychology, 1942, 16, 63-88.

FESTINGER, L. A theory of cognitive dissonance. Evanston, IL: Row, Peterson, 1957.

FISHER, R. A. Statistical methods for research workers. London: Oliver & Boyd, 1938.

FLEMING, E., & ANTONNEN, R. Teacher expectancy or my fair lady. American Educational Research Journal, 1971, 8, 241-252.

FLOWERS, C. E. Effects of an arbitrary accelerated group placement on the tested academic achievement of educationally disadvantaged students. (Doctoral dissertation, Columbia University, 1966). Dissertation Abstracts International, 1966, 27, 991-A. (University Microfilms No. 6610288)

GAGE, N. L. Forward to J. D. Elashoff and R. E. Snow (Eds.) Pygmalion Reconsidered. Worthington, OH: Charles A. Jones, 1971.

GIBBONEY, R. A., & LANGSDORF, M. The Career Intern Program: Final Report, Volume I: An Experiment in Career Education that Worked. NIE Papers in Education and Work, No. 7. Elkins Park, PA: EDO 142795, 1971.

GLASS, G. V. Integrating findings: The meta-analysis of research. Review of Research in Education, 1977, 5, 351-379.

GOLDSMITH, J. S., & FRY, S. The test of a high expectancy prediction on reading achievement and IQ of students in grade ten. Referred to as "submitted to American Educational Research Journal" in Baker and Crist, 1971.

GOOD, T. L. Which pupils do teachers call on? Elementary School Journal, 1970, 70, 190-198.

GREENFIELD, D., BANUAZIZI, A., & GAGNON, J. An evaluation of the second year of Project STILE (Student-Teacher Interactive Learning Environment). Unpublished report prepared for the Division of Education, Commonwealth of Massachusetts, 1979.

HASTDORF, A., & CANTRIL, H. They saw a game: A case study. Journal of Abnormal and Social Psychology, 1954, 49, 129-134.

HESS, R., SHIPMAN, V., BROPHY, J. & BEAR, R. The Cognitive Environments of Urban Preschool Children. Chicago: University of Chicago Graduate School of Education, 1968.

JENSEN, A. How much can we boost IQ and scholastic achievement? Harvard Educational Review, 1969, 39, 1-123.

JENSEN, A. Bias in mental testing. New York: Free Press, 1980.

JOSE, J., & CODY, J. Teacher-pupil interaction as it relates to attempted changes in teacher expectancy of academic ability achievement. American Educational Research Journal, 1971, 8, 39-49.

KELLAGHAN, T., MADAUS, G. F., ARASIAN, P. W. The Effects of Standardized Testing. Boston: Klumer Nijhoff, 1982.

KERMAN, S. Teacher expectations and student achievement. Phi Delta Kappan, June 1979, 716-718.

KESTER, S. W. The communication of teacher expectations and their effects on the achievement and attitudes of secondary school pupils. (Doctoral dissertation, University of Oklahoma, 1969). Dissertation Abstracts International, 1969, 30, 1434-A. (University Microfilms No. 6917653)

KIRK, R. E. Experimental design: procedures for the behavioral sciences (2nd ed.). Belmont, CA: Brooks/Cole, 1979.

KLEINFIELD, J. Instructional style and the intellectual performance of Indian and Eskimo students. Final Report. No I-J-027, Office of Education, U.S. Department of HEW, 1972.

KLEINHESSELINK, R. R., & EDWARDS R. E. Seeking and avoiding belief discrepant information as a function of its perceived refutability. Journal of Personality and Social Psychology, 1975, 59, 250-253.

KOHL, H. Great expectations. In R. E. Snow & J. D. Elashoff (Eds.), Pygmalion Reconsidered. Worthington, OH: Charles A. Jones, 1971.

LEACOCK, E. B. Teaching and learning in city schools. A comparative study. New York: Basic Books, 1969.

LIGHT, R. J., & SMITH, P. V. Accumulating evidence: Procedures for resolving contradictions among different research studies. Harvard Educational Review, 1971, 41, 429-471.

MAXWELL, M. L. A study of the effects of teachers expectations on the IQ and academic performance of children. (Doctoral dissertation, Case Western Reserve, 1970). Dissertation Abstracts International, 1971, 31, 3345-A. (University Microfilms No. 7101725)

MAZER, G. E. Effects of social class stereotyping on teacher expectation. Psychology in the Schools, 1971, 8(4): 373-383.

MENDOZA, S., GOOD, T., & BROPHY, J. Who talks in junior high classrooms? Report Series 68, Research and Development Center for Teacher Education. Austin: University of Texas, 1972.

MILLER, C. J., McLAUGHLIN, J., & CHOMSKY, N. Socioeconomic class and teacher bias. Psychological Reports, 1969, 23, 806.

MILLER, H. L. Hard realities and soft social science. Public Interest, 1980, 59, 67-83.

MOSTELLER, F., & BUSH, R. Selected quantitative techniques. In G. Lindzey (Ed.), Handbook on social psychology, Vol. I: Theory and method. Cambridge, MA: Addison-Wesley, 1954.

MOYNIHAN, D. P. et al. The Negro family: The case for national action. Washington, DC: Department of Labor, 1965.

PALARDY, J. M. What teachers believe—What children achieve. Elementary School Journal, 1969, 69, 370-374.

PELLEGRINI, R., & HICKS, R. Prophecy effects and tutorial instruction for the disadvantaged child. American Educational Research Journal, 1972, 9, 413-419.

PILLEMER, D. B., & LIGHT, R. J. Synthesizing outcomes: How to use research evidence from many studies. Harvard Educational Review, 1980, 50, 176-195.

RIST, R. C. Student social class and teacher expectancies: The self-fulfilling prophecy in ghetto education. Harvard Educational Review, 1970, 40, 411-451.

RAUDENBUSH, S. W. Magnitude of teacher expectancy effects on pupil IQ as a function of the credibility of expectancy induction. Journal of Educational Psychology, 1983.

ROSENTHAL, H. The effect of teacher expectancy upon the achievement and intelligence scores of adult students. Dissertation Abstracts International, 1975, 35, 7017-7018.

ROSENTHAL, R. On the social psychology of the self-fulfilling prophecy: Further evidence for Pygmalion effects and their mediating mechanisms. MSS Modular Publications. New York: Module 53, 1974.

ROSENTHAL, R. Combining results of independent studies. Psychological Bulletin, 1978, 85, 185-193.

ROSENTHAL, R. & JACOBSON, L. Pygmalion in the classroom. New York: Holt, Rinehart & Winston, 1968.

ROSENTHAL, R., & RUBIN, D. B. Pygmalion reaffirmed. In J. D. Elashoff, R. E. Snow (Eds.), Pygmalion reconsidered. Worthington, OH: Charles A. Jones, 1971.

ROSENTHAL, R., & RUBIN, D. B. Interpersonal expectancy effects: The first 345 studies. Behavioral and Brain Sciences, 1978, 3, 377-386.

ROSENTHAL, R., & RUBIN, D. B. Comparing effect sizes of independent studies. Psychological Bulletin, 1982, 92, 500-504. (a)

ROSENTHAL, R., & RUBIN, D. B. A simple general purpose display of experimental effect. Journal of Educational Psychology, 1982, 74, 2, 166-169 (b)

ROWE, M. B. Science, Silence and Sanctions. Science and Children, 1969, 6, 11-13.

RUTTER, M., MAUGHM, B., MORTIMORE, P., & OUSTEN, J. Fifteen thousand hours: Secondary schools and their effects on children. Cambridge, MA: Harvard University, 1979.

RYAN, W. Blaming the victim. New York: Pantheon, 1971.

SEAVER, W. B. Effects of naturally induced teacher expectancies on the academic performance of children in primary grades. Unpublished doctoral dissertation, Northwestern University, 1971.

SMITH, M. L. Teacher expectations. Evaluation in Education, 1980, 4, 53.

TERRY, J. T. Student performance and school related attitudes as a function of teacher expectation and behavior. Unpublished doctoral dissertation, Boston College, 1977.

THORNDIKE, R. L. Review of Pygmalion in the classroom. American Educational Research Journal, 1968, 5, 708-711. Reprinted in Elashoff and Snow, 1971.

WALLEN, R. Ego-involvement as a determinant of selective forgetting. Journal of Abnormal and Social Psychology, 1942, 37, 20-39.

WINER, B. J. Statistical principles in experimental design. New York: McGraw-Hill, 1971.

YEE, A. Interpersonal attitudes of teaching advantaged and disadvantaged pupils. Journal of Human Resources, 1968, 3, 327-345.

YOUNG, L. The New York Street Academy. Case study for the National Institute of Education. Cambridge, MA: Huron Institute, 1982.

ZANNA, M. P., SHERAS, P. L., & COOPER J. Pygmalion and Galatea: The interactive effects of teacher and student expectancies. Journal of Experimental Social Psychology, 1975, 11, 279-287.

19

The Impact of Leisure-Time Television on School Learning
A Research Synthesis

Patricia A. Williams, Edward H. Haertel,
Geneva D. Haertel, and Herbert J. Walberg

To integrate empirical findings concerning the impact of leisure time television viewing on student achievement in grades K-12, 274 correlations were assembled or calculated from 23 educational and psychological review articles, doctoral dissertations, statewide assessments, national surveys, articles from refereed journals, technical reports, books, and unpublished papers. For each study, characteristics of the sample, type of outcome, quality of the study, method of collecting viewing data, mean hours of viewing, and strength and direction of observed relationships were coded. The overall correlation of hours of televiewing and achievement is negative but small (−.05). Regardless of the sample size, year and location of the research, the effect remains consistent. The overall effect, however, is not constant across the range of viewing times. The effects are slightly positive for up to 10 hours of viewing a week, but beyond 10 hours the effects are negative and increasingly more deleterious until viewing time reaches 35 to 40 hours, beyond which additional viewing has little effect. Females and high IQ children are more adversely affected than other groups.

The influence of mass media on social processes is undisputed. Historically, each of several forms of media, including novels, movies, comic books, and television, have been identified simultaneously as villain and redeemer Morgan & Gross, in press, p. 2). During the past 30 years television has

This research was supported by a grant from the National Institute of Education to the last author, but points of view expressed in this article are not necessarily those of the NIE.

From Patricia A. Williams et al., "The Impact of Leisure-Time Television on School Learning: A Research Synthesis," 19 (1) *American Educational Research Journal* 19-50 (Spring 1982). Copyright 1982 American Educational Research Association, Washington, D.C. Reprinted by permission.

clearly been cast in such a dual role. It has been regarded by some proponents as a curative for environmental limitations and a stimulus to creativity. Opponents of TV, however, claim it produces shortened attention spans and a decreased ability to process written information. Public debate over the costs and benefits of television viewing has been an impetus to conducting empirical research studies. Most recently, television, more than any other form of media, has been identified as a potential contributing factor in the decline in achievement test scores (Harnischfeger & Wiley, 1976). In the light of such controversy a research synthesis was conducted on the impact of leisure-time television on the school learning of children in grades K–12. Walberg (1980) identified the television as one of 10 factors that influence school achievement. For purposes of this study, only television's impact was examined, as its effects are of more immediate concern to the educational community.

The fact that television affects school achievement is not challenged, but research efforts to examine these effects have uncovered inconsistent results among studies and even within single studies. The variety of research methods, sample sizes, criterion measures, and statistics reported have led to conflicting interpretations of the effects of television viewing on children's school achievement. The disparate nature of these studies is made explicit by taking a historical perspective on the types of research designs employed. Early studies compared students who had access to television with students from homes where television was unavailable. Later studies related the amount of time spent in leisure-time television viewing and school achievement. Examples of discrepant results are easily found and can be exemplified by discussing a few representative studies. Greenstein (1954) examined the relationship between TV viewing and school grades by comparing third- through sixth-grade children who watched TV with those who did not. Results indicated that the performance of the viewers was consistently higher than that of the nonviewers. Similarly, Schramm, Lyle, and Parker (1961) in a comparison of Radiotown and Teletown (the latter had TV, the former did not) reported significant differences in vocabulary test scores of first graders, favoring students in Teletown. These differences were found for high- and medium-IQ students from each town, but not for the low-IQ students. Results showing little impact of television were reported by Himmelweit, Oppenheim, and Vince (1958). They suggested that on the whole, school performance of viewers was level with or only slightly lower than that of the nonviewers.

In contrast, researchers have also reported negative relationships between amount of television viewing and achievement. Scott (1956) found that those children who viewed more television achieved less proficiency in total achievement than those children who viewed less. In an investigation of fifth-grade students LaBlonde (1966) reported that measured achievement and televiewing bore an inverse relationship to each other: the higher the achievement test score, the less time spent watching television. Morgan and Gross (1980) found that heavier television viewing was significantly related to lower achievement scores, with reading comprehension being the area most negatively and significantly associated with television viewing. Additional negative relations concerning the influence of leisure viewing was provided by Hornik (1978). This study, conducted in El Salvador, examined the impact of TV use on cognitive growth in reading skills of seventh-through ninth-grade students. Following three separate groups over 2- to 3-year periods revealed consistent negative effects on reading improvement for all three groups, and even a negative effect on general ability for one cohort.

Further disparity among studies is created by the great variety of methods used for measuring televiewing. These methods range from a simple question (How much time do you spend watching television?) to elaborate diaries requesting information on all activities a student engages in between leaving school and bedtime. While some studies obtained viewing estimates from students, others used parents' estimates of their child's viewing time. Occasionally, student estimates were validated by personal interviews with the parent or the child.

In the light of differences in research design, results and methods of collecting data, the corpus of studies relating televiewing to achievement has left several questions unanswered. First, there is agreement that TV affects achievement, but what is the magnitude and direction of the effect? Second, are girls affected more than boys or vice versa? Third, are younger children more susceptible to the effects of televiewing? Are certain subject areas affected more than others? Is there a differential effect on high and low achievers? Is there a differential effect for students with high IQs and low IQs? Finally, has the impact of televiewing changed over the years?

To answer these and other questions the tools of research synthesis were applied. These techniques included the work of Glass (1978) on meta-analysis, as well as contributions by Gage (1978), Jones and Fiske (1953), Light and Smith (1971), and Rosenthal (1976). Using these techniques, the research relating leisure-time television viewing to school learning was synthesized. In this synthesis no new data were collected. Instead the data points were correlation coefficients relating television to school achievement. By employing these techniques it was possible to relate the magnitude and direction of the televiewing-achievement relationship to characteristics of the studies like grade level, geographical location, and sex of the sample. In addition, methodological factors such as use of significance tests, assumptions of linearity, and use of random sampling were examined. By employing the techniques of research synthesis, it was possible to explore the substantive and methodological characteristics of research on the relation of leisure television viewing to learning.

METHOD

Sample of Studies

A search was made of *Review of Educational Research, Review of Research in Education*, and *Annual Review of Psychology* for the years 1967–1979; *Current Index of Journals in Education* (CIJE) for the years 1974–1979; and a computer search of *Psychological Abstracts*, ERIC, and CIJE for the years 1963–1978 for published articles, books, and unpublished technical reports. Additional studies were identified in bibliographies of studies located in these indexes as well as through suggestions from other researchers. Studies that reported empirical findings concerning the impact of leisure-time television viewing on student achievement in grades K–12 were selected. Thirty-two studies were located, but only 23 could be used. Studies were discarded for the following reasons: inadequate descriptive statistical information to permit calculation of effect sizes or correlations (e.g., Ridder [1963]; Witty, [1966, 1967]); effects were limited to a single program rather than the effects of total leisure-time viewing (e.g., Sesame Street Evaluations); and studies such as Hornik (1978), which examined access to TV, because recent acquisition of a TV was confounded with socioeconomic status. The 23 studies included: four doctoral dissertations, three statewide assessments, two national surveys, articles from refereed journals, technical reports, books, and unpublished papers. They represented findings in England, Japan, Canada, and five geographical regions of the United States. Though income and racial group were not coded and used in the analyses, high-, middle-, and low-income students as well as white, black, Oriental, and Hispanic students were represented in these studies. The search and selection procedures yielded 274 effects from a combined student population of 87,025.

A summary of the key features of the 23 studies is presented in the Appendix. Information on each study includes sample size and description, dependent measure, substantive results, control variables, test for curvilinearity, and determination of viewing time and method of collecting data.

The studies synthesized spanned a period of 26 years, with the first conducted in 1954 and the most recent in 1980. Sample sizes in these studies ranged from 67 students to 33,233 in a national survey. The criterion measures employed included not only standardized achievement-test scores, but also criterion-referenced tests, grade-point averages, percentiles, and teacher ratings. The types of data analysis employed include methods as simple as use of cross-tabulations and frequencies to more complicated techniques such as cross-lagged panel correlations. Researchers used several diverse methods for collecting viewing information, including diaries, program checklists, interviews, or a single item embedded in a larger questionnaire. Table I contains a list of the 23 studies synthesized, the mean correlation standard deviation calculated from each study and the number of correlations each study contributed to the analyses.

Coding Information

Information coded for each effect included author's name, year of study, dependent measures, basic methodology, sample characteristics, quality of the study, statistic reported, presence of controls, determination of viewing time, correlation, and mean hours of viewing for comparison. Dependent measure refers to the type of achievement reported, that is, reading, language arts, vocabulary, spelling, mathematics, social studies, science, general intelligence, total school achievement, and study skills. Type of information collected refers to whether the data were achievement test scores (raw scores on a locally standardized test or standardized scores), grade point average, individual course grades, IQ scores, reading group, grade equivalents, percentiles, teacher ratings, or ranked achievement scores.

Basic methodology was coded as either true experiment, quasi-experiment, or survey. Sample characteristics included age, sex (coded as male, female, or mixed), IQ (coded as high, medium, low, or unrestricted if levels were not reported), prior achievement (coded as high, medium, low, or unrestricted), geographical location, and grade levels (grouped into class intervals, i.e.,

TABLE I

Mean and Standard Deviation of Correlations, and Number of Correlations Coded, For Each Study in the Synthesis

Study	X	SD	N
Anderson & MacGuire (1978)	−.09	.09	12
Childers & Ross (1973)	−.08	.00	1
Furu (1971)	−.16	.05	3
Gadberry (1977)	−.17	.07	7
Greenstein (1954)	−.26	.00	1
Heideman (1957)	.05	.23	8
Himmelweit, Oppenheim, & Vince (1958)	−.15	.21	16
Kohr (1979)	−.11	.04	8
LaBlonde (1966)	−.28	.19	10
Lyle & Hoffman (1972)	−.02	.08	6
Mayeske et al. (1969)	.00	.12	24
Morgan & Gross (1980)	−.08	.12	36
Nelson (1963)	−.22	.00	1
Perney, Freund, & Barman (1976)	.00	.19	4
Rhode Island Assessment 4–8 (1977a)	−.01	.12	40
Rhode Island Assessment 17 (1977b)	−.15	.00	1
Schramm, Lyle, & Parker (1961)	.18	.20	5
Scott (1956)	−.14	.06	4
Haertel & Wiley (1979)	−.02	.07	72
Slater (1963)	−.16	.07	4
Tan & Gunther (1979)	.10	.00	1
Texas Assessment (1977)	−.08	.11	8
Thompson (1964)	−.15	.19	2

primary [grades K–3], elementary [4–6], junior high [7–8], and high school [9–12]).

Quality of the study included indications of sample size (grouped according to the following categories: 0–60, 61–100, 101–250, 251–500, 501–1,000, and above 1,000); use of significance tests, whether or not linearity was assumed, if random sampling was employed; and the statistic reported for the comparison (percentages, means, and standard deviations, simple correlations, part correlations, partial correlations, simple regression coefficients, F ratios, t-tests, Chi-squares, frequencies or cross-tabulations, or normalized S).

In addition, presence of controls indicated whether or not IQ, prior achievement, or sex had been used as a covariate or as blocking variables in the studies reported.

Two variables were coded to provide information on how estimates of viewing time were determined for each study. First, information was coded indicating who provided the estimates of hours of viewing (parent, child, or both). Second, the method used to collect the viewing data was coded as diary, questionnaire completed by the child, questionnaire completed by the parent, program checklist, ownership of TV or residence in a TV reception area, or combination of methods.

The final variable, mean hours of viewing, was coded for each comparison indicating the number of hours viewed per weekday, per weekend, and per week. Most studies did not report all three. Whatever information was available was coded. Occasionally it was necessary to calculate average viewing times of a study or a comparison. In the analyses, hours of viewing were broken down as follows: 0–10, 10.1–15, 15.1–20, 20.1–25, 25.1–30, 30.1–35, and over 35.

To summarize statistically the results of the various studies, it was necessary to express all of these results in terms of some common scale or metric. Because televiewing and achievement are both continuous variables, a natural choice was to use product-moment correlations, as suggested by Glass (1978). Unfortunately, only 7 of the 23 studies reported actual product-moment correlations computed between televiewing and educational outcomes. (Correlations were nonetheless reported in more of the studies than any other single statistic. The next largest category was comprised of six studies reporting means and standard deviations.) For those studies reporting statistics other than correlations, it was necessary to estimate the correlation using whatever data were available. In most cases, the conversion formulas presented by Glass could be used for this purpose, and for the few remaining statistics, comparable conversion formulas were found or derived.

For purposes of this research synthesis, correlation coefficients had one important limitation: The correlation expresses only the *linear* relationship between two variables. There was reason to believe, based on some of the studies included, that the relationship between viewing and achievement might be curvilinear in form (Greenstein, 1954; Kohr, 1979; Mayeske, 1969). Thus, individual correlations might not be adequate summaries of the information available from some of the studies. This could be seen most clearly in those studies where mean achievement scores were reported for a series of viewing-time levels (e.g., less than 10 hours per week, 10–15 hours per week, etc.). It was evident that in some such cases, the graph of achievement as a function of televiewing was not a straight line. The problem of representing these more complex relationships so that they could be summarized across studies might have been intractable, except for one important fact: unlike most of the variables of concern in education, weekly hours of televiewing were automatically measured on a ratio scale, with a true zero point (no viewing at all) and equal-interval units (e.g., hours). Thus, average amounts of viewing were directly comparable across studies in a way that average scores on the various achievement tests used in different studies were not.

Because levels of televiewing were comparable in this way, it was possible to use a series of several correlation coefficients to describe a curvilinear relationship between televiewing and achievement. Where achievement scores were reported for a series of televiewing levels, a correlation was estimated using the first and second categories, another correlation was estimated using the second and third, then the third and fourth, and so forth. Each of these represented the strength of the televiewing-achievement relationship for a different televiewing level. In other words, if a graph were drawn showing the relation of achievement to viewing time, the series of correlations would tell the steepness of adjacent sections of the graph. To identify the various correlations with specific sections of that graph, the mean viewing time across each adjacent pair of categories was coded along with the corresponding estimated correlation. In the same way, a mean viewing time was coded for the remainder of the 277 of the correlations or estimated correlations from the various studies. Thus, even though each individual correlation could only represent a linear relationship, by identifying these individual correlations with different locations on the televiewing-achievement curve they could be used together to describe a relationship that might not be linear.

Data Analysis

Once coding was completed, a series of statistical analyses were performed to determine which of the coded study and sample characteristics were related to the size of the viewing-achievement correlations. Most of these analyses addressed substantive questions, such as whether televiewing effects are the same for males and females or whether televiewing's effect on achievement is larger in the lower ranges of IQ. Some, however, addressed methodological questions with a bearing on the research synthesis itself, for example, whether there are systematic differences in the size of correlations estimated by different methods or whether studies of poorer quality suggest a different relationship between televiewing and achievement than studies that used better methods. In all of these analyses, the coded correlation coefficients comprised the dependent variable. For example, means of correlation coefficients and F tests of differences among these means were calculated. Other coded characteristics of studies and samples served as independent variables.

Stem-and-Leaf Display and Elimination of Outliers

As a preliminary to more formal analyses, the 277 correlations were

FIGURE 1. *Stem and leaf and five-point summary of correlations between achievement and amount of television viewing.*

```
  .6
  .6
  .5
  .5 |0
  .4 |7
  .4
  .3 |5
  .3 |0 1 1 2 4
  .2
  .2 |0 1 1 3 4
  .1 |6 6 6 7 8 8 8 9
  .1 |0 0 0 1 1 2 2 2 2 4 4
  .0 |5 5 5 6 6 6 6 6 7 7 7 7 7 7 8 8 8 8 8 8 8 9 9 9
  .0 |0 0 0 0 0 0 0 0 0 1 1 1 1 2 2 2 2 2 2 2 3 3 3 3 3 3 3 3 4 4 4 4 4 4 4 4 4 4 4
 -.0 |1 1 1 1 1 1 2 2 2 2 2 2 2 2 3 3 3 3 3 3 3 4 4 4 4 4 4 4 4
 -.0 |5 5 5 5 5 5 5 5 6 6 6 6 6 6 6 6 7 7 7 7 7 7 7 7 7 7 7 7 7 7 8 8 8 8 8 8 9 9 9 9 9
 -.1 |0 0 0 0 0 0 0 0 0 1 1 1 1 1 1 1 1 1 1 1 1 2 2 2 2 2 2 2 2 2 2 2 2 2 3 3 3 3 3 3 3 3 4 4 4 4 4
 -.1 |5 5 5 5 6 6 6 6 7 7 7 8 8 8 8 8 8 8 8 8 8 9 9 9 9 9
 -.2 |0 0 0 0 0 0 1 1 1 1 1 2 2 2 3 3 3 3
 -.2 |5 5 5 6 7 9 9
 -.3 |0 1
 -.3
 -.4
 -.4 |6 6 6 6 7 7 8
 -.5
 -.5 |6
 -.6
 -.6
 -.7
 -.7
 -.8
 -.8
 -.9
 -.9 |8
```

	Five-Point Summary (original)	Five-Point Summary (omitting outliers)
*	-.98	-.56
H	-.13	-.13
M	-.06	-.06
H	.02	.02
*	.50	.35
N	= 277	N = 274

displayed in a stem-and-leaf diagram as described by Tukey (1977). This display is shown in Figure 1. In addition to providing all the information of a histogram, the stem-and-leaf diagram displays the actual value of each correlation to two decimal places. The first digit (the stem) appears to the left of the vertical line, and the second digit (the leaf) appears to the right. For example, the leaves "01124" to the right of the stem ".3" represent five correlations: .30, .31, .31, .32, and .34. Also displayed in Figure 1 is the 5-point summary of distribution, consisting of minimum (*), first quartile (H), median (M), third quartile (H), and maximum (*).

Figure 1 shows that the majority of the correlations lie between −.30 and +.20, but the range extends all the way from −.98 to +.50. To determine whether some of the extreme values should be rejected as outliers, a test by Pearson and Stephens (1964) was applied. Under the assumption that the sample of coefficients was drawn from a normally distributed population, the null hypothesis that the three extreme values, −.98, .47, and .50, were from the same population could be rejected at the .05 level of significance. On this basis, these correlations were dropped from the sample, and subsequent analyses were based on an N of 274. The 5-point summary of the sample of 274 is also displayed in Figure 1.

Two types of independent variables. Following preliminary inspection of the correlation coefficients, the relationship of correlation size to each of the independent variables were considered. The independent variables were considered in two categories. Some independent variables such as age, sex, and the subject area in which achievement was measured, varied among different correlations coded for the same study. Thus, a single study might report findings for 11-year-olds and 15-year-olds, for males and females, or for reading and mathematics achievement. Independent variables of this type are referred to as correlation-level variables. The N values, means, and standard deviations of correlations were calculated for each value of all correlation-level variables. Other independent variables (e.g., year of the study, geographic region, or method of collecting viewing information) varied from study to study but took on only a single value for all correlations coded for a single study.[1] Independent variables of this type are referred to

---

[1] Three independent variables took on only a single value for all correlations coded for a single study with the exception of one study. Lyle and Hoffman (1972) employed different methods of collecting viewing and achievement data for first graders than for sixth- or tenth-grade students, so that codes for the type of information collected on the dependent measure, method of determining viewing, and person providing viewing information all varied within that study only. For this reason, the Lyle and Hoffman study was treated as two separate studies in all study-level analyses, one at the first-grade level and the other at grade levels 6 and 10. The study-level data set therefore included 24, not 23 observations.

as study-level variables. To examine independent variables in this second category, an additional data set was created with only one observation for each study. This second data set included all study-level variables, together with the average viewing-achievement correlation for each study. Using this data set, values of N, means, and standard deviations of the average correlations were calculated for all study-level variables. For example, one value of the study-level variable "geographic region" was "midwest." There were five studies in the midwest, so the mean and standard deviation of the average correlations for these five studies were tabulated.

The correlation-level tabulations revealed that some of the coded characteristics were present for six or fewer of the 274 correlations, and on this basis these characteristics were dropped from further consideration. All of the independent variables dropped pertained to specific types of statistical controls for prior achievement or for IQ.

Analyses of variance. The relationship of each independent variable to the size of the correlations was tested for significance using analysis of variance (ANOVA). Because the average size of the correlations differed greatly from study to study ($F[22,251] = 4.98$, $p < .001$), study was used as a blocking variable in the ANOVAs for correlation-level variables. That is, the main effect of study was removed before examining the main effect for the independent variable being analyzed. This procedure helped to minimize the problem of confounding study and other variables, and the problem of lack of statistical independence among correlations coded for the same study. For the study-level variables, ordinary one-way ANOVAs were performed with study as the unit of analysis. One final series of ANOVAs was performed, to examine the relationship between amount of viewing and correlation size under various conditions. For each correlation-level variable where the one-way ANOVA was significant, a two-way ANOVA was performed, the factors being that variable and hours of televiewing. Study was again used as a blocking variable.

Graphing the viewing-achievement relationship. When the correlations were grouped into categories according to weekly hours of viewing, analysis of variance revealed statistically significant differences among the mean correlations at different levels. This suggested that the relationship between viewing and achievement was in fact nonlinear. For example, the mean correlation for samples viewing less than 10 hours per week was .07, suggesting that achievement improved as televiewing increased from 0–10 hours. For samples where the mean viewing time was between 30 and 35 hours per week, the mean correlation was −.09, suggesting that in that range, increased viewing had a deleterious effect upon achievement. To determine more precisely the form of the achievement-viewing relationship, a polynomial regression was used to fit correlation size as a function of weekly hours of viewing. Linear and quadratic terms were both significant; higher-order terms were not. The coefficient of determination from this regression was

.11. The regression function was interpreted as describing the *slope* of the viewing-achievement relationship as a function of amount of viewing. Using this expression for the slope, it was possible (using calculus) to obtain an estimate of the viewing-achievement relationship itself. However, while the shape of the viewing-achievement relationship could be determined, the size of the effect was not shown by this analysis. The strength of the relationship between televiewing and achievement may be inferred, however, from the original tabulations of televiewing-achievement correlations for different viewing levels described earlier. Identical analyses were also performed for the smaller samples of correlations for males only and for females only, on the basis of a significant interaction between sex and viewing found in the two-way ANOVA for sex.

RESULTS

The stem-and-leaf diagram of all coded correlations revealed that the median televiewing-achievement correlation was −.06, with 50 percent of the correlations falling between −.13 and +.02. Of a total of 277 correlations, 95 were zero or positive and 182 were negative. The stem-and-leaf shows that overall, televiewing appears to have a slightly negative effect on school achievement.

The results reported below elaborate on this finding in two ways. First, analyses of study characteristics produced no evidence that findings differed for studies done in different times or places, or that televiewing-achievement correlations varied according to methodological characteristics of the studies. Second, analyses of sample characteristics did reveal statistically significant differences in televiewing effects on achievement for males versus females and for high- versus middle- or low-IQ students. Evidence was also found that the effect of televiewing on achievement is not linear, and that small amounts of viewing may in fact be related to increased achievement, but excessive viewing is detrimental.

Examinations of both kinds of questions, concerning study characteristics and sample characteristics, began with tabulations of numbers, means, and standard deviations of correlations. These were followed by analyses of variance for each characteristic. Descriptive statistics, *F*-ratios and significance levels from all of these analyses are reported in Table II.

Analyses of Study Characteristics

The first results reported in Table II concern the locations of the various studies. No significant difference was found in the average televiewing-achievement correlations for studies in different regions of the United States or in Canada, England, or Japan. An additional analysis, not reported in Table II, concerned the years in which various studies were done. To determine whether the mean televiewing-achievement correlations differed between earlier and more recent studies, mean correlations for studies were

TABLE II

Means and Standard Deviations of Correlations, Numbers of Correlations, and F Tests for All Independent Variables

	$\bar{X}$	SD	N	$F(df_1 df_2)$	P
a) Location of the Study					
Geography					
Northeast	−.08	.10	2	1.83 (9,14)	.3753
East	−.13	.04	5	...	...
Midwest	−.14	.16	1	...	...
South	.10	.00	1	...	...
West	−.07	.06	4	...	...
Canada	.05	.19	2	...	...
Japan	−.16	.00	1	...	...
Entire U. S.	−.01	.01	2	...	...
Not specified	−.08	.00	1	...	...
England	−.15	.00	1	...	...
b) Methodological Characteristics					
Research Design					
Quasi-experiments	−.10	.19	4	.09 (1,22)	.7619
Surveys	−.08	.09	20	...	...
Sample Size					
1 (Low–100)	−.11	.14	5	.228 (3,20)	.8756
2 (101–500)	−.08	.14	9	...	...
3 (501–2,000)	−.10⁻	.06	4	...	...
4 (200–high) over 2,000	−.06	.06	6	...	...
Random Sampling					
Yes	−.09	.09	14	.088 (1,22)	.7690
No	−.08	.14	10	...	...
c) Study Characteristics					
Statistic Reported					
Means and standard deviations	−.09	.10	6	.581 (7,15)	.7613
Simple correlations	−.10	.12	7	...	...
Partial correlations	−.08	.00	1	...	...
F ratios	−.02	.10	2	...	...
T tests	.02	.22	2	...	...
Chi-square or contingency coefficient	−.22	.00	1	...	...
Frequencies or crosstabs	−.07	.08	3	...	...
Normalized *S*	−.16	.01	1	...	...
Linearity Assumed					
No	−.10	.09	9	.152 (1,22)	.7001
Yes	−.08	.12	15	...	...
Use of Significance Tests					
Yes	−.09	.12	21	.002 (1,22)	.9692
No	−.08	.06	3	...	...
Dependent Measure:					
Type of information collected					
Raw Achievement Scores	−.12	.03	3	.883 (8,15)	.5524
Standardized Achievement Scores	−.04	.05	5	...	...
GPA	−.13	.13	6	...	...
IQ Scores	.08	.15	2	...	...

TABLE II—*Continued*

	$\bar{X}$	SD	N	$F(df_1 df_2)$	P
Grade Equivalent	−.08	.18	3	...	...
Percentiles	−.08	.00	1	...	...
Teacher Rating	−.08	.10	2	...	...
Not Specified	−.16	.00	1	...	...
Ranked Achievement Scores	−.16	.00	1	...	...

d) Method of Obtaining Viewing Information

	$\bar{X}$	SD	N	$F(df_1 df_2)$	P
Person Responding					
Child	−.11	.10	19	3.138 (2,21)	.0642
Parent	−.05	.11	3	...	...
Both	−.09	.10	2	...	...
Method of Collecting Data					
Questionnaire by child	−.09	.10	12	1.432 (5,18)	.2636
Questionnaire by parent	.09	.13	2	...	...
Interview with child	−.16	.00	1	...	...
Interview with parent	−.02	.00	1	...	...
Program checklist	−.12	.12	5	...	...
Combination of methods	−.11	.09	3	...	...

e) Achievement Measure

	$\bar{X}$	SD	N	$F(df_1 df_2)$	P
Subject Area					
Reading	−.06	.16	66	.46 (8,243)	.8843
Language arts	−.12	.16	21	...	...
Vocabulary	−.01	.14	51	...	...
Spelling	−.06	.08	8	...	...
Mathematics	−.05	.11	60	...	...
Science	−.21	.04	2	...	...
General intelligence	−.03	.05	4	...	...
Total school achievement	−.08	.14	52	...	...
Study skills	−.06	.18	10	...	...

f) Population Characteristics

	$\bar{X}$	SD	N	$F(df_1 df_2)$	P
Age					
5	−.00	.19	4	0.75 (11,240)	0.6919
6	.04	.16	20	...	...
7	−.03	.07	12	...	...
8	−.07	.09	33	...	...
9	−.01	.13	36	...	...
10	−.15	.19	42	...	...
11	−.04	.11	28	...	...
12	−.14	.05	5	...	...
13	−.06	.14	66	...	...
14	−.04	.13	13	...	...
15	−.08	.05	3	...	...
16	−.08	.06	3	...	...
17	−.06	.11	9	...	...
Grade Level					
Primary	−.02	.13	65	1.69 (3,248)	.1688
Elementary	−.07	.16	110	...	...
Junior High	−.06	.13	71	...	...
High School	.05	.11	28	...	...

(Continued)

TABLE II—*Continued*

	$\bar{X}$	SD	N	$F(df_1 df_2)$	P
Sex					
Male	−.04	.15	35	6.70 (1,62)	.0120
Female	−.13	.18	35	...	...
IQ					
High	−.14	.21	22	3.50 (2,249)	.0317
Medium/unrestricted	−.05	.13	233	...	...
Low	−.04	.13	19	...	...
Mean Viewing Time Per Week (hours)					
1 (0–10)	.07	.09	45	6.26 (6,245)	.0001
2 (10.1–15)	−.11	.21	23	...	...
3 (15.1–20)	−.09	.14	72	...	...
4 (20.1–25)	−.05	.12	59	...	...
5 (25.1–30)	−.10	.10	36	...	...
6 (30.1–35)	−.09	.09	24	...	...
7 (over 35)	−.03	.14	15	...	...

regressed on the year the studies were reported. No significant relationship was found between year of study and televiewing-achievement correlation size. In conclusion, the televiewing-achievement relationship was not found to vary according to either the time or the place the study was performed.

Various statistical characteristics of studies were also examined. These included the designation of the study as a quasi-experiment or survey; sample size; whether there was random sampling from a well-defined population; the type of reported statistic from which correlation estimates were derived; whether linearity of the televiewing-achievement relationship was assumed in the study; and whether significance tests were reported. Of these six indicators of the size, type, and quality of the different studies, none was found to be related to the size of televiewing-achievement correlations.

The last three study-level variables reported in Table II pertained to the collection of achievement and televiewing information. These were the type of information used to indicate achievement (raw achievement test score, derived score, teacher rating, etc.); the person(s) providing viewing information (parent and/or child); and the method of collecting viewing information (questionnaire, interview, program checklist, or a combination of methods). None of these variables yielded statistically significant F-ratios.

An objection sometimes raised to quantitative research integrations is that the quality of the primary studies synthesized is not taken into account. Critics argue that the results of one well-designed study are more credible than those of many poorly executed studies. The examination of study characteristics in this synthesis, however, yielded no evidence that methodological characteristics of studies were related to their reported outcomes. Thus, the inclusion of all the available studies in the substantive analyses appears to be justified.

Analyses of Sample Characteristics

The study characteristics discussed in the last section were each examined, treating study as the unit of analysis. That is, each study was treated as a single data point, and the average of all televiewing-achievement correlations coded for a given study was the dependent variable. The sample characteristics discussed below were examined treating each of the 274 individual televiewing-achievement correlations as a data point, and using study as a blocking variable. (This distinction was discussed in the section on data analysis.) The first of the sample characteristics, achievement subject area, refers to the dependent measure employed. The other sample characteristics, age, grade level, sex, IQ, and mean viewing time per week, all refer to the students in the original studies.

As shown in Table II, no significant differences were detected in the relationship of televiewing to achievement in different content areas, and no significant differences were found for children at different age or grade levels. Significant F-ratios were obtained, however, for sex, IQ, and mean viewing time per week.

In examining the effect for sex, correlations for mixed-sex samples were not used. The remaining correlations represented 7 of the 23 studies. The mean televiewing-achievement correlation for males was $-.04$, and for females was $-.13$, indicating a significantly greater impact of televiewing upon achievement for girls than for boys ($F[1,62] = 6.70, p < .05$).

In examining the effect for IQ, correlations for samples where IQ was unrestricted were pooled with those for medium-IQ samples. Thus, the three levels were high, medium/unrestricted, and low. Mean televiewing-achievement correlations for low- and medium/unrestricted-IQ levels were approximately $-.05$, but for the high IQ levels, the mean was $-.14$, indicating a significantly greater impact of TV viewing on achievement for higher IQ ranges ($F[2,249] = 3.50, p < .05$).

A significant effect for mean viewing time per week was also found. This indicated that the impact of televiewing on achievement depends on the amount of television viewed ($F[6,245] = 6.26, p < .001$). From Table II it appeared that up to 10 hours per week, watching more television had a positive influence on achievement, but beyond 10 hours per week, increased viewing had a negative impact.

In summary, analyses of sample characteristics taken one at a time revealed significant main effects for sex, IQ, and viewing. Subsequent analyses were to probe possible interactions among these factors. In particular, sex-by-viewing and IQ-by-viewing interactions were examined in two-way analyses of variance, again blocking on study.[2]

---

[2] There were insufficient data to examine the sex by IQ interaction because only a single study (Morgan & Gross, in press) controlled simultaneously for both sex and IQ.

The 70 televiewing-achievement correlations for single-sex samples included none for which viewing averaged less than 15 hours per week. Thus, only five of the seven viewing levels were included in the sex-by-viewing ANOVA. This analysis showed, in addition to significant main effects for sex and viewing, a significant interaction between these two variables ($F[4,54] = 9.61$, $p < .001$). The interaction indicates that the shape of the curve relating televiewing and achievement differs for males and females.

The problem of empty cells in the IQ by viewing ANOVA could not be solved by simply dropping some viewing levels, as was done in the sex-by-viewing analysis. All seven viewing levels were represented for the medium/unrestricted IQ range, but many viewing levels were missing for the low- and high-IQ ranges. (As a result, only four degrees of freedom were available for testing the IQ by viewing interaction.) The IQ-by-viewing interaction was significant ($F[4,239] = 3.78$, $p < .01$), as were the main effects for both viewing and IQ. This significant interaction indicates that the form of the viewing-achievement relationship differs for different levels of IQ.

Form of the Televiewing-Achievement Relationship

As described in the section on data analysis, the form of the relationship between televiewing and achievement could be estimated from the mean correlations at different viewing levels. Results of this estimation are displayed in Figure 2. This figure shows how achievement on a hypothetical composite achievement test varies as a function of weekly hours of televiewing. While it is not possible to determine the mean or standard deviation of this hypothetical test, it is clear that achievement increases as with televiewing up to 10 hours per week, and then decreases steadily, leveling off at 35-40 hours per week. Given that the overall average televiewing-achievement correlation is only $-.05$, it appears that the actual size of the effect is small.

The same analysis was run for the smaller set of correlations on male samples and on female samples, to clarify the sex-by-viewing interaction reported above. Because viewing times for all of these samples were 15 or more hours per week, the forms of the separate relationships below this viewing level could not be determined. It appeared, however, that increased viewing beyond 15 hours per week up to about 30 hours was more deleterious for females than for males; beyond 30 hours per week, the effects of additional viewing were small, and comparable for the two sexes. No further analysis was made of the viewing by IQ interaction, because of insufficient data.

DISCUSSION

This synthesis of 23 research studies indicated that there is a slight negative relationship between television viewing and achievement. The effect was

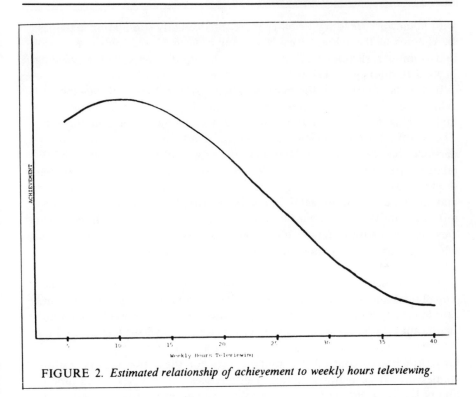

FIGURE 2. *Estimated relationship of achievement to weekly hours televiewing.*

found in large, national surveys and statewide assessments as well as small studies in single schools, in different regions of the United States and abroad, in studies spanning a period of 26 years, using a variety of achievement measures and research methodologies. Televiewing does influence achievement, but its effect is small, and it appears unlikely that television alone is responsible for a nationwide decline in measures of achievement. Televiewing accounts for little variance in achievement: It is neither the "villain" nor the "redeemer" some have claimed.

The research synthesis also showed that the influence of television on achievement depends on the amount of viewing time. Up to 10 hours per week of viewing may actually enhance achievement slightly. Beyond 10 hours, achievement diminishes with increased viewing up to 35 or 40 hours per week, and beyond that level, additional viewing apparently has little further impact. This pattern may reflect differences in the selectiveness of light versus heavy viewers. It is easy to imagine that in homes where children view less than 10 hours of television per week, parents exercise substantially more control over what is watched than in homes where children view several hours of television daily. Another hypothesis would be that it is only beyond 10 hours per week that televiewing begins to interfere significantly with homework, reading, or other more intellectually stimulating activities. In as much as the average weekly viewing of 6- to 11-year-olds is 25 hours and 41 minutes (Ratner et al., 1966, p. 51), the negative impact of televiewing beyond 10 hours per week is clearly a matter of concern.

It was also found that the negative relationship between televiewing and achievement is much stronger for girls than for boys, and for children of high intelligence than for those of average or below average intelligence. The reasons for the televiewing-achievement relationship are not well understood; one can only speculate as to the origins of these sex- and ability-related differences. They may reflect differences in the kinds of activities displaced by television viewing or in the kinds of programs viewed (cartoons may have a different impact than documentaries, for example), or they may reflect the influence of other, unknown variables, correlated with television viewing and causally linked to academic achievement. In the latter case, television viewing may have no direct, causal influence on achievement at all.

It is clear that more research on television and achievement is called for. The studies included in this synthesis were primarily cross-sectional and cannot clearly establish firm causal influences. It is also notable that while significant differences were found in effects for males versus females and for different levels of intelligence, only one study, conducted by Morgan and Gross (in press), controlled simultaneously for these two factors. Future studies should be planned to detect differences between sexes and among ability levels, to model possibly curvilinear relationships, and to elucidate various causal mechanisms through the use of longitudinal designs.

REFERENCES

ANDERSON, C. C., & MAGUIRE, T. O. The effect of TV viewing on the educational performance of elementary school children. *Alberta Journal of Educational Research*, 1978, *24*(3), 156–163.

CHILDERS, P., & ROSS, J. The relationship between viewing television and student achievement. *Journal of Educational Research*, 1973, *66*(7), 317–319.

FURU, T. *Function of television for children and adolescents.* Tokyo: Sophia University, 1971.

GADBERRY, S. *Television viewing and school grades: A cross-lagged longitudinal study.* Paper presented at the Society for Research in Child Development, 1977. (ERIC Document Reproduction Service, No. ED 140 973).

GAGE, N. L. *The scientific basis of the art of teaching.* New York: Teachers College Press, 1978.

GLASS, G. V. Integrating findings: The meta-analysis of research. In L. S. Shulman (Ed.), *Review of research in education (Vol. 5).* Itasca, Ill.: Peacock, 1978.

GREENSTEIN, J. Effects of television upon elementary school grades. *Journal of Educational Research*, 1954, *48*, 161–176.

HAERTEL, E. H., & WILEY, D. E. *Social and economic differences in elementary school achievement.* Chicago: ML-GROUP for Policy Studies in Education, CEMREL, Inc., 1978.

HAERTEL, E. H., & WILEY, D. E. Social and economic differences in elementary school achievement; Part II (Study of the sustaining effects of compensatory education on basic skills). In R. H. Hinckley (Ed.) *Report No. 4: Student home environment, educational achievement, and compensatory education.* Santa Monica Calif.: System Development Corp., 1979.

HARNISCHFEGER, A., & WILEY, D. E. Achievement test scores drop. So what? *Educational Researcher,* 1976, *5*(3), 5–12.

HEIDEMAN, P. J. *A study of the relationship between televiewing and reading abilities of eighth grade students.* Unpublished doctoral dissertation, University of Minnesota, 1957.

HIMMELWEIT, H. T., OPPENHEIM, N. A., & VINCE, P. *Television and the child.* London: Oxford Press, 1958.

HORNIK, R. Television access and the slowing of cognitive growth. *American Educational Research Journal,* 1978, *15*(1), 1–15.

JONES, L. V., & FISKE, D. Models for testing the significance of combined results. *Psychological Bulletin,* 1953, *50*(3), 375–382.

KOHR, R. L. *The relationship of homework and television viewing to cognitive and noncognitive student outcomes.* Paper presented at the annual meeting of the National Council for Measurement in Education, San Francisco 1979.

LaBLONDE, J. *A study of the relationship between television viewing habits and scholastic achievement of fifth grade children.* Unpublished doctoral dissertation, University of Minnesota, 1966.

LIGHT, R. J., & SMITH, P. V. Accumulating evidence: Procedures for resolving contradictions among different research studies. *Harvard Educational Review,* 1971, *41,* 421–471.

LYLE, J., & HOFFMAN, H. R. Children's use of television and other media. In E. A. Rubenstein et al. (Eds.), *Television and social behavior (Vol. 4).* Washington, D.C.: U.S. Government Printing Office, 1972.

MAYESKE, G. W., WISLER, C. E., BEATON, JR., A. E., WEINFELD, F. D., COHEN, W. M., OKADA, T., PROSHEK, J. M., & TADLER, K. A. *A study of our nation's schools.* U.S. Department of Health, Education, & Welfare, Office of Education, 1969.

MORGAN, M., & GROSS, L. Television and educational achievement and aspirations. In National Institute of Mental Health (Eds.), *Television and behavior: Ten years of scientific progress and implications for the 80's (Vol. 7),* in press.

NELSON, R. J. *Relationships of reported television viewing to selected characteristics reported by superior high school students.* Unpublished doctoral dissertation, University of Wisconsin, 1963.

PEARSON, E. S., & STEPHENS, M. A. The ratio of range to standard deviation in the same normal sample. *Biometrika,* 1964, *51,* 484–487.

PERNEY, J., FREUND, J., & BARMAN, A. *Television viewing: Its relationship to early school achievement.* Evanston, Ill.: National College of Education, 1976. (ERIC Document Reproduction Service, No. ED 153 723).

RATNER, M., HELLEGERS, J. F., STERN, G. P., OGG, R. C., ADAIR, S., ZACHARIAS, L., McNEIL, D., FREUNDLICH, T., & NIEMASIK, J. *FTC staff report on television advertising to children* (Federal Trade Commission). Washington, D.C.: U.S. Government Printing Office, 1966.

RHODE ISLAND STATEWIDE ASSESSMENT PROGRAM. *Highlights Report: Norm referenced assessment of 4th and 8th graders.* Providence, RI: Rhode Island Department of Education, 1977. (a)

RHODE ISLAND STATEWIDE ASSESSMENT PROGRAM. *Highlights report: Norm referenced assessment of 17 year old students.* Providence, RI: Rhode Island Department of Education, 1977. (b)

RIDDER, J. M. Pupil opinions and the relationship of television viewing to academic achievement. *Journal of Educational Research,* 1963, *57*(4), 204–206.

ROSENTHAL, R. *Experimenter effects in behavioral research.* New York: Irvington Publishers, 1976.

SCHRAMM, W., LYLE, J., & PARKER, E. B. *Television in the lives of our children.* Stanford: Stanford University Press, 1961.

SCOTT, L. Television and school achievement. *Phi Delta Kappan,* 1956, *38,* 25–28.

SLATER, B. *An analysis and appraisal of the amount of televiewing, general school achievement, and socio-economic status of third grade students in selected public schools of Erie County, New York.* Unpublished doctoral dissertation, State University of New York at Buffalo, 1963.

TAN, A. S., & GUNTHER, D. Media use and academic achievement of Mexican-American high school students. *Journalism Quarterly,* 1979, *56*(4), 827–831.

TEXAS ASSESSMENT PROJECT. *Achievement in reading and mathematics 6th grade.* Austin, Texas: Texas Education Agency, 1978.

THOMPSON, G. Children's acceptance of television advertising and the relation of televiewing to school achievement. *Journal of Educational Research,* 1964, *58*(4), 171–174.

TUKEY, J. W. *Exploratory data analysis.* Reading, Mass.: Addison-Wesley, 1977.

WALBERG, H. J. A psychological theory of educational productivity. In F. H. Farley & N. Gordon (Eds.), *Psychology and Education.* Chicago & Berkeley: National Society for Study of Education and McCutchan Publishing, 1980.

WITTY, P. Studies of mass media—1949–1965. *Science Education,* 1966, *50*(2), 119–126.

WITTY, P. Children of the television era. *Elementary English,* 1967, *44,* 528–535.

AUTHORS

PATRICIA A. WILLIAMS, Graduate Student, University of Wisconsin, Madison, Wisconsin 53706. *Specializations:* Evaluation research; instructional media of technology.

EDWARD H. HAERTEL, Assistant Professor, School of Education, Stanford University, Stanford, California 94305. *Specialization:* Educational and psychological measurement.

GENEVA D. HAERTEL, Educational Consultant, 675 Sharon Park Drive #317, Menlo Park, California 94025. *Specialization:* Educational psychology.

HERBERT J. WALBERG, Research Professor of Education, University of Illinois, Box 4348, Chicago, Illinois 60680. *Specializations:* Social psychology and productivity of education; measurement, evaluation and statistical analysis.

APPENDIX

Description of Studies Included in the Research Synthesis

Author: Anderson and MacGuire   Year: 1978

Sample Size and Description: The study employed 102 subjects in grades three and four and 198 subjects in grades five and six from a metropolitan city in Western Canada.

Dependent Measure: Results were reported on reading, vocabulary, and mathematics subtests of a locally constructed achievement test.

Substantive Results: The number of TV programs viewed appeared to have only a marginal negative relationship with achievement, the strongest being with vocabulary.

Control Variables: No control variables were used in the tabulations for the research synthesis.

Test for Curvilinearity: Linearity not assumed.

Determination of Viewing Time and Method of Collecting Data: The extent of TV viewing was determined by the frequency with which TV programs were watched. Students responded to a survey which listed programs broadcast in the area, by marking the programs viewed each week.

Author: Childers and Ross   Year: 1973

Sample Size and Description: The study employed 100 middle elementary pupils.

Dependent Measure: Results were reported on grade point average calculated across all subject areas.

Substantive Results: The relationship between television viewing hours, IQ, and achievement scores with grade point average showed that there was no significant relationship between the amount of hours a child spends watching television and his/her grades in school.

Control Variables: IQ and prior achievement were used in the tabulations for the research synthesis.

Test for Curvilinearity: Linearity assumed.

Determination of Viewing Time and Method of Collecting Data: Questionnaires were filled out by the student indicating how many hours of television were viewed on an average week night.

Author: Furu   Year: 1971

Sample Size and Description: This study employed a random sample of 1,303 fourth-, seventh-, and tenth-grade students in Tokyo, Japan.

Dependent Measure: Grade point averages were calculated across all subject areas.

Substantive Results: The school achievement score of the high TV group was lower than that of the low TV group for every grade (4th, 7th, 10th). The effects of the interaction of intelligence and TV was not significant for any grade. A significant effect from heavy viewing was found only in the low intelligence seventh-grade group and in the high intelligence 10th-grade group.

Control Variables: No control variables were used in the tabulations for the research synthesis.

Test for Curvilinearity: Linearity assumed.

Determination of Viewing Time and Method of Collecting Data: In the fourth and seventh grade, students filled in time-scale sheets to show the amount of TV viewing from Thursday through Sunday. A weighted mean score for each day was used as the measure of viewing time. In the 10th grade, the viewing time for weekends was ascertained by direct questions. An estimated total for weekdays, Saturdays, and Sundays was used as the measure.

Author: Gadberry   Year: 1977

Sample Size and Description: This longitudinal study employed 90 subjects from three age groups (6 to 7, 8 to 9, and 10 to 11) from suburban Long Island public schools.

Dependent Measure: Student performance was measured at two time points in this cross-lagged panel design. The dependent measure was grade point average calculated across all subject areas.

Substantive Results: Viewing amount affects school grades in a negative direction for all ages, both sexes and high and low achievers. Results indicate a small but nonsignificant negative relationship.

Control Variables: Sex and prior achievement were used in the tabulations for the research synthesis.

Test for Curvilinearity: Linearity assumed.

Determination of Viewing Time and Method of Collecting Data: Both diary method and an aided recall method were used at different points in the study. These yielded information on programs viewed, which was used to determine total viewing time.

Author: Greenstein   Year: 1954

Sample Size and Description: This study involved 67 fifth-grade students followed over six semesters. Students were divided into two groups: those who had access to television (experimental) and those who did not (control). Assignment to the TV and non-TV groups did vary if a student gained access during the course of the study. The study was conducted in a Chicago elementary school in a lower- and middle-income community.

Dependent Measure: Grade point average calculated across all subject areas was the dependent variable.

Substantive Results: Grades of the TV group were consistently higher than the non-TV group in reading, for up to 6 hours of daily viewing. For more than 6 hours the differences were negligible. Oral composition grades of the TV group were significantly better than the non-TV group. There were no significant differences in grades in written composition. The means were consistently higher for the TV group in all subject areas except penmanship.

Control Variables: No control variables were used in the tabulations for the research synthesis.

Test for Curvilinearity: Linearity not assumed.

Determination of Viewing Time and Method of Collecting Data: Questionnaires were completed by the child. Students estimated their viewing time for each weekday. Interviews were conducted to determine the validity of the students' estimates.

Author: Heideman   Year: 1957

Sample Size and Description: This study employed a simple random sample of eighth-grade pupils from the five junior high schools in St. Paul, Minnesota. The total sample included 199 individuals.

Dependent Measure: Grade equivalent scores on vocabulary and reading comprehension subtests from a standardized reading achievement test were the dependent measures.

Substantive Results: There were no significant differences between the high-televiewing and low-televiewing groups for either sex on any reading score when IQ and/or socioeconomic status were not controlled. For boys, when IQ was controlled there were significant differences between the means of the low televiewers and high televiewers on overall reading ability, but not for vocabulary and reading comprehension. For girls, there were no significant differences between the means of the high and low viewers on any reading variable when IQ was controlled.

Control Variables: Sex and IQ were used in the tabulations for the research synthesis.

Test for Curvilinearity: Linearity assumed.

Determination of Viewing Time and Method of Collecting Data: Average viewing time was computed from daily minutes of television recorded across three inventories. These inventories listed all of the programs telecast over the four local stations and were completed by students for each of 3 weeks.

Author: Himmelweit, Oppenheim, and Vince   Year: 1958

Sample Size and Description: The main study involved 1,845 matched pairs of viewers and nonviewers in primary and secondary modern schools in England, subjects were matched on the basis of sex, age, intelligence, and social class.

Dependent Measure: Teachers compared the performance of viewers and nonviewers in their classes on reading in class, written English, arithmetic, and general science.

Substantive Results: Results suggested that overall the school performance of viewers was equal to or slightly lower than that of their matched controls. Altogether, 47 percent of the controls were rated as performing better than viewers matched with them, and 36 percent of the viewers were doing better than the controls. Overall, there was a trend, although not statistically significant, indicating better academic performance on the part of the controls, viewers school attainment was sometimes a little poorer, but there were no sharp differences in the patterns of performance from one subject area to another.

Control Variables: IQ was used in the tabulations for the research synthesis.

Test for Curvilinearity: Linearity assumed.

Determination of Viewing Time and Method of Collecting Data: Children were asked to keep a diary for 1 day a week. They recorded everything they did between school and bedtime. Estimate of total viewing time was determined from entries in the diary.

Author: Kohr   Year: 1979

Sample Size and Description: The study involved a random sample of 10,037 students from three grade levels: 5, 8, and 11. Students came from 113 school districts broadly representative of the state of Pennsylvania. There were 453 elementary schools, 151 middle or junior high schools, and 128 senior high schools. The paper reports on secondary analyses of data collected in the Pennsylvania Educational Quality Assessment Program.

Dependent Measure: Scores on reading and mathematics subtests from a standardized achievement test.

Substantive Results: Student-level analyses yielded little evidence of linear or nonlinear relationships between viewing and cognitive or noncognitive outcomes, except that there was a substantial drop in achievement when students indulged in 5 or more hours of television viewing per school night. School-level analyses showed strong negative relationships between television viewing and cognitive achievement, particularly at ages 8 and 11.

Control variables: Sex was used in the tabulations for the research synthesis.

Test for Curvilinearity: Linearity not assumed.

Determination of Viewing Time and Method of Collecting Data: Students responded to a questionnaire. Estimates of the amount of television viewing from the time students got home from school until going to bed were indicated by marking one of the appropriate response categories: (1) about 1 hour or less, (2) about 2 hours, (3) about 3 hours, (4) about 4 hours, and (5) about 5 hours or more.

Author: La Blonde   Year: 1966

Sample Size and Description: This study employed a random sample of fifth grade children registered in the public schools of St. Paul, Minnesota from high-, average- and low-income areas.

Dependent Measures: The dependent measures were scores on reading, mathematics, language arts, and study skills subtests and overall achievement from a standardized achievement test.

Substantive Results: Measured achievement and televiewing bear an inverse relationship to each other. Comparisons indicate a negative and significant relationship when girls were considered separately. When boys were considered separately there was a negative and nonsignificant relationship in all areas except reading where results indicated a negative and significant relationship.

Control Variables: Sex was used in the tabulations for the research synthesis.

Test for Curvilinearity: Linearity assumed.

Determination of Viewing Time and Method of Collecting Data: Data were obtained by means of a Television Viewing Log, which contained a listing of all the television shows scheduled for the area that week. Students underlined the programs they watched. An estimate of viewing time was calculated for each child.

Author: Lyle and Hoffman   Year: 1972

Sample Size and Description: This study involved a random sample of first-, sixth- and tenth-grade students from a racially mixed school district in California. The total sample included 1,694 students.

Dependent Measure: Results for first-grade students were reported as teacher ratings of overall achievement. Intelligence test scores were reported for sixth- and tenth-grade students.

Substantive Results: In the first and sixth grades, little difference in amount of televiewing was indicated among ability groups. In the tenth grade, however, there was some evidence that brighter students watched less TV.

Control Variables: Sex was used in the tabulations for the research synthesis.

Test for Curvilinearity: Linearity assumed.

Determination of Viewing Time and Method of Collecting Data: For first graders, personal interviews were conducted. For sixth- and tenth-grade students a program log listing all programs broadcast in the area was employed. Students marked the programs they had watched.

Author: Mayeske et al.   Year: 1969

Sample Size and Description: The study employed a random sample of 33,233 students from throughout the United States in grades six, nine, and 12.

Dependent Measure: Average composite achievement scores (across all subject areas) from a standardized achievement test were the dependent measure.

Substantive Results: A curvilinear relationship was found between TV viewing and the achievement composite. The nature of this relationship altered at the different grade levels. The trend was for achievement levels of students who said they watched television not at all, very little, or very much to be lower than the achievement levels of the students who said they watched TV an intermediate number of hours.

Control Variables: No control variables were used in the tabulations for the research synthesis.

Test for Curvilinearity: Linearity not assumed.

Determination of Viewing Time and Method of Collecting Data: Students responded to a questionnaire by indicating the approximate number of hours spent each day viewing television.

Author: Morgan and Gross   Year: in press

Sample Size and Description: This random sample was composed of 602 students in the sixth through ninth grades attending a public school in suburban/rural New Jersey.

Dependent Measure: The dependent measures were scores on reading, mathematics, and language subtests from a standardized achievement test.

Substantive Results: This analysis consistently revealed significant negative correlations between amount of viewing and achievement in reading, mathematics, and language. The magnitude of these correlations remained the same when controlled for social class, sex, grade in school, but were reduced when IQ was held constant. Language usage and structure and reading comprehension remained negative and significant when controlled for IQ. Simple correlations of viewing with mathematics scores dropped to almost zero when IQ was held constant.

Control Variables: Sex and IQ were used in the tabulations for the research synthesis.

Test for Curvilinearity: Linearity not assumed.

Determination of Viewing Time and Method of Collecting Data: Television viewing data were collected by means of a questionnaire. Students responded to the question, Altogether, about how many hours a day do you spend watching television, including morning, afternoon and evening?

Author: Rhode Island Statewide Assessment   Year: 1977a

Sample Size and Description: The study involved approximately 2,785 4th grade and 3,985 8th grade students randomly sampled from Rhode Island elementary and junior high schools. The sample was proportionately representative of the community size, sex, and racial distributions of the state. Nonpublic and public schools were sampled.

Dependent Measure: Standardized achievement test scores on vocabulary, reading comprehension, spelling, combined language skills, study skills, and combined mathematics skills were the dependent variables.

Substantive Results: For fourth graders, watching 2-3 hours of TV a day had the strongest effect. This effect was positive. Students in the fourth grade who watched 2-3 hours achieved significantly more than other fourth graders. By contrast, eighth graders who watched more than 4 hours a day showed the strongest effect on achievement. This effect was negative, they achieved less. The authors conclude that in general, TV watching did not have a strong effect on achievement.

Control Variables: No control variables were used in the tabulations for the research synthesis.

Test for Curvilinearity: Linearity assumed.

Determination of Viewing Time and Method of Collecting Data: Students responded to questionnaires by indicating the amount of time spent watching television each day.

Author: Rhode Island Statewide Assessment   Year: 1977b

Sample Size and Description: The study involved 3,702, 17-year-olds randomly sampled from Rhode Island high schools. The sample was proportionately representative of the community size, sex, and racial distributions of the state. Nonpublic and public schools were sampled.

Dependent Measure: The dependent measure was total test score on a criterion-referenced achievement test.

Substantive Results: There was a $-.15$ correlation between number of hours spent watching television and total test scores. The correlation was significant at the .001 level.

Control Variables: No control variables were used in the tabulations for the research synthesis.

Test for Curvilinearity: Linearity assumed.

Determination of Viewing Time and Method of Collecting Data: A questionnaire was administered to students requesting the amount of viewing time for each day.

Author: Nelson   Year: 1963

Sample Size and Description: The sample involved 200 above-average high school students: 100 who graduated in 1962 (trial group) and 100 who graduated in 1963 (cross-validation group). They were representatives of 41 high schools located in the state of Wisconsin.

Dependent Measure: The dependent measure was grade point average calculated across all subject areas.

Substantive Results: There was little relationship between amount of regular televiewing and high school grade point averages among these high school students.

Control Variables: IQ and prior achievement were used in the tabulations for the research synthesis.

Test for Curvilinearity: Linearity not assumed.

Determination of Viewing Time and Method of Collecting Data: A questionnaire and a program checklist were distributed. The total amount of time each student viewed programs regularly was determined from summing the time assigned to those programs watched on a regular basis. The amount of time each student indicated he or she had viewed the previous day was compared with the amount of time allotted to programs viewed by him or her on that day. Yearly interviews with students and their parents were used to verify responses.

Author: Perney, Freund, and Barman   Year: 1976

Sample Size and Description: The sample consisted of 202 kindergarten children from two suburban school districts north of Chicago. The two school districts contained a cross-section of several different racial/ ethnic backgrounds.

Dependent Measure: The dependent measures were scores on quantitative and verbal ability subtests from two standardized achievement tests.

Substantive Results: Total amount of television viewed correlated negatively with quantitative scores, but correlated positively with verbal scores for both girls and boys. Both effects were significant for girls and nonsignificant for boys.

Control Variables: Sex was used in the tabulations for the research synthesis.

Test for Curvilinearity: Linearity assumed.

Determination of Viewing Time and Method of Collecting Data: A parent questionnaire was constructed to collect information concerning the television viewing habits of the children and their families (types and amount of shows watched, and conditions under which viewing was done).

Author: Schramm, Lyle, and Parker   Year: 1961

Sample Size and Description: The study involved 256 first-grade students from two Canadian communities—Radiotown and Teletown (the latter had TV, the former did not). The towns were similar in most other respects.

Dependent Measure: Scores from the vocabulary subtests of the Stanford-Binet Intelligence test were used.

Substantive Results: When Radiotown and Teletown were compared on a general vocabulary test, viewers in both high and average intelligence groups scored significantly higher than corresponding groups of non-viewers. There was no difference between viewers and nonviewers in the below average intelligence group.

Control Variables: IQ was used in the tabulations for the research syntheses.

Test for Curvilinearity: Linearity assumed.

Determination of Viewing Time and Method of Collecting Data: Questionnaires were sent to the parents to determine viewing time.

Author: Scott   Year: 1956

Sample Size and Description: The sample consisted of 407 students within four randomly selected elementary schools. The study was confined to 15 sixth- and seventh-grade classes.

Dependent Measure: Scores on reading, mathematics, language, and spelling subtests from a standardized achievement test were used.

Substantive Results: Those children who viewed more television achieved less proficiency, as measured by standardized tests, in mathematics and reading and were significantly inferior in total achievement to those children who viewed less.

Control Variables: No control variables were used in the tabulations for the research synthesis.

Test for Curvilinearity: Linearity assumed.

Determination of Viewing Time and Method of Collecting Data: A program checklist was distributed for two 1-week periods. On each school day children checked those programs that were actually viewed since the prior day at school.

Author: Slater   Year: 1963

Sample Size and Description: This study employed a simple random sample of 150 students from Erie County, New York. The sample was proportionately representative of the school population of the entire county, namely city school students, village school students, and town school students.

Dependent Measure: Ranked standardized achievement scores on reading, spelling, mathematics, and total school achievement were the dependent measures.

Substantive Results: There was a negative relationship between TV watching and achievement for every variable. Reading was significant at the .05 level. Spelling and mathematics were nonsignificant at the .05 level.

Control Variables: No control variables were used in the tabulations for the research synthesis.

Test for Curvilinearity: Linearity assumed.

Determination of Viewing Time and Method of Collecting Data: Average viewing time was computed from a TV inventory which listed all the TV programs available for those hours when children were not in school. During a 2 week period the TV inventory was sent home each night to be marked by the students and their parents.

Author: Haertel and Wiley   Year: 1979

Sample Size and Description: A nationally representative cluster sample of roughly 15,000 pupils in grades 1–6 were tested. Parents were interviewed in the home to obtain income, TV viewing, and other background information.

Dependent Measure: Scores on a standardized achievement test were used. Students at each grade level took tests of vocabulary, reading comprehension, mathematics concepts, and mathematics computation.

Substantive Results: Significant differences in viewing among racial groups were found with blacks watching more hours of TV than nonblacks. A curvilinear relationship between viewing and achievement emerged, especially in grades 4–6, with maximum achievement associated with moderate viewing. At the lower-grade levels, very slight positive relationships were found.

Control Variables: No other factors were controlled in the tabulations used for the research synthesis.

Test for Curvilinearity: Separate means were reported for each range of reported daily viewing: curvilinearity was not tested formally, but was not assumed either.

Determination of Viewing Time and Method of Collecting Data: Home-based parent interview-structured questionnaire items on amount of viewing time on weekdays.

Author: Tan and Gunther   Year: 1979

Sample Size and Description: The study employed 74 Mexican-American members of a predominantly Mexican-American high school in a large, industrial southern city.

Dependent Measure: Grade point average calculated across all subject areas was the dependent measure.

Substantive Results: There was no relationship between total use of English-language mass media and academic performance. However, there was a significant negative relationship between grade point average and TV use for entertainment.

Control Variables: No control variables were used in the tabulations for the research synthesis.

Test for Curvilinearity: Linearity assumed.

Determination of Viewing Time and Method of Collecting Data: Questionnaires were distributed to students, who responded to the item How much time do you now spend daily watching television? (hours). Average hours of daily viewing were computed from the responses.

Author: Texas Assessment Project   Year: 1978

Sample Size and Description: This study involved a random sample of approximately 10,400 sixth-grade students. The sampling plan was designed to provide a proportionate representation of ethnic groups, and a cross-section of different types of school districts.

Dependent Measure: Scores on reading and mathematics subtests of a standardized achievement test were used.

Substantive Results: A relationship was found between amount of viewing time and performance on achievement tests. Students who reported watching up to 2 hours of TV a day scored at the national average or above on all tests. Those who reported watching more than 4 hours of TV scored below national norms. Those who watched more than 5 hours attained the lowest scores on all tests.

Control Variables: No control variables were used in the tabulations for the research synthesis.

Test for Curvilinearity: Linearity not assumed.

Determination of Viewing Time and Method of Collecting Data: Students responded to an item on a questionnaire by marking the approximate numbers of hours of television viewed the previous night, none, 1 hour or less, 1–2 hours, 2–3 hours, 3–4 hours, 4–5 hours, 5–6 hours, 6 hours or more.

Author: Thompson   Year: 1964

Sample Size and Description: The sample was composed of 100 third-grade children selected from the schools of a central Pennsylvania community. These children were typical of the average third-grade class in variables such as age, IQ, and average achievement. The average status level of the group was lower-middle-class with an over proportion in the professional and technical group and an under proportion in the operative and kindred workers group.

Dependent Measure: The dependent measure was total school achievement as assessed by total achievement test scores.

Substantive Results: There was a significant negative correlation between hours of viewing and total achievement. When mental age was held constant, the correlation with total achievement dropped to an insignificant level.

Control Variables: Mental Age was used in the tabulations for the research synthesis.

Test for Curvilinearity: Linearity assumed.

Determination of Viewing Time and Method of Collecting Data: Viewing time was assessed by an individual interview with the child.

20

Time and Method Coaching for the SAT

Samuel Messick and Ann Jungeblut

An exhaustive review of studies of coaching for the Scholastic Aptitude Test (SAT) revealed them to be methodologically flawed in a variety of ways. Despite these flaws and the attendant noise obscuring the results, some definite regularities emerged relating the size of score effects associated with coaching to the amount of student contact time entailed in the coaching programs. Rank-order correlations between these two variables were upwards of .7 for both SAT-V(Verbal subscale) and SAT-M(Math subscale). The relationship proved to be nonlinear, however, with arithmetically increasing amounts of score effect being associated with geometrically increasing amounts of student contact time, which in these data may also be serving as a proxy for increasing curriculum emphases on content knowledge and skill development as opposed to item review and practice. Thus, within the limitations of the available fragmentary data, there appear to be diminishing returns in SAT coaching effects, especially for SAT-V. According to the logarithmic models fit to the data, the student contact time required to achieve average score increases much greater than 20 to 30 points (on a 200- to 800-point scale) for both SAT-V and SAT-M rapidly approaches that of full-time schooling.

The controversy over whether or not the Scholastic Aptitude Test (SAT) is coachable is fueled by both misconception and miscommunication. The misconception centers mainly around the nature of the SAT, whereas the miscommunication centers mainly around the nature of coaching.

The SAT is not a measure of subject-matter attainment, such as the typical educational achievement test in biology or American history, nor is it a measure of innate intelligence or fixed endowment. The SAT measures developed abilities of verbal and mathematical reasoning and comprehension that are acquired gradually over many years of experience and use in both school and nonschool settings. By virtue of this gradual development, these intellective skills appear to be relatively difficult to improve markedly through brief courses of intervention in the final year or 2 of high school, when the SAT is typically taken. But since these abilities are learned, albeit in manifold ways through both education and experience, one would expect high-quality instruction over extended periods of time to improve them and hence to increase SAT scores. Thus, the question of the degree to which the SAT is coachable depends on what is meant by *coaching*, a point about which there has been not only marked contention but lax communication. Some writers restrict their usage of the term to practice on sample items and last-minute cramming (cf. Pike, 1978), whereas others include under the same rubric virtually full-time instruction at specialized preparatory schools for periods of 6 months or more (cf. Slack & Porter, 1980).

In an effort to uncover some regularities in the results of coaching studies that go beyond a simple scorecard of significant and nonsignificant findings or a conglomerate averaging of score effects from different coaching programs, we review all of the available studies of coaching for the SAT regardless of the way the term is interpreted. We view the issue as being much more complicated than the simplistic question of

We wish to thank Donald Alderman, Albert Beaton, John Carroll, Robert Linn, Frederic Lord, Donald Powers, Ledyard Tucker, and Bary Wingersky for their careful review of the manuscript and their many helpful comments. Special thanks go to John Tukey, whose suggestion that coaching effects be examined in terms of score gain per contact hour provided the impetus for this analysis.

Requests for reprints should be sent to Samuel Messick, Educational Testing Service, Princeton, New Jersey 08541.

From Samuel Messick and Ann Jungeblut, "Time and Method Coaching for the SAT," 89(2) *Psychological Bulletin* 191-216 (March 1981). Copyright 1981 by the American Psychological Association. Reprinted by permission of the author and publisher.

whether or not coaching works for the SAT. Rather, the key questions are how much student time devoted to what kinds of coaching experiences yield what level of score improvements in comparison with the level of experiential growth that would have occurred anyway without those coaching experiences. This latter point, that coaching effects must be evaluated relative to the experiential growth in ability that may occur regardless of the coaching program, underscores the need for comparable control groups of uncoached students in studies of coaching effectiveness but comparison with equivalent control groups has by no means been the rule. Since this point is critical in interpreting the import of experimental findings, the summaries of the various coaching studies draw special attention to the strengths and limitations of the study designs. Before these studies are examined in detail, however, further clarification of both the nature of the SAT and the nature of coaching is offered.

Coaching for Developed Abilities and Subject-Matter Learning

The SAT was developed as a measure of academic abilities to be used toward the end of secondary school as a standardized supplement to the high school record and letters of recommendation typically available to college admissions officers. The SAT was explicitly designed to differ from achievement tests in subject-matter fields in the sense that its content is drawn from a wide variety of substantive areas, not tied to a particular course of study, curriculum, or program. It assesses intellectual processes of comprehension and reasoning that are exercised to some degree in all subject-matter areas at all levels of schooling, as well as in response to real-life situations. The item content of the SAT attempts to sample the sort of generic cognitive skills underlying performance in college: reading with comprehension, understanding vocabulary, verbal reasoning, computational skills, quantitative reasoning, and problem solving.

There is a progression or ordering of educational tests ranging from measures of scholastic abilities at one pole, with content drawn from a variety of substantive areas, to measures of academic mastery at the other pole, with content specialized by subject-matter field (cf. Anastasi, 1980; Snow, 1980). The SAT falls toward the first extreme it taps general cognitive processes that develop gradually over many years of experience and use both inside the classroom and in everyday life, and these processes should therefore be relatively difficult to enhance markedly through brief courses of intervention. The typical educational achievement test falls toward the other extreme— it taps specific knowledge and skills acquired through the normal course of classroom instruction or independent study, and such knowledge and skill should therefore be relatively responsive to instructional intervention, even in brief courses. Similarly, there is a progression of types of preparation for taking examinations ranging from simple practice on sample items at one extreme to intensive instruction aimed at developing ability and knowledge at the other extreme. What has come to be called *coaching* is here considered to fall anywhere in the broad range between these two extremes of practice and instruction, entailing some combination of test familiarization, drill-and-practice with feedback, training in strategies for specific item formats and for general test taking (including advice on pacing, guessing, and managing test anxiety), subject-matter review, and skill-development exercises. There is little question that the verbal and mathematical abilities measured by the SAT are learned, but there are large questions about how they can be taught. Thus the functional characteristics of any SAT coaching programs that prove to be effective would have important implications for educational practice.

The effect of coaching or special preparation programs on SAT performance has become a question of increasing concern to students, their parents, secondary schools, and colleges. A recent survey conducted in seven Northeastern states (Alderman & Powers, 1980) indicated that perhaps as many as one third of the secondary schools in the area offer a program of special preparation for SAT-V(Verbal subscale), with programs in SAT-M(Math subscale) probably at least as numerous. Commercial or proprietary coaching programs are also quite widely available in urban and suburban communities (Federal Trade Commission [FTC], 1978). Studies have been conducted periodically over the past 30 years to investigate the effects of both school-based and proprietary programs on student performance on the SAT. The results of these studies are examined with particular attention to problems of reseach design.

Problems of Method and Interpretation in SAT Coaching Studies

In the evaluation of coaching effectiveness, a key feature of research design is random assignment of examinees to coaching treatment groups and noncoaching control groups, for only with random assignment can we consider treatment effects to be independent of prior status on any of a host of personal or background characteristics. With random assignment, no systematic differences are expected between the experimental and control groups initially, and if effective control conditions are maintained, the only systematic difference that will eventuate is that one group will have received coaching and the other will not. In the absence of randomization, there is an inevitable equivocality in the interpretation of the results because some unmeasured personal characteristics might have influenced both the student's participation in the coaching program and that program's apparent effectiveness. That is, certain personal factors characteristic of students attending a particular coaching program, such as motivation or career aspirations, may be responsible, at least in part, for subsequent SAT performance that *appears* to be the result of the coaching experience. Thus the effects of selection or of self-selection are confounded with effects of the coaching treatment in nonrandomized studies. Consequently, selection factors afford plausible rival explanations for the results or for part of the results that might otherwise be identified as coaching effects. Selection factors include all systematic differences, whether measured or unmeasured, between the experimental and control groups that are correlated with the dependent variable, in this case SAT performance—except, of course, that the experimental group received the coaching treatment, whereas the control group did not. If these systematic differences result from student choice of the treatment rather than from experimenter choice of the student, they are called self-selection factors.

In nonrandomized designs, researchers usually attempt to control statistically, using regression techniques like analysis of covariance, for those potential selection factors that have been measured. Attempts are also frequently made to analyze the data in alternate ways to assess the sensitivity or robustness of the findings under various plausible assumptions. However, there is no way to adjust statistically for selection factors that have not been assessed. Since very few of the studies reviewed here employ random assignment and those that do have other problems of maintaining realistic control conditions, the specter of selection bias arises continually as a plausible alternative interpretation of apparent coaching effects.

As our review underscores, the available studies of coaching for the SAT are methodologically flawed in various and divergent ways. Most are subject to the problem of selection bias just discussed, which severely compromises interpretations of the source or determinants of score effects. Others were subject to disturbances of student motivation or of control conditions, which very likely introduced biases in estimating the size of score effects. Still others were based on small samples of coached students, which resulted in estimated score effects that were imprecisely bounded. Several studies suffered from combinations of two or more of these problems. In searching for regularities among the findings, especially between the size of score effects and key characteristics of the coaching programs, we attempt to discount studies having likely biases in their score estimates while at the same time trying to take into account the greater variability of estimates from studies with small sample sizes. Although the statistical significance of results is documented (see Table 1), the issue of coaching is addressed more in terms of estimation of score effects than of rejection of the null hypothesis. Finally, we turn to the problem of interpreting the determinants or sources of the educed relationships and confront once again the pervasive confounding influence of selection bias.

Although there was considerable variation in the score increases observed for particular groups of students and for particular coaching programs, the studies conducted in the 1950s and 1960s as well as two more recent studies (Alderman & Powers, 1980; Evans & Pike, 1973) yielded average score increases relative to control groups of about 9 points on SAT-V and about 13 points on SAT-M, on a score scale ranging from 200 to 800 points with a standard deviation of about 100 points (Messick, 1980). If the average effects for two commercial coaching schools studied by the FTC (1979; see also Stroud, 1980) are added, the average SAT-V increase becomes 14 points and the average SAT-M increase becomes 15 points. Studies lacking any control groups whatsoever yielded larger adjusted score effects—on the average, 38 points on SAT-V and 54 points on SAT-M—but since they differed from control group studies not only in design characteristics but in critical program characteristics as well, their interpretation is especially problematic.

Studies With No Control Groups

Three studies—those by Pallone in 1961, by Marron in 1965, and by Coffman and Parry in 1967—lacked any control group for evaluating unusual patterns of score change. Pallone examined the effects of short- and long-term intensive developmental reading courses on SAT scores of students in a private school for boys. The courses were undertaken "for students in their final year of precollege work, including a large number of high school graduates who were completing a year of post-high school study in preparation for entrance into the U.S. government academies" (p. 655). According to Pallone, to improve the skills measured by the SAT, "not 'coaching' methods, but instruction of a developmental nature in reading and vocabulary skills was indicated. Improvement in scores could be expected only if the basic skills measured by the test were first strengthened" (pp. 654–655). This pro-

gram provided focused instruction to strengthen reading achievement along with intensive practice in reading skills, including such special skills as skimming and critical reading, as well as a brief analysis of typical verbal analogy test items. Approximately 20 students participated in a 6-week summer pilot program that met for 90 minutes daily. An average score increase of 98 points was obtained on SAT-V from the March to August SAT administrations. The long-term program covered a 6-month period with daily meetings of 50 minutes each. For some 80 students who completed this long-term course, an average SAT-V increase of 109 points was reported over a 12-month period from pretest to posttest, although the difference in mean scores in Pallone's Table 3 (p. 656) is only 84. The students who participated in the summer program also completed the long-term reading course, and their mean increase in Verbal score over 12 months was almost 122 points, or an average of about 24 points over the increase reported after the summer course. The special quality of the sample and the lack of control groups severely limit the implications of these findings vis-à-vis coaching. Furthermore, the instructional focus on skill development and the intensive and long-term nature of the programs put Pallone's efforts close to what ordinarily would be considered "instruction," in contradistinction to "coaching," as Pallone himself insisted.

In the absence of control groups of similar students at this preparatory school who were not taking Pallone's course, it is difficult to assess the import of these score gains. Pallone (1961) suggested comparing them with normal expectations of gains of about 35 points on SAT-V during the final secondary school year, which would yield an instructional or program effect of about 83 points for the summer pilot program (prorated for the 5 months between pre- and posttests) and about 74 points for the long-term program (which had 12 months between pre- and posttests). Or, if the difference in mean scores is taken as 84 as in Pallone's Table 3, the long-term instructional effect is about 49 points. This is not a very satisfactory comparison, however, since Pallone's students were not representative of students in their final year of high school who take the SAT. In a recent review article on the SAT, Slack and Porter (1980) suggested comparing Pallone's results with average gains in national administrations of junior- to senior-year retesters having the same initial average score levels as Pallone's students, which yields prorated instructional effects of 85 and 79 (or 54) points, respectively, for the summer and long-term programs. Again, this is not a very satisfactory comparison because Pallone's private school students were not a representative sample of the national population of test repeaters. Pike (1978) suggested comparing Pallone's results with average gains of control students in superior schools from other studies of proprietary programs, and this comparison leads to instructional effects of about 75 and 53 (or 28) points, respectively, for the summer and long-term programs. If compared with score gains of control students in other coaching studies who had average initial score levels roughly comparable to Pallone's groups, the adjusted instructional effects are 80 and 65 (or 40) points, respectively.

The point is that in the absence of comparable control groups, no generally satisfactory estimate of instructional effects can be obtained. If an average is taken across the four adjustments just suggested, the resulting estimates of instructional effects are 81 and 68 (or 43) points, respectively, for the summer and long-term programs. These values are very likely still overestimates, however, because none of the comparisons can take into account the highly self-selected nature of Pallone's (1961) private school students, many of whom were completing a post-high-school year particularly motivated to increase their chances of entering service academies or selective colleges. Nevertheless, given the overall size of the effects, even with somewhat larger adjustments, it seems likely that Pallone's intensive summer and long-term efforts at "instruction of a developmental nature" succeeded in strengthening basic skills measured by the SAT.

Marron (1965) examined SAT score gains for students at 10 well-known preparatory schools that specialized in preparing high school graduates for admission to the service academies and selective colleges. The instructional programs entailed "six months of full-time exposure to course content that is directly related to the verbal and mathematics College Board tests (both Aptitude and Achievement)" (p.1). A special administration of SAT-V and SAT-M at all 10 schools served as the pretest, whereas the posttest was a regular SAT administration 6 months later. It should be noted that if the level of motivation and effort on a special pretest that did not count for college admission was not comparable to that on the regular posttest, the instructional effects in Marron's study would likely be overestimated. This issue did not arise for Pallone (1961) because both pre- and posttests in his study were regular SAT administrations.

Since significant differences were obtained among the 10 schools with respect to both the pretest scores and the posttest scores and these latter differences remained significant in analyses of covariance adjusting for pretest levels, the overall results were reported separately for groups of schools having nonsignificant differences within group. Score gains on SAT-V were 77 points for Group 1 (2 schools, $N = 83$), 56 points for Group 2 (6 schools, $N = 600$), 47 points for Group 3 (1 school, $N = 5$), and 35 points for Group 4 (1 school, $N = 26$); the weighted average SAT-V increase over all groups was 58 points. Score increases for SAT-M were 83 points for Group 1 (4 schools, $N = 232$), 78 points for Group 2 (3 schools, $N = 405$), and 72 points for Group 3 (3 schools, $N = 78$); the weighted average SAT-M increase over all groups was 79 points. Again, in the absence of control groups, it is difficult to appraise the size of these instructional effects.

Marron (1965) suggested comparing the SAT score gains with the gains considered typical for males in their senior year in secondary school, which he reported based on College Board data as 40 points for SAT-V and 43 points for SAT-M over a 10-month testing interval. Prorated for the 6-month testing interval in Marron's study, this yields an adjusted weighted average of 34 points for SAT-V and 53 points for SAT-M. As was done for Pallone's (1961) results, the suggested adjustments of Slack and Porter (1980) and Pike (1978) were also applied to Marron's figures, along with an adjustment based on score gains of control students in other coaching studies who had average initial score levels roughly comparable to the scores of Marron's groups. Taking the average of all four of these adjustments, the resulting weighted average values are 35 points for SAT-V and 54 points for SAT-M. But again, none of these adjustments is very satisfactory because none of the suggested comparisons takes into account that Marron's students were highly self-selected, thereby leaving important factors of differential motivation and growth uncontrolled. In any event, the relevance of Marron's study to the issue of coaching is arguable, since 6 months of full-time exposure to course content directed at verbal and mathematical knowledge and skills would ordinarily be considered instruction.

In an attempt to explore further the effects of developmental reading instruction on SAT-V scores, especially in light of Pallone's (1961) findings, Coffman and Parry (1967) studied three groups of college freshmen who took the SAT-V before and after completing a course in accelerated reading. The course was described as stressing speed of reading with relative accuracy. Pre- and posttest scores based on special administrations of the SAT were available for two small groups of 10 and 9 students who elected to take an 8-week course that met 6 hours each week. Pre- and posttest SAT-V scores were also available for 25 students whose course met 3 hours a week for 15 weeks. For students in the 8-week course, SAT-V scores increased 3.5 points in one group and 9.9 in the other. A 28.9 mean loss was observed for the group taking the 15-week course, possibly because of problems of test administration and score equating, since time constraints dictated the use of a shortened SAT-V for that group. It may also reflect problems in the motivation of students who take a special SAT when they are already in college, as may the relatively modest score increases in the other two groups   although all of these students were presumably motivated to enroll in the course, which explicitly entailed taking the SAT. Again, the lack of control groups seriously impairs the usefulness of these results.

Studies With Nonequivalent Control Groups

A second methodological weakness obtains in four other coaching studies: Although each incorporated control groups, the control students attended different schools from those providing special preparation for experimental students or else were drawn from other extrinsic sources such as test-score files, thus confounding coaching effects with school effects and with myriad other self-selection factors.

Dyer (1953) studied seniors at two highly selective independent schools for boys—225 students at one school served as the treatment group, and 193 students at the other school served as the control group. The students at both schools took a special pretest SAT and, 6 months later, a regular SAT, which served as the posttest. The experimental group completed 12 verbal practice exercises in 30- to 60-minute sessions and 5 math practice exercises in 60- to 90-minute sessions. The control variables in an analysis of covariance were initial SAT scores, number of years each student had been enrolled in school, and the number and level of foreign language and mathematics courses taken in the senior year. The estimated increase in score for the treatment group over the control group was 4.6 points in Verbal and 12.9 points in Math. When the students were divided into those who were not taking mathematics courses as seniors and those who were, the no-math boys who were coached gained over 29 points more than those who were not coached. In contrast, it was found that the boys taking mathematics who were coached gained 3.3 points more than those taking mathematics who were not coached. These findings provide the first example in studies of coaching of an interaction between size of effects and student background characteristics, alerting us to the more general possibility that coaching programs, like other forms of teaching, may have differential effects for different kinds of students.

French (1955) conducted a coaching study employing dual treatment and control groups at three schools: The 158 students at School A pursued their regular courses with no attempt at special preparation for the SAT and served as a control group for coaching in both Verbal and Math; the 110 students at School B served as a treatment group for Verbal and as a control group for Math; the 161 students at School C served as a treatment group for both Verbal and Math. The special preparation program in Verbal at School B differed from the one at School C in that the former primarily emphasized vocabulary for a total of 4½ hours, whereas the latter reviewed 10 verbal exercises more representative of SAT-V skills. The pretest was a special administration of the SAT, with a regular administration 6 months later serving as a posttest. An analysis of covariance, using pretest scores as the control variable and posttest scores as the dependent or outcome variable, showed an advantage in Verbal score for the coached groups of 18 points at School C and 5 points at School B (the one with the vocabulary coaching program). The score increase in Math was 6 points when compared with scores of School A and 18 points when compared with scores of School B. When broken down by sex and current enrollment in math courses, the SAT-M data indicated that coached boys not studying math at the time of coaching showed greater increases over control students than did coached boys who were studying math, by about 4 points in one school and 10 in the other. This pattern of higher coaching effects for boys not currently studying math is consistent with the Dyer results. In contrast, coached girls not studying math at the time showed *smaller* increases over control students than did coached girls who were studying math. Coached girls currently studying math exhibited score increases of about 20 and 30 points over the noncoached girls currently studying math in the two control schools, whereas the coached girls not studying math exceeded their noncoached counterparts in the two math control schools by only 1 and 4 points. The interaction between size of coaching effects and current enrollment in math courses thus appears in these data to be moderated by the student's sex.

Dear (1958) undertook a study to determine whether longer periods of coaching in small groups—two class periods a week for 6 weeks and for 12 weeks—were likely to be more effective than the shorter term coaching studied by Dyer (1953) and by French (1955). In Dear's study, six public and four private secondary schools were chosen randomly from a list of schools in which at least 15 students had taken the May SAT as juniors. A treatment group from each school was selected at random from students who volunteered for coaching. A second group of nine schools drawn at random from the same geographical region—the New York–New Jersey–Greater Philadelphia area—served as control schools. Three students were selected from each school from each of three ability levels—90 coached students and 81 control students. Of these, 71 coached and 79 uncoached students took the SAT at regular administrations in May and again ten months later in March. The coaching program began in mid-November and continued through mid-March, with weekly coaching sessions supplemented by 1 additional hour of homework each week. Most students repeated the SAT in January (8 months after the pretest), which was halfway through the coaching period, and again in March (10 months after the pretest). The January results showed about a 22-point advantage for 60 coached students on Math, but a 2.5-point disadvantage on Verbal (relative to the average adjusted score increase of the control group). The March advantage for the coached students on Math was about 24 points. The Verbal score results, unfortunately, were not determined because of a significant difference in the slopes of the regression lines for the coached and uncoached groups. In contrast to Dyer's (1953) results, the greatest coaching gains on SAT-M were for students currently studying math, but no comparison can be made with French's (1955) finding of a sex-moderated interaction, since the Dear sample was not broken down for separate analyses by sex of student.

An ambitious investigation of the effects on student test performance of commercial coaching for the SAT was undertaken by the FTC in 1978, with extensively revised statistical analyses being issued the following year (FTC, 1979). Students enrolled in two New York City area commercial coaching schools during the 3 testing years of 1974 to 1977 served as the experimental or treatment group, and a random sample from College Board test-score files of uncoached persons who took the SAT during the same 3-year period in the same greater New York metropolitan area served as a control group. Six subgroups were examined: (a) high school juniors taking the SAT for the first time in April 1975 (76 coached and 607 uncoached students); (b) juniors taking the SAT for the first time in April 1976 (247 coached, 617 uncoached); (c) seniors taking the SAT for the second time in November 1975 (98 coached, 396 uncoached); (d) seniors taking the SAT for the second time in November 1976 (177 coached, 387 uncoached); (e) all high school students taking the SAT for the first time on any test date during the 3-year period (417 coached, 1,763 uncoached); and (f) all high school students taking the SAT for the second time during this period (316 coached, 1,267 uncoached). Statistical analyses were actually based on smaller samples than these largely because of missing student descriptive data.

When demographic and personal characteristics of the experimental and control groups were contrasted, it was found that the coached group was significantly higher than the uncoached group in high school class rank, parental income, most recent English grades, most recent math grades, and number of years of math taken. In addition, the coached group included significantly more nonpublic school students than the uncoached group. Although statistical adjustments were made for these and other preexisting group differences for which measures were available, there was no way to take into account unmeasured factors also likely to differentiate the groups, such as motivation or level of parental education. In the absence of random assignment of students to coached and uncoached groups and especially in view of the large and extensive differences confounded in the nonrandomized groups ultimately analyzed, any score effects derived from these data must be interpreted as combined coaching/self-selection effects.

The FTC used multiple regression techniques to control for group differences on the Preliminary Scholastic Aptitude Test

(PSAT)—or on the first SAT when two were taken—as well as for differences on several relevant background variables. Although they found negligible effects for students at one commercial coaching school, statistically significant effects were obtained for students at the other school, where the impact for SAT-Verbal was estimated to be 30 and 27 points, respectively, for first- and second-time SAT takers over the pooled time periods. Score effects of 19 and 28 points, respectively, were estimated for SAT-Math over the same periods. The program at the school in which students exhibited significant average score increases (School A) involved 10 4-hour sessions for a total of 40 hours of coaching, whereas that at the school showing negligible overall effects (School B) involved a total of 24 hours of coaching. Again, because of uncontrolled differences between the coached and uncoached groups, these estimated score increases of 20 to 30 points for both SAT-V and SAT-M at one coaching school represent combined coaching/self-selection effects.

Two major reanalyses of the FTC (1978, 1979) data were subsequently undertaken to address a broader set of issues with more powerful analytical techniques. A third reanalysis (National Education Association, 1980) reexamined some of the same ground covered by the FTC analysis but in a relatively primitive fashion, adding neither novel findings nor better controlled or more precise estimates. In the first major reanalysis, Stroud (1980) applied an analysis of covariance type of model that differed from the FTC analysis in two important respects: The FTC analysis used a pooled regression equation across both coached and uncoached students using, along with other variables, verbal pretests and background measures (such as PSAT-V and English grades) in predicting score effects on SAT-V but quantitative pretests and background variables (such as PSAT-M and math grades) in predicting SAT-M effects. In contrast, Stroud employed a regression equation defined by the performance of uncoached students only and, in addition, included both verbal and quantitative pretests and background variables in predicting coaching effects for each area on the SAT. This analysis is not only more precisely controlled through the inclusion of additional covariates, but it more appropriately contrasts the performance of coached students with predicted score levels they would have expected had they been uncoached students with their same values on predictor variables. This approach results in valid estimates with fewer assumptions and facilitates straightforward examination of interactions (Cochran, 1968).

Stroud's (1980) reanalysis indicates that, given their background characteristics and pretest levels, students enrolled in one of the two coaching schools studied by the FTC (School A) obtained significantly higher SAT scores than did uncoached students by about 20 to 35 points in both Verbal and Math—the same neighborhood as the FTC estimates. The estimated effects for students at the other school (School B) averaged about 5 points in Verbal and 7 in Math and were not statistically significant. These are estimated combined effects due to coaching and self-selection, since it is not possible, as noted previously, to estimate coaching and self-selection effects separately with these data. Stroud also investigated the possibility of interactions between size of effects and the student background variables included as covariates. No interactions were uncovered at Coaching School A for either SAT-V or SAT-M. At Coaching School B, however, statistically significant and independent interactive effects were obtained on SAT-V for race and self-reported parental income. On the average, even though their number was quite small ($N = 13$), black students at School B exhibited significantly larger coaching/self-selection effects on SAT-V than nonblacks, and students reporting low family income exhibited significantly larger coaching/self-selection Verbal effects than those reporting high family income (Messick, 1980, pp. 46–51). In contrast to the findings of Dyer (1953) and French (1955), no differential score effects were uncovered for SAT-M, either as a function of years of math taken or of sex or of any of the other covariates.

In the second major reanalysis of the FTC data, Rock (1980) employed a statistical model that takes account of differential rates of growth in SAT scores over time, if they

occur, for the coached and noncoached groups. If growth is occurring in the dependent variable (i.e., in the verbal and mathematical abilities measured by the SAT), then one of the key ways in which nonrandomized treatment and control groups might differ prior to any coaching intervention is in the rate of this intellectual growth. The statistical growth model employed by Rock does not adjust for self-selection factors or other group differences on background variables unrelated to differential growth, as analysis of covariance can. However, it does correct for those self-selection effects embodied in differential group growth that were not predicted from the available covariates used (Bryk & Weisberg, 1977). Since direct application of the model requires estimation of differential growth rates from time series data, even if only linearly from two testing occasions prior to coaching, only students having three test scores could be considered. For the treatment or experimental group, Rock included only those students at the largest coaching school (School A) for whom three test scores were available, a PSAT and two administrations of the SAT. The control group included only those uncoached students for whom these same three test scores were also available. The treatment group numbered 192 students and the control group, 684.

The coached students performed better than the uncoached students on the PSAT and were higher as well in high school rank-in-class and family income. As would be expected, the coached students also scored higher than their uncoached cohorts on the first SAT administration—but in the case of the Verbal area scored differentially higher. That is, during the period from taking the PSAT to taking the initial SAT, prior to attendance at the coaching school, the verbal skills of the students who subsequently were to be coached appeared to grow more rapidly than those of the uncoached students. In Math, however, both the coached and uncoached students showed similar group growth rates during this preintervention period. When the confounding effects of differential group growth rates were controlled for, the estimated coaching/self-selection effect for SAT-V dropped to about 17 points, whereas that for SAT-M, by virtue of not exhibiting differential group growth rates in these data, remained at about 30 points. Thus, by taking differential group growth rates into account, the estimated SAT-V effect was reduced to about half that in the FTC (1979) report or the Stroud (1980) re-analysis. Furthermore, the fact that Rock's estimate of the Verbal effect is substantially less than the Math effect is consistent with earlier findings and with expectations that Math, being generally more curriculum re-lated than Verbal, might be more responsive to coaching or special preparation.

Studies With Matched Control Groups

A third methodological problem occurs in studies in which control and experimental students, although from the same school, are not assigned randomly but are matched on selected measures, thereby still permitting systematic differences between the groups on other nonassessed variables.

Frankel (1960), in the first study ever published on the effects of commercial coaching on SAT scores, selected 45 high school students who had taken commercial coaching courses and matched them with 45 control students from the same high school on the basis of (a) having taken the same two reg-ular SAT administrations to serve as pretest and posttest, (b) having pretest scores within 10 points of each other on both Verbal and Math, and (c) being of the same sex. Within each pair, one student had taken a com-mercial coaching course involving roughly 30 hours of coaching in classes of about 25 students during the 7- to 8-month period between pre- and posttests. In brief, Frankel found an 8.4 point advantage for coached students on Verbal and a 9.4 point advantage on Math.

Whitla (1962) compared the score in-creases of 52 students who had attended a 10-hour course in improved study habits, reading skills, and math concepts at a pro-prietary school in Boston with the score in-creases of a comparable group of 52 students from the same area who had not taken a coaching course. All of the students had taken a regular SAT in March or May of

their junior year and, in addition, took a spe-cial SAT in the fall of their senior year when the study began; the January regular SAT administration provided the posttest. The average Verbal and Math scores of the two groups were within 1 point of each other on the spring SAT and within 2 points on the fall pretest, suggesting that the two groups were not only well matched in terms of initial level but also in terms of growth rate over this period. Whitla found an 11-point ad-vantage for the coached group on Verbal but a 5-point disadvantage on Math when the posttest was compared with the fall pretest; there was a 10-point advantage on Verbal and a 7-point disadvantage on Math when compared with the spring SAT. Note that the term *disadvantage* does not signify a score decrease on the part of the coached group, but rather a failure of their scores to increase as much as those of the control group.

Studies With Randomized Control Groups

Three coaching studies have used a ran-domized design. The first one, by Roberts and Oppenheim (1966), utilized the PSAT as both pretest and posttest. In contrast to earlier coaching studies that involved highly selective and effective private schools and specialized or suburban public schools, the Roberts and Oppenheim study was under-taken to investigate whether students re-ceiving less adequate instruction might es-pecially benefit from special preparation. Data were collected from 18 predominantly, if not entirely, black secondary schools in rural and urban Tennessee. In 6 schools coaching consisted of special instruction in verbal material, in 8 schools coaching was for mathematics, and in 4 schools no special instruction was provided. Within the treat-ment schools students were assigned ran-domly to coached and uncoached groups. The instruction was provided in 15 half-hour sessions over a 4- to 6-week period. The re-sults showed small increases for the coached groups over the control groups: about 1½ (1.44) points on PSAT-V and less than 1 (.81) point on PSAT-M, increases that cor-respond to about 14 points on SAT-V and 8 points on SAT-M. This advantage of coached over control groups, however, was due as much to score decreases on the part of the control students, possibly signaling problems in motivation or attrition, as to score increases on the part of the coached students.

A second randomized study, conducted by Evans and Pike (1973; Pike & Evans, 1972), examined intensive coaching efforts in the math area. A sample of 509 students in 12 schools participated in the study. The coached students received 21 hours of instruction and 21 hours of homework, over a 7-week period, directed at one of the following item types: Regular Math (RM), Data Sufficiency (DS), or Quantitative Comparisons (QC). Three randomly chosen groups of students were defined in each school: one to be instructed in QC, one in either RM or DS, and one as a control group. These groups took the SAT first in October, which served as a pretest, and again in December (posttest) and the following April (delayed posttest). The pretest and posttest were special administrations of the SAT, whereas the delayed posttest was a regular administration. The three experimental groups were given special preparation during November and December, and the control group received instruction after the December posttest and prior to the April delayed posttest. On this schedule, all groups received instruction in test-taking skills—becoming familiar with test directions, pacing, and appropriate strategies for guessing and using partial information. All groups also had instruction in math content—numerical facts, numerical and basic algebraic skills, and in particular mathematical areas such as inequalities. In addition, there was practice on one of the item types for students in each respective experimental group. The study revealed score increases beyond those experienced by the control group for each of the three experimental groups coached on a particular item type—11 SAT-M score points for QC, 19 points for DS, and 25 for RM. However, because the Evans and Pike (1973) study was designed to investigate the relative susceptibility of three item formats to special instruction, it is difficult to say just how large the effects would be in terms of coaching for SAT-M. Their best estimate of

score increases reflective of coaching for all four groups over the total period from October to April was about 25 points. The average increase over the control group for the three experimental item-type groups, weighted according to their respective sample sizes, was 16.5 points over the period from the October pretest to the December posttest. Pike (1978) later conjectured that, still keeping within the total 21 hours of special preparation, a judicious combination of instruction for both RM and DS, the two major item types then in SAT-M, would be expected to yield coaching or special preparation effects of about 33 points.

In the third randomized study, Alderman and Powers (1980) investigated the effectiveness of existing secondary school programs that had been initiated by the schools to improve the performance of students on the SAT-V scale. Students at each of eight schools for whom PSAT scores were available were randomly assigned to a special preparation group or to a control group. Access to the same preparation course was delayed for control students for the purpose of this study. A special administration of a retired form of the SAT was used as the posttest. Across the eight schools the overall increase in SAT-V attributable to special preparation was about 8 points, which is statistically significant at the .05 level. The actual effects ranged from −3 points at one school to 28 at another. Differences in effectiveness among the coaching programs were not statistically significant from school to school, however, and the best statistical estimate of the range was from 4 to 16 points. Nor, apparently, did the control groups react in comparable fashion from school to school, possibly reflecting differences in motivation or seriousness in approaching a special SAT that did not count for college admissions. The largest school effect of 28 points, for example, resulted in part from a control-group decrease almost equal in magnitude to the treatment-group increase (−11 score points in going from the converted PSAT to the SAT for the control group versus 13 score points for the treatment group, which yields a 28-point school effect when covariance adjustments are made). An attenuated form of this pattern occurred at two other schools, whereas the remaining five schools showed varying degrees of score increase for both treatment and control groups.

Another, more subtle methodological problem has emerged in the process of reviewing these coaching studies having randomized control groups, namely, the problem of engendering and maintaining realistic motivation for taking the posttest SAT, especially for uncoached control students. Developing realistic motivation and effort for taking pre- and posttests is a common requirement of all coaching studies. However, the three experiments that employed randomized control groups also used as the posttest a special administration of the SAT or PSAT rather than a regular administration, so that the control students would not have scores counting on their record before having access to special preparation. But by virtue of not counting for college admissions, these special administrations may have been viewed to some degree as practice tests, thereby eliciting less motivation and effort than would a regular SAT administration. As in the study by Roberts and Oppenheim (1966), warning signals suggesting this possibility were noted in the Alderman and Powers (1980) study. As discussed earlier, control groups in three schools were found to exhibit score *decreases* in going from a regular PSAT to a special SAT, even though the expectation is for a score *increase* from an October PSAT to a spring SAT of upwards of 10 or 12 points—this is the basal estimate provided by national administration samples. Such control-group score decreases substantially complicate the interpretation of intercept differences as estimates of coaching effects (Messick, 1980, pp. 20–22).

As noted, control-group scores also decreased in the Roberts and Oppenheim (1966) study, which similarly employed a special administration posttest, in that case a special PSAT. Unlike Alderman and Powers (1980), who used a regular administration of the PSAT as a pretest, the Roberts and Oppenheim pretest PSAT was a special administration as well. None of the nonrandomized coaching studies reviewed earlier displayed control-group score decreases, and the posttest in all of those studies was a reg-

ular administration of the SAT—although Dyer (1953), French (1955), and Whitla (1962) did use special pretest administrations and thereby introduced the possibility of other biases. The remaining randomized study, conducted by Evans and Pike (1973), employed special administration SATs as both pretest and posttest, but their delayed posttest was a regular SAT administration. Pike's (1978) subsequent interpretation of score increases from posttest to delayed posttest as reflecting the long-term consolidation or continuance of gains due to coaching becomes jeopardized from this vantage point by the plausible rival interpretation that those score gains instead reflect increases in motivation and effort in going from a special administration to a regular one.

Comparison of Results Across Studies of Coaching

For numerous reasons, including the diversity of design limitations and the differences in sample sizes, it is difficult to compare results across these several studies in a meaningful way (cf. Pike, 1978). Table 1 represents one such attempt for those studies having some type of control group. The size of coaching effects reported there were calculated uniformly as follows: When analysis of covariance was performed, the reported values are intercept differences between the experimental and control regression lines, weighted in the case of multiple experimental or control groups by their respective sample sizes. In four studies not reporting analyses of covariance, the values in Table 1 are average score increases of experimental over control groups, again weighted in the case of multiple experimental or control groups by their respective sample sizes. Two of these latter studies (by Frankel, 1960, and by Whitla, 1962) involved statistical matching, and two (by Roberts & Oppenheim, 1966, and by Evans & Pike, 1973) involved randomization. Averaging these results over all of the studies in Table 1, weighting in each case by the size of the experimental sample, yields 14.3 points for Verbal and 15.1 points for Math (the unweighted averages are 10.4 for Verbal and 13.0 for Math).

For those studies having no control groups,

a summary is provided in Table 2. The special preparation programs summarized there focus on verbal or mathematical content knowledge and skill development and entail the largest amounts of student contact time of any of the studies reviewed, which would ordinarily lead one to characterize them as instruction rather than coaching. These programs range from 45 hours of student contact time over 6 weeks to 48 hours over 8 weeks to roughly 100 hours over 6 months to virtually full-time over 6 months or approximately 600 hours (assuming six 50-minute periods a day for 24 weeks). The 45-, 48-, and 100-hour programs were devoted solely to special preparation in Verbal, whereas the full-time programs involved both Verbal and Math preparation, presumably with each receiving roughly equal 300-hour coverage. In contrast, the most intensive of the control-group studies summarized in Table 1 were 40 hours of student contact time divided, presumably equally, between Verbal and Math (Stroud, 1980) and 21 hours over 7 weeks devoted to special preparation in Math only (Evans & Pike, 1973); in addition, School H in Alderman and Powers (1980) entailed 45 hours of student contact time over 10 weeks in Verbal preparation only.

In the absence of control groups, instructional or program effects were estimated in Table 2 in the manner described earlier— that is, by adjusting the average score gains reported in each study by the average of four adjustments, those suggested by (a) the authors of the original articles, (b) Slack & Porter (1980), and (c) Pike (1978), as well as (d) the average score gains of control students in other coaching studies who had roughly comparable initial score levels. Averaging these estimates over all the studies in Table 2, weighting in each case according to group size, yields 38 points for SAT-V and 54 points for SAT-M (the unweighted averages are 39 points for Verbal and 53 points for Math). Given that the adjustments were dubious and provisional and that the students in each program were highly self-selected, these values are still probably overestimates of program effects. But their general magnitude suggests that the verbal and mathematical reasoning skills measured by

the SAT may be enhanced to a measurable degree by long-term and intensive instruction, at least for highly motivated students.

Granted that there is some overlap or blurring of the distinction between coaching studies in Table 1 and instructional studies in Table 2, the two types seemed sufficiently different to warrant separate treatment. Accordingly, overall averages were not computed for the total combined set of studies because possible differences in impact might thereby be obscured. In contrast, Slack and Porter (1980) have chosen to combine both types of studies in a single table and to report overall weighted average score increases of coached groups over uncoached control groups or, when control groups were not utilized, over norm comparison groups. This assumes that the adjustments applied to the score gains in studies lacking control groups were large enough to correct appropriately for the experiential growth of self-selected students that would have occurred regardless of the program. And indeed, the adjustments made by Slack and Porter, being derived from normative data of dubious relevance to the preparatory school students in question, were smaller than those based on the average of four adjustments as applied in our Table 2. Because of this and various oversights in their table, the combined weighted averages of 29 points for SAT-V and 33 points for SAT-M that they report are more like 22 and 28 points, respectively (Messick, 1980, pp. 24–26). Such combined averaging is misleading not only because the adjustments may be questionable, but because the combined averages obscure important differences between the special preparation programs in the two types of studies. As indicated earlier, a comparison of the brief program descriptions in Tables 1 and 2 reveals that the programs in studies lacking control groups happened also to be quite long-term and intensive with respect to student contact time, whereas the programs in control-group studies were relatively short-term and nonintensive. The former programs also entailed organized curriculum content and skill development as well as test review, whereas the latter programs tended to emphasize test review and practice exercises.

Rather than averaging across these two

Table 1
Average Difference Between Experimental and Control Groups in Studies of SAT Coaching Interventions

Study/design	Sample characteristics			Characteristics of the special preparation	SAT-Verbal			SAT-Math		
	School	Level	Sex		Difference[a]	Significance level[b]	Experimental/control N	Difference[a]	Significance level[b]	Experimental/control N
Dyer (1953)/control, different school	Private	High school seniors	M	12 30-60-min sessions for Verbal; 5 60-90-min sessions for Math	4.6	<.05	225/193	12.9	<.01	225/193
French (1955)/control, different school	Public	High school seniors	M and F	10 Verbal and 10 Math coaching sessions using ETS item materials	18.3	<.01	161/158	6.2	<.01	161/158
French (1955)/control, different school	Public	High school seniors	M and F	4½ hours of vocabulary coaching, 10 sessions of Math coaching using ETS item materials	5.0	<.05	110/158	18.0	<.01	161/110
Dear (1958)/control, same and different schools	Public and private	High school seniors	M and F	Approximately 6 weekly 2-hour, 2-person coaching sessions plus 1 hour of homework each week	-2.5	ns	60/526	21.5	<.01	60/526
Dear (1958)/control, same and different schools	Public and private	High school seniors	M and F	Approximately 12 weekly 2-hour, 2-person coaching sessions plus 1 hour of homework each week				23.6	<.01	71/116
Frankel (1960)/control, same school statistically matched	Public	High school seniors	M and F	10 3-hour, 25-person coaching sessions	8.4	ns	45/45	9.4	ns	45/45
Whitla (1962)/control, statistically matched	Public and private	High school seniors	M and F	Proprietary coaching school. 5 2-hour sessions plus homework in Verbal and Math	11.0	ns	52/52	-5.3	ns	50/50
Roberts & Oppenheim (1966)/randomized	Public	High school juniors	M and F	7½ hours of programmed instruction in test taking and in Verbal and Math content	14.4[d]	<.05	154/111	8.1[d]	ns	188/122
Evans & Pike (1973)/randomized	Public	High school juniors	M and F	Test-taking skills and math content, 7 3-hour sessions, 21 hours of homework	No coaching for SAT-Verbal			16.5	<.05	288/129
Alderman & Powers (1980)/randomized	Public and private	High school juniors	M and F	Varied strategies, at eight schools, emphasizing reading and analogies. 5-45 hours	8.4	<.05	239/320	No coaching for SAT-Math		

Table 1 (continued)

Study/design	Sample characteristics			Characteristics of the special preparation	SAT-Verbal			SAT-Math		
	School	Level	Sex		Difference[a]	Significance level[b]	Experimental/control N	Difference[a]	Significance level[b]	Experimental/control N
FTC (1979; see also Stroud, 1980)/control, test-score files	Public and private	High school juniors and seniors	M and F	School A: 40 hours commercial coaching	31.7[e]	<.01	393/1729	24.9[e]	<.01	393/1729
				School B: 24 hours commercial coaching	5.2[e]	ns	163/1729	7.5[e]	ns	163/1729
Average weighted by size of experimental sample					14.3[f]			15.1[f]		

Note. SAT = Scholastic Aptitude Test, M = male; F = female; ETS = Educational Testing Service; *ns* = nonsignificant.
[a] The coaching effects are intercept differences between regression lines for experimental and control groups or (for Frankel, 1960; Whitla, 1962; Roberts & Oppenheim, 1966; and Pike & Evans, 1972) average score increases of experimental over control groups, both weighted in the case of multiple experimental or control groups by their respective sample sizes.
[b] As shown for coaching effects reported in original text.
[c] Not calculated; variances and regression slopes differed significantly for experimental and control groups.
[d] This study employed the Preliminary Scholastic Aptitude Test as both pre- and posttest; the averages shown have been converted to the SAT score scale ranging from 200 to 800 points.
[e] Weighted mean score effects pooling juniors and seniors across test administration years from Stroud's reanalysis of Federal Trade Commission (FTC) data.
[f] If Rock's (1980) estimates for FTC School A of 16.9 for SAT-Verbal and 30.6 for SAT-Math (N = 192) are substituted for Stroud's (1980) estimates, the weighted averages become 9.7 for Verbal and 14.5 for Math.

types of studies, which inevitably precipitates arguments about the appropriate size of the score effects to be included from the uncontrolled studies, let us instead *rank* all the studies in order of the reported treatment versus control group contrasts and when control groups are not available in order of the reported score increases. That is, for SAT-V, Pallone's (1961) long-term and summer programs would be ranked 1 and 2, respectively, followed by Marron's (1965) four groups, and so forth. This procedure grants that the score effects in the studies lacking control groups are larger in an ordinal sense than those in the control-group studies, but it takes no position with respect to how much larger. If the programs are then also ranked in terms of the number of student contact hours involved and a Spearman rank-order correlation coefficient computed, the rank correlation is found to be .62 across 24 studies for SAT-V and .74 across 15 studies for SAT-M. Both coefficients are significant at the .01 level. If 5 particularly suspect studies showing signs of probable biases in the score effects estimated are deleted from the calculations for SAT-V, the new correlation is .77 across 19 studies, which is also significant at the .01 level. In this latter calculation, Schools A, B, and D from Alderman and Powers (1980) were eliminated because of control-group score decreases, as was the Roberts and Oppenheim (1966) study for the same reason, and the Coffman and Parry (1967) study was dropped because of treatment-group score decreases and other indications of the low relevance to the SAT of both the accelerated reading program studied and the samples of enrolled college students employed. Further, if the Rock (1980) estimate taking account of differential group growth rates is substituted for the Stroud (1980) estimate of SAT-V effects at School A in the FTC (1979) study, the resulting rank correlations are .60 across 24 studies and .76 across 19 studies. If one suspect study, namely, Roberts and Oppenheim, is deleted from the calculations for SAT-M, the new correlation is .71, which is also significant at the .01 level. These rank-order correlations are summarized in Table 3. It should be noted that although the various coaching programs required dif-

Table 2
Adjusted Average Score Gains in Studies of SAT Instructional Interventions Without Control Groups

Study	Sample characteristics			Characteristics of the special preparation	SAT-Verbal		SAT-Math	
	School	Level	Sex		Adjusted average score increase[a]	N	Adjusted average score increase[a]	N
Pallone (1961)	Private	High school seniors and graduates	M	90-min. daily instruction and practice in developmental reading skills over 6 weeks	81	20+		
Pallone (1961)	Private	High school seniors and graduates	M	50-min. daily instruction and practice in developmental reading skills, with stress on logical inference and analogic analysis over 6 months	68 (43)[b]	80−		
Marron (1965)	Private	High school seniors and graduates	M	Full-time daily sessions aimed at verbal and mathematical content and test-taking skills over 6 months	Group 1 54 Group 2 33 $\rbrace$ 35 Group 3 24 Group 4 12	83 600 5 26	Group 1' 59 Group 2' 53 Group 3' 46	232 405 78
Coffman & Parry (1967)[c]	Public	College freshmen	M and F	6-hours weekly of instruction in accelerated reading over 8 weeks	4[d]	19		
Average weighted by size of experimental sample					38 (36)[b]		54	

Note. SAT = Scholastic Aptitude Test; M = male; F = female.

[a] To estimate instructional or program effects, average score increases in the Pallone (1961) and Marron (1965) studies were adjusted by the average of four adjustments, those suggested by (a) the authors of the original articles—Pallone suggested 35 points on SAT-Verbal as normal expectation of gains during the final year of secondary school (15 points for the 5-month interval between tests in the short-term program), and Marron suggested 24 and 26 points, respectively, for SAT-Verbal and SAT-Math as typical gains for high school seniors over 6 months; (b) Slack and Porter (1980)—average gains in national administrations of junior-to-senior year retesters having the same initial average score levels as Pallone's and Marron's groups; (c) Pike (1978)—average gains of control students in superior schools from other studies of proprietary programs; as well as, (d) average gains of control students in other studies who have average initial score levels roughly comparable to those of Pallone's and Marron's groups.

[b] Due to discrepancies in Pallone's tables, there is some uncertainty as to whether the average adjusted score effect in his long-term program should be 68 points or 43 points (see page 195).

[c] The 15-week program in Coffman and Parry was not included because the 29-point mean decrease in scores was considered atypical and possibly indicative of motivational and test-administration problems.

[d] The two 8-week programs in Coffman and Parry were combined, but adjustments were made only by the Slack and Porter procedure, which attenuated by only a few points an already tenuous effect. None of the suggested comparison groups of SAT takers appeared to provide even remotely reasonable yardsticks for gauging score gains of students already enrolled in a college not requiring the SAT.

ferent and usually unknown amounts of homework, this rank-correlation procedure tacitly assumes that the amount of homework in each case was roughly proportional to the number of student contact hours, so that the overall orderings would not be markedly changed if homework were taken into account.

In interpreting these sizable monotonic relationships between student contact time and score effects, it must be remembered that these are rank-order correlations between average values of different samples or groups, and correlations between averages are typically much higher than correlations between individual differences within groups. Furthermore, these rank correlations are dominated by the relative consistencies between the two types of studies with respect to the ranking variables—that is, the control-group studies are all relatively low in both student contact time and score effects, whereas the uncontrolled studies are all relatively high in both student contact time and score effects. It must also be remembered that the relatively high-contact programs entailed structured curricula emphasizing content knowledge and skill development, whereas the relatively low-contact programs emphasized test review and practice. With this confounding of program characteristics in mind, it appears that increases in student contact time (possibly serving as a proxy for increasing curriculum emphases on content knowledge and skill development) are systematically associated on the average with increases in SAT scores. However, even though the time dimension is covered in only a fragmentary fashion by the available studies, when the magnitude of (adjusted) score effect is plotted against student contact time, the relationship does not appear to be linear. Since the form of this relationship might enable us to predict the rough magnitude of score effects expected to be associated with coaching programs entailing given levels of student contact time, these data plots warrant careful examination.

Diminishing Returns in Coaching Effects

Attempting to approximate the general form of the function relating score effects

to student contact time in coaching programs is difficult with the available data for two reasons: One is the fragmentary way in which the time dimension is covered by the existing studies, especially in the range between 30 hours and 300 hours, the latter representing half-time devoted to either Verbal or Math coaching in a 6-month full-time preparatory school program; the other is the inevitable variability or noise present in studies having methodological flaws. Barring the collection of new data, little can be done about the first difficulty. But with respect to the second, we can attempt to mute the effect of noise to some extent by excluding from consideration, at least initially, data from studies already identified as being particularly suspect—namely, data from Roberts and Oppenheim (1966), from Coffman and Parry (1967), and from Schools A, B, and D of Alderman and Powers (1980). Although these suspect data points will not be used to fit any functions, they will be plotted subsequently to see how aberrant they are with respect to functions based on the remaining data.

For somewhat different reasons, the data for Pallone's (1961) summer and long-term programs will also be excluded initially and subsequently plotted in relation to identified functions in the same way. Here the primary reason is uncertainty about how to estimate student contact time for these programs. Pallone's long-term program is described as 50 minutes of daily instruction over 6 months or approximately 100 hours, but since the students were also attending preparatory school full-time during this period, it seems more appropriate in the absence of control groups to estimate their contact time for Verbal preparation at 300 hours, as was done for Marron's (1965) preparatory school students. There is also some uncertainty, arising from discrepancies in Pallone's own tables, as to whether the average adjusted score effect for his long-term program is 68 points or 43 points (see Table 2). Moreover, the summer program is described as 90 minutes of daily instruction over 6 weeks, or approximately 45 hours, but since the students might also have been attending other summer preparatory courses during this period, it is impossible in the absence of information

Table 3
Correlations Between Rank Order of Score Effect and Rank Order of Student Contact Time for Studies of SAT Interventions With and Without Control Groups

Verbal[a]

Study	Student contact time (hours)	Rank[*] time	Rank score effect
Dyer (1953)	10 [b]	13	15
French (1955)			
Verbal and Math	8.3[c]	14	8
Vocabulary	4.5	19	14
Dear (1958)	6	15.5	18
Frankel (1960)	15	9	12
Whitla (1962)	5	17.5	11
Alderman & Powers (1980)[d]			
School C	10.5	12	19
School E	6	15.5	17
School F	5	17.5	16
School G	11	11	9
School H	45	6.5	10
Pallone (1961)			
Short	45	6.5	2
Long	100	5	1
Marron (1963)			
Group 1	300	2.5	3
Group 2	300	2.5	4
Group 3	300	2.5	5
Group 4	300	2.5	6
FTC (1979; Stroud, 1980)			
School A	20	8	7[e]
School B	12	10	13[e]
Rank-order correlation			.77 (19 studies)[f]
Roberts & Oppenheim (1966)[g]	3.8		
Alderman & Powers (1980)			
School A	7		
School B	10		
School D	10		
Coffman & Parry (1967)[h]	48		
Rank-order correlation			.64 (24 studies)[f]

Math[a]

Study	Student contact time (hours)	Rank time	Rank score effect
Dyer (1953)	8.3[c]	11.5	9
French (1955)[i]	8.3	11.5	10.5
Dear (1958)			
Long	12	9.5	6
Short	6	13	7
Frankel (1960)	15	8	12
Whitla (1962)	5	14	14
Evans & Pike (1973)			
Group QC	21	5	10.5
Group DS	21	5	8
Group RM	21	5	4
Marron (1965)			
Group 1	300	2	1
Group 2	300	2	2
Group 3	300	2	3
FTC (1979; Stroud, 1980)			
School A	20	7	5[e]
School B	12	9.5	13[e]
Rank-order correlation			.71 (14 studies)
Roberts & Oppenheim (1966)[g]	3.8		
Rank-order correlation			.74 (15 studies)

Table 3 (*continued*)

Note. SAT = Scholastic Aptitude Test; QC = Quantitative Comparisons; DS = Data Sufficiency; RM = Regular Math.

ᵃ When only a total student contact time was available, it was assumed that half the time was devoted to Verbal and half to Math.

ᵇ Each of 12 exercises was estimated to require a 50-min. class period.

ᶜ Each of 10 exercises was estimated to require a 50-min. class period.

ᵈ Schools A, B, and D were suspect because of control-group score decreases and hence were omitted in these calculations based on 19 studies; they are included in the later calculations based on all 24 studies.

ᵉ Ranks based on weighted mean score effects pooling juniors and seniors across test administration years from Stroud's reanalysis of Federal Trade Commission (FTC) data.

ᶠ If the Rock (1980) estimate taking account of differential group growth rate is substituted for the Stroud (1980) estimate of SAT-Verbal effects at School A in the FTC study, the resulting correlations are .76 across 19 studies and .60 across 24 studies.

ᵍ Roberts and Oppenheim was suspect because of control-group decreases and hence was omitted from the calculations for Verbal based on 19 studies and for Math based on 14 studies.

ʰ Coffman and Parry was suspect because of treatment-group score decreases and other indications of motivational problems and hence was omitted from the calculations based on 19 studies. The 25-week program was dropped altogether because of the treatment-group score decreases, and the two 8-week programs were combined, yielding a weighted average score effect of 6.5.

ⁱ Each of five double-length exercises was estimated to require two 50-min. class periods.

ʲ French's Math coaching group was contrasted with two control groups, one in a school having no coaching and one in a school having vocabulary coaching; these two comparisons were combined, yielding a weighted average score effect of 11.

about their programs to estimate what the effective student contact time for Verbal preparation might have been. If a control group had been available of similar students attending the same summer school but who were not taking Pallone's course, then the average net score increase for Pallone's students over the control students could have been associated with the 45 hours of student contact time in Pallone's course description. In addition, since Pallone's summer course was a *pilot* program involving only about 20 students, it seemed prudent to give it little or no weight in fitting functions.

With these exclusions, 17 data points remain for SAT-V score effects and 14 data points for SAT-M effects (see Table 3). When these (adjusted) values are plotted separately for Verbal and Math scores as a function of their associated student contact times, the resulting arrays appear nonlinear. This may be demonstrated by contrasting the linear function that best fits all of the Verbal (or Math) data points with the linear function that best fits only those data points toward the low end of the time dimension, that is, all but the full-time programs. If the overall relationship were approximately linear, these two regression lines would be quite similar to each other. But their slopes, as we shall see later, indeed differ by a factor of 4 or 5, which makes an enormous difference over a time range of 300 hours.

Given this broad time range and the fact that the data points are clustered at the two extremes, the nature of the nonlinear relationship is better revealed analytically than visually. The linear least squares regression equation for the 17 Verbal studies is $V = 7.336 + .079T$, where V is SAT-V score effect and T is time in hours ($N = 17, r = .66$). This equation is dominated by Marron's (1965) four Verbal groups at 300 hours of student contact time, for which the predicted score effect of 31 points is close to their adjusted weighted average (see Table 2). But the predicted values at the low end of the time scale are out of line with the data— e.g., the predicted score effect for 1 hour of contact time is 7.4 points; for 10 hours, 8.1 points; for 20 hours, 8.9 points; for 30 hours, 9.7 points; for 50 hours, 11.3 points. The linear regression equation for the 13 data points toward the low end of the time scale, ignoring Marron's four groups for the moment, is $V = 4.322 + .335T$, ($N = 13$, $r = .37$). The predicted values toward the low end of the scale are now more in line with the data (e.g., 4.7 score points for 1 hour of contact time, 7.7 for 10 hours, 11.0 for 20 hours, 14.4 for 30 hours, 21.1 for 50 hours), but the predicted values toward the high end are out of line (e.g., the predicted score effect for 300 hours of contact time is 105 points, which is three times as large as the adjusted weighted SAT-V effect for Marron's four groups and almost twice as large as their unadjusted weighted average). Thus, the regression line based on data from coaching programs entailing less than 50 hours of student contact time projects an expected score effect for programs of 300 contact hours that is two to three times higher than the average effect actually associated with those 300-hour programs in practice. Consequently, as student contact time increases, there appear to be diminishing returns in SAT-V score effects associated with coaching.

A similar picture emerges for SAT-M. The linear regression equation for the 14 Math studies is $M = 12.699 + .134T$, ($N = 14$, $r = .89$). Again, this equation is dominated by Marron's (1965) three Math groups at 300 hours of student contact time, for which the predicted score effect of 53 points is close to their adjusted weight average (see Table 2). But once more the predicted values at the low end of the time scale are out of line with the data—for example, 12.8 score points for 1 hour, 14.0 for 10 hours, 15.4 for 20 hours, 16.7 for 30 hours, and 19.4 for 50 hours. The linear regression equation for the 11 data points toward the low end of the time scale, ignoring Marron's three groups momentarily, is $M = 4.900 + .713T$, ($N = 11$, $r = .49$). The predicted values toward the low end of the scale, as they were for Verbal, are now more in line with the data (e.g., 5.6 score points for 1 hour, 12.0 for 10 hours, 19.2 for 20 hours, 26.3 for 30 hours, and 40.5 for 50 hours), but those toward the high end of the scale are out of line (e.g., the predicted score effect for 300 hours of contact time is 219 points, which is over four times as large as the adjusted weighted SAT-M effect for Marron's three Math groups

and nearly three times as large as their unadjusted weighted average). Clearly, as student contact time increases, there appear to be diminishing returns in SAT-M score effects as well.

As is frequently the case in situations with diminishing returns, a logarithmic transformation of the time dimension provides a much better representation of the functional relationships, as is seen in Figure 1 for SAT-V and Figure 3 for SAT-M. In this formulation, all logs are to the base 10. The solid line in Figure 1 is the regression of SAT-V score effect on student contact time in log hours, $L(T)$, based on all 17 data points discussed previously; its equation is $V = -6.587 + 15.155L(T)$, ($N = 17$, $r = .70$). The dashed regression line in Figure 1 is based on the 13 data points toward the low end of the time scale, omitting the values for Marron's (1965) four Verbal groups; its equation is $V = -7.768 + 16.418L(T)$, ($N = 13$, $r = .47$). In contrast to the discrepant regression lines obtained when a linear fit in real time was attempted for 17 and 13 data points, these two regression lines in log time are very similar to each other—for example, the predicted SAT-V score effect corresponding to 300 hours of student contact time (2.477 log hours) is 31 points by the first equation and 33 points by the second. It should be noted that these predicted values, even though based on an unweighted least squares solution, closely correspond to the adjusted score effect for Marron's largest group ($N = 600$) and that his other three more deviant groups entailed much smaller sample sizes ($N = 83$, 5, and 26 in descending order of score effect). According to these logarithmic functions, an estimated zero SAT-V score effect is obtained at somewhat less than 3 hours, suggesting that additional data points in this region may require more curvature in the function or, more likely, that a threshold or critical mass of coaching effort must be attained before positive score effects are exhibited.

The triangle in Figure 1 corresponds to Rock's (1980) estimate of the SAT-V score effect taking differential group growth rates into account for students at School A in the FTC (1979) study. Even though these two logarithmic regression equations were based

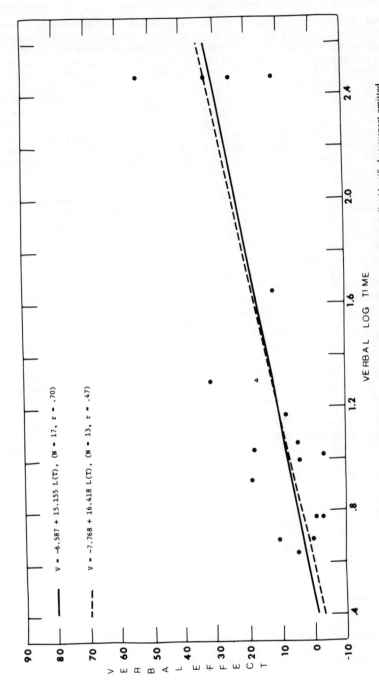

Figure 1. Regressions of SAT-Verbal score effects on student contact time in logs, with those studies identified as suspect omitted.

on Stroud's (1980) estimate for School A, the Rock estimate is clearly more consistent with both regression lines. The regression equation substituting Rock's estimate of the SAT-V effect for School A in the FTC data for Stroud's estimate is $V = -7.544 + 15.221 L(T)$, ($N = 17$, $r = .74$), which is very similar to the regression equation based on Stroud's estimate but, by virtue of the greater congruence of Rock's value, reflects a somewhat higher correlation among the data points.

Figure 2 expands the data base represented in Figure 1 by adding the data points excluded initially. The five circles in Figure 2 correspond to the five suspect data points of Roberts and Oppenheim (1966), Coffman and Parry (1967), and Schools A, B, and D from Alderman and Powers (1980). It can be seen that these points are somewhat noisier than the rest, the correlation between SAT-V effect and log time being .59 for 22 data points but .70 for 17 points. However, as is apparent in Figure 2, the regression equation based on 22 data points does not differ dramatically from the other equations: $V = -2.405 + 12.566L(T)$, ($N = 22$, $r = .59$).

Finally, the squares in Figure 2 correspond to the two discrepant estimates of adjusted SAT-V effects for Pallone's (1961) long-term program (see Table 2). When plotted at 300 hours (2.477 log hours), as previously argued, the smaller of these estimates (43) is quite consistent with the logarithmic regression system for 13, 17, and 22 data points, whereas the larger estimate (68) is deviant but not incompatible. The logarithmic regression equation for the 23 data points including the 43-point estimate at 300 hours of student contact time is $V = -4.025 + 14.253L(T)$, ($N = 23$, $r = .66$); substituting the larger 68-point estimate at 300 hours for the smaller value, the equation becomes $V = -6.673 + 17.089L(T)$, ($N = 23$, $r = .66$). The first equation is quite similar to the three plotted in Figure 2 and the second equation is not markedly different. As compared with the Figure 2 estimates of 33, 31, and 29 points for a benchmark 300 hours of student contact time, the regression equations including Pallone's data yield 31 and 36 points. Even

when Pallone's estimated score effects are plotted at 100 hours of student contact time (tacitly treating Pallone's course in isolation from other verbal preparation likely accruing from full-time school attendance), the respective regression lines are still quite comparable to those shown in Figure 2: For 43 score-effect points, $V = -3.618 + 14.166L(T)$, ($N = 23$, $r = .62$), and for 68 score-effect points, $V = -4.973 + 16.051L(T)$, ($N = 23$, $r = .59$). These equations yield estimates of 31 and 35 points, respectively, for the benchmark of 300 hours of student contact time. Nevertheless, if plotted at 100 hours, these data points for Pallone's long-term program are quite deviant, particularly the larger value of 68 points, but the reported score effect for Pallone's summer pilot program appears to be aberrant in this logarithmic formulation for any plausible range of adjustments for experiential growth or any plausible range of student contact time. In sum, the logarithmic regression system relating SAT-V score effect to log contact time based on 17 data points appears to be quite robust under the addition of the noisier values available from a half-dozen other studies all of which are questionable for one reason or another.

The solid line in Figure 3 is the regression of SAT-M score effect on student contact time in log hours based on 14 data points (see Table 3); its equation is $M = -14.072 + 26.646L(T)$, ($N = 14$, $r = .91$). The dashed regression line in Figure 3 is based on the 11 data points toward the low end of the time scale, omitting the values for Marron's (1965) three Math groups; its equation is $M = -7.911 + 20.775L(T)$, ($N = 11$, $r = .51$). In contrast to the marked discrepancy in regression lines obtained when a linear fit in real time was attempted for 14 and 11 points, these two regression lines in log time are very similar to each other— although they are not quite as consonant as the corresponding lines in the Verbal data, as might be expected because of the smaller samples of data points. For example, the predicted SAT-M effect corresponding to 300 hours of student contact time (2.477 log hours) is 52 points by the first equation and 44 points by the second, an 8-point difference, which is a far cry from the 166-point

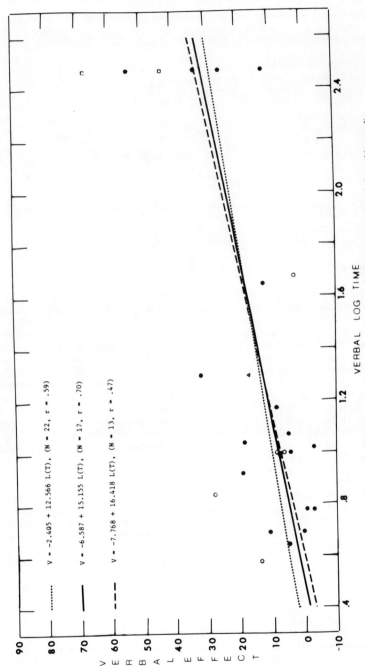

Figure 2. Regressions of SAT-Verbal score effects on student contact time in logs for all Verbal coaching studies.

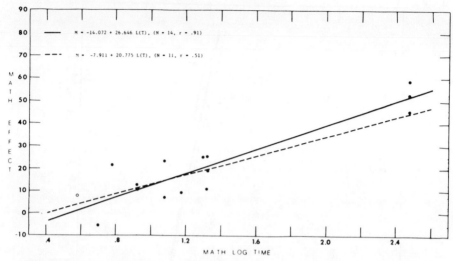

Figure 3. Regressions of SAT-Math score effects on student contact time in logs for all Math coaching studies.

discrepancy in the same 300-hour estimates based on a linear fit in real time to 14 and 11 data points. The one circle in Figure 3 represents the Roberts and Oppenheim (1966) data, which can be seen to be quite consistent with these logarithmic regressions; the regression equation including this additional data point is $M = -12.451 + 25.763L(T)$, $(N = 15, r = .91)$. Again, according to these logarithmic functions, an estimated zero SAT-M score effect is obtained at around 3 hours or somewhat less, indicating that the threshold of coaching effort needed for positive score effects, if such be its import, is roughly comparable for Verbal and Math—although the slope of the Math function is more than half again as steep as that of the Verbal function.

In regard to appraising the goodness of fit of the data points to the proposed logarithmic model, it can be seen in Figures 1 and 2 that the largest residuals for SAT-V are associated with Marron's (1965) Groups 1 and 4, with Stroud's (1980) estimate for FTC (1979) School A, and with three of the five suspect studies. This is attested to by noting that the root-mean-square residual for 22 data points is 10.9, which is reduced to 10.5 by eliminating the five suspect stud-

ies, further reduced to 8.4 by dropping Marron's four groups, and still further reduced to 6.6 by substituting Rock's (1980) FTC School A estimate for Stroud's. The goodness of fit for SAT-M as revealed in Figure 3 is even better. The root-mean-square residual for 14 data points is 7.3 whereas that for 11 data points is 7.6. Although it would be desirable to evaluate the size of residuals in relation to the standard error of their associated score-effect estimate, many of the studies did not report standard errors, nor could they be readily calculated from the information given. Nonetheless, there was some indication that deviations from the model were at least partially a function of sampling error because the larger residuals tended to be associated with studies having smaller sample sizes. The rank-order correlation between the absolute value of SAT-V residuals and the size of their corresponding treatment-group sample was $-.30$ for the regression model based on 17 studies (still using Rock's estimate), whereas the rank-order correlation for SAT-M residuals based on 14 studies was $-.56$. Although the former coefficient is not statistically significant, the latter value is. Overall, then, the proposed logarithmic model, however adventitious it may appear at first glance, offers a plausible hypothesis for the relationship between increasing student contact time and increasing score effects in programs of coaching and instruction for the SAT.

To recapitulate briefly, substantial rank-order correlations were noted between SAT score effects in coaching studies and the level of student contact time entailed in each coaching program (see Table 3). This regularity of monotonic relationship appears not to be linear, however, but approximately logarithmic, at least within the limitations of the fragmentary data. If this suggested logarithmic relationship has substance, then each additional increase in SAT scores associated with coaching may require geometrically increasing amounts of student contact time and of all the curricular effort that contact time may be proxy for. For example, according to the logarithmic function for SAT-V based on 17 data points, an average score increase of 10 points on a 200- to 800-point scale would be expected to be associated with approximately 12 hours of student contact time in a Verbal coaching program, but 20 score points would require 57 hours, 30 score points would require 260 hours, and for 40 SAT-V score points a total of 1,185 hours would be required (although the latter extrapolation is far beyond the range of the data). Similarly, for the SAT-M function based on 14 data points: An average score increase of 10 points would be expected to be associated with approximately 8 hours of student contact time, but 20 score points would require 19 hours, 30 score points would require 45 hours, and to attain 40 SAT-M score points would require a total of 107 hours. The fact that Math entails less student contact time than Verbal for a given amount of score increase is consistent once again with the expectation that Math, being more curriculum related than Verbal, should be relatively more responsive to instructional intervention.

It must be emphasized that these functions apply to existing data and that the available studies all involved students who to a large degree were motivated to increase their test scores through coaching or special preparation. Such motivated students are likely to have been highly task oriented, and under such circumstances it is not unreasonable that student contact time should be directly related to average test score increases. We have also cautioned that increases in student contact time are confounded in these studies with increasing curriculum emphases on content knowledge and skill development, so that other program characteristics that contact time may be proxy for should also be taken into account in interpreting the relationship and in shaping expectations. Indeed, the terms *time* and *method* were paired in the title of this article partly to underscore that student contact time and aspects of coaching method are confounded in the available coaching studies and partly to highlight the importance of recurrent flaws in experimental method that serve to obscure the functional role of contact time in understanding coaching effects. Speaking of methodological flaws, we must finally also consider the possible role of selection bias in interpreting the basis of the observed relationship, because many of the longer-term programs—such as the preparatory schools in Marron's (1965) study and the commercial coaching schools in the FTC (1979) study—were not only associated with larger score effects but were also highly subject to self-selection bias.

With these caveats in mind, it appears likely that improvement of the comprehension and reasoning skills measured by the SAT, when it occurs, is a function of the time and effort expended and that each additional score increase may require increasing amounts of time and effort, probably geometrically increasing amounts. If this is the case, the time required to achieve average score increases much greater than 20 to 30 points (on a 200- to 800-point scale) rapidly approaches that of full-time schooling, especially in Verbal; hence it quickly becomes unfeasible to augment the already full-time requirements of secondary school with sufficient additional contact time devoted to coaching to obtain large improvements in comprehension and reasoning skills over those afforded by a high school education. As a consequence, the soundest long-range mode of preparation for the SAT would appear to be a secondary school program that integrates the development of thought with the development of knowledge.

References

Alderman, D. L., & Powers, D. E. The effects of special preparation on SAT-verbal scores. *American Educational Research Journal*, 1980, *17*, 239–253. (Also, CB RDR 78-79, No. 4, and ETS RR 79-1, Princeton, N.J.: Educational Testing Service, 1979.)

Anastasi, A. Abilities and the measurement of achievement. In W. B. Schrader (Ed.), *New directions for testing and measurement— Measuring achievement: Progress over a decade.* San Francisco: Jossey-Bass, 1980.

Bryk, A. S., & Weisberg, H. I. Use of the nonequivalent control group design when subjects are growing. *Psychological Bulletin*, 1977, *84*, 950–962.

Cochran, W. G. The use of covariance in observational studies. *Applied Statistics*, 1968, *17*, 270–275.

Coffman, W. E., & Parry, M. E. Effects of an accelerated reading course on SAT-V scores. *Personnel and Guidance Journal*, 1967, *46*, 292–296.

Dear, R. E. *The effect of a program of intensive coaching on SAT scores* (ETS RB 58-5). Princeton, N.J.: Educational Testing Service, 1958. (Reported in French, J. W., & Dear, R. E. Effect of coaching on an aptitude test. *Educational and Psychological Measurement*, 1959, *19*, 319–330.)

Dyer, H. S. Does coaching help? *College Board Review*, 1953, *19*, 331–335. (Reported in French, J. W., & Dear, R. E. Effect of coaching on an aptitude test. *Educational and Psychological Measurement*, 1959, *19*, 319–330.)

Evans, F. R., & Pike, L. W. The effects of instruction for three mathematics item formats. *Journal of Educational Measurement*, 1973, *10*, 257–272.

Federal Trade Commission, Boston Regional Office. *Staff memorandum of the Boston Regional Office of the Federal Trade Commission: The effects of coaching on standardized admission examinations.* Boston, Mass.: Author, September 1978.

Federal Trade Commission, Bureau of Consumer Protection. *Effects of coaching on standardized admission examinations: Revised statistical analyses of data gathered by Boston Regional Office of the Federal Trade Commission.* Washington, D.C.: Author, March 1979.

Frankel, E. Effects of growth, practice, and coaching on Scholastic Aptitude Test scores. *Personnel and Guidance Journal*, 1960, *38*, 713–719.

French, J. W. *The coachability of the SAT in public schools* (ETS RB 55-26). Princeton, N.J.: Educational Testing Service, 1955. (Reported in French,

J. W., & Dear, R. E. Effect of coaching on an aptitude test. *Educational and Psychological Measurement*, 1959, *19*, 319–330.)

Marron, J. E. *Preparatory school test preparation: Special test preparation, its effect on College Board scores and the relationship of affected scores to subsequent college performance.* West Point, N.Y.: Research Division, Office of the Director of Admissions and Registrar, United States Military Academy, 1965.

Messick, S. *The effectiveness of coaching for the SAT: Review and reanalysis of research from the fifties to the FTC* (ETS RR 80-8). Princeton, N.J.: Educational Testing Service, 1980.

National Education Association: *Measurement and testing: An NEA perspective.* Washington, D.C.: Author, 1980.

Pallone, N. J. Effects of short-term and long-term developmental reading courses upon S.A.T. verbal scores. *Personnel and Guidance Journal*, 1961, *39*, 654–657.

Pike, L. W. *Short-term instruction, testwiseness, and the Scholastic Aptitude Test: A literature review with research recommendations* (CB RDR 77-78, No. 2, and ETS RB 78-2). Princeton, N.J.: Educational Testing Service, 1978.

Pike, L. W., & Evans, F. R. *The effects of special instruction for three kinds of mathematics aptitude items* (CB RDR 71-72, No. 7, and ETS RB 72-19). Princeton, N.J.: Educational Testing Service, 1972.

Roberts, S. O., & Oppenheim, D. B. *The effect of special instruction upon test performance of high school students in Tennessee* (CB RDR 66-7, No. 1, and ETS RB 66-36). Princeton, N.J.: Educational Testing Service, 1966.

Rock, D. A. *Disentangling coaching effects and differential growth in the FTC commercial coaching study* (ETS RR 80-11). Princeton, N.J.: Educational Testing Service, 1980.

Slack, W. V., & Porter, D. The Scholastic Aptitude Test: A critical appraisal. *Harvard Educational Review*, 1980, *50*, 154–175.

Snow, R. E. Aptitude and achievement. In W. B. Schrader (Ed.), *New directions for testing and measurement—Measuring achievement: Progress over a decade.* San Francisco: Jossey-Bass, 1980.

Stroud, T. W. F. *Reanalysis of the Federal Trade Commission study of commercial coaching for the SAT* (ETS RR 80-10). Princeton, N.J.: Educational Testing Service, 1980.

Whitla, D. K. Effect of tutoring on Scholastic Aptitude Test scores. *Personnel and Guidance Journal*, 1962, *41*, 32–37.

21

Evaluating the Effectiveness of Coaching for SAT Exams
A Meta-Analysis

Rebecca DerSimonian and Nan Laird

A current controversy in the educational literature is whether or not coaching programs are effective in raising SAT examination scores. Two recent papers[1,2] have addressed this issue by reviewing the relevant literature, and summarizing the evidence from various studies on coaching effectiveness. The first paper, by Slack and Porter, comes to the unqualified conclusion that training "can effectively help students to raise their scores." Their results have been criticized on several grounds, and in particular because they utilized evidence from studies of questionable scientific merit. The second paper, by Messick and Jungeblut, takes a different and somewhat more cautious approach to the problem of how to combine the evidence, arriving nonetheless at a conclusion that could also be regarded as favorable to coaching, "some definite regularities emerged relating the size of score effects associated with coaching to the amount of student contact time entailed in the coaching programs."

A main difficulty in summarizing the evidence from these studies stems from the diverse nature of the studies. Some are carefully controlled randomized comparisons, while others are simple before-and-after comparisons that use national norms to estimate any improvement attributable to maturation. Because of differing sample sizes and study populations, each study has a different level of sampling error as well. Thus, a central problem in combining these studies is the assignment of weights reflecting the relative value of the information in that study. The Slack and Porter paper weighted studies by the size of the coached group, disregarding other study characteristics. The Messick and Jungeblut study used an unweighted analysis to estimate the size of the effect as a function of the student contact time in the coaching program.

Here we reanalyze the studies cited in Slack and Porter and Messick and Jungeblut using an approach to summarizing the evidence from several studies that

This work was supported in part by a grant from the Mellon Foundation, and in part by Grant 5T32 CA09337-03 from the National Cancer Institute.

From Rebecca DerSimonian and Nan Laird, "Evaluating the Effectiveness of Coaching for SAT Exams: A Meta-Analysis," *Harvard Educational Review.* Copyright © 1982 by President and Fellows of Harvard College. All rights reserved.

TABLE 1a Uncontrolled and Controlled Studies: Observed Gain Attributed to Coaching, Estimated Sampling Variances, and the Resulting Significance Levels

| | Verbal | | | | | Math | | | | |
| | Points Gained W | Number of Students | | Sampling Variance D | P-Value P | Points Gained W | Number of Students | | Sampling Variance D | P-Value P |
Study		Coached n_x	Uncoached n_y				Coached n_x	Uncoached n_y		
Uncontrolled										
Pallone 1[a, b]	81	20	—	120	<.001	—	—	—	—	—
Pallone 2[a, b]	68	80	—	30	<.001	—	—	—	—	—
Marron 1[a, b]	54	83	—	29	<.001	59	232	—	10	<.001
Marron 2[a, b]	33	600	—	4	<.001	53	405	—	6	<.001
Marron 3[a, b]	24	5	—	480	n.s.	46	78	—	31	<.001
Marron 4[a, b]	12	26	—	92	n.s.*	—	—	—	—	—
Coffman[a, b]	4	19	—	126	n.s.	—	—	—	—	—
Controlled										
Lass[a]	3	38	38	126	n.s.	11	38	38	126	n.s.
Dyer 1[a, b]	4.6	225	193	23	n.s.*	29	74	74	65	<.001
Dyer 2[a]	—	—	—	—	—	3	165	165	29	n.s.*
French 1[a, b]	18.3	161	158	30	<.001	6.2	161	158	30	n.s.*
French 2[a, b]	5	110	158	37	n.s.*	18	161	110	37	<.01
French 3[a]	47	173	173	28	<.001	15	165	165	29	<.01
Dear 1[a, b]	-2.5	60	526	45	n.s.	23.6	71	116	54	<.01
Dear 2[a, b]	—	—	—	—	—	21.5	60	526	45	<.01
FTC 1[b]	31.7	393	1729	8	<.001	24.9	393	1729	7	<.001
FTC 2[b]	5.2	163	1729	16	n.s.	7.5	163	1729	16	n.s.

*P-Value inconsistent with that cited by Slack and Porter.
a. Cited by Slack and Porter.
b. Cited by Messick and Jungeblut.

is quite distinct from that used in the previous papers on this topic. Our approach is to combine the results of different studies in order to estimate an overall average level of coaching effectiveness, and the degree to which coaching effectiveness may vary in different situations. We do this by assuming that there is a distribution of coaching effects associated with a population of possible coaching programs. The observed effects from different studies provide information that we use to estimate this distribution. We then explore the nature of this distribution by taking into account differences in study design and implementation.

One of the principle advantages of this approach is that we have an objective method of weighting studies that can be made progressively more general by incorporating study characteristics into the analysis. The general method and its relation to other methods for combining studies is later described in detail.

DATA BASE

Porter and Slack used the results of 16 studies evaluating coaching for the SAT verbal exams, and 13 studies evaluating coaching for the SAT math exams. They restricted their analysis to studies published prior to 1968. Messick and Jungeblut included studies published prior to 1980, but excluded two SAT verbal and two SAT math studies utilized by Slack and Porter. We utilized all the studies reported in either Slack and Porter or Messick and Jungeblut, giving a total of 19 verbal and 17 math evaluations. These are reported in Table 1.

The points gained are taken from information reported in Slack and Porter or Messick and Jungeblut, with the latter paper given preference if there was a disagreement in the assessment of points gained. Disagreement for uncontrolled studies arises from the use of different methods for estimating the points gained in a hypothetical equivalent control group using statistics published by ETS. For controlled studies the points gained were generally the improvement in the coached group minus the improvement in the uncoached group.

Table 1 also reports the number of students in the study groups. For four math and two verbal studies, Dyer 1 and 2, Lass, and French 3, the number in the uncoached group was not reported; hence it was assumed to be equal to the number in the coached group. It is important to note that many studies given in Table 1 are actually separate reports on subgroups of students in one program evaluation. In the math studies Messick and Jungeblut reported the Dyer studies 1 and 2 as one study combined, whereas they were kept separate by Slack and Porter, since one group was taking senior math, while the other was not.

Standard errors for the points gained were not reported in either Slack and Porter or Messick and Jungeblut for any of the studies. A few standard errors can be found in the original articles. Ideally, we would use the reported standard errors as measures of the sampling variation in each study. Since this information was not always available, we now describe the method used to estimate the sampling variances given in Table 1. We regard the observed effect of coaching, W, as a difference, $\Delta X - \Delta Y$. For all studies ΔX is the observed gain in the coached group.

TABLE 1b   Matched and Randomized Studies: Observed Gain Attributed to Coaching, Estimated Sampling Variances, and the Resulting Significance Levels

| | Verbal | | | | | Math | | | | |
| | | Number of Students | | | | | Number of Students | | | |
Study	Points Gained W	Coached n_x	Uncoached n_y	Sampling Variance D	P-Value P	Points Gained W	Coached n_x	Uncoached n_y	Sampling Variance D	P-Value P
Matched										
Frankel[a, b]	8.4	45	45	107	n.s.	9.4	45	45	107	n.s.
Whitla[a, b]	11	52	52	92	n.s.	−5.3	50	50	96	n.s.
Randomized										
Roberts[a, b]	14.4	154	111	37	.01	8.1	188	122	32	n.s.
Alderman[b]	8.4	239	320	18	.05	–	–	–	–	–
Evans[b]	–	–	–	–	–	16.5	288	129	27	.01

*P-Value inconsistent with that cited by Slack and Porter.
a. Cited by Slack and Porter.
b. Cited by Messick and Jungeblut.

For controlled studies ΔY is the observed gain in the uncoached group, and for uncontrolled studies it is the expected gain in the uncoached group. This is somewhat of a simplification, since some investigators with control groups may have used covariance analysis, rather than the difference in average gains, to estimate the effect of coaching. In this case our approximation of the sampling variance of W is overstated by about 6%.

We denote the sampling variance of the observed effect of a study by D. Statistics published by ETS give the standard deviation of an individual test score as 100, and the correlation between two repeat test scores for an individual as .88.[4] The variance of a change in an individual's scores is, therefore, $S^2 = 2400$. Thus, $S^2_{\Delta X} = S^2/n_x$, and $S^2_{\Delta Y}$, $= S^2/n_y$ if study has a control group, where n_x and n_y are the number of students in each group. We assume $S^2_{\Delta Y} = 0$ in studies with no control group, since here ΔY can be thought of as the population mean. Therefore, D is $S^2 (1/n_x + 1/n_y)$ if there is a control group, and is S^2/n_x if there is no control group. D is reported in Table 1 under the heading Sampling Variance. We also give the significance level calculated using this estimated D.

In three verbal studies and two math studies the significance levels we calculated do not agree with those reported by Slack and Porter or Messick and Jungeblut. We identify these studies in Table 1 by a star. All the disagreements are such that our calculations give a nonsignificant level when it is reported to be significant by Slack and Porter. In one case, the Dyer verbal study, the original 1953 article[5] reported a nonsignificant level that agrees with our calculation, but not with that of Slack and Porter. In 1959 French and Dear[6] report this same study result as significant.

In addition to points gained, sample size, and investigator, we also utilize information as to whether or not the study was uncontrolled, matched, randomized, or controlled, but unrandomized and unmatched. Other characteristics of these studies can be found in the original articles, or in summary form in Messick and Jungeblut.

A RANDOM EFFECTS APPROACH TO META-ANALYSIS

Glass[7] refers to meta-analysis as "the statistical analysis of a large collection of analysis results from individual studies for the purpose of integrating the findings." Such analyses are becoming increasingly popular in many scientific disciplines, including education, psychology,[8,9] medicine,[10,11] and public health. Attendant with the growth of meta-analyses is focus on the methodological aspects of meta-analysis,[12,13] as well as considerable skepticism,[14] about the validity of combining results from studies that may differ radically in design, execution, and results.

Light and Smith[15] review several approaches to combining evidence from studies, including descriptive approaches, approaches that yield some type of quantitative summary statistic, and a mixed qualitative-quantitative approach they call "taking a vote." Another popular approach (with a large literature) is to combine the p-values from different studies to yield a single p-value.[16] This has the drawback of not yielding an estimate of the size of the effect.

The meta-analyses of Slack and Porter and Messick and Jungeblut both yield quantitative summary measures of coaching effectiveness. The former takes a simple average of coaching effectiveness over all studies, weighting inversely according to sample sizes. The latter combines selected studies in an unweighted regression analysis of coaching effect versus a measure of the coaching program's contact hours, where the study selection process is done on a qualitative, rather than a quantitative basis. Both of these approaches are examples of a statistical technique known as "pooling."[17,18]

The general idea behind pooling is that each study yields an observation about a common unknown treatment effect of interest. The key assumption is that the treatment effect is constant across studies, although other parameters can vary. Each observed treatment effect is subject to measurement error, which may differ in level across studies. Each observed treatment effect may also be subject to bias, although how to handle this problem is treated less often, since bias generally cannot be quantified. Most methodological discussions of pooling focus on when is it safe to pool, and, if safe, how to take the weighted average (or other summary statistic).

In deciding whether or not it is safe to pool, or to delete specific studies before pooling, one can make qualitative decisions by a detailed study review and the establishment of criteria, such as delete all uncontrolled studies. A second step is to go further to do a quantitative assessment of whether or not the assumption of a constant treatment effect is supported by the data. This is done by comparing the total variation in observed treatment effects with the sum of the within-study error variances. A large discrepancy between these two measures of overall variation is taken as a sign that the treatment effect of interest may vary from study to study; thus pooling is unsafe.

To make this discussion more concrete, we consider the verbal studies given in Table 1. Calculating the unweighted sample variance of the observed coaching effects from the first column of figures, we have $S_T^2 = 571$. Taking the unweighted average of the within-study variances from the fourth column of figures, we have $S_W^2 = 76$. Here S_T^2 is the total variance in the observed effects, and S_W^2 is the average within-study variance. If the effect of coaching were constant across studies, *and if we assume no study bias,* these two variances should be approximately equal. Their difference is a measure of between-study variation. Here we are forced to conclude, to no one's surprise, that either the studies are biased, or the effectiveness of coaching varies from study to study, or both. We say that this result is no surprise because a simple examination of the size of the observed study effects compared to their estimated standard errors suggests that a common treatment effect is not a tenable hypothesis. For instance, the 95% confidence intervals for the Coffman and Pallone 1 verbal studies (based on the estimated variances) are far from overlapping.

With such a large difference in the total observed variation and the total sampling variation, many investigators would conclude that pooling is unsafe. To proceed further requires a more sophisticated model, such as that used by Messick and Jungeblut, who assumed that the size of the effect was related to contact hours. However, they did not take sampling variability or study bias into account in any systematic way. Our approach to combining the results from different studies is to quantify not only the overall level of effect, but to also estimate the variability of effectiveness across studies. We do this by using a random effects model for the effect of coaching. The basic idea is to decompose the observed effect of coaching for each study, W_i, into two independent components, as

$$W_i = T_i + e_i$$

where T_i is the true gain attributable to coaching by the ith study, and e_i is the sampling error. The variance of e_i is the usual sampling variance (D_i), and is normally calculated from the observed data in the ith sample. The true gain, T_i, represents the quantity of interest to the investigator.

This true gain associated with each study will depend upon numerous factors, including the characteristics of the coaching program and its implementation (such as contact hours, materials used, etc.), as well as the design and execution of the evaluation of the program, i.e., use of controls, randomization, and so on. For certain factors, such as student population, this distinction is not sharp, as program effectiveness may vary for different groups of students.

To explicity account for this variation in true gains, we use a random effects model, which assumes

$$T_i = \mu + \delta_i \qquad [1]$$

where μ is a mean gain over a population of possible coaching evaluations, and δ_i is the deviation of the ith study's effect from that mean. We regard our studies as a sample from this population, and use their observed gains to estimate μ as well as var $(\delta) = \sigma^2$. A similar model was used by Cochran,[19] also in the context of combining results from related experiments. Here σ^2 measures the variation in gains across program evaluations. If our studies were many different evaluations of only one particular coaching program, σ^2 would represent the variance in the biases that arise as a result of the use of different protocols for evaluation.

Alternatively, we might investigate the coaching effectiveness of many different programs, but carry out a series of studies according to a common protocol; i.e., a randomized, controlled study on a carefully specified population of students. In this case, σ^2 would measure the degree to which the gain of a coaching program depends upon the special characteristics of the program. Clearly, it is this last situation we wish to be in, for here variation in study results can be linked to aspects of the program, and progress is made toward understanding the phenomenon of interest. Unfortunately, studies designed and executed according to a common protocol are generally few in number, and do not represent the totality of information we have at our disposal.

In the simple model just described, σ^2 has components of variation that are due to differences in coaching programs, as well as differences in methods of evaluation.

Part of the purpose of this article is to decompose the overall variation into components that will enable us to separate out biases in methods of evaluation from real variation in program effectiveness. We do this by enriching the simple model in equation 1 to reflect characteristics of the studies. The next section considers the specific models in some detail.

MODELS

Letting W_i denote the observed effect of coaching in the ith study, we shall generally assume that W_i is normally distributed, with mean T_i, and sampling variance D_i, $i = I \ldots ,N$, where N is the number of studies. The assumption of normality seems reasonable since W_i is some type of average for each study, so that the central limit theorem can be applied. For much of our work, we shall further assume that T_i is normally distributed in the population of studies. The different models presented below specify the nature of this normal distribution. For some models, however, we estimate the parameters of the distribution of the T_i without relying on the normality assumption.

We use three different models for the distribution of true gains. For Model 1 we use the simple specification presented in the previous section, namely each T_i has mean μ and variance σ^2. Under the normality assumption, we then have

$$W_i = \mu + \delta_i + e_i$$

where δ_i and e_i are independent, zero mean normals with variances σ^2 and D_i. This simple model ignores any dependence between different evaluations of the same program, as well as any covariate information about the program, or its evaluation.

Model 2 takes into account the fact that many of these different studies are actually done by the same investigator. There are four investigators who report results from more than one evaluation. These different evaluations usually represent minor differences in program implementation, such as different subgroups of students, and so on. For Model 2 we index the programs by $\ell = 1, \ldots L$ and the evaluations of the programs by $j = 1, \ldots N_\ell$, where the ℓth program has N_ℓ evaluations.

Here we write

$$T_{\ell j} = P_\ell + S_{\ell j}$$

where each P_ℓ is normal with mean μ and variance σ_P^2, and each $S_{\ell j}$ is normal with mean 0 and variance σ_S^2. The P_ℓs are the program effects, and $S_{\ell j}$ are the study effects. Assuming all P_ℓs and $S_{\ell j}$s are independent, we have

$$\text{var}(T_{\ell j}) = \sigma_P^2 + \sigma_S^2$$

$$\text{cov}(T_{\ell j}, T_{\ell' j'}) = 0 \quad \ell \neq \ell'$$

and

$$\text{cov}\,(T_{\ell j},\,T_{\ell j'}) = \sigma_P^2 \text{ for all } \ell$$

Here μ is the overall level of program effectiveness, and σ_P^2 measures the variation in program effectiveness. Unfortunately, type of evaluation is confounded with program effectiveness, thus σ_P^2 has a component due to method of evaluation. Our estimate of σ_S^2, however, gives us some handle on the variation arising from differences in program implementation. The overall mean μ differs from μ in Model 1, in that it is a mean over a population of coaching programs, rather than a mean over a population of coaching program evaluations.

The purpose of Model 3 is to take explicit account of biases arising from uncontrolled, unrandomized evaluations. Here studies are divided into three groups: uncontrolled, controlled but not randomized or matched, and randomized or matched controlled studies. A separate mean and variance is calculated for each group. Because of the relatively small number of studies in each group, we do not take correlation between studies into account in this analysis as in Model 2, but treat all studies as independent.

For Models 1 and 3 we also calculate nonparametric estimates of the mean gain and the variance of the gain, which do not rely on the assumption of a normal distribution for the true gains.

ESTIMATION AND COMPUTATION

We estimate the overall effects and variance components in these models using maximum likelihood. We compute the estimates iteratively using the EM algorithm.[20] As a by-product of the method of computation empirical Bayes estimates[21] of the individual study and program effects are available, as well as their estimated variances.

Estimates of the standard errors of the estimated mean gains are readily calculated, since these estimated mean gains are linear combination of W_is.

RESULTS:
ESTIMATING THE DISTRIBUTION OF GAINS

Table 2 reports the estimated parameters in the distribution of coaching effects from Model 1. The overall level of coaching effectiveness is about 22 points for both math and verbal scores, but the estimated variance in the effects are large: 477 for the verbal scores, and 282 for math scores. Such large variances reflect the large discrepancies in estimates of effectiveness reported by the various studies.

When we account for possible correlation in the study results, using Model 2 we find the mean program effect is slightly lower, about three to four points. For the verbal studies the two components of variation, σ_P^2 and σ_S^2, are about equal, while

TABLE 2   Estimated Parameters Under Model 1

	Verbal Scores	Math Scores
Mean gain, $\hat{\mu}$	22.8	21 1
SE of $\hat{\mu}$	5.3	4.4
Variance of coaching effects, $\hat{\sigma}^2$	477	282

TABLE 3   Estimated Parameters Under Model 2

	Verbal Scores	Math Scores
Mean gain, $\hat{\mu}$	19.3	17.7
SE of $\hat{\mu}$	6.6	5.1
Program variance, $\hat{\sigma}_p^2$	272	175
Study variance, $\hat{\sigma}_s^2$	243	66

σ_P^2 is about three times σ_S^2 for the math studies. These estimated variances imply a correlation of .53 for verbal studies of the same program, and a corresponding correlation of .73 for math studies. These figures are quite compatible with the observed gains reported in Table 1, where we see that the results for multiple studies by one investigator are generally more consistent for math scores than for verbal scores.

A breakdown of the studies into the uncontrolled, the controlled, and the matched and randomized groups for Model 3 is very revealing. Table 4 reports the estimated mean gains and variances of the effects for each group of studies separately. The difference in the estimated mean gains is striking, and remarkably consistent for both verbal and math studies. The matched and randomized studies show mean gains of about 10 points, with controlled, but unmatched and unrandomized studies showing mean gains of 15 points. The uncontrolled studies show mean gains four to five times the corresponding mean gains of the matched and randomized studies. By comparing the estimated mean gains to their corresponding standard errors reported in Table 4, it is clear that the mean effects estimated from the controlled and the matched and randomized studies are not significantly different. For math scores the mean gain for the uncontrolled studies is clearly different from the controlled and matched and randomized studies, and marginally so (from a statistical viewpoint) for the verbal scores.

Not only are there striking differences in the estimated mean gains, but the estimated variances of coaching effectiveness for the three types of evaluations differ considerably for the verbal scores. Variation in the assessment of coaching effectiveness from uncontrolled studies is almost 80 times the corresponding variation in matched or randomized studies, and about three times that found in

TABLE 4   Estimated Parameters Under Model 3

	Verbal Studies			Math Studies		
	Uncontrolled Studies	Controlled Unmatched Unrandomized	Matched or Randomized	Uncontrolled Studies	Controlled Unmatched Unrandomized	Matched or Randomized
Mean gain, $\hat{\mu}$	40.6	15.3	10.1	53.8	15.6	9.8
SE of $\hat{\mu}$	10.1	5.5	3.5	2.6	2.6	3.8
Variance of coaching effects $\hat{\sigma}^2$	615	208	8	9	32	9

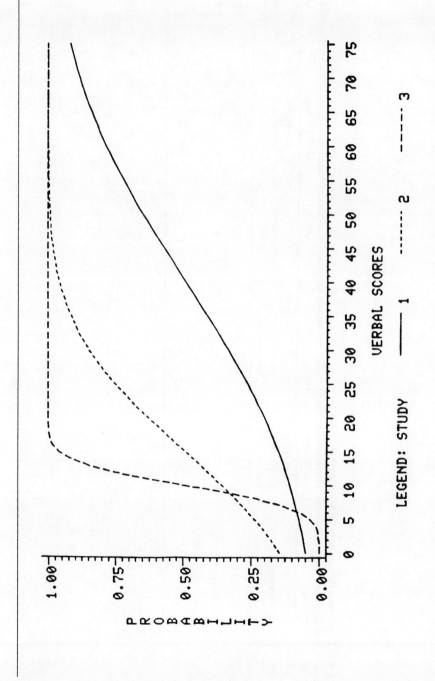

Figure 1

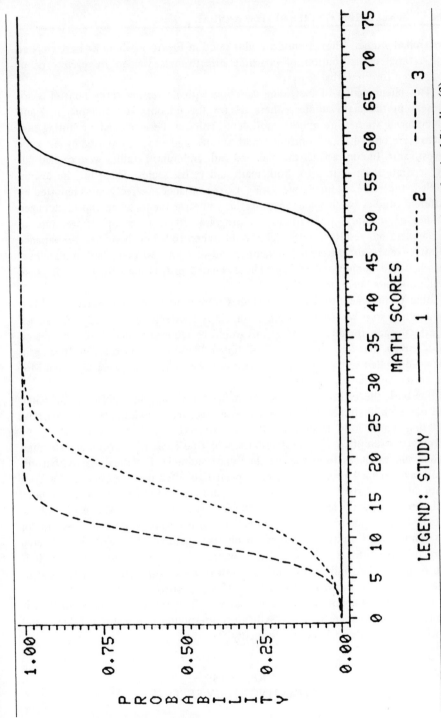

Figure 2: Distribution of Effects in Uncontrolled (1), Controlled but Unrandomized (2), and Randomized Studies (3)

controlled studies. These results are illustrated in Figure 1, where we have graphed the estimated distribution of coaching effectiveness yielded by each type of evaluation for the verbal scores.

This phenomenon of increasing variation with decreasing study control is not present in the math studies, where σ^2 for the uncontrolled and matched and randomized studies are almost equivalent. This can be explained by noting that there were only three uncontrolled math studies, and all were reported by the same investigator. In contrast, all the matched and randomized studies were carried out by separate investigators for both math and verbal scores. Thus, for the uncontrolled studies σ^2 is actually measuring σ_S^2, the variance in effectiveness reported by different studies by the same investigator, while for the matched and randomized studies σ^2 measures the variation in program effectiveness, σ_P^2. If we were to extrapolate our results from Model 2 to the uncontrolled math studies, the variance in effectiveness for different programs would be about 30, compared to $\sigma_P^2 = 9$ for matched and randomized studies. The estimated distributions for the math score evaluations are illustrated in Figure 2.

Four of the uncontrolled verbal studies were done by one investigator, and two by another, so if we were to again extrapolate the results of Model 2, the variance in effectiveness for different programs would be reduced to about 300, compared to $\sigma_P^2 = 8$ for matched and randomized studies. We would also expect the mean gain for uncontrolled verbal studies to be reduced somewhat if we were to account for the correlations among studies.

For both the verbal and the math studies the mean gain reported by matched and randomized studies do indeed suggest a positive, if modest, effect on coaching differing significantly from zero ($P < .01$ for verbal, $P < .05$ for math). If the normality assumption for the distribution of true gains is correct, the estimated means and variances from the matched and randomized studies suggest that virtually all coaching programs can be expected to offer positive benefits for both math and verbal studies, although the real gains are likely to be less than 15 points, and almost certainly less than 20. Referring back to Table 1, we see that all the matched and randomized studies observed positive gains in this range, except for the Whitla math study. It showed an observed gain of -5.3, with an estimated standard error of 9.8, which is quite compatible with a positive true gain. It is worth noting that individually only one out of four math studies and two out of four verbal studies showed statistically significant positive results (Table 1b).

Table 5 gives the nonparametric estimates of the means and variances for Models 1 and 3. They compare very well with the corresponding estimates in Tables 2 and 4, which are calculated assuming normality.

RESULTS: ESTIMATING STUDY EFFECTS

In Tables 6 and 7 we present empirical Bayes estimates of the individual studies under Models 1 through 3. Even though the assumptions underlying Models 1

TABLE 5 Nonparametric Estimates for Models 1 and 3

	Verbal Studies				Math Studies			
	All Studies	Uncontrolled Studies	Controlled Unmatched Unrandomized	Matched or Randomized	All Studies	Uncontrolled Studies	Controlled Unmatched Unrandomized	Matched or Randomized
Model 1								
Mean gain, $\hat{\mu}$	22.0				21.3			
Variance, $\hat{\sigma}^2$	482				280			
Model 3								
Mean gain, $\hat{\mu}$		39.0	14.7	10.3		54.3	16.3	10.1
Variance, $\hat{\sigma}^2$		630	234	0		6	57	3

TABLE 6   Gains in Verbal Studies, Empirical Bayes Estimates

Study	Observation W	Model 1	Model 2	Model 3
Uncontrolled				
Pallone 1	81	69.4	72.2	74.5
Pallone 2	68	65.3	66.5	66.7
Marron 1	54	52.2	51.5	53.4
Marron 2	33	32.9	33.0	33.0
Marron 3	24	23.4	28	31.2
Marron 4	12	13.7	17	15.7
Coffman	4	7.9	6.9	10.2
Controlled				
Lass	3	7.1	6.1	7.6
Dyer 1	4.6	5.4	5.2	5.7
French 1	18.3	18.6	18.8	17.9
French 2	5.0	6.3	7.3	6.6
French 3	47	45.7	44.5	43.3
Dear 1	− 2.5	− .3	− .8	.6
FTC 1	31.7	31.6	31.3	31.1
FTC 2	5.2	5.8	6.0	5.9
Matched				
Frankel	8.4	11.0	10.2	10.0
Whitla	11.0	12.9	12.2	10.2
Randomized				
Roberts	14.4	15.0	14.7	10.9
Alderman	8.4	8.9	8.7	9.5

through 3 are quite different, the resulting study estimates are remarkably similar; the largest discrepancy occurring for small studies showing relatively large or small gains (i.e., Coffman in verbal studies and Whittla and Dyer 1 in math studies). These estimated effects could be used in subsequent regression analyses aimed at correlating effect size with program characteristics.

DISCUSSION

Our analysis of studies of coaching effectiveness for SAT scores has demonstrated that a large part of the variation in results from different studies can be explained by taking into account the type of control group. When coached students are simply compared to national norms (uncontrolled studies), the mean gains are around 40 to 50 points for verbal and math studies. For controlled but unmatched and unrandomized studies the mean gain is about 15 points for both math and verbal scores, and is reduced to about 10 points for the matched and randomized studies. The estimated variances in the gains due to coaching also differ according to the method of control, with uncontrolled studies tending to show more variation

TABLE 7   Gains in Math Studies, Empirical Bayes Estimates

Study	Observation W	Model 1	Model 2	Model 3
Uncontrolled				
Marron 1	59	57.7	57.6	56.4
Marron 2	53	52.3	52.6	53.3
Marron 3	46	43.6	46.7	51.8
Controlled				
Lass	11	14.1	13.2	14.7
Dyer 1	29	27.5	22.2	19.8
Dyer 2	3	4.7	6.5	9.2
French 1	6.2	7.6	8.5	10.9
French 2	18	18.4	16.5	16.7
French 3	15	15.6	14.6	15.3
Dear 1	23.6	23.2	22.6	18.4
Dear 2	21.5	21.4	21.4	18.0
FTC 1	24.9	24.8	24.1	23.0
FTC 2	7.5	8.2	9.3	10.3
Matched				
Frankel	9.4	12.6	11.9	9.8
Whitla	− 5.3	1.4	1.1	8.5
Randomized				
Roberts	8.1	9.4	9.2	9.4
Evans	16.5	16.9	16.6	11.5

in the effects attributed to coaching as well as a higher level overall. By contrast, matched and randomized studies report very consistent results.

Some caution should be used in interpreting these results, since some confounding may arise as a result of different evaluation techniques being used to study different coaching programs. For example, most of the uncontrolled studies used male students in private schools, while the controlled and matched and randomized studies tended to use both males and females in a mixture of public and private schools.[22] Differences in student contact hours may also confound the results. In theory, more complicated models could be developed to account for these differences, but given the limited data and uneven reporting, the payoff is likely to be small. A separate issue is bias arising from the use of results from published studies, but at present there seems to be no alternative.

Meta-analyses of the type that we have done in this article are likely to become more popular in many disciplines as evidence from various sources accumulates on a common subject. Such analyses would be facilitated by better reporting from investigators about all aspects of their investigations, including study design and analysis, as well as features of the intervention and study population. Such a reporting scheme for clinical trials in medicine has recently been proposed by Chalmers et al.[23] and DerSimonian et al.[24] The technology of meta-analysis itself could be improved by further work on model selection and validation. In some disciplines methods for taking subjective assessments of experts into account might be desirable, especially where there is little objective data.

REFERENCE NOTES

1. SLACK, W., & PORTER, D. The Scholastic Aptitude Test: A critical appraisal. Harvard Educational Review, 1980, 50(2), 154-175.

2. MESSICK, S., & JUNGEBLUT, A. Time and method in coaching for the SAT. Psychological Bulletin, 1981, 89(2), 191-216.

3. JACKSON, R. The Scholastic Aptitude Test: A response to Slack and Porter's "Critical appraisal." Harvard Educational Review, 1980, 50(3), 382-400.

4. ANGOFF, W. H., & DYER, H. S. The Admissions Testing Program. In W. H. Angoff (Ed.), The College Board Admissions Testing Program. New York: College Entrance Examination Board, 1971.

5. DYER, H. S., Does Coaching Help? College Board Review, 1953, 19, 331-335.

6. FRENCH, L. W., & DEAR, R. E. Effect of coaching on an aptitude test. Educational and Psychological Measurements, 1959, 19, 319-330.

7. GLASS, G. V Primary, secondary, and meta-analysis of research. Educational Researcher, 1976, 5(10), 3-8.

8. SMITH, M. L., & GLASS, G. V Meta-analysis of psychotherapy outcome studies. American Psychologist, 1977, 32, 752-760.

9. BRAUN, P., KOCHANSKY, G., SHAPIRO, R., GREENBERG, S., GUDEMAN, J. E., JOHNSON, S., & SHORE, M. F., Overview: Deinstitutionalization of psychiatric patients: A critical review of outcome studies. American Journal of Psychiatry, 1981, 138(6), 736-749.

10. BAUM, M. L., ANISH, D. S., CHALMERS, T. C., SACKS, H. S., SMITH, H., & FAGERSTROM, R. M. Trials of antibiotic prophylaxis in colon surgery: Evidence against further use of no-treatment controls. New England Journal of Medicine, 1981, 305, 795-799.

11. GILBERT, J., McPEEK, J. B., and MOSTELLER, F., Progress in surgery and anesthesia: Benefits and risks of innovative therapy. In B. A. Barnes, J. P. Bunker, F. Mosteller (Eds.), Costs, risks, and benefits of surgery, New York: Oxford University Press, 1977, 124-169.

12. ROSENTHAL, R., Combining results of independent studies. Psychological Bulletin, 1978, 85(1), 185-193.

13. ELASHOFF, J. D., Combining results of clinical trials. Gastroenterology, 1978, 75, 1170-1174.

14. GOLDMAN, L., & FEINSTEIN, A. R. Anticoagulants and myocardial infarction. The problem of pooling, drowning and floating. Annals of Internal Medicine, 1979, 90, 92-94.

15. LIGHT, R. J., & SMITH, L. V. Accumulating evidence: Procedures for resolving contradictions among different research studies. Harvard Educational Review, 1971, 41(4), 429-471.

16. ROSENTHAL, Combining results.

17. ELASHOFF, Combining results.

18. GOLDMAN & FEINSTEIN, Anticoagulants and myocardial infarction.

19. COCHRAN, W. A. The combination of estimates from different experiments. Biometrics, 1954, 101-129.

20. DEMPSTER, A. P., LAIRD, N. M., & RUBIN, D. B., Journal of the Royal Statistical Society Series B, 1977, 39(1), 1-38.

21. EFRON, B., & MORRIS, C. Stein's paradox in statistics. Scientific American, 1977, 236, 119-127.

22. MESSICK & JUNGEBLUT, Time and method in coaching for the SAT.

23. CHALMERS, T. C., SMITH, H., BLACKBURN, B., SILVERMAN, B., SCHROEDER, B., REITMAN, D., & AMBROZ, A. A method for assessing the quality of a randomized control trial. Controlled Clinical Trials, 1981, 2, 31-49.

24. DerSIMONIAN, R., CHARETTE, J., McPEEK, B., & MOSTELLER, F. Reporting in comparative clinical trials. New England Journal of Medicine, 1982.

22

The Effects of Psychological Intervention
on Recovery from Surgery and Heart Attacks
An Analysis of the Literature

Emily Mumford, Herbert J. Schlesinger, and Gene V Glass

Abstract: A quantitative review of 34 controlled studies demonstrates that, on the average, surgical or coronary patients who are provided information or emotional support to help them master the medical crisis do better than patients who receive only ordinary care. A review of 13 studies that used hospital days post-surgery or post-heart attack as outcome indicators showed that on the average psychological intervention reduced hospitalization approximately two days below the control group's average of 9.92 days. Most of the interventions were modest and, in most studies, were not matched in any way to the needs of particular patients or their coping styles. Beyond the intrinsic value of offering humane and considerate care, the evidence is that psychological care can be cost-effective. (*Am J Public Health* 1982; 72:141–151.)

Introduction

Most studies of the effects of psychotherapy on utilization of medical services have considered ambulatory patients in office practices and health maintenance organizations (HMOs). However, there is also evidence that the patient's emotional status may influence the time it takes to recover from acute episodes of severe illness or from surgery. Such findings have obvious relevance for health care planning and financing.

The literature documents many ways in which psychological factors can influence health and the use of medical services, and three of these have particular relevance for patients in medical crisis: 1) emotional factors may influence the course of existing disease and recovery from medical crisis;[1,2] 2) the patient's emotional response to his/her disease may influence prescribing by the physician;[3] and 3) the patient's response to symptoms and to medical advice can influence the patient's subsequent management of his/her own disease.[8-12]

Impact of Emotions on Disease and Recovery

Kimball found that, of 54 adult patients admitted for open heart surgery, mortality was highest among patients

From the Departments of Psychiatry and Preventive Medicine, University of Colorado School of Medicine, Denver; the Denver V.A. Medical Center; and the School of Education, University of Colorado, Boulder. Address reprint requests to Emily Mumford, PhD, Department of Psychiatry, Box C-268, University of Colorado School of Medicine, 4200 E. 9th Avenue, Denver, CO 80262. Dr. Mumford is professor of psychiatry and preventive medicine at the University of Colorado School of Medicine. Dr. Schlesinger is Chief, Psychology Service, Denver VA Medical Center, and professor, Department of Psychiatry, University of Colorado School of Medicine. Dr. Glass is professor, School of Education, University of Colorado School of Medicine.

Editor's Note: See also related editorial, p 127 this issue.

who had been identified as "depressed" prior to surgery, although these patients were not at more risk on the basis of age, rating of cardiac functioning, or duration of illness.[13] Sime studied 57 women admitted for abdominal surgery and found that high levels of preoperative fear were associated with slower recovery, greater use of analgesics, and more negative emotions.[14]

Low morale was a significant predictor of death in the study by Garrity and Klein that assessed 48 patients for anxiety, hostility, and depression as compared with calmness and cheerfulness five days following admission to intensive coronary care. Of the 12 patients who died within six months of discharge, 10 had been characterized as suffering from unresolved emotional distress, and previous physical status did not explain the excess death rate among the depressed patients.[15]

Zheutlin and Goldstein studied 38 patients suffering major cardiac insult and reported that the combination of one Minnesota Multiphasic Personality Inventory (MMPI) scale and a cardiac status index predicted more than 70 per cent of the variance in patient recovery as assessed in a cardiac work evaluation unit.[16] Bruhn, Chandler, and Wolf found that 17 patients with myocardial infarctions who subsequently died had significantly higher MMPI depression scores than did survivors.[17]

Physician's Decision about Treatment

Kinsman, Dahlem, et al, have studied the patient's style of emotional response to asthma as it influences medical decisions about treatment.[6,7] Patients who scored high on a scale of "panic-fear symptomatology" tended to be kept in the hospital longer than low-scoring patients although objective measures of airway limitation did not indicate greater physiologic distress. These patients were often sent home on higher dosages of medication than were patients who had scored lower on the "panic-fear" scale. The differences in

From Emily Mumford et al., "The Effects of Psychological Intervention on Recovery from Surgery and Heart Attacks: An Analysis of the Literature," 72(2) *American Journal of Public Health* 141-151 (February 1982). Copyright 1982 American Public Health Association. Reprinted by permission.

medication were not explainable by objectively determined physical status.[6,18] High panic-fear patients may intimidate doctors into allowing unnecessary hospitalizations. Patients extremely low on panic-fear may, in denying symptoms, seek medical care only when in acute distress and at a point when hospitalization is required.[7,19]

Patient's Response to Medical Advice

Clinicians believe that a hopeful and cooperative patient tends to have a smoother and swifter recovery than a depressed and uncooperative patient. Yet the hospital experience, as it is currently structured, may interfere actively with the patient's willingness and ability to cooperate effectively to achieve recovery. Not told what to expect next, and admonished to rely on the experts, patients and their families are disadvantaged when they strive to cooperate. Some benefits from psychologically-informed intervention in the studies to be reviewed may reflect correction of defects in the social system in which recovery and recuperation are expected to take place. Preparatory education and restructuring delivery experiences enhance the ability of obstetrical patients to cooperate with their physicians.[20,21] The literature we analyze here suggests similar benefits from emotional and social support for patients recovering from medical and surgical crisis.

Materials and Methods

Meta-Analysis of Psychological Intervention

With the help of a Medlars search (1955–1978) and subsequent pursuit of key references through the Citation Index, we located 34 controlled, experimental studies in the published and unpublished literature that tested the effects of providing psychological support as an adjunct to medically required care for patients facing surgery or recovering from heart attack.[3,4,23-55]

The term "psychological intervention" covers a wide range of activities performed by psychiatrists, psychologists, surgeons, anesthesiologists, nurses, and others intended to provide information or emotional support to patients suffering disabling illness or facing surgery. These activities range from special programs to quite simple and inexpensive modifications of, or additions to, required medical procedures.

For example, in a study of the influence of psychological preparation for surgery, the evening before surgery 25 male patients discussed their concerns and fears in a small group led by a nurse. They were told what to expect and how to aid in their own recuperation. This group was contrasted with a randomly selected control group of 25 male patients who underwent similar surgical procedures with only the routine care. The experimental patients slept better, experienced less anxiety the morning of surgery, and recalled more details but fewer fearful or unpleasant images from the day of surgery. They suffered less postoperative urinary retention, required less anesthesia and pain medication, returned more rapidly to oral intake, and were discharged sooner than the control patients.[4]

In each of the studies reviewed, the recovery of patients who received information or emotional support in preparation for surgery, or during recovery from surgery or from heart attack, was compared with that of a control group not provided the special intervention. The Appendix Table summarizes the circumstances and findings of each study with the following information:

- patients sampled
- medical or surgical problem
- nature of intervention and provider
- sampling method used in the study
- size of experimental and control groups
- description of the outcome indicators
- effect size (ES) of the outcome indicators

The effect size (ES) of the outcome indicators is a standardized measure, the average difference between the treatment and control group on the outcome variable divided by the standard deviation of the control group. The ES can be interpreted in terms of the improvement or loss that the average member of the control group would experience if given the experimental treatment. A positive ES in the Appendix tables signifies the difference favors the group receiving the psychological intervention.[22]

Results

The ESs for all 210 outcome indicators in the 34 studies average +.49; the intervention groups do better than the control groups by about one-half standard deviation. These findings are consistent across studies; only 31 (15 per cent) of the 210 outcome comparisons were negative and 8 of the negative ESs are contributed by one study.[33]

Table 1 is based only on the 180 ESs derived from well-controlled studies that reported standard deviations. We exclude measures from studies that did not either randomly assign or carefully match experimental and control patients. We also exclude measures from studies that provided neither standard deviations nor statistics that allowed for their estimation.

Table 1 analyzes the ESs within 10 outcome categories segregating psychological self-reported "pain" variables and other-rated, physiological or "medical" variables. The ESs based on external indicators are, for the most part, larger than those for the self-ratings and average +.45 compared with +.35. The highest ESs are for cooperation with treatment, speed of recovery, and fewer post-hospital complications (events). One can conclude that in general cooperation with treatment influences both speed and uneventfulness of recovery, an observation also made by Ley in his review of studies of the effects of different types of pre-operative communications on various outcome variables.[56]

The "psychological interventions" described in the Appendix Table can be categorized in terms of their intended mode of action. Some studies tested educational methods and approaches designed to provide patients with information about their conditions and what to expect. Other studies tested various psychotherapeutic approaches intended to provide reassurance, to soften irrational beliefs, or in general

TABLE 1—Average Effect Sizes within 10 Outcome Categories

	Mean	S.D.	N*
Self Ratings			
1. Pre-op. anx., pain.	+.32	.73	6
2. Post-op. anx., pain.	+.38	.59	32
ES =	+.35		
Other Rating and External Indicators			
3. Cooperation with treatment	+.60	.40	11
4. Pre- & Post-op. pain-distress (other rated)	+.44	.46	43
5. Post-op. physiological indicators	+.28	.50	25
6. Post-op. narcotics, hypnotics, etc.	+.17	.42	13
7. Speed recovery	+.80	.50	17
8. Post-op. complications	+.38	.47	13
9. Post-hosp. course (events)	+.60	.34	10
10. Days in hospital	+.25	.28	10
ES =	+.45		N = 180
Grand ES =	+.43		

* Most studies included more than one outcome indicator category.

to offer emotional support and relieve anxiety. Some studies offered interventions of both types. In the Appendix Table, reading down the third column "Nature of Experimental Group Intervention," one observes that psychotherapeutic approaches (ES +.41; s_{ES} .65; N 87) seem rather more effective than educational approaches (ES +.30; s_{ES} .51; N 56) which are also effective. A combination of both approaches seems clearly superior to either alone (ES +.65; s_{ES} .45; N 40).

A subset of the outcome indicators is particularly important for its cost implications. Thirteen studies reported 14 comparisons of the number of days hospitalized for the intervention and control groups. Ten of these studies provide adequate data for meta-analysis. The average difference in days of hospitalization for the 10 comparisons weighted equally is about two days in favor of the intervention group.* Table 2 summarizes these findings. It can be argued that studies with larger numbers of patients should be given more weight in deriving a composite. Reasoning also that a mean should be weighted inversely to its variance error, weighting each by the sample size would be appropriate. The average difference weighted for sample size and size of standard error equals 2.37 days, slightly higher than the unweighted average. Hence a reasonable estimate of the true difference between intervention and control groups favors the intervention group by more than two days.

Is this difference statistically reliable? The estimate of about two days shorter hospitalization for patients having psychological intervention is based on data from approximately 2,000 intervention and control patients across the four comparisons. Seven studies gave the standard deviation of hospital stay. The average standard deviation is 4.75 days and t = 7.32, significant at any reasonable level. If we

---

*One study not included in the analysis reported simply "shorter stay" for patients given information compared with control patients.[57]

analyze the findings using the study as the unit of analysis a significant t of 3.42 results.

We attempted to include the entire population of interest, i.e., all published and unpublished controlled experimental studies of the effects of psychological intervention in medical crisis.** One might suspect that unpublished studies would be more likely to contain negative results than would published studies. Smith attempted to study whether published studies are biased in favor of positive findings. She found that the average ES obtained by meta-analysis of data from published articles is about one-third larger than the ES from theses and dissertations that used comparable outcome indicators and subjects.[58] Two of the studies included in the Appendix Table are unpublished.[1,42] The effect sizes for one are slightly negative, for the other quite positive.

Discussion

It is important to recognize that these favorable effects prevail even though the interventions were mostly modest and not tailored to the needs of any individual patient. Since patients differ in the way they cope with emotional and physical threat, they might be expected to benefit most from interventions designed to complement their particular coping styles. The apparent superiority of providing both educational and emotional support may simply reflect increased chances of meeting the needs of more patients when two different types of intervention are offered.

A few studies offer evidence that the benefits of intervention are enhanced when the type of support provided is matched to the individual coping style of the pa-

---

**After we had completed our analysis, another study was published finding a 12-day shorter hospital stay for a treatment group compared with a control group of elderly patients operated on for repair of fractured femurs. Twice as many patients in the treatment group returned home rather than to another institution.[59]

TABLE 2—Duration of Hospitalization for Intervention and Control Groups for Fourteen Studies

Author(s) Medical Problem	Intervention Group		Control Group			
	Average days hospitalized	N	Average days hospitalized	N	Difference (Δ)	Standard Error [*]
Archuleta, Plummer & Hopkins[1] (1977) Major surgery	7.49	248	6.90	267	-.59	.43
Fortin & Kirouac[26] (1976) Major surgery	6.44	37	6.35	32	.09	.50
Langer, Janis & Wolfer[28] (1975) Major surgery	5.64	15	7.60	15	1.96	.37
Gruen[3] (1975) Myocardial infarction	22.50	35	24.90	35	2.40	1.43
Surman, et al[35] (1974) Cardiac surgery	13.40	20	17.00	20	3.60	[**]
Schmitt and Wooldridge[4] (1973) Elective surgery	9.70	25	11.80	25	2.10	1.07
Lindeman and Stetzer[39] (1973) Elective Surgery						
Adults	6.70	90	6.65	86	-.05	.45
Children	2.11	19	3.00	11	.89	.69
Lindeman and Van Aernam[40] (1971) Major surgery	6.53	126	8.44	135	1.91	.62
DeLong[42] (1971) Abdominal Surgery	6.17	31	7.18	33	1.01	.50
Andrew[44] (1970) Hernia surgery	6.91	22	6.78	18	.13	.95
Healy[a45] (1968) Abdominal surgery	—	181	—	140	5.00	[**]
Egbert et al.[a5] (1964) Abdominal Surgery	—	51	—	46	2.70	1.06
Kolouch[b51,52] (1962, '64) Elective Surgery	6.86	197	12.40	"many thousands"	5.54	.10

[*] Standard Error of the difference between the means equals $S_p \cdot \sqrt{\frac{1}{n_i} \cdot \frac{1}{n_c}}$ where S_p is the pooled standard deviation.
[**] Data insufficient to calculate Standard Error.

tient.[14,25,40,42,59] A patient who copes reasonably well with the help of denial may find detailed explanations about impending surgery or cardiac damage burdensome while another patient who copes with stress by seeking information and mastery could be reassured and helped by the same explanation.[42]

Surgical intervention or treatment on a coronary care unit may be viewed as a crisis as Whitehead defined it, "a dangerous opportunity." Analogous to the risks and benefits of medical and surgical interventions, the hospital experience itself may also be a dangerous opportunity for the patient's survival and subsequent social and emotional adjustment. The patient regaining his/her balance following a medical crisis can change direction and assume new and potentially better patterns of adaptation.[60-65] On the other hand, if the dangerous opportunity is not seized, needless incapacity may result. Survivors of heart attack range from the cardiac cripple to those whose emotional and social lives have been turned for the better.

The elaborate services provided in the surgical recovery room or the coronary care unit leave little to chance. They contrast markedly with the minimal attention systematically provided to educate patient and family for recuperation following hospitalization. In an action-oriented society, reports of the considerable effectiveness of modest interventions may command less attention than reports of the modest effects of more flamboyant interventions.

It is often argued that the medical care system cannot afford to take on the emotional status of the patient as its responsibility. Time is short and costs are high. However, it may be that medicine cannot afford to ignore the patient's emotional status assuming that it will take care of itself. Anxiety and depression do not go away by being ignored. The psychological and physiological expressions of emotional upheaval may be themselves disastrous for the delicately balanced patient or may lead to behavior that needlessly impedes recovery when surgery or medical treatment was otherwise successful.

Usually advances in medical knowledge call for large investments in training, personnel, and equipment if patients are to benefit. Thus, a measure that promises to benefit patients and to save money at the same time is newsworthy.

REFERENCES

1. Archuleta V. Plummer OB. Hopkins KD: A demonstration model for patient education: A model for the project "Training Nurses to Improve Patient Education." Boulder. Project Report: Western State Commission for Higher Education. June 1977.
2. Gersten JC. Langner TS. Eisenberg JG. et al: An evaluation of the etiologic role of stressful life-change events in psychological disorders. J Health Soc Behav 1977; 18:228–244.
3. Gruen W: Effects of brief psychotherapy during the hospitalization period on the recovery process in heart attacks. J Consult Clin Psychol 1975; 43:223–232.
4. Schmitt FE. Woolridge PJ: Psychological preparation of surgical patients. Nurs Res 1973; 22:108–116.
5. Egbert LD, Battit GE, Welch CE. et al: Reduction of postoperative pain by encouragement and instruction of patients. N Engl J Med 1964; 270:825–827.
6. Dahlem NW. Kinsman RA. Horton DJ: Requests for as-needed medications by asthmatic patients: relationships to prescribed oral corticosteroid regimens and length of hospitalization. J Allergy Clin Immunol 1979; 63:23–27.
7. Kinsman RA. Dahlem NW. Spector SL. et al: Observations on subjective symptomatology. coping behavior. and medical decisions in asthma. Psychosom Med 1977; 39:102–119.
8. Barofsky I: Medication Compliance: A Behavioral Management Approach. Thorofare. NJ: Charles B. Slack. 1977.
9. Becker MH. Maiman LA. Kirscht JP: The health belief model and prediction of dietary compliance: a field experiment. J Health Soc Behav 1977; 18:348–366.
10. Sackett DL. Haynes RB: Compliance with Therapeutic Regimens. Baltimore: Johns Hopkins University Press. 1976.
11. Eichhorn RL. Andersen RM: Changes in personal adjustment to perceived and medically established heart disease: A panel study. J Health Hum Behav 1962; 3:242–249.
12. Stimson G. Webb B: Going to See the Doctor. London: Routledge and Kegan Paul. 1975.
13. Kimball CP: Psychological responses to the experience of open heart surgery. In: Moos RH (ed): Coping With Physical Illness. New York: Plenum. 1977. pp 113–133.
14. Sime AM: Relationship of pre-operative fear. type of coping. and information received about surgery to recovery from surgery. J Pers Soc Psychol 1976; 34:716–724.
15. Garrity TF. Klein RF: Emotional response and clinical severity as early determinants of six month mortality after myocardial infarction. Heart Lung 1975; 4:730–737.
16. Zheutlin S. Goldstein SG: The prediction of psychosocial adjustment subsequent to cardiac insult. J Clin Psychol 1977; 33:706–710.
17. Bruhn JG. Chandler B. Wolf S: A psychological study of survivors and nonsurvivors of myocardial infarction. Psychosom Med 1969; 31:8–19.
18. Jones NF. Kinsman RA. Dirks JF. et al: Psychological Contributions to Chronicity in Asthma: Patient Response Styles Influencing Medical Treatment and Its Outcome. Psychophysiology Research Laboratories. Dept. of Behavioral Science. National Jewish Hospital and Research Center. 3800 E. Colfax Avenue. Denver. Co. 80206. January 1979. Report No. 46.
19. Kinsman RA. Luparello T. O'Banion K. et al: Multidimensional analysis of the subjective symptomatology of asthma. Psychosom Med 1973; 35:250–267.
20. Enkin MW. Smith SL. Derner SW. et al: An adequately controlled study of effectiveness of PPM training. In: Morris N (ed): Psychosomatic Medicine in Obstetrics & Gynecology. Basel: S. Karger. 1972.
21. Scott JR. Rose NB: Effect of psychoprophylaxis (Lamaze preparation) on labor and delivery in primiparas. N Engl J Med 1976; 294:1205–1207.
22. Glass GV: Integrating findings: the meta-analysis of research. Rev Res Educ 1977; 5:351–379.
23. Flaherty GG. Fitzpatrick JJ: Relaxation technique to increase comfort level of postoperative patients: a preliminary study. Nurs Res 1978; 27:352–355.
24. Finesilver C: Preparation of adult patients for cardiac catheterization and coronary cineangiography. Int J Nurs Studies 1978; 15:211–221.
25. Felton G. Huss K. Payne EA. et al: Preoperative nursing intervention with the patient for surgery: outcomes of three alternative approaches. Int J Nurs Stud 1976; 13:83–96.
26. Fortin F. Kirouac S: A randomized controlled trial of preoperative patient education. Int J Nurs Stud 1976; 13:11–24.
27. Auerbach SM. Kendall PC. Cuttler HF. et al: Anxiety. locus of control. type of preparatory information. and adjustment to dental surgery. J Consult Clin Psychol 1976; 44:809–818.
28. Langer EJ. Janis IL. Wolfer JA: Reduction of psychological stress in surgical patients. J Exp Soc Psychol 1975; 11:155–165.
29. Melamed BG. Siegel LJ: Reduction of anxiety in children facing hospitalization and surgery by use of filmed modeling. J Consult Clin Psychol 1975; 43:511–521.
30. Wolfer JA. Visintainer MA: Pediatric surgical patients' and parents' stress responses and adjustment as a function of psychologic preparation and stress-point nursing care. Nurs Res 1975; 24:244–255.
31. Visintainer MA. Wolfer JA: Psychological preparation for surgical pediatric patients: the effects of childrens' and parents' stress responses and adjustment. Peds 1975; 56:187–202.
32. Johnson PA. Stockdale DF: Effects of puppet therapy on palmar sweating of hospitalized children. Johns Hopkins Med J 1975; 137:1–5.
33. Rahe RH. O'Neil T. Hagan A. et al: Brief group therapy following myocardial infarction: eighteen-month follow-up of a controlled trial. Int J Psych Med 1975; 6:349–358.
34. Field PB: Effects of tape-recorded hypnotic preparation for surgery. Int J Clin Exp Hypn 1974; 22:54–61.
35. Surman OS. Hackett TP. Silverberg EL. et al: Usefulness of psychiatric intervention in patients undergoing cardiac surgery. Arch Gen Psychiatry 1974; 30:830–835.
36. Vernon DTA. Bigelow DA: Effect of information about a potentially stressful situation on responses to stress impact. J Pers Soc Psychol 1974; 29:50–59.
37. Vernon DTA. Bailey WC: The use of motion pictures in the psychological preparation of children for induction of anesthesia. Anesthesiology 1974; 40:68–72.
38. White WC. Akers J. Green J. et al: Use of imitation in the treatment of dental phobia in early childhood: a preliminary report. J Dent Child 1974; 41:26–30.
39. Lindeman CA. Stetzer SL: Effects of preoperative visits by operating room nurses. Nurs Res 1973; 22:4–16.
40. Lindeman CA. Van Aernam B: Nursing intervention with the presurgical patient: the effects of structured and unstructured preoperative teaching. Nurs Res 1971; 20:319–332.
41. Aiken LH. Henrichs TF: Systematic relaxation as a nursing intervention technique with open heart surgery patients. Nurs Res 1971; 20:212–217.
42. DeLong RD: Individual differences in patterns of anxiety arousal. stress-relevant information and recovery from surgery. Diss AB Int B Sci Eng 1971; 32:554B–555B. (Dissertation. U. of Ca. Los Angeles. 1970).
43. Layne OL. Yudofsky SC: Postoperative psychosis in cardiotomy patients. N Engl J Med 1971; 284:518–520.
44. Andrew JM: Recovery from surgery with and without preparatory instruction. for three coping styles. J Pers Soc Psychol 1970; 15:223–226.
45. Healy KM: Does preoperative instruction make a difference? Am J Nurs 1968; 68:62–67.
46. Lazarus HR. Hagens JH: Prevention of psychosis following open-heart surgery. Am J Psychiatry 1968; 124:1190–1195.
47. Cassell S: Effect of brief puppet therapy upon the emotional responses of children undergoing cardiac catheterization. J Consul Psychol 1965; 29:1–8.
48. Cassell S. Paul MH: The role of puppet therapy on the emotional responses of children hospitalized for cardiac catheterization. J Peds 1967; 71:233–239.
49. Mahaffy PR: The effects of hospitalization on children admitted for tonsillectomy and adenoidectomy. Nurs Res 1965; 14:12–19.

50. Dumas RG, Leonard RC: The effect of nursing on the incidence of postoperative vomiting. Nurs Res 1963; 12:12–15.
51. Kolouch FT: Role of suggestion in surgical convalescence. Arch Surg 1962; 85:144–145.
52. Kolouch FT: Hypnosis and surgical convalescence: a study of subjective factors in postoperative recovery. Amer J Clin Hypn 1964; 7:120–129.
53. Bonilla KB, Quigley WF, Bowers WF: Experiences with hypnosis on a surgical service. Milit Med 1961; 126:364–370.
54. Vaughan GF: Children in hospital. Lancet 1957; 12:1117–1120.
55. Goldie L: Hypnosis in the casualty department. Brit Med J 1956; 2:1340–1342.
56. Ley P: Psychological studies of doctor-patient communication. In: S Rachman (ed): Contributions to Medical Psychology. Elmsford NY: Pergamon Press, 1977, 1:9–42.
57. Putt AM: One experiment in nursing adults with peptic ulcers. Nurs Res 1970; 19:484–494.
58. Smith ML: Publication bias and meta-analysis. Eval in Ed 1980; 4:22–24.
59. Levitan SJ, Kornfeld DS: Clinical and cost benefits of liaison psychiatry. Am J Psychiatry 1981; 138:790–793.
60. Moos RH (ed): Coping with Physical Illness. New York, NY: Plenum Publishing Co., 1977.
61. McFadden ER, Luparello T, Lyons HA, et al: The mechanism of action of suggestion in the induction of acute asthma attacks. Psychosom Med 1969; 31:134–143.
62. Kennedy JA, Baksk H: The influence of emotions on the outcome of cardiac surgery: a predictive study. Bull NY Acad Med 1966; 42:811–845.
63. Klein R, Dean A, Willson M, et al: The physician and postmyocardial infarction invalidism. JAMA 1965; 194:123–128.
64. Aldes JH, Stein SP, Grabin S: A program to effect vocational restoration of "unemployable" cardiac cases. Dis Chest 1968; 54:518–522.
65. Rosenberg SG: Patient education leads to better care for heart patients. HSMHA Health Rep 1971; 86:793–802.

ACKNOWLEDGMENTS

The work reported here was supported in part by the National Institute of Mental Health, Division of Mental Health Service Programs, under Contracts NIMH 278-77-0049 (MH) and MHSC-78-0037 (MH) and by The John D. and Catherine T. MacArthur Foundation. We wish to thank Suzannah Hillyard Krause for assistance in assembling the bibliography and preparing the tables.

APPENDIX

APPENDIX TABLE—The Effects of Psychologically-Informed Intervention on Recovery from Medical Crisis[a]

Study: Authors and Date	Patients Sampled: Medical Problem or Procedure	Nature of Experimental Group Intervention; Duration; Provider	Sampling Method: n_1 = size of experimental group[b] n_2 = size of control group[b]	Outcome Indicators	Outcome Effect Size: (ES) (+ favors Experimental Group)
Flagherty & Fitzpatrick[23] (1978)	Adults: Major surgery	Relaxation technique at 1st attempt to get out of bed, post-op. nurse	Random: n_1 = 21 n_2 = 21	a. Post-op. Demerol	+ .76
				b. Incision Pain	
				1. Intensity	+ .95
				2. Distress	+2.70
				c. Change in blood pressure	
				1. Systolic	+ .03
				2. Diastolic	− .10
				d. Change in pulse rate	+ .27
				e. Change in respiration	+ .80
Finesilver[24] (1978)	Adults: Cardiac catheterization and coronary cineangiography	Specific information and emotional support, 2 sessions: 1. At admission 2. Day before surgery; by investigator	Random: n_1 = 20 n_2 = 20	a. Medication administered during surgery[c]	+1.22
				b. Mood adjective checklist	
				1. Well-being	+ .04
				2. Happiness	+ .14
				3. Fear	+ .11
				4. Helplessness	+ .19
				5. Anger	+ .16
				c. Distress during hospitalization (nurse's rating)	+ .74
				d. Cooperation during catheterization (nurse's rating)	+ .17
				e. Post-catheterization rating by patients of how "upset" they were by procedure	+ .24
Archuleta, Plummer and Hopkins[1] (1977)	Adults: Major surgery	Preoperative teaching by nurse plus 5 min. reinforcement.	Random: n_1 = 248 n_2 = 267 In 11 hospitals	a. Days hospitalized	− .15
				b. Analgesics used	− .09
				c. Forced vital capacity	− .10
				d. Maximal midexpiratory flow	+ .02
				e. Forced expiration volume at 1 second	− .05
Felton, Huss, Payne et al.[25] (1976)	Adults: 1st time major surgery under general anesthesia	1. Preoperative information by nurse, photographs and films, average time 88 min.	Random: n_1 = 25 n_2 = 25	a. Days hospitalized[d]	—
				b. Ventilatory function	
				1. 24 hrs. post-op	+ .05
				2. 48 hrs. post-op	− .38
				3. 72 hrs. post-op.	− .25

APPENDIX TABLE—Continued

Study: Authors and Date	Patients Sampled: Medical Problem or Procedure	Nature of Experimental Group Intervention; Duration; Provider	Sampling Method: n_1 = size of experimental group[b] n_2 = size of control group[b]	Outcome Indicators	Outcome Effect Size: (ES) (+ favors Experimental Group)
				c. Heart or circulatory complications[c]	+ .60
				d. Multiple affect adjective checklist (anxiety)	+ .28
				e. Personal orientation inventory	
				1. Inner-directedness	+1.53
				2. Self-regard	+ .87
				3. Acceptance of aggression	+ .33
		2. Therapeutic communication approach by nurse, average time 62.5 min.	Random: n_1 = 12 n_2 = 25	a. Days hospitalized	0.00
				b. Ventilatory function	
				1. 24 hrs. post-op.	0.00
				2. 48 hrs. post-op.	− 0.48
				3. 72 hrs. post-op.	− .71
				c. Heart or circulatory complications	+1.45
				d. Multiple affect adjective checklist (anxiety)	+ .17
				e. Personal Orientation Inventory	
				1. Inner-directedness	0.00
				2. Self-regard	− .53
				3. Acceptance of aggression	− .85
Fortin and Kirouac[26] (1976)	Adults: Major surgery	Preoperative education and training by nurses 1 session per week starting 15–20 days before hospitalization	Random: n_1 = 37 n_2 = 32	a. Inpatient ambulatory activity	+ .43
				b. Activities of daily living	
				1. 10 days post-op.	+ .83
				2. 33 days post-op.	+ .79
				c. Days before return to work or usual level of activity	+ .42
				d. Analgesics	+ .63
				e. Absence of pain and nausea at discharge	+ .69
				f. Satisfaction with hospitalization[d]	—
				g. Days hospitalized	+ .05
				h. Days lost from work in 33 post-op. days[d] Exper. = 23.8 days Control = 26.0 days	—
				i. Readmission or death	0.00
Auerbach, Kendall, Cuttler, et al.[27] (1976)	Adults: Dental surgery	Audio-tape of specific information about surgery by dental student	Random: n_1 = 29 n_2 = 19	a. State anxiety	
				1. Immediately after intervention	− .38
				2. Immediately after surgery	+ .22
Gruen[3] (1975)	Adults: Myocardial Infarction	Eclectic Verbal: Psychiatrist, ½ hr. a day for 5–6 days "to awaken hope"	Random: n_1 = 35 n_2 = 35	a. Days hospitalized	+ .23
				b. Days in intensive care	+ .49
				c. Days on monitor	+ .36
				d. Number of patients with congestive heart failure	+ .40
				e. Congestive heart failure, days per patient	− .02
				f. Number of patients with arrythmias	+ .50
				1. Ventricular	+ .50
				2. Supraventricular	+ .85
				g. Nurse ratings	
				1. Chest pain	+ .09
				2. Other pain	− .41
				3. Depression	+ .25
				4. Anxiety	− .16
				5. Refusals of treatment	− .28
				6. Weakness, exhaustion	+ .48
				h. Physician ratings	
				1. Depression	+ .33
				2. Anxiety	− .05
				3. TMAS Bendig Score	+ .06
				4. ST Anxiety Inventory	+ .14
				5. MAACL Anxiety	+ .14
				i. Nowlis Adjective Checklist	
				1. Anxiety	+ .09

APPENDIX TABLE—Continued

Study: Authors and Date	Patients Sampled: Medical Problem or Procedure	Nature of Experimental Group Intervention: Duration: Provider	Sampling Method: n_1 = size of experimental group[b] n_2 = size of control group[b]	Outcome Indicators	Outcome Effect Size: (ES) (+ favors Experimental Group)
				2. Surgency	+ .65
				3. Elation	+ .32
				4. Affection	+ .54
				5. Sadness	+ .32
				6. Vigor	+ .30
				j. Four-month follow-up	
				1. Anxiety	+ .71
				2. Retarded activity	+ .42
Langer, Janis and Wolfer[28] (1975)	Adults: Major Surgery	Combination RET (Ellis) and learning theory (Kanfer). psychologist. 20 minutes	Random: n_1 = 15 n_2 = 15	a. Nurses ratings	
				1. Anxiety	+ .51
				2. Ability to cope	+1.15
				b. Per cent of subjects requiring[c]	
				1. Sedatives	+ .90
				2. Pain relievers	+1.15
				c. Days hospitalized[d]	—
				Exper. = 5.64 days	
				Control = 7.60 days	
	Adults: Major Surgery	Preparatory information only. psychologist 20 minutes	Random: n_1 = 15 n_2 = 15	a. Nurses ratings	
				1. Anxiety	+ .62
				2. Ability to cope	+ .30
				b. Per cent of subjects requiring[c]	
				1. Sedatives	+ .63
				2. Pain relievers	+ .42
				c. Days hospitalized[d]	—
				Exper. = 7.2 days	
				Control = 7.6 days	
Melamed and Siegel[29] (1975)	Children: Tonsils. hernia. urinary surgery	Film: "Ethan Has an Operation". 12 min.: Actors	Matched: n_1 = 30 n_2 = 30	a. Measures taken post-intervention. but immediately pre-op.	
				1. Anxiety scale of Personality Inventory for Children	+ .67
				2. Behavior Problems Checklist (not taken)	—
				3. Palmar Sweat Index	+ .75
				4. Hospital Fears Rating Scale	+ .75
				5. Observer Rating of Anxiety	+ .60
				Observer Rating of Anxiety	0.00
				Observer Rating of Anxiety	0.00
				b. Measures taken 20 days Post-op.	
				1. Anxiety Scale of Personality Inventory for Children	+ .50
				2. Behavior Problems Checklist	+ .80
				3. Palmar Sweat Index	+ .60
				4. Hospital Fears Rating Scale	+ .75
				5. Observer Rating of Anxiety	+ .60
				Observer Rating of Anxiety	0.00
				Observer Rating of Anxiety	0.00
Wolfer and Visintainer[30] (1975): Visintainer and Wolfer[31] (1975)	Children: Elective surgery	"Psychologic preparation and support" by same nurse 1 hour across 6 points in time during hospitalization	Random: n_1 = 45 n_2 = 35	a. During blood test	
				1. Anxiety	+ .70
				2. Cooperation	+ .60
				b. During pre-op. medication	
				1. Anxiety	+1.32
				2. Cooperation	+1.20
				3. Pulse rate	+1.07
				c. During transport to O.R.	
				1. Anxiety	+ .52
				2. Cooperation	+ .51
				d. While in O.R.	
				1. Anxiety	+ .58
				2. Cooperation	+ .63
				e. Ease of fluid intake	+ .43
				f. Minutes to first voiding	+ .85
				g. Recovery room medication	+ .65
				h. Post-hospital adjustment	+ .90
Johnson and	Children:	Puppet therapy 1 time pre-	Random:	a. Palmar Sweat Index Change Score	

APPENDIX TABLE—Continued

Study: Authors and Date	Patients Sampled: Medical Problem or Procedure	Nature of Experimental Group Intervention; Duration; Provider	Sampling Method: n_1 = size of experimental group[b] n_2 = size of control group[b]	Outcome Indicators	Outcome Effect Size (ES) (+ favors Experimental Group)
Stockdale[32] (1975)	Assorted surgery	operation, mean duration 13.4 min. by "The experimenter"	n_1 = 22 n_2 = 21	1. From pre-therapy to immediate post-therapy	+ .27
				2. From pre-therapy to night after surgery	+ .23
Rahe, O'Neil, Hagan, et al.[33] (1975)	Adults: Mycardial infarction	Four to six group therapy sessions, psychiatrist, during early rehabilitation	Mostly random, well-matched n_1 = 36 n_2 = 21	a. Number of coronary disease events 18-month follow-up post-infarction:	
				1. Coronary insufficiency	+ .61
				2. By-pass surgery	+ .63
				3. Reinfarction	+ 1.16
				4. Mortality	+ .58
				b. Knowledge of etiological factors in heart disease	+ .79
Field[34] (1974)	Adults: Orthopedic surgery	Hypnotherapy recording by "Research Assistant" who interviewed patient, 20 minutes plus interview	Random: n_1 = 30 n_2 = 30	a. Nervousness (rated by physician)	+ .37
				b. Speed of recovery	+ .06
Surman, Hackett, Silverberg, et al.[35] (1974)	Adults: Cardiac surgery	One or more therapeutic interviews, including teaching of autohypnosis 60–90 minutes	Random: n_1 = 20 n_2 = 20	a. Post-op. Complications	
				1. Delirium	+ .15
				2. Cardiac failure	+ .11
				3. Hepatic dysfunction	+ .60
				4. Arrhythmias	0.00
				b. Post-op. Medication	
				1. Narcotic doses	.41
				2. Morphine units	.30
				3. Darvon doses	− .02
				4. Sleep medication	.11
				5. Valium amount	+ .16
				c. Patient's State 5 days post-op.	
				1. Anxiety	− .14
				2. Pain	− .40
				3. Depression	− .75
				d. Days hospitalized[d] Exper. = 13.4 days Control = 17.0 days	—
Vernon and Bigelow[36] (1974)	Adult Males: Hernia repair surgery	Information recording re: hernia surgery and recovery heard twice pre-surgery plus encouragement to ask questions (investigator not specified)	Random: n_1 = 20 n_2 = 20	a. Pre-op.	
				1. Mood[c]	
				(1) Fear	0.00
				(2) Worry or fear of pain	+ .78
				2. Patient's confidence in doctors and nurses	+ .27
				b. Post-op.	
				1. Mood[c]	
				(1) Anger	+ .14
				(2) Depression	+ .36
				(3) Fear	+ .16
				2. Confidence in doctors & nurses	+ .22
Vernon and Bailey[37] (1974)	Children: Minor elective surgery	Film showing children going through induction of anesthesia without fear, approximately 45 min. by MD investigator	Random: n_1 = 19 n_2 = 19	a. Global Mood Scale, fear rating	
				1. Entering surgical suite	+ 1.11
				2. Entering operating room	+ 1.10
				3. First minute of surgery	+ .70
				4. Until surgical anesthesia level reached	+ .50
				5. Anesthesiologist's rating of patient's fear	+ .46
Schmitt and Wooldridge[4] (1973)	Adult males: Elective surgery	Nurse investigator's small group therapy session evening before surgery. 1 hour for 19 experimental subjects; and added individual 15 to 60 min. session with nurse the morning of surgery.	Random: n_1 = 25 n_2 = 25	a. Self-report of anxiety on morning of surgery	+ 1.73
				b. Ability to void post-op.	+ 1.50
				c. Post-op. blood pressure	+ 1.10
				d. Amount of analgesics used	+ .78
				e. Number of days to resume oral intake	+ .21
				f. Days hospitalized post-op.	+ .55
Lindeman and	Adults: Elective	Pre-op. visits by operating	Random:	a. Days hospitalized	− .02

APPENDIX TABLE—Continued

Study: Authors and Date	Patients Sampled: Medical Problem or Procedure	Nature of Experimental Group Intervention: Duration: Provider	Sampling Method: n_1 – size of experimental group[b] n_2 – size of control group[b]	Outcome Indicators	Outcome Effect Size: (ES) (+ favors Experimental Group)
Stetzer[39] (1973)	surgery	room nurses; reassurance and information	n_1 = 90 n_2 = 86	b. Analgesics used within 48 hrs. post-op.	– .22
				c. Problems in emerging from anesthesia	+ .23
				d. Anxiety pre-op.	+ .09
				e. Anxiety post-op.	+ .19
	Children:	Structured pre-op. teaching by nurses	Random: n_1 = 19 n_2 = 11	a. Days hospitalized	+ .30
				b. Analgesics used within 48 hrs. post-op.	– .56
				c. Problems in emerging from anesthesia	+ .36
				d. Anxiety pre-op.	+ .21
				e. Anxiety post-op.	+ .46
Lindeman and Van Aernam[40] (1971)	Adults: Chest and abdominal surgery	Structured pre-op. teaching by nurses	Random: n_1 = 126 n_2 = 135	a. Days hospitalized	+ .34
				b. Analgesics used within 48 hrs. post-op.	– .02
				c. Maximal expiratory flow rate	+ .47
				d. Vital capacity	– .35
				e. One second forced expiratory volume	+ .35
Aiken and Henrichs[41] (1971)	Adult males: Heart surgery	Modified systematic desensitization (Wolpe and Lazarus) Nurses, plus 15 min. tape recorded relaxation exercise	Matched: n_1 = 15 n_2 = 15	a. Psychosis post-op.	+ .87
				b. Anesthesia time	+ .72
				c. Units of blood	+ 1.00
				d. Degrees of hypothermia	+ 1.03
				e. Duration of hypothermia	+ .62
				f. Mortality (3.15 = 3.15)	0.00
				g. Minutes on bypass machine	+ 1.41
DeLong[42] (1971)	Adults, female: Elective abdominal surgery	Specific information about condition, surgery and recovery given by psychologist	Random: n_1 = 31 n_2 = 33	a. Days hospitalized	+ .54
				b. Physical recovery	+ .65
Layne and Yudofsky[e 43] (1971)	Adults: Intracardiac surgery	Therapeutic interview evening before surgery	Sample of convenience: n_1 = 42 n_2 = 19	a. Psychosis post-op.[c] Exper. = 10% Control = 22%	+ .51
Andrew[e 44] (1970)	Adult males: Hernia surgery	Informational tape recording. 8 minutes, by psychologist	Sampling method unclear: n_1 = 22 n_2 = 18	a. Days hospitalized	– .04
				b. Amount of medication	+ .11
Healy[e 45] (1968)	Adults: Abdominal surgery	Preparation for post-surgical experience, by nurse	Sampling method unclear: n_1 = 181 n_2 = 140	a. "Discharge earlier than norm"[cg]	+ 3.28
				b. Narcotics required[d]	—
				c. Post-surgical complications	+ .92
Lazarus and Hagens[e 46] (1968)	Adults: Open-heart surgery	Interview 1 hr. plus consultation with staff and changes in recovery room procedures	Sample of convenience: groups in two different hospitals n_1 = 21 n_2 = 33	a. Per cent patients with psychosis post-op.[c]	+ .65
Cassell[47] (1965); Cassell and Paul[h 48] (1967)	Children: Cardiac catheterization	Puppet therapy before and after catheterization; child clinical psychologist.	Random: n_1 = 20 n_2 = 20	a. Disturbance during catheterization	+ .82
				b. Willingness to return to hospital 1. 3 days post-op.	+ .08
				2. 30 days post-op.	+ .23
				c. Behavior adjustment post-hosp. 1. 3 days	+ .08
				2. 30 days	+ .05
				d. Days 1 and 3 observation 1. Mood	+ .40
				2. Anxiety	+ .36
				3. Anxiety	+ .86
Mahaffy[i 49] (1965)	Children: Tonsilectomy and ad-	Information and support to mothers by nurse at admis-	Random: n_1 = 21	a. Post-op. 1. Ability to take fluids orally	+ 1.95

APPENDIX TABLE—Continued

Study: Authors and Date	Patients Sampled: Medical Problem or Procedure	Nature of Experimental Group Intervention: Duration; Provider	Sampling Method: n_1 – size of experimental group[b] n_2 – size of control group[b]	Outcome Indicators	Outcome Effect Size: (ES) (+ favors Experimental Group)
	noidectomy	sion and when child returns from recovery room.	$n_2 = 22$	2. Vomiting	+1.12
				3. Crying before bedtime	+1.01
				4. Crying after bedtime	+ .90
				b. Post-hospital Questionnaire	
				1. Fever	+ .84
				2. Called doctor to home	+ .52
				3. How long before child "recovered"	+ .79
				4. Child's behavior worries mother	+ .83
				5. Child's sleep disturbed	+1.31
				6. Fear of doctors and nurses	+ .36
				7. Fear of leaving mother	+ .28
				8. Crying	+ .30
Dumas and Leonard[e] [50] (1963)	Adult females: Gynecologic surgery	Nurse visited one hour before surgery, accompanied patient to surgery and remained until the patient was on OR table.	Unspecified: $n_1 = 31$ $n_2 = 31$ Total over 3 experiments	a. Post-op. vomiting[c]	+1.10
Kolouch[e] [51,52] (1962, 1964)	Adults: Elective surgery	Hypnotherapy prior to surgery and suggestion while patient still under anesthesia; by surgeon investigator.	Sampling method unclear: 100 cases selected by experimenter	a. Post-operative analgesics[d] b. Days hospitalized[f]	— + .70
Egbert, Battit, Welch, et al.[5] (1964)	Adults: Abdominal surgery	Information and reassurance by the anesthesiologist night before surgery plus visit by the same anesthesiologist post-surgery	Random: $n_1 = 51$ $n_2 = 46$	a. Amount post-op. morphine[j] b. Amount of pain[j] c. Days hospitalized	+ .51 + .40 + .67
Bonilla, Quigley and Bowers[e] [53] (1961)	Adult males: Knee surgery	Hypnotherapy pre-surgery by operating surgeon, 100 minutes total except for post-surgical hypnotism needed for 2 patients	Consecutive cases for each group: $n_1 = 9$ $n_2 = 40$	a. Average rehabilitation time[k] b. Post-op. narcotic[d]	+1.31 —
Vaughan[e] [54] (1957)	Children: Strabismus surgery	Reassurance and explanations by surgeon on admission for 15–25 minutes, repeat visits by surgeon 3rd and 5th days post-op., for 10–15 min.	Matched: $n_1 = 20$ $n_2 = 20$	a. Disturbed behavior[c] 1. Immediate post-op. 2. 7 days post-op. 3. 26 weeks post-op.	+ .37 + .90 +1.15
Goldie[e] [55] (1956)	Adults and Children: Requiring surgery or orthopedic procedure in ER	Hypnosis treatment as adjunct to or substitute for anesthesia; the physician handling the patient.	Sample of convenience: $n_1 = 210$ $n_1 = 178$	a. Administration of general or local anesthetic for[c] 1. Incisions 2. Removal of foreign body 3. Suturing 4. Reducing fracture or dislocation	+ .31 + .89 + .47 +1.34

FOOTNOTES TO APPENDIX TABLE

[a] Some authors published more than one article about the same studies and from these, only non-duplicated findings are reported. Studies that tested the effect of emotional support for a mother on recovery of child-patient were included. Studies that tested the effect of support for a mother of a child-patient on the subsequent comfort of the mother were not included.

[b] The group sizes for some studies change slightly for different outcome variables.

[c] Values transformed from percentages to metric numbers by probit transformation.

[d] Means and standard deviations needed to compute ES not available in published study.

[e] These ESs are derived from studies that did not assign patients to experimental and control groups randomly or through adequate matching or are approximated through probit transformation. They are excluded from the analysis reported in Table 2.

[f] Only the outcome variables listed were reported in sufficient detail to permit computing ES.

[g] This largest ES for hospital stay was computed from probit transformed dichotomous data. The author does not describe how the "norm" for expected hospital stay was determined. The analysis reported in Table 2 omits this finding.

[h] Three outcome measures relating to recall of surgery are omitted. The ESs are large and favor the intervention group but the benefit of recall is uncertain. The same findings are reported in Cassell's study.[47]

[i] Author reports findings for five types of surgery but data are sufficient to permit computing ES for only two—hernia and thyroid. We present the average ES for these two as a conservative estimate of the effects obtained.

[j] Authors report 24-hour morphine usage for five post-op. days and four measures of post-op. pain. Since the ESs are quite similar and redundant, we substitute the average ES for each set. The S.D.s needed to compute the ESs could be estimated from the data presented.

[k] S.D. could be estimated from other data to compute ES.

23

Effects of Psycho-Educational Intervention on Length of Hospital Stay

A Meta-Analytic Review of 34 Studies

Elizabeth C. Devine and Thomas D. Cook

It is by now commonplace to note the national need to contain hospital costs and to suggest that one way to achieve this is by reducing the average length of hospital stay. A recent review of studies on "psychological interventions" shows that these interventions can reduce the average hospital stay of surgical and heart attack patients (Mumford, Schlesinger, & Glass, 1981). Salient among the components of these interventions are such activities as providing information about the procedures and events the patient may experience, teaching skills to reduce pain, and providing psychosocial support. Since the interventions require less than an hour to administer and do not require expensive technology, they would presumably be cost effective if they do succeed in reducing hospital stay by the two days that Mumford and associates have claimed. Evidence that these interventions consistently reduce hospital stay would also provide support for the importance of psycho-educational nursing care, since it would have been demonstrated that these interventions improve patient recovery.

Our review is based on 34 studies and was conducted simultaneously with the work of Mumford and associates, which involved only 13 studies measuring the length of hospital stay. The purposes of the present article are (1) to achieve more stable estimates of the extent to which the interventions reduce hospital stay, and (2) to rule out empirically five plausible threats to validity (Cook & Campbell, 1979; Glass, McGaw, & Smith, 1981) that, with their small sample size, Mumford et al. could not address.

Before embarking on these two tasks, we want to make a minor point about terminology. Since the interventions we shall examine include components that are obviously educational, we prefer to label them as "psycho-educational" rather than "psychological," and will henceforth use that label.

Possible Sources of Bias

A perennial problem in reviewing literature is the possibility that estimates of the magnitude of an effect will be inflated if only published sources are considered.

This research was funded in part by the Center for Urban Affairs and Policy Research, Northwestern University.

From Elizabeth C. Devine and Thomas D. Cook, "Effects of Psycho-Educational Intervention on Length of Hospital Stay: A Meta-Analytic Review of 34 Studies," *American Journal of Nursing* (September/October 1983). Copyright ©1983, the American Journal of Nursing Company. Reprinted by permission.

Glass et al. (1981) note: "To omit dissertations and fugitive research is to assume that the direction and magnitude of effect is the same in published and unpublished works." That this assumption is often wrong has been frequently documented, for studies published in journals yield larger estimates of the average effect than do studies contained in theses or dissertations (Glass et al., 1981). This is not surprising, for the size of an effect is related to statistical significance levels and such levels constitute one of the criteria by which editors decide to publish papers.

For surgical patients in the nation at large, the average length of hospital stay has been declining in recent years (Commission on Professional and Hospital Activities, Note 1). Given this fact, we need to probe whether the effect of psycho-educational interventions continues to be observed now that the average hospital stay is less, and whether a ceiling effect may be operating to attenuate more recent results.

It is customary that only physicians have discharging privileges in most hospitals; they must thus be considered as a possible source of bias. If physicians are aware of the experimental condition to which their patients have been assigned and want a particular study to show effects, then this lack of blinding to treatment assignment might lead to spurious or inflated estimates of treatment effectiveness. For this reason we also examine effect size from studies where the discharging physicians were or were not blind to treatment assignment.

Mumford and associates restricted their analyses involving effect size to studies in which experimental and control patients were initially randomly assigned or were carefully matched. The purpose of this restriction was presumably to rule out threats to internal validity. Even when random assignment takes place, however, differential attrition from a study can still occur. A selection bias then results, making it difficult to interpret any group differences in the outcome variable. The fourth issue we examine is whether estimates of the size of effect are systematically related to an assessment of internal validity based on knowledge of both attrition rates and the nature of subject assignment to conditions.

It is also important to consider the extent to which the effects of psycho-educational interventions might be attributable to a Hawthorne effect—i.e., to the attention paid to patients by the hospital staff or by researchers rather than to the purportedly causal elements in the interventions. Indeed, Westermeyer (1982) has called attention to this possibility in discussing the results of Mumford et al., implying that study participation may bring extra patient-staff interaction or a feeling on the part of the patient that he or she had a special status that, quite apart from the actual content of the interventions, might lead to observed effects. The final issue we consider is whether a Hawthorne effect can explain the results attributed to psycho-educational interventions.

In summary, this report will examine whether the reduction in hospital stay associated with psycho-educational interventions is restricted to studies that (1) are published, (2) have an early publication date, (3) involve physicians who are aware of the experimental conditions, (4) have flawed internal validity, or (5) where a Hawthorne effect may be operating. In addition to addressing these issues through blocking on the relevant variables, we shall also use our 34 studies to provide a more stable (and probably less biased) estimate of the size of effect than appeared in the review by Mumford and associates.

METHODS

To meet the two goals of providing a more stable and less biased estimate of the size of effect a meta-analysis was conducted. Meta-analysis refers to a set of techniques used for the quantitative review of studies with overlapping substantive content. The techniques used in meta-analysis and the strengths and limitations of quantitative reviews are discussed elsewhere (see Glass et al., 1981; Cook & Leviton, 1980).

To identify studies for review a rigorous search was undertaken. In addition to examining the bibliography of every study or review paper that was located, we used a computer to search Dissertation Abstracts (1961-1981), Psychological Abstracts (1967-1981), and MEDLARS (1974-1981) under surgical-patient and relating this to psychological stress, preoperative intervention, coping behavior, patient education, and therapeutic relationship. This process revealed over 100 studies. They were then individually examined for possible inclusion in this review. Admitted were studies in which there was (1) an intervention that was educational or psychological, (2) a population of surgical patients, (3) an experimental design that included treatment and control groups, and (4) a measure of length of stay that permitted size of effect estimates to be calculated. Of the 34 studies 18 were conducted by nurses. The rest were conducted by physicians or psychologists.

Of the 13 studies in the review by Mumford and associates, 10 are in our sample. One was omitted because it did not involve surgical patients (Gruen, 1975); another did not provide sufficient data for calculating size of effect estimates (Healey, 1968); and by our standards the third had an inadequate control group derived not from patients in the same hospital as the treated subjects, but from national length-of-stay statistics on teaching and nonteaching hospitals provided by the Commission on Professional and Hospital Activities (Kolouch, 1962).

In this report we shall use two indicators of the size of effect: One in the traditional measure of effect size (ES) first developed by Cohen (1969) and popularized by Glass (1977; Glass et al., 1981). ES depends on knowledge of a standard deviation (ES $= \dfrac{\text{mean } X_c - \text{mean } X_e}{Sd_c}$).[1] The second in the percentage difference in days of hospitalization between control and experimental groups, which we call PD (PD $= \dfrac{\text{mean } X_c - \text{mean } X_e}{\text{mean } X_c} \times 100$). The ES and PD measures are related, of course, having the same numerator. Since the PD measure does not require knowledge of a standard deviation, sample sizes are slightly larger when it is used than when the ES measure is used. For our meta-analysis PD values are calculated for 32 studies and ES values for 28. Since some studies include more than one experimental group, there are 65 comparisons in all between treatment and control groups. Of these, PD values are calculated for 61, and ES values for 55.

An important decision in meta-analysis is whether to use a sample of studies or a sample of comparisons. On one hand, analyses based on a sample of comparisons are not advantageous because they give a disproportionate weight to studies with more treatment groups and thus with more comparisons with controls. They also neglect instances where theory was used to predict that some treatments would produce larger effects than others, for such treatments are considered equivalent to treatments where smaller effects were expected. On the other hand, analyses based on all possible comparisons increase the sample size for study and take cognizance of all the available tests of a relationship. Because it is not clear in the present case that either a sample of studies or comparisons is to be preferred, we report two sets of analyses: one with a sample of all treatment-control comparisons, and the other with each study providing only one ES or PD value. For the studies with multiple experimental groups, the decision rule for selecting the single treatment is as follows. When predictions were made, we sampled only the treatment predicted to be the most effective; if no prediction was made and the design was factorial, we sampled the treatment that combined the most individual components of the intervention; and in all other instances we took the mean of the various experimental treatment groups as the single indicator of length of stay. Therefore, four analyses are presented. Estimates of mean effect size (mean ES) and mean percentage difference (mean PD) are reported for a sample of studies as well as a sample of comparisons.

The literature on psycho-educational interventions with surgical patients spans many years. The earliest study in our review was published in 1964 and the latest in 1981. The interventions have been administered by nurses, physicians, psychologists, pastoral counselors, and social workers. While most have involved face-to-face interactions, printed and taped materials have also been used both alone and in combination with face-to-face interactions. A wide range of patients and hospital settings have been used. The surgeries for which the patients were scheduled included broad categories (e.g., elective, abdominal, and orthopedic) as well as specific types (e.g., inguinal hernia repair, cholecystectomy, and coronary artery bypass grafting). The hospital settings included major medical centers, veteran's administration hospitals, and HMO affiliated hospitals, as well as community hospitals with and without religious affiliations. The interventions have involved such activities as providing the patient with information about what to expect in the way of procedures, pain, sensations, and activities; teaching the patient exercises that should promote recovery by preventing complications or reducing anxiety (e.g., the stir-up regime or relaxation exercises); and providing interactions with a health care provider that are designed to reduce patients' anxiety or to enhance their ability to cope with the hospitalization experience.

RESULTS

Magnitude Estimates

Mumford et al. found a mean ES value of .25. With our larger sample of studies, the mean ES values are almost double that estimate irrespective of whether the analysis is based on a sample of studies (.48) or of comparisons (.49). Mumford et al. found that hospital stay was reduced by almost two days (equivalent to a mean PD = 19.1%). Our estimates are smaller. We found an average decrease of 1.64 days for the sample of studies (mean PD = 16.0%) and of 1.21 days for the sample of comparisons (mean PD = 13.4%). Separate analyses of the 18 studies conducted by nurses result in similar estimates of effect. Mean ES values are .54 (sample of studies) and .50 (sample of comparisons); mean PD values are 16.4% (sample of studies) and 13.3% (sample of comparisons).

Table 1 summarizes the studies included in our data analysis. Although there are differences between Mumford et al. and ourselves in magnitude of effect estimates, the direction of findings is the same in both reviews. In this sense we replicate the findings of Mumford and associates. However, our estimates do differ from theirs, being larger using the ES measure and smaller using PD—an apparent anomaly that we discuss later.

Ruling Out Alternative Explanations

Sources of potential bias are explored by partitioning the population of studies into those that do and do not contain the potentially biasing elements. The mean ES and mean PD values for the respective subsets are then examined to determine if the effect is absent or greatly diminished in the less biased studies. In the following results, statistical testing is not done for two reasons. First, the conceptual need is to determine whether any effect is still apparent once sources of bias are not operating; this is not the same as testing whether the presence of a potential source of bias makes a difference when contrasted with a situation where the source of bias is not operating. We want to know whether there is an effect in unbiased tests; not whether bias adds to the effect estimates. Second, no widely accepted procedure for statistically testing the difference in effect sizes from independent studies currently exists (Hedges, 1982), although work in this area is in progress (Hedges & Olkin, Note 2). Hence, even if it were advisable to conduct statistical tests comparing effect sizes, this cannot yet be done.

To what extent do these estimates of the reduction in hospital stay depend on sampling biases associated with the editorial decision to publish? We coded each study as to whether it was published or not. Although the effect size estimates are

TABLE 1   Summary of 34 Studies Included in Meta-Analysis

Author, Date, and Surgical Condition	Publication Source	Subject Assignment	Experimental Group(s)		PD	Side of Effect	ES
			N	Days Less of Hospitalization			
Best (1981) orthopedic	D	R	40	1.33	28.4	+	.57
Christopherson and Pfeiffer (1980) coronary artery bypass	J	NR	17	2.50	18.8	+	.42
			18	2.10	15.8	+	.35
Risser et al. (1980) upper abdominal	J	NR	9	2.70	18.9		f
Hill (1979) cataract	D	R	10	.06	1.9	+	.08
			10	− .12	− 3.8	−	.15
				− .18	− 5.6	−	.23
Pickett (1979) cholecystectomy	D	NR	16	.12	1.6		f
			16	.01	.1		f
Dziurbejko and Larkin (1978) gynecologic	J	R	7	4.44	39.6	+	.88
			7	2.86	25.7	+	.56
Johnson et al. (1978b) Experiment 1[g] cholecystectomy	J	R	13	1.07	16.7		1.27
			12	.58	9.1	+	.69
			14	.52	8.1	+	.62
			14	.39	6.1	+	.46
			14	.19	2.5	+	.19
Johnson et al. (1978a) Experiment 1[g] cholecystectomy	J	NR	10	1.15	18.0	+	1.36
			9	1.15	18.0	+	1.36
			8	1.06	16.0	+	1.26
			11	1.16	18.2	+	1.38
			13	.84	13.2	+	1.00
Johnson et al. (1978a) Experiment 2[g] hernia	J	NR	8	.53	14.7	+	.59
			9	.29	8.0	+	.32
			10	.53	14.7	+	.59
			11	.14	3.9	+	.16
			12	.63	17.5	+	.70

TABLE 1 Continued

Author, Date, and Surgical Condition	Publication Source	Subject Assignment	Experimental Group(s)		Size of Effect	
			N	Days Less of Hospitalization	PD	ES
Van Steenhouse (1978) cardiac	D	R	18	− .83	− 7.7	− .20
			18	− .33	− 3.1	− .08
Archuleta et al. (1977) elective	B	NR	248	− .59	− 8.6	− .15
Ortmeyer (1977) orthopedic	D	R	30	.80	12.1	+ .39
			30	.60	9.1	+ .29
Wilson (1977) cholescystectomy; and hysterectomy	D	R	18	.80	10.2	+ .58
			18	1.10	14.0	+ .80
			17	1.02	12.9	+ .74
Felton et al. (1976) major	J	R	25	3.00	21.4	f
			12	0.00	0.0	f
Fortin and Krowac (1976) hernia; cholescystectomy; and hysterectomy	J	R	37	.09	1.4	+ .04
Surman et al. (1974) cardiac	J	R	20	4.30	21.9	f
Davis (1973) general	D	R	13	1.53	23.4	+ .40
Lindeman and Setzer (1973) elective: pediatric and adult	J	R	19	.89	29.7	+ .30
			90	− .05	− 0.8	− .02
Schmitt and Wooldridge (1973) elective	J	R	25	2.89[h]	24.4	+ .48
Solomon (1973) thoracic	D	R	8	6.51	42.4	+1.10
Lindeman (1972) elective	J	R	158	2.01	23.2	+ .42
Florell (1971) orthopedic	D	NR	70	1.77	29.0	+ .77
			30	1.20	19.7	+ .52
Lucas (1975) cardiac	D	R	9	2.22	17.4	+1.08
			9	.56	4.4	+ .27

(continued)

TABLE 1 Continued

Author, Date, and Surgical Condition	Publication Source	Subject Assignment	Experimental Group(s)		Size of Effect	
			N	Days Less of Hospitalization	PD	ES
Cohen (1975) hernia, and cholescystectomy	D	R	40	f	f	+ .12
			37	f	f	+ .34
			39	f	f	+ .21
Hart (1975) cardiac	D	R	20	− .20	− 1.6	− .21
Hegyvary and Chamings (1975) abdominal hysterectomy	J	R	20	.90	12.0	+ .63
			30	.30	4.1	+ .28
Langer et al. (1975) elective, 6 types	J	R	15	1.40	18.4	f
			15	1.96	25.8	f
			15	.40	5.3	f
Budd and Brown (1974) cardiac	J	NR	16	3.80	22.1	f
Lindeman and Van Aernam (1971) elective	J	NR	107	1.91	22.6	+ .25
Andrew (1970) hernia	J	NR	22	.46	6.8	+ .20
Chapman (1970) hernia	J	R	17	1.99	25.2	+ .46
			18	1.60	20.3	+ .37
Delong (1970) cholescystectomy; and abdominal hysterectomy	J	R	31	1.05	14.7	+ .52
Johnson (1965) cholescystectomy; and abdominal hysterectomy	B	R	14	1.14	13.1	+ .78
Egbert et al. (1964) abdominal	J	R	51	2.70	f	+ .54

greater for published studies than for dissertations, Table 2 shows that the differences do not appear to be large.

To what extent does the size of effect depend on when a research report or dissertation was published? Table 2 shows the size of effect estimates for three time periods: 1970-1973, 1974-1977, and 1978-1981. For the percentage difference measure, effects are greatest in the earliest period, next most in the latest period, and least in the middle. For the effect size measure, the effects are greatest in the latest period, next most in the earliest period, and least in the middle. These results suggest that the effect is still found in the most recent years even though hospital stays have declined in these years nationwide.

To what extent do the results depend on physician awareness of the subject's treatment condition? Only 12 of our studies reported that the patient's physician was unaware of the group assignment of subjects. In the other studies the awareness level of physicians was not reported, making it unclear whether they knew of the assignment. We compared effect estimates from studies explicitly reporting that physicians were kept blinded with estimates from those that did not make this claim. By three of four measures, larger effects were obtained when it was explicit that the physicians were blind to treatment assignment. As Table 2 shows, the mean ES values were .71 versus .33 for studies and .63 versus .36 for comparisons; the mean PD values were 17.8% versus 15.1% for studies and 12.8% versus 13.9% for comparisons. Thus, it seems that physician awareness of group assignment has not spuriously caused the effect attributed to psycho-educational interventions.

Our sample consisted of 23 studies with random assignment of subjects, and 10 with a quasi-experimental design.[2] As Table 2 shows, the method of subject assignment is not systematically related to the size of effect estimates. However, the internal validity of a study cannot be judged by subject assignment alone since systematic attrition can operate even with random assignment. Therefore, we conducted a further test. Studies were rated as higher in internal validity if they used random assignment, if the overall attrition was less than 15%, and if the difference in attrition between groups was less than 10%. Studies not meeting these criteria were rated as lower in internal validity. As Table 2 shows, for three of the four measures the size of effect estimates are larger for studies with higher internal validity. This suggests that the effectiveness of psycho-educational interventions does not depend on internal validity threats spuriously inflating the results.

To what extent does the extra attention or special status resulting from study participation explain these findings? Seven of the studies included a placebo control group in which patients received as much attention from the researcher as experimentals—indeed, in one instance (Davis, 1973) they even received more—and they were presumably aware of their participation in a research study. In four cases this was the only source of controls (Delong, 1970; Hill, 1979; Langer, Janis, & Wolfer, 1975; Van Steenhouse, 1978). In the other three, there was both a placebo and a usual care control group (Davis, 1973; Lucas, 1975; Solomon, 1973). In the analyses previously reported, which included these three studies, the intervention was contrasted with the length of stay of controls receiving usual care. However, for

TABLE 2   Average Size of Effect Estimates by Publication Form, Publication Date, Physician Blinding, Subject Assignment, and Internal Validity

| | Studies | | | | All Comparisons | | | |
| | ES | | PD | | ES | | PD | |
	Mean	N	Mean	N	Mean	N	Mean	N
Publication Form								
Journal or Book	.51	(16)	17.2	(20)	.57	(33)	14.9	(40)
Dissertation	.45	(12)	14.2	(12)	.36	(22)	10.4	(21)
Publication Date								
1970-1973	.47	(10)	22.6	(10)	.44	(13)	21.6	(13)
1974-1977	.28	(8)	11.0	(11)	.36	(15)	10.6	(19)
1978-1981	.63	(8)	15.1	(10)	.57	(25)	11.3	(28)
Physician Blinded								
Yes	.71	(11)	17.8	(11)	.63	(26)	12.8	(28)
Questionable	.33	(17)	15.1	(21)	.36	(29)	13.9	(33)
Subject Assignment[a]								
Random	.48	(21)	16.7	(22)	.42	(39)	13.2	(41)
Nonrandom	.54	(6)	15.0	(9)	.68	(15)	13.9	(19)
Internal Validity[a]								
Higher	.54	(18)	18.2	(20)	.47	(31)	14.2	(36)
Lower	.41	(8)	12.6	(11)	.57	(23)	12.0	(19)

NOTE: a. One study did not report subject assignment (Andrew, 1970). It is excluded from this analysis.

the analyses that follow, ES and PD values were recalculated in order to contrast the intervention with the placebo controls from these three studies and the placebo controls from the four studies that had only placebo controls. The mean ES values for the studies where the intervention is contrasted with a placebo control group are .36 (n = 6, sample of studies) and .15 (n = 10, sample of comparisons). The average decrease in hospital stay for these studies is .77 days based on a sample of studies (n = 7; mean PD = 9.7%) and .55 days based on a sample of comparisons (n = 10; mean PD = 6.2%). These estimates are distinctly smaller than those obtained from contrasting the intervention with usual care, and they suggest that much of the effect reported by Mumford et al. and by ourselves in earlier analyses may be attributable to a Hawthorne effect.

DISCUSSION

Is the Effect Valid?

The present analyses revealed that the relationship between psycho-educational interventions and decreased hospital stay does not totally depend on whether the research was published, when it was published, whether the physician was aware of treatment assignment, or whether threats to internal validity inflated relationships. Because of this we can be all the more confident that the interventions discussed here probably do shorten hospital stays.

However, the size of effect estimates were much smaller when placebo controls were used instead of usual care controls. At first glance this suggests the viability of an alternative interpretation based on the Hawthorne effect. Before accepting this conclusion, two relationships should be noted. First, great variability exists in the size of effect estimates for research using placebo controls. Those studies result in some of the higher estimates obtained (DeLong, 1971; Langer et al., 1975; Lucas, 1976), as well as some of the lower ones (Hill, 1979; Van Steenhouse, 1978). Thus, while the estimates of average effect are much lower in studies using placebo controls, this is not a necessary nor a consistent finding.

Second, there was great variability in the content of the placebo interventions. In one study the placebo was a brief tape recording about the preadmission process, the facilities, the physical environment, and the rules of the hospital (Delong, 1971). In another study, involving cardiac surgery patients, the placebo was an interview discussing the patient's decision to have surgery, physical limitations imposed by the disease, what the patient had been told by the doctors and nurses, and any questions that the patient brought up (Van Steenhouse, 1978). This suggests not only that the content of the placebo treatments varied, but also that they may sometimes have functioned as an attenuated form of the psycho-educational treatment. Indeed, Solomon (1973) and Van Steenhouse (1978) explicitly noted this.

A partial test of the influence of different types of placebos can be made by reviewing the three studies with both placebo and usual care control groups. In Solomon (1973) the placebo involved a tour of the intensive care unit, while the experimental treatment was a psychotherapeutic interview combined with the same tour. Solomon explicitly noted that, in addition to providing attention, the tour may also have decreased fears by providing information about what to expect in the hospital. In Davis (1973) the placebo involved several pastoral visits whose effects were contrasted with those of an experimental treatment based on a specific crisis intervention technique. The author noted that patients in the pastoral visit placebo group frequently talked about their operations and other matters in a way that could be interpreted as seeking support or help in a crisis. The researcher made no note that such discussion was discouraged. In Lucas (1976) the placebo was a brief interview with an interested psychologist, and the researcher noted that conversation was specifically guided away from the operation, recovery, or the future. This was presumably to create a placebo group with minimal overlap with the content of the psycho-educational treatment.

In the first two cases above, the placebo groups had shorter average hospital stays than the usual care controls (5.9 days in Study 1 and 1.1 days in Study 2), and the treatment groups had shorter average hospital stays than placebo groups (.6 days in Study 1 and .4 days in Study 2). In the third study, where placebo and treatment groups were less similar, the placebo and treatment groups differed (2.22 days in treatment 1 and .56 days in treatment 2), but the placebo and usual care groups did not differ at all. The implication of such results is that where the placebo and treatment groups receive somewhat comparable treatment content, results do not differ much in the extent to which length of hospital stay is reduced; but where treatments are more dissimilar, the differences in hospital stay are greater. It seems likely, therefore, that the small difference we have noted between treatment and placebo groups in the outcome variable is due, at least in part, to the similarity between the two groups in the information and psychosocial support conveyed to patients in some studies.

The relationship between publication data and the two measures of effect is somewhat puzzling since the largest PD values were found in the 1970-1973 time period, and the largest ES values were found in the 1978-1981 time period. This difference is probably due to the fact that later studies are conducted with more homogeneous patient populations. This should decrease the variance in length of stay and thus inflate ES estimates, thereby masking any relationship between ES and date of publication. However, a time-bound decrease in variance would be less likely to influence PD estimates and to mask a true relationship between publication date and size of effect.

The implication is that with the passage of time, the psycho-educational interventions have had a smaller effect on the length of hospital stay. Is this decrease large enough to significantly diminish the potential policy relevance of the finding under discussion? Of the studies published in or after 1978, most demonstrated a decrease in average hospital stay for patients receiving psycho-educational interventions (see Table 1). The average decrease in these studies was 1.31 days (n = 10; mean PD = 15.1%) for a sample of studies and .90 days (n = 28; mean PD = 11.3%) for a sample of comparisons. These estimates are lower than the averages for the total sample, but they do not completely obscure the effect and a decrease in hospital stay of about one day is still achieved. It is especially worth noting that the most recent study in our sample (Best, 1981) was conducted in a hospital that was not experiencing an empty bed problem and that subscribed to a formal policy of patient education. Nonetheless, a decrease in hospital stay of 1.33 days (PD = 28.4%) was found despite the ongoing education and the lack of pressure to keep patients in the hospital longer.

How Large is the Effect?

The estimate of effect size in this review is almost double that of Mumford and associates (.49 versus .25), while our estimate of percentage decrease in days of hospitalization is lower (14.7% versus 19.1%). Why should this be so?

First consider the percentage decrease in hospital stay. We recalculated the average difference in days between treatment and control groups for the studies reported in Table 1 of Mumford and associates, omitting Gruen's (1975) study, which did not involve surgical patients, and Kolouch's (1962) study because of the extreme nonequivalence of its control group. The average difference in hospitalization between experimental and controls is 1.44 days (mean PD = 14.5%). This is much closer to our own estimates of 1.64 days (mean PD = 16.0%, sample of studies) or 1.21 days (mean PD = 13.4%, sample of comparisons).

Next, consider the difference between our estimate of mean ES and Mumford and associates'. Our review has many more studies with patients scheduled for only one type of surgery than does the review by Mumford and associates (41% versus 15%). As one might expect, the variance in hospital stay is lower for a specific surgery than for a collection of different surgeries, and this may explain why the effect size measure (whose denominator is a standard deviation) is higher in our meta-analysis than in that of Mumford and associates.

Despite these differences in size of effect estimates, it is important to note two things. First, the direction of findings is the same in both reviews. Second, since our sample included a broader range of hospitals, patients, types of surgery, modes of treatment delivery, and health care providers, the phenomenon under review is demonstrated across a more heterogeneous sample of persons, settings, and times. Such robustness implies that psycho-educational interventions may be particularly useful in reducing health care costs, since their effectiveness is not likely to be contingent upon particular hospitals, surgeries, care givers, and so on.

Implications for Nursing

Psycho-educational nursing care is a well-accepted component of the nursing role as prescribed (American Nursing Association, 1973; Bird, 1955; Joint Commission on Accreditations of Hospitals, 1981; Sutherland, 1981).

This review has documented the effectiveness of psycho-educational interventions in reducing the length of hospital stay, and thus has documented the potential effectiveness of systematic patient education. Since the experimental interventions were compared with care as usual, the present review also suggests that, at least in some clinical settings, there is a need to improve the psycho-educational care that is given.

The potential cost saving to the nation would be enormous if psycho-educational interventions could be consistently implemented with all surgical patients and if, as we expect, a reduction in hospital stays resulted. But who should deliver these interventions? Nurses are not unique in their ability to achieve reductions in hospital stay when they administer the intervention, for psychologists, physicians, and pastoral counselors have also been among the treatment givers in studies resulting in a reduction in hospital stay.

From a policy perspective, however, nurses are available in large numbers in all hospitals. Moreover, they are uniquely available to patients, given the round-the-clock nature of nursing care. But, before we accept that nurses are the ideal treatment providers, we have to note that this may appear to be prescribing a new task for professionals who are already overburdened, and whose numbers are not likely to increase dramatically in the immediate future. However, against this is the position that a comprehensive protocol for psycho-educational nursing care would not involve a new task for nurses. Rather, it would involve the systematic administration of an intervention that is already prescribed as a nursing function and is probably already being practiced with varying degrees of sophistication and time commitment. Consequently, the increase in nursing time that would be required is probably less than a total of one hour per patient. And, it is against this standard that the expected benefit in terms of patient recovery, as well as patient and nurse satisfaction, should be judged.

NOTES

1. Glass et al. (1981) provide formulas for estimating ES values from certain statistical values.

2. Andrew (1970) did not report the manner of subject assignment. This study is excluded from the analyses on subject assignment and internal validity.

REFERENCE NOTES

1. Commission on Professional and Hospital Activities. Personal communication, March 1982.

2. Hedges, L., & Olkin, I. Synthesis of Independent Research Studies: The Literature and Statistical Procedures. Papers presented at the meeting of the American Educational Research Association, New York, March 1982.

REFERENCES

American Nurses Association. Standards of nursing practice. Kansas City: American Nurses Association, 1973.

ANDREW, J. M. Recovery from surgery with and without preparatory instruction, for three coping styles. Journal of Personality and Social Psychology, 1970, 15, 223-226.

ARCHULETA, V., PLUMMER, O. B., & HOPKINS, K. D. A demonstration model for patient education: A model for the project "Training Nurses to Improve Patient Education." Boulder, CO: Western State Commission for Higher Education, 1979.

BEST, J. K. Reducing length of hospital stay and facilitating the recovery process of orthopedic surgical patients through crisis intervention and pastoral care. Unpublished doctoral dissertation, Northwestern University, 1981.

BIRD, B. Psychological aspects of preoperative and postoperative care. American Journal of Nursing, 1955, 55, 685-687.

BUDD, S., & BROWN, W. Effect of a reorientation technique on post cardiotomy delirium. Nursing Research, 1974, 23, 341-348.

CHAPMAN, J. S. Effects of different nursing approaches on psychological and physiological responses. Nursing Research Reports, 1970, 5(1), 5-7.

CHRISTOPHERSON, B., & PFEIFFER, C. Varying the timing of information to alter preoperative anxiety and postoperative recovery in cardiac surgery patients. Heart and Lung, 1980, 9, 854-861.

COHEN, F. Psychological preparation, coping, and recovery from surgery. (Doctoral dissertation, University of California, Berkeley, 1975). Dissertation Abstracts International, 1976, 37, 454B.

COHEN, J. Statistical Power Analysis for the Behavioral Sciences. New York: Academic Press, 1969.

COOK, T. D., & CAMPBELL, D. T. Quasi-Experimentation: Design and analysis issues for field settings. Chicago: Rand McNally, 1979.

COOK, T. D., & LEVITON, L. C. Reviewing the literature: A comparison of traditional methods with meta-analysis. Journal of Personality, 1980, 48, 449-472.

DAVIS, H. S. The role of a crisis intervention treatment in the patient's recovery from elective surgery. (Doctoral dissertation, Northwestern University, 1973). Dissertation Abstracts International, 1973, 36, 3490B.

DELONG, R. D. Individual differences in patterns of anxiety arousal, stress-relevant information and recovery from surgery. (Doctoral dissertation, University of California, Los Angeles, 1970). Dissertation Abstracts International, 1971, 32, 554B.

DZIURBEJKO, M. M., & LARKIN, J. C. Including the family in preoperative teaching. American Journal of Nursing, 1979, 79, 1892-1894.

EGBERT, L. D., BATTIT, G. E., WELCH, C. E., & BARLETT, M. K. Reduction of postoperative pain by encouragement and instruction of patients. New England Journal of Medicine, 1964, 270, 825-827.

FELTON, G., HUSS, K., PAYNE, E. A., & SRSIC, K. Preoperative nursing intervention with the patient for surgery: Outcomes of three alternative approaches. International Journal of Nursing Studies, 1976, 13, 83-96.

FLORELL, J. L. Crisis intervention in orthopedic surgery. (Doctoral dissertation, Northwestern University, 1971). Dissertation Abstracts International, 1971, 32, 3633B.

FORTIN, F., & KIROUAC, S. A randomized controlled trial of preoperative patient education. International Journal of Nursing Studies, 1976, 13, 11-24.

GLASS, G. V. Integrating findings: The meta-analysis of research. Review of Research in Education, 1977, 5, 351-379.

GLASS, G. V, McGAW, B., & SMITH, M. L. Meta-analysis in social research. Beverly Hills, CA: Sage, 1981.

GRUEN, W. Effects of brief psychotherapy during the hospitalization period on the recovery process in heart attacks. Journal of Consulting and Clinical Psychology, 1975, 43, 223-232.

HART, R. R. Recovery of open heart surgery patients as a function of a taped hypnotic induction procedure. (Doctoral dissertation, Texas Technical University, 1975). Dissertation Abstracts International, 1976, 36, 5259B.

HEALY, K. M. Does preoperative instruction make a difference? American Journal of Nursing, 1968, 68, 62-67.

HEDGES, L. Estimation and testing for differences in effect size: A comment on Hsu. Psychological Bulletin, 1982, 91, 691-693.

HEGYVARY, S. T., & CHAMINGS, P. A. The hospital setting and patient care outcomes. Journal of Nursing Administration, 1975, March-April, 29-32; May, 36-42.

HILL, B. J. Sensory information, behavioral instructions and coping with sensory alteration surgery. (Doctoral dissertation, Wayne State University, 1979). Dissertation Abstracts International, 1979, 40, 2381B.

Joint Commission on Accreditation of Hospitals. Accreditation manual for hospitals, 1981 edition. Chicago: Joint Commission on Accreditation of Hospitals, 1981.

JOHNSON, J. E. The influence of purposeful nurse-patient interaction on the patient's postoperative course. In Exploring progress in medical-surgical nursing practice ANA 1965 Regional Clinical Conferences. New York: American Nurses Association, 1966.

JOHNSON, J. E., FULLER, S. S., ENDRESS, M. P., & RICE, V. H. Altering patients' responses to surgery: An extension and replication. Research in Nursing and Health, 1978a, 1, 111-121.

JOHNSON, J. E., RICE, V. H., FULLER, S. S., & ENDRESS, M. P. Sensory information, instruction in a copying strategy, and recovery from surgery. Research in Nursing and Health, 1978, 1, 4-17.

KOLOUCH, F. T. Hypnosis and surgical convalescence: A study of subjective factors in postoperative recovery. American Journal of Clinical Hypnosis, 1964, 7, 120-129.

LANGER, E. J., JANIS, I. L., & WOLFER, J. A. Reduction of psychological stress in surgical patients. Journal of Experimental and Social Psychology, 1975, 11, 155-165.

LINDEMAN, C. A. Nursing intervention with the presurgical patient. Nursing Research, 1972, 21, 196-209.

LINDEMAN, C. A., & STETZER, S. I. Effect of preoperative visits by operating room nurses. Nursing Research, 1973, 22, 4-16.

LINDEMAN, C. A., & VAN AERNAM, B. Nursing intervention with the presurgical patient— the effects of structured and unstructured preoperative teaching. Nursing Research, 1971, 20, 319-332.

LUCAS, R. H. The affective and medical effects of different preoperative interventions with heart surgery patients. (Doctoral dissertation, University of Houston, 1975). Dissertation Abstracts International, 1976, 36, 5763b.

MUMFORD, E., SCHLESINGER, H. J., & GLASS, G. V. The effects of psychological intervention on recovery from surgery and heart attacks: An analysis of the literature. American Journal of Public Health, 1982, 72, 141-151.

ORTMEYER, J. A. Anxiety and repression coping styles, and treatment approaches in the integration of elective orthopedic surgical stress. (Doctoral dissertation, Northwestern University, 1977.) Dissertation Abstracts International, 1978, 38, 5536A.

PICKETT, C. Locus of control and intervention strategies with surgical patients. (Doctoral dissertation, Virginia Polytechnic University, 1979). Dissertation Abstracts International, 1978, 38, 5536.

RISSER, N. L., STRONG, A., & BITHER, S. The effect of an experimental teaching program on post-operative ventilatory function: A self-critique. Western Journal of Nursing Research, 1980, 2, 484-500.

SCHMITT, F. E., & WOOLDRIDGE, P. J. Psychological preparation of surgical patients. Nursing Research, 1973, 22, 108-116.

SOLOMON, A. J. The effect of a psychotherapeutic interview on the physical results of thoracic surgery. (Doctoral dissertation, California School of Professional Psychology, San Francisco, 1973). Dissertation Abstracts International, 1973, 34, 2319B.

SURMAN, O. S., HACKETT, T. P., & SILVERBERG, E. L. Usefulness of psychiatric intervention in patients undergoing cardiac surgery. Archives of General Psychiatry, 1974, 30, 830-835.

SUTHERLAND, M. Education in the medical care setting: Perceptions of selected registered nurses. Health Education, 1981, 11, 25-27.

VAN STEENHOUSE, A. L. A comparison of three types of presurgical psychological intervention with male open heart surgery patients. (Doctoral dissertation, Michigan State University, East Lansing, 1978). Dissertation Abstracts International, 1978, 39, 1449A.

WESTERMEYER, I. Education and counseling in hospital care. American Journal of Public Health, 1982, 72, 127-128.

WILSON, J. F. Determinants of recovery from surgery: Preoperative instruction, relaxation training and defensive structure. (Dissertation, University of Michigan, Ann Arbor, 1977). Dissertation Abstracts International, 1977, 38, 1476b.

24

Meta-Analysis of Research on Class Size and Its Relationship to Attitudes and Instruction

Mary Lee Smith and Gene V Glass

Features of 59 studies of this relationship were coded and quantified and 371 findings were transformed into a common metric for statistical integration. Analysis, based on a logarithmic model, revealed a substantial relationship between class size and teacher and pupil attitudes as well as instruction. Favorable teacher effects (workload, morale, attitudes toward students) are associated with smaller classes as are favorable effects on students (self-concept, interest in school, participation). Smaller classes are associated with greater attempts to individualize instruction and better classroom climate. The results complement those of a previous meta-analysis that showed positive effects of class size on achievement.

In earlier papers (Glass & Smith, 1978, 1979), we presented the results of a statistical integration of the research on the relationship between class size and achievement, identifying 80 studies and translating their separate results into a common metric. When this metric was summarized, a substantial relationship between class size and achievement was demonstrated. Those studies that employed rigorous controls yielded results which, taken together, showed that:

> As class-size increases, achievement decreases. A pupil, who would score at about the 63rd percentile on a national test when taught individually, would score at about the 37th percentile in a class of 40 pupils. The difference in being taught in a class of 20 versus a class of 40 is an advantage of ten percentile ranks .... Few resources at the command of educators will reliably produce effects of that magnitude. (1978, p.i.)

The present study is a companion piece to the 1979 study. The same literature search produced documents for both studies. The documents were described and categorized on the same set of characteristics, and the same

From Mary Lee Smith and Gene V Glass, "Meta-Analysis of Research on Class Size and Its Relationship to Attitudes and Instruction," 17(4) *American Educational Research Journal* 419-433 (Winter 1980). Copyright 1980, American Educational Research Association, Washington, D.C. Reprinted by permission.

procedures were used to quantify the outcomes generated in the documents. The statistical techniques were modified slightly as noted below because of the intervening development of improved techniques.

CODING CHARACTERISTICS OF THE STUDIES

Once the documents were identified and obtained, various characteristics of the research studies were coded or given quantitative descriptions. These features included the year the study was published, the source of the study, subject taught, duration of instruction, number of pupils, groups, and instructors; training, experience, and gender of instructors; age and ability of pupils, method of assigning pupils to groups, metric of outcome measure and domain of effect (see Table I).

QUANTIFICATION OF EFFECTS

A simple statistic was desired that would describe the relationship between the class size and its effects as determined by a study. No matter how many class sizes are compared in a study, the data can be reduced to some number of paired comparisons, a smaller class against a larger class. Certain differences in the findings must be attended to if the findings are later to be integrated. The most obvious differences involve the actual numbers of pupils in what are designated "smaller" and "larger" classes and the scale properties of the measure of effect. The actual class sizes compared must be preserved and become an essential part of our descriptive measure. The measurement scale properties can be handled by standardizing all mean differences in the effect (teaching process, affective outcomes) dividing by the within-group standard deviation. The eventual measure of relationship is straightforward and unobjectionable:

$$\Delta_{S-L} = \frac{\bar{X}_S - \bar{X}_L}{\hat{\sigma}},$$

where:

$\bar{X}_S$ is the estimated mean effect of the *smaller* class which contains S pupils;

$\bar{X}_L$ is the estimated mean effect of the *larger* class which contains L pupils; and

$\hat{\sigma}$ is the estimated within-class standard deviation assumed to be homogeneous across the two classes.

The resulting effect measures or Δ's (deltas) are in a common metric which may then be summarized across studies. The Δ's are standardized mean differences for a given pair of class sizes and as such are similar to z-scores. If one assumes normality of the distribution, it is possible to interpret a Δ_{S-L} of +1 to mean that the average pupil in the smaller class would score at the 84th percentile of the larger class.

TABLE I
Domain of Effects

Student Attitudes
  Attitudes toward teachers[a]
  Attitudes toward school or class[a]
  Self-concept[a]
  Mental health[a]
  Attitude toward educational program
  Motivation[a]
  Preference for class size[a]
  Attitude toward life[a]
Individualization
  Teacher knowledge of pupils[c]
  Amount of individual student-teacher interaction[c]
  Number or variety of activities[c]
  Amount of seatwork or students working on individual tasks[c]
  Amount of work in small groups[c]
  Teacher attention to individual students[c]
  Adaptation of teaching to individuals[c]
  Building foundation for independent work[c]
  Conferences with parents[c]
Student Participation in Learning
  Participation in discussions or lesson[a]
  Generation of and response to questions[a]
  Interest and enthusiasm for classwork[a]
  Attendance[a]
  Study habits[a]
  Student directedness[c]
  Student engagement[a]
  Difficulty in learning[a]
  Attention[a]
  On-task behavior[a]
Enrichment
  Creative activities[c]
  Dramatics[c]
  Divergent thinking[a]
  Use of manipulative materials[c]
Classroom Behavior
  Aggression[a]
  Off-task behavior[a]
  Apathy[a]
  Friction[a]
  Difficulty[a]
  Discipline[a]
  Dependence[a]
  Anxiety[a]
  Teacher control[c]
  Good behavior[a]
  Frustration[a]
  Character development[a]

TABLE I—*Continued*

Interpersonal Regard
  Peer group links[a]
  Student social interaction[a]
  Cohesiveness[c]
  Friendly teacher-student relationship[c]
  Sociometric choice[a]
Open Education
  Freedom of movement in the classroom[c]
  Student choice of activities[c]
  Informality[c]
  Social interaction[c]
Quality of Instruction
  Creative instruction[c]
  Use of teaching aids[c]
  Teacher organization and planning[b]
  General quality[c]
  Amount of material covered[c]
  Task structuring[c]
  Positive evaluation[c]
  Varied learning activities[c]
  Innovation[c]
Teacher Attitude
  Morale[b]
  Attitude toward students[b]
  Perceptions and satisfaction[b]
  Expectations for performance[c]
  Workload[b]
  Absences[b]
  Professional growth[b]
School Climate
  General climate[c]
  Innovations and adaptations in the school[c]
  Use of school space[c]

Note. Superscript numbers indicate the more general classification of effects.
[a] student effects
[b] teacher effects
[c] instructional effects

When a researcher failed to report means and standard deviations for class-size effects, it was necessary to solve for Δ's by using the F, t, χ^2, or correlational statistics and formulas documented elsewhere (Glass, 1978; Glass & Smith, 1979). Probit transformations were used on categorical data and data reported in percentages.

INTEGRATING RESULTS "DIFFERENT EFFECTS"

Those who flinch at the integration of results from reading tests and math tests will find the integration of all nonachievement effects even more disturbing. These effects range from the extent of individualized instruction in the classroom to student's attitude toward life. But what these variables have in common is that each has been chosen by a class size researcher as a hypothesized effect of varying class size. These researchers had in mind that each of these variables related in some way to the quality of education. Despite their uniqueness, each variable can be scaled so that one end represents educational improvement or the desired state of education. At the coarsest level of aggregation, these effects answer the question, "Are small classes better learning environments than large classes?"

We moved away from this coarse level of aggregation to a more specific one in which effects were separated into (1) affective effects on pupils, (2) effects on teachers, and (3) effects on instructional environments and processes (see Table I). This system for scaling and categorizing effects was one of several we tried out in an attempt to find contingent (interactive) class size effects. None of the other methods revealed such interactions, and they will not be reported here. At the most specific level were 10 categories of outcome, already presented in Table I, representing student attitudes, individualization of instruction, student participation in learning, enrichment activities, classroom behavior, interpersonal regard, "open education," general quality of instruction, teacher attitude, and school climate. Unfortunately, several of these more specific categories had insufficient data to detect interactions with the class size effects. Those which had sufficient data produced results consistent with those of the more general grouping described above and thus are not reported here.

STATISTICAL ANALYSIS

The overall advantage of small classes over large classes cannot be represented simply by an average of Δ_{S-L}. Both the small class size and the large class size represent a wide range of values. Many techniques have been employed to state the overall magnitude of Δ_{S-L} as a function of the size of the respective classes and the differences in the two class sizes which were compared. After developing and evaluating these techniques, the one selected was the logarithmic model, which best represented the relationship of class sizes and achievement effects (Barton & Glass, 1979).

The use of the logarithmic model arose from the expectation that class size and nonachievement effects might be related in something of a nonlinear fashion, reasoning that one pupil with one teacher acquires an interest in the subject of intensity A, two pupils develop somewhat less intense interest, three even less, and so on. Furthermore, the drop in interest from one to two pupils could be expected to be larger than the drop from two to three, which in turn is probably larger than the drop from three to four, and so on. A logarithmic curve represents one such relationship:

$$z = \alpha - \beta \log_e C + \epsilon, \tag{1}$$

where C denotes class size.

In formula (1), α represents the effect for a "class" of one person, because $\log_e 1 = 0$, and β represents the speed of decrease in effect as a class size increases.

Formula (1) cannot be fitted to data directly because z is not measured on a common scale across studies. This problem can be circumvented by calculating Δ_{S-L} for each comparison of a smaller and a larger class within a study. Then, from formula (1), one has

$$
\begin{aligned}
z_S - z_L = \Delta_{S-L} &= (\alpha - \beta \log_e S + \epsilon_1) - (\alpha - \beta \log_e L + \epsilon_2) \\
&= \beta(\log_e L - \log_e S) + \epsilon_1 - \epsilon_2 \tag{2} \\
&= \beta \log_e(L/S) + \epsilon.
\end{aligned}
$$

The model in formula (2) is particularly simple and straightforward. The values of Δ_{S-L} are merely regressed onto the logarithm of the ratio of the larger to the smaller class size, forcing the least squares regression line through the origin.

The solution for the least squares estimate of β as follows:

$$\hat{\beta} = \frac{\Sigma(\Delta_{S-L})(\log_e L/S)}{\Sigma(\log_e L/S)^2} \tag{3}$$

Once β is estimated from the data Δ_{S-L} and $\log_e(L/S)$, estimates of the outcomes variable z can be obtained for the full spectrum of the class size continuum by plotting the curve

$$\hat{z} = \hat{\beta} \log_e C. \tag{4}$$

The fit of the log model to the data can be examined by inspecting the scatterdiagram of Δ_{S-L} and $\log_e(L/S)$ for departures from linearity. Furthermore, if z is assumed to be normally distributed, then $\hat{z}$ can be transformed into percentile units that can be more readily understood by many readers.

The statistical model adopted for analysis of the data in this report is an improvement over the methods used to analyze the data in our earlier work on class size and achievement (Glass & Smith, 1978). In the former analysis, achievement was regressed onto a trivariate linear combination of L, S, and

S^2. The equation was fit by the method of least squares estimation. This method seemed reasonable, and it was suited to the anticipated curvilinear relationship between class size and achievement. However, it permitted no simple representation of the relationship in two dimensions where it might be easily seen and understood. Our attempt to reduce the four dimensional regression space to a plane was accomplished nonarbitrarily, but the solution by means of one or more "pivot points" seemed problematic: (1) there was more than one point that satisfied the conditions of "pivot point" and the reasons for choosing one over the others was unclear, (2) it was difficult to determine how well determined by data the line was that resulted from constraining the four dimensional regression surface into two dimensions; and (3) the entire business was clumsy and inelegant. The logarithmic model described above had none of these shortcomings, and in addition, it fit the data with a slightly smaller residual error mean square than the three parameter regression model.

FINDINGS

Despite the large range in class sizes, there was a substantial average value for Δ_{S-L}, amounting to almost one-half standard deviation across all types of nonachievement effect. This finding indicates that "smaller is better" even before we use the logarithmic model to define precisely what "smaller" is. The comparable finding for the achievement data—the uncorrected average Δ_{S-L}—was .011, a remarkable difference.

The subsequent findings are presented in a series of figures depicting curves of the magnitude of effect related to class size, first for the data as a whole and then for different parts of the data set. The metric used to display the effects consists of percentile ranks derived from standard-score equivalents. For convenience of interpretation, the curves have been standardized so that a class size of 30 represents the 50th percentile of effects.

THE DATA AS A WHOLE

Figure 1 plots the curve of effects calculated for class sizes 5 through 70 for the data as a whole. Table II contains the equivalent calculations. In column one, the class sizes against which the effects are calculated appear. Column two contains the values of $\hat{z}$, the class-size effects, calculated as follows: $\hat{z} = \hat{\beta}(\log_e C)$, where $\hat{\beta}$ is the estimated regression slope of Δ onto $\log_e(L/S)$, and C is class size. The third column is for z' and is the adjustment of the class-size effect so that a class size of 30 is the anchor point, at the 50th percentile of effects. The fourth column is the series of percentile equivalents for z'. Across the 371 Δ_{S-L}, the average is .49 and the standard deviation is .70. The value of $\hat{\beta}$ is .47.

These findings indicate that there is a beneficial effect on the general quality of the educational environment resulting from decreasing class size.

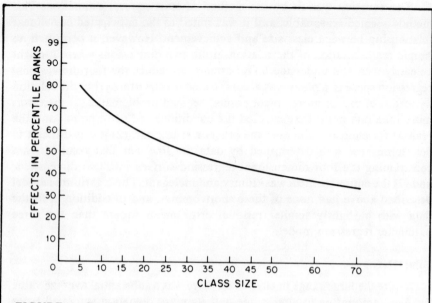

FIGURE 1. Graph of the relationship of class size and effects on attitudes and instruction (the data as a whole). $n_{\Delta_{S-L}} = 371$. $\hat{\beta} = .47$.

TABLE II

The Calculation of Class Size Effects for the Data as a Whole

Class Size	$\hat{z}$	z'	Percentile Rank
5	.76	.84	80th
10	1.08	.52	70th
15	1.27	.33	63rd
20	1.41	.19	58th
25	1.51	.09	54th
30	1.60	0	50th
35	1.67	−.07	47th
40	1.73	−.13	45th
50	1.83	−.23	41st
60	1.92	−.32	38th
70	2.00	−.40	37th

$$\beta = .47$$
$$\Delta_{S\,L} = .49$$
$$\sigma_{\Delta_{n\,L}} = .70$$
$$n_{\Delta_{n\,L}} = 371$$

Because the benefits experienced by the average pupil in a class of 30 pupils is set equal to the 50th percentile, the results indicate that if this pupil were placed in a class of size 20, he would experience nonachievement benefits superior to 58 percent of the pupils who are taught in classes of size 30. In a class of 10 pupils, he would benefit more than 70 percent of the pupils in classes of 30, though he started out at the median (50th percentile) of such classes. On the other hand, increasing his class from 30 to 40 pupils would result in a decline in nonachievement benefits; 55 percent of the pupils in classes of 30 pupils would now experience greater benefits than he. In a class of 60 pupils, this hypothetical average student would gain benefits exceeding only 38 percent of the pupils in classes of 30 pupils. Even at this coarsest level of aggregation, class size does make a difference. Figure 2 shows the effects of class size on achievement compared to its effects on attitudes and instruction.

The next task is to subdivide the data into more meaningful portions and to plot the class-size curve for each subset. This task answers questions about the interaction of class-size effects with different features of the studies. Unfortunately, we have many more such questions than the data can answer.

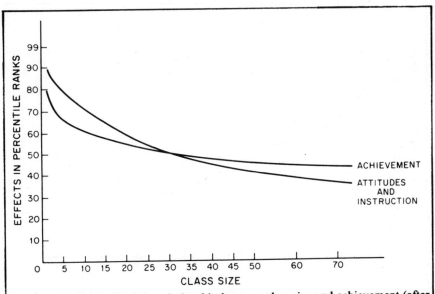

FIGURE 2. Graph of the relationship between class size and achievement (after Glass & Smith, 1979 and Barton & Glass, 1979) and the relationship between class size and attitudes and instruction (after Figure 1).

We cannot say, for instance, whether the class-size effect is different for boys and girls because the distribution of gender was constant across the studies and seldom were results reported separately for boys and girls. We cannot determine whether the class-size effect is different for teachers with different levels of experience because the researchers usually failed to record teacher experience. What we do have are answers to the following interactions: the class-size effect for various outcome classifications, pupil ages, and the sources, dates, and the internal validity of the studies.

OUTCOME CLASSIFICATIONS

Figure 3 contains the curves for effects related to class size for pupil affective effects, teacher effects, and instructional effects, respectively. The largest of the effects was on teachers. Thus, the truism is given empirical support: teachers feel better and feel they perform better in smaller classes. The effects on pupils is positive but not as dramatic as the effect of teachers. The $\hat{\beta}$ for 172 values of Δ_{S-L} is .47. The effect on instructional processes and environments is the same as the effect on pupil affect ($\hat{\beta} = .47$ for 155 Δ_{S-L}).

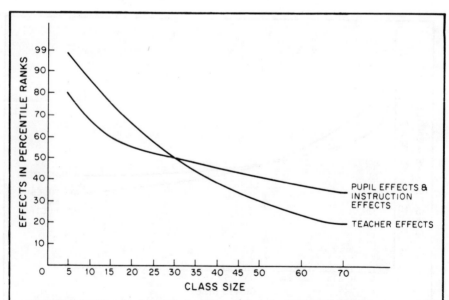

FIGURE 3. Graph of the relationship of class size and affective effects on pupils ($n_{\Delta_{S-L}} = 172$, $\beta = .47$); effects on teachers ($n_{\Delta_{S-L}} = 30$, $\beta = 1.03$), and effects on instructional process ($n_{\Delta_{S-L}} = 155$, $\beta = .47$).

The effects were arranged in more specific categories (see Table I), but five of these categories had insufficient data to estimate the logarithmic model. The results for the remainder are presented in Table III and support the conclusions reached above.

PUPIL AGE

The data were categorized by age of pupils and arranged in three groups: (1) 12 years and under; (2) 13 to 17; and (3) 18 and over. The class-size effect curve was plotted for each age group (see Figure 4).

These curves show definite differences in the class-size effect for the three age groups. The effect was greatest for pupils 12 years and under ($\hat{\beta} = .52$), somewhat less for pupils 13 to 17 ($\hat{\beta} = .47$), and least for pupils 18 and over ($\hat{\beta} = .38$). Thus the class-size effect does interact with pupil age.

FEATURES OF THE STUDIES

An important finding of the meta-analysis of class size and achievement was that well-designed studies produced quite different results from studies with minimal controls. The studies dealing with nonachievement effects were subdivided according to the method used by the researcher to assign subjects to experimental conditions (i.e., randomized, matched, "repeated measures" and uncontrolled).

Although all experimental methods produced positive class-size effects, there were insufficient data to estimate separately the logarithmic model for studies with "repeated measures" ($n = 18$). Otherwise, more pronounced results emanated from uncontrolled studies ($\hat{\beta} = .57$) than from studies using randomization ($\hat{\beta} = .44$) or matching ($\hat{\beta} = .49$) as the method of assigning

TABLE III

The Values of $\hat{\beta}$, Numbers of $\Delta_{S \cdot L}$ for Five Categories of Effect, with Differences in Effect Between Class Sizes of 10 and 40

Category of Effect	$n_{\Delta_{S \cdot L}}$	$\hat{\beta}$	Differences (Percentile Ranks)
Student Attitude	58	.43	29
Individualization	59	.36	19
Student Participation	109	.42	23
Enrichment	3	.70	—[a]
Pupil Behavior	17	.79	—[a]
Interpersonal Regard	19	.59	—[a]
Open Education	4	2.28	—[a]
Quality of Instruction	45	.31	17
Teacher Attitude	40	2.29	74
School Climate	7	2.11	—[a]

[a] Where nothing is recorded in column 3, there were insufficient data to estimate effects.

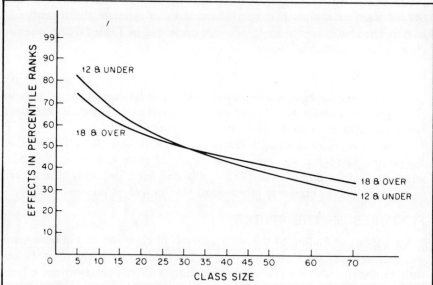

FIGURE 4. Graph of the relationship of class size and effects on attitudes and instruction for pupils of different age groups.

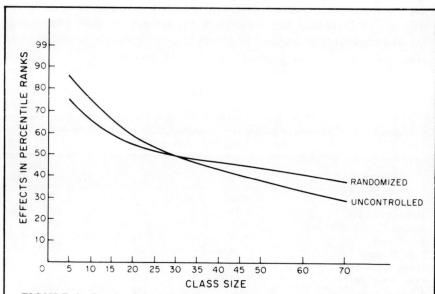

FIGURE 5. Graph of the relationship of class size and effects on attitudes and instruction for studies using randomization versus uncontrolled studies (studies using matching or repeated measures produced intermediate effects and are not plotted).

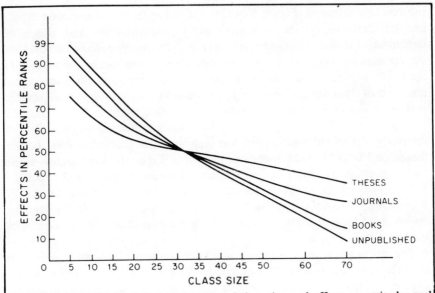

FIGURE 6. Graph of the relationship of class size and effects on attitudes and instruction for four sources of publication.

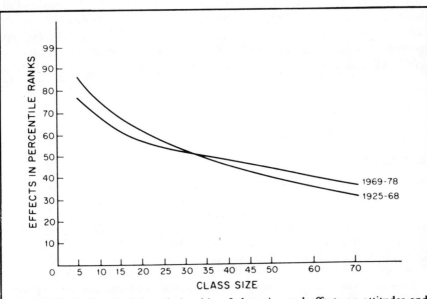

FIGURE 7. Graph of the relationship of class size and effects on attitudes and instruction for studies done 1925–1968 and 1969–1978.

subjects to treatments. Figure 5 depicts the curve for two contrasting experimental methods: effects of studies using randomization and effects of
uncontrolled studies. One explanation is that the poorly designed studies are
not credible and the overall class-size effect is inflated because 60 percent of
the effects come from uncontrolled studies. The more optimistic view is that
the effect of class size on the quality of education is a robust effect, detectable
even with less sophisticated and powerful research methods.

To find out whether the class-size effect was conditional on the source of
the study, the model was determined separately for journal articles, books,
theses, and unpublished papers and plotted in Figure 6. A difference in the
class-size effect was found in decreasing order from unpublished papers ($\hat{\beta}$
= 1.13) to books ($\hat{\beta}$ = .82) to journal articles ($\hat{\beta}$ = .54) to theses ($\hat{\beta}$ = .35).
We made no attempt to explain this ranking except to highlight the need for
reviewers to look at all sources of study lest a biased estimate of effects be
made.

The median year of publication was 1969 and the studies were so divided
to see if the class-size effect was greater in the more recent research (see
Figure 7). This was not the case. The class-size effect was greater in studies
published before 1969 ($\hat{\beta}$ = .59) than later ($\hat{\beta}$ = .42). The direction of results
was the same, the magnitude of relationship differed. This is a less suspicious
finding than if the direction differed.

In sum, reducing class size has beneficial effects both on cognitive and
affective outcomes and on the teaching process itself. These relationships
have not in the past been apparent because of an inability to deal with either
the class sizes or the effects precisely and quantitatively. Using meta-analysis
permits us to unravel the complexity and reveal the small but consistent
effects of class size.

REFERENCES

BARTON, M. A., & GLASS, G. V *Integrating studies that have quantitative independent
variables.* Paper presented at the annual meeting of the American Educational
Research Association, San Francisco, April 1979.

GLASS, G. V Integrating findings: The meta-analysis of research. In L. Shulman
(Ed.), *Review of research in education* (vol. 5). Itasca, Ill.: Peacock, 1978.

GLASS, G. V, & SMITH, M. L. *Meta-analysis of research on the relationship of class size
and achievement.* (No. OB-NIE-G-78-0103, Dr. L. S. Cahen, Project Director). San
Francisco: Far West Laboratory for Educational Research and Development,
1978.

GLASS, G. V, & SMITH, M. L. Meta-analysis of the research on class size and
achievement. *Educational Evaluation and Policy Analysis,* 1979, *1,* 2–16.

AUTHORS

MARY LEE SMITH, Assistant Professor, Laboratory of Educational Research, P.O. Box 249, University of Colorado, Boulder, Colorado 80309. *Specializations*: evaluation and research methodology, naturalistic inquiry, counseling psychology.

GENE V GLASS, Professor, Laboratory of Educational Research, P.O. Box 249, University of Colorado, Boulder, Colorado 80309. *Specialization*: statistics and psychoanalysis applied to education.

25

Identifying Features of
Effective Open Education

Rose M. Giaconia and Larry V. Hedges

The identification of general effects for open education is complicated by the fact that open education is not a single, well-defined treatment. Open education programs usually share some common philosophical assumptions about the nature, development, and learning of children. But open education programs differ widely in both the types and number of features of open education that are actually implemented (Horwitz, 1979). Some open education programs emphasize open space as the salient feature of a good open education program; other programs emphasize teaching practices and the role of the child; still other programs emphasize some combination of open space and teaching practices.

These naturally occurring variations in open education programs would not hinder efforts to draw general conclusions about the efficacy of open education if a consistent treatment effect could be identified across all the empirical studies of open education programs. Marshall (1981) examined several of the recent reviews of the effectiveness of open education and concluded that the results are inconclusive in spite of the increasingly sophisticated methodology used in successive reviews. A more recent synthesis of research (not examined by Marshall) used even more sophisticated statistical methods (Hedges, Giaconia, & Gage, Note 1). These investigators also concluded that open education produced a variety of effects across program implementations. Some open education programs produced particularly large positive effects for student outcomes such as self concept, reading achievement, creativity, locus of control, mathematics achievement, and favorable attitude toward school. Yet other open education programs yielded large negative effects for these same student outcomes.

Marshall (1981) argued that one reason for the variability in outcomes associated with open education is that the term "open education" does not uniquely define a treatment. She argued that open classrooms may vary in the extent to which they implement various component features of open education. Variations in the effectiveness of open education may therefore be due to variations in the specific

This research was supported by the Spencer Foundation. We thank N. L. Gage for his advice and encouragement.

From Rose M. Giaconia and Larry V. Hedges, "Identifying Features of Effective Open Education," original manuscript. Copyright © 1983 by Sage Publications, Inc.

component features of openness that are implemented in various classrooms. Marshall suggested that future research on the effectiveness of open education should "consider the separate component dimensions of open education" (p. 181) and attempt to relate these separate dimensions (features) to educational outcomes.

This article reports an attempt to relate the observed variability in the features of open education that were implemented in different open education programs to the observed variability in program effects. In order to achieve this end, this article (1) suggests a strategy for identifying effective versus less effective open education programs by use of an unbiased estimate of effect size rather than the statistical significance of results reported; (2) identifies features of open education that may or may not be present in open education programs; and (3) determines which of these features distinguish more effective from less effective open education programs.

THE OPEN EDUCATION DEBATE

The relative merits of open and traditional education have been a subject of debate since the time of Socrates (Broudy & Palmer, 1965). Over the years a plethora of terms have emerged for innovative educational programs that all seem to share some common philosophical assumptions and observable features of open education, e.g., progressive education, informal education, free school, open space school, open corridor school, integrated day plan, alternative school, and so on. In recent times anecdotal evidence and logical analysis have yielded to empirical research as evidence in the open versus traditional education debate. Proponents of both open and traditional education have tried to bolster their claims about the efficacy of open or traditional education with systematic empirical studies of open education programs. Horwitz (1979) identified over 200 of these empirical studies.

The persistence of the open education debate and the large number of empirical studies that have been generated by this debate both suggest the importance of attempts to search for meaningful ways to summarize the empirical findings. Three of these recent attempts will be reviewed briefly: a review by Horwitz (1979), a meta-analysis by Peterson (1979), and a meta-analysis by Hedges, Giaconia, and Gage (Note 1). A fourth review, a meta-analysis by Hetzel, Rasher, Butcher, and Walberg (Note 2), will not be discussed because the sample of studies, methods, and results parallel those of Peterson (1979).

THE REVIEW BY HORWITZ

Horwitz (1979) identified about 200 empirical studies that evaluated open education programs. Most of these studies involved comparisons of an open education program with a traditional education program. Studies were included in the review if the educational treatment had either been explicitly labeled by the term "open" or if it had been described as having characteristics generally ascribed to open education, such as flexibility of space, student choice of activity, richness of learning materials, integration of curriculum areas, and more individual and small-group than large-group instruction.

Nine student outcome variables were reported in this review: academic achievement, self concept, attitude toward school, creativity, independence and conformity, curiosity, anxiety and adjustment, locus of control, and cooperation.

Horwitz used a box score method to summarize findings across the studies. That is, for each student outcome variable, he tallied the number of studies whose results could be classified as either "open better," "traditional better," "mixed results," or "no significant differences." Conclusions were drawn about the effects of open education on the basis of which category received the most tallies. Horwitz found that in many instances the studies showing no significant differences or mixed results outnumbered those studies showing open better or traditional better.

For the student outcome variables academic achievement, self concept, anxiety and adjustment, and locus of control, the no significant differences category received the most tallies. For the student outcome variables attitude toward school, creativity, independence and conformity, curiosity, and cooperation, the open better category contained the largest number of studies.

Horwitz concluded, "At this time, the evidence from evaluation studies of the open classroom's effects on children is not sufficiently consistent to warrant an unqualified endorsement of that approach to teaching as decidedly superior to more traditional methods" (p. 83).

THE META-ANALYSIS BY PETERSON

Peterson (1979) completed a meta-analysis of the studies reviewed by Horwitz and other studies that she located. She used only those 45 studies that contained enough information to permit calculation of effect sizes (means and standard deviations of open and traditional education groups). Peterson did not retrieve the doctoral dissertations reviewed by Horwitz and found that the abstracts of these dissertations often contained too little information to compute effect sizes. Thus, Peterson's sample of 45 studies was only about one-fourth as large as Horwitz's original sample.

Peterson's rationale for undertaking a meta-analysis of a sample of the same studies that Horwitz had already reviewed was to eliminate two major problems inherent in the box score or vote-counting method that Horwitz used. First, the box score procedure may tend to compound the problem of the low statistical power of many studies of the effects of open education. Sample sizes in most studies of teaching (including studies of open education) are small, and effects for any single teaching variable are expected to be small (Gage, 1978, pp. 26-27). The statistical test for a treatment effect in the study therefore has a large probability of incorrectly yielding no statistically significant difference between open and traditional education when a true difference may have existed. In general, the box score or vote-counting procedure tends to compound such errors and has a high probability of failing to detect effects when sample sizes or treatment effects (or both) are small (Hedges & Olkin, 1980).

Second, the box score method used by Horwitz provided no indication of the magnitude of the open education treatment effect. Glass (1978) argued that the box score procedure does not allow the research integrator to determine whether a treatment "wins by a nose or a walkaway." Glass recommended calculating an "effect size" for each study as a measure of the strength of the treatment effect.

Glass's effect size is really a sample estimate of the difference between the experimental and control group means expressed in standard score units. Hedges (1981) has described the statistical model implicit in effect-size calculation. He pointed out that the goal of effect-size calculation for a given experiment is to estimate the population effect size

$$\delta = \frac{\mu_E - \mu_C}{\sigma}$$

where μ_E is the population mean of the scores in the experimental (open education) group

μ_C is the population mean of the scores in the control (traditional education) group,

and σ is the population standard deviation of the scores within the two groups.

Peterson used Glass's procedure, which consists of estimating the population effect size δ by

$$\frac{\text{mean } X_E - \text{mean } X_C}{S_C}$$

where mean X_E = sample mean of the experimental (open education) group,

mean X_C = sample mean of the control (traditional education) group,

S_C = standard deviation of the control group.

Effect sizes can be interpreted as the difference between the average (mean) performance in the experimental and control groups, expressed in standard score units. Thus the effect size may be interpreted as the z-score for the average person in the experimental group relative to the average performance of persons in the control group. In this article effect sizes have been calculated so that a positive effect size implies that the open education group received higher (more desirable) scores; i.e., the average individual in the open education group received a higher (more desirable) score than the average person in the traditional education group. Thus, a positive effect size of .50 suggests that the average score of a student in the open education group is one-half a standard deviation higher than that of the average student in the traditional education group.

Alternatively, because z-scores can be translated into percentile ranks, an effect size can be interpreted as the percentile rank of the performance of the average person in the experimental group relative to the average control subject's performance. For example, an effect size of +.50 indicates that the average performance in the experimental group is one-half of the standard deviation higher than the average performance in the control group. Similarly, an effect size of +.50 indicates that if we consider the performance of the average person in the control group to be at the fiftieth percentile, the performance of the average person in the experimental group is at the sixty-ninth percentile. A complete discussion of the interpretation of effect sizes is available in Glass (1978).

Peterson computed an estimate of effect size for each study using Glass's procedure. She then averaged the effect sizes for all studies on each of the following student outcome variables: composite achievement, mathematics achievement, reading achievement, creativity, problem-solving, self-concept, attitude toward school, attitude toward teacher, curiosity, locus of control, anxiety, and independence. She based conclusions about the effects of open education on both the direction and magnitude of the average effect sizes; a positive effect size meant average performance was higher in the open education groups, while a negative effect size indicated that average performance was higher in the traditional education groups.

Peterson noted that for most of the student outcomes, effect sizes were quite small, indicating little advantage for either open or traditional education. Average effect sizes for mathematics achievement, reading achievement, and composite achievement were negative and showed about one-tenth of a standard deviation (or slight) advantage for the traditional education groups. Average effect sizes for locus of control and anxiety were near zero, showing no advantage for either open or traditional education.

For the student outcomes creativity, attitude toward school, and curiosity, average effect sizes were positive and indicated an advantage for open education students between one-tenth and one-fifth of a standard deviation. Independence and attitude toward teacher yielded relatively larger effect sizes that showed an advantage for the open education students of between one-third and one-half of a standard deviation.

Peterson concluded (about the main effects of open education), "although a more direct or traditional approach appears to be better than a more open approach for increasing students' achievement, an open approach appears to be better than a more direct approach for increasing students' creativity, independence, curiosity, and favorable attitudes toward school and learning" (p. 67).

THE META-ANALYSIS BY HEDGES, GIACONIA, AND GAGE

The limitations of previous reviews of research on open education led us to undertake a meta-analysis of the research on open education. A detailed report of this meta-analysis is given in Hedges, Giaconia, and Gage (Note 1). This meta-analysis was designed to improve upon the meta-analysis by Peterson in at least three ways. First, doctoral dissertations were retrieved and used in the analysis.

Peterson had excluded these from her analysis. There were about 90 of these dissertations and they constituted over half of the total sample of studies used in the current analysis.

Second, the statistical analyses were based on improved statistical theory for effect size analyses. For example, the development of statistical theory for effect-size estimation (Hedges, 1981) led to the conclusion that Glass's estimator was biased, tending to overestimate the true (population) effect size. Hedges et al. used an unbiased estimator of effect size given by

$$c_m \frac{\text{mean } X_E - \text{mean } X_C}{S_{pooled}}$$

where mean X_E = sample mean of the experimental (open education) group,
mean X_C = sample mean of the control (traditional education) group,
S_{pooled} = pooled estimate of the within-group standard deviation, i.e.,

$$S_{pooled}^2 = \frac{(n_E - 1)S_E^2 + (n_C - 1)S_C^2}{n_E + n_C - 2}$$

c_m = constant for m degrees of freedom, where $m = n_E + n_C - 2$.

The exact formula for c_m is given by Hedges (1981), but a good approximation is given by

$$1 - \frac{1}{4m - 1}$$

where $m = n_E + n_C - 2$.

Another improvement in the statistical methodology was the use of a statistical test for the homogeneity of effect sizes that was developed by Hedges (1982a). This procedure tests whether the obtained effect-size estimates could have arisen by chance in samples from populations with the same underlying (population) effect size. Thus, the test of homogeneity of effect size asks whether the variability in effect-size estimates is greater than would be expected if all the studies shared a common underlying effect size. The test yields a chi-square statistic and is much like the omnibus F-test for differences between means in multigroup analyses of variance. Details of this homogeneity test and formulas for computation of its chi-square statistic are given in Hedges (1982a).

The third way in which the meta-analysis by Hedges and his coworkers improved upon the meta-analysis by Peterson was by taking into account various character-istics of each study. These characteristics of each study included *subject* character-istics, *experimental design* characteristics, *experimenter* characteristics, and *experi-mental context* variables. A team of faculty and graduate student readers read each study and coded data on several variables. Table 1 is a listing of the major variables that were coded. The reason for coding this information was to examine the relationship between characteristics of studies and effect size.

TABLE 1   Characteristics of Studies Coded for Initial Data Analysis

Subject characteristics

Grade level
Sex ratio of pupils
Ethnicity of pupils
Socioeconomic status of pupils

Experimental design characteristics

Type of design (random assignment experimental, quasi-experimental, mixed)
Method of measuring independent variable
Duration of teaching
Number of schools
Number of teachers
Number of pupils
Are open teaching methods used?
Is open space used?
Number of instructional personnel (teachers and aides) used in each class
Number of grades in each classroom
Degree and type of matching

Experimenter characteristics

Mandatory versus voluntary teacher participation
Approximate percentage of teachers who volunteered
Commitment of the investigator (pro-neutral/or against open education)

Experimental context variables

Form of the publication
Year of publication
Clarity of the research report
Quality of the research report

The sample used contained 153 studies and included most of the studies reviewed by Horwitz. A few studies that had been published after Horwitz's bibliography was prepared were added. Several studies that Horwitz had reviewed were excluded because complete reports could not be obtained, because the studies did not compare open education students to any other group, or because it appeared that the open education group was not receiving any open education treatment (i.e., the treatment did not include any elements of open instruction or open space).

Identified were 38 student outcome variables, average effect sizes were reported for 16 of these: achievement motivation, adjustment, anxiety, attitude toward school, attitude toward teacher, cooperativeness, creativity, curiosity, general mental ability, independence and self-reliance, locus of control, self-concept, language skills achievement, mathematics achievement, reading achievement, and miscellaneous achievement.

The unbiased estimator of effect size (Hedges, 1981) was used to compute an estimate of effect size for each study on each dependent variable. If more than one measure of an outcome variable was reported for the same sample of students in a study, we calculated an effect size for each measure and averaged them. The average effect size was used as the estimate of effect size for the group of students on that dependent variable. For example, if scores on two reading comprehension tests were reported for the sixth graders in a study, an effect-size estimate was calculated using the means and standard deviations reported for each test, and the average of the two effect sizes was used for the purposes analysis. This ensured that all of the effect sizes used in our statistical analyses were independent. Some studies reported data on more than one comparison between open and traditional education students. For example, a study might report the results of three comparisons between (three) open and (three) traditional classes at different grade levels. Because different classrooms and different students are involved in each of the comparisons, the effect sizes derived from the comparisons are independent. Thus, the total number of independent *comparisons* (independent effect size estimates) exceeds the number of *studies* used in the meta-analysis. Since the comparisons for any particular dependent variable are statistically independent, they each contribute independent information about the effect of open education. When a study did not report enough information to permit calculation of an effect size, only the direction of effect (favors open, favors traditional, or favors neither) was recorded.

The data analysis strategy was first to estimate an average effect size across studies on each dependent variable. The final 16 dependent variables were believed to represent fundamentally different constructs, so no attempt was made to combine results across these constructs. The next step in the data analysis was to test whether the effect-size estimates for each dependent variable were internally homogeneous. The statistical test for assessing whether a series of effect size estimates differ by more than sampling fluctuations and the details of the test procedure are given in Hedges (1982a). The results of those initial analyses are reported in Table 2.

The average effect sizes for the student outcomes adjustment, attitude toward school, attitude toward teacher, curiosity, and general mental ability were all positive and showed an advantage for the open education group of about one-fifth of a standard deviation. The direction of the effect for the majority of studies also favored open education for these student outcomes.

The average effect sizes were near zero for the student outcomes locus of control, self-concept, and anxiety. The direction of the effect for the majority of the studies favored traditional education for locus of control and anxiety. For self-concept, the direction of effect for the majority of studies favored open education.

For cooperativeness, creativity, and independence, average effect sizes were positive and indicated an advantage for open education of between one-fourth and one-third of a standard deviation. The majority of the studies showed a direction of effect that favored open education for all of these student outcomes.

TABLE 2   Summary of the Results of the Meta-Analysis

	Number of Comparisons[a]	Number of Studies[b]	Effect Sizes				Percentage of Comparisons		
			Mean	SD	Homogeneity Statistics	df	Open	Traditional	Neither
Academic Achievement									
Language	34	33	-.069	.569	201.76**	33	33	63	4
Math	64	57	-.037	.388	311.36***	63	43	52	5
Reading	73	63	-.083	.362	313.88***	72	42	54	4
Miscellaneous	23	25	-.153	.430	105.65***	22	38	55	7
Nonachievement Outcomes									
Achievement Motivation	10	8	-.262	.296	24.39*	9	29	57	14
Adjustment	19	9	.170	.577	36.46*	18	58	42	0
Anxiety	29	19	-.010	.611	226.08***	28	49	51	0
Attitude toward school	68	50	.169	.452	423.63***	67	68	31	1
Attitude toward teacher	20	17	.199	.497	260.02***	19	67	25	8
Cooperativeness	7	8	.229	.442	18.53*	6	80	10	10
Creativity	21	22	.286	.419	72.63***	20	69	19	12
Curiosity	5	7	.165	.430	37.65***	4	57	29	14
General Mental Ability	13	16	.183	.440	83.27***	12	59	36	5
Independence	26	22	.278	.667	161.37***	25	68	30	2
Locus of Control	19	16	.007	.346	64.44***	18	46	50	4
Self-Concept	84	60	.071	.418	295.24***	83	53	41	6

NOTES: a. Number of statistically independent effect size estimates.
    b. Number of studies in which at least the direction of the effect could be determined.
*p < .01
**p < .001

456

The average effect sizes for language achievement, mathematics achievement, reading achievement, and miscellaneous achievement were negative, but near zero, indicating no particular advantage for either open or traditional education. The direction of effect for the majority of studies, however, favored traditional education.

The large number of significant heterogeneity test statistics, indicating fundamentally *different* effect sizes across studies, led to a search for a model or models to explain the variation in effect sizes using the characteristics of studies that had previously been coded. A procedure described in Hedges (1982b) was used to search for models that depended on study characteristics and were adequate to explain the variability in the effect sizes. This search was disappointing in that no consistent pattern of well-fitting models emerged. For example, the average effect sizes of well-designed and poorly designed studies did not differ consistently.

The general conclusion of the global analysis was that some of the claims of proponents of open education had been supported, but that open education did not produce consistent effects across the different student outcomes. Open education made its strongest showing for the student outcomes creativity, cooperativeness, independence and self reliance, attitude toward teacher, curiosity, attitude toward school, and adjustment. Open education made its weakest showing for reading, mathematics, and language achievement.

SUMMARY OF THE GLOBAL REVIEWS OF OPEN EDUCATION

Table 3 summarizes the results reported in the three reviews of open education by Horwitz, Peterson, and Hedges et al.

Two major conclusions seem warranted from the results reported in Table 3. First, in general, open education is somewhat more effective than traditional education for nonachievement outcomes. Traditional education is only slightly more effective than open education for the traditional academic achievement measures. For many student outcomes there are near zero differences between open and traditional education.

Second, these general conclusions about the effectiveness of open education must be tempered by the fact that the variability of the effects of open education programs is often quite high. The ranges of effect size reported by Peterson for each student outcome were quite large. For example, mathematics achievement yielded an average effect size of $-.14$, but the range was -1.01 to $+.41$. Similarly, the standard deviations of effect size reported by Hedges et al. were large. For example, mathematics achievement yielded an average effect size near zero ($-.037$), but the standard deviation was .388.

RATIONALE FOR THE FURTHER STUDY

The wide variability in the numbers and types of features of open education that are implemented in open education programs has been documented by both

TABLE 3 Summary of the Results Reported in Three Reviews of Open Education

Student Outcomes	Review by Horwitz (1979) Percentage of Studies Classified as:					Meta-Analysis by Peterson (1979)			Meta-Analysis by Hedges, Giaconia and Gage (1981)		
	No. of Studies	Open Better	Traditional Better	Mixed Results	No Significant Difference	No. of Studies	Effect Size M	Effect Size Range	No. of Comparisons	Effect Size M	Effect Size SD
Academic Achievement Composite	102	14	12	28	46	25	-.12	-.78 to +.41	—	—	—
Language Achievement	—	—	—	—	—	—	—	—	34	-.069	.569
Math Achievement	—	—	—	—	—	18	-.14	-1.01 to +.58	64	-.037	.338
Reading Achievement	—	—	—	—	—	20	-.13	-.72 to +.44	73	-.083	.362
Miscellaneous Achievement	—	—	—	—	—	—	—	—	23	-.153	.430
Problem Solving	—	—	—	—	—	1	.98	—	—	—	—
General Mental Ability	—	—	—	—	—	—	—	—	13	.183	.440
Achievement Motivation	—	—	—	—	—	—	—	—	10	-.262	.296
Adjustment	22	31	0	50	19	—	—	—	19	.170	.577
Anxiety	17	18	29	6	47	5	.07	-.62 to +.69	29	-.010	.611
Attitude toward school	57	40	4	25	32	15	.12	-.43 to +.48	68	.169	.442
Attitude toward teacher	—	—	—	—	—	—	.42	+.29 to +.56	20	.199	.497
Cooperativeness	9	67	0	11	22	—	—	—	7	.229	.442
Creativity	33	36	0	30	33	11	.18	-.23 to +.50	21	.286	.419
Curiosity	14	43	0	36	21	3	.13	-.17 to +.52	5	.165	.430
Independence	23	78	4	9	9	3	.30	+.07 to +.55	26	.278	.667
Locus of Control	24	25	4	17	54	5	.03	-.34 to +.70	19	.007	.346
Self-Concept	61	25	3	25	47	14	.16	-.14 to +1.45	84	.071	.418

researchers and reviewers of open education (see Horwitz, 1979). Similarly, the wide variability in the sizes of effects produced by different open education programs has been shown by the ranges and standard deviations in Table 3. Further, the statistical test of homogeneity, when applied to the effect sizes computed in the most recent meta-analysis (by Hedges et al., Note 1), showed that for every student outcome variable, the variability in effect sizes was greater than could be accounted for by random sampling variability. Thus, while the average effect sizes across studies were in most cases quite small, some studies produced particularly large positive or particularly large negative effect sizes. Some factor or factors other than chance were contributing to the variability in effect sizes across studies.

The present study examined the relation of the observed variability in effect sizes to the observed variability in the numbers and types of open education features implemented.

METHODS

The 153 studies of open education that were used in the previous meta-analysis (Hedges et al., Note 1) served as the data base. For each of the 16 student outcomes, studies were sorted into one of three categories on the basis of the magnitude and direction of the unbiased estimate of effect size for the study.

Larger effect studies were the one-third of the studies with the largest positive effect sizes. Smaller effect studies were the one-third of the studies with the smallest effect sizes, including those less than zero. Medium effect studies were the one-third of the studies remaining after the larger effect and smaller effect studies had been identified. Only larger and smaller effect studies were used in the subsequent analyses. Larger and smaller effects could have been defined on the basis of some arbitrary value of effect size, for example, by defining small effects as those smaller than $-.2$. We chose to define large and small effects (more and less effective open education programs) in *relative* terms. Thus, our question was how the relatively more effective of existing programs differed from the relatively less effective programs.

There was usually not sufficient data in the reports of studies to distinguish variations in the features of different open education programs reported within the same study. Therefore, in the present analysis only one effect size per study (on each dependent variable) was used. If more than one independent effect size was calculated for a study, the median of the effect sizes for that study was used for classification as a larger, medium, or smaller effect study.

Since statistical significance depends on sample size, a high degree of statistical significance is not equivalent to a large effect magnitude. Indeed, the reason for effect size indices stems from the need for an index of effect magnitude that is independent of sample size. Therefore, we sorted the studies into larger effect (more effective) versus smaller effect (less effective) categories on the basis of effect size rather than statistical significance of the reported result. Sorting the studies into larger effect and smaller effect categories for each student outcome variable separately was more theoretically justifiable than trying to identify *generally* (across student outcomes) effective versus generally ineffective open education programs. Effect sizes are invariant with respect to linear transformation (Hedges, 1982a). Therefore, if a set of outcome measures are approximately linearly equatable (highly correlated), effect sizes provide an index of treatment effect that is independent of the particular measure of the outcome variable. In a sense, effect sizes based on a set of linearly equatable measures will provide comparable estimates of the effect of open education. But because different student outcomes are not linear transformations of each other (e.g., measures of reading achievement are not linear transformations of measures of mathematics achievement, that is, they are not perfectly correlated), there is little reason to believe that effect sizes on one outcome will be comparable in magnitude to effect sizes calculated on another outcome.

Description of Outcome Variables

The student outcome variables used in this study were those for which there were at least seven studies in each of the larger effect and smaller effect categories. Note that some dependent variables with more than 21 independent *comparisons* did not meet this requirement. The outcome variables that did have at least 21 studies were self-concept, creativity, attitude toward school, reading achievement, mathematics achievement, and language achievement.

Table 4 summarizes the number of larger effect and smaller effect studies that were compared for each of the six student outcome variables. It also lists the mean effect sizes and standard deviations for each student outcome variable. For many student outcome variables, the difference between the mean effect size for the larger effect studies and the smaller effect studies is about one standard deviation.

Self-Concept. Self-concept was broadly defined to include self-appraisal, self-security, or self-acceptance in both academic and general life situations. Reported were 15 different measures of self-concept in the 32 larger effect and smaller effect studies. Most of these measures of self-concept were group-administered, student self-report inventories. Most of the measures contained items dealing with general self-concept, self-concept in academic situations, as well as physical self-concept. Although the measures of self-concept were fairly homogeneous with respect to item formats and item content, there are reasons to suspect that construct interpretations from such a large set of different measures should be made cautiously. Shavelson, Huber, and Stanton (1976), in a review of studies of self-concept, argued that there is a general lack of an agreed-upon definition of self-concept, a lack of adequate validation of interpretations of self-concept measures, and a lack of empirical data on the equivalence of the self-concept measures currently being used.

Creativity. Creativity was defined to include the fluency, flexibility, originality, and elaboration dimensions of behavior in both the verbal and figural domains. Used were 6 different measures of creativity by the 14 larger effect and smaller effect studies. Most of these studies reported scores for the Torrance Tests of

TABLE 4   Average Effect Sizes for All Studies, Large Effect Studies
and Small Effect Studies

Student Outcome	All Comparisons Across All Studies			Large Effect Studies			Small Effect Studies		
	M	SD	n^a	M	SD	n^b	M	SD	n
Self-Concept	.071	.418	84	.641	.423	16	−.347	.249	16
Creativity	.286	.419	21	.724	.187	7	−.169	.234	7
Favorable attitude toward school	.169	.442	68	.730	.279	13	−.329	.253	13
Reading achievement	−.083	.362	73	.344	.315	17	−.498	.136	17
Mathematics achievement	−.037	.388	64	.387	.204	14	−.616	.239	14
Language achievement	−.069	.569	34	.494	.434	8	−.590	.147	8

NOTES: a. n equals number of comparisons; some studies yielded more than one comparison per student outcome; e.g., separate effect sizes were computed for each grade level within a study.

b. n equals number of studies; one effect size per study (per student outcome was used in computing means and standard deviations.

Creative Thinking. Most of the measures of creativity that were used required the student to produce either ideas, figures, or drawings in response to a verbal or figural stimulus. Only one measure (Pennsylvania Assessment of Creative Tendency) was a self-report inventory that measured attitudinal factors supporting creative behavior. Thus, the measures reported for creativity were fairly homogeneous with respect to the construct that they purport to measure.

Favorable Attitude Toward School. Favorable attitude toward school was defined to include favorability toward, interest in, or appreciation of various aspects of school life, such as learning, peer relations, physical environment, structuring of tasks, teacher's role, and school and classroom policies. Reported were 18 different measures in the 26 larger and smaller effect studies. Most of these measures of attitude toward school were student self-report inventories, and many were instruments developed by the investigator for his or her particular study of open education.

The measures of attitude toward school differed widely in the extent to which they emphasized the various aspects of school life (e.g., physical environment, teacher relations), and in the breadth of coverage of the aspects of school life. Thus, the measures used for attitude toward school were fairly heterogeneous and it is not clear that they are all measuring the same construct.

Reading Achievement. Reading achievement represented a summary measure of several reading subskills, such as reading comprehension and vocabulary. Reported were 12 different measures of reading achievement in the 34 larger effect and smaller effect studies.

Mathematics Achievement. Mathematics achievement represented a summary measure of mathematics subskills such as computation, concepts, reasoning, and problem-solving. Used were 10 different measures of mathematics achievement in the 28 larger effect and smaller effect studies.

Language Achievement. Language achievement represented a summary measure of language subskills, such as spelling, usage, and capitalization and punctuation. Reported were 8 different measures of language achievement in the 16 larger effect and smaller effect studies.

All of the achievement measures for reading, mathematics, and language were quite homogeneous. Most of these measures were subtests of standardized achievement batteries, for which extensive reliability and validity data had been gathered. Thus, the interpretation of effects across the different reading, mathematics, and language measures is probably less ambiguous than the interpretation of effects across the different attitude toward school measures.

Description of the Design Characteristics of Studies

Nine different design characteristics on which the larger effect and smaller effect studies could differ were identified. These characteristics included some of the subject variables, experimental design variables, experimental variables, and context variables on which Hedges et al. collected information for their meta-analysis. An analysis of the design features of the larger and smaller effect studies yielded no systematic differences in study design. Therefore, we concluded that design characteristics alone did not explain the differences in effect size. A report of these analyses can be found in Giaconia and Hedges (Note 3).

Descriptions of the Features of Open Education Programs

The careful identification of a complete and representative set of features of open education programs on which to compare larger effect and smaller effect studies was crucial to this study. Two major decisions had to be made: which features of open education would be included in the analysis and how information about these features would be coded.

The first decision involved a tradeoff between compiling an exhaustive, detailed list of features that would fully capture all of the nuances of different open education programs, and the practical constraint that most studies included too little information about the open education treatment to conduct this fine-grained analysis.

The features of open education used in this study to compare larger effect and smaller effect studies were based partly on the general categories proposed by Traub, Weiss, Fisher, and Musella (1972), partly on the categories described by Walberg and Thomas (1972), and largely on general impressions gathered in the course of reading the 153 studies reviewed in the meta-analysis by Hedges et al. (Note 1).

Traub et al. developed a teacher questionnaire (Dimensions of Schooling) that categorized several features that were found to distinguish open education programs from traditional education programs. Two criteria were used by Traub and his coworkers in identifying these features of open education programs. First, the feature could not contradict any of the assumptions about the way children behave, develop, and learn that Barth (1969) had identified as central to open education. Second, the feature had to be present in two or more programs that could be easily ranked in degree of openness. This process led to the formulation of ten dimensions of schooling.

Walberg and Thomas (1972) identified eight themes of open education that they used as the starting point for the development of a 50-item open-education observation scale and a parallel teacher questionnaire. The eight themes proposed by Walberg and Thomas were based largely on the ten themes that Bussis and Chittenden (1970) had arrived at from their interviews with open education teachers.

Seven general features of open education were identified for use in this study: role of the child in learning, diagnostic evaluation, materials to manipulate, individualized instruction, multiage grouping of students, open space, and team teaching.

Table 5 gives the definitions of each of these seven features of open education programs. The table also lists key words or descriptive statements reported in some of the studies that are examples of each of the seven features.

Table 6 shows the correspondence among the features of open education identified for this study, the dimensions of schooling described by Traub et al., and the open education themes reported by Walberg and Thomas. The table shows some evidence of convergence among the three sets of features, although some of the features differ in specificity and some of the categories do not overlap perfectly.

A second decision, after choosing which features of open education on which to compare larger effect and smaller effect studies, was how to code information in the 72 studies. The choice was between coding only the presence or absence of a feature in each open education program and coding qualitative aspects of each feature. The former approach was chosen because most of the studies contained too little information for a finer-grained analysis and because the number of studies examined for any one student-outcome variable was small.

RESULTS AND DISCUSSION

One way to assess the relationship between the seven features and effect size is to compare the average number of features implemented in larger and smaller effect studies. Table 7 reports the mean number of features of open education that were implemented in larger effect and smaller effect studies for each student outcome variable. The results of t-tests for the difference between means are also shown.

For the nonachievement outcomes of self-concept, creativity, and favorable attitude toward school, the more effective programs had a larger number of features (on the average) than the less effective programs. The opposite was true for the

TABLE 5 Descriptions of the Features of Open Education on Which
Larger Effect and Smaller Effect Studies Were Compared

Feature: Role of Child in Learning

Definition: Child is active in guiding her own learning; child actively chooses materials, methods, and pace of learning; role of teacher as resource person; less teacher-centered instruction and more student-centered instruction.

Indicators and descriptive statements:

—voluntary action on the part of the child
—active agent in his or her own learning process
—self-motivated learning
—student initiates activities
—active participant rather than recipient of commands
—trust in the student's ability to choose his or her own learning experiences
—child-centered environment
—child's freedom and responsibility for his or her learning and development
—democratic learning atmosphere
—student sets rate of learning
—high degree of child contribution to the learning environment
—teacher as resource person
—teacher is authoritative not authoritarian

Feature: Diagnostic Evaluation

Definition: Purpose of evaulation is to guide instruction; little or no use of conventional tests, but extensive use of work samples, observation, and written histories of the student.

Indicators and descriptive statements:

—charting of progress toward specific individual goals
—evaluation used to facilitate and guide learning
—child's performance not compared to that of other children
—teacher's record-keeping combines constant jotting in class and thoughtful writing about each child
—less standardized concept of student progress
—nongraded approach to evaluate student's performance

Feature: Materials to Manipulate

Definition: Presence of diverse set of materials to stimulate student exploration and learning.

Indicators and descriptive statements:

—sensory materials
—exploration and discovery-oriented materials
—use of natural materials

—rich material environment
—alternative modalities for learning

—diversity of materials
—abundance of instructional aids
—tactile confrontation with manipulative materials
—real world materials

achievement outcomes of reading, mathematics, and language achievement; the less effective programs had more features than the more effective programs. The difference in number of features between larger and smaller effect studies was

TABLE 5   Continued

Feature: Individualized Instruction

Definition: Instruction based on the individual needs and abilities of each student; individualization of rate of, methods, and materials for learning; small group as opposed to large instruction.

Indicators and descriptive statements:

—individualized instruction
—individualized approach
—individualized work
—environment responsive to individual learned needs
—individualizing the curriculum

—individualized goal setting
—learning in accord with their own rate and style
—small group or individual instruction

Feature: Multiage Grouping of Students

Definition: Grouping students for instruction in which grade labels are not applied; two or more grades may be housed in the same area.

Indicators and descriptive statements:

—family grouping
—nongraded school
—heterogeneous age grouping
—children from different grades work together in same classroom

—ungraded classrooms
—vertical grouping
—continuous progress education

Feature: Open Sapce

Definition: Physical environment of the classroom involving flexible use of space and furnishings.

Indicators and descriptive statements:

—open area classroom
—open space architecture
—flexible school architecture
—open instructional area
—activity centers
—fluid space
—decentralized classroom

—pod facility school
—open plant facility
—no interior walls or movable walls
—school without walls
—flexible seating arrangements
—physically unstructured

Feature: Team Teaching

Definition: The sharing in planning and conducting instruction offered to the same group of students by two or more teachers; use of parents as teaching aides.

Indicators and descriptive statements:

—team teaching organization
—team teaching units
—teachers work together in teams with a team leader
—large spaces with two or more teachers

largest for the outcomes of self-concept and creativity, where the more effective programs had an average of one to two more features than the less effective programs.

TABLE 6   Comparison of the Categories of Open Education Features
Proposed in Three Studies

Giaconia and Hedges *Open Education Features*	*Traub, Weiss, Fisher,* *and Musella* *Dimensions of Schooling*	*Walberg and Thomas (1972)* *Open Education Themes*
Role of child in learning	Student control; setting instructional objectives; role of teacher	Provisioning for learning; humaneness, respect, openness, and warmth
Diagnostic evaluation	Student evaluation	Diagnosis of learning events; evaluation of diagnostic information
Materials to manipulate	Materials and activities	Provisioning for learning; humaneness, respect, openness and warmth
Individualized instruction	Individualization of learning	Instruction, guidance, and extension of learning
Multiage grouping of students	Composition of classes; structure for decision-making	Provisioning for learning
Open space	Physical environment	–
Team teaching	–	–
–	Time scheduling	–
–	–	Seeking opportunities for professional growth
–	–	Self-perception of teacher

Because some of the seven features are represented more often in conceptualizations of open education, it is useful to examine the occurrence of each of the features individually. The percentages of larger effect and smaller effect studies for which each feature of open education was present or absent were determined. A chi-square test or Fisher's Exact Test was computed for each feature in order to determine the relationship between the classification of a study as larger effect or smaller effect, and the presence or absence of an open-education program feature. A chi-square statistic (χ^2) was computed when the total number of larger effect and smaller effect studies was greater than 30; Fisher's Exact Probability was computed when the total number of studies was less than 30.

The χ^2 tests reported for each open education feature are not independent of each other, because some of the features of open education covary. But undue reliance should not be placed on either the magnitude or statistical significance of these values in any event. It is more important to look for patterns in the ways the larger effect and smaller effect studies are distributed across categories, regardless of statistical significance.

TABLE 7   Differences Between Larger Effect and Smaller Effect Studies in the
Mean Number of Features of Open Education that Were Implemented

	Larger Effect Studies			Smaller Effect Studies			
Student Outcomes	M	SD	n	M	SD	n	t
Self-Concept	6.12	.81	16	3.88	1.78	16	4.60[*]
Creativity	4.71	1.80	7	3.71	1.38	7	1.17
Favorable attitude toward school	4.15	1.68	13	3.92	1.75	13	0.34
Reading achievement	4.47	1.46	17	4.53	1.46	17	−0.12
Mathematics achievement	4.43	1.02	14	4.71	1.77	14	−0.52
Language achievement	4.75	1.75	8	5.00	1.69	8	−0.29

NOTE: Maximum number of features is 7.

   [*]$p < .01$

Table 8 reports the percentages of larger and smaller effect studies for which each feature of open education was present.

For the nonachievement outcomes, the first four features (role of the child, diagnostic evaluation, materials to manipulate, and individualized instruction) tended to differentiate the studies that yielded larger effects from the studies that yielded smaller effects. The open education programs that produced larger effects on these nonachievement outcomes were much more likely to include these four features than the programs producing smaller effects. For example, *all* of the more effective programs on the outcome of self-concept included these four features and the vast majority of larger effect studies on the outcomes creativity and favorable attitude toward school included these four features. On the other hand, only about half of the studies yielding smaller effects on nonachievement outcomes included the first four features. Overall, the larger effect studies were about 30% more likely than the smaller effect studies to have included each of the first four features.

For the achievement outcomes the pattern of differences between larger and smaller effect studies in the inclusion of the first four features was not the same as for the nonachievement outcomes. With the exception of the materials to manipulate feature, the more effective programs were no more likely to include these features than were the less effective programs.

Comparisons on these first four features of the more effective programs on the nonachievement outcomes and the more effective programs on the achievement outcomes showed that the programs that were more effective in producing academic achievement were only slightly less likely to include each of the first four features than were the more effective programs on nonachievement outcomes. On the other hand, the programs that were less effective in producing academic

TABLE 8   Percentages of Larger (L) and Smaller (S) Effect Studies on Each Outcome Variable with Each Open Education Feature[a]

		Self Concept	Creativity	Favorable Attitude Toward School	Self Concept/ Creativity Average[b]	Non-Achievement Average[b]	Reading Achievement	Mathematics Achievement	Language Achievement	Achievement Average[b]
Role of the child	L	100	86	85	93.0	90.3	75	71	86	77.3
	S	50**	67	69	58.5	62.0	75	69	88	77.3
Diagnostic evaluation	L	100	100	73	100.0	91.0	82	80	86	82.7
	S	46**	50*	50	48.0	44.3	77	83	83	81.7
Materials to manipulate	L	100	80	82	90.0	87.3	77	67	83	75.7
	S	27**	50	56	38.5	44.3	50	54	67	57.0
Individualized instruction	L	100	83	80	91.5	87.7	85	83	86	84.7
	S	44**	67	75	55.5	62.0	77	86	100	87.7
Multiage grouping	L	81	83	46	82.0	70.0	71	57	57	58.3
	S	75	33	46	54.0	51.3	65	79	75	73.0
Team teaching	L	67	40	36	53.5	47.7	73	62	71	68.7
	S	69	57	62	63.0	62.7	50	54	38	47.3
Open space	L	87	71	54	79.0	70.7	75	71	88	78.0
	S	81	71	85*	76.0	79.0	94	79	88	87.0

NOTES: a. Studies for which there was no information on a particular feature and for which an informed judgment could not be made were excluded from the analysis for that feature. Median percentage of cases excluded for all features, for all student outcomes, was 7% of total sample.

b. This column is an unweighted average, calculated for descriptive purposes. No significance tests were performed.

*p < .10, **p < .01 for chi-square test or Fisher's Exact Test.

468

achievement were more likely to include each of the first four features than were the less effective programs on the nonachievement outcomes.

The last three features reported in Table 8 (open space, multiage grouping, and team teaching) did not consistently differentiate between more effective and less effective open education programs. This was true for both achievement and non-achievement outcomes.

The observed relationship between the first four features and program effectiveness on nonachievement outcomes is understandable given the relationship between these features as educational treatments and the outcomes as psychological constructs. Some elements of these features would probably be a part of any systematic intervention designed to influence self-concept, creativity, or attitude. Indeed, the reason that the first four features are most central to conceptions of open education is that most conceptualizations of open education have emphasized outcomes such as self-concept, attitude, and creativity.

For example, the self-concept measures used in these studies assess self-appraisal, self-security, and self-acceptance. And, the feature called diagnostic evaluation emphasizes the positive progress of each child. Therefore, the child experiences positive self-referenced evaluations rather than potentially negative norm-referenced evaluations. Given this experience it is plausible that children will rate themselves more positively on measures of self-appraisal, self-security, and self-acceptance. Similarly, the feature called individualized instruction is indicated by individualized goal setting and learning in accordance with the child's own rate and style. Because children do not experience potentially negative norm-referenced evaluations, it again seems plausible that children will rate themselves positively on the measures of self-concept used in the studies.

On the other hand, the relationship between the first four features of open education and academic achievement as measured by standardized tests is more tenuous. For example, although individualized goal setting may lead to greater mastery of goals set by the child, this may not lead to greater mastery of the objectives required for success on a standardized achievement test.

The last three features of open education programs (open space, multiage grouping, and team teaching) are administrative or organizational features. The relationship between these features and outcome is probably indirect. For example, open space may be *conducive* to the child's self-initiation of activities and learning. But the effects of open space per se are probably less direct in this regard than the effects of an open education program where the role of the child as self-initiator of learning is an explicit part of the program. Therefore, it is not surprising that these features are not strongly related to program effectiveness for either achievement or nonachievement outcomes. While these features are often included in open education programs, they are not often central to conceptualizations of open education programs.

Effectiveness Across Outcomes

The analyses described in this article involved the examination of programs that produced particularly large or small effects on dependent variables considered separately. It might be argued that the more effective open education programs will be more effective than the average program across outcome variables. That is, the open education programs that produce the largest effects on one dependent variable will produce similarly large effects on other dependent variables. The question of effectiveness across outcomes was examined using data from the studies that measured more than one outcome variable. Approximately half of the studies in our sample reported data on both achievement and nonachievement outcomes. The programs that were more effective in producing self-concept and creativity had average effect sizes on reading, mathematics, and language achievement that were substantially (.1 to .3 standard deviations) lower than the average across all studies reported in Hedges et al. (Note 1). Similarly, the studies that produced the larger effects on the outcomes of reading and mathematics achievement had average effect sizes on self-concept that were near the average for all open education programs. The open education programs that produced the larger effects on reading and mathematics achievement produced effects on creativity that were .2 to .3 standard deviations smaller than the average open education program. Thus these data do not support the notion of program effectiveness across outcomes. On the contrary, these data suggest that effectiveness on nonachievement outcomes does not co-occur with effectiveness on achievement outcomes and vice versa. In particular it seems that the programs that are most effective in producing creativity and self-concept are substantially less effective in producing academic achievement.

Descriptions of the Features of Traditional Education

We examined two major sources of variation in studies of open education that might be related to variations in the effectiveness of open education programs: study design characteristics and the features of open education that were implemented. Variations in the nature of the traditional education program to which the open education program was compared in computing effect sizes are a third plausible explanation for variations in the effectiveness of open education programs. Just as open education is not a single well-defined treatment, neither is traditional education: Indeed, much of the effort in research on teaching has been devoted to identifying variations within traditional education programs that are more and less effective.

But systematic comparisons of the features of traditional education and their relation to the relative effectiveness of the open education programs were hindered by the fact that most studies provided no explicit description of the traditional education program. Those studies that did describe the traditional education program often did so by pointing out how the traditional program lacked a particular feature present in the open education program. For example, if the open education program was described as one involving the flexible use of space and furnishings, the traditional educational program was described as one in which the students' desks were arranged in rows. While such descriptions serve to illustrate that the open and traditional programs were different in some respects, they may not capture all the salient features of the traditional education program.

Thus, future research comparing open and traditional education programs could benefit from more explicit descriptions of the features of both the open and traditional programs.

CONCLUSION

The results of this review support the view that open education programs *can* produce greater self-concept, creativity, and positive attitude toward school. The open education programs that have produced superior effects on nonachievement outcomes are characterized by the four features that we have described as the role of the child in learning, diagnostic evaluation, manipulative materials, and individualized instruction. Although these four features are often central to theoretical conceptions of open education, researchers have sometimes focused on more concrete features such as open-space architecture or multiage grouping. Our results suggest that multiage grouping, open space, and team teaching do not distinguish more effective open education programs from less effective programs. Therefore, future reviews of the effectiveness of open education cannot ignore the types of open education programs.

The call for more studies of open education may seem ill-advised, given the burgeoning body of open education studies. But what are needed are studies to systematically test the causal efficacy of various configurations of the open education features that have been shown in this study to be related to larger program effects. Studies of this sort can determine the relative contribution of each feature to overall program effects. This information can then be used to identify a set of necessary and sufficient features of effective open education programs.

Our results do not support the efficacy of any combination of program features in producing academic achievement. The program features do not appear to differentiate open education programs that produce superior academic achievement. Furthermore, the programs that produce large effects on nonachievement outcomes produce smaller than average effects on academic achievement. This might suggest that the superior effects on self-concept and creativity are obtained with the concomitant penalty of smaller effects on academic achievement. One caveat is that diagnostic evaluation was in all (100%) of the programs that produced large effects on self-concept and creativity. Therefore these students were not accustomed to competitive testing situations. For this reason, the students may have performed poorly on the standardized achievement tests that were used as dependent variables.

This study has also illustrated a strategy for educational researchers to use when faced with a body of literature that shows a high degree of inconsistency in results. That is, an effect size for each study can be computed. The two extreme groups of studies on effect size can be compared and contrasted on both study design characteristics and dimensions or features of the treatment variable in question. The characteristics or features that distinguish the extreme groups of studies become candidates for variables that explain variation in the outcomes of studies. Such an approach works best when the effect sizes across studies are not homogeneous; that is, cannot be considered to be estimates of the same population effect size.

REFERENCE NOTES

1. Hedges, L. V., Giaconia, R. M., & Gage, N. L. Meta-analysis of the effects of open and traditional instruction. Stanford, CA: Stanford University Program on Teaching Effectiveness Meta-Analysis Project, Final Report, Volume 2, 1981.
2. Hetzel, D. C., Rasher, S. P., Butcher, L., & Walberg, H. J. A quantitative synthesis of the effects of open education. Paper presented at the meeting of the American Educational Research Association, Boston, 1980.
3. Giaconia, R. M., & Hedges, L. V. Identifying features of effective open education programs. Paper presented at the meeting of the American Educational Research Association, Los Angeles, April 1981.

REFERENCES

BARTH, R. S. Open education assumptions about learning. Educational Philosophy and Theory, 1969, 1(2), 29-39.

BROUDY, H. S., & PALMER, J. R. Exemplars of teaching method. Chicago: Rand McNally, 1965.

BUSSIS, A. M., & CHITTENDEN, E. A. Analysis of an approach to open education. Princeton, NJ: Educational Testing Service, 1970.

GAGE, N. L. The scientific basis of the art of teaching. New York: Teachers College Press, 1978, 26-27.

GLASS, G. V Integrating findings: The meta-analysis of research. In L. S. Schulman (Ed.) Review of Research in Education (Vol. 5). Itasca, IL: Peacock, 1978.

HEDGES, L. V. Distribution theory for Glass's estimator of effect size and related estimators. Journal of Educational Statistics, 1981, 6, 107-128.

HEDGES, L. V. Estimating effect size from a series of independent experiments. Psychological Bulletin, 1982, 92. (a)

HEDGES, L. V. Fitting categorical models to effect sizes from a series of experiments. Journal of Educational Statistics, 1982, 7. (b)

HEDGES, L. V., & OLKIN, I. Vote-counting methods in research synthesis. Psychological Bulletin, 1980, 88, 359-369.

HORWITZ, R. A. Psychological effects of the "open classroom." Review of Educational Research, 1979, 49, 71-86.

MARSHALL, H. H. Open classrooms: Has the term outlived its usefulness? Review of Educational Research, 1981, 51, 181-192.

PETERSON, P. L. Direct instruction reconsidered. In P. L. Peterson & H. L. Walberg (Eds.), Research on teaching. San Francisco: McCutchan, 1979.

SHAVELSON, R. J., HUBNER, J. J., & STANTON, G. C. Self-concept: Validation of construct interpretations. Review of Educational Research, 1976, 46, 407-441.

TRAUB, R. E., WEISS, J. FISHER, C. W., & MUSELLA, D. Closure on openness: Describing and quantifying open education. Interchange, 1972, 3, 69-84.

WALBERG, H. J., & THOMAS, S. C. Open education: An operational definition and validation in Great Britain and United States. American Educational Research Journal, 1972, 9, 197-208.

26

Effects of Ability Grouping on Secondary School Students

A Meta-Analysis of Evaluation Findings

Chen-Lin Kulik and James A. Kulik

This article reports results from a meta-analysis of findings from 52 studies of ability grouping carried out in secondary schools. In the typical study the benefits from grouping were small but significant on achievement examinations—an average increase of one-tenth standard deviations on examination scores, or an increase from the 50th to the 54th percentile for the typical student in a grouped class. The size of achievement effect differed in different types of studies of grouping, however. Studies in which high-ability students received enriched instruction in honors classes produced especially clear effects, for example, while studies of average and below average students produced near-zero effects. The benefits of grouping were also clear in the area of student attitudes. Students in grouped classes developed more positive attitudes toward the subjects they were studying than did students in ungrouped classes.

Does ability grouping—the practice of organizing classrooms in graded schools to combine children who are similar in ability—have positive or negative effects on school children? The question should be a familiar one to teachers and educational researchers. Few questions about classroom organization have been around for so long; few have stirred so much controversy; and few have inspired so much research.

The practice of ability grouping goes back to the last century (Otto, 1950). Its roots are often traced to W. T. Harris's plan, initiated in St. Louis in 1867, of rapidly promoting groups of bright students through the elementary grades. This plan represented a first step toward ability-grouped classrooms, but the Santa Barbara Concentric Plan of the turn of the century more

The material in this report is based on work supported by the National Science Foundation under Grant No. SED 79-20742. Any opinions, findings, and conclusions or recommendations expressed in this report are those of the authors and do not necessarily reflect the views of the National Science Foundation.

From Chen-Lin Kulik and James A. Kulik, "Effects of Ability Grouping on Secondary School Students: A Meta-Analysis of Evaluation Findings," 19 (3) *American Educational Research Journal* 415-428 (Fall 1982). Copyright 1982, American Educational Research Association, Washington, D.C. Reprinted by permission.

nearly anticipated modern practice. In the Santa Barbara Plan, each grade was divided into A, B, and C sections, and each mastered the same fundamentals for each subject, but the A's did more extensive work than the B's, and the B's more than the C's. Today thousands of American schools follow this model of homogeneous grouping.

In schools in many countries, ability groups are even more distinct than they are in American schools (Yates, 1966). In England, for example, many pupils attend rigidly "streamed", or ability grouped, primary and junior schools, and then continue on to either grammar or secondary modern schools, depending on their ability. This sorting process has served England's highly selective university system for more than a half century. In most other countries of the Eastern and Western worlds, students of different ability levels are sent to different types of secondary schools and effectively segregated from each other.

In 1916 the first serious attempt was made to study homogeneous grouping with something resembling controlled experimentation. In that year, Guy M. Whipple studied a gifted class consisting of 13 boys and 17 girls, chosen on teacher recommendation from the fifth and sixth grades of a school in Urbana, Illinois. Numerous studies followed soon after so that by 1936, when the National Society for the Study of Education published a yearbook on grouping of pupils, seven or eight comprehensive reviews were available on the topic (Whipple, 1936). One of these reviews alone contained 140 references, including 108 reports of experimental studies (Billett, 1932). In the years since, researchers have continued to study grouping, and reviewers have tried to make sense of their findings.

The central message from these reviews, however, is that nothing has been established with certainty. The earliest reviewers and the most recent have lamented the lack of clear evidence on the effectiveness of ability grouping. But the emphasis of the reviewers has changed over the years. In the 1950s reviewers often concluded that grouping can be especially beneficial for high-aptitude students. In today's era of equal educational opportunity, the tide has gradually turned against ability grouping. Today's reviews often focus on possible negative effects of the practice, especially for disadvantaged students and especially in the areas of self-concept and achievement motivation.

These different reviewer reactions reflect the split in the larger society in opinions about grouping. For the most part, teachers overwhelmingly support the practice of ability grouping (National Education Association, Note 1). In most surveys at least 75 percent of teachers say that they favor teaching in homogeneous classes. Teachers prefer the practice because homogeneous groups of pupils seem to be easier to teach. Teachers have fewer individual differences to contend with, and they feel that students learn more from instruction aimed at the right level. Some policymakers and administrators, however, bitterly criticize the practice of grouping. They complain that grouping is popular because it appeals to a basic need to stratify society and to segregate persons into ingroups and outgroups. In their view, grouping does not foster better learning, but confers unnecessary distinction on those in the fast tracks while placing a stigma on those in the slow groups.

It is impossible for any single review to cover all aspects of ability grouping. Like other reviews, this one has a specific focus. It covers experimental studies that separate students within a school into classes differing in average ability level, where ability level is measured by an IQ test, a reading test, or by past achievement. This review does not cover studies of interschool grouping (where students are assigned to different types of schools on the basis of test scores); studies of intraclass grouping (where students are grouped and regrouped within a classroom for instruction in particular subjects); studies of rapid promotion; and studies of nongraded or individualized instruction. This review is further limited to studies at the secondary school level.

Unlike early reviews, which used narrative and boxscore methods to synthesize research findings, this review employs an objective and quantitative approach. The method is called "meta-analysis," or the analysis of analyses. The term was first used by Glass (1976) to describe the statistical analysis of a large collection of results from individual studies to integrate findings. Meta-analysts use objective search procedures to locate as many studies of an issue as possible. They then describe these studies in quantitative or quasi-quantitative fashion in as many respects as they can, both by features and outcomes of the studies. Finally, meta-analysts use statistical methods to describe outcomes and to relate study features to these outcomes.

Among the major questions that meta-analysis will be used to answer are the following: What are the effects of ability grouping in the typical study? Does grouping have different effects on different types of students; for example, students of high, average, and low aptitude? Does grouping have different effects for different types of instructional outcomes; for example, for attitudinal and achievement outcomes? Finally, do the effects of grouping vary as a function of type of study—with the methodological features, types of settings, and type of grouping practice?

METHODS

This section describes the procedures used in locating studies, coding study features, and quantifying outcomes of studies.

Locating Studies

The first step in this meta-analysis was to collect numerous studies that examined effects of grouping on secondary school children.[1] We began the

---

[1] A complete list of studies used in the analyses described in this article is available from Chen-Lin C. Kulik, Center for Research on Learning and Teaching, The University of Michigan, 109 E. Madison Street, Ann Arbor, Michigan 48109.

collection process by computer searching three data bases through Lockheed's DIALOG Online Information Service: *ERIC*, a data base on educational materials from the Educational Resources Information Center, consisting of the two files *Research in Education* and *Current Index to Journals in Education; Comprehensive Dissertation Abstracts;* and *Psychological Abstracts.* We developed special sets of key words for the three different data bases. The bibliographies in articles located through the computer searches provided a second source of studies for the meta-analysis.

In all, our bibliographic searches yielded more than 700 titles. Most of the articles, however, failed in one way or another to meet the criteria established for the analysis. We reduced the initial pool of 700 titles to 180 potentially useful documents on the basis of information about the articles contained in titles or abstracts. We then obtained copies of these 180 documents and read them in full. A total of 52 of the 180 reports contained data that could be used in the meta-analysis.

The guidelines used to reduce the initial pool of titles to the final set of studies were of three sorts. First, the studies had to take place in secondary school classrooms. We did not include in our analysis studies carried out at elementary or postsecondary levels, nor did we include studies describing laboratory analogs of groupings. Second, studies had to report on measured outcomes in both grouped and ungrouped classes. We excluded from our analysis studies without control groups and studies with anecdotal reports of outcomes. And third, studies had to be free from crippling methodological flaws. We did not use results from studies in which treatment and control groups were clearly different in aptitude. Nor did we use results from studies in which a criterion test was unfairly "taught" to one of the comparison groups.

In addition, we established guidelines to ensure that each study was counted only once in our analysis. When several papers described the same study, we used the most complete report for our analysis. When the same instructional outcome was measured with several instruments in a single paper, we pooled the results from the instruments to obtain a composite measure. Finally, when a single paper reported findings separately for different school subjects, we pooled results from the various subjects to obtain a composite result. These guidelines prevented studies with many measures and many subgroups from exerting a disproportionate influence on overall results.

Describing Characteristics of Studies

The 52 studies used in this analysis were of many different types. To describe the main features of the studies, we initially defined 15 variables. Three of the variables described the types of grouping procedures used in the studies: whether the grouping was based on a specific aptitude (i.e., a mathematics or reading test) or on a measure of general aptitude; whether special materials appropriate for ability level were used in the different groups; and whether group assignments lasted for the duration of the experiment or changed during the term (i.e., grouping was flexible). The next five variables described aspects of the experimental design of the studies: random versus nonrandom assignment of students to comparison groups; control for teacher effects by using the same teachers for both experimental and control groups; control for historical effects by use of concurrent experimental and control groups; control for scoring bias through use of objective examinations; and control of author bias through use of standardized examinations. Five other variables described features of the course settings, including duration of the program, class level of students, subject matter, average ability level of students, and level of skills tested on examinations. Finally, two variables described publication features of the study: the manner of publication and the year of publication.

One of the study features initially selected for coding—level of skill measured on the achievement examination—proved to be of little use because studies showed almost no variation on this feature. Almost all the examinations used in the 52 studies contained items measuring both lower level and higher order skills. Because there was little variation on this feature, it could not possibly explain observed variation in study outcomes. Therefore this variable was dropped from the study at an early point, leaving 14 variables that might explain variation in outcome of grouping studies.

Quantifying Outcomes

The 52 studies contained findings on effects of grouping in four major areas: student achievement, self-concept, attitude toward subject matter, and attitude toward school. Achievement outcomes were based on examinations administered to students in both grouped and ungrouped classes. Favorability of self-concept and of attitudes toward school and school subjects were based on self-report responses to questionnaire items or scales.

To quantify outcomes in each of these areas, we used the Effect Size (ES), defined as the difference between the means of two groups divided by the standard deviation of the control group (Glass, 1976). For studies that reported means and standard deviations for both experimental and control groups, we calculated ES from the measurements provided. For less fully reported studies, we calculated ES from statistics such as t and F, using procedures described by Glass, McGaw, and Smith (1981).

To make our study more similar to traditional reviews, we also examined the direction and significance of differences in instructional outcomes in grouped and ungrouped classes. On the basis of results, we classified each outcome on the following 4-point scale: 1 = difference favored the ungrouped class and statistically significant; 2 = difference favored the ungrouped class but not statistically significant; 3 = difference favored the grouped class but not statistically significant; and 4 = difference favored the grouped class and statistically significant.

In our previous meta-analyses of research on programmed, audiotutorial, and computer-based instruction (Kulik, Cohen, & Ebeling, 1980; Kulik, Kulik, & Cohen, 1979, 1980), we reported that different effect-size measures agreed remarkably well when applied to the same data set. This also turned out to be the case in the present analysis. For 38 of the studies with data on achievement outcomes, for example, we were able to calculate both ES and scores on the 4-point scale reflecting direction and significance of observed differences. The correlation between the two indices was .83. The correlation between size of effect as measured by ES and examination difference as measured in percentage points was .77. Because these correlations were so high, we were able to write regression equations for "plugging" missing data on specific effect-size measures. For example, if a study did not report standard deviations for groups but did report final examination averages in percentage terms, we were able to use the number of percentage points separating experimental and control groups to estimate ES.

RESULTS

In this section we first describe the performance on achievement examinations of students from grouped and ungrouped classes, and then examine the effects of grouping on student attitudes and on self-concepts.

Achievement

In 36 of the 51 achievement studies, the examination performance of students from grouped classes was better than the examination performance of students from ungrouped classes; in 14 other studies, examination performance was better in the ungrouped classes; and in one study, there was no difference between grouped and conventional classes. A total of 10 of the comparisons reported a statistically significant difference in results from the two teaching approaches. Results of eight of these studies favored grouping, and results of two studies favored conventional instruction. These box score results therefore tended to favor grouping.

By using the index of ES, we were able to describe the influence of grouping with greater precision. The average ES in the 51 studies was .10; the standard deviation of ES was .32; and its standard error was .045. It is statistically unlikely that an ES of this size would be found if there were no overall difference in examination performance of students from grouped and ungrouped classes ($t = 2.22$, $df = 50$, $p < .05$).

The average ES of .10 implies that in a typical class, performance of ability-grouped students was raised approximately one-tenth of a standard deviation unit. To interpret this effect more fully, it is useful to refer to areas of the standard normal curve. Using this guideline, we see that students from grouped classes performed at the 54th percentile on their examinations, whereas students who received only conventional instruction performed at the 50th percentile on the same examinations. Or put another way, 54 percent of the students from grouped classes outperformed the average student from the ungrouped classes. J. Cohen (1977) referred to effects of this magnitude as small in size.

Although the effect of grouping was small in the typical study, the size of effect varied from study to study (Figure 1). Effects ranged in size from high positive (e.g., an increase in achievement scores of about one standard deviation unit in a study by Howell, 1962, and an increase of about two-thirds standard deviation units in a study by Simpson & Martison, 1961) to high negative (e.g., a decrease in achievement of about one standard deviation unit in a study by Stoakes, 1964). Although this variation in size of effect was not so great as in other meta-analyses that we have conducted (e.g., Cohen, Kulik, & Kulik, 1982; Kulik, Kulik, & Cohen, 1980; Ebeling,

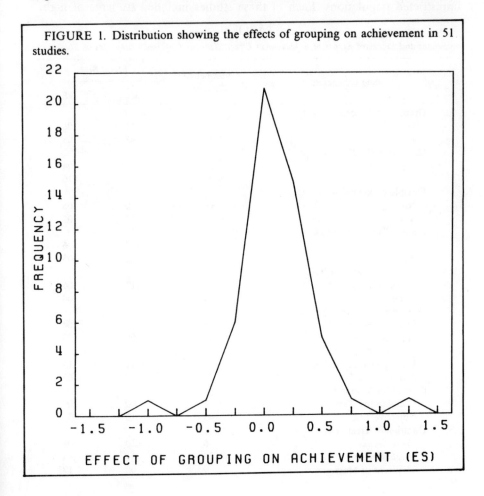

FIGURE 1. Distribution showing the effects of grouping on achievement in 51 studies.

Note 2), there was still enough variation for us to suspect that factors other than grouping played a role in determining experimental outcomes.

Further analyses showed that studies with certain features consistently reported more positive effects on student achievement (Table I). An especially important feature was the nature of the population studied. Effects were largest in the 14 studies of programs designed for talented and gifted students; these students accomplished more in special "honors" programs than they did in mixed-ability classrooms. Effects were near zero in the four programs designed especially for academically deficient students; such students learned as much in mixed-ability classrooms as they did in homogeneous classrooms. Finally, effects were also near zero in the 33 studies that compared effects of multitrack versus mixed-ability classrooms on unrestricted populations.

We carried out a further analysis of the effects in the 33 studies of unrestricted populations. Each of these studies included students of high,

TABLE 1

Means and Standard Errors of Achievement Effect Sizes for Different Categories of Studies

Coding Categories	Number of Studies	Effect Size	
		M	SE
Grouping by Specific Ability			
No	36	.11	.06
Yes	15	.08	.05
Material Tailored to Groups			
No	30	.07	.04
Yes	21	.15	.10
Flexible Grouping			
No	46	.10	.05
Yes	5	.12	.05
Random Assignment to Groups			
No	38	.14	.06
Yes	13	−.01	.05
Control for Instructor Effect			
Different Instructor	37	.12	.06
Same Instructor	14	.07	.04
Control for Historical Effect			
Different Semester	6	.17	.04
Same Semester	45	.09	.05
Control for Author Bias			
Locally Developed Test	9	.11	.14
Standardized Test	42	.10	.05
Control for Scoring Bias			
Nonobjective Test	6	.00	.09
Objective Test	45	.12	.05
Duration of Treatment			
5–18 Weeks	6	.20	.08
19–36 Weeks	34	.11	.05
37 Weeks or More	9	.00	.17

Class Level			
Jr. High	33	.05	.12
Sr. High	18	.20	.08
Subject Matter			
Math	14	.05	.04
Science	3	.18	.22
Social Science	4	.1:	.21
Reading	7	.02	.09
Composite	23	.15	.09
Target Group**			
Academically Deficient	4	.02	.18
Representative of Population	33	.02	.04
Talented and Gifted	14	.33	.11
Source of Study*			
Unpublished	7	.22	.10
Dissertations	22	.03	.07
Published	22	.19	.07
Study Year			
Before 1951	9	.24	.07
1951–1960	9	.15	.10
1961–1970	27	.07	.07
1971–1980	6	−.01	.03

* Difference in *ES* for categories of this variable significantly greater than zero, $p < .05$.
** $p < .01$.

middle, and low ability, and in each study students were assigned to both homogeneous and heterogeneous classes. In 19 of the 33 studies, the investigators reported results in enough detail so that we could calculate separate measures of effect size for students at each ability level, and thus determine whether effects of multitrack programs were strongest on high-, middle-, or low-ability students. The effects turned out to be similar at each ability level. The average effect size was .00 for students in the high-ability classes; −.06 for students in the middle-ability classes; and .002 for students in low-ability classes. There is no significant difference among these three effect sizes, and none of them is large enough to be considered significantly different from zero.

A second feature that was significantly related to effect size was the source of the study. Effects reported in journal articles and in ERIC documents were stronger than effects reported in dissertations. There was also a tendency for effects reported in early studies to be somewhat stronger than effects in studies from more recent years. This apparent historical trend might be attributable, however, to the greater emphasis in an earlier era on setting up and evaluating honors programs rather than multitrack educational systems.

Self-concept

Fifteen studies reported results on student self-concept. In seven studies self-concept was higher for students in grouped classrooms; in six studies self-concept was higher for students from ungrouped classrooms; and in two studies self-esteem was equal for the two groups. In two studies the effect of grouping was statistically significant and positive; two studies showed a statistically significant negative effect on student self-concept. The average *ES* in these studies was .01, with a standard deviation of .40 and a standard error of .107. This effect was a trivial one.

Attitudes Toward Subject Matter

Eight studies reported results on student attitudes toward the subject matter taught in grouped and ungrouped classrooms. In each of these eight studies grouping was used only for teaching a specific subject matter; for example, mathematics or English composition, and not for an entire school program. In seven of the studies, student attitudes were more positive in the grouped class, and in three of these seven studies the difference between grouped and ungrouped classes was statistically significant. The average *ES* was .37, with a standard deviation of .32 and a standard error of .12. Even though the number of studies available was small, results were consistent enough for us to conclude with statistical confidence ($t = 3.08$, $df = 7$, $p <$ .02) that grouping had a positive effect on student attitudes toward the subject being taught.

Attitudes Toward School

Another 11 studies reported results on attitudes of students toward the school they were attending. In eight of the studies the students from grouped classes expressed more favorable attitudes toward their schools; in the other three studies the attitudes of the students from ungrouped classes were more favorable. In two of the studies the effect of grouping on student attitudes toward school was statistically significant and positive; no study reported a statistically significant, negative effect on school attitudes. The average *ES* in these studies was .09, with a standard deviation of .23 and a standard error of .072. This effect is a very small one at best, and was not large enough to be considered statistically reliable ($t = 1.22$, $df = 10$).

DISCUSSION

The practice of ability grouping has had a long and a sometimes stormy history. When first introduced as a way of individualizing instruction in large schools at the turn of the century, ability grouping excited the imagination of teachers, administrators, and educational researchers. In the years since then, teachers have continued to support the practice, but the reputation of ability grouping has waxed and waned among educational researchers and administrators. In the 1950s, for example, researchers and administrators praised grouping as a way of ensuring quality education for the nation's gifted, but in today's era of equal educational opportunity, many condemn grouping as a practice that denies quality education to students from disadvantaged backgrounds.

Reviewers have never lacked an adequate pool of research studies with which to answer the basic question about ability grouping: What effect does it have on students? What reviewers have lacked, however, is a way of reading the message that the research studies hold. Until quite recently objective methods were not used in research synthesis. Reviewers have therefore had to use narrative and box score methods to pull together findings from different studies. These methods are notoriously subjective, and conclusions from reviews that use them often turn out to be unreliable.

Meta-analysis, on the other hand, provides an objective technique for research synthesis. Its emphasis on quantification keeps reviewers from projecting personal needs onto the vast inkblot of educational research. With meta-analysis, reviewers must stick to the main trends in research findings. They cannot minimize or talk away the overall thrust in a set of results, and they cannot magnify anomalous findings into major principles. Meta-analysis imposes on reviewers the strict discipline of quantitative proof.

What meta-analysis established about grouping seems clear enough. Meta-analysis showed that students gained somewhat more from grouped classes than they did from ungrouped ones. The benefits of grouping tended to be slight in the area of achievement—an average increase of one-tenth standard deviation on achievement examinations, or an increase from the 50th to the 54th percentile for the typical student in a grouped class. The benefits were somewhat greater in the attitudinal area. Students in grouped classes clearly developed more positive attitudes toward the subjects they were studying. Grouping practices, however, did not appear to influence students' attitudes toward themselves and their schools.

Although grouping had only a small overall effect on student achievement, one subgroup of studies produced especially clear effects. In this type of study students of high ability, or "gifted" students, were put into a special honors class for enriched instruction in their secondary school subjects. Studies of this type usually reported significant results, and they usually reported effects on achievement that were medium in size. High-ability students apparently benefited from the stimulation provided by other high-aptitude students and from the special curricula that grouping made possible.

Other types of studies reported only trivial effects on student achievement. Most studies that compared achievement in multitrack and single-track schools, for example, reported no significant effects of grouping. Students learned as much in the heterogeneous classrooms as in the homogeneous ones. And this was as true of the students assigned to the high-aptitude classes in a grouped school as it was of the students who ended up in the slow classes. Studies that dealt only with low-ability students—assigned either to special remedial classes or to heterogeneous ones—also reported no examination differences associated with grouping.

Our conclusions about student achievement were generally consistent with the conclusions drawn by narrative reviewers. Like nearly every other reviewer, we found that grouping generally has small effects on student achievement. We noted, however, that special honors programs often had beneficial effects on the performance of gifted and talented students. Ekstrom (1961) and others also noted the effectiveness of honors classes in their reviews of grouping research. Finally, we pointed out that ability grouping had only trivial effects on the achievement of average and below average students. This finding is consistent with the conclusions of some recent reviewers who are critical of grouping (Findlay & Bryan, 1971), but it does not support the view of other recent reviewers who claim that grouping has unfavorable effects on the achievement of low-aptitude students. The effect of grouping is near-zero on the achievement of average and below average students; it is not negative.

We also found that effects reported in journal articles were stronger than those reported in dissertations. This result was not surprising. Smith (1980) recently summarized findings on this question from 12 meta-analyses carried out at the University of Colorado. In each of the 12 studies, the average effect size for journal articles was stronger than the average effect size for dissertations, and in the typical meta-analysis, the journal effect was .16 standard deviation units higher than the dissertation effect. Summarizing results from three meta-analyses conducted at The University of Michigan, J. A. Kulik (Note 3) also reported that the average journal effect was .16 standard deviation units higher than the typical effect reported in dissertations. The result of this meta-analysis agrees perfectly with these earlier summaries.

The effects of grouping were clearer on student attitudes than on student achievement. Students assigned to grouped classes for work in certain subject areas (e.g., mathematics or English composition) responded more favorably to these subjects than did similar students assigned to heterogeneous classes. Effects were positive in nearly all the studies of attitudes toward subject matter, and in the typical study these attitudinal effects were medium in size. Effects of grouping on attitudes toward school and on self-concept were also positive, but these effects were smaller and less consistent.

Our conclusions about attitudinal effects are therefore different from the conclusions reported in most narrative reviews. Many narrative reviewers did not consider attitudinal outcomes at all in their reviews, and those who did tended to emphasize the negative effects of grouping on the attitudes and self-concepts of low-ability students. Such conclusions, however, were based primarily on anecdotal and uncontrolled studies. The controlled studies that we examined gave a very different picture of the effects of grouping on student attitudes. Students seemed to like their school subjects more when they studied them with peers of similar ability, and some students in grouped classes even developed more positive attitudes about themselves and about school.

This meta-analysis thus confirmed some common beliefs about the effects of grouping, and it showed that other common beliefs are not supported by the facts. More important, however, this meta-analysis provided precise, quantitative estimates of the size of grouping effects, based on a large number of diverse studies. We believe that these estimates give researchers and policymakers alike a new starting point for planning future policy and research in this area.

REFERENCE NOTES

1. National Education Association, Research Division. *Ability grouping* (Research Summary 1968-53). Washington, D.C.: National Education Association, 1968.
2. EBELING, B. J. *Programmed instruction in secondary education: A meta-analysis of evaluation findings.* Paper presented at the annual meeting of the American Educational Research Association, Los Angeles, April 1981.
3. KULIK, J. A. *Integrating findings from different levels of instruction.* Paper presented at the annual meeting of the American Educational Research Association, Los Angeles, April 1981.

REFERENCES

BILLETT, R. O. *The administration and supervision of homogeneous grouping.* Columbus, Oh.: Ohio State University Press, 1932.

COHEN, J. *Statistical power analysis for the behavioral sciences* (Rev. ed.). New York: Academic Press, 1977.

COHEN, P. A., KULIK, J. A., & KULIK, C.-L. C. Educational outcomes of tutoring: A meta-analysis of findings. *American Educational Research Journal,* 1982, *19,* 237–248.

EKSTROM, R. B. Experimental studies of homogeneous grouping: A critical review. *The School Review,* 1961, *69,* 216–226.

FINDLAY, W. G., & BRYAN, M. M. *Ability grouping: 1970, status, impact and alternatives.* Athens, Ga.: University of Georgia, Center for Educational Improvement, 1971. (ERIC Document Reproduction Service No. ED 060 595)

GLASS, G. V Primary, secondary, and meta-analysis of research. *Educational Researcher,* 1976, *5,* 3–8.

GLASS, G. V, McGAW, B., & SMITH, M. L. *Meta-analysis in social research.* Beverly Hills, Calif.: Sage, 1981.

HOWELL, W. J. Grouping of talented students leads to better academic achievement in secondary school. *Bulletin of NASSP,* 1962, *46,* 67–73.

KULIK, J. A., COHEN, P. A., & EBELING, B. J. Effectiveness of programmed instruction in higher education: A meta-analysis of findings. *Educational Evaluation and Policy Analysis,* 1980, *2,* 51–64.

KULIK, J. A., KULIK, C.-L. C., & COHEN, P. A. Research on audio-tutorial instruction: A meta-analysis of comparative studies. *Research in Higher Education,* 1979, *11,* 321–341.

KULIK, J. A., KULIK, C.-L. C., & COHEN, P. A. Effectiveness of computer-based college teaching: A meta-analysis of findings. *Review of Educational Research,* 1980, *50,* 525–544.

OTTO, H. J. Elementary education—III. Organization and administration. In W. S. Monroe (Ed.), *Encyclopedia of educational research.* New York: MacMillan, 1950.

SIMPSON, R. E., & MARTISON, R. A. *Educational programs for gifted pupils: A report to the California legislature prepared pursuant to Section 2 of Chapter 2385, Statutes of 1957.* Sacramento, Calif.: California State Department of Education, 1961. (ERIC Document Reproduction Service No. ED 100 072)

SMITH, M. L. Publication bias and meta-analysis. *Evaluation in Education: An International Review Series,* 1980 *4*(1), 22–24.

STOAKES, D. W. An educational experiment with the homogeneous grouping of mentally advanced and slow learning students in the junior high school (Doctoral dissertation, University of Colorado, 1964). *Dissertation Abstracts International,* 1965, *25,* 5654. (University Microfilms No. 65-04218)

WHIPPLE, G. M. (Ed.). *The grouping of pupils* (Thirty-fifth Yearbook, Part 1, National Society for the Study of Education). Chicago: University of Chicago Press, 1936.

YATES, A. (Ed.). *Grouping in education.* New York: John Wiley & Sons, 1966.

AUTHORS

CHEN-LIN C. KULIK, Assistant Research Scientist, Center for Research on Learning and Teaching, 109 E. Madison Street, Ann Arbor, MI 48109. *Specializations:* Research synthesis; individualized instruction; psychological measurement.

JAMES A. KULIK, Research Scientist, Center for Research on Learning and Teaching, 109 E. Madison Street, Ann Arbor, MI 48109. *Specializations:* Research synthesis; educational evaluation.

27

Reading Instruction
A Quantitative Analysis

Susanna W. Pflaum, Herbert J. Walberg, Myra L. Karegianes, and Sue P. Rasher

Concerned with the need for documenting the effects of instructional method on reading achievement, Huey, after the turn of the century (1908), wrote "we have thus far been content with trial and error, too often allowing the publishers to be our jury, and a real rationalization of the process of inducting the children into the practice of reading has not been made. . . . We have come to the place where we need to pass in review all the methods that have been tried in all the centuries of reading and to learn any little that we can from each" (p. 9). Some 70 years later, in discussing investigations of different instructional methods, Farr and Roser (1979) concluded, "Regardless of the quantity of research, however, there are no definitive answers to the question of the best program because the results of various studies support different programs, and nothing conclusive can be shown about which programs are superior" (p. 426). That nothing conclusive has resulted from the research on instructional methods is reflected in other texts written for teachers of reading; for example, Durkin (1974), Fry (1977), Mangrum and Forgan (1979), and others concluded that few important differences between methods are detectable. In terms of practical application, the issue of method preference is an important one and should be resolved given the need for schools to choose among the variety of programs available and given the clear differences between various approaches to reading instruction.

Our examination of research on instructional methods in reading reveals that there is far less emphasis, especially in the last few years, on method research than may be generally assumed. The proportion of instructional method studies summarized in the *Reading Research Quarterly* annual survey of research in reading to the total number of studies in reading research was about 13 percent between the years 1965 and 1978. During the latter half of that period, the proportion of instructional studies was even lower, about nine percent, compared with the earlier half of the period when 18 percent of the studies were investigations of instructional methods. The decrease in the number of research studies on reading instruction may reflect the view held among reading educators that there are no important differences among methods in promoting achievement.

The sources for the belief that there are few achievement differences attributable to instructional method are the large-scale reviews of the late 1960's. Chall (1967) reviewed older work comparing instructional effects in programs that contained no phonics instruction with those containing a supplementary phonics program. Generally, she concluded that phonics as a supplement resulted in higher achievement than no phonics. More important in reference to modern instruction in reading was her finding that early and intensive phonics produce better word reading and slightly better paragraph reading compared with later and less intensive phonics instruction.

In addition to the work by Chall, another important research synthesis of beginning reading instructional methods from the "Cooperative Research Program in First-Grade Reading Instruction" (Bond & Dykstra, 1967) attracted considerable interest. The 27 studies, using approximately the same design and the same analyses, measured achievement gains at the end of the first grade from various inno-

Susanna W. Pflaum is Associate Professor, College of Education, University of Illinois at Chicago Circle, Box 4348, Chicago IL 60680. Specializations: Reading; Reading behaviors of disabled readers.

Herbert J. Walberg is Research Professor of Urban Education, University of Illinois at Chicago Circle. Specializations: Social psychology of education; measurement, evaluation, and statistical analysis.

Myra L. Karegianes is English Department Chairperson, Juarez High School. Specializations: Writing and Reading Research.

Sue Pinzur Rasher is Research Associate, College of Education, University of Illinois at Chicago Circle. Specializations: Evaluation research, data analysis, multivariate analysis.

From Susanna W. Pflaum et al., "Reading Instruction: A Quantitative Analysis," 9(7) *Educational Researcher* 12-18 (July 1980). Copyright © 1982 by the American Educational Research Association. Reprinted by permission of the publisher.

vative approaches to beginning reading, each of which was compared with the traditional basal program. The innovative approaches included the basal-plus-phonics treatment, the linguistic approach, the initial-teaching-alphabet (i.t.a.) approach, the language-experience method, and a phonic-linguistic program. Overall, those programs that stressed systematic study of sound-symbol relationships tended to produce higher achievement in some areas than did the basal alone. Generally speaking, however, the significant differences were relatively small in terms of practical educational value, often amounting to only about 1 or 2 months grade-equivalence differences. On the other hand, using a different covariance model, Guthrie and Tyler (1978) reported from these first-grade data that structural linguistics and supplementary phonics-plus-basal produced higher achievement than did the basal programs. Also, these sound-symbol-focused approaches produced greater gains than the language-experience method.

Some of the first-grade studies were extended through the second grade, and in summarizing the results of the second year, Dykstra (1968) found that the i.t.a., phonic-linguistic and linguistic approaches produced higher word recognition and spelling than the basal alone or basal-plus-phonics programs. Using these data, Lohnes and Gray (1972) reported that the variance in achievement was largely accounted for by general intelligence thereby leaving little opportunity for method differences to emerge. Thus, the repeated finding that sound-symbol emphases produced higher beginning reading achievement appears to be important. Also, it makes it difficult to understand why text writers maintain that method makes little difference.

Beyond the initial stages of reading instruction, there has been very little comparison of instructional methods, and therefore little review of the area. Although over half of the 244 studies included in the survey of methods and materials reported by Maxwell (1972) were conducted at the primary grade levels, there were a number of studies that investigated methods and materials used at grade levels above three. Overall, there were few differences between experimental and control groups and no direction for teacher choice. In regard to instructional method applied to remedial instruction, the literature is largely negative: for example, 25 studies investigating specialized treatments which were intended to remove disabled learner's supposed deficits in visual processing were not effective in improving reading (Hammill, 1972), nor have psycholinguistic training programs proved effective (Hammill, Goodman, & Wiederholt, 1974).

Although reviews and syntheses of investigations in beginning reading methods appear to support focused instruction emphasizing sound-symbol training, reading educators have not embraced the findings. There is, however, an increase in phonics instruction at earlier points in schooling contained in many of the newer basal programs during the last decade, indicative, according to Popp (1975), of publisher response to the research. Beyond the early levels of reading, there is little direction from research about methods of instruction. And in reference to disabled readers, there is simply no evidence that particular treatments are effective.

This study uses quantitative techniques by Glass (1978) to synthesize the literature on instructional methods in reading. We were interested in finding (1) if the reading educators' view of no important difference in beginning reading methods is valid, (2) if there are additional directions from the research conducted with older developmental and with disabled readers to be obtained from extant research to add to research summaries involving beginning teaching, and (3) if there are instructional method differences across factors of subject type, treatment characteristics, different achievement measures, and design and analysis characteristics.

Method

Study Selection

Thirteen annual issues (Vols. 1-13) which summarize investigations in reading from the *Reading Research Quarterly* for the years 1965 and 1977-1978 inclusive were used as the source for the reading studies analyzed in this research synthesis.

Of the 13 summaries, 665 are investigations of instructional method. About 20 percent, 132, of these were randomly chosen for inclusion in the synthesis. Because 67 (50.5 percent) lacked sufficient length of instructional time (fewer than five sessions), lacked a comparison control group, or lacked inferential statistics, a method for study substitution was devised involving random selection among the remaining pool of studies. Of 199 studies examined, the final sample consisted of 97 studies, including 341 different comparisons of experimental versus control treatments. The final sample was about 15 percent of the population of instructional method studies. This number was actually much higher considering the rate of exclusion; using the rate of unacceptable studies found with the 196 studies examined as the base, the basal sample represents 30 percent of the total population.

Variables

To code the data, a system for characterizing study factors was devised and used with each of the 341 comparisons. On the code sheet were six subject variables (number of students for the comparison and classifications of sex, race, family income, reading achievement, ability level, and grade level); for treatment characteristics (length of sessions in minutes, number of sessions per week, number of weeks, and number of treatment teachers), there were 10 variables which rated various study analysis controls (for IQ, income, entering achievement, pretest, measures of investigation, the reliability of implementation, assignment procedures to treatments, objectivity, representatives of the sample, and the purity of the treatment delivery), and 12 different outcome measures. To code the instructional method, the rating indicated the degree to which the treatment included a particular method: not used, used somewhat as a major feature of instruction (i.e., when the method was one of three major features of instruction), or used as the exclusive treatment (i.e., when a treatment method was the only one the experimental group received). The definition of each instructional method type together with the frequency of inclusion appear in Table I. Thirteen of the 30 methods were represented by fewer than three studies. None of the methods was represented by more than 10. As with the other variables, the instructional method variables were operationally defined and applied by two raters, both of whom were familiar with reading instruction. The definitions were discussed at length and initially used together. When studies were examined individually, differences in interpretation were discussed and reconciled. In coding the studies, we designated as control treatments the conditions the original researcher described as control treatments. These were instructional approaches common to reading instruction for that level. For example, control conditions at the elementary grade levels were, in nearly every instance, eclectic basal readers.

Methods of Analysis

Two sets of analyses were carried out to estimate the consistency and magnitude of the experimental methods of teaching reading. The sign of every comparison of experimental versus control groups on all study outcome measures was coded "1" if the experimental group was superior and "0" if the control group was superior. (When more than one experimental treatment was included in a study, we coded each experimental treatment versus the control group). Counts of these two categories, either unweighted or weighted by

study, estimate the frequency of superiority and inferiority of experimental methods across all studies compared with control methods and by various classifications of methods of teaching, methodological threats to research validity, student characteristics, and measured outcomes. The strength of this vote-counting method is that it permits the inclusion of all studies that report the sign of the results even if detailed statistics are lacking.

A second method, however, estimates the *magnitude* of the superiority or inferiority of the experimental method by calculating "effect sizes" (Glass, 1978) which are the differences between the experimental group mean and the control group mean (in the first step) divided by the standard deviations of the control groups (in the second step), or other more complicated estimates of the comparison that can be derived from F and T ratios and probabilities (see Glass, 1978). These effect sizes express the magnitude of the superiority or inferiority of the experimental group compared to the control group in units of standard deviation of the control group. Thus, even though the outcome measures differ vastly across comparisons, calculation of effect sizes permit estimates of experimental impacts in a universal metric across all studies or across classifications of studies for studies with explicit statistics. Effect sizes as well as their averages can be readily converted to percentiles using common tables of normal deviates; for example, an effect size of +1 implies that the experimental group scored on average at the 84th percentile of the control group whose mean percentile is 50, and effect sizes of −2 and 0 convert to percentiles of 5 and 50, respectively.

Weighting Procedure

Some studies may have only an experimental group, a control group, one reading outcome measure, and no classifications of students, say, by sex or grade; such studies yield one vote and one effect size. Other studies re-

port a host of statistics that yield many votes and effect sizes. To simply tabulate all comparisons across studies would allow studies with many breakdowns and outcome measures to weigh more heavily in the analysis.

To overcome this problem and to meet the canons of statistical inference that allow only one degree of freedom (or vote) for each piece of completely independent information, each vote (or effect size) was weighted inversely to the number of votes (or effect sizes) in the study from which it was calculated. This procedure yields the appropriate number of degrees of freedom and weighs each study equally. It applies not only to the overall estimates of experimental effects but also to classifications of studies by teaching methods or experimental rigor.

Results

Three-fourths (73) of the 97 studies showed that the experimental groups were superior to the control groups. The binomial probability (Dixon & Massey, 1969) of the evidence under the hypothesis of an even 50-50 split in the population of studies from which the sample studies were drawn is less than one in 1,000; thus, it may be concluded that experimental reading methods in the sample of studies more often produce superior results.

Only 31 of the 97 studies in the sample reported means and standard deviations or other explicit statistics on which effect sizes could be calculated. The mean and standard deviation of the effect sizes is .603 and .967; a T-test of 3.47 shows that the probability of the evidence, given the null hypothesis, is less than 1 in 1,000.

The mean effect size of .6 converts to a percentile of 73. Thus, the typical control group performance on the reading outcome measures is at the 50th percentile, and the experimental groups score, on average, 23 percentile points higher than the average of the control groups.

Rosenthal (in press) and Smith (in press) note that calculating effect sizes from published

TABLE I

Classified Studies

Method	Definition	Statistics			
		Frequency	Mean Effect Size	Standard Deviation	F
Eclectic Basal					
Major Feature	Uses mixed methodology in	7	.86 (4) [a]	1.28	0.42
Exclusive Feature	basal program — beginning	1			
Sound-Symbol Blending					
Major	Single sounds-letters are	5	1.62 (3)	1.94	4.11*
Exclusive	taught separately and blended together	1	—	—	
Sound-Symbol Analytic					
Major	Sound-symbol correspon-	5	.56 (2)	.00	.00
Exclusive	dences taught within word context	3	— [b]	—	—
Language Experience					
Major	Use of student-produced	1	—	—	—
Exclusive	materials for reading instruction	3	—	—	
Altered Orthography					
Major	Use of special symbols	2	1.53 (2)	3.11	1.02
Exclusive	representing actual phonemes of language	7	—	—	
Pacing of Vocabulary					
Major	Rate of new words introduced	1	—	—	—
Exclusive	controlled	1	—	—	—
Individualized Book Reading					
Used Somewhat	Independent reading and	1	—	—	.71
Major	reporting on books	6	.01 (2)	.47	
Exclusive		3	.39 (1)	—	
Individualized Mastery System					
Used Somewhat	Instruction and progress	1	—	—	.00
Major	monitored through mastery	4 (1)	1.62	.00	
Exclusive	of skills	1 (1)	.69	.00	
Meaning Vocabulary Development					
Major	Meaning of words taught	1	—	—	
Exclusive		1	—	—	
Comprehension Skill Development					
Used Somewhat	Instruction in comprehension	2	1.62 (1)	.00	.00
Major	focusing on component skills	4	.62 (2)	.00	
Advanced Phonic Skills					
Used somewhat		1	—	—	
Text Organizers					
Used somewhat	Instruction on overall struc-	1	—	—	.04
Major	ture of discourse	3	.73 (2)	.00	
Syntax Training					
Major	Instruction focusing on	2	—	—	.47
Exclusive	sentence structure	1	− .05 (1)	—	
Rate Training					
Used somewhat	Instruction on speed reading,	1	—		
Major	skimming, scanning	2	—		
Exclusive		2	—		
Study Skills Training					
Used somewhat	Instruction on study techniques	2	—		
Major	such as SQ3R, outlining, etc.	3	—		

(continued)

Table I Classified Studies Cont.

Method	Definition	Frequency	Mean Effect Size	Standard Deviation	F
Reading in Different Content Areas	Instruction on how to read in science, social studies, etc.				.00
Used somewhat		1	—	—	
Major		1	.57 (1)	—	
Exclusive		1	—	—	
Tutoring	Instruction in a one-to-one setting				.11
Used somewhat		1	—	—	
Major		5	.90		
Exclusive		4	—	—	
Impress Method	Students repeat reading with adults in intensive sessions				.34
Major		1	—	—	
Exclusive		1	.04 (1)	—	
Counseling	Students discuss personal matters with adult				
Major		2	—		
Exclusive		2	—		
Black Studies	Special instruction on black history, culture, etc.				.07
Major		1	.34 (1)	—	
Listening During Reading	Students listen to tapes as they read text				.19
Major		1	1.02 (1)	—	
Listening	Listening to stories they do not read				
Major		1	—		
Auditory Perceptual Training	Instruction in auditory discrimination and processing				.11
Major		4	.78 (3)	.99	
Visual Perceptual Training	Instruction in visual processing and perception				.03
Major		4	—	—	
Exclusive		4	.69 (3)	1.11	
Oral Reading Training	Instruction in improvement of oral reading				.19
Exclusive		1	1.02 (1)	—	
High Intensity Silent Reading	Students read silent for a designated time period (SSR)				
Reading		1	—		
Exclusive					
Reinforcement	Students receive some type of reinforcement based on performance				.00
Major		1	.60 (1)	—	
Exclusive		1	.51 (1)	—	
Grouping	Method of grouping is featured				
Major		1	—		
Exclusive		1	—		
Teacher Aide	The effects of use of teacher aides in reading				
Major		1	—		
Motor Training	Instruction in coordination				.17
Major		5	.79 (4)	1.07	
Other					4.62*
Used somewhat		2	3.56 (1)	—	
Major		11	.53 (5)	.78	
Exclusive		16	.29 (5)	.67	

* $p < .05$; ** $p < .01$; [a] Number is frequency of studies for which effect sizes could be calculated; [b] Fewer than two studies.

studies may produce upwardly biased estimates of mean effects because nonpositive and nonsignificant studies may be less likely to be published. Smith's comparison of analyses of studies in a variety of areas suggests that published studies may produce mean effect sizes up to one-third greater than the mean of unpublished studies. Reducing the effect size of .6 in the present synthesis by a third results in a lower bound, adjusted value of .4 and a corresponding experimental-group percentile of 65, which is 15 percentile points higher than the control group mean.

Table II.shows that about 13 percent of the effect sizes are negative; 60 percent are between 0 and 1; and a quarter are greater than 1 (corresponding to the 84th percentile). Thus, by either vote counts from 97 studies or effect sizes from 31 studies, all weighted equally; experimental methods of teaching reading in general, as they have been employed in the present sample of studies, yield, in the majority of cases and on the average, results that are superior to the control methods used and that are both statistically and educationally significant.

Results by Classification

Analyses of variance on all variables show no significant difference by method on the direction tests. There are two significant differences in the analyses using effect sizes (Table I). The sound-symbol blending method mean effect size is significantly higher than the mean for other experimental treatments, as is the category "other" treatments. In the latter case, the significant effect may be explained by the unusually large effect size in the "used somewhat" subcategory.[1]

None of the subject variables is significant.[2] However, of interest is the distribution of study by grade level. The great majority of these randomly selected studies are investigations of beginning reading methods rather than instructional studies of older readers, a finding similar to Maxwell's (1972); 57 studies are at kindergarten and grade one and two levels. We assume that this is a fair representation of reading method research. Another prevailing subject characteristic is that the research is evenly distributed between those including subjects of a range of reading ability and those including only poor readers.

Although the length of treatment variables is not significant, there is a tendency for the two larger treatment duration categories to have higher mean effect sizes than the shorter categories: weeks 1-10, .29; weeks 11-20, .24; weeks 31-40, .98; 41 weeks or more, 1.61.

No variables on treatment teachers or study control variables are significant. However, there was a tendency for the effect size to be greater if the investigator was thought an advocate of the method or conducted the research ($\bar{X} = 1.17$, SD = 1.57), than if he or she appeared to have greater objectivity ($\bar{X}$ =

.45, SD = .70). Finally, no dependent measure variable is significant.

Discussion

There were three purposes for this study. One was to test the prevailing view among reading educators that different methods for teaching reading cause few differences in achievement. The study suggests, when the individual methods are considered, that this view is largely correct except for the apparent superiority of the sound-symbol blending method. There is, in addition, the strong finding that experimental treatments, overall, are superior to control treatments.

The second purpose was to examine if differences existed among methods for teaching older readers and for remediating disabled readers. The view that clearly superior, specific methods for these groups do not exist is supported by the results. Again, it is clear from the strength of the direction and effect size analyses that carefully planned and executed instructional methods, as the experimental treatments as a whole may be regarded, are superior to traditional approaches.

The third purpose was to find if methods varied across subject, teacher, research procedure, or dependent measure. The finding that experimental treatments produce significantly higher achievement is generally applicable across pupil and teacher variables, different research methods, design characteristics, and outcome types.

The size of the difference between experimental and control methods, even under the more conservative estimate, amounts to about 15 percentile points experimental advantage on average over that of control methods, a difference that is both statistically and educationally significant and that demonstrates that specially designed instruction generally tends to produce more learning than less systematic instruction, assuming that control treatments may be less well thought out or operationalized compared with experimental

TABLE II

Frequency Distribution of Effect Sizes

	Frequency	Percent
3.5 - 3.9	2	6.5
3.0 - 3.4	0	—
2.5 - 2.9	0	—
2.0 - 2.4	0	—
1.5 - 1.9	3	9.7
1.0 - 1.4	3	9.7
0.5 - 0.9	8	25.8
0.0 - 0.4	11	35.5
-0.0 - -0.4	3	9.7
-0.5 - -0.9	1	3.2
Total	31	100.1

treatments. The possibility that the greater effects found with the experimental treatments are due to experimental bias and Hawthorne effects may rise as alternative hypotheses but these counter-interpretations or threats to experimental validity are not significant and must be discounted.

One specific treatment, sound-symbol blending, made a significantly greater impact on reading than the other experimental treatments. This finding supports the earlier evidence from beginning reading research on the superiority of regular systematic phonics instruction (Bond & Dykstra, 1967; Guthrie & Tyler, 1978). With the different technique for synthesizing research used in this study, this support for systematic phonics appears to be a strong one. Furthermore, the mean effect size of this method is comparatively larger than that of the other phonics method, sound-symbol analytic; specifically, the synthesis of separate sounds associated with letters appears to be superior to analysis of sound-symbol associations within words. We must be cautious, however, because significant effect size on sound-symbol blending may be due to chance in the testing of many effects.

Conclusion

Applied to instruction, the results suggest that new, innovative methods, on average, produce greater effects than traditional methods. We interpret this finding as the result of focused instruction in reading. Additional syntheses of research are likely to confirm these overall findings. It may be, however,

that additional investigation within a particular method may demonstrate differences within that method for different pupil achievement levels. Finally, an issue not addressed here, which may be important concerns possible differences teacher use of different methods.

In regard to decisions about choice of reading methods, it seems that the particular method is not the critical factor. Instead, analysis suggests that reading specialists and teachers emphasize systematic, focused methods of teaching that are more often found in experimental studies and innovative programs than in the ordinary reading instruction.

Notes

[1] In Table I, only the categories indicating extent of use of the treatment are listed for each treatment type; thus, some treatment types may list only "major feature."

[2] Readers interested in statistical information on all variables may write the first author for more detailed data.

References

Bond, G.L., & Dykstra, R. The cooperative research program in first-grade reading instruction. *Reading Research Quarterly*, 1967, *2*, complete volume.

Chall, J. *Learning to read: The great debate*. New York: McGraw-Hill, 1967.

Dixon, W.J., & Massey, F.J. *Introduction to statistical analysis*. New York: McGraw-Hill, 1969.

Durkin, D. *Teaching them to read* (2nd ed.). Boston: Allyn & Bacon, 1974.

Dykstra, R. Summary of the second-grade phase of the cooperative research program in primary reading instruction. *Reading Research Quarterly*, 1968, *4*, 49-70.

Farr, R., & Roser, N. *Teaching a child to read*. New York: Harcourt Brace, 1979.

Fry, E.B. *Elementary reading instruction*. New York: McGraw-Hill, 1977.

Glass, G.V Integrating findings: The meta-analysis of research. In L.S. Shulman (Ed.), *Review of Research in Education* (Vol. 5). Itasca, Ill.: F.E. Peacock, 1978.

Guthrie, J. T., & Tyler, S.J. Cognition and instruction of poor readers. *Journal of Reading Behavior*, 1978, *10*, 57-78.

Hammill, D.D. Training visual perceptual processes. *Journal of Learning Disabilities*, 1972, *6*, 552-559.

Hammill, D.D., Goodman, L., & Wiederholt, J.L. Visual-motor processes: Can we train them? *The Reading Teacher*, 1974, *27*, 469-478.

Huey, E.B. *The psychology and pedagogy of reading*. New York: Macmillan, 1908.

Lohnes, P.R., & Gray, M.M. Intelligence and the cooperative reading studies. *Reading Research Quarterly*, 1972, *7*, 466-476.

Mangrum, C.T., II, & Forgan, H.W. *Developing competencies in teaching reading*. Columbus, Oh.: Charles E. Merrill, 1979.

Maxwell, M.J. Results of the survey of the literature on methods and materials in reading. In F.P. Greene (Ed.), *Twenty-first Yearbook of the National Reading Conference. Investigations relating to mature reading*, 1972, *1*, 203-211.

Popp, H.M. Current practices in the teaching of beginning reading. In J.B. Carroll & J.S. Chall (Eds.), *Toward a literature society: The report of the Committee in Reading of the National Academy of Education*. New York: McGraw-Hill, 1975.

Rosenthal, R. Combining probabilities and the file-drawer problem. *Evaluation in Education*, in press.

Smith, M.L. Publication bias and meta-analysis. *Evaluation in Education*, in press.

28

Effect of Intravenous Streptokinase on Acute Myocardial Infarction
Pooled Results from Randomized Trials

Meir J. Stampfer, Samuel Z. Goldhaber,
Salim Yusuf, Richard Peto, and Charles H. Hennekens

INTRACORONARY infusion of streptokinase in patients with acute myocardial infarction is an exciting and innovative technique for reperfusion of the ischemic myocardium,[1-4] but its net benefits have not yet been reliably estimated.

Intravenous infusion of streptokinase is less invasive, less expensive, and easier than intracoronary infusion, and its effects have already been studied in randomized trials. Inevitably, when several trials address the same or a similar question, they are unlikely to yield identical results, and in these circumstances an overview of the results of all the strictly randomized trials can be useful.[5-7] Although the play of chance may well produce distortions in one direction or another in particular trials, such effects are likely to cancel each other out when several trials are viewed together. In this analysis, we therefore examine the mortality results from all eight identified randomized trials that have tested intravenous streptokinase in acute myocardial infarction. As we will show, the results suggest that this therapy, given early, significantly reduces mortality over subsequent weeks.

From the Channing Laboratory and Cardiovascular Division, Department of Medicine, Brigham and Women's Hospital and Harvard Medical School, the Department of Cardiology, Oxford, and the Nuffield Department of Medicine, Radcliffe Infirmary, Oxford. Address reprint requests to Dr. Hennekens at 55 Pond Ave., Brookline, MA 02146.

Dr. Stampfer was supported by a National Institute of Environmental Health Sciences National Research Service Award (5T32 ES 07069), Dr. Goldhaber by a National Research Service Award Training Grant (HL 07049), and Dr. Hennekens by a Research Career Development Award (HL 00286).

METHODS

Selection of Trials for Pooling

Initially, we included all published trials in which subjects were randomized to intravenous-streptokinase treatment or to a control group receiving either placebo or anticoagulation. Mortality was used as an end point, with a follow-up period of approximately 40 days for increased comparability. We then examined more closely comparable trials that also met the following more stringent criteria: a reasonably similar treatment protocol using a uniform loading dose of 250,000 IU followed by continuous infusion therapy, and initiation of therapy within 24 hours of onset of symptoms.

Statistical Techniques

Patients admitted to one trial are likely to differ systematically from those admitted to another, and so one should compare patients in one trial only with other patients in that trial and not with patients in other trials. Therefore, to provide an overview of several trials, we have employed the statistical methods that are commonly used in a single study to obtain an overall estimate across different levels (or strata) of a confounding variable — for example, across different age groups. In our analysis we treat each separate trial as one stratum. Information from each stratum is then combined to provide an estimate of the mean overall effect without the need to compare patients in one trial directly with those in another. For any one trial, we define the risk ratio as the proportion of deaths in streptokinase-treated patients divided by that among the controls. We calculated a weighted average of these risk ratios by assigning a weight to the risk ratio derived from each individual study. Each trial's assigned weight is proportional to the precision of that trial's results (the inverse of the variance of the risk ratio).[8] Thus, each trial's contribution to the overall result is directly related to the amount of information it provides. For example, a large trial would carry more weight than a smaller trial. The formula is

From Meir J. Stampfer et al., "Effect of Intravenous Streptokinase on Acute Myocardial Infarction: Pooled Results from Randomized Trials," 307 (19) *New England Journal of Medicine* (November 4, 1982). Reprinted by permission of the *New England Journal of Medicine*.

Table 1. Characteristics of Randomized Trials of Intravenous Streptokinase in Acute Myocardial Infarction.

TRIAL	DURATION OF SYMPTOMS	LOADING DOSE	INFUSION DOSE	PERIOD	PLACEBO CONTROLS?	FOLLOW-UP PERIOD	MORTALITY		RISK RATIO (95% CONFIDENCE LIMITS)	TWO-TAILED P VALUE
							DRUG GROUP	CONTROLS		
	hours	thousands of IU	hours			days	no. dead total			
1st European trial, 1969[12]	72	1250	104	72	No	HS	20/83 (24.1%)	15/84 (17.9%)	1.35 (0.74–2.45)	0.32
2d European trial, 1971[13] *	24	250	100	24	No	HS †	69/373 (18.5%)	94/357 (26.3%)	0.70 (0.53–0.92)	0.01
Finnish study, 1971[14]	72	600	Varied	Varied	No	42	22/219 (10.0%)	17/207 (8.2%)	1.22 (0.67–2.24)	0.51
Italian study (CCU), 1971[15] *	12	250	150	12	No	40	19/164 (11.6%)	18/157 (11.5%)	1.01 (0.55–1.85)	0.97
2d Frankfurt study, 1972[16] *	12	250	200	2.5	Yes	HS	13/102 (12.7%)	29/104 (27.9%)	0.46 (0.26–0.81)	0.007
Australian trial (CCU), 1973[17] *	24	250	100	17	No	40 ‡	21/264 (8.0%)	23/253 (9.1%)	0.88 (0.50–1.54)	0.64
						90 §	26/264 (9.8%)	32/253 (12.6%)	0.78 § (0.48–1.27)	0.31
British study (CCU), 1976[18] *	24	250	100	24	Yes	42 ‡	43/302 (14.2%)	44/293 (15.0%)	0.95 (0.64–1.40)	0.79
						6 mo §	48/302 (15.9%)	52/293 (17.7%)	0.90 § (0.63–1.28)	0.55
European Study Group (CCU), 1979[19] *	12	250	100	24	Yes	21 ‡	18/156 (11.5%)	30/159 (18.9%)	0.61 (0.36–1.04)	0.07
						6 mo §	25/156 (16.0%)	50/159 (31.4%)	0.51 § (0.34–0.77)	0.001

*Trial meets criteria for comparable protocol. CCU denotes coronary-care unit.   †The mean hospital stay (HS) was 43 days.
‡The primary follow-up period was longer; these data are derived from published reports.   §More prolonged follow-up of the same trial participants, pooled separately (see text).

$$\hat{RR}_w = \mathrm{Exp} \, [\Sigma \, w_i \, \ln RR_i]/\Sigma \, w_i.$$

where $\hat{RR}_w$ denotes the estimated overall risk ratio, i the trial number, RR_i the risk ratio in the ith trial, and w_i weight, which is the inverse of the variance of RR_i.

In pooling, one implicitly assumes that there is a uniform effect and that differences in the results of individual trials can reasonably be attributed to the play of chance. We applied a chi-square test of heterogeneity[9] and found that the data were compatible with this assumption of a uniform risk ratio, since no statistically significant difference emerged (P = 0.20). We tested the pooled risk ratio for significance[10] and calculated 95 per cent confidence limits.[11]

RESULTS

We have found eight trials[12-19] that meet our initial inclusion criteria (Table 1). The apparent risk ratios in these eight trials vary between 0.46 and 1.35, but there was a tendency for larger trials to indicate a protective effect (i.e., a risk ratio of less than unity), so that the weighted average of these risk ratios is significantly (P = 0.01) less than unity (0.80, with 95 per cent confidence limits of 0.68 to 0.95). This suggests a reduction of about 20 per cent in mortality among patients treated with streptokinase, as compared with controls.

If from this overall analysis we exclude the two studies whose protocols differed most markedly from the others (the First European Working Party Trial[12] and the Finnish study,[14] in which patients were enrolled with a duration of symptoms of up to 72 hours and the dosage regimens differed substantially), then the pooled risk ratio among the six remaining more comparable studies becomes even more significantly less than unity (0.74, with 95 per cent confidence limits of 0.62 to 0.89; P = 0.001).

Most of the early studies were conducted before the advent of coronary-care units. However, four of the more recent studies included only patients in coronary-care units.[15,17-19] Pooling only the mortality from the early weeks of these four studies yields a non-significant risk ratio (0.85, with 95 per cent confidence limits of 0.66 to 1.10; P = 0.23). However, three of these four studies[17-19] reported on more extended follow-up (Table 1), and pooling the results for these three trials at six months (three months for the Australian Study) again yielded a significant risk ratio (0.71, with 95 per cent confidence limits of 0.56 to 0.91; P = 0.008).

There are four additional trials (with results generally favoring streptokinase) that are not listed in Table 1 because the treatment assignment was not by strict randomization.[16,20-22]

DISCUSSION

These results suggest that intravenous streptokinase therapy after acute myocardial infarction reduces mortality over the subsequent few weeks by about 20 per cent. This statistically significant finding is stronger when the six most comparable studies are analyzed separately. Moreover, there is some (albeit inconclusive) suggestion of a protective effect of streptokinase even beyond the sixth week, since with longer follow-up the decreased mortality in the streptokinase-treated coronary-care patients became somewhat more pronounced.

The use of total mortality as the end point includes, of course, any fatal effect of treatment. Not all trials reported on side effects, but those that did found an increased incidence of chills and local bleeding among the streptokinase-treated patients. However, serious complications were not common; typically only 1 to 2 per cent required a reduction of the dose of streptokinase or cessation of the infusion.

Clinical trials often require very large numbers of participants to demonstrate unequivocally a clinically important difference between the treatment and control groups. For example, suppose streptokinase truly reduces mortality from 20 per cent to 16 per cent at six weeks (i.e., leads to 20 per cent fewer deaths). In that case, a trial with about 3800 patients would be required to have a 90 per cent probability of demonstrating such a difference with statistical significance. Trials that are too small are often misinterpreted as demonstrating no effect if the result does not achieve statistical significance (the Type II, or beta, error).[23] By pooling, one may use the information from all randomized trials, whether or not their results attained some conventional level of statistical significance. Such pooling should result in a more precise overall estimate of the effects of treatment (with tighter confidence limits on the range of plausible values for the true risk ratio).

There is a sense, of course, in which the results of pooled analyses may not be as reliable as those of a single trial of the same total size. Trials are most appropriately pooled when the populations studied, treatment regimens, and end points are similar.[21] In all eight studies considered here, the populations consisted of patients thought to have acute myocardial infarction, the treatment was with intravenous streptokinase, and mortality was the primary end point. However, treatment regimens and control groups did differ from study to study, as shown in Table 1. Furthermore, these studies spanned a 15-year period. However, if criteria for including trials are too selective, the results can be very misleading. For this reason, we included all randomized trials in our initial analysis, despite differences in types of patients studied, treatment regimens, and periods of follow-up. However, when we considered only studies with more uniform procedures, the results were similar.

A major limitation of the current pooling study is the uncertain value of applying past results to current medical practice.[25] Almost all the studies of intravenous streptokinase were carried out before widespread use of antiarrhythmic therapy, beta blockade, nitrates, calcium-channel blocking agents, and various other such treatments. On the other hand, intravenous streptokinase may be even more efficacious when combined with modern management.

There is a growing recognition of the need for a large-scale trial of intracoronary streptokinase.[26-29] Our results from pooling past trials of intravenous streptokinase suggest that further studies should be directed not only toward evaluating intracoronary streptokinase but also toward comparing intracoronary with intravenous streptokinase in the treatment of acute myocardial infarction.

We are indebted to Kelly Hallet for expert and patient preparation of the manuscript.

REFERENCES

1. Rentrop P, Blanke H, Karsch KR, et al. Acute myocardial infarction: intracoronary application of nitroglycerin and streptokinase. Clin Cardiol. 1979; 2:354-63.
2. Rentrop P, Blanke H, Karsch KR, Kaiser H, Köstering H, Leitz K. Selective intracoronary thrombolysis in acute myocardial infarction and unstable angina pectoris. Circulation. 1981; 63:307-17.
3. Mathey DG, Kuck K-H, Tilsner V, Krebber H-J, Bleifeld W. Nonsurgical coronary artery recanalization in acute transmural myocardial infarction. Circulation. 1981; 63:489-97.
4. Mason D, ed. Symposium on intracoronary thrombolysis in acute myocardial infarction. Am Heart J. 1981; 102:1123-208.
5. Simon TL, Ware JH, Stengle JM. Clinical trials of thrombolytic agents in myocardial infarction. Ann Intern Med. 1973; 79:712-9.
6. Van de Loo J, Verstraete M. Fibrinolytic treatment of acute myocardial infarction: a question still open. Thromb Diath Haem. 1973; 59: Suppl:203-12.
7. Shaw LW, Cornfield J, Cole CM. Statistical problems in the design of clinical trials and interpretation of results. Thromb Diath Haem. 1973; 59: Suppl:191-202.
8. Rothman KJ, Boice JD Jr. Epidemiologic analysis with a programmable calculator. Bethesda, Md.: United States Department of Health, Education, and Welfare. Public Health Service. National Institutes of Health. 1979. (DHEW publication no. (NIH)79-1649).
9. Sheehe PR. Combination of log relative risk in retrospective studies of disease. Am J Public Health. 1966; 56:1745-50.
10. Mantel N, Haenszel W. Statistical aspects of the analyses of data from retrospective studies of disease. JNCI. 1959; 22:719-48.
11. Miettinen O. Estimability and estimation in case-referent studies. Am J Epidemiol. 1976; 103:226-35.
12. Amery A, Roeber G, Vermeulen HJ, Verstraete M. Single-blind randomised multicentre trial comparing heparin and streptokinase treatment in recent myocardial infarction. Acta Med Scand. 1969; 505: Suppl:5-35.
13. European Working Party. Streptokinase in recent myocardial infarction: a controlled multi-centre trial. Br Med J. 1971; 3:325-31.
14. Heikinheimo R, Ahrenberg P, Honkapohja H, et al. Fibrinolytic treatment in acute myocardial infarction. Acta Med Scand. 1971; 189:7-13.
15. Dioguardi N, Mannucci PM, Lotto A, et al. Controlled trial of streptokinase and heparin in acute myocardial infarction. Lancet. 1971; 2:891-5.
16. Breddin K, Ehrly AM, Fechler L, et al. Die kurzzeitfibrinolyse beim akuten myokardinfarkt. Dtsch Med Wochenschr. 1973; 98:861-73.
17. Bett JHN, Biggs JC, Castaldi PA, et al. Australian multicentre trial of streptokinase in acute myocardial infarction. Lancet. 1973; 1:57-60.
18. Aber CP, Bass NM, Berry CL, et al. Streptokinase in acute myocardial infarction: a controlled multicentre study in the United Kingdom. Br Med J. 1976; 2:1100-4.
19. European Cooperative Study Group for Streptokinase Treatment in Acute Myocardial Infarction. Streptokinase in acute myocardial infarction. N Engl J Med. 1979; 301:797-802.
20. Schmutzler N, Heckner F, Kortge P, et al. Thrombolytic therapy of recent myocardial infarction. I. Introduction, plan of trial, general clinical results. German Med Monthly. 1966; 11:308-14.
21. Schmutzler R, Fritze E, Gebauer D, et al. Fibrinolytic therapy in acute myocardial infarction. Thromb Diath Haem. 1971; 47: Suppl:211-6.
22. Gormsen J. Biochemical evaluation of standard treatment with streptokinase in acute myocardial infarction. Acta Med Scand. 1972; 191:77-85.
23. Freiman JA, Chalmers TC, Smith H, Kuebler RR. The importance of beta, the type II error and sample size in the design and interpretation of the randomized control trial: survey of 71 "negative" trials. N Engl J Med. 1978; 299:690-4.
24. DeSilva RA, Hennekens CH, Lown B, Casscells W. Lignocaine prophylaxis in acute myocardial infarction: an evaluation of randomized trials. Lancet. 1981; 2:855-8.
25. Goldman L, Feinstein AR. Anticoagulants and myocardial infarction: the problems of pooling, drowning, and floating. Ann Intern Med. 1979; 90:92-4.
26. Muller JE, Stone PH, Markis JE, Braunwald E. Let's not let the genie escape from the bottle — again. N Engl J Med. 1981; 304:1294-6.
27. Sobel BE, Bergmann SR. Coronary thrombolysis: some unresolved issues. Am J Med. 1982; 72:1-4.
28. Kolata G. New heart attack treatment discussed. Science. 1981; 214:1229-30.
29. $12 million clinical trial OKd by heart institute council. NIH Week. 1982; 2(24):3-4.

29

The Experimental Evidence for Weight-Loss Treatment of Essential Hypertension
A Critical Review

Melbourne F. Hovell

Abstract: The empirical evidence concerning the therapeutic effects of weight loss for hypertension treatment was reviewed. Interventions were critically reviewed for strength of measures and experimental design. Six of 21 intervention studies proved to be methodologically strong. However, only one study was considered a randomized clinical trial, testing the combined effects of weight reduction and pharmacological treatment of hypertension. Average blood pressure decrease obtained from the methodologically strongest studies was −21 mmHg and −13 mmHg, for systolic and diastolic measures, respectively. This magnitude change suggests that weight loss may be a clinically and statistically significant treatment. Confounding and bias variables, such as adherence to diet, medication, salt consumption, etc., were discussed and future areas of research were outlined. It was concluded that weight loss appears to be an effective and safe treatment of hypertension. (*Am J Public Health* 1982; 72:359–368.)

Introduction

Blood pressure chronically above 140/90 mmHg predisposes individuals to cardiovascular disease and mortality.[1-5] Veterans Administration Hospital Trials and the National Heart, Lung and Blood Institute's Hypertension Detection and Follow-Up Trial (HDFP) indicated that reducing blood pressure (including borderline hypertension) reduces disease and mortality rates.[6-12] Thus, vigorous treatment of elevated blood pressure appears an effective and critical public health service.

However, "treatment" may consist of components independently or jointly responsible for blood pressure reduction. The HDFP experimental group received stepped-care medication prescriptions in conjunction with counseling to change other risk factors (e.g., smoking, weight), and usual-treatment controls were referred to private physicians.[12] Although both groups were prescribed antihypertensive medication, not all in either group received medication (referred care=54.3 per cent to 70.3 per cent; stepped care=75.4 per cent to 86.3 per cent at five years). The blood pressure, morbidity and mortality differences between groups may have been due to nonpharmacological components of treatment.

Investigators have reported therapeutic effects from relaxation, biofeedback, meditation, blood-pressure monitoring, and other nonpharmacologic treatments of hypertension.[13-18] These nonmedication-treatments shed light on possible behavioral factors involved in the etiology, and control of hypertension, and are less dangerous than antihyperten-

sive medication.[19] One nonpharmacological procedure—weight loss—offers special promise for decreasing blood pressure.[20-22]

This paper critically reviews empirical evidence that weight loss decreases blood pressure with special attention to experimentally controlled analyses. This paper does not detail various definitions of hypertension or excess weight, nor are micro level measurements of blood pressure or body weight/composition considered. These are discussed elsewhere.[22-28]

Prevalence of Hypertension and Overweight

Using different standards and measures, researchers have estimated that a large portion of the adult US population is greater than "ideal" weight. The Metropolitan Life Insurance Group has estimated that, for adults over 30 years, 30 per cent of the men and 40 per cent of the women are 20 per cent or more above "desirable" weight.[29] The Build and Blood Pressure Study[1] reported that 6 per cent of males and 11 per cent of females ages 15 to 69 years were 20 per cent or greater than a population standard mean weight for sex and height. Others have reported similar estimates.[30-33]

Prevalence estimates for hypertension (140/90 or greater) range from 10 per cent to more than 30 per cent, depending on age, race and sex.[34-36] The National Health Survey found about 16 per cent of Whites and 33 of Blacks with blood pressure above 160/95 mmHg, after age adjustment.[37] Prevalence of overweight hypertensive persons is most important. Screening of one million people showed 50 per cent higher prevalence of hypertension among self-reported overweight individuals than among those of normal weight.[38] Overweight adults were more prevalent among hypertensive persons.[36-60] In a comprehensive review by Chiang, Perlman, and Epstein,[20] from 20 per cent to 33 per cent of all hypertensive adults were overweight.

Address reprint requests to Melbourne F. Hovell, PhD, MPH, Laboratory for the Study of Behavioral Medicine, Department of Psychiatry, Stanford University School of Medicine, Stanford, CA 94304. This paper, submitted to the Journal June 18, 1981, was revised and accepted for publication October 6, 1981.

From Melbourne F. Hovell, "The Experimental Evidence for Weight-Loss Treatment of Essential Hypertension: A Critical Review," 72(4) *American Journal of Public Health* 359-368 (April 1982). Copyright 1982 American Public Health Association. Reprinted by permission.

Association between Blood Pressure and Body Weight

Most studies of the relationship of elevated blood pressure to excess weight show that the higher the weight, the higher the blood pressure.[61-68] Correlations between weight and blood pressure ranged from .21 to .42 for adults less than 75 years in a number of US studies, and similar findings were reported in Europe.[36-38,69,70] An Australian investigation reported correlations of .21 to .35, depending on age and sex, for persons not under treatment for hypertension. For men under 49 years, the relatively high prevalence of systolic hypertension was independent of age after adjusting for weight.[66] The authors concluded that weight gain contributed significantly to elevated blood pressure. However, this relationship is not universal. Boyle and coworkers[48,64] found the expected positive relation for Whites, but not for Blacks in Charleston, South Carolina. Weisner, et al,[61] found small statistically significant correlations (e.g., .18, .19) between weight and blood pressure when controlling for age. The authors concluded that obesity was only a minor determinant of blood pressure. Similarly, Ballantyne and coworkers[62] found a positive association only for non-smoker males from an untreated hypertensive population. It also appears that selected societies and social groups which have a narrow range of body weight and/or few persons with high blood pressure show little or no association.[39-52,71] These reports serve to temper conclusions concerning weight and blood pressure.

Overall, observational studies argue that excess body weight is related to high blood pressure levels. However, as cross-sectional correlational studies, they do not establish that weight change produces blood pressure change.

Weight Change Association

A few longitudinal analyses have reported data showing correspondence between weight change and subsequent blood pressure change.[50,72-75] Kannel and associates[69] presented information on over 5,000 participants followed for 12 years. Comparing individuals with greatest relative weight gains and those with greatest weight loss showed corresponding increases and decreases in blood pressure, respectively, for obese and nonobese men and women, although statistically significant only for males. For men over 25 years and gaining weight, an increased risk of developing hypertension (160/95 mmHg) was reported. In another Framingham report,[72] a 16-year longitudinal assessment was made for weight and blood pressure change. Considering relative weight and weight change by sex and age groups, this study found statistically significant positive regression coefficients between relative weight change and blood pressure change. For each 10 unit change in relative weight, a 6.6 mmHg and 4.5 mmHg change in systolic pressure was observed for men and women, respectively. For each 10 per cent increase in relative weight, there was a 30 per cent increase in incidence of coronary disease for males. For each 10 per cent decrease in relative weight, there was a 20 per cent decrease in incidence of coronary disease. Slightly smaller relationships were found for women.

Another study examined weight change and blood pressure change over six years, where a 10 Kg change in relative weight corresponded to a 3.9 mmHg and 2.7 mmHg change in systolic and diastolic pressures.[76] Regression coefficients were roughly .41 and .73 for systolic and diastolic readings. However, in one age stratum, a nonsignificant negative relationship (B = -1.03) was obtained. Thus, this investigation found similar results, but a weaker and less consistent relationship between weight change and blood pressure change, perhaps because the study included only women.

These studies provide valuable information concerning weight and blood pressure change. However, they continue to fall short of sufficient information to draw firm conclusions about the effects of weight loss on blood pressure, especially for individuals with hypertension. The proportion of hypertensive persons was not reported and probably small, and, the proportion of persons losing weight tended to be small. In one study,[76] each age stratum showed an overall average gain in weight after six years. Finally, these studies did not report the effect, if any, of weight loss on blood pressure for initially hypertensive persons. The relationships observed seem to reflect weight gain and change in normotensive blood pressure. Even if the positive relationship holds for weight loss among hypertensive persons, studies of a "correlational" design cannot rule out possible confounding unmeasured variables. Hypertensive persons may experience various illnesses and medical treatments, which may result in both decreased weight and blood pressure. For such patients it might be erroneous to attribute blood pressure change to weight change.

Weight Loss Interventions

The best evidence of possible benefits from weight loss must come from experimentally controlled interventions, with hypertensive persons. Only from results of a randomized clinical trial can one be confident that outcomes observed are representative.[77] Twenty-one intervention studies were reviewed and rated for measurement and experimental design quality. From these assessments, studies closest to "ideal" were isolated from others as the primary basis for drawing conclusions about weight loss in the treatment of hypertension.

Methodology

Table 1 lists the variables considered in judging the quality of blood pressure measurement and the arbitrary ratings assigned. In clinical research, many samples are limited to persons representing extremes within the population and so may be expected to "regress" toward the mean following initial measures.[78] One method of reducing this bias is to use repeated measures. Employing trained personnel (ideally "blind" to the study purpose) strengthens the accuracy and consistency of observations. Thus, repeated measures, trained personnel, and similar measurement variables were examined. Similar standards were employed for weight measures, although rated somewhat·differently (Table 2).

TABLE 1—Blood Pressure Measurement Criteria and Point Ratings

Criteria	Points
Repeated measures across calendar time	4
Repeated measures within each visit	2
Explicit observer reliability checks	3
Consistent assessment procedures (e.g., same arm, place, conditions, etc.)	2
Explicitly noted trained personnel	1
Observers experimentally blind to the study purpose and/or group assignment	3
Procedures to reduce expectation bias (e.g., random zero muddler sphygmomanometer)	2

TABLE 3—Research Design Criteria and Point Ratings

Criteria	Points
Inclusion of control group or condition	4
Random allocation of participants to groups	3
Measurement of controls concurrent in time	2
Equal "treatment" of experimental and control participants, except for the experimental variable under study	2
Consistent procedure (adherence to protocol)	1
Inclusion of adherence measures	1
Inclusion of follow-up assessment	1
Unbiased representative sample from a known population	1
Specification of sample characteristics (e.g., race, sex, age, SES, etc.)	1
Experimenters blind to group assignment and/or measures	2

Table 3 shows the standards used to judge the quality of each study's research design. Inclusion of a control group and random allocation were weighted relatively high, while fewer points were assigned for experimenters' being blind to groups or outcomes, adherence measures, and other variables.

These ratings reflect only critical measurement and design features. Other procedures may strengthen a study, while idiosyncratic biases may weaken an otherwise strong analysis. Such details are discussed for selected studies.

Results

Table 4 depicts overall scores assigned for measurement and design variables, and presence or absence of selected key procedures for each study. Most (67 per cent) of the interventions employed repeated measures of blood pressure and weight. Only two in some way blinded persons recording blood pressure, and only one for weight. No report noted explicit reliability checks for either blood pressure or weight. This is surprising for studies published recently, as blood pressure is subject to considerable variability increasing measurement difficulty[78] and even trained observers are subject to measurement errors.[100,101]

Only four reports for blood pressure and five for weight measures achieved more than half the possible total scores for these ratings.

TABLE 2—Body Weight Measurement Criteria and Point Ratings

Criteria	Points
Repeated measures across calendar time	4
Explicit reliability checks[*]	1
Consistent assessment procedures	2
Observers experimentally blind to study purpose and/or group assignments	3
Calculation of relative weight, considering height and sex	1

*Only one point, rather than three as for blood pressure, was assigned for explicit reliability checks of weight based on the assumption that weight is more accurately measured than blood pressure.

Only seven reports included comparison groups or other control procedures, and only three included random allocation (Table 5). Most studies were pre-post measures of treatment procedures for clinic patients. Of the seven including "control" groups, one[89] controlled only for weight loss and not blood pressure, the major outcome to be controlled. Only four studies earned a score greater than half the possible total score for research design.

Nonrandom control procedures are subject to selection bias, where confounding variables (e.g., age, sex, treatment sensitivity) may not be equally distributed among groups. Literature controls suffer from the additional weakness that measures are not obtained at the same time, thus failing to control for the effects of unknown events which occur simultaneously with treatment as explanations for blood pressure change. Linder and Blackburn[89] employed a literature control procedure for their weight loss intervention.

In behavioral science small sample experimental designs have been well developed,[102] where an individual or group serves as its own control. Keys and associates[88] conducted premeasures, repeated measures during a diet intervention, and finally measures during a partial return toward baseline diet. Weight and blood pressure decreased and increased coincident with intervention and return to baseline, respectively. Master and Oppenheimer described the same sequence for one patient.[91] These studies do not provide adequate evidence to warrant generalization to the population at large. However, they do present strong cases for believing that weight loss was responsible for the blood pressure observed.

For an adequate test, not only must one group receive treatment while the control does not but, in addition, all other relevant interventions and experiences should be balanced among groups. This is especially difficult with patients reporting to a clinic for "help". Hypertensive patients are no exception. One of the most carefully designed and experimentally controlled studies reviewed[93] found nonsignificant differences between groups' changes in blood pressure, probably due to differential adjunctive treatment. Experimental participants received diets for weight loss, while control patients were referred to private physicians. The experimental group lost significantly more weight than the control, and blood pressure decreased in both groups. How-

TABLE 4—Methodological Ratings

	Measurement								Design	
	Sample Variable						Total Score		Sample Variable	Total Score
	Repeat. Meas.		Observ. Blind		Reliab. Ck.					
Reference	BP	WT	BP	WT	BP	WT	BP (17 poss)	WT (11 poss)	Control Proc.	(18 poss)
78	+	+	–	–	–	–	4	4	–	1
79	–	–	–	–	–	–	0	0	–	0
80	–	–	–	–	–	–	0	0	+	6
81	+	+	–	–	–	–	4	4	–	0
82	–	–	–	–	–	–	0	0	–	0
83	+	+	–	–	–	–	9	7	+	7
84	+	+	–	–	–	–	4	4	+	0
85	–	–	–	–	–	–	0	0	–	0
86	+	+	+	–	–	–	10	7	–	0
87	+	+	–	–	–	–	4	4	+	11
88	+	+	–	–	–	–	4	5	+ (wt)	6
89	+	+	–	–	–	–	4	4	–	0
90	+	+	–	–	–	–	4	4	–	0
91	–	–	–	–	–	–	0	0	–	0
92	+	+	+	+	–	–	10	8	+	11
93	+	+	–	–	–	–	10	7	+	11
94	+	+	–	–	–	–	6	5	–	0
95	+	+	–	–	–	–	5	5	–	0
96	–	–	–	–	–	–	0	0	–	0
97	+	+	–	–	–	–	7	7	+	13
98	–	–	–	–	–	–	1	1	–	0

ever, only the control group enjoyed an increase in hypotensive prescriptions. Similarly, Tyroler, et al, reported a decrease in hypotensive medications for the experimental group and an increase in prescription for their control group.[98] In this instance, blood pressure differences remained statistically significant for the systolic measure.

Failure to adhere to treatment regimens and unequal distribution among experimental groups for participants not

TABLE 5—Summary Results of "Controlled" Studies

| | Random Allocation | | | |
| | Control | | Intervention | |
Reference	BP Change mm Hg	WT Change kgs	BP Change mm Hg	WT Change kgs
92	−11.2/−5.3	−2.2	−11.9/−6.9	−5.1
93	−6.9/−2.5	−0.7	−37.4/−23.3	−9.5
97	−12.0/−8.0	−1.8	−18.0/−13.0	−8.16

	Nonrandom Allocation			
83	0.5/1.3	−1.8	−33.0/−16.0	−15.0
87	NA	NA	−5.5/−2.0	−12.7
88	NA	−10.0	−18.2/−14.9	−19.5

| Overall Crude Mean Change | | | |
| Control | | Intervention | |
BP mm Hg	WT kgs.	BP mm Hg	WT kgs.
−7.4/−3.6	−3.3	−20.7/−12.7	−11.7

fully adhering are serious flaws in clinical trials.[103-105] Efforts to assess adherence, as well as sustain it, strengthen intervention studies. The Linder and Blackburn study[89] attempted to assess adherence. Blood acetone concentrations from expired air and laboratory physical fitness measures were obtained as indications of diet and exercise compliance. These measures provided only a "some-versus-none" estimate; the degree of adherence was not assessed. It is not clear that such measures were sufficiently sensitive to diet and physical activity behavior. Without validation, it is not known to what degree an individual might adhere to the behavioral prescriptions and fail these tests (false negatives) or vice versa (false positives).

The use of these data also raised concern about possible reactivity in this analysis. Patients were threatened with discharge for poor compliance. Such a contingency may have increased dropouts and raises an ethical question for persons receiving treatment. Despite these reservations, this study served as a model for attempting to assess adherence.

Can Weight Loss "Cause" Decreased Blood Pressure?

Inspection of results reported by the six methodologically strongest analyses[84,88,89,93,94,98] provides the best estimate of effects of weight loss on blood pressure. Table 5 illustrates mean weight and blood pressure changes for each study and overall mean changes for all six studies. For the studies using nonrandom allocation, substantial weight loss (−12.7 to −19.5 kgs) was achieved; more modest decreases were observed in controls (−1.8 to −10.0 kgs). Each intervention group concurrently enjoyed mean decreases in blood pressure (−5.5/−2.0 to.−33/−16 mmHg), but the one control group obtained a small increase in blood pressure (0.5/1.3 mmHg).

Weight changes among the studies employing random allocations[93,94,98] followed the same pattern, with greatest decreases for intervention groups (−5.1 to −9.5 kgs) and relatively small decreases in control groups (−0.7 to −2.2 kgs). The same trend was observed for blood pressure changes. Intervention groups' blood pressures decreased from −11.9/−6.9 to −37.4/−23.3 mmHg, while control's decreased only from −6.9/−2.5 to −12.0/−8.0 mmHg.

Collapsing these changes into crude means shows about −21 mmHg systolic and −13 mmHg diastolic change corresponding to about −12 kgs decrease in weight for intervention groups. Similarly, about −7 mmHg systolic and −4 mmHg diastolic blood pressure changes corresponded to approximately −3 kgs of weight in controls. Most studies found statistically significant differences for all or some comparisons. It is interesting that weight loss was achieved by controls and, here too, blood pressure decreased. These results seem to indicate that decreased weight results in decreased blood pressure. However, inspection of individual studies shows some as equivocal.

Fletcher[84] analyzed 155 obese women attending a medical clinic. Of these, 38 had systolic hypertension and 30 had diastolic hypertension. All were prescribed weight reducing diets (600-1000 cal). Analyses were conducted only for women completing four months of treatment, and only for women who lost 6.3 kgs or more compared to those who lost

less than 6.3 kgs. Thus, not only were groups not allocated at random, but considerable self-selection probably occurred. This left group equivalence for diet adherence, as well as other variables, questionable. Dropouts were ignored and, if "treatment failures" (those not losing weight or decreasing in blood pressure) were more prevalent among dropouts, results could have been biased, making weight loss seem to lower blood pressure.

Defending this analysis, groups had similar age, weight, and initial blood pressures. Moreover, the majority of the dropouts occurred in persons within normal blood pressure categories, which may indicate that obese hypertensive persons are more likely to remain in weight loss treatment than obese normotensive persons.

Perhaps all research is removed from the usual or in vivo environment. However, its value depends, in part, on the degree to which analyses are conducted under situations approximating the community at large. The report by Keys, et al,[88] may be questioned as an unusual laboratory test. Thirty-two normotensive young men, ages 20–33 years, underwent semistarvation under laboratory conditions. Changes from baseline, starvation diet, and return toward baseline were compared. Not surprisingly, with a mean decrease of 14.95 kgs for normal weight men, other changes including modest decreases in blood pressure were observed. To their credit, the authors reported no serious side effects. Nevertheless, it is unclear to what extent these results relate to weight loss in a "free living" situation or for blood pressure change in overweight hypertensive persons. Their results do point out that weight loss in nonobese persons may reduce blood pressure, raising a question about therapeutic benefits of moderate weight loss in normal weight hypertensive volunteers.

No study is perfect, but the analysis reported by Reisen and associates[94] comes the closest among the interventions reviewed. One hundred twenty-one obese hypertensive patients participated in two analyses: a pre-post test of weight reduction in patients not receiving hypotensive medications, and random allocation of patients prescribed antihypertensive medication to a weight loss strategy or control group. Control and weight loss plus medication-treatment groups were reported receiving the same medication and dosage. A dietitian regularly interviewed all patients concerning diet and encouraged patients to adhere to their respective treatments. Blood pressure was measured using an automatic machine, thereby reducing observer bias and drift. Repeated measures for each clinic visit yielded individual means provided reasonable estimates of true blood pressures. Weight and blood pressure analyses were adjusted for age, sex, initial levels, and initial per cent overweight. Moreover, the level of sodium excretion was measured for the two diet groups and the medication control. Three relatively modest criticisms for this study are: 1) the 14 dropouts (relatively few) were not included in the analysis; 2) no experimenter blinding procedures were used; and 3) subjects were recruited from a patients population, thereby potentially limiting generalization.

As noted earlier, Reisen, et al,[94] found decreased weight and blood pressure in the diet only and diet plus medication groups, and relatively little weight loss and decrease in blood pressure for the medicated control group. These differences proved statistically significant, and neither salt consumption nor medication prescriptions appeared to differ among groups. Thus, weight loss, in conjunction with medication treatment, appears to be a more effective means of lowering blood pressure in overweight hypertensive patients than medication alone. Further, the decrease in blood pressure for unmedicated hypertensive patients suggests that weight loss may be an effective treatment alternative to medication.

Collateral Changes

Blood pressure changes associated with weight loss may be a function of collateral changes in hypotensive medication consumption. The controlled studies, except for Keys, et al,[88] either did not make clear whether participants were prescribed medication[84,89] or explicitly noted that the majority were. Both Ramsay, et al,[93] and Tyroler, et al,[98] noted changes in medication prescriptions. This raises the possibility that weight loss intervention inadvertently results in increases prescriptions and lowered blood pressure. In absence of prescription data, this cannot be ruled out.

Not only may prescriptions change, so may the amount of medication consumed, and consumption may increase or decrease. For interventions reviewed, too little information concerning medication adherence was reported to eliminate possible confoundings. The safest conclusion to draw is that weight loss in conjunction with pharmacological treatment seems to lower blood pressure.

High salt intake has been associated with increased blood pressure[106] and salt restriction can decrease pressures.[107,108] Dahl and associates[107] suggest that weight loss may have its hypotensive effect via incidental salt restriction with reduced food intake. Studies reviewed do not fully rule out this possibility. However, contrary evidence was reported by Reisen, et al,[94] were salt excretion did not change with weight loss. This also was supported in the review by Tobian.[108]

Weight loss may be achieved by consuming fewer calories than needed for usual activity levels, by increasing physical activity, or both. These studies concentrated on calorie reduction for weight loss. With the exception of the Linder and Blackburn analysis,[89] none reported measuring physical activity. It is possible that changes in physical activity my have accentuated (e.g., increased activity) or compromised the effects of the diet instruction. Changes in physical activity within control groups also could confound results. It seems unlikely that participants in weight loss programs greatly increase their activity level, but this cannot be ruled out. Future studies could provide valuable information by measuring and/or controlling activity levels.

Incidental salt reduction with calorie restriction may be the mechanism of blood pressure control, as noted earlier. However, there may be other ways by which salt or other factors confound the possible effects of weight loss on blood pressure. Noppa[76] reported that only about 1 per cent to 18 per cent of the blood pressure variance was determined by weight change, depending on age. Tyroler, et al,[98] noted that only a small part of the blood pressure decrease seemed

attributable to weight loss. They suggested that psychotherapeutic benefits of treatment contributed to the hypotensive results. Given decreased blood pressure simply from monitoring,[14,110] relaxation, and biofeedback procedures,[16] it seems possible that weight loss intervention has effects for reasons over and above weight decreases. Perhaps social interaction between caretaker and patient has a direct effect on physiology,[111] reducing "stress" and blood pressure. Future research should explore the effects of usual components of weight loss treatments.

Although adherence to medication is a recognized concern,[109] it seems implausible that the blood pressure changes reported in studies reviewed were a function of collateral increases in medication; increased adherence does not appear to limit the practical value attributable to weight loss. However, the limited evidence showing blood pressure decrease with weight loss, in absence of salt restriction, is insufficient to determine separate effects of these variables. If lowered blood pressure is due to salt reduction, then patients may be subjected to possible emotional and financial expense from weight loss treatment, when simple salt restriction might be as effective. Additional studies are needed to tease out the separate and combined effects of weight and salt reduction.

Replication and Generalization

Replication determines reliability of an association. The generalizability of an association is demonstrated by replication under varying circumstances. Most of the 21 intervention studies reviewed showed a positive association between weight loss and blood pressure decrease. Table 6 reveals that these reports were distributed across four different age groups in both males and females. Although foreign research was not systematically sampled, this survey shows positive results in England, Israel and the US. These replications, uncontrolled and controlled, present a compelling argument for the generalization that weight loss reduces blood pressure. Failure to conduct analyses by socioeconomic status and the questionable function of weight change among Blacks tempers this conclusion.

Potential Therapeutic Value of Weight Loss

Estimated Incidence Reduction

Tyroler and associates[98] presented an enticing analysis of the seven-year incidence of diastolic hypertension and relative risk for weight change. Across initial weight groups, they obtained an incidence for diastolic hypertension of 16.8 per cent. Over half (58.3 per cent) of individuals gaining more than 4.5 kgs and initially overweight, were hypertensive (diastolic). Comparing the incidence of overweight persons who gained 4.5 kgs or more with normal weight persons who gained less than 4.5 kgs (including persons losing weight), the relative risk of diastolic blood pressures above 105 mmHg was 6.9. Comparing various initial weight and weight change groups showed relative risks of diastolic hypertension almost universally above 1.5. Thus, many

TABLE 6—Distribution of Weight and Blood Pressure Outcomes by Age, Sex and Country

	Wt. Decrease	NR*	Total	Systolic Decrease	NR	Total	Diastolic Decrease	NR	Total
	N = 18	3	21	N = 16	5	21	N = 15	6	21
Age (years)									
20–30	3			3			2		
31–40	4			4			4		
41–50	6			6			6		
51+	3			2			2		
NR	2			1			1		
Sex									
M & F	11			8			7		
M	3			3			3		
F	3			4			4		
NR	1			1			1		
Country									
United States	14			11			10		
England	3			4			4		
Israel	1			1			1		
NR	0			0			0		

*Some studies did not report (NR) weight change, blood pressure change, or the age or sex of participants.

people were becoming hypertensive, especially among weight gainers initially overweight. Assuming a causal relationship, these investigators estimated that a 41 per cent reduction in the incidence of diastolic hypertension could be achieved, providing at least one-third of their cohort received treatment, that treatment decreased weight in those initially overweight and prevented weight gain in those of normal weight. Two tentative conclusions might be drawn from these estimates: 1) almost half of expected hypertension cases may be prevented by weight loss and prevention of weight gain in normotensive persons; and 2) enormous effort and community resources are necessary to reduce weight gain in one-third of the adult population. Tyroler and associates[98] offer a tantilizing possibility and challenge.

Expectations for Effective Weight Loss Intervention

Within the weight loss literature, behavior modification is held as an effective weight loss intervention.[112,113] However, as noted by Wooley and associates,[114] these treatments offer no panacea. The degree of weight loss is about 4.5 to 6.8 kgs, with relatively poor maintenance beyond one year for behavioral treatments. Indeed Graham and coworkers[115] showed only a modest mean weight loss (3.32 kgs) 4.5 years after treatment.

However, the weight changes reported for the 21 studies reviewed here hint at greater effectiveness among hypertensive patients (crude mean weight loss of 12.5 kgs). Perhaps overweight hypertensive persons are more responsive to weight loss treatment than are normotensive overweight, as suggested by the fewer dropouts among hypertensive patients reported by Fletcher.[84] Reported weight loss of 4.5 kgs to 13.5 kgs justifies hope of achieving moderate weight loss. It should be noted that mean weight losses of 4.5 kgs approaches the more "effective" level reported by Tyroler and associates[98] for which estimates of decreased risk of hypertension were made.

Future Research

This review suggests a number of areas for further investigation. A randomized clinical trial of the effects of weight loss in overweight borderline hypertensive patients not taking hypotensive medication is needed to separate the effects of weight loss alone from weight loss plus medication. A controlled trial testing weight loss while salt consumption is held constant and analysis of salt reduction without weight loss in obese hypertensives could provide data illuminating the various diet treatment options. Based on Keys, et al.[88] and other studies reviewed, where weight loss in nonobese persons resulted in blood pressure decreases, it may be useful to test the value of moderate weight reduction in normal weight hypertensive volunteers, especially those with borderline hypertension. Component analyses of weight loss intervention may be valuable as well. Such studies may be able to identify "caring" procedures and/or sensitizing effects which could aid nonobese hypertensives or obese hypertensives unable to lose weight. A tantilizing hypothesis, worthy of experimental test, concerns the possible behavioral-psychological differences for weight loss among hypertensive versus normotensive overweight persons. Obese hypertensive patients, concerned about high blood pressure, may be more "motivated" to follow weight loss instructions than the overweight, normotensive patients.

The interventions reviewed provided no information concerning long-term efforts of weight loss intervention. Weight loss tends to be fragile, with limited maintenance. The long-term success of weight loss among hypertensive persons and the permanence of blood pressure reduction is another area of needed research. In conjunction with maintenance analyses, assessment of changes in morbidity and mortality would provide important estimates of the ultimate health benefits. Providing weight loss can be maintained, a large scale community trail, including morbidity and mortality measures, may be appropriate. Finally, a primary prevention test of weight loss/maintenance, in persons at risk for development of hypertension, seems warranted.

Conclusions

The National High Blood Pressure Education Program Coordinating Committee[116] published formal recommendations concerning the dietary management of hypertension:

". . . . For borderline hypertension in subjects with excess weight, or in those overweight subjects with drug intolerance, weight reduction has been suggested as a reasonable first step in treatment, with careful monitoring of progress by the patient's physician . . ."

This review of uncontrolled and controlled treatment studies supports the Committee's recommendations, with the best evidence provided by one methodologically well designed study.[94] For practical purposes, weight loss appears an effective adjunctive therapy when combined with pharmacological treatment to reduce blood pressure in overweight hypertensive patients, and may offer similar benefits to nonmedicated patients.

REFERENCES

1. Society of Actuaries: Build and Blood Pressure Study, vol 1. Chicago, 1959.
2. McGee D, Gordon T: The results of the Framingham study applied to four other US-based epidemiologic studies of cardiovascular disease. In: The Framingham Study, An Epidemiological Investigation of Cardiovascular Disease, Pub. No. (NIH) 76-1083. Washington DC: US Dept of Health, Education, and Welfare, April 1976, section 31.
3. Pooling Project Research Group: Relationship of blood pressure, serum cholesterol, smoking habit, relative weight and ECG abnormalities to incidence of major coronary events, final report of the Pooling Project. J Chronic Dis 1978; 31:201-306.
4. Shurtleff D: Some characteristics related to the incidence of cardiovascular disease and death, Framingham Study 18 year follow-up. In: The Framingham Study, An Epidemiological Investigation of Cardiovascular Disease, Pub. No. (NIH) 74-599. Washington DC: US Dept of Health, Education, and Welfare, 1974, section 30.
5. Gordon T, Kannel WB: Predisposition to atherosclerosis in the head, heart, and legs—the Framingham Study. JAMA 1972; 221:661-666.
6. Veterans Administration Cooperative Study Group on Antihypertensive Agents: Effects of treatment of morbidity in hypertension—results in patients with diastolic blood pressure averaging 115 through 126 mmHg. JAMA 1967; 202:1028-1034.
7. Veterans Administration Cooperative Study Group on Antihypertensive Agents: Effects of treatment on morbidity in hypertension, II—results in patients with diastolic blood pressure averaging 90 through 114 mmHg. JAMA 1970; 213:1143-1152.
8. The Hypertension Detection and Follow-up Program: Hypertension, Detection and Follow-up Program Cooperative Group. Prev Med 1976; 5:207-215.
9. The Hypertension Detection and Follow-up Program: A progress report, Hypertension Detection and Follow-up Program Cooperative Group. Cir Res 1977; 40 (Suppl. 1):106-109.
10. Patient participation in a hypertension control program: Hypertension, Detection and Follow-up Program Cooperative Group. JAMA 1978; 239:1507-1514.
11. Therapeutic control of blood pressure after one year in the

12. Hypertension Detection and Follow-up Program: Hypertension, Detection and Follow-up Program Cooperative Group. Prev Med 1979; 8:2-13.
12. Hypertension Detection and Follow-up Cooperative Group: Five year findings of the Hypertension Detection and Follow-up Program, I—reduction in mortality of persons with high blood pressure, including mild hypertension. JAMA 1979; 242:2562-2571.
13. Surwit R, Hager J, Feldman T: The role of feedback in voluntary control of blood pressure in instructed subjects. J Appl Behav Anal 1977; 10:625-631.
14. Laughlin K, Fisher L, Sherrard D: Blood pressure reductions during self-recording of home blood pressure. Amer Heart J 1979; 98:629-634.
15. Taylor C, Farquhar J, Nelson E: Relaxation therapy and high blood pressure. Arch Gen Psychiatry 1977; 34:339-342.
16. Black H: Nonpharmacologic therapy for hypertension. Amer J Med 1979; 66:837-842.
17. Shapiro A, Schwartz G, Ferguson D: Behavioral methods in the treatment of hypertension—a review of their clinical status. Ann Intern Med 1977; 86:626-636.
18. Frumkin K, Nathan R, Prout M: Nonpharmacologic control of essential hypertension in man—a critical review of the experimental literature. Psychosom Med 1978; 40:294-320.
19. Perry H, Goldman A, Lavin M, et al: Evaluation of drug treatment in mild hypertension—VA-NHLBI feasibility trail. Ann NY Acad Sci 1978; 304:267-288.
20. Chiang B, Perlman L, Epstein F: Overweight and hypertension, a review. Circ 1969; 39:403-421.
21. Sims E, Phinney S, Vaswani A: The management of hypertension associated with obesity. Int J Obes 1978; 2:117-125.
22. Brozek J, Chapman C, Keys A: Drastic food restriction-effect on cardiovascular dynamics in normotensive and hypertensive conditions. JAMA 1948; 137:1569-1574.
23. Heller R, Rose G, Pedoe T: Blood pressure measurement in the United Kingdom Heart Disease Prevention Project. J Epidemiol Community Health 1978; 32:235-238.
24. Souchek J, Stamler J, Dyer A, et al: The value of two or three versus a single reading of blood pressure at a first visit. J Chronic Dis 1979; 32:197-210.
25. Seltzer CC, Stoudt HW, Bell B, et al: Reliability of relative body weight as a criterion of obesity. Am J Epidem 1970; 92:339-350.
26. Seltzer CC, Mayer J: A simple criterion of obesity. Postgrad Med 1965; 38:A101-107.
27. Florey CV du: The use and interpretation of Ponderal index and other weight-height ratios in epidemiological studies. J Chronic Dis 1970; 23:93-103.
28. Womersley J, Durnin JV: A comparison of the skinfold method with extent of overweight and various weight-height relationships in the assessment of obesity. Brit J Nutr 1977; 38:271-284.
29. Metropolitan Life Insurance Company of New York: New weight standards for men and women. Statistical Bulletin/Metropolitan Life Insurance Company 1959; 40:1-10.
30. Christakis G: The prevalence of adult obesity. In: Bray GA (ed): Obesity in Perspective. Bethesda: DHEW Pub. No (NIH) 75-708, 1973.
31. Albrink MJ: Obesity. In: Beeson PB, MdDermott W (eds): Textbook of Medicine. Philadelphia: W. B. Saunders, 1975, pp 1375-1386.
32. Kolata GB: Obesity—a growing problem. Science 1977; 198:905-906.
33. Knittle JL, Ginnsberg-Fellner F, Brown RE: Adipose tissue development in man. Am J Clin Nutr 1979; 30:762-766.
34. Kannel WB, Dawber TR: Hypertension cardiovascular disease—the Framingham Study. In: Onesti G, Kim KE, Moyer J (eds): Hypertension—Mechanics and Management. New York: Grune and Stratton, 1971.
35. Hypertension Detection and Follow-up Program Cooperative Group: The Hypertension Detection and Follow-up Program—a progress report. Cir Res 1977; 40 (suppl. 1):106-109.

36. Epstein FH, Francis T, Hayner N, *et al:* Prevalence of chronic diseases and distribution of selected physiologic variables in a total community, Tecumseh, Michigan. Amer J Epidem 1965; 81:307–322.

37. National Center for Health Statistics: Hypertension in Adults 25–74 Years of Age: United States 1971–1975. National Health Survey series 11, No. 221, US Department of Health and Human Services, Public Health Service, Office of Research, Statistics, and Technology, National Center for Health Statistics, Hyattsville, MD, April 1981, Pub. No. (PHS) 81-1671.

38. Stamler R, Stamler J, Riedlinger WF, *et al:* Weight and blood pressure, findings in hypertension screening of 1 million Americans. JAMA 1978; 240:1607–1610.

39. Whyte H: Behind the adipose curtain. Amer J. Cardiol 1965; 15:66–80.

40. Whyte H: Blood pressure and obesity. Circulation 1959; 19:511–515.

41. Shaper A: Blood pressure studies in East Africa. *In:* Stamler J, Stamler R, Pullman TN (eds): The Epidemiology of Hypertension. New York: Grune and Stratton, 1967, pp 139–145.

42. Keys A, Aravanis C, Blackburn HW, *et al:* Epidemiological studies related to coronary heart disease: characteristics of men aged 40–59 in seven countries. Acta Med Scand (suppl. 460), 1967.

43. Palmai G: Skinfold thickness in relation to body weight and arterial blood pressure. Med J Aust 1962; 2:13–15.

44. Boe J, Humerfelt S, Wedervang G: Blood pressure in a population—blood pressure readings and height and weight determinations in the adult population of the City of Bergen. Acta Med Scand (suppl. 321), 1957.

45. Doyle AE, Lovell RRH: Blood pressure and body build in men in tropical and temperate Australia. Clin Sci 1961; 20:243–247.

46. Aleksandrow D: Studies on the epidemiology of hypertension in Poland. *In:* Stamler J, Stamler R, Pullman TN (eds): The Epidemiology of Hypertension. New York: Grune and Stratton, 1967, pp 82–97.

47. Hunter JD: Diet, body build, blood pressure and serum cholesterol levels in coconut-eating polynesians. Fed Proc 1962; (suppl 11) 21:36–43.

48. Boyle E, Briffey W, Nichman M, *et al:* Epidemiological study of hypertension among racial groups in Charleston County, South Carolina—the Charleston Heart Study, Phase II. *In:* Stamler J, Stamler R, Pullman TN (eds): The Epidemiology of Hypertension. New York: Grune and Stratton, 1967, pp 193–203.

49. McDonough J, Garrison G, Hames C: Blood pressure and hypertensive disease among Negroes and Whites in Evans County, Georgia. *In:* Stamler J, Stamler R, Pullman TN (eds): The Epidemiology of Hypertension. New York: Grune and Stratton, 1967, pp 167–187.

50. Miall WE, Bell RA, Lovell HG: Relation between change in blood pressure and weight. Brit J Prev Sco Med 1968; 22:73–80.

51. Robinson SC, Brucer M, Mass J: Hypertension and obesity. J Lab Clin Med 1939; 25:807–822.

52. Thomas CB, Cohen BH: Familiar occurrence of hypertension and coronary artery disease; with observations concerning obesity and diabetes. Ann Intern Med 1955; 42:90–127.

53. Chiang BN, Ting N, Li YB, *et al:* Maximal exercise responses in middle aged hypertensive and normotensive Chinese males: a preliminary report. Chin Med J (Taiwan) 1967; 14:239–250.

54. Larimore JW: A study of blood pressure in relation to types of body habitus. Arch Intern Med 1923; 31:567–572.

55. Marks HH: Influence of obesity on morbidity and mortality. Bull NY Acad Med 1960; 36:296–308.

56. Huber EG: Systolic blood pressures of health adults in relation to body weight. JAMA 1927; 88:1554–1557.

57. Green MB, Beckman M: Obesity and hypertension. New York J Med 1948; 48:1250–1284.

58. Master AM, Jaffee HL, Chesky K: Relationship of obesity of coronary disease and hypertension. JAMA 1953; 153:1499–1501.

59. Padmavati S, Gupta S: Blood pressure studies in rural and urban groups in Delhi. Circulation 1959; 19:395–405.

60. Stamler J, Berkson DM, Lindberg HA, *et al:* Racial patterns of coronary heart disease—blood pressure, body weight and serum cholesterol in Whites and Negroes. Geriatrics 1961; 16:382–396.

61. Weisner RL, Fuchs RJ, Kay TD, *et al:* Body fat—its relationship to coronary heart disease, blood pressure, lipids and other risk factors measured in a large male population. Amer J Med 1976; 61:815–824.

62. Ballantyne D, Devine BL, Fife R: Interrelation of age, obesity, cigarette smoking and blood pressure in hypertensive patients. Brit Med J 1978; 1:880–881.

63. Noppa H, Bengtsson C, Bjorntorp P, *et al:* Overweight in women, metabolic aspects. Acta Med Scand 1978; 203:135–141.

64. Boyle E: Biological patterns in hypertension by race, sex, body weight and skin color. JAMA 1970; 213:1637–1643.

65. Symonds B: The blood pressure of healthy men and women. JAMA 1923; 80:232–236.

66. Brennan PJ, Simpson JM, Blacket RB, *et al:* The effects of body weight on serum cholesterol, serum triglycerides, serum urate and systolic blood pressure. Aust N Z J Med 1980; 10:15–20.

67. Sive PH, Medalic JH, Kahn HA, *et al:* Correlation of weight-height index with diastolic and with systolic blood pressure. Brit J Prev Soc Med 1970; 24:201–204.

68. Society of Actuaries: Blood Pressure Study, 1979. Chicago, 1980.

69. Kannel WB, Brand N, Skinner JJ: The relation of adiposity to blood pressure and development of hypertension—the Framingham Study. Ann Intern Med 1967; 67:48–59.

70. Bjerkedal T: Overweight and hypertension. Acta Med Scand 1957; 159:13–26.

71. Epstein FH, Eckhoff RD: Epidemiology of high blood pressure—geographic distributions and etiological factors. *In:* Stamler J, Stamler R, Pullman TN (eds): The Epidemiology of Hypertension. New York: Grune and Stratton, pp 155–160.

72. Ashley FW, Kannel WB: Relation of weight change to changes in atherogenic traits—the Framingham Study. J Chronic Dis 1974; 27:103–114.

73. Johnson BC, Karunas TM, Epstein FH: Longitudinal change in blood pressure in individuals, families and social groups. Clin Sci Mol Med 1973; 45:35s–45s.

74. Rabkin SW, Mathewson FA, Msu P: Relation of body weight to development of ischemic heart disease in a cohort of young North American men after a 26 year observation period—the Manitoba Study. Amer J Cardiol 1977; 39:452–458.

75. Hsu P, Mathewson FA. Rabkins SW: Blood pressure and body mass index patterns, a longitudinal study. J Chronic Dis 1977; 30:93–113.

76. Noppa H: Body weight change in relation to incidence of ischemic heart disease and change in risk factors for ischemic heart disease. Amer J Epidem 1980; 111:693–704.

77. Lilienfeld A, Lilienfeld DE: Foundations of Epidemiology. New York: Oxford University Press, 1980, pp 256–275.

78. Sheppard DS: Reliability of blood pressure measurements—implications for designing and evaluating programs to control hypertension. Presented at the National Conference of High Blood Pressure Control, Houston March 24, 1980.

79. Adlersberg D, Coler HR, Laval J: Effect of weight reduction on course of arterial hypertension. Journal of Mount Sinai Hospital 1946; 12:984–992.

80. Alexander JK: Effects of weight reduction on the cardiovascular system. *In:* Bray GA (ed): Obesity in Perspective. Washington DC: DHEW Pub. No. (NIH) 75-708, 1973, pp 233–236.

81. Benedict FG, Roth P: Effects of a prolonged reduction in diet on 25 men—influence on basal metabolism and nitrogren excretion. Proc Nat Acad Sci 1918; 4:149–152.

82. Evans FA, Strang JM: The treatment of obesity with low caloric diets. JAMA 1931; 97:1063–1069.

83. Fellows HH: Studies of relatively normal obese individuals

during and after dietary restrictions. Amer J Med Sci 1931; 181:301–312.

84. Fletcher AP: The effect of weight reduction upon the blood pressure of obese hypertensive women. Quart J Med 1954; 23:331–346.

85. Genuth SM, Castro JH, Vertes V: Weight reduction in obesity by outpatient semistarvation. JAMA 1974; 230:987–991.

86. Green MB, Beckman M: Obesity and hypertension. NY State J Med 1948; 48:1250–1253.

87. Jung RT, Shetty PS, Bernard M, et al: Role of catecholamines in hypotensive response to dieting. Brit Med J 1979; 1:12–13.

88. Keys A, Henschel A, Taylor HL: The size and function of the human heart at rest, semi-starvation and in subsequent rehabilitation. A J Physiol 1947; 150:153–169.

89. Linder PG, Blackburn GL: Multidisciplinary approach to obesity utilizing fasting modified by protein-sparing therapy. Obesity Bariat Med 1976; 5:198–216.

90. Martin L: Effect of weight-reduction on normal and raised blood pressures in obesity. Lancet 1952; 2:1051–1053.

91. Master AM, Oppenheimer ET: A study of obesity—circulatory, roentgenray and electrocardiographic investigations. JAMA 1929; 92:1652–1656.

92. Preble WE: Obesity—observations on one thousand cases. Boston Med Surg J 1923; 188:617–621.

93. Ramsay LE, Ramsay MH, Hettiarachchi J, et al: Weight reduction in a blood pressure clinic. Brit Med J 1978; 2:244–245.

94. Reisen E, Abel R, Modan M, et al: Effect of weight loss without salt restriction on the reduction of blood pressure in overweight hypertensive patients. N Engl J Med 1978; 298:1–6.

95. Salzano JV, Gunning RV, Mastopaulo TN, et al: Effect of weight loss on blood pressure. J Amer Diet Ass 1958; 34:1309–1312.

96. Stamler J, Farinaro E, Mojonnier LM, et al: Prevention and control of hypertension by nutritional-hygienic means. JAMA 1980; 243:1819–1823.

97. Terry AH: Obesity and hypertension. JAMA 1923; 81:1283–1284.

98. Tyroler HA, Heyden S, Hames CG: Weight and hypertension—Evans County studies of Blacks and Whites. In: Paul O (ed): Epidemiology and Control of Hypertension. Miami: Symposia Specialists, 1975, pp 177–201.

99. Wilcox RG: Serum lipid concentrations and blood pressure in obese women. Brit Med J 1978; 1:1513–1515.

100. Kelly MB: A review of the observational data collection and reliability procedures reported in the Journal of Applied Behavior Analysis. J Appl Behav Anal 1977; 10:97–101.

101. Kazdin A: Artifact, bias and complexity of assessment—the ABCs of reliability. J Appl Behav Anal 1977; 10:141–150.

102. Hersen M, Barlow D: Single Case Experimental Designs. Strategies for Studying Behavior Change. New York: Pergamon Press, 1976.

103. Sackett DL: The magnitude of compliance and noncompliance. In: Sackett DL (ed): Compliance with Therapeutic Regimens. Baltimore: The Johns Hopkins University Press, 1976, pp 9–25.

104. Goldsmith CH: The effects of differing compliance distributions on the planning and statistical analysis of therapeutic trials. In: Sackett DL (ed): Compliance with Therapeutic Regimens. Baltimore: The Johns Hopkins University Press, 1976, pp 137–151.

105. Feinstein AR: Compliance bias and the interpretation of therapeutic trials. In: Sackett DL (ed): Compliance with Therapeutic Regimens. Baltimore: The John Hopkins University Press, 1976, pp 152–168.

106. Tobian L: Dietary salt (sodium) and hypertension. A J Clin Nutr 1979; 32:2659–2662.

107. Dahl LK, Silver L, Christie RW: The role of salt in the fall of blood pressure accompanying reduction in obesity. N Engl J Med 1958; 258:1186–1192.

108. Tobian L: The relationship of salt to hypertension. A J Clin Nutr 1979; 32:2739–2748.

109. Dunbar JM, Marshall GD, Hovell MF: Behavioral strategies for improving compliance. In: Haynes RB, Taylor DW, Sackett DL (eds): Compliance in Health Care. Baltimore: The Johns Hopkins University Press, 1979, pp 174–192.

110. Hovell MF, Black DR, Rogers T, et al: A behavioral systems intervention for hypertensive patients. Presented at the 88th Annual Convention of the American Psychological Association, Montreal, September 1980.

111. Christian JJ: The potential role of the adrenal cortex as affected by social rank and population density on experimental epidemics. Amer J Epidem 1968; 87:255–264.

112. Abramson E: Behavioral approaches to weight control—an updated review. Behav Res Ther 1977; 15:355–364.

113. Williams BJ, Martin S, Foreyt JP, (eds): Obesity—Behavioral Approaches to Dietary Management. New York: Brunner/Mazel, 1976.

114. Wooley SC, Wooley OW, Dyrenforth SR: Theoretical, practical and social issues in behavioral treatments of obesity. J Appl Behav Anal 1979; 12:3–26.

115. Graham LE, Taylor CB, Hovell MF: Five year follow-up to a behavioral weight loss program II—maintenance, adherence and physical activity. (In preparation.)

116. National High Blood Pressure Education Program Coordinating Committee: Statement on the Role of Dietary Management in Hypertension Control. Bethesda: NIH, 1979.

ACKNOWLEDGMENTS

This paper was prepared while the author was serving as a postdoctoral scholar in epidemiology, School of Public Health, University of California, Berkeley. The advice and editorial assistance of L. Syme, B. Cann, F. Hovell, C. Cauchi, W. Winkelstein, W. Reeves and coworkers at Stanford are acknowledged and appreciated. Preparation of this manuscript was supported, in part, by grants (Behavioral Factors in Cardiovascular Disease Etiology No. HL7365, University of California, Berkeley; and Recruitment and Adherence contract No. 71-2161-L) from the National Heart, Lung, and Blood Institute, DHHS.

30

A Review and Critique of Controlled Studies of the Effectiveness of Preventive Child Health Care

William R. Shadish, Jr.

There is considerable controversy over the value of preventive child health care. Much of this controversy seems generated in spite of empirical evidence, rather than because of it. In a review of 38 controlled empirical studies, significant support was found for the general effectiveness of preventive child health care. Specific interventions for specific problems had most support, while the effectiveness of broad-scale interventions was less clear. Many methodological problems were found in most studies. On the basis of the evidence, it might be concluded that preventive child health care has been given only the weakest of tests, but those tests are encouraging.

> *Children need continuing and comprehensive medical attention aimed at prevention*
> (Harvard Child Health Project, 1977)

> *Pediatric care has little impact on children's health*
> (Ghez & Grossman, Note 1)

These statements are endpoints of a continuum of opinions concerning preventive child health care. Some authors suggest that such preventive care is effective and should be central to a comprehensive approach to child health. Such persons favor increases in health services to children, including federally mandated programs like Early and Periodic Screening, Diagnosis

This work is a revised version of a report previously published by the Health Care Financing Administration prepared under grant #18-97265/5-01 from the Health Care Financing Administration, Department of Health, Education and Welfare and Robert Wood Johnson Foundation grant #4429, to the Center for Health Services and Policy Research. Requests for reprints should be sent to Department of Psychology, Northwestern University, Evanston, Illinois, 60201.

From William R. Shadish, Jr., "A Review and Critique of Controlled Studies of the Effectiveness of Preventive Child Health Care," 2(1) *Health Policy Quarterly* 24-52 (Spring 1982). Copyright © 1982 Human Sciences Press. Printed by permission of the publisher.

and Treatment (EPSDT), and the Child Health Assurance Program (CHAP). Other authors suggest that such efforts may not be worth the money. They are cautious in recommending increased health services *carte blanche,* preferring to see more and better evidence that such services are worthwhile. Unfortunately, though some authors are remarkably clear in their critiques, others fail to address basic definitional issues. Thus, what could be a direct and candid exchange of viewpoints and evidence is often a morass of unfocused opinion.

A major factor in this confusion is lack of attention to the relevant empirical literature. A central thesis of the present article is that views are proliferating among both advocates and critics in spite of the evidence rather than because of it. There are few sound analyses of the empirical literature, but a plethora of poorly grounded opinion. In this article, both opinion and evidence will be presented with the goal of abandoning poorly grounded conclusions and identifying more valid and productive ones for further research.

PREVENTION

Many terms are used in the preventive health care literature, and some conventions are common regarding their usage. One distinction is between efficacy and effectiveness. To quote Starfield (1977a):

> Efficacy denotes the degree to which diagnostic and therapeutic procedures used in practice can be supported by scientific evidence of their usefulness under optimum conditions. Whether or not these procedures are applied adequately in practice, and whether they produce the intended results when so applied are matters of effectiveness. (p. 71)

Efficacy is necessary to, but not sufficient for, effectiveness. This article focuses on effectiveness. It is often of most concern to policymakers, who accept the efficacy of procedure under ideal conditions, but have to deal with less than ideal conditions in implementing it.

Prevention is not easily defined. Wallace and Oglesby (1972) list 43 service categories that are aspects of preventive maternal and child health care. They include family planning, poison control programs, immunization, treatment of otitis media, and mass screening programs. In fact, this diversity is apparent whenever authors attempt to define prevention (e.g. Mechanic, 1978). Schweitzer (1975) thus notes:

> The term "preventive medicine" does not represent a single act of diagnosis and treatment; rather it represents a bundle of services that have to be analyzed both singly and jointly to account for differing diagnostic and treatment parameters. (p. 23)

Preventive child health care has been criticized in varying degrees (Mechanic, 1978; Ghez & Grossman, Note 1) as untested or ineffective (though dental, prenatal, and infant care are seldom questioned). Criticisms of specific activities have also been made. For example, some authors have suggested that, with few or no exceptions, screening procedures cannot be justified or are untested (Bailey, Kiehl, Akram, Loughlin, Metcalf, Jain, & Perrin, 1974; Bernick, 1977a, 1977b; Eggertsen, Schneeweiss & Bergman, 1980; Frankenburg, 1973; Holland, 1974; Holt, 1974; White, 1975). Other authors have suggested that physical examinations are of dubious worth (Braren & Elinson, 1972; Yankauer & Lawrence, 1955; Yankauer & Lawrence, 1956; Yankauer, Lawrence, & Ballou, 1957; Yankauer, Frantz, Drislane, & Katz, 1962).

Finally, just as there is variation in preventive activities, there is variation in the outcome variables that have been used in evaluating child health care. Some authors argue forcefully that equity in the distribution of health services should be a clear and paramount goal for national child health policy (Schorr, 1978), in light of existing inequities in distribution (German et al., 1976). Other authors suggest cost-benefit or cost-effectiveness analysis of preventive care (Bay, Flathman, & Nestman, 1976; Schweitzer, 1975), though this is difficult and rarely done (Lave & Lave, 1978). The most frequent criterion for evaluating preventive health services is health status, including broad mortality and specific morbidity indices. It is difficult, however, to argue that one of these three kinds of variables is more important than another. The choice of an outcome variable is at least in part a value judgement and a political act, and in part a statement of the practical options open to the researcher.

PREVENTION AND EMPIRICAL LITERATURE

Two observations suggest that much has been written about preventive child health care that is not well grounded in empirical literature. First, until recently there were no methodologically critical reviews of literature directly concerned with preventive child health care. (The 1979 report of the Canadian Medical Association Task Force on the Periodic Health Examination has a small relevant section).

Second, many statements about preventive child health care do not afford the empirical literature adequate presentation. These statements frequently occur in the context of policy papers, which can have an important impact on policymakers. Thus, Marmor (1977a, 1977b) discusses prevention in the context of national health insurance, as do Ghez and Grossman (Note 1). The author's purpose usually is not to provide any comprehensive review of the literature regarding prevention. Rather, it is to support or oppose a particular policy. Citations and references are used selectively to make the author's case. The results of such articles, however, do not always reflect the available empirical evidence. This is true in the case of preventive child care.

Empirical research should not be the only factor to enter into a policy decision. The democratic process demands multiple inputs from multiple constituencies, of which evidence from the scientific community is only a small part (Cook & Cook, 1977). The evidence, however, should be given a fair presentation. An examination of a sample of policy statements will illustrate their difficulties as vehicles for fair presentation of evidence.

Policy statements make many points in limited space. Thorough presentation of references is usually sacrificed. Ghez and Grossman (Note 1) present more references than most authors, yet they cite only nine references in support of their critique of pediatric care. Not all are empirical studies, and not all are cited in published form. Schorr (1978), an avowed advocate of child health care, cites only two references in regards to routine child health services to support her broad conclusion that "the evidence is clear that personal health services are important and, when delivered properly, can contribute significantly to health and well-being" (p. 371).

Policy statements are prone to interpret things as consistent with the case being made. Consider what Marmor says about preventive care (1977a):

> Economists Burton Weisbrod and Ralph Andreano conclude that preventive care can increase costs without significantly raising the level of health. They attribute apparent cost-savings in the Kaiser-Permanente plan (which is often cited as a model of the medical and financial efficacy of prevention) "to various factors, many of which are unrelated to preventive care." (p. 84)

One is tempted to infer that Andreano and Weisbrod made these conclusions and attributions after an empirical analysis of either preventive care or of the Kaiser-Permanente plan. Reference to the original work (Andreano & Weisbrod, 1974) leaves a different impression:

> Nevertheless, there is little if any evidence that either the organizational change or the emphasis on preventive care actually lowers cost. The apparent cost-saving in the Kaiser Permanente Groups has been attributed to various factors, many of which are unrelated to preventive care, and mass innoculation and screening programs have been attacked as being wasteful and uneconomic. Even the annual physical checkup has been criticized for consuming large amounts of physician time and detecting conditions that are aided by early treatment only occasionally. (p. 35)

Those authors then provide one reference in support of what they say. Andreano and Weisbrod have not analyzed either preventive care or Kaiser Permanente. They do not make the attributions about Kaiser Permanente that Marmor states. Rather, they seem to be quoting from another source. Finally, they do not conclude that preventive care can increase costs, but that there is little evidence that it lowers cost.

As another example, Ghez and Grossman (Note 1) cite Kessner (1974) as an empirical study that allegedly supports the case that pediatric care is ineffective: "Kessner finds that source of care has no effect on prevalence of the three health conditions" (pp. 18-19). It is not clear what this statement has to do with the effectiveness of pediatric care itself. If source of care has no effect, it could be that all sources are equally effective or equally ineffective. Kessner's study, in fact, was not aimed at assessing preventive care, but rather at assessing "the health status of a selected population,...differences in provider performance, organization, and attitude, and...information about the strengths and weaknesses of the tracer method" (p. xiv). Ironically, Kessner notes the possibility that the "data may well be used inappropriately to...draw very broad conclusions about the delivery of health services" (p. xv).

Finally, policy advocates rarely cite contradicting evidence. Ghez and Grossman (Note 1), for example, report evidence of decreases in infant mortality in Mississippi, cited in a paragraph by Davis and Schoen (1978, p. 176), in support of a case that prenatal care is effective. They fail to report a case from the same book in the very next paragraph which some would say opposes their conclusion that pediatric care is ineffective.

There is tremendous pressure today to provide "policy relevant" answers to pressing questions. This can easily have a deleterious effect on the quality of any presentation. Such pressures can lead to the difficulties just cited. All this occurs as part of an honest effort to provide quick, relevant answers to policymakers' questions about "what is known." Incomplete or inadequate presentation of the empirical literature is an unfortunate but frequent result.

REVIEW OF EMPIRICAL LITERATURE

The preventive child health literature was initially identified by a computer search of the *Medlars* and *Dissertation Abstracts International* databanks. Copies of original (non-foreign language) sources were obtained and abstracted, as were relevant references from each article. This process resulted in over 150 abstracted articles and books.

Of these articles, 38 receive particular attention. These 38 were selected using a number of criteria. The article had to address an activity relevant to preventive child health efforts; this excluded a number of articles which dealt with such points as adult prevention. The topic of the study had to assess the effectiveness of a procedure in a field setting, rather than efficacy in an ideal setting. The study had to report empirical data; this excluded opinion, advice to the practitioner, program descriptions, and reviews of the literature. Finally, each had to include a control condition of some kind, in addition to a treatment condition. Use of these criteria excluded many articles that reviews with other criteria might find relevant (e.g., Agustin, Stevens, & Hicks, 1973).

The 38 articles were abstracted further. The results of that process are presented in Table 1. The first column of the table lists the study by first author's name and date of publication. The second column categorizes the experimental design according to the following system:

1. Random assignment of subjects to control or experimental condition.
2. Study used seperate experimental and control groups, but method of assignment to groups was either unspecified or nonrandom.

3.   Study used some sort of within subjects control condition, e.g., time series or longitudinal data.

The third column lists the independent variables under study, and the fourth column presents the results for each dependent variable. While it would have been useful to use more sophisticated methods to synthesize literature, such as meta-analysis (Glass, 1976), these methods were of limited utility in the present case due to poor reporting of statistics in the 38 articles.

Overall Results

The value of preventive child health care in general has been questioned by some authors (e.g., Ghez & Grossman, Note 1). It is not clear that it is fair to make such a sweeping critique, however, in view of the many varied activities that fall under the rubric of prevention. Nonetheless, since a broad challenge has been put by some, it is justified to examine the literature in Table 1 as a whole to provide a broad answer.

The bulk of the evidence suggests that prevention does have a beneficial effect on the dependent variables reported by the authors. Only four studies could reasonably be interpreted to suggest that it has no effect (Braren & Elinson, 1972; Gordis & Markowitz, 1971; Klein, Roghmann, Woodward, & Charney, 1973; Moore & Frank, 1973). On the other hand, at least 15 studies could be interpreted as suggesting that prevention has a positive effect (Alpert, Heagarty, Robertson, Kosa, & Haggerty, 1968; Beiner, 1975; Brown, 1975; Crawford, 1970; Gordis, 1973; Kurtzmann, Freed, & Goldstein, 1974; Leodolter, 1978; MacCready, 1974; Muhler, 1968; Perrin, Charney, MacWhinney, McInery, Miller, & Nazarian, 1974; Spencer, 1974; Vaughn, 1968; Webb, Khazen, Hanley, Partington, Percy, & Rathborn, 1973; Williams, 1975; Department of Public Health, Note 2). Positive effect is defined as unambiguous change on the only measure reported, or beneficial change on most or all measures reported. Admittedly, such attempts to classify magnitude of effects are crude and judgmental at best. However, the fact that the number of strong positive effects so greatly outnumbered the no effect findings would suggest that were the judgments made by other people with other means, the results might still have favored positive conclusions.

The remaining 20 studies fall somewhere in between. At one extreme are studies like that by Yankauer and colleagues, which

Table 1

38 Empirical Studies

Author	Design	Independent Variable	Results
A. Comprehensive Care			
Alpert, et al., (1968)	1	Comprehensive care program versus the usual medical care	As compared to the controls, the experimental group had fewer hospitalizations, operations and illness visits and more health visits.
Gordis (1973)	2	Census tracts in Baltimore with a comprehensive care program versus tracts without such programs	Incidence of rheumatic fever decreased over time in experimental tracts to level below control tracts.
Gordis & Markowitz (1971)	1	(a) Comprehensive versus regular care, in infants from birth to one year	(a) No effect on immunization levels, use of medication, mortality or morbidity.
	1	(b) Continuous care versus traditional care over 15 months, in children with history of rheumatic fever	(b) No effect on compliance with physicians' recommendations, as determined by periodic urine tests for penicillin.
Kaplan et al., (1972)	2	Health care project versus traditional care	The project produced an improvement in school attendance, but a small effect compared to other factors.
Klein et al., (1973)	2	Neighborhood health care center users versus non-users versus comparison sample	During the second year of operation, admission rate of health center users was only 33 versus 67 per thousand for the comparison group. Comparing first two years, hospital days

Table 1 (continued)

Author	Design	Independent Variable	Results
			per thousand dropped by half for users. The author concludes that the center did not affect child admissions, but noted users behaved differently than nonusers on the dependent variables.
Leodolter (1978)	3	Austria's Mother-Child Health Pass-port Program	Over several years, Austria's infant mortality, perinatal mortality, and maternal mortality all de-creased while the program was in effect.
Moore & Frank (1973)	3	Comprehensive health services to children	No relationship between levels of use of services and school absenteeism.
Morehead et al., (1971)	2	OEO Neighborhood health centers versus four other types of health services providers	OEO centers did generally well on adequacy of care constructed from chart reviews, including child care.
Vaughn (1968)	2	Comprehensive care project for mothers and infants versus Dade county total versus women with no prenatal care	Project statistics indicated lower maternal mortality, stillbirth, neonatal mortal-ity and premature births for comparison groups, particularly for women with no prenatal care.

B. Dental Care

| Brown (1975) | 3 | Comprehensive home and office dental care | Dental caries decreased over time; dental cleanli-ness increased; gingival health was unchanged. Some data to suggest that such preventive efforts are cost-effective. |

Table 1 (continued)

Author	Design	Independent Variable	Results
Kurtzmann et al., (1974)	3	Mobile dental clinic in underserved area.	57.4% of children treated had never visited a dentist, providing some evidence for positive effect on distribution of care. Authors note greatly improved dental status (by priority ratings) over time.
Muhler (1968)	1	Six separate studies comparing controls with some combination of home and/or office dentifrice and care	In all six studies, the effectiveness of such care was supported by reduction in number of dental caries.

C. Health Education

Author	Design	Independent Variable	Results
Beiner (1975)	2	36 health education lectures to adolescent males, including dental education	Experimental subjects exceeded controls in lung and respiratory functioning, physical strength, dental health, amount of exercise; they also smoked and drank less than controls.
Ezell (1975)	2	American Dental Association dental health program versus traditional dental health program	Both programs increased oral health attitudes and behaviors; the ADA program increased oral health behaviors more than the traditional program.
Williams (1975)	2	Preventive dental health education program versus no program	Plaque accumulation decreased in program participants.

Table 1 (continued)

Author	Design	Independent Variable	Results
D. Iron Deficiency Anemia			
Brigety & Pearson (1970)	2	Dietary supplementation of iron versus diet plus medicinal supplementation, in children at risk for anemia	One third of all subjects' hematocrit values increased, while two thirds remained the same. No differences between diet and diet plus iron groups.
Crawford (1970)	3	Liquid ferric iron coupled with low weight carbohydrate (Niferex) to treat 52 anemic children	Hematocrit increased in 47 of 52 children.
Starfield & Scheff (1972)	3	Medical care for anemia as determined by interview and chart review	53 low hemoglobin values found. 24 abnormal values not recognized. Of 29 recognized abnormalities, only 23 were diagnosed. Only 14 of the 53 were recognized, diagnosed, treated and reassessed.
E. Lead Poisoning			
Byers (1959)	3	Intravenous or intramuscular edathamil calcium disodium to treat identified cases of increased lead burden	Half of the patients returned to normal on tests of psychological function; but half did not, particularly if re-exposed to lead.
Pueschel et al., (1972)	3	Screen and treat for lead in a high risk area; follow up 1½ years later Treatment included both chelation therapy and environmental interventions	8% of children had high lead burden. Of those found 1½ years later, 75% had changed environmental contributing factors. Of those found and treated after initial screen, they had increased IQ and Sequin Formboard tests, but no change in Bender Gestalt test.

Table 1 (continued)

Author	Design	Independent Variable	Results
F. Otitis Media			
Ensign et al., (1960)	2	Sulfamethoxypyridazine (Kynex) to prevent otitis media in Indian children at risk	None of the study group who took the medication regularly had earaches or draining ears, but 12.6 per cent of the control group without previous draining ears had otitis media. Less success in children with destroyed or mutilated eardrums. Successful in children with previous draining ears, and in children who took medication as prescribed.
Maynard et al., (1972)	2	Ampicillin prophylaxis for otitis media in Alaskan Eskimo children at risk	Incidence of otitis media less in experimental group than in matched control. No difference in acute respiratory disorders. Best success in children who took medicaton as prescribed.
Perrin et al., (1974)	1	Sufisoxazole versus placebo as prophylaxis for otitis media	Experimental condition significantly decreased otitis media compared to placebo, for suburban children with recurrent history.
G. Tonsillectomy/ Adenoidectomy			
Mawson et al., (1968)	1	Adenotonsillectomy in children	For dependent variables of catarrh, mouth breathing, snoring, coughing, both experimental and control groups decreased over time, but experimental group decreased more.

Table 1 (continued)

Author	Design	Independent Variable	Results
McKee (1963)	1	Tonsillectomy and adenoidectomy	Respiratory illnesses decreased in experimental group but not control. Of non-respiratory illnesses, only otitis media decreased in experimental group.
Roydhouse (1970)	2& 1 for three total groups	Adenotonsillectomy	Principal benefits is reduction in throat disease and otitis media. Increase in cough and chest infection for operated children as well as decrease in severity of colds and increase in gastrointestinal problems.

H. Mental Health

Author	Design	Independent Variable	Results
Runquist (1976)	2	Once a week mental health consultation to teachers for problems with their students	No change in teachers' attitudes to children nor in child's deviant behavior. Increases in child's socialized behavior and in parent/teacher contact. Decrease in number of outside referrals of problem children.

I. Screening

Author	Design	Independent Variable	Results
Currier (1977)	3	EPSDT screen and referral	A drop of 13% occurred in the referral rate for health problems during a 6-month period among those who were screened a second time or more.
Department of Public Health, Portsmouth Virginia, (Note 2)	2	Screening and counseling versus screening versus no treatment controls	Controls exceeded experimentals in number of physician visits and prescriptions, number of hospital visits and hospital days, costs of physician visits and prescriptions, and total health costs.

Table 1 (continued)

Author	Design	Independent Variable	Results
MacCready (1974)	3	PKU screening	After program had been in effect for several years, PKU admissions dropped to zero.
Spencer (1974)	3	PKU screens	After introduction of screens, no new PKU admissions between 1968 and 1974.
Webb et al., (1973)	3	PKU screening	PKU admissions for retardation decreased to zero for children born after program started. Says costs of screen less than estimated cost of treating PKU aftermath.

J. Physical Examinations

Author	Design	Independent Variable	Results
Anderson (1970)	3	A sample of routine physical examinations by pediatricians in private practice of infants in first year of life	1.9% yielded significant abnormalities over the year. 3.9% yielded significant abnormalities at their initial exam.
Braren & Elinson (1972)	2	Single physical exam (stratified by age, one grouping being 0-19 years)	Exam did not seem to affect mortality assessed nine years later.
Yankauer & Lawrence (1955)	3	Physical exam of 1st graders who had exam in kindergarten Excludes conditions which could be identified by non-physicians	5.5% had not had exam in last year. 21% had adverse conditon. 2% had adverse condition neither known or treated. Only 1 child had serious condition requiring prompt attention.

Table 1 (continued)

Author	Design	Independent Variable	Results
Yankauer & Lawrence (1956)	3	As above with annual physical exams through fourth grade	14% developed adverse conditions in 3 years. 38% of these were neither known nor under care. Only 1% had conditions that could not have been discovered by other means than a physician's examination.
Yankauer et al., (1957)	3	As above	2% had severe or moderate handicap that could be completely or partially treated, but were not under care. Most adverse conditions were either irremediable, only slightly handicapping or already under care.
Yankauer et al., (1962)	3	Physical exam of first graders who were supposed to have exam within last year	21% had adverse condition, 3% of which were neither known nor under care.

suggest minimal benefit, if any. At the other extreme are studies which report quite a few benefits, but also fail to find benefits on a number of other variables (e.g., Mawson, Adlington, & Evans, 1968; McKee, 1963). What unifies the 20 is that they all show at least some benefit. Every attempt was made to classify studies conservatively, not assigning a study to a category implying more benefit unless the reported evidence warranted it. This conservative bias was deliberate so as to avoid the probability of finding a positive effect unless the evidence clearly supported it.

Moreover, these general positive results hold over different types of interventions and problems. Table 1 presents studies categorized into ten different preventive focuses: (A)

Comprehensive Care, (B) Dental Care, (C) Health Education, (D) Iron Deficiency Anemia, (E) Lead Poisoning, (F) Otitis Media, (G) Tonsillectomy/Adenoidectomy, (H) Mental Health, (I) Screening, and (J) Physical Examinations. Only for comprehensive care and for physical examinations is the data less clearly supportive of success (some reasons for this will be discussed in the next section).

The conclusions are basically consistent with previous reviews of dental care (Andlaw, 1978), anemia (Starfield, 1977b), otitis media (Starfield, 1977c), mental health (President's Commission on Mental Health, 1978), screening (Bailey et al., 1974; Eggertsen et al., 1980; Frankenburg, 1973; Reis et al., Note 3; though see Holt, 1974, for a dissenting view), and physical examinations (Canadian Task Force on Periodic Health Examination, 1979).

Prevention, therefore, seems to have at least a small positive effect with children, if we can believe the reports of these researchers. However, such a conclusion is neither complete nor critical, because methodological, strategic, and tactical problems mitigate interpretation of the results of these 38 studies.

PROBLEMS WITH THE 38 EMPIRICAL STUDIES

In the preceding review, the authors' reports of outcome were accepted at face value, in general, as accurately reflecting the conditions and results of the study. Yet a closer analysis of these studies suggests that, in some cases, the author's conclusions are not very credible, and that in other cases, interpretation of results is considerably more equivocal than acknowledged.

One factor accounting for this equivocality is poor methodology. Such factors as use of control groups, method of assignment to groups, measurement, and assessment of program implementation, are aspects of methodology that are crucial for the inferences that may be made (Campbell & Stanley, 1963). These factors are as important in health services research as in any other field of scientific endeavor (Davis & Schoen, 1978). The profound effects of inadequate attention to methodology in health services can be seen in the devastating critiques of California's Medi-Cal Copayment Experiment (1974).

Another factor which must be accounted for in interpreting results concerns strategic and tactical aspects of research practice. Choosing to plan and conduct evaluations using certain control groups, subjects, and interventions can dramatically affect the chances of detecting successful outcome.

Some might view the analysis that follows as methodologically sophisticated but practically naive, since legal, financial, and political constraints can limit the quality of research attainable in "real world" situations. These constraints notwithstanding, however, an explicit contention of this discussion is that these problems are overstated, and cannot account for the poor quality of research found in Table 1.

Experimental Design

An experimental design that randomly assigns subjects to conditions is the ideal for studying the impact of an intervention (Campbell & Stanley, 1963; Cook & Campbell, 1979). However, for any design good research practice requires assessing the plausibility of conclusions in light of the strengths and weaknesses of the design. This is commonly done by examining the plausibility of various "threats to validity," a term coined by Campbell and Stanley (1963) to describe plausible competing explanations for an observed effect. It is informative to examine a few of these threats in regards to the 38 empirical studies to assess how well competing explanations could explain the effects ascribed to preventive child health care in Table 1.

Seventeen studies examined only one group of children, using the children as their own control (Design 3 in Table 1; e.g., Currier, 1977; MacCready, 1974). This kind of design is subject to a number of uncontrolled rival hypotheses that might explain observed changes on the dependent variable. When one can show that these potential alternative explanations are not really plausible in the study's circumstances, then causal inferences are strengthened even with this weak design. A few examples will illustrate this.

History is a rival explanation in designs of type 3 that suggests that some other change-producing event occurred in addition to the treatment. In the Currier (1977) evaluation of EPSDT in Michigan, it is reasonable to suggest that other events have occurred which might affect the health of children, such as other federal or state programs, or efforts by local physicians' organizations to attend to the needs of children more concertedly. Conscientious researchers are virtually obligated to point this out.

Maturation is a rival explanation in type 3 designs which suggests that biological or psychological processes which systematically vary over time in a subject are responsible for observed changes. Some have suggested, for example, that diseases occur less frequently as children age. Currier (1977) suggests that EPSDT caused the drop in referral rate at reinterviews. It is plausible to suggest that the children were simply older, and older children have fewer diseases.

A similar line of reasoning can be applied to the studies using a control group without random assignment (Design 2), called the non-equivalent control group design (Campbell & Stanley, 1963). It can control for history and maturation, but is subject to a different set of threats to validity, including regression artifacts and a host of interactions between selection into groups and such variables as maturation. The Klein et al. (1973) study will illustrate this point. They compared users with nonusers of a neighborhood health care center. Users select themselves into treatment, and nonusers select themselves into the control condition. One might assume that there are one or more underlying variables which control this self-selection process. It is plausible to suggest, for example, that persons who are more conscientious about their health will take the time and effort to go to treatment. This has been referred to as "creaming" (Cook & Campbell, 1979), and has been noted in educational evaluations for quite a while. If people who use the health center are more conscientious they might be healthier than those who are less conscientious. This would account for Klein et al.'s observation that users were at lower risk than nonusers for hospitalization.

A detailed analysis of rival hypotheses requires intimate knowledge of the experimental conditions. The original researcher is in the best position to do this analysis. *Post-hoc* analyses like the present one have the more difficult task of suggesting from one article what is and is not plausible. Therefore, it is the original researcher who should take responsibility for the task.

Randomized designs are often feasible in medical research, as witnessed not only in Table 1 but also by their prevalence in the literature (Boruch, McSweeny, & Soderstrom, 1978). Though political, legal, and ethical problems are often raised by randomized experiments, routine appeal to these problems as an excuse not to randomize is more common than warranted (Boruch, 1975; Boruch, Ross, & Cecil, 1979). It is likely that randomization could have been used more than is apparent in Table 1.

This is not to say that randomized experiments are always preferred. Weaker designs are often sufficient, particularly when alternative hypotheses are not plausible. A control group is less needed in PKU screening studies, for example, since it is not likely that children have stopped being susceptible to the disorder. Similarly for lead poisoning, it is not plausible to suggest that children would have gotten better without treatment.

Yet the present review does not suggest that the researchers chose nonrandomized designs because rival hypotheses were not plausible. Rather, it seems more the case that no attention at all was paid to alternate explanations for effect. This is simply poor research practice. Whatever designs are used, increased attention to the sophisticated use of experimental and quasi-experimental designs holds great promise for improving the practice of health services research (Cook & Campbell, 1979; Fitzgerald, Hormuth, & Cook, in press).

It is difficult to say what biases have been introduced to estimates of the success of preventive child health interventions by the use of quasi-experimental designs (i.e., Designs 2 & 3). Some studies suggest that quasi-experimental designs tend to find success more often than the experimental designs (Gilbert, McPeek, & Mosteller, 1978). Others have found essentially no differences in success rates between the two kinds of designs (Glass & Smith, 1978). If Gilbert et al.'s conclusions hold, then preventive child health care may in fact be somewhat less successful than the data suggest.

Attrition

Subjects who originally agree to participate in research drop out as time progresses, for many reasons. Such attrition can be a serious research problem. For example, when subjects have been initially randomized to conditions, attrition for differential reasons can damage the comparability of the groups at post-test.

Subjects who are not assigned to a desirable treatment may be disappointed or angry and drop out. Remaining control subjects may experience these same feelings of resentment, and we do not know what effect this may have on results. Control subjects might leave the study to obtain desirable medical care elsewhere, leaving control subjects who are less conscientious about their medical care and, as suggested previously, less healthy.

It is important, therefore, to assess the magnitude of attrition and the reasons that account for it. Gordis and Markowitz (1971) report exactly 50% attrition in both experimental and control groups, yet made no attempt to account for this. It is unusual to find such precisely identical rates of attrition. More frequently one finds differential attrition rates (Alpert et al., 1968); these authors do note their intent to discern eventually the influence of differential attrition upon the final results of the study. Such an exercise is important and useful, but seldom actually done.

Attrition is also a problem in single group designs. In the Currier (1977) study, for example, nearly 80% of the original subjects did not return for reinterview. It seems plausible to suggest that the 20% that did return were again those who were more conscientious about their health. They would then have fewer referrals at rescreen because they were healthier, not because EPSDT had any effect.

At a minimum, authors should examine and report differences between dropouts and subjects on whatever variables are available and relevant, such as socioeconomic status, education, and health attitudes. This was rarely done in any of the 38 studies. Strategies for dealing with attrition are presented in. Riecken, Boruch, Campbell, Caplan, Glennan, Pratt, Rees, and Williams (1974).

Measurement

Boruch and Gomez (1977) discuss the problems posed for evaluations by poor measurement. Briefly put, they show that less reliable and less sensitive measures can lead to relatively insensitive experiments that are not likely to find effects even with very strong treatments.

None of the authors of the 38 studies report the reliability of the measures they used. We can guess that reliability data is available for some of the measures, like the intelligence tests reported by Pueschel, Kopito, and Shwachman (1972). On the other hand, reliability of the scoring of the Bender Visual Motor Gestalt test used by Pueschel is frequently low: This would decrease the chance of finding a significant effect for this variable, and explain why Pueschel et al. found no effect with the Bender. It is not clear how reliable are such variables as clinical diagnosis, hematocrit values, and hospitalization rate.

It may seem logical to point out that the more relevant a measure is to a treatment, the more likely it is to show change. We can wonder how relevant to the treatment are such variables as school attendance to health project use (Kaplan, Lave, & Leinhardt, 1972), or mortality to a single physical examination administered nine years previously (Braren & Elinson, 1972).

Choosing irrelevant criteria is poor strategy for assessing treatment effect. Better strategy is to use substantive theory, prior data, and pilot tests, to select more relevant criteria (Boruch & Gomez, 1977).

In a broader context, we must examine the validity of a dependent variable as an indicator of the construct of interest. In this regard, the 38 studies usually have included reasonably direct indicators of health, the exception being the questionable validity of school attendance as a measure of health status.

Finally, a number of the 38 studies used only one such indicator. A number of methodologists (e.g., Riecken et al., 1974) suggest using multiple indicators for each construct—advice well worth following to increase the sensitivity of an experiment.

On the whole, despite poor reporting of reliability and validity, the 38 articles do not seem to have significant problems with sensitivity, in that most reported some changes on the measures. A number of cases reporting no differences (e.g., Braren & Elinson, 1972; Kaplan et al., 1972) may be a function of irrelevant or invalid measurement rather than ineffective treatment, however.

Statistics

All of the 38 studies faced the task of choosing a method for analysis and of reporting that analysis. All the studies report at least some descriptive statistics such as percentages. Fewer studies, however, report inferential statistics, such as chi-square tests, and t-tests, to assess the statistical significance of an observed difference. More importantly, inferential statistics were not always reported in an optimally useful manner. For example, it is not clear if the small number of statistically significant differences reported by Beiner (1975) represent all the tests he conducted, or are a small subset of the 156 items he noted were evaluated by a computer. This makes an important difference, as one would expect about 7-8 significant differences in 156 variables by chance alone at the .05 alpha level.

To facilitate future reviews of the literature, reporting of statistics ought to include significance (either dichotomous at the .05 level, or the exact level), the exact value of an inferential statistic, a relevant contingency table, or a correlation between treatment and outcome (Glass, 1977). The more detail is reported, the easier it is for future reviewers to determine the magnitude of effects using such techniques as meta-analysis (Glass, 1977).

As far as the 38 studies go, since so few reported inferential statistics, it may be that the apparent success of preventive interventions is no greater than what would be expected by chance. Such a sobering perspective will hopefully encourage researchers to report and conduct their analyses with more thoughtfulness in the future.

Treatment Implementation

On the whole, the 38 studies failed to assess or report the implementation of the treatments they studied. Two major problems in interpreting results stem from this. First, with some broadly defined treatments such as comprehensive care, little knowledge is available to suggest exactly what activities were conducted under the treatment. Lacking this knowledge, it is hard to replicate the results, or to know exactly what aspect of the treatment was responsible for what effects. It remains possible that the comprehensive care project of Alpert et al. (1968) was different in implementation from that of Gordis (1973), Gordis & Markowitz (1971), and Vaughn (1968), thus accounting for differences in outcome. The same comments hold for the authors' discriptions of control conditions, such as "regular care."

The second problem raised by failure to assess implementation is that it is not possible to know if a given treatment produced poor results because it doesn't work, or because it was not administered. Starfield and Scheff's (1972) research on prevention of anemia, and Ensign, Urbanich, and Moran (1960), and Maynard, Fleshman, and Tschapp's (1972) work with otitis media clearly show that prevention ot these problems is clearly related to the extent that treatment is implemented.

Assessment of implementation is only recently receiving attention from investigators (Boruch & Gomez, 1977; Sechrest & Redner, 1979; Rossi, Note 4). Starfield and Scheff's (1972) work, and the tracer method (e.g. Kessner, 1974) are practical approaches to assessing implementation of health services. The results of those studies provide critical process information about when, where, how, and why treatment fails to be given, and should be sobering reading for all health services researchers.

Strategic and Tactical Choices in Research

As research is planned and implemented, choices about what treatment to examine, what control groups to use, and what subjects to investigate, all constrain the interpretation of results. Often, an interpretation that the treatment did or did not work is less a statement about effectiveness of prevention than it is about these choices. A few examples will illustrate.

One conclusion drawn from Table 1 was that less clearly supportive results were obtained for comprehensive care and for physical examinations. Both comprehensive care and physical examinations are multi-faceted interventions, whereas the remaining eight categories of prevention deal with more narrowly defined interventions. It is notoriously difficult to evaluate large scale, comprehensive interventions (Weiss & Rein, 1969). For example single variables are unlikely to be sensitive to the diffuse effects of complex interventions. Some aspects of these interventions may be better implemented than others.

Evaluation of broad-aimed programs, therefore, requires special expertise. The developing literature in evaluation research can be fruitfully applied to broad-aimed health services programs (Cronbach, et al. 1980; Cook, in press). Health services researchers interested in such evaluation would do well to familiarize themselves with this literature.

Researchers must also be concerned with the construct validity of the treatment, that is, with what the treatment is. Gordis (1973) suggests he is studying comprehensive care. In fact, the author noted that the study used incidence of rheumatic fever as an outcome variable in part because "the comprehensive care programs in Baltimore have previously been shown to be heavy utilizers of throat cultures" (p. 331). It would appear, then, that the construct was not really comprehensive care, but the treatment of rheumatic fever. Calling this a study of comprehensive care, then, may be a misleading choice of labels.

Similarly, Yankauer and colleagues (1955, 1956, 1957, 1962) exclude from physical examinations any condition detected at the previous annual exam, or which does not need a physician to detect it. While this may be an eminently sensible approach to physicals, it may not represent the construct of physical examinations as routinely practiced by physicians.

Choice of control condition can artificially make a treatment appear better or worse. If the researcher compares one treatment to an ostensibly similar treatment, detecting differences between treatments may be more difficult than if treatment were compared to no treatment controls. In this light, it is less surprising that Gordis and Markowitz (1971) found no effect when comparing comprehensive care to traditional care, if the two are highly similar in essential treatment elements.

The decision to match control subjects to treatment subjects can make a treatment appear harmful or useful, depending on the nature of the population from which the sample of subjects were drawn. In the evaluation of the Head Start educational interventions, for example, matching of treatment with control subjects contributed significantly to making Head Start look like it hurt children (Campbell & Erlebacher, 1970).

Finally, choice of subjects will also affect treatment outcome. One would expect, for example, that virtually any dental care intervention might have an effect on children who have had little previous access to care (Kurtzmann et al., 1974). Similarly for iron deficiency anemia, the Crawford (1970) study found strong effects when treating anemic children, while the other relevant studies used children at risk for anemia, and showed less positive findings.

Discussion

The methodological quality of the 38 studies is mediocre on the whole, and extremely poor in some cases. Given this, the lack of attention to assessing the plausibility of rival hypotheses is unfortunate. It would appear that there are some legitimate competing explanations for some of the findings (e.g., the Currier study). Nonetheless, this rather cursory examinination does not seem to suggest that all the significant findings could be explained away. In fact, it seems that some of the nonsignificant findings may themselves be an artifact of insensitive measurement. On the whole, then, the credibility of these findings is not high; on the other hand, there does not seem to be enough reason to suggest the studies are totally inconclusive. It is probably most accurate to say that preventive child health care has, in general, been given only the weakest of tests, but that those tests are somewhat encouraging. Prevention is still a good idea.

CONCLUSIONS

It is unfortunate that a more definitive statement cannot be made about the effectiveness of preventive child health care. However, it is quite possible to begin to accumulate more useful evidence. For example, secondary and meta-analysis (Boruch & Wortman, 1978; Glass, 1977) could yield useful information from existing data sets; and future primary studies could use more rigorous methodologies (Davis & Schoen, 1978; Green, 1977; Sackett & Holland, 1975).

A major focus of future research, though, ought to be the implementation of preventive care. Many times when prevention seems to fail, it was actually never delivered (Ensign et al., 1960; Hansen, 1975; Kessner, 1974; Lin-Fu, 1970; Starfield & Scheff, 1972; Webb et al., 1973). The challenge is to identify at what point implementation of the treatment fails, and then to identify how that situation can be remedied. And sometimes when prevention fails, the patient simply may have failed to carry out the doctor's orders. We need also, therefore, to form and study models of preventive health behavior (e.g., Langlie, 1976).

In view of the evidence, then, neither strong advocacy of nor strong opposition to preventive child health care seem warranted. A more cogent position would be to recognize that it probably works, in many cases, more demonstrably in small, specific interventions than in broad-aimed, difficult-to-evaluate programs. Truly understanding the empirical roots of this position provides a realistic basis for discussing and evaluating preventive child health care policy.

REFERENCE NOTES

1. Ghez, G., & Grossman, M. *Preventive care, care for children, and national health insurance.* Paper presented at the American Enterprise Institute Conference: "National Health Insurance: What Now, What Later, What Never?" Washington, D.C., October 4-5, 1979.
2. Department of Public Health. *Evidence of cost-effectiveness of EPSDT.* Unpublished manuscript, City of Portsmouth, Virginia, 1973.
3. Reis, J., Hughes, E., Pliska, S., McCain, L., Cordray, D., Held, P., Prince, T., & Kerr, P. *An assessment of the validity of the results of HCFA's Demonstration and Evaluation Program for the Early and Periodic Screening, Diagnosis, and Treatment Program (EPSDT): A metaevaluation* (Working Draft). Unpublished manuscript, Center for Health Services and Policy Research, Northwestern University, Evanston, Ill., June 30, 1979.
4. Rossi, P.H. *The challenge and opportunities of applied social research.* Presidential address to the American Sociological Association, August 28, 1980.

REFERENCES

Agustin, M.S., Stevens, E., & Hicks, D. An evaluation of the effectiveness of a children and youth project. *Health Services Reports*, 1973, *88*, 942-946.
Alpert, J.J., Heagarty, A.L., Robertson, L., Kosa, J., & Haggerty, R.J. Effective use of comprehensive pediatric care: Utilization of health resources. *American Journal of Diseases of Children*, 1968, *116*, 529-533.

Anderson, F.B. Evaluation of the routine physical examination of infants in the first year of life. *Pediatrics,* 1970, *45,* 950-960.

Andlaw, R.J. Oral hygiene and dental cares—A review. *International Dental Journal,* 1978, *28,* 1-6.

Andreano, R., & Weisbrod, B. *American health policy: Perspectives and choices.* Chicago: Rand McNally, 1974.

Bailey, E.N., Kiehl, P.S., Akram, D.S., Loughlin, H.H., Metcalf, T.J., Jain, R., & Perrin, J.M. Screening in pediatric practice. *Pediatric Clinics of North America,* 1974, *21,* 123-165.

Bay, K.S., Flathman, D., & Nestman, C. The worth of a screening program: An application of a statistical decision made for the benefit evaluation of screening projects. *American Journal of Public Health,* 1976, *66,* 145-150.

Bernick, K. Issues in pediatric screening. In Harvard Child Health Project, *Children's medical care needs and treatment* (Vol. 2). Cambridge, Mass.: Ballinger Publishing Co., 1977. (a)

Bernick, K. Screening for hearing impairments. In Harvard Child Health Project, *Children's medical care needs and treatment* (Vol. 2). Cambridge, Mass.: Ballinger Publishing Co., 1977. (b)

Beiner, K.J. The influence of health education on the use of alcohol and tobacco in adolescence. *Preventive Medicine,* 1975, *4,* 252-257.

Boruch, R.F. On common contentions about randomized field experiments. In R.F. Boruch & H.W. Riecken (Eds.), *Experimental testing of public policy: The proceedings of the 1974 social science research council conference on social experiments.* Boulder, Colorado: Westview Press, 1975.

Boruch, R.F., & Gomez, H. Sensitivity, bias, and theory in impact evaluations. *Professional Psychology,* 1977, *8,* 411-434.

Boruch, R.F., McSweeny, A.J., & Soderstrom, E.J. Randomized field experiments for program planning, development, and evaluation: An illustrative bibliography. *Evaluation Quarterly,* 1978, *2,* 655-695.

Boruch, R.F., Ross, J., & Cecil, J.S. (Eds.). *Proceedings and background papers: Conference on ethical and legal problems in applied social research.* Evanston, Illinois: Northwestern University, 1979.

Boruch, R.F., & Wortman, P.M. An illustrative projection secondary analysis. *New Directions for Program Evaluation,* 1978, *4,,* 89-110.

Braren, M., & Elinson, J. Relationship of a clinical examination to mortality rates. *American Journal of Public Health,* 1972, *62,* 1501-1505.

Brigety, R., & Pearson, H. Effects of dietary and iron supplementation on hematocrit levels levels of preschool children. *Journal of Pediatrics,* 1970, *76,* 757-760.

Brown, J.P. Dental treatment for handicapped patients: I. The efficacy of a preventive program for children; II. Economics of dental treatment: A cost benefit analysis. *Australian Dental Journal,* 1975, *20,* 316-325.

Byers, R.K. Lead poisoning: Review of the literature and report on 45 cases. *Pediatrics,* 1959, *23,* 585-603.

California's Medi-cal Copayment Experiment. *Medical Care,* 1974, *12,* 1051-1058.

Campbell, D.T., & Erlebacher, A. How regression artifacts in quasi-experimental evaluations can mistakenly make compensatory education look harmful. In J. Hellmuth (Ed.), *Compensatory education: A national debate (Vol. 3, The Disadvantaged Child).* New York: Brunner/Mazel, 1970.

Campbell, D.T., & Stanley, J.C. *Experimental and quasi-experimental designs for research.* Chicago: Rand-McNally, 1963.

Canadian Task Force on Periodic Health Examination. The periodic health examination. *The Canadian Medical Association Journal,* 1979, *121,* 3-45.

Cook, T.D. An evolutionary perspective on a dilemma in the evaluation of ongoing social programs. In M.B. Brewer & B.E. Collins (Eds.), *Festschrift for Donald T. Campbell.* San Francisco, California: Jossey-Bass, in press.

Cook, T.D., & Campbell D.T. *Quasi-experimental: Design and analysis issues for field settings.* Chicago: Rand-McNally, 1979.

Cook, T.D., & Cook, A.F.L. Comprehensive evaluation and its dependence on both humanistic and empiricist perspectives. In R.S. French, (Ed.), *Humanists and policy studies: Relevance revisited.* Washington, D.C.: George Washington University, Division of Experimental Programs, 1977.

Crawford, O.W. Oral treatment of iron deficiency anemia. *Illinois Medical Journal,* 1970, *137,* 60-63.

Cronbach, L.J., et al. *Toward reform of program evaluation.* San Francisco, California: Jossey-Bass, 1980.

Currier, R. Is early and periodic screening, diagnosis, and treatment (EPSDT) worthwhile? *Public Health Reports,* 1977, *52,* 527-536.

Davis, K., & Schoen, C. *Health and the war on poverty.* Washington, D.C.: The Brookings Institution, 1978.

Eggertsen, S.C., Schneeweiss, R., & Bergman, J.J. An updated protocol for pediatric health screening. *The Journal of Family Practice,* 1980, *10,* 25-37.

Ensign, P.R., Urbanich, E.M., & Moran, M. Prophylaxis for otitis media in an Indian population. *American Journal of Public Health,* 1960, *50,* 195-199.

Ezell, O.E. Evaluation of the American Dental Association's prevention-oriented program in a school health education setting (Doctoral Dissertation, The University of Tennessee, 1975). *Dissertation Abstracts International,* 1975, 1322-1323A. (University Microfilms No. 7518958).

Fitzgerald, N.M., Hormuth, S.E., & Cook, T.D. Quasi-experimental methods for community psychology research. In E.C. Susskind & D.C. Klein (Eds.), *Knowledge-building and community psychology.* New York: Holt, Rinehart, and Winston, in press.

Frankenburg, W.K. Pediatric screening. *Advances in Pediatrics,* 1973, *20,* 149-175.

German, P.S., Skinner, E.A., Shapiro, S., & Salkever, D.S. Preventive and episodic health care of inner-city children. *Journal of Community Health,* 1976, *2,* 92-106.

Gilbert, J.P., McPeek, B., & Mosteller, F. Statistics and ethics in surgery and anesthesia. *Science,* 1978, *78,* 684-689.

Glass, G.V. Primary, secondary and meta-analysis of research. *Educational Researcher,* 1976, *5,* 3-8.

Glass, G.V. Integrating findings: The meta-analysis of research. *Review of Research in Education,* 1977, *5,* 351-379.

Glass, C.V., & Smith, M.L. Reply to Eysenck. *American Psychologist,* 1978, *33,* 517-518.

Gordis, L. Effectiveness of comprehensive-care programs in preventing rheumatic fever *New England Journal of Medicine,* 1973, *289,* 331-335.

Gordis, L., & Mardowitz, M. Evaluation of effectiveness of comprehensive and continuous pediatric care. *Pediatrics,* 1971, *48,* 766-776.

Green, L.W. Evaluation and measurement: Some dilemmas for health education. *American Journal of Public Health,* 1977, *67,* 155-161.

Hansen, H. Prevention of mental retardation due to PKU: Selected aspects of program validity. *Preventive Medicine,* 1975, *4,* 310-321.

Harvard Child Health Project. *Report of the Harvard Child Health Project Task Force.* Cambridge, Massachusetts: Ballinger Publishing Co., 1977.

Holland, W.W. Taxing stock. *Lancet,* 1974, *2,* 1494-1497.

Holt, K.S. Screening for disease—infancy and childhood. *The Lancet,* 1974, (November 2), 1057-1061.

Kaplan, R.S., Lave, L.B., & Leinhardt, S. The efficacy of a comprehensive health care project: An empirical analysis. *American Journal of Public Health,* 1972, *62,* 924-930.

Kessner, D.M. *Contrasts in Health Status (Vol. 3, Assessment of medical care for children).* Washington, D.C.: Institute of Medicine, 1974.

Klein, M., Roghmann, K., Woodward, K., & Charney, E. The impact of the Rochester Neighborhood Health Center on hospitalization of children, 1968 to 1970. *Pediatrics,* 1973, *51,* 833-839.

Kurtzmann, C., Freed, J.R., & Goldstein, C.M. Evaluation of treatment provided through two universities' mobile dental project. *Journal of Public Health Dentistry,* 1974, *34,* 74-79.

Langlie, J.K. A new look at preventive health behavior (Doctoral dissertation, University of Wisconson-Madison, 1975). *Dissertation Abstracts International,* 1976, 8341A. (University Microfilms No. 76-6095).

Lave, J.R., & Lave, L.B. Cost-benefit concepts in health: Examination of some prevention efforts. *Preventive Medicine,* 1978, 7, 414-423.

Leodolter, I. The mother-child health passport: Austria's successful weapon against infant mortality. *Preventive Medicine,* 1978, 7, 561-563.

Lin-Fu, J.S. Childhood lead poisoning...an eradicable disease. *Children,* 1970, 17, 2-9.

MacCready, R.A. Admissions of phenylketonuria patients to residential institutions before and after screening programs of the newborn infant. *Journal of Pediatrics,* 1974, 85, 383-385.

Marmor, T. Children and national health insurance. In *Report of the Harvard Child Health Project Task Force (Vol. 3, Developing a better health care system for children).* Cambridge, Mass.: Ballinger Publishing Company, 1977. (a)

Marmor, T. Rethinking national health insurance. *The Public Interest,* 1977, 46, 73-95. (b)

Mawson, S.R. Adlington, P., & Evans, M. A controlled study evaluation of adenotosillectory in children. *Journal of Laryngology & Otolarygology,* 1968, 82, 963-979.

Maynard, J.E., Fleshman, J.K., & Tschapp, C.F. Otitis media in Alaskan children: Prospective evaluation of chemoprophylaxis. *Journal of the American Medical Association,* 1972, 219, 597-599.

McKee, W.J.E. Controlled study of the effects of tonsillectomy and adenoidectomy in children. *British Journal of Preventive Social Medicine,* 1963, 17, 49-69.

Mechanic, D. Approaches to controlling the cost of medical care: Short-range and long-range alternatives. *New England Journal of Medicine,* 1978, 298, 249-254.

Moore, G.T., & Frank, K. Comprehensive health services for children: An exploratory study of benefit. *Pediatrics,* 1973, 51, 17-21.

Morehead, M.A., Donaldson, R.S., & Seravalli, M.R. Comparisons between OEO neighborhood health centers and other health care providers of ratings of the quality of health care. *American Journal of Public Health,* 1971, 61, 1294-1306.

Muhler, J.C. Mass treatment of children with a stannous fluoride-zirconium silicate self-administered prophylactic paste for partial control of dental caries. *Journal of the American College of Dentists,* 1968, 35, 45-57.

Perrin, J.M., Charney, E., MacWhinney, J.B., McInery, T.K., Miller, R.L., & Nazarian, L.F. Sulfisoxazole as chemoprophylaxis for recurrent otitis media. *New England Journal of Medicine,* 1974, 291, 664-667.

President's Commission on Mental Health. Report of the task panel on prevention. In *Report to the President from the President's Commission on Mental Health.* Washington, D.C.: U.S. Government Printing Office, 1978.

Pueschel, S.M., Kopito, L., & Shwachman, H. Children with an increased lead burden: A screening and follow-up study. *Journal of the American Medical Association,* 1972, 222, 462-466.

Riecken, H.W., Boruch, R.F., Campbell, D.T., Caplan, N., Glennan, T.K., Pratt, J.W., Rees, A., & Williams, W. *Social experimentation: A method for planning and evaluating social intervention.* N.Y.: Academic Press, 1974.

Roydhouse, N. A controlled study of adenotonsillectomy. *Archives of Otolaryngology,* 1970, 92, 611-616.

Runquist, M.P. Mental health consultation to day care: An experiment in primary prevention (Doctoral dissertation, University of Nebraska-Lincoln, 1975). *Dissertation Abstracts International,* 1976, 4177B. (University Microfilms No. 76-2057).

Sackett, D.L., & Holland, W.W. Controversy in the detection of disease. *The Lancet,* 1975, August 23, 357-359.

Schorr, L.B. Social policy issues in improving child health services: A child advocate's view. *Pediatrics,* 1978, 62, 370-376.

Schweitzer, S.O. Cost effectiveness of early detection of disease. *Health Services Research,* 1975, Spring, 22-32.

Sechrest, L., & Redner, R. Strength and integrity of treatments in evaluation studies. In *How well does it work? Review of criminal justice evaluation, 1978.* Washington, D.C., U.S. Department of Justice, Law Enforcement Assistance Administration, National Institute of Law Enforcement and Criminal Justice, National Criminal Justice Reference Service, 1979.

Spencer, D.A. Untreated phenylketonuria. *Lancet,* 1974, *June 29,* 1351.

Starfield, B. Efficacy and effectiveness of primary medical care for children. In *Report of the Harvard Health Project Task Force (Vol. 2, children's medical care needs and treatment).* Cambridge, Mass.: Ballinger, 1977. (a)

Starfield, B. Iron deficiency anemia. In *Report of the Harvard Child Health Project Task Force (Vol. 2, children's medical care needs and treatment).* Cambridge, Mass.: Ballinger, 1977. (b)

Starfield, B., & Scheff, D. Effectiveness of pediatric care: The relationship between processes and outcome. *Pediatrics,* 1972, *49,* 547-552.

Vaughn, B.J. Maternal and infant care projects: Results in Dade County Florida. *Southern Medical Journal,* 1968, *61,* 641-645.

Wallace, H.M., & Oglesby, A.C. Preventive aspects of maternal & child health, *Preventive Medicine,* 1972, *1,* 554-558.

Webb, J.F., Khazen, R.S., Hanley, W.B., Partington, M.S., Percy, W.J.A., & Rathborn, J.C. PKU screening—is it worth it? *Canadian Medical Association Journal,* 1973, *108,* 328-329.

Weiss, R.S., & Rein, M. The evaluation of broad-aim programs: A cautionary case and a moral. *Annals of the American Academy of Political and Social Science,* 1969, *385,* 133-142.

White, K.L. Prevention as a national health goal. *Preventive Medicine,* 1975, *4,* 247-251.

Williams, L.B. A study of the results of a preventive dental health program with fourth and fifth grade students in the Tulsa Public Schools (Doctoral dissertation, the University of Tulsa, 1975). *Dissertation Abstracts International,* 1975, 661B. (University Microfilms No. 7516849).

Yankauer, A., & Lawrence, R.A. A study of periodic school medical examinations. *American Journal of Public Health,* 1955, *45,* 71-78.

Yankauer, A., & Lawrence, R.A. A study of periodic school medical examinations: II. The annual increment of new "defects." *American Journal of Public Health,* 1956, *46,* 1553-1562.

Yankauer, A., Lawrence, R.A., & Ballou, L. A study of periodic school medical examinations: III. The remediability of certain categories of "defects." *American Journal of Public Health,* 1957, *47,* 1421-1429.

Yankauer, A., Frantz, R., Drislane, A., & Katz, S. A study of case-finding methods in elementary schools: I. Methodology and initial results. *American Journal of Public Health,* 1962, *52,* 656-662.

31

Synthesis of Results in Controlled Trials of Coronary Artery Bypass Graft Surgery

Paul M. Wortman and William H. Yeaton

The annual rate of coronary artery bypass graft surgery (CABGS) in the United States is now over 100,000 per year and still growing (Harrison, 1981), despite the fact that evaluations of its efficacy have often resulted in contradictory findings (Paton, 1980). For example, a recent NIH consensus conference, while generally endorsing the procedure, noted a number of areas in which there is inconclusive evidence of the effectiveness of over half of all CABGS relative to medical interventions (Special Report, 1981). There are now dozens of published studies dealing with the effectiveness of this technology, though considerable confusion remains in assessing its overall impact. The problem confronting both physicians and patients is how to synthesize the results of these reports.

Recent methodological advances in data aggregation or synthesis techniques offer a potentially valuable means of evaluating the outcomes of controlled clinical trials comparing CABGS with medical interventions. For instance, Glass and his colleagues have used data aggregation techniques to compare various therapy approaches to psychological problems (Glass, McGaw, & Smith, 1981; Smith & Glass, 1977), to contrast drug and nondrug approaches to therapy (Smith, Glass, & Miller, 1980), and to assess the benefits attributable to psychological interventions for surgery and coronary problems (Mumford, Schlesinger, & Glass, 1982). Chalmers and his colleagues have aggregated the results of clinical trials in which antibiotic prophylaxis was used in colon surgery (Baum, Anish, Chalmers, Sacks, Smith, & Fagerstrom, 1981), and have synthesized the evidence from individual studies meant to evaluate the use of anticoagulants for acute myocardial infarctions (Chalmers, Matta, Smith, & Kunzler, 1977). Gilbert, McPeek, and Mosteller (1977) have utilized data-synthesis techniques to quantify the difference in proportion of

Authors' Note: The authors wish to express their appreciation to Fred Bryant, Katherine Halvorsen, Gregg Jackson, Janet Landman, Hillary Murt, Emil Posavac, Lee Sechrest, and Bob Wolfe for their comments on earlier drafts of this report. Thanks also are due to Jack Langenbrunner for initial coding and retrieval of studies. The work on this report was supported by grants from the National Institute for Education (NIE-G-79 0128) and the National Center for Health Services Research (HS-04849-01).

From Paul M. Wortman and William H. Yeaton, "Synthesis of Results in Controlled Trials of Coronary Artery Bypass Graft Surgery," original manuscript. Copyright © 1983 by Sage Publications, Inc.

survivors between groups using innovative and standard surgical and anesthetic procedures. DeSilva, Lown, Hennekens, and Casscells (1981) examined the outcomes of randomized clinical trials in which lignocaine was used prophylactically to prevent fibrillation in acute myocardial infarction.

The purpose of this article is to utilize data-synthesis techniques to compare the results of (CABGS) and nonsurgical (medical) interventions for coronary artery disease. Since previous evidence from evaluation of other medical interventions indicates that the research design utilized in the trial is often an important determinant of the results found (e.g. Wortman, 1981), data were aggregated separately for trials in which random selection had been used to assign patients to surgical and medical conditions (i.e., randomized clinical trials [RCTs]) and those controlled trials that had not used random assignment (quasi-experiments).

SELECTION OF STUDIES

Three sources were utilized to identify a list of studies from which controlled trials of CABGS could be selected. First, recent reviews of the literature by McIntosh and Garcia (1978) and Buccino and McIntosh (1979) were consulted for pertinent references. Second, the reference section of each article chosen for data synthesis was scrutinized for pertinent references. Third, a MEDLARS II search of 1970 to 1978 produced a large list of studies from which pertinent CABGS studies were chosen. An article was chosen if its title suggested that some version of bypass graft surgery had been tested and its results reported. Reports including only abstracts were omitted, as were studies reporting descriptions of CABGS, or describing specialized results that did not appear to include either mortality or survival rates. Articles appearing in books were omitted, as were articles using either the same or extensively overlapping subject samples (e.g., early studies for which a follow-up study was available, and studies in which a specialized subset of patients had also been included in a more inclusive study). In cases where there was difficulty in selecting a study by reading the title, the complete article was examined to determine its appropriateness.

From these three sources, a final list of 90 studies was compiled. Each of these studies was classified on the basis of its research design following criteria established by Campbell and Stanley (1963). Studies using preexperimental or case study designs that did not utilize a control group were excluded. Also, those designs utilizing historical controls, such as a medically treated group monitored for a portion of time not coincident with treatment implementation in the surgery group, were excluded from the data synthesis. A recent article (Sacks, Chalmers, & Smith, 1982) examined a number of medical therapies, including bypass surgery, and found that historical controls consistently overestimated the effectiveness of the treatment. Only quasi-experiments using concurrent controls and RCTs were selected for further examination. These screening procedures reduced the sample of studies available to 25. The studies utilized in the analysis are listed in the Appendix, which includes 9 RCTs and 16 quasi-experiments.

TABLE 1   Data from Controlled Trials of CABGS

Appendix Study Number	Surgery		Medical		
	Percentage Survival	Percentage Mortality (# deaths/N)	Percentage Survival	Percentage Mortality (# deaths/N)	Percentage Crossover
			RCT		
1.	?	7.0	?	20.0	0.0
2.	89.0	8.6	92.0	6.2	?
3.	93.5	5.2	84.1	12.2	18.6
4.	90.0	7.8	78.0	16.3	16.3
5.	94.4	5.5	86.6	11.7	6.7
6.	89.0	9.9	88.0	9.5	36.1
7.	?	4.5	?	10.0	45.0
8.	86.0	12.0	87.0	10.0	18.0
9.	86.0	?	83.0	?	?
			Quasi-Experiment		
10.	?	15.0	?	10.0	0.0
11.	?	5.7	?	11.4	11.4
12.	?	4.8	?	19.0	4.8
13.	77.5	15.0	48.5	29.8	8.8
14.	70.0	25.9	45.0	47.4	?
15.	75.0	13.0	5.0	57.1	?
16.	?	5.8	?	21.2	12.1
17.	?	6.9	?	0.0	?
18.	53.0	?	31.0	?	?
19.	95.0	5.7	56.0	42.9	8.6
20.	85.0	?	83.0	?	4.7
21.	92.0	11.9	81.0	17.6	0.0
22.	75.0	18.0	45.0	40.6	0.0
23.	98.2	?	75.9	?	4.3
24.	?	14.0	?	38.0	0.0
25.	50.0	50.0	62.0	35.7	?

COMBINING RESULTS

Two related but separate results were collected systematically from the studies reporting quasi-experimental and randomized clinical trials of CABGS (Table 1). First, survival data taken from the surgical and medical groups were coded for the longest follow-up period given in the study. These data were obtained from relevant tables and material in the text, or estimated from survival curves presented in graphic form. In all cases but one, it was possible to verify that a survival analysis had been conducted by examination of a written statement in the article to that effect (in that one instance, the dependent variable was reported as "percent survival," though it was not possible to determine if conditional probabilities had been used in the survival analysis).

Second, mortality rates (number of deaths divided by number of patients in the group at the beginning of the study) were also recorded, using the total number of deaths through the longest follow-up period as the basis of calculation. In 13 studies it was possible to record both survival and mortality rates. When sufficient information was available in the article, deaths in the surgical group occurring prior to operation were not counted in either the surgical or medical groups. In this way, it was possible to avoid the biasing procedure of counting all deaths prior to a potential operation as medical deaths, since these patients may not have been formally assigned to that treatment condition. Following this procedure, deaths in the surgical and medical groups were excluded when calculating mortality rates even when these deaths were used in the survival rate calculations. (There were very few instances of this, however.) For purposes of consistency, those patients who crossed over from the medical to the surgical group (crossovers), but who died subsequent to operation, were considered as an endpoint at the time of surgery—when sufficient information was given in the article to follow this procedure—since this was the most frequent practice used in the controlled trials of CABGS.

When possible, both survival and mortality data were taken from individual studies, since these two outcomes were not exactly complementary within a given study, though their sum typically approximated unity. Since various methods of calculating survival rates were utilized in different studies (e.g., life table, actuarial, and the Kaplan & Meier [1958] methods), survival results based on the same data would not, in general, be equal. Furthermore, methods that yield a survival rate for a given time period based on the conditional probability of surviving during previous time periods produce different values than methods that do not use conditional probabilities. For these and other reasons we used both survival and mortality data in our analyses.

Thus each individual article yielded either a percentage survival or a percentage mortality (or both) for surgical and medical groups (Table 1). Two difference scores were calculated by subtracting the survival rate in the medical condition from the survival rate in the surgical condition, and by subtracting the mortality rate in the surgical condition from the mortality rate in the medical condition in each of the individual studies utilizing information from the longest follow-up periods reported (Table 2). Positive survival and mortality difference scores therefore suggested relative benefit to the surgical group. These difference scores were aggregated to estimate the direction and degree of benefit attributable to the medical and surgical groups.

Results from individual studies were combined in two ways: First, the mean difference and the sample standard deviation of differences were calculated for both survival and mortality data. Second, the mean difference and the estimated standard deviation of the population standard deviation of differences were calculated using the approach prescribed by Gilbert, McPeek, and Mosteller (1977; see Table 3). In the latter approach, the difference between the proportion of survivors in two contrasted groups was used in the analysis. This difference is analogous to the difference between the proportion of those who die in medical and surgical

TABLE 2   Differences in Survival and Mortality Percentage Between Surgical and Medical Groups in RCTs and Quasi-Experiments

	Differences	
Appendix Study Number	Percentage Survival (Surgery)- Percentage Survival (Medical)	Percentage Mortality (Medical)- Percentage Mortality (Surgical)
	RCT	
1.	—	13.0
2.	− 3.0	− 2.4
3.	9.4	7.0
4.	12.0	8.5
5.	7.8	6.2
6.	1.0	− .4
7.	—	5.5
8.	− 1.0	− 2.0
9.	3.0	—
	Quasi-Experiment	
10.	—	− 5.0
11.	—	5.7
12.	—	14.2
13.	29.0	14.8
14.	25.0	21.5
15.	70.0	44.1
16.	—	15.4
17.	—	− 6.9
18.	22.0	—
19.	39.0	37.2
20.	2.0	—
21.	11.0	5.7
22.	30.0	22.6
23.	22.3	—
24.	—	24.0
25.	−12.0	−14.3

groups (mortality difference) in our data aggregation scheme. However, use of the Gilbert and associates procedure to estimate the difference in *survival* rates between medical and surgical groups is not as analogous given the manner in which survival rates were typically calculated (namely, using conditional probabilities based on the number of patients at risk in a given interval).

Table 3 displays the mean and standard deviation of differences in survival and mortality rates between surgical and medical groups for RCTs and quasi-experiments. These means and standard deviations have been calculated in two ways: as a sample statistic and as a sample estimate of the population difference using the previously mentioned methods of Gilbert and associates (1977). The method used

TABLE 3   Data Synthesis of Percentage Differences Between
Surgical and Medical Groups

	Survival Data		Mortality Data	
	Gilbert, McPeek & Mosteller (1977) Estimate	Sample Statistic Estimate	Gilbert, McPeek, & Mosteller (1977) Estimate	Sample Statistic Estimate
RCTs				
M.	4.2	4.2	4.4	4.4
S.D.	approx. 0	5.6	approx. 0	5.5
Number of studies	7	7	8	8
Quasi-Experiments				
M.	23.8	23.8	13.8	13.8
S.D.	19.1	22.0	13.7	16.9
Number of studies	10	10	13	13

to calculate standard deviation gives roughly similar results; means are calculated in exactly the same manner in both methods. The determination of the sample standard deviation for our data set yields values consistently greater than the Gilbert and associates technique of estimating the true or population standard deviation.

RESULTS

Evidence from both RCTs and quasi-experiments suggests that there is a relative benefit to patients who have undergone CABGS in that differences between mortality and survival rates in medical and surgical groups consistently favor the surgical group. However, the magnitude of the benefit is quite discrepant depending on the source of the evidence. As shown in Table 3, the average benefit to the surgical group is 4% to 5% based on results from RCTs, while the average benefit to the surgical group is approximately 14% to 24% based on results from quasi-experiments.[1] Inspection of Table 3 also suggests that there is little difference in the means and standard deviations for the survival versus the mortality data in RCTs, though the choice of survival or mortality data makes a considerable difference in the absolute size of the means and standard deviations for the quasi-experimental studies. In quasi-experiments, the mean for the survival data is 10 percentage points larger than that for mortality, while the estimates of standard deviations are substantially higher for the quasi-experiments than for the RCTs.

Biostatisticians typically examine the reduction in mortality as an overall measure of effectiveness (Gore, 1981). Viewed in this perspective (see Table 4), surgery produces over one-third lowering in the mortality rate (4.4/120 = 36.7%) for RCTs, and nearly cuts the rate in half (13.8/28.5 = 48.5%) for quasi-experiments. The former figure is generally considered a clinically significant effect. And even the latter is within the 95% confidence interval for RCTs. However, in both cases the interval does include zero. A power analysis for the RCTs revealed that for a significance level of .05 and a power of .80, over 1100 patients would be needed to detect the observed effect. This is nearly equal to the total for all the patients in all the RCTs.

Another perspective of the discrepancy in results between studies utilizing RCTs and quasi-experiments is that of effect size. Glass et al. (1981) have recommended use of the average effect size statistic whereby a difference between means of two groups within a study is divided by an appropriate standard deviation (e.g., the standard deviation of the control group), then all of these effect size values are averaged. In the data synthesis presented here, an effect-size-like statistic can be calculated by determining the average difference between means of surgical and medical groups, and dividing by the standard deviation of differences. Viewed in this way, the between-groups difference shown in Table 3 is consistently greater in the quasi-experiments than in the RCTs. However, the degree to which effect size estimates are greater in quasi-experiments depends on whether mortality data or survival data are used, as well as the choice of estimate for the standard deviation. Nevertheless, the pattern is the same as that just noted for the percentage reduction in mortality. Effect sizes for RCTs are about 0.8, while those for quasi-experiments average about 1.0.

Table 4 displays a summary of means by experimental condition, design, and type of outcome measure, and additionally presents overall means irrespective of design. The overall survival mean in surgical groups after a follow-up of approximately four years was 82.3%, while in medical groups the analogous result was 66.5% over a comparable time period. For a mean follow-up period of approximately two years, the average mortality in surgical groups was 12.0%; in medical groups the analogous result for a comparable time period was 22.2%. Results broken down by design type are discussed below.

Additional data were compiled from the controlled trials of CABGS for purposes of clarifying the above findings. When there were follow-up reports to the initial study, pertinent baseline and descriptive information were taken from the original study if these results were not available in later reports. Additional data included crossover information, operative mortality rates, and diagnostic severity. The average rate of crossovers from the medical to the surgical group was 20.7% (152 crossovers/736 patients) in RCTs, and 5.1% (48 crossovers/942 patients) in quasi-experiments. The mean operative mortality was 4.6% (49 deaths/1076 patients) in the RCTs, and 8.3% (53 deaths/636 patients) in the quasi-experiments. The average percentage of one- two- and three-vessel disease for the surgical and medical groups, respectively, in RCTs was 16.2%, 33.1%, 49.6%; and 16.8%, 37.7%, 44.0%.[2] The average percentage of one-, two-, and three-vessel disease for the surgical and medical groups, respectively, in quasi-experiments was 13.5%, 26.7%, 64.8%, and 13.8%, 28.8%, 63.3%.

Correlation coefficients were calculated between mortality rate *differences* and the rate of crossovers in both RCTs and quasi-experiments. The correlation was

TABLE 4   Summary Table of Mean Percentages of Mortality and Survival
in Surgical and Medical Groups

	Average of Longest Follow-Up Period	Mean Follow-Up	Number of Studies	Surgical Groups	Medical Groups	Difference
RCTs						
Survival	just over 4 years	–	7	89.7	85.5	4.2
Mortality	–	just over 2 years	8	7.6	12.0	4.4
Quasi-Experiments						
Survival	nearly 4 years	–	10	77.1	53.2	23.9[*]
Mortality	–	nearly 2 years	13	14.7	28.5	13.8
Overall Mean						
Survival	approx. 4 years	–	17	82.3	66.5	15.8
Mortality	–	approx. 2 years	21	12.0	22.2	10.2

[*] The difference between survival percentage in the surgical and medical groups (23.9%) varies slightly from the average difference shown in Table 3 (23.8%) due to rounding error.

equal to −.52 for RCTs (based on 7 studies), and +.17 (based on 9 studies) for quasi-experiments. Thus the greater the number of crossovers, the smaller the difference in mortality rates for RCTs, and vice versa for quasi-experiments. A correlation coefficient of −.50 (5 studies) was found between survival rate *differences* and the rate of crossovers in RCTs, and +.41 (6 studies) for quasi-experiments. Again, the interpretation is similar to the one for mortality differences. Calculation of mean mortality using the total combined number of deaths in all studies divided by the number of patients in all studies yielded the following results: RCT surgery groups, 7.0%; RCT medical groups, 11.5%—a difference of 4.5%; quasi-experimental surgery groups, 13.4%; quasi-experimental medical groups, 31.0%—a difference of 17.6%. Both the mean and median year of publication in RCTs were 1978, while in quasi-experiments the mean and median were 1976 and 1975 (actually, midyear 1975), respectively.

DISCUSSION

Results from this synthesis of controlled trials comparing surgical and medical interventions for coronary artery disease suggest that the degree of benefit attributable to the surgical group depends heavily on the design used in the trial. When quasi-experimental designs are utilized, the benefit is very large (i.e., about 14% to 24%). When RCTs are examined, the benefit—while clinically significant—is considerably reduced (i.e., about 4% to 5%) at the longest follow-up period, and the effect size is consistently smaller. These findings do not vary according to the method of analysis chosen. While it is true that bypass graft surgery seems to produce a consistent benefit, and that the overall mean results favor a surgical intervention, the large effects for nonramdomized, controlled trials compared to the smaller benefit for RCTs may account for the remaining confusion in assessing this technology.

Is it possible to reconcile these differences? The additional data from the controlled trials of CABGS allow interpretation of the difference in benefit found in quasi-experiments and RCTs. For example, the slightly higher operative mortality rate in quasi-experiments argues against an interpretation suggesting that the higher mortality at follow-up might be due to superior operative techniques that simply postponed the point at which death would be counted (namely, in the follow-up period rather than the perioperative period). Additionally, longer follow-up periods in the quasi-experiments could be related to a larger benefit to the surgical group in these trials, since the effect of operative mortality in the surgical group is to delay any advantage to this group until some time after both the operations. However, both the average follow-up time and the average of the longest follow-up period were greater in the studies utilizing RCTs than in those using quasi-experiments.

Another factor considered in interpreting the difference in benefit in quasi-experiments and RCTs is the distribution by risk categories in the surgical and medical groups in these two types of trials. Within a given design type, the prevalence of one-, two-, and three-vessel disease in surgical and medical groups was quite comparable. In contrast, the data on diagnostic severity indicate that there is a slightly greater prevalence of one- and two-vessel disease in both surgical and medical groups in RCTs than quasi-experiments, while the percentage of three-vessel disease patients is moderately higher in both the surgical and medical groups of quasi-experiments. The presence of relatively more patients having higher risk in the quasi-experiments argues against a simple patient selection mechanism whereby quasi-experiments would be burdened with the highest risk patients, with a resulting small benefit attributable to this burden. From a different perspective, there is evidence to suggest that surgery is relatively more beneficial to patients with three-vessel disease (Read, Murphy, Hultgren, & Takaro, 1978), and the data available from RCTs reviewed in this report (two RCTs provided survival rates and three provided mortality rates by presence of one-, two-, and three-vessel disease; only two quasi-experiments provided this information) indicated a 7% to 12% benefit to the surgery group as compared to the medical group in this subset of patients.

The relatively high average rate of crossovers found in RCTs (20.7%) also has direct relevance to estimates of the benefit of surgical as compared to medical interventions. Since it is typically patients in the medical group at greatest risk who cross over to the surgical group (most often those complaining of severe angina), these patients are, in effect, dropped from the medical group. The common methodological response to the crossover problem was to count these medical patients as an endpoint at the time they received an operation, and thus not to contaminate the surgical group with patients randomly assigned to the medical condition. Consequently, the medical group is freed of patients who might otherwise have died, and the difference between surgical and medical group mortality and survival rates is diminished. Indeed, the correlational evidence, though based on a small number of studies, indicated that a consistent negative relationship existed in RCTs (relatively large crossover rates were associated with benefits to the medical group; relatively small crossover rates were associated with benefits to the surgical group).

The extent to which this difference between medical and surgical groups is underestimated because of the crossover problem is unknown, though the maximum extent of the bias can, at least, be roughly gauged.[3] In a report of the National Cooperative Study Group (1978), medical patients who later received surgery can be compared with medical patients without later surgery (Figure 3 in the NCSG report) to assess the survival rates of crossovers and noncrossovers. The difference in survival rates between the crossover group of medical patients and the noncrossover group of medical patients ranged from approximately 8% at six months, to approximately 12% at three years, both favoring the crossover group. However, there was an early difference of between 5% to 10% in survival rates favoring the crossover group. Thus while inferences must be made with caution, it would appear that from several different perspectives, the problem of crossovers would account for only a small proportion of the difference between results in RCTs and quasi-experiments.

While the crossover problem is minimal in quasi-experimental trials (an average of 5.1%), the threat of selection bias looms heavily. Only one quasi-experiment matched patients in medical and surgical groups on a case-by-case basis, and researchers' efforts to demonstrate that the groups were equivalent by statistically equating differences in clinical history and personal characteristics were apparently not sufficient to eliminate the biased benefit attributable to surgery.

When the mortality results in RCTs are pooled using raw data rather than percentages (Goldman & Feinstein, 1979), so that differences in the size of studies is removed as a source of bias, the average mortality difference between surgical and medical groups is increased only slightly from 4.4% to 4.5%, and the percentage reduction in mortality increased by less than 2% (4.5/11.5 = 39.1%). The use of analogous pooling procedures in quasi-experiments increases the average mortality difference from 15.7% to 17.6%. Thus the primary finding of a differential impact of surgery in RCTs versus quasi-experiments is preserved, though the magnitude of the differential impact is altered slightly.

If quasi-experiments were more recent than RCTs, surgical results in quasi-experiments would be expected to show a substantial superiority over those obtained in RCTs, since the surgical procedures would be relatively perfected after years of refinement and experience. In fact, the temporal pattern of RCTs and quasi-experiments was exactly the opposite as evidenced by the later mean and median year of publication in RCTs, a result consistent with the pattern of evaluation of other medical technologies (Wortman, 1981).

As Table 4 indicates, surgical outcomes were better (a 12.6% survival rate difference) for patients in RCTs than in quasi-experiments. This result was dwarfed by the over 30% difference in survival outcomes for medically treated patients. This finding is consistent with the results reported by Sacks et al. (1982) in which historical controls were found to do much worse than controls in RCTs. Since the focus of the studies in this data synthesis was on a surgical procedure, little information was reported on the medical group concerning treatment protocol, drugs used, patient compliance, and the like. Without this information it is difficult to make very informed hypotheses to explain this large difference, other than those noted earlier concerning increased severity and lower crossover rate for medically treated patients in quasi-experiments. While these factors might account for some of the discrepancy between design results, it is also likely that there were well-developed protocols that were more conscientiously followed for medically treated patients in the RCTs. Thus, while it is likely that improved surgical procedures may have characterized the more recently conducted RCTs, there also was a greater improvement in the care for the medically treated control patients.

Another factor that might influence the difference between surgical and medical groups is any change in the composition of the samples receiving both treatments over the time frame during which CABGS has been implemented. As evidence accumulates that certain subgroups of patients are very likely to benefit from the operation (e.g., those with left main artery problems), patients fitting these classifications must be systematically excluded from clinical trials for ethical reasons.[4] Exclusion of these patients leaves only patients where reasonable doubt exists regarding the benefits of surgery, that is, those patients in whom potential benefit is most difficult to discriminate. If such exclusions occur, the difference found in any trial designed to compare surgical and medical interventions will be underestimated. In the studies examined, for example, there was a greater number of patients with three-vessel disease in quasi-experiments. These are generally the most severely ill patients, and it is felt that surgery is beneficial for such patients. However, it should be noted that the evidence for this is not conclusive (Special Report, 1981).

Finally, there are unknown factors that may influence the degree of benefit attributable to a surgical intervention. Since the design utilized in a center or a set of centers has not been randomly assigned to that center, there is a system-wide selection factor whose influence must be assessed. As an example, centers where RCTs have been conducted probably have taken the necessary steps to ensure that medical protocols are closely followed (no study reported this data), thereby increasing survival rates in the medical group and decreasing differences between surgical and medical rates. Certainly, if the relative completeness of information reported in the RCTs as compared to the quasi-experiments used in this data synthesis is any indication of the overall quality in which a trial was conducted, then we would argue that such a general methodological superiority favoring RCTs is quite plausible. Without information on possible selection bias regarding which centers receive (or adopt) which design strategy, or the extent to which treatments have ·been implemented as planned, a priori superiority of RCTs relative to quasi-experiments must be assumed based on inherent features of the design that allow greater inferential power.

In summary, the results of this data synthesis of the scientific literature emphasize the critical role of the research design in making inferences regarding the benefit of CABGS relative to medical treatment. A number of factors, such as the operative mortality rate and the length of follow-up, were examined and dismissed as likely influences on this major result. Other factors, such as the temporal pattern of conduct of RCTs and quasi-experiments, the risk categories of patients assigned to RCTs and quasi-experiments, and the rate of crossovers, could account for some of the difference between results in RCTs and quasi-experiments. Given the clinically meaningful reduction in mortality for RCTs, these sources of systematic bias lend support for a higher rate of effectiveness. Most importantly, however, it is clear that quasi-experiments considerably overestimate the effect of coronary artery bypass graft surgery. In particular, the control groups used in such studies account for most of the difference.[5] Thus concurrent, but nonrandomized, controls seem to suffer from the same problems in patient selection found in other research examining historical control groups.

NOTES

1. Cohen (1977) has argued that the difference between proportions is not an appropriate measure of the magnitude of effect shown. Instead, he recommends use of the arc sine transformation. When the data were transformed, the survival and mortality differences between surgical and medical groups in RCTs were decreased by .4% and increased by 1.5%, respectively, while the survival difference between surgical and medical groups in quasi-experiments was increased by 2.9% and the mortality difference was decreased by .5%. Given the essential equivalence of the transformed and untransformed data, the raw data are presented for interpretive ease.

2. The sum of the percentage of one-, two-, and three-vessel disease for patients in the medical and surgical groups in RCTs and quasi-experiments may not add to 100% due to the methods of reporting the outcomes within individual studies. To illustrate, authors may report only the percentage of three-vessel disease patients, or other classifications such as left-main artery (LMA) could make up a portion of the total percentage within a given study. In three RCTs and four quasi-experiments LMA patients were included in disease categories. In both types of studies the percent of LMA patients was about the same (i.e., between 7 and 8%). However, three quasi-experiments were composed entirely of LMA patients. Since surgery is generally considered efficacious in such patients, it is important to consider the impact of including these studies. When the data from these three quasi-experiments were omitted, the results were essentially unchanged.

3. It is possible to estimate the effect of crossovers on the mean of a given medical group under the strict assumption that only those medical patients with the greatest risk of dying will cross over to receive surgery. If one assumes a normal distribution of survival probabilities with mean = 0 and standard deviation = 1, and if a further assumption is made that the lowest 21%

of the tail is truncated (this figure corresponds to the 21% average crossover rate of RCTs found in our study and to the common practice of considering crossovers as an endpoint at the time they receive surgery), elementary algebra and integral calculus reveal that the mean of the resulting distribution has been increased to .36. This value serves as an upper bound of the effect of crossovers since it assumes that *only* those medical patients with the worst prognosis actually cross over, an assumption only approximated in evaluations of CABGS. See Yeaton and Wortman (1982) for a more elaborate discussion of this estimation procedure.

4. The reverse is also possible. Patient subgroups for which the treatment appears ineffective may also be eliminated. The European Coronary Surgery Study Group (1982) just reported a five-year decrease in mortality for bypass patients of 7.2 percent (16.2% minus 9.0%). (Our analysis used the 7.0 percent decrease reported in a previous interim article.) This is the most recent and largest RCT, involving 768 patients (although 30 were "lost" for our purposes). No patients with single-vessel disease were included, whereas about one-sixth of the patients in the other RCTs had single-vessel disease. Moreover, approximately 60 percent had either three-vessel or left main artery disease. The latter group often was not included in other RCTs since surgery has been determined to be quite effective for such patients. Thus the European Coronary Surgery Study Group dealt with a more severely ill patient population than previous reports. Since the articles generally did not report mortality rates within severity categories, it is difficult to adjust for differences in patient mix. In retrospect, one would recommend not only that such information be made available, but also that such studies block or stratify on this variable. This analysis strategy would prevent the a posteriori subgroup analysis and the "fishing" problems they pose for appropriate statistical inference.

5. This problem may also apply to RCTs. The European trial (1980, 1982) has recently been criticized for having a higher mortality rate in the medical (control) patients than found in similar patients in other studies (Whalen et al., 1982).

APPENDIX:
ARTICLES USED IN DATA SYNTHESIS

RCTs

1. Bertolasi, C. A., Tronge, J. E., Carreno, C. A., Jalon, J. & Vega, M. R. Unstable angina—Prospective and randomized study of its evolution, with and without surgery. American Journal of Cardiology, 1974, 33, 201-208.
2. Conti, C. R., Hodges, M., Hutter, A., Resnekov, L., Rosati, R., Russell, R., Schroeder, J., & Wolk, M. Unstable angina—A national cooperative study comparing medical and surgical therapy. Cardiovascular Clinics, 1977, 8, 167-178.
3. European Coronary Surgery Study Group. Prospective randomized study of coronary artery bypass surgery in stable angina pectoris: Second interim report. Lancet, 1980, 2, 491-495.
4. Kloster, F. E., Kremkau, E. L., Ritzmann, L. W., Rahimtoola, S. H., Rosch, J., Kanarek, P. H. Coronary bypass for stable angina: Prospective randomized study. New England Journal of Medicine, 1979, 300, 149-157.
5. Mathur, V. S. & Guinn, G. A. Prospective randomized study of the surgical therapy of stable angina. Cardiovascular Clinics, 1977, 8, 131-144.

6. National Cooperative Study Group. Unstable angina pectoris: National cooperative study group to compare surgical and medical therapy. II. In-hospital experience and initial follow-up results in patients with one, two, and three vessel disease. American Journal of Cardiology, 1978, 42, 839-848.

7. Neill, W. A., Ritzmann, L. W., Okies, J. E., Anderson, R. P. & Seldon, R. Medical versus urgent surgical therapy for acute coronary insufficiency: A randomized study. Cardiovascular Clinics, 1977, 8, 179-187.

8. Norris, R. M., Agnew, T. M., Brandt, P.W.T., Graham, K. J., Hill, D. G., Kerr, A. R., Lowe, J. B., Roche, A.H.G., Whitlock, R.M.L., & Barratt-Boyers, B. G. Coronary surgery after recurrent myocardial infarction: Progress of a trial comparing surgical with nonsurgical management for asymptomatic patients with advanced coronary disease. Circulation, 1981, 63, 785-792.

9. Read, R. C., Murphy, M., Hultgren, H., & Takaro, T. Survival of men treated for chronic stable angina pectoris: A cooperative randomized study. Journal of Thoracic and Cardiovascular Surgery, 1978, 75, 1-12. Medicine, 1975, 293, 1329-1333.

QUASI-EXPERIMENTS

10. Aronow, W. S., & Stemmer, E. A. Two-year follow-up of angina pectoris: Medical or surgical therapy. Annals of Internal Medicine, 1975, 82, 208-212.

11. Bender, H. V., Fisher, R. D., Faulkner, S. L., & Gottlieb, C. F. Unstable coronary artery disease. Comparison of medical and surgical treatment. Annals of Thoracic Surgery, 1975, 19, 521-528.

12. Berk, G., Kaplitt, M., Padmanabhan, V., Frantz, S., Morrison, J., & Gulotta, S. J. Management of preinfarction angina. Evaluation and comparison of medical versus surgical therapy in 43 patients. Journal of Thoracic and Cardiovascular Surgery, 1976, 71, 110-177.

13. Campeau, L., Corbara, F., Crochet, D., & Petitclerc, R. Left main coronary artery stenosis: The influence of aortocoronary bypass surgery on survival. Circulation, 1978, 57, 1111-1115.

14. Demots, H., Bonchek, L. I., Rosch, J., Anderson, R. P., Starr, A., & Rahimtoola, S. H. Left main coronary artery disease: Risks of angiography, importance of coexisting diseases of other coronary arteries and effects of revascularization. American Journal of Cardiology, 1975, 36, 136-141.

15. Faulkner, S. L., Stoney, W. S., Alford, W. C., Thomas, C. S., Burrus, G. R., Frist, R. A., & Page, H. L. Ischemic cardiomyopathy: Medical versus surgical treatment. Journal of Thoracic and Cardiovascular Surgery, 1977, 74, 77-82.

16. Hultgren, H. N., Pfeifer, J. F., Angell, W. W., Lipton, M. J., & Bilisoly, J. Unstable angina: Comparison of surgical and medical management. American Journal of Cardiology, 1977, 39, 734-740.

17. Kouchoukos, N. T., Oberman, A., Russell, R. O., Jr., & Jones, W. B. Surgical versus medical treatment of occlusive disease confined to the left anterior descending coronary artery. American Journal of Cardiology, 1975, 35, 836-842.

18. Manley, J. C., King, J. F., Zeft, H. J., & Johnson, W. D. The "bad" left ventricle: Results of coronary surgery and effect on late survival. Journal of Thoracic and Cardiovascular Surgery, 1976, 72, 841-848.
19. Matloff, J. M., Sustaita, H., Chatterjee, K., Chaux, A., Marcus, H. S., & Swan, H.J.C. The rationale for surgery in preinfarction angina. Journal of Thoracic and Cardiovascular Surgery, 1975, 69, 73-81.
20. McNeer, J. F., Starmer, C. F., Bartel, A. G., Behar, V. S., Kong, Y., Peter, R. H., & Rosati, R. A. The nature of treatment selection in coronary artery disease. Experience with medical and surgical treatment of a chronic disease. Circulation, 1974, 49, 606-614.
21. Rogers, W. J., Smith, L. R., Oberman, A., Kouchoukas, N. T., Mantle, J. A., Russell, R. O., Jr., Rackley, C. E. Coronary revascularization surgery. Feasibility after myocardial surgery. Postinfarction Surgery, 1981, 36-49.
22. Talano, J. V., Scanlon, P. J., Meadows, W. R., Kahn, M., Pifarre, R., & Gunnar, R. M. Influence of surgery on survival in 145 patients with left main coronary artery disease. Circulation (Supplement I), 1975, Vols. 51 and 52, 1-105-1-111.
23. Tyras, D. H., Kaiser, G. C., Barner, H. B., Pennington, D. G., Codd, J. E., & Willman, V. L. Left main equivalent: Results of medical and surgical therapy. Circulation (Supplement II), 1981, 64, 11-7-11-10.
24. Vismara, L. A., Miller, R. R., Price, J. E., Karam, R., DeMaria, A. N., & Mason, D. T. Improved longevity due to reduction of sudden death by aortocoronary bypass in coronary atherosclerosis. Prospective evaluation of medical versus surgical therapy in matched patients with multivessel disease. American Journal of Cardiology, 1977, 39, 919-924.
25. Yatteau, R. F., Peter, R. H., Behar, V. S., Bartel, A. G., Rosati, R. A., & Kong, Y. Ischemic cardiomyopathy: The myopathy of coronary artery disease: Natural history and results of medical versus surgical treatment. American Journal of Cardiology, 1974, 34, 520-525.

REFERENCES

BAUM, M. L., ANISH, D. S., CHALMERS, T. C., SACKS, H. S., SMITH, H., Jr., & FAGERSTROM, R. M. A survey of clinical trials of antibiotic prophylaxis in colon surgery: Evidence against further use of no-treatment controls. New England Journal of Medicine, 1981, 305, 795-799.
BUCCINO, R. A., & McINTOSH, H. D. Aortocoronary bypass grafting in the management of patients with coronary artery disease. American Journal of Medicine, 1979, 66, 651-666.
CAMPBELL, D. T., & STANLEY, J. C. Experimental and quasi-experimental designs for research on teaching. In N. L. Gage (Ed.) Handbook of research on teaching. Chicago: Rand McNally, 1963.
CHALMERS, T. C., MATTA, R. J., SMITH, H., Jr., & KUNZLER, A. Evidence favoring the use of anticoagulants in the hospital phase of acute myocardial infarction. New England Journal of Medicine, 1977, 297, 1091-1096.
COHEN, J. Statistical power analysis for the behavioral sciences (Rev. ed.). New York: Academic Press, 1977.

DeSILVA, R. A., LOWN, B., HENNEKENS, C. H., & CASSCELLS, W. Lignocaine prophylaxis in acute myocardial infarction: An evaluation of randomized trials. Lancet, 1981, ii, 855-858.

GILBERT, J. P., McPEEK, B., & MOSTELLER, F. Progress in surgery and anesthesia: Benefits and risks of innovative surgery. In J. P. Bunker, B. A. Barnes, & F. Mosteller (Eds.) Costs, risks, and benefits of surgery. New York: Oxford University Press, 1977.

GLASS, G. V, McGAW, B., & SMITH, M. S. Meta-analysis in social research. Beverly Hills, CA: Sage, 1981.

GOLDMAN, L. & FEINSTEIN, A. R. Anticoagulants and myocardial infarction. The problems of pooling, drowning, and floating. Annals of Internal Medicine, 1979, 90, 92-94.

GORE, S. M. Assessing clinical trials—trial size. British Medical Journal, 1981, 282, 1687-1689.

HARRISON, D. C. Coronary bypass: The first 10 years. Hospital Practice, 1981, 16, 49-56.

KAPLAN, E. L., & MEIER, P. Nonparametric estimation from incomplete observations. Journal of the American Statistical Association, 1958, 53, 457-481.

McINTOSH, J. R., & GARCIA, J. A. The first decade of aortocoronary bypass grafting, 1967-1977: A review. Circulation, 1978, 57, 405-431.

MUMFORD, E., SCHLESINGER, H. J., & GLASS, G. V The effects of psychological intervention on recovery from surgery and heart attacks: An analysis of the literature. American Journal of Public Health, 1982, 72, 141-151.

National Cooperative Study Group. Unstable angina pectoris: National Cooperative Study Group to compare surgical and medical therapy. II. In-hospital experience and initial follow-up results in patients with one, two and three vessel disease. American Journal of Cardiology, 1978, 42, 839-848.

PATON, B. C. Who needs coronary bypass surgery? Human Nature, September 1978, 76-83.

READ, R., MURPHY, M., HULTGREN, H., and TAKARO, T. Survival of men treated for chronic angina pectoris. A cooperative randomized study. Journal of Thoracic and Cardiovascular Surgery, 1978, 75, 1-16.

SACKS, H., CHALMERS, T. C., & SMITH, H. Randomized versus historical controls for clinical trials. American Journal of Medicine, 1982, 72, 233-240.

SMITH, M. L., & GLASS, G. V Meta-analysis of psychotherapy outcome studies. American Psychologist, 1977, 32, 752-760.

SMITH, M. L., GLASS, G. V, & MILLER, T. I. The Benefits of Psychotherapy. Baltimore: Johns Hopkins University Press, 1980.

Special Report. National Institute of Health Consensus Development Conference Statement. New England Journal of Medicine, 1981, 304, 680-684.

WORTMAN, P. M. Randomized clinical trials. In P. M. Wortman (Ed.) Methods for evaluating health services. Beverly Hills, CA: Sage, 1981.

YEATON, W. H., & WORTMAN, P. M. Differential attrition: Estimating the effect of crossovers on the evaluation of a medical technology. Technical report. Ann Arbor, MI: Institute for Social Research, 1982.

32

Lessons Learned from Past Block Grants
Implications for Congressional Oversight

U.S. General Accounting Office

The Omnibus Budget Reconciliation Act of 1981 created nine new block grants from the consolidation of more than 50 categorical grants and two already existing block grants. Up until 1981, the only block grants in existence were

- Partnership for Health Act (PHA),
- Omnibus Crime Control and Safe Streets Act (referred to as LEAA, for Law Enforcement Assistance Administration, the agency created to administer the legislation),
- Comprehensive Employment and Training Act (CETA),
- Community Development Block Grants (CDBG), and
- Title XX Social Services.

The 1981 legislation and proposals for 1982 have heightened the interest of the Congress and others in whether experience under the older block grants can prove useful in the congressional oversight of the newly established programs.

The Chairman of the Subcommittee on Oversight of the House Committee on Ways and Means asked us to review the five block grants listed above and identify information that might be helpful in evaluating current programs. While the objective traditionally associated with block grants is to fund broadly defined functional areas with the greatest flexibility for grantees and the fewest Federal requirements, a review of these five block grants shows some diversity among them with regard to what attaining this objective means in practice.

The Chairman asked us to examine the legislation and evaluations related to the older block grants to see if experience can help inform the current debate. We were asked to answer questions related to four issues. The first issue is whether the range and type of informational and accountability requirements imposed under each of the block grants have been adequate. The second issue is whether the poor and other disadvantaged groups have received their share of services under block grants compared to categorical grants. Under the third issue, we examine how administrative costs differ under block grants and categoricals. The fourth issue concerns

From the U.S. General Accounting Office, "Lessons Learned from Past Block Grants: Implications for Congressional Oversight," GAO/IPE-82-8.

the Federal evaluation activities—evaluation being one mechanism for achieving accountability—that were implemented for the five programs.

WHAT IS A BLOCK GRANT?

Block grants are often contrasted with two other funding mechanisms: categorical grants and general revenue sharing. The differences among the three are sometimes clearer in the abstract than in the implementation. For the purposes of definition, however, we can place block grants somewhere between categorical grants and general revenue sharing by the scope of restrictions or conditions they impose on grant recipients. At the one extreme, categorical grants provide funding for specialized purposes and narrowly defined activities. Typically, the Federal role in administering them is active and includes specifying application requirements, negotiating awards, monitoring the progress of the funded activities, and evaluating effects. At the other extreme, general revenue sharing provides funds to local governments for almost any use, including initiating new programs, stabilizing local taxes, and generally supporting government programs. In addition, the Federal Government imposes almost no conditions on the recipients beyond requirements to hold proposed-use hearings, conduct audits, and comply with civil rights requirements. Block grants have comparatively fewer constraints than categorical grants, but they give recipients narrower latitude than general revenue sharing. Overall, however, block grants give recipients wide latitude in making administrative arrangements and in choosing services within a functional area.

Five features distinguish block grants from other forms of assistance.

(1) Federal aid is authorized for a wide range of activities within a broadly defined functional area.
(2) Grantees are allowed considerable discretion in identifying problems, designing programs and allocating resources.
(3) Federally imposed administrative, fiscal reporting, planning, and other requirements are kept to the minimum necessary to insure that national goals are accomplished.
(4) The amount of Federal aid a grantee receives is calculated from a statutory formula rather than being the decision of Federal administrators.
(5) The initial recipient of block grant funds is usually a general purpose governmental unit, such as a city or State. (ACIR, 1977a, p. 6)

In practice, it may be difficult to classify a program as either a block or a categorical grant, and the problem is compounded by some misconceptions. Block grants are often accompanied by grant program consolidation and, recently, they have been accompanied by reductions in appropriations. Although both consolidation and budget reduction have occurred in the block grants created by the Omnibus Budget Reconciliation Act of 1981, neither is a defining characteristic of block grants. Grant consolidations can combine administrative functions to reduce the number of separate programs and give recipients more discretion than they previously enjoyed. The same features that usually accompany a discretionary grant program—application requirements, competitive selection of grantees, little discretion for recipients in the program design—usually remain under simple consolidations. In contrast, block grants redistribute power and authority and may or may not be accompanied by a reduction in the number of Federal programs.

Similarly, block grants can have higher or lower appropriations than their predecessor categorical programs. While the block grants enacted in 1981 typically had appropriations cuts of the order of 25 percent, most of the earlier block grants were enacted with increased appropriations. The term "block grant" refers to the manner in which power and decisionmaking are distributed, not to the dollar resources that are made available.

GENERAL DESCRIPTIONS OF THE FIVE BLOCK GRANTS

The five block grant programs that were in existence long enough to provide experience useful to current congressional needs are listed in Table 1. The oldest, PHA, was established 16 years ago in 1966. The most recent, Title XX Social Services, was established in 1975. Four Federal agencies administered the five programs. Outlays in fiscal year 1981 ranged from a low of $23 million for PHA to a high of $4 billion for CDBG. In the following short histories, we describe the establishment and subsequent evolution of each of the five programs.

Partnership for Health Act

The Partnership for Health Act of 1966 (Public Law 89-749) was originally designed to reorganize Federal categorical health programs by consolidating nine grant programs into one. The first Hoover Commission had urged health program consolidation in the 1940's, and subsequent commissions in intergovernmental relations and health services also supported it. President Lyndon Johnson criticized the proliferation of individual categorical grants as rigid, inefficient, and unable to meet the Nation's health needs. Early in 1966, he submitted a sweeping legislative program for public health that included a block grant for health services.

Although the States used PHA funds to support mental health, general health, tuberculosis control, and other public health activities, the breadth and goals of PHA coverage were never realized. PHA outlays dropped from $90 million in fiscal year 1972 to $23 million in fiscal year 1981. (OMB, 1982, p. 21) The reasons for PHA's decline are several. The legislative and executive branches disagreed over the extent of Federal requirements and oversight for the program. Was the grant to support any public health activity that a State or a local government undertook, or was it to further national public health needs, and where should the line between the two be drawn? (ACIR, 1977a, p. 17)

Moreover, in the early years of PHA, the States resisted the attempts of Federal officials to intervene in grant activities in response to congressional concerns about

TABLE 1   The Structural and Fiscal Characteristics of the Five Original Block Grants

Year Enacted	Federal Agency	Services Provided	Categorical Programs Consolidated	Outlays $ Million FY 1981	Distribution Formula	Primary Recipient
Partnership for Health (PHA), 1966	HHS	Public health	9	23	Population, financial need	States
Omnibus Crime Control and Safe Streets (LEAA), 1968	LEAA	Law enforcement, criminal justice	0	316	Population	States
Comprehensive Employment and Training (CETA), 1973	DOL	Manpower	17	2,231	Unemployment previous year funding level, low income	General purpose local and states
Community Development Block Grants (CDBG), 1974	HUD	Community and economic development	6	4,042	Population, overcrowded and old housing, poverty, population growth lag	General purpose local
Title XX Social Services, 1975	HHS	Social	2	2,646	Population	States

SOURCE: ACIR, Block Grants: A Comparative Analysis (Washington, D.C.: 1977), p. 7, and The Partnership for Health Act: Lessons from a Pioneering Block Grant (Washington, D.C.: 1977), p. 10. FY 1981 outlays from OMB Budget of the Government of the United States 1983. Special Analysis H (Washington, D.C.: 1982), p. 21; figures exclude categorical components of CDBG, and LEAA. See also 88 Stat. 2337.

the program. Almost all the early disputes were resolved in favor of the States. By 1972, the U.S. Department of Health, Education, and Welfare (HEW, now HHS) decided to eliminate the requirements for the submission of State plans. The regulations were changed to require only State assurances that a detailed plan had been prepared and met all applicable Federal requirements. (ACIR, 1977c, pp. 32, 37) The pertinent congressional committees favored greater controls; that these controls were not accepted strengthened congressional preference for enacting new categorical health grants. The Advisory Commission on Intergovernmental Relations concluded that

> In summary, the failure to achieve an effective operational balance between the concerns of the states and those of the federal government ultimately produced a program with meager funding, only a few really powerful supporters . . . , and an uncertain future. In other words, state dominance fostered federal disinterest. (ACIR, 1977a, p. 17)

PHA, which had been renamed Health Incentive Grants for Comprehensive Public Health Services, was abolished with the enactment of new block grants in the Omnibus Budget Reconciliation Act of 1981, when it was combined with seven other programs in the new Preventive Health and Health Services Block Grant.

Omnibus Crime Control and Safe Streets Act

The Omnibus Crime Control and Safe Streets Act of 1968 (Public Law 90-351) was enacted as a block grant to provide decentralized aid to State and local governments for a variety of activities that would promote crime control and criminal justice system improvement, including assistance to police, prosecutors, courts, corrections, and probation and parole. In addition to its block grant titles, the Act authorized the creation of the Law Enforcement Assistance Administration to oversee the action programs, and it funded discretionary grants and other component programs. President Johnson proposed the legislation as categorical aid in the context of heightened public concern over the increased crime rates and civil disorders of 1967 and 1968. The program engendered early controversy, however, when many States and local governments purchased unneeded and sophisticated police equipment.

As the program evolved under LEAA, the Congress added more and more requirements. Additional provisions were written for correctional programs, for example, and a separate juvenile delinquency program was enacted. The mandatory annual comprehensive plans that the States submitted for LEAA review and approval became more voluminous. This stringency, however, resulted in strong complaints from State program directors that often centered on the LEAA guidelines for comprehensive plans. They were considered by many to be "restrictive, incomplete, repetitive, and overly detailed." (ACIR, 1977a, p. 26) Many felt that the plan requirements actually hindered substantive planning and that the plans themselves had become compliance documents rather than a means for improving the administration of the criminal justice system.

As the States became more impatient with the requirements of the program, broader Federal attempts to integrate the fragmented criminal justice system and so produce a coordinated police-courts-corrections attack on crime were also largely unsuccessful. Rates of reported crime increased periodically. There was frustration in the Congress with continued problems of State administration, while the support of local governments for the program was tempered by their not directly receiving block grant funds from Washington even though they were the dominant providers of many of the services. In addition, intense State and local rivalries continued. The program lacked a united constituency. The constant criticisms from all these quarters, combined with other factors such as persistently high crime rates, so increased LEAA's vulnerability that it was given no appropriations after fiscal year 1980.

Comprehensive Employment and Training Act

Since the average unemployment rate was less than 5 percent in the last half of the 1960's, the objective of Federal employment and training programs was to aid people who had the greatest problems in getting and keeping jobs—the poor, members of minority groups, the young, the inadequately educated. The Congress enacted numerous categorical programs aimed at helping these individuals become competitive in the job market. By 1967, responsibility for these programs was spread across 17 categorical programs and several Federal agencies. (ACIR, 1977b, p. 5) Legislative proposals for comprehensive reform led to enactment of the Comprehensive Employment and Training Act of 1973 (Public Law 93-203) to coordinate planning and delivery of services for the unemployed. (ACIR, 1977b, p. 9)

CETA transferred substantial authority from Federal agencies to more than 400 "prime sponsors," most of which were city and county governments, with State governments being given authority for sparsely populated areas. Prime sponsors were to design and administer flexible systems of employment and training services that could match the needs of the unemployed with program resources. With the 1974 economic recession, however, CETA's clientele changed. More and more people lacked not job skills but simply jobs. The Congress responded with appropriations for additional jobs in the public sector by creating a second CETA categorical program for public service employment. The specific designation of funds for public service jobs is what leads us to classify these components of CETA as categorical rather than block grants.

The pressure for creating more jobs continued, so that between fiscal years 1974 and 1977, public service employment accounted for most of the enormous increases in CETA's total appropriations. (Mirengoff and Rindler, 1978, p. 19) Over the years, however, complaints about fraud and abuse in the program increased.

Although various reforms were enacted, the public service job programs were phased out in 1981. The CETA block grant program had barely begun to emerge from years of having been overshadowed by the public service jobs programs when proposals were circulated to replace CETA with some other program.

Community Development Block Grant

The Community Development Block Grant (Public Law 93-383) replaced urban renewal, model cities, and four other related categorical programs that had been administered by the Department of Housing and Urban Development (HUD). It was enacted amid a consensus favoring grant reform for community development. The Conference of Mayors, the National League of Cities, and others endorsed the block grant concept before any bill was introduced. (Conlan, 1981, p. 9) As of 1981, CDBG funds had been authorized for many activities including housing rehabilitation, maintenance of social service facilities, and general public improvements and economic development. Large counties, all central cities of metropolitan areas, and suburban cities with populations of more than 50,000 are entitled to apply for block grants in an amount calculated by formulas that considered levels of population, housing overcrowding, population growth lag, old housing, and poverty.

CDBG was the first block grant to completely bypass the States in fund allocations. Local governments had been the primary participants and the major partner with HUD in categorical programs for community development. Indeed, their strength in this respect may have prevented a battle with State governments for control of the block grant funds before CDBG's enactment. (ACIR, 1977a, pp. 32, 36; Conlan, 1981, p. 9) While no major Federal program is without controversy, CDBG has not been given the same degree of criticism in the Congress as the four other block grants. This may explain its growth in budget authority from $1.8 billion in fiscal year 1976 to $3.7 billion in fiscal year 1981.

The Omnibus Budget Reconciliation Act of 1981 created a new block grant from a companion program of discretionary grants to small cities that is administered by States or, at a State's option, by the Federal Government. In another major change, the legislation modified the application process. Instead of submitting a detailed application that is subject to comprehensive HUD review, the recipient must submit a statement of, among other matters, its community development objectives and projected use of funds. The recipient must also make certain assurances and certifications relative to the use of such funds. Although the Secretary's role in authorizing the awarding of funds is limited, the legislation does provide that the required assurances and certifications should be made in a manner that is satisfactory to the Secretary.

Title XX Social Services

Title XX of the Social Security Act (Public Law 93-647) was enacted to provide Federal reimbursement to States for providing services to eligible working parents for child care, for training disabled adults in rehabilitation centers, for providing homemaker help for elderly people living alone, and the like. The program began as a block grant to States and replaced authorizations for services to welfare recipients formerly funded by titles IVA and VI of the Social Security Act. Many assisted under Title XX also received cash assistance under Aid to Families with Dependent Children and Supplemental Security Income.

Title XX was enacted in 1975 partly to help control the vast growth of Federal spending for social services from $282 million in 1967 to $1.7 billion in 1972. (Spar, 1981, p. 5) Much of this increase was accounted for by a shift from full State financing for institutional programs in mental health and retardation, corrections, and some education programs. To control these costs, the Congress capped at $2.5 billion the social service titles that were later to become Title XX. State ceilings calculated from a simple population formula were also established. HEW's efforts to publish regulations for the ceilings and otherwise tighten controls on the expenditure of Federal funds met widespread adverse reaction from State and local politicians, program administrators, advocacy groups, unions, national organizations, and provider agencies. They rallied against the proposed regulations along with the Congress, which acted twice to prevent the promulgation of the regulations. (Slack, 1979, pp. 10-11; Spar, 1981, pp. 6-7) The controversy culminated in the 1975 passage of Title XX into law.

Title XX was amended and the Social Services Block Grant Act was enacted in its place as part of the 1981 legislation. The purpose of this block grant is to consolidate Federal funding assistance for Title XX Social Services and to increase the flexibility the States have in using funds. Many requirements that had been imposed on States were eliminated by this legislation, including the specifications that a portion of funds be used for services for welfare recipients and that most services be limited to families with incomes below 115 percent of their State's median income. (U.S. Congress, House, 1981, p. 992) Appropriations were reduced from $2.9 billion in fiscal year 1981 to $2.0 billion in fiscal year 1982.

The Instability of Early Block Grants

These short histories show the instability of the original block grants. LEAA has been abolished. PHA was merged into a large new block grant. The block grant component of CETA has an uneven history and there are pending proposals to eliminate it and substitute a new program. The Title XX Social Services program was amended and became the major component of the new Social Services Block Grant. Only the CDBG entitlement program continues intact and similar to its original form.

1981 LEGISLATION AND NEW PROPOSALS

In 1981, the President proposed six block grant programs consolidating more than 80 separate grant programs. The original proposals resembled President Nixon's special revenue sharing proposals of 1971 more closely than they did the existing block grants. (Barfield, 1981, p. 29; ACIR, 1977a, pp. 4-5) "Special revenue sharing" refers to a program with so few Federal strings that it falls between general revenue sharing and block grants. We describe the requirements of the block grants enacted in the Omnibus Budget Reconciliation Act of 1981 in chapter 2, but we summarize their characteristics in Table 2.[1]

In 1982, the Administration plans to propose seven new block grants and expand three of those enacted in 1981.[2] For the longer term, the President proposed in his state of the Union message a "turnback" program consisting of

> the return of some $47 billion in Federal programs to State and local government, together with the means to finance them and a transition period of nearly 10 years to avoid unnecessary disruption. (GSA, 1982, p. 80)

The States would draw upon a $28 billion trust fund as they assumed responsibility for more than 40 grant programs:

> Turnback of these programs to States would be optional through FY 87. If states elect to withdraw from the Federal grant programs before then, their trust fund allocations would be treated as super revenue sharing and may be used for any purpose. (Fact Sheet, 1982, p. 2)

One official, speaking for the "new federalism" of the Administration, summarized the overall direction of these proposals as follows:

> The existing and proposed block grants are part of a logical progression from a federally dominated categorical grant-in-aid system to the State oriented system proposed under the New Federalism. . . . Block grants are a mid-way point in this necessary transfer of authority and responsibility from the Federal Government to the States.[3]

OBJECTIVES, SCOPE,
AND METHODOLOGY

The original block grants and those enacted in 1981 provided the material we analyzed in the four issues areas specified in meetings with the staff of the Subcommittee on Oversight of the House Committee on Ways and Means. The areas we examined derived from the following questions:

(1) How has block grant legislation attempted to balance the competing goals of flexibility and accountability?
(2) Have the poor and members of other disadvantaged groups been served equally under block grants and categorical programs?
(3) Have there been savings in administrative costs under block grants compared to categorical grants?
(4) What are the extent and the nature of evaluative information available to the Congress under block grants?

TABLE 2 The Structural and Fiscal Characteristics of 1981 Block Grants

Program	Federal Agency	Services Provided	First Year Authorization in $ Millions	Distribution Formula	Primary Recipient	Effective Date
Community Development (small cities)	HUD	Housing rehabilitation, community development	1,082.0	Population, overcrowded and old housing, poverty population growth lag	States and general purpose local governments	October 1, 1981 (State administration continues as option)
Low Income Home Energy Assistance	HHS	Energy assistance	1,880.0	FY 1981 ratio to state under Home Energy Assistance Act	States	October 1, 1981
Social Services	HHS	Training, day care, family planning, child abuse, elderly, handicapped services	2,400.0	Population	States	October 1, 1981
Elementary and Secondary Education	Education	Education	3,937.0	School-aged population	State and local education agencies	July 1, 1982
Primary Care	HHS	Primary health services for medically underserved populations	302.5	FY 1982 ratio to state for community health centers	States	October 1, 1982 (State administration continues as option)
Alcohol, Drug Abuse, and Mental Health	HHS	Alcohol and drug abuse prevention and treatment, mental health services	491.0	FY 1981 ratio to state for mental health, FY 1980 for alcohol and drug abuse	States	Optional in FY 1982

TABLE 2   Continued

Program	Federal Agency	Services Provided	First Year Authorization in $ Millions	Distribution Formula	Primary Recipient	Effective Date
Community Services	HHS	Poverty programs	389.0	FY 1981 ratio to state under Equal Opportunity Act	States	Optional in FY 1982
Maternal and Child Health	HHS	Maternal and child health services, rehabilitation and treatment for handicapped children	373.0	FY 1981 ratio to state for consolidated programs	States	Optional in FY 1982
Preventive Health and Health Services	HHS	Comprehensive public health and emergency medical services, education for populations at risk	95.00	FY 1981 ratio to state for 8 categorical programs, state population	States	Optional in FY 1982

SOURCE: Omnibus Budget Reconciliation Act of 1981, Public Law 973-35.

One method we used to address these issues is the evaluation synthesis, in which existing evaluation studies are assembled, their results synthesized, and their methodologies assessed. The evaluations thus serve as our data base for addressing the specific congressional questions we were asked. In performing this synthesis, we limited our literature review to reports, studies, and data sources that are national in scope. These included evaluations prepared by GAO and other Federal agencies and by nongovernmental sources. Where necessary, we supplemented and confirmed the evaluation data through agency officials responsible for administering the programs. We used the synthesis technique to address the questions on targeting to disadvantaged groups and on administrative costs.

We analyzed the legislative provisions and the Federal regulations for the older and the newly created block grants and present the results of this analysis. However, we made no attempt to verify the degree of compliance with these provisions at the State and local levels.

We conducted interviews with directors of Federal units responsible for evaluating block grant programs and with others who are also knowledgeable about the programs' operations and evaluations. For block grants for which there was more than one evaluation office, we interviewed at least the officials at the unit with the largest budget and the clearest mandate for evaluation. Our reliance on interview data is heaviest in our discussion of Federal block grant evaluations.[4]

There are two major limitations to our methodology. First, changes under way in the 1980's, if they persist, could lead to experiences under the block grant programs that are totally different from earlier experience. For example, increasing economic constraints and fiscal conservatism could increase the pressure for a reduction in Federal requirements. Second, relying on a universe of only five early block grant programs provides no firm basis from which to draw conclusions. There is, however, no reason to assume that the conditions that influenced the earlier programs will not be as important in the 1980's or that experience under the five programs does not reflect either the realities of implementation or those of Federal accountability.

SUMMARY

Extensive interest in the block grant mechanism is evidenced by the recent consolidation of more than 50 categorical and 2 former block grants into 9 new block grant programs. Since the Congress exercises oversight of these programs, any information on problems or key issues relevant to block grant implementation and administration is useful.

These issues of the legislative requirements imposed in enacted block grants derive from the need to have minimal provisions constraining flexibility and, at the same time, to insure that measures exist for documenting what the expenditure of public funds is accomplishing. We discuss how these requirements have been imposed, what changes have occurred in them over time, and the problems of drawing inferences from experience for understanding the way the new block grants might operate.

We also looked at whether people who are poor or members of minority groups receive their share of services under block grants. We attempted to answer whether block grants have been equitable, compared to categorical grants, in serving specially identified groups. We examined the three older block grants, which were intended, at least in part, to target services, and we relate our findings to new block grants.

NOTES

1. Our discussion of the Elementary and Secondary Education block grant treats chapters 1 and 2 of that grant as block grants. There is some debate whether chapter 1 should be considered a block grant. We believe it bears sufficient similarity to other 1981 block grants and to our definition of block grants to do so.

2. The new consolidations are in vocational and adult education, education for the handicapped, employment and training, rehabilitation services, child welfare, rental rehabilitation, and combined welfare administration. The proposed expansions are in primary care; services for women, infants, and children; and energy and emergency assistance. (OMB, 1982, pp. 7-8)

3. Statement of Dr. Robert J. Rubin, HHS, before the Subcommittee on Intergovernmental Relations of the Senate Committee on Governmental Affairs, May 11, 1982.

4. We designed the major areas of inquiry in these interviews to find out what approaches agencies had taken in evaluating block grants; what organizational structures, resources, and mandates existed for conducting evaluations; what major evaluation activities had actually occurred; what barriers had been faced in evaluating the programs; and what uses had been made of evaluation findings.

Have the Poor and Other Disadvantaged Groups Been Served Equally Under Block Grants and Categorical Programs?

To what degree do block grants focus services on the poor and minority groups? It has been argued that with the passage of time fewer poor and minorities would participate in block grant programs compared with the categorical programs that preceded them. Advocacy groups for the poor and civil rights organizations that believe that federally administered categorical programs are better able to target social welfare assistance have expressed concern about the argument. (Ad Hoc Coalition, 1981, pp. I-6, I-7)

Much of the controversy derives from the philosophy that power should be turned back to State and local governments (as we discussed in chapter 1). From the concerns of advocacy groups, one could predict that under block grants targeting to the poor and minorities would decline over time.

In this chapter, we examine the record of CDBG, CETA, and Title XX Social Services in targeting services to the poor and minority groups. LEAA and PHA are not included in the analysis because they were not intended to be targeted specifically to the poor or minorities.

The targeting objectives of CDBG, CETA, and Title XX are not their only legislative objectives, however. One other objective of block grants is to increase local flexibility and decisionmaking. There are also multiple programmatic goals such as the CDBG objective of aiding in the prevention or elimination of slums or blight. The difficulty these multiple goals pose for evaluation purposes is that they make the standard of comparison unclear. For example, if CDBG has multiple objectives, what percentage of CDBG benefits should be targeted to lower income people? Clearly 100 percent is too high because some funds should be used to combat slums and blight. This limitation must be emphasized or the false conclusion will be reached that all funds should benefit disadvantaged groups.[1]

In the following section, we identify the studies reviewed to assess targeting; then we discuss each of the three programs separately. For each program, we examine the legislative basis for targeting and the targeting data for income and, where available, for race. At the end of the chapter, we review the grants enacted in 1981.

STUDIES USED TO ASSESS TARGETING

In Table 3 we list eight basic evaluation studies on block grant targeting. Some comprise a series of reports. In the table, we have also indicated who conducted each study and the time period for data collection. Our main criterion for selecting studies was that all report quantitative data on income targeting for the block grant programs nationwide. Operationally, that excluded case studies of targeting in one community and one State and studies that did not report quantitative data on targeting.[2] We made an exception with the University of Pennsylvania review of a sample of neighborhoods in nine cities because the cities are scattered geographically, the research design was well constructed for looking at targeting, and the sample of individuals within each city was large.

CETA TARGETING

The Legislative Background

Even though the creation of CETA as a block grant shifted employment and training decisions from Federal to State and local officials, its central goal remained the same as its predecessor manpower programs. Its purpose was to "provide job training and employment opportunities." (Pub. L. No. 93-203, sec. 2) Title I authorized the CETA block grant specifically

> to establish a program to provide comprehensive manpower services throughout the Nation. Such program shall include the development and creation of job opportunities and training, education, and other services needed to enable

TABLE 3   List of Studies Reported

Block Grant	Title and Series	Source	Data Collection Period
CETA	Sixth Annual Report	National Commission for Employment Policy	July 1973-Sept. 1979
	CETA: Manpower Programs Under Local Control	William Mirengoff and Lester Rindler	July 1973-Sept. 1977
CDBG	Community Development Strategies Evaluation	University of Pennsylvania	1970-1979
	Targeting Community Development	The Brookings Institution	July 1974-Sept. 1978
	Fourth Annual Community Development Block Grant Report (and others in a series of six)	U.S. Department of Housing and Urban Development	July 1974-Sept. 1980
	Second Year Community Development Block Grant Experience	National Association of Housing and Redevelopment Officials	July 1974-June 1976
	Meeting Application and Review Requirements for Block Grants Under Title I of the Housing and Community Development Act of 1974	U.S. General Accounting Office	July 1974-June 1975
Title XX	Annual Report to the Congress on the Social Security Act (separate report for FY 1979 and FY 1980)	U.S. Department of Health and Human Services	Oct. 1978-Sept. 1980

NOTE: Originally Table 7.

individuals to secure and retain employment at their maximum capacity. (Pub. L. No. 93-203, sec. 101)

While the block grant allowed prime sponsors considerable latitude in choosing which groups to serve, it required them to give assurances that they would, to the maximum extent feasible, serve those "most in need," including "low-income persons and persons of limited English-speaking ability." (Pub. L. No. 93-203, sec. 105(a)(1); see also Mirengoff and Rindler, 1978, p. 196) Because abuses were perceived in the public service employment titles of CETA, eligibility requirements were tightened in order to focus services on the disadvantaged unemployed. By

1978, eligibility had also been tightened for the block grant program itself, now redesignated as CETA titles IIB and IIC. (GAO, 1982, p. 111)

The standards for assessing the targeting of CETA services to people with low incomes are made more complex by the fact that the legislation intends that there be other recipients of CETA block grant services, including

> handicapped individuals, persons facing barriers to employment commonly experienced by older workers, and persons of limited English-speaking ability. (Pub. L. No. 95-524, sec. 103(a)(5)(A))

Evaluation Results

The two studies on CETA that we examined (see Table 3) both used the DOL Management Information System, which collects data each year on the characteristics of participants in CETA programs. It also reported fiscal year 1974 data for the manpower programs that preceded CETA.[3] In Table 4 we present a variety of characteristics of participants in the CETA block grant, comparing them to those of participants in the manpower programs that preceded CETA.

Our overall finding is that on the whole block grant participants were only slightly less economically needy than the preblock grant manpower program participants. The first six characteristics in Table 4 for purposes of targeting can be considered indicators of "economic need." Blacks and Spanish-speaking are included in this list because they are disproportionately represented in the total population of economically needy people. There was a drop of 10 percentage points (see column 4) in the percent of participants who were "economically disadvantaged," from 87 percent under the categorical programs in fiscal year 1974 to 77 percent in the first year of CETA. However, other measures fail to show a consistent direction of change in the economic need of participants. The table also shows that the percent of participants who were black and the percent who received AFDC and public assistance increased slightly between fiscal years 1974 and 1975. These findings suggest that on an overall dimension of "economic need" there was only a slight decrease in the economic need of participants under the CETA block grant mechanism compared with the prior categorical manpower programs. Modest changes in clientele of the order detected in the targeting studies may be explained by the fact that the CETA legislation identified other intended recipients.

On the question of minority group targeting, Table 4 shows that blacks and the Spanish-speaking were equally likely to be participants under CETA and the prior categorical programs.

Finally, comparing data on CETA participants in fiscal years 1975 and 1979, we find no consistent change. Three of the five available characteristics show less targeting in fiscal 1979 and two show less targeting in fiscal 1975.[4] (The data are in note 4.) While these data do not support concerns that fewer and fewer disadvantaged citizens would be participating in the CETA program over time, this finding is difficult to interpret because of changes in the national economy and the 1978 CETA amendments.

TABLE 4   Percentage of CETA Block Grant Participants with Selected Characteristics Compared with Pre-CETA Categorical Program Participants[a]

Characteristics	Categorical Programs FY 1974 (1)	CETA Block Grant[a]		Change	
		FY 1975 (2)	FY 1977 (3)	FY 1974-1975 (4)	FY 1974-1977 (5)
Economically disadvantaged[b]	87	77	78	-10	- 9
AFDC and public assistance	23	27	26	+ 4	+ 3
Black	37	39	35	+ 2	- 2
Spanish-speaking[c]	15	13	14	- 2	- 1
Unemployed	76[d]	62	74	-14[d]	- 2[d]
Receiving Unemployment Insurance	5	4	7	- 1	+ 2
Female	42	46	48	+ 4	+ 6
Under 22 years old	63	62	52	- 1	-11
Less than 12 years of school	66	61	50	- 5	-16

NOTE: Originally Table 8.
SOURCE: Adapted fom NCEP, *Sixth Annual Report* (Washington, D.C.: 1980), pp. 112-13.
a. Title I of CETA as originally enacted.
b. Based on the poverty level as determined by OMB.
c. Estimated.
d. Not available for FY 1974, this figure had to be obtained from a different and possibly noncomparable DOL source. Consequently, comparison of this figure with later CETA statistics should be made only with caution.

In summary, when we compare the block grant with the categorical programs that existed before its enactment, we find some decrease in targeting under CETA to the economically needy, although trends are inconsistent across the measures. Overall, targeting to the needy did not change materially between 1975 and 1979. There was little change in targeting of the block grant to Black and Spanish-speaking participants compared with the predecessor categorical programs.

CDBG TARGETING

The Legislative Background

The Community Development Block Grant program for large cities has emphasized social targeting to families of low and moderate incomes. The 1974 legislation cited as its "primary objective"

> the development of viable urban communities, by providing decent housing and a suitable living environment and expanding economic opportunities, principally for persons of low and moderate income. (Pub. L. No. 93-383, sec. 101(c))

The Act also includes language in three of seven detailed objectives indicating that they are intended principally for people of low and moderate income. In addition, the legislation provides that communities must "give maximum feasible priority to activities which will benefit low- or moderate-income families or aid in the prevention or elimination of slums or blight." (Pub. L. No. 93-383, sec. 104(b)(2))

Although the legislation established social targeting as an important CDBG objective, there were two other equal objectives: (1) "the prevention or elimination of slums or blight" and (2) meeting "other community development needs having a particular urgency." (Pub. L. No. 93-383, sec. 104(b)(2)) While not citing them as primary objectives, the Act refers to other CDBG goals such as "to streamline programs and improve the functioning of agencies" and "the restoration and preservation of properties of special value for historic, architectural, or esthetic reasons." (Pub. L. No. 93-383, sec. 101(b) and (c)) Evaluation results for the targeting of CDBG to low and moderate income groups will, therefore, have to be judged in terms of the multiple objectives of the legislation.

There has been considerable controversy since the Act's passage regarding what constitutes "maximum feasible priority" in targeting activities to benefit low- or moderate-income people. (U.S. Congress, House, 1977, p. 21) The Senate passed but the conference deleted a provision to set a 20 percent limit on expenditures not "of direct and significant benefit to families of low or moderate income, or to areas which are blighted or deteriorating." (Dommel, 1980, p. 12) In the beginning, HUD did not define "maximum feasible priority" quantitatively or instruct its staff on how to determine whether programs under CDBG met the requirement. Two years after CDBG was enacted, we found widely varying interpretations of this requirement among HUD area office staff. (GAO, 1976, p. 10; see also Dommel, 1980, pp.

13-14). The initial regulations did define "low and moderate income," considering it income less than or equal to 80 percent of the local standard metropolitan statistical area median income.[5]

During the Carter Administration, HUD worked to increase targeting of CDBG to lower income families. This involved in part initiatives by HUD administrators, demonstrating that changes occur in programs by means other than congressional action. (Dommel, 1980, pp. 14-21)

Evaluation Results for Income

The only study whose data allow comparisons of CDBG with the earlier categorical programs on income targeting is that conducted by the University of Pennsylvania, but it has two serious limitations. First, it represents a sample of only nine cities. Second, its inquiry was limited to housing rehabilitation, which represents only about 28 percent of all CDBG expenditures. (HUD, 1981, p. 59) However, housing rehabilitation seems to be a typical CDBG activity in terms of the degree to which it targets benefits to low and moderate income census tracts. This is demonstrated by 1979 data that show that two major activity groups had more targeting while three had less targeting to low and moderate income tracts than the "housing rehabilitation and related activities" group. (HUD, 1981, pp. 52-53, 59, A94) The issue is still unresolved and it cannot be assured that the Pennsylvania results represent all CDBG activities nationwide.

Keeping these limitations in mind, we can see in Table 5 (comparing columns 1 and 3) that CDBG housing rehabilitation aid was more targeted to low and moderate income recipients than earlier categorical programs in six of the seven cities for which comparisons could be made. (In Pittsburgh, the numbers are essentially the same.) A median of 96 percent of households receiving CDBG assistance had low and moderate incomes compared with 78 percent for the earlier categorical programs. The comparison group of 1970-74 categoricals (column 3) represents rehabilitations financed under other public funding sources in that time period.[6] "Low and moderate income" is defined according to HUD regulations discussed above.[7]

Table 5 also allows the comparison of CDBG with categorical programs contemporaneous with CDBG. This group includes rehabilitation aid under section 312 of the 1964 Housing Act and numerous State and local programs in six of the nine cities.[8] Comparing the first and second columns of the table thus shows that CDBG was more targeted to low and moderate income recipients in all seven cities for which the comparison can be made. The median of 97 percent of households that received CDBG aid had low and moderate incomes compared with 70 percent for the contemporaneous categorical programs.

Four other CDBG studies we examined included larger samples of communities and a cross-section of activities rather than housing rehabilitation alone. Their weaknesses are not present in the University of Pennsylvania study; all were based on planned benefits rather than actual benefits and all lacked any direct measure of

TABLE 5   Percentage of Recipient Households with Low and Moderate
Income by Funding Source

	CDBG 1975-1979 (1)	Categoricals 1975-1979 (2)	Categoricals 1970-1974 (3)
Birmingham	94	—	83
Corpus Christi	100	93	78
Denver	99	70	—
Memphis	97	87	91
New Haven	79	51	63
Pittsburgh	71	62	73
San Francisco	—	—	—
St. Paul	96	89	78
Wichita	100	38	95

Median
CDBG versus Categoricals 1970-1974
   CDBG   96%
   Categoricals 78%

CDBG versus Categoricals 1975-1979
   CDBG   97%
   Categoricals 70%

NOTE: Originally Table 9.
SOUCE: Stephen Gale *et al.*, "Community Development Strategies Evaluation: Social Targeting," draft report, University of Pennsylvania, Philadelphia, October 1980, table 4.4.

the income of the beneficiaries. In developing another report on determining who
benefits from the community development block grant programs, we are able to
cite some improvements that could be made in CDBG benefit data and reporting
processes.[9]

In Table 6 on the next page, we compare the University of Pennsylvania findings
with those of the four other studies. Excluding the University of Pennsylvania
study, we estimate that from 54 to 66 percent of CDBG benefits are allocated to
low and moderate income persons.

Change over time in targeting for the CDBG programs can be examined in the
Brookings and HUD studies as shown in Table 6. The Brookings study shows that
targeting increased from 1975 to 1978 while the HUD findings show essentially no
change for two years but an increase by 1978. These increases are apparently
attributable to the policy changes introduced in the Carter Administration, as we
noted earlier. Going beyond the period covered by the table, the Brookings research
shows a slight decrease in targeting in 1979 and 1980 while the HUD study finds a
slight increase.[10] In summary, CDBG data show that participation by the poor
increased over time under the block grant mechanism but did so presumably
because of greater Federal influence.

TABLE 6   Percentage of CDBG Benefits Allocated to Low and Moderate
Income Groups by Study and Fiscal Year

Study	1975	1976	1977	1978
The Brookings Institution[a]	54	56	60	62
National Association of Housing and Urban Development Officials	59	55	–	–
University of Pennsylvania[b]		(median 96)		
U.S. Department of Housing and Urban Development	64	62	61	66
U.S. General Accounting Office	56			

NOTE: Originally Table 10.
SOURCE: Brookings: Paul R. Dommel et al., Targeting Community Development (Washington, D.C.: U. S. Department of Housing and Urban Development, 1980), p. 161. NAHRO: Robert L. Ginsburg, "Second Year Community Development Block Grant Experience: A Summary of Findings of the NAHRO Community Development Monitoring Project," Journal of Housing, February 1977, pp. 81-82. University of Pennsylvania: Stephen Gale et al., "Community Development Strategies Evaluation: Social Targeting," draft report, University of Pennsylvania, Philadelphia, 1980, table 4.4. HUD: HUD, Fourth Annual Community Development Block Grant Report (Washington, D.C.: 1979), p. II-7. GAO: GAO, Meeting Application and Review Requirements for Block Grants Under Title I of the Housing and Community Development Act of 1974, CED-76-106 (Washington, D.C.: 1976), p. 13.
a. Data for later years are available but not reported here in order to make the time periods of the different data collections more comparable.
b. Not reported separately by fiscal year. Includes only housing rehabilitation funded wholly by CDBG in fiscal years 1975-1978.

In our 1981 report on CDBG, we found that some cities provided assistance under this grant for nonessential or cosmetic home repairs. One city was cited where 31 of the 200 most recent CDBG-aided loans (or 15.5 percent) went to people whose annual incomes exceeded $30,000. (GAO, 1981a, p. 20) While this represents only a case study of rehabilitation loans in one city, the findings are not inconsistent with findings in the studies in Table 6. They estimate that up to 34-46 percent of CDBG resources (excluding the University of Pennsylvania results) benefit entire communities rather than any particular income group. Our 1981 study included site visits but was not intended to be a systematic study of the allocation of CDBG benefits to income groups. Neither it nor the other studies we have discussed above suggest widespread targeting problems with CDBG.

In summary, the University of Pennsylvania analysis shows that 96 percent of households aided in residential rehabilitation by CDBG had low and moderate incomes compared with 78 percent for the categorical programs that preceded CDBG. Furthermore, 97 percent of CDBG-aided households and 70 percent of

TABLE 7   Percentage of Population That Is Minority and Percentage of Recipient Households That Are Minority by Funding Source

	Minority Population 1970 (1)	CDBG 1975-1978 (2)	Categoricals 1975-1978 (3)	1975-1978 (4)
Birmingham	47	31	–	33
Corpus Christi	43	100	92	91
Memphis	44	93	80	98
New Haven	31	37	65	59
Wichita	14	55	14	30

NOTE: Originally Table 11.
SOURCE: Stephen Gale et al., "Community Development Strategies Evaluation: Social Targeting," draft report, University of Pennsylvania, Philadelphia, October 1980, tables 4.10 and 4.12.

current categorically aided households had low and moderate incomes. This study concluded that

the proportion of CDBG rehabilitation assistance reaching targeted households equals or exceeds the proportions of other rehabilitation programs that predate or are contemporaneous with CDBG.[11]

If the University of Pennsylvania research is not considered, estimates derived from the other studies of all CDBG activities suggest that 54 to 66 percent of CDBG benefits were targeted to people with low and moderate incomes. Analysis of CDBG trends over time suggests a slight increase in targeting rather than the cumulative reduction of targeting that some observers have feared.

Evaluation Results for Race

The CDBG legislation has no provisions for targeting benefits to minority groups but, because minorities are more likely than nonminority groups to have low incomes and to live in substandard housing, the extent to which they benefit from CDBG is germane to the program's objectives. The University of Pennsylvania study collected data on race in a survey of current residents of CDBG-aided dwelling units. In Table 7, we present data on targeting to minority groups for the five cities for which the data were sufficient. (Gale, 1980, p. 48)

Comparing the block grant recipients in 1975-78 with the earlier categorical grant recipients (that is, columns 2 and 4) shows no consistent pattern of difference in the allocation of rehabilitation assistance to minority groups. Minorities are served equally when compared with the earlier categorical grants. Using categorical programs in 1975-78 for comparison (that is, columns 2 and 3) produces the same results.[12]

TABLE 8   Percentage of CDBG Funds Allocated to Low and Moderate Income
Groups by Type of City, Level of Community Distress, and
Program Year

City type and Distress Level	Number of Jurisdictions	1979	1980
Central Cities			
Low distress	10	61	61
High distress	19	63	64
Satellite Cities			
Low distress	8	52	53
High distress	4	60	55
Total			
Low distress	18	55	57
High distress	23	62	62

NOTE: Originally Table 12.
SOURCE: Paul Dommel, et al., "Implementing Community Development" draft manuscript,
U.S. Department of Housing and Urban Development, Washington, D.C., 1982,
p.104.

In short, the results on racial targeting based on the University of Pennsylvania study are limited to only five cities and show no strong patterns. However, the findings of that study also show that the proportion of minority group members receiving CDBG benefits in four of the five cities is higher than the proportion of minority group members in the overall population (comparing columns 1 and 2). Birmingham, Alabama, is the only city in which the percentage of minority recipients—under both categorical and block grants—is smaller than the minority population.

Targeting and the CDBG Allocation Formula

In this concluding section, we use the Brookings targeting data to illustrate the impact of the legislative formula that allocates block grant funds. For locally operated programs such as CDBG, if the formula allocates more funds to communities where most of the lower income people live, greater targeting to the poor is likely to occur. Table 8 presents data to illustrate the differing record of cities in targeting CDBG benefits. Distress is measured by an index combining poverty levels, age of housing, and population change.

The table shows that "the more distressed communities tended to allocate a higher level of benefits to lower income groups than did better-off communities in the sample." (Dommel, 1982, p. 102) Also, the targeting is measurably higher in central cities than in satellite cities.

While a complete explanation of these differences would include the influence of methodological factors, the results show differing performances in targeting of

CDBG benefits to low and moderate income persons. Satellite cities and cities with low distress achieve less targeting than central cities and cities with high distress. Suburban jurisdictions appeared to be susceptible to more fluctuation in targeting and their programs were more easily diverted from the social targeting objective of the law. (Dommel, 1982, p. 110)

These results show in part the impact of the CDBG allocation formula. If the formula were structured so as to exclude from CDBG eligibility some suburban and low distress communities, it is likely that targeting CDBG funds to low and moderate income persons would increase.[13]

Of course, many elements must be weighed in constructing any allocation formula. When the law is targeting benefits to people with low and moderate incomes, the allocation formula it specifies will be critical in achieving targeting.

TITLE XX TARGETING

The Legislative Background

The Title XX Social Services program was directed largely toward the poor. Title XX provided that

States must expend an amount equal to at least 50 percent of the Federal share of their expenditures for persons who are eligible for Aid to Families with Dependent Children (AFDC), Supplementary Security Income (SSI), Medicaid and for family members or other persons whose needs are taken into account in determining the eligibility of an AFDC or SSI recipient. (HHS, 1981, p. 2)

This 50 percent requirement was eliminated in the Social Services block grant.

People became eligible for Title XX services in one of three ways:

(1) *Income eligibles.* States determined how poor people had to be in order to receive services. The highest income level a State could serve and receive Federal reimbursement for was 115 percent of the State median income, adjusted for family size. Eligibility criteria could vary for different types of service but could not exceed the 115 percent limitation. The Omnibus Budget Reconciliation Act of 1981 removed income eligibility limits, although the States may provide their own income limitations.

(2) *Income maintenance recipients.* States could provide Title XX social services to supplement cash assistance provided under AFDC and SSI. Title XX provided services while AFDC and SSI provided cash assistance. Categories of certain persons—such as migrant workers, drug addicts, and runaways—could also be served without an individual means test.

(3) *Services without regard to income.* People needing three services could be aided whether their income was low or high—protective services for children or adults, information and referral, and family planning. (HHS, 1981, pp. 3-4)

Evaluation Results for Income

Even though Title XX eligibility was based primarily on income, data on the income of recipients are not available. In fact, lack of adequate data has been a problem with Title XX since its inception. (Ad Hoc Coalition, 1981, p. II-8) Even so, data from the Social Services Reporting Requirements (SSRR) allow for some analysis of the targeting issue.

One evaluation of the SSRR data on the eligibility of Title XX recipients indicated reason for some confidence in this information. The eligibility of people who are categorically eligible may be verified through Medicaid cards or local welfare agency files. There is, however, greater variability in procedures for those who claim eligibility based on income. Some States simply asked applicants to sign declarations while others went so far as to verify income through the Social Security office. Providers can jeopardize fund reimbursement with errors in eligibility determinations, which seemed to make most service providers cautious. (One America, 1980, pp. 45-46)

Weaknesses in the SSRR data, however, make the counts of services and recipients not totally valid for national summaries. The validity of national statistics is reduced because many States lump all clients into one recipient category (primary recipients) and some States use their own classifications.[14]

With these limitations, data on the number and percent of primary recipients of Title XX services by type of eligibility for fiscal year 1979 were

Income	2,894,654	40
Income maintenance (AFDC, SSI)	2,808,648	39
Without regard to income	1,508,832	21
Total	7,212,134	100%

These figures show that 79 percent of the primary recipients were eligible by virtue of having low incomes—40 percent for income eligibles plus 39 percent for income maintenance recipients. This 79 percent targeting estimate includes some people with incomes up to 115 percent of the State median income adjusted for family size. This was true, however, in only 16 States, only 2 of which provided all or even most of their services at maximum levels. (HHS, 1980, p. 14, and 1981, p. 10)

The category "without regard to income" may include many who would have met the eligibility criteria had they been applied. Many in this category also received information and referral services that have very low unit costs, thereby not detracting significantly from the overall targeting achieved under the program. In short, although services provided "without regard to income" increased from 13 percent to 21 percent of the total primary recipients between fiscal years 1976 and 1979, the actual share of social services the needy received appears to have been greater than these figures suggest.

In summary, the data show that roughly 79 percent of the primary recipients of Title XX Social Services obtained services because of their low incomes. The remainder received legally authorized protective services, information and referral, and family planning assistance without regard to income.

TARGETING UNDER THE 1981 BLOCK GRANTS

The Omnibus Budget Reconciliation Act, contains more targeting provisions than the enabling legislation of the pre-1981 block grants. Six of the nine block grants enacted in 1981 provide services to people with low incomes as well as other categories of recipients. The Social Services block grant, in contrast, relaxes some of the targeting provisions of the older Title XX Social Services program.

Three of the six new grants with low income targeting provisions prescribe specific income limitations. First, the Low Income Home Energy Assistance block grant generally restricts eligibility to households whose incomes are less than 150 percent of the State poverty level or 60 percent of the State median income, as well as those receiving AFDC, SSI, food stamps, or Veterans' and Survivors' pension benefits. Next, the Maternal and Child Health grant provides health assessments, follow-up and diagnostic services, treatments, immunizations, and other health services to mothers who have children and whose incomes are below the nonfarm official poverty line, although other services authorized under the block grant are not limited to this class of recipient. Finally, the Community Services grant provides for

> a range of services and activities having a measurable and potentially major impact on the causes of poverty in the community or those areas of the community where poverty is a particularly acute problem [and] . . . activities designed to assist low income participants. (Pub. L. No. 97-35, sec. 675)

The legislation defines the poverty line as a criterion of eligibility in community services programs.

The three other block grants with targeting objectives do not define the eligibility of individual recipients as specifically. The Primary Care grant aids "medically underserved" populations, defined by such criteria as ability to pay, infant mortality rates, and the availability of health professionals. The Elementary and Secondary Education block grant targets services to the "educationally deprived," which includes people with low incomes and migrants as well as handicapped children. Under the new CDBG small cities block grant, States must give "maximum feasible priority" to activities that benefit low and moderate income families or aid in the prevention of slums and blight but in most cases may channel funds away from these activities to meet other urgent community needs.

The Omnibus Budget Reconciliation Act contains definitions of target populations but generally does not link these provisions to mechanisms that States might use to achieve targeting, such as sub-State allocation formulas. Chapter 2 of the

Elementary and Secondary Education grant is one of the few block grants enacted in 1981 to address the connection between distribution formulas and targeting. This legislation specifies that States will distribute funds to local education agencies according to their relative enrollments, with these funds adjusted to

> provide higher per pupil allocations to local education agencies which have the greatest numbers or percentages of children whose education imposes a higher than average cost per child, such as
>
> (1) children from low-income families,
> (2) children living in economically depressed urban and rural areas, and
> (3) children living in sparsely populated areas. (Pub. L. No. 97-35, sec. 565(a))

However, there is no requirement that the local education agencies use these funds for these children.

Three grants may make changes in their distribution formulas to facilitate targeting. The Alcohol, Drug Abuse, and Mental Health, Maternal and Child Health, and Preventive Health and Health Services grants require the Secretary of HHS to report to the Congress on alternative distribution formulas within one year after enactment of the Omnibus Reconciliation Act. The Act instructs the Secretary to take into account State financial resources, which are likely to be influenced by the size of a State's low-income population, and the number of low-income mothers and children.

Provisions requiring grantees to fund previously supported projects are another mechanism that may affect targeting in the short run, although not always in the same direction. Programs that served low-income clients before a grant took effect are likely to continue to serve them through organization inertia. For example, the Primary Care and Community Services grants require grantees to maintain sub-grantees' pre-block grant funding levels for several fiscal years after the block grant's effective date. Primary Care specifies that grantees are to receive 100 percent of the previous fiscal year's funding in the first year; grantees under Community Services are to receive 90 percent. The Preventive Health grant and the Alcohol, Drug Abuse, and Mental Health grant also provide that subgrantees are to continue to receive funding in the first fiscal year of the grant but do not specify the amount.

One long-run implication of these differences is that as the States establish their own criteria for the form and content of annual reports, efforts to study targeting nationwide will be impaired. In the past, data reported by grantees tended to be the primary source for annual reports to the Congress and, thus, the bases for determining social targeting. In the future, unless the States succeed in establishing comparable data collection and reporting procedures in all relevant topical areas, the quality and scope of targeting data will vary from State to State. In the absence of uniform data, it may be difficult to determine the amount of targeting on a nationwide basis under these block grants.

SUMMARY

CDBG, CETA, and Title XX all have the objective of focusing services on the economically needy. A review of the data suggests that they in fact targeted services to their designated groups as shown below:

— three of every four participants in CETA were economically disadvantaged,

— 54 to 66 percent or more of CDBG benefits were targeted to people of low and moderate incomes, and

— about 79 percent of the primary recipients of Title XX Social Services were eligible because of their low incomes.

The failure to reach 100 percent targeting to the poor may indicate multiple legislative objectives rather than program deficiencies, and therefore these figures are difficult to interpret.

Another approach to studying targeting, possible despite some methodological problems with the data, was to compare CETA and CDBG to their predecessor categorical programs. Thus,

— CETA showed a slight decrease in targeting to the poor under the block grant but, in general, the characteristics of the people served were similar, and

— CDBG rehabilitation assistance showed better targeting to low and moderate income groups under the block grant in six of seven cities.

CDBG was targeted more to lower income recipients compared to selected current categorical programs. While limited to only seven cities and examining only one component of the CDBG program, the comparisons of housing rehabilitation assistance show that a median of 97 percent of recipients of CDBG assistance had low and moderate incomes compared with 70 percent under current categorical programs.

The data available also allowed us to examine change in order to determine whether or not targeting to the poor diminished. Data on income targeting for CETA and CDBG suggest no such decline in benefits to the poor. This could be interpreted as a strength of block grants or as a result of their recategorization.

With regard to targeting by race and ethnicity, there were no consistent differences between the block grants and the categorical grants.

Some of the same CDBG data illustrate the impact of the allocation formula on eventual targeting to low and moderate income groups. We found that data from 1979 and 1980 show that satellite cities and cities with low distress achieved less targeting of CDBG funds than central cities and high distress cities.

The review of targeting for these three programs indicates that people with low incomes and people in minority groups have received services about equally often under block and categorical grants. The reasons for these findings are less clear. Perhaps the existing clientele from the prior categorical programs help prevent dilution of targeting. Also, statutory requirements, imposed either by the State or by the Federal Government designating who is to be served, whether generally or specifically, may have contributed to the targeting we have observed. There were numerous targeting requirements associated with the CDBG, CETA, and Title XX programs.

Will the 1981 block grant yield similar findings? Some factors are common to the earlier grants. Six of the nine new block grants have the objective of serving a disadvantaged clientele and specify in some detail who is to be served. One even incorporates targeting in its distribution formula. In the short run, continuing to fund certain subgrantees at levels comparable to those under the categorical programs may have mixed effects on targeting. The programs that previously served low-income populations may, through inertia, continue to do so.

A major difference between the old and the new block grants is the more prominent role of the States in 1982. States have had power in the early block grants, but primary power was held by the local and Federal governments under CDBG and CETA (except in balance-of-State areas).

The ability to draw conclusions at a national level about targeting under the new block grants requires comparable national data. Although some voluntary efforts are under way, Federal agencies are not requiring that uniform data be collected on the 1981 block grants. In the absence of uniform data, it may be difficult to determine the amount of targeting on a nationwide basis under these block grants.

NOTES

1. Another major methodological concern has to do with assumptions that are required in analyzing the targeting data under block grants. When participants in block grants are compared with participants in the early categorical programs, it is assumed that they differ only with respect to the type of grant mechanism, but other factors, such as historical differences, may obscure the comparison. This problem may be partly overcome by comparing block grant participants with participants in contemporaneous categorical programs, but there is a disadvantage in that the categorical programs may have legislative objectives that differ from those of the block grant. Slight differences in objectives may be more significant than differences in the mechanism.

2. We were unable to obtain a copy of the National Urban League report on CDBG targeting. We excluded a Southern Regional Council report on targeting that did not present quantitative findings.

3. DOL obtains these data from prime sponsor reports following a detailed manual. We did not independently audit the data, but program officials stated that analyses indicate that the descriptive statistics are reliable.

4. Data for the CETA block grant (title I, later redesignated titles IIB and IIC) are as follows:

Characteristic	FY 1975	FY 1979	Change
AFDC and public assistance	27%	26%	−1%
Economically disadvantaged	77	71	−6
Black	39	33	−6
Unemployed	62	77	+15
Receiving Unemployment Insurance	4	5	+1
Spanish-speaking	13	n.a.	n.a.

The definition of "economically disadvantaged" changed in fiscal 1979; in this table, we use the earlier definition for both fiscal years in order to make the data comparable. Our data source here is NCEP, 1980, pp. 112-13.

5. CDBG amendments in 1977 change "low or moderate income" to "low and moderate income" to reflect the congressional intention that not all benefits go to people of moderate income. In this report, we have used the two phrases interchangeably.

6. These comparisons principally include aid under section 312 of the Housing Act of 1964 and section 115 of the urban renewal program. Section 312, originally intended for use in urban renewal areas, provides loans for rehabilitating residential properties at a 3 percent interest rate for up to 20 years. Section 115 provided grants of up to $3,500 to very low income homeowners in urban renewal areas to bring single-family dwellings up to safe and decent conditions; section 115 grants were terminated with the enactment of CDBG. Section 312 loans continued as an active program until the enactment of the Omnibus Reconciliation Act of 1981. (Gale, 1980, p. 52)

7. The University of Pennsylvania researchers assembled HUD statistics on standard metropolitan statistical area family income for each sample city and for each year. This made it possible to aggregate data from different years.

8. This comparison group also includes some programs in which CDBG funds were used to defray administrative costs or to subsidize interest rates. Thus, this is not a pure comparison group and could be more precisely, if awkwardly, called "partially or non-CDBG funded, post-1975."

9. The findings are reported in a study tentatively entitled "HUD Needs to Better Determine the Extent of Community Block Grants' Lower Income Beneficiaries."

10. See Dommel, 1982, p. 100. The HUD data are problematic because the sample of cities was changed significantly. (HUD, 1981, p. 50)

11. Gale, 1980, p. iii. The conclusion summarizes targeting on a variety of dimensions but is consistent with the income data.

12. The Brookings researchers also examined the allocation of benefits to blacks and Hispanics by analyzing "minority areas"—census tracts in which 30 percent or more of the residents were black or Hispanic in 1970. Thirty of the 41 jurisdictions had one or more minority areas. Data for these 30 cities in 1975 and 1978 show that

Overall, over the 4 years the minority tracts did better than the nonminority tracts. . . . In the first year, 34 percent of the tracts that were not heavily minority were allocated activities, compared with 58 percent of the heavily black tracts and 42 percent of the heavily Hispanic tracts. In the fourth year, 40 percent of the tracts that were not heavily minority received activities, compared with 77 percent of the black tracts and 69 percent of the Hispanic tracts. (Dommel, 1980, p. 175)

Although the number of tracts receiving benefits increased between 1975 and 1978, the number of minority tracts that were assisted grew faster than other tracts. The Brookings data are difficult to interpret because about one-fourth of the jurisdictions were deleted (for not having any "minority areas") and because an area in which whites constituted up to 70 percent of the population could still be designated "minority area." The Brookings data are best at showing change, and that change shows a trend toward more activities and more dollars (except for Hispanics in 1978) in minority tracts over time.

13. An analysis of HUD data shows that 55 percent of the CDBG funds in cities that had none of the categorical programs that preceded CDBG benefited low and moderate income groups compared with 63 percent in cities that had had categorical programs. This suggests that had CDBG been limited to funding only cities that had participated in categorical programs, CDBG would show better targeting toward low and moderate incomes. The method of analysis may have exaggerated the differences. See HUD, 1980, pp. III-7, III-8.

14. It is also a weakness of the Social Services Reporting Requirements that it cannot measure either the success or the effect of Title XX services. Not suprisingly, One America found data on client outcomes to be the least quantifiable and least used. Its report was apparently a factor in the decision not to implement data collection on goal status. (One America, 1980, pp. 35-36, 44)

REFERENCES

Ad Hoc Coalition on Block Grants. Block Grants Briefing Book. Washington, DC: 1981.
ACIR (Advisory Commission on Intergovernmental Relations). Block Grants: A Comparative Analysis. Washington, DC: 1977a.
––– The Comprehensive Employment and Training Act: Early Readings from a Hybrid Block Grant. Washington, DC: 1977b.
––– The Partnership for Health Act: Lessons from a Pioneering Block Grant. Washington, DC: 1977c.
BARFIELD, CLAUDE. Rethinking Federalism: Block Grants and Federal, State, and Local Responsibilities. Washington, DC: American Enterprise Institute for Public Policy Research, 1981.
CONLAN, TIMOTHY J. "Back in Vogue: The Politics of Block Grant Legislation." Intergovernmental Perspective, 7 (1981), 8-15.
DOMMEL, PAUL R., et al. "Implementing Community Development." Draft manuscript, U.S. Department of Housing and Urban Development, Washington, DC, 1982.
–– Targeting Community Development. Washington, DC: U.S. Department of Housing and Urban Development, 1980.
Fact Sheet: Federalism Initiative. Washington, DC: The White House, January 27, 1982.
GALE, STEPHEN, et al. "Community Development Strategies Evaluation: Social Targeting." Draft report, University of Pennsylvania, Philadelphia, October 1980.
GAO (U.S. General Accounting Office). CETA Programs for Disadvantaged Adults–What Do We Know About Their Enrollees, Services, and Effectiveness? IPE-82-2. Washington, DC: 1982.
––– The Community Development Block Grant Program Can Be More Effective in Revitalizing the Nation's Cities, CED-81-76. Washington, DC: 1981.
––– Meeting Application and Review Requirements for Block Grants Under Title I of the Housing and Community Development Act of 1974, CED-76-106. Washington, DC: 1976.
GSA (General Services Administration). Weekly Compilation of Presidential Documents. Washington, DC: U.S. Government Printing Office, February 1, 1982. Vol. 18, No. 4.
HHS (U.S. Department of Health and Human Services). Annual Report to the Congress on Title XX of the Social Security Act: Fiscal Year 1980. Washington, DC: 1981.
––– Annual Report to the Congress on Title XX of the Social Security Act: Fiscal Year 1979. Washington, DC: 1980.
HUD (U.S. Department of Housing and Urban Development). Sixth Annual Community Development Block Grant Report. Washington, DC: 1981.
––– Fifth Annual Community Development Block Grant Report. Washington, DC: 1980.
MIRENGOFF, WILLIAM, and LESTER RINDLER. CETA: Manpower Programs Under Local Control. Washington, DC: National Academy of Sciences, 1978.
OMB (U.S. Office of Management and Budget). Budget of the Government of the United States, 1983. Special Analysis H. Washington, DC: 1982.
One America, Inc. The Social Services Reporting Requirements: A Management Review of the Validity and Use of the Data Reported. Washington, DC: 1980.

SLACK, IRIS J. Title XX at the Crossroads. Washington, DC: American Public Welfare Association, 1979.

SPAR, KAREN. Title XX of the Social Security Act: Program Description, Current Issues. Washington, DC: Congressional Research Service, 1981.

United States Congress, House of Representatives. Omnibus Budget Reconciliation Act of 1981. Conference Report 97-208, Book 2. Washington, DC: The White House, February 18, 1981.

——— Community Development Block Grant Program: Staff Report of the Committee on Banking, Finance, and Urban Affairs Subcommittee on Housing and Community Development. Washington, DC: U.S. Government Printing Office, 1977.

33

The Relation of Teaching and Learning
A Review of Reviews of Process-Product Research

Hersholt C. Waxman and Herbert J. Walberg

The central acts of education are teaching and learning, and it is worth our best efforts to study their causal connections. Of course, long before Plato's accounts of the Socratic method in the *Republic* and the *Dialogs* the insights and methods of sagacious teachers had been celebrated in East, South, and West Asia. Since Plato, many historical exemplars of teachers and their effects on students may be noted (Broudy,

[1] The work of the second author on this review was supported by grants from the National Institute of Education and the National Science Foundation. Any shortcomings and all opinions in this review, however, are attributable only to the authors.

1963). Since modern behavioral research began (perhaps dating from John B. Watson's, 1919, Chicago-school paper, "Psychology as the Behaviorist Views It," and his declaration on how a dozen healthy infants might be led to behave), the number of empirical studies of teaching have been growing rapidly. As early as 1950, Domas and Tiedeman chronicled research on teacher competence in 117 pages of annotated references. The number of double-columned pages in the first *Handbook of Research on Teaching* is 1,218 (Gage, 1963); 1,400 additional pages were thought necessary for the *Second Handbook* (Travers, 1973) only a decade later.

In view of the long history of humanistic inquiry and the large amount of positivistic research in recent decades, it is reasonable to ask what is known about the relation be-

HERSHOLT C. WAXMAN is a graduate student, University of Illinois at Chicago, College of Education, Box 4348, Chicago, IL 60680. He received his B.E. and M.E. at the University of Illinois, Chicago and his areas of specialization and interest include research on teaching and causal modeling.

HERBERT J. WALBERG is a Research Professor, University of Illinois, Chicago, College of Education. He received his B.E. at Chicago State, his M.E. at University of Illinois, Urbana, and his Ph.D. at University of Chicago. His specializations include social psychology, and productivity of education; measurement, evaluation, and statistical analysis. Dr. Walberg has recently edited a book (with P. L. Peterson), *Research on Teaching*, and *Improving Educational Standards and Productivity*.

From Hersholt C. Waxman and Herbert J. Walberg, "The Relation of Teaching and Learning: A Review of Reviews of Process-Product Research," 1(2) *Contemporary Education Review* 103-120 (Summer 1982). Copyright 1982, American Educational Research Association. Reprinted by permission

tween what the teacher does and what the student learns—the question addressed by the "process-product paradigm." Because 19 review articles have assessed evidence on the paradigm in the last decade, it would seem useful before writing the 20th review or conducting new primary studies to (1) examine critically the prior reviews; (2) describe their methods; (3) compare and contrast their conclusions; (4) attempt to synthesize them; and (5) point to new directions and methods for both future reviews and primary research.

We acknowledge at the outset that research on the paradigm is described as "chaotic," "disappointing," "embarrassingly small," "fruitless," and based on the "personal preferences" or "commitments" of the researchers (Doyle, 1977; Dunkin & Biddle, 1974; Gage, 1972, 1978; Rosenshine, 1979; Rosenshine & Furst, 1973). Other criticisms of the paradigm focus on the weaknesses of the observational systems, the criteria used to assess teacher effectiveness, the instability of measurements, weak research designs and methodological and statistical problems (Berliner, 1976, 1980; Brophy, 1979; Heath & Nielson, 1974; Shavelson & Dempsey-Atwood, 1976).

Fenstermacher (1978) attacks the paradigm on the grounds that it "lacks a normative theory of education," adding that it "does not incorporate a conception or justification of what is ultimately worth knowing and doing, it includes no view or defense of right conduct or moral integrity, nor does it give consideration to or argument for the ethical obligations and reasonable expectations of persons who act in specific, historical, social, political, and economic settings" (p. 175). Winne and Marx (1977) argue that this research on teaching "has been devoid of postulating a reasonable psychological foundation mapping out why certain events of teaching should influence particular learning processes in students which are manifested later in observable behavior such as test responses" (p. 670). In short, process-product research, according to some critics, has not dealt with the theoretical assumptions of why a particular style of teaching influences student learning, nor has it addressed values questions.

Popkewitz, Tabachnick and Zeichner (1979), moreover, argue that the paradigm

has certain limitations for educational inquiry and for understanding the phenomena of teacher education. It crystalizes the conduct of research to make inquiry a self-sustaining activity that has lost its generative power and critical stance. A consequence is a conservative orientation to the tasks of professional preparation and a distortion of the phenomena under study. (p. 52)

Doyle (1977) also attacks the process-product paradigm because he contends that there are problems of productivity, methodology and theory attributable to the researcher's failure to analyze the theoretical grounds used for "selecting variables or for interpreting available findings" (p. 164). A final noteworthy criticism of the paradigm is that it has "generally failed to generate practical solutions to teaching and learning problems" (Forman & Chapman, 1979, p. 37).

Some validity is to be found in these points but, contrary to such discouraging characterizations of the paradigm, it should also be noted that, notwithstanding the difficulty of field research in natural settings, a large number of studies with moderate technical adequacy have accumulated—some by the critics themselves. To the extent that the samples and conditions are varied, and the usual measurement and statistical problems abound, and consistent results across studies still emerge robustly, the findings need to be seriously assessed and carefully reviewed. (Correlational studies, however, without experimental follow-up or causal modeling require extra skepticism, as noted by Fiedler, 1975, and by Noble & Nolan, 1976, because of possible exogenous and reverse causation as noted below.)

With respect to normative values and theory, if the causal and measurement questions could be settled, and if the general public, school boards, parents, educators, students, and other groups were to place a dollar or other utility value on goals, and if the costs of the educational materials and services were known, linear programming, which has been used in defense, business, and industry for 35 years and is increasingly employed in the public sector, could be routinely employed to allocate educational resources efficiently for maximum learning benefit. Thus the short- and moderate-term problem in research on teaching to improve student learning seems to be descriptive rather than prescriptive, because theoretical, ethical, and normative issues are beside the point if questions remain unanswered about the causal efficacy of teaching means in relation to learning ends. It may be further argued that, because education is a profession or practical discipline like medicine or agriculture, the research aims of prediction and control must take precedence over theoretical insight and understanding; if more intensive, "high-quality" treatments produce no benefit beyond usual practices, they have little rational utility no matter what their theoretical or ethical acceptability.

Reviewing Reviews: A Rationale

For these reasons and notwithstanding the valid criticism of the process-product paradigm, this aspect of research on teaching is likely to remain among the highest priorities in educational psychology and research. Because a large number of studies and assessments of the research are available, it seems timely to examine, compare, assess and summarize the results.

Until recently, the standards for reviewing in the behavioral sciences have remained inexplicit, varied, and vague. Jackson's (1980) examination of 87 review articles in prominent educational, psychological, and sociological review journals reveals only 12 that had any statement of explicit methods employed. Light and Smith (1971), moreover, note the lack of systematic effort to consolidate information across studies. Only in the last several years has the insight from the natural sciences—that scientific norms and methods of parsimony, generality, explicitness, comprehensiveness, and quantificiation may be used in research assessment and reviews—begun to enter behavioral research. We will describe several recent standards for reviews of literature and assess the recent reviews of research on the process-product paradigm by these standards in an effort to help improve both future reviews and primary studies.

Selection of Reviews

A systematic collection of a decade of re-

search reviews published from 1970 through 1979 on teaching behaviors that affect student learning was conducted by searching the *Current Index to Journals in Education, Review of Educational Research, Review of Research in Education, The Second Handbook of Research on Teaching*, and publications of the National Society for the Study of Education. Reviews cited in the references in all these sources were also examined. Critical, evaluative reviews that systematically attempted to summarize research findings using a categorization or conceptual organization concerning at least two teaching variables and treating at least three studies were included.

Several categories of publication were excluded. For closely similar reviews published by the reviewer in two or more places, only the review with the earliest publication date was selected. Also excluded were such papers as Barr and Dreeben (1977), Joyce (1978), and Doyle (1977) because they deal primarily with paradigms or approaches for studying the effects of teaching rather than reviewing studies. Reviews found in classroom texts, such as Gage and Berliner (1975) and Good and Brophy (1977), were also excluded because they are primarily expositions of research studies for students rather than systematic, critical reviews of the research literature. Reviews such as Glass et al. (1977) on teacher indirectness and others that included only single teacher variables were also excluded. The search and selection procedure resulted in 19 reviews.

Selection of Studies for Review

Research reviews themselves should have explicit criteria in their search and selection procedures so that they can be accurately replicated and so that the limits of generalizability can be specified (Jackson, 1980). Table I includes the rationale for the selection of studies in the 19 reviews. Three reviews mention no explicit selection criteria (Bennett, 1978; Berliner & Rosenshine, 1977; Harris, 1979), and many of the others are discrepant, vague, and arbitrary. For example, Brophy (1979) merely included "a few sets of findings [drawn mostly from the author's work] . . . to illustrate the kinds of relations that are being discovered" (p.

TABLE 1
Theoretical Rationales for Selecting Studies

Bloom (1976)
We have summarized the studies we could locate on the relation between cues provided a class and the achievement of the students (p. 117). [W]e have summarized the relation between the rewards and reinforcement provided by the instructor and the achievement of students (p. 120). [W]e are fortunate that about 20 studies of classroom situations have included measures of participation (p. 123). [T]he only evidence we can find that relates learning to the effects of feedback and correctives is based on the developing literature on mastery learning. (p. 125)

Borich (1979)
The present studies were selected as illustrative of the type of studies from which competency statements could be derived; no inference should be made that this selection is exhaustive, although it is believed to be representative. (p. 78)

Brophy (1979)
A few sets of findings [drawn mostly from the author's work] are summarized to illustrate the kinds of relations that are being discovered. (p. 734)

Brophy & Evertson (1976)
In this chapter, we will briefly review the findings of others who have looked at the relationships between teacher characteristics and student learning in the early elementary grades. (p. 125)

Cruickshank (1976)
All the studies selected for discussion herein have essentially the same major purpose—to investigate the notion of teacher effectiveness or teacher effects. That is, they either explore relationships between what have been termed presage, context, or process variables, and desired student outcomes, or attempt to determine whether different educational treatments had different effects on desired student outcomes, usually student improvement. (p. 57)

Dunkin & Biddle (1974)
Thus, all of the studies reviewed here have involved systematic observation of teaching in classrooms. To say that these studies involved "observation" means that the investigator actually looked at the processes of classroom interaction—although his observations may have taken place through mechanical means such as audio or videotape recordings. To say that these observations were "systematic" means that instruments were developed for noting or measuring events that took place in those classrooms observed—and usually that a number of different classrooms or lessons were studied. (p. 3)

Gage (1978)
My coworkers and I focused entirely on four major, relatively large-scale correlational studies of teaching. (p. 38)

Good (1979)
The purpose of this paper is to present tenable conclusions from recent process-product studies. (p. 52)

Medley 1977)
Four criteria were used in deciding whether or not a relationship should be included in this review: (1) The study from which a relationship came had to be designed so that the relationship was generalizable to some population of teachers larger than the sample studies. (2) The relationship had to be both reliable enough to be statistically significant and large enough to be practically significant. (3) The measure of teacher effectiveness had to be based on long-term pupil gains in achievement areas recognized as important goals of education. (4) The process measure had to specify the behaviors exhibited in such a way that they could be reproduced as desired. (p. 5)

Rosenshine (1971a)
This review focuses upon 19 investigations which have used category systems in an attempt to determine specific relationships between what a teacher does and what pupils learn. It is offered as a sympathetic review. The studies

discussed in this review are those which investigators used the natural setting of the classroom to find relationships between specific teaching behaviors and pupil achievement. (p. 52)

Rosenshine (1971b)
The major purpose of this book is to report the results of all available studies in which teacher behavior was studied in relation to student achievement. (p. 12)

Rosenshine (1977)
Between 1972–1976, six major correlational studies have been reported along with three major experimental studies. Yet, it is hard to summarize these studies because of differences in topic and particularly in the SES background of the students studied. Three of these covered the same context—primary grade reading and mathematics for children from low SES backgrounds—and because of this common focus only those studies were selected for this review. (p. 115)

Rosenshine (1978)
The studies that have been published since 1973 have been more promising in terms of suggesting productive instructional strategies; it is these studies that are reviewed here. (p. 38)

Rosenshine & Furst (1973)
Nine variables appear to have yielded the most significant and/or consistent results across the 50-odd studies in which naturally occurring behavior was related to measures of student growth (adjusted by regression for relevant pretest measures). (pp. 155–156)

Soar (1977)
Differences in measures of classroom behavior, measures of pupil outcome, differences in methods of analysis, and differences in the groups studied, to name a few sources of differences, make integration of the results of different studies difficult. In contrast, this paper is an attempt to integrate results from four studies of ours in which there were greater degrees of parallelism across studies than is usually found. (p. 96)

Stallings & Hentzell (1978)
Four observation evaluations conducted as SRI International (Follow Through, California Early Childhood Education, Teaching Basic Reading Skills in Secondary Schools, & Women and Math) will be highlighted in this paper. (p. 6)

---

734).[2] On the other hand, Rosenshine (1971b) indicated that he reported results "of all available studies in which teacher behavior was studied in relation to student achievement" (p. 12). None of the reviews discussed their search procedures, and only one review (Medley, 1977) explicitly listed the criteria for the inclusion and exclusion of studies.

As indicated in Table I, many reviews merely indicated the number of studies or type of studies included in their review

[2] The authors learned from a personal communication that this review was written by invitation, which may be satisfactory explanation for the selection of studies for review. There may be similar reasons for seemingly arbitrary decisions by reviewers that are unmentioned in their publications.

(Bloom, 1976; Dunkin & Biddle, 1974; Gage, 1978; Rosenshine, 1971b; Rosenshine & Furst, 1973; Stallings & Hentzell, 1978). Another common theme prevalent in the rationales of several reviews is selecting research studies that had "the same major purpose," "common focuses," "greater degrees of parallelism," or were "compatible with other research" (Brophy & Evertson, 1976; Cruickshank, 1976; Rosenshine, 1977; Soar, 1977, pp. 96–103). Finally, an additional focus which was discussed in some reviewers' rationales was that studies were included because they were "promising" or "illustrative" (Borich, 1979; Brophy, 1979; Rosenshine, 1978).

As one might expect, as a consequence of the somewhat haphazard and arbitrary selection processes, any two reviews chosen at

TABLE II
The Coverage of 13 Studies in 5 Reviews

Reviews	Tikunoff, Berliner & Rist (1975)	Brophy, Evertson (1974)	Gage (1976)	McDonald (1976)	Stallings & Kaskowitz (1974)	Ward & Tikunoff (1975)	Soar (1973)	Soar (1966)	Soar & Soar (1972)	Soar & Soar (1973)	McDonald & Elias (1976)	Good & Grouws (1975)	Gall et al. (1975)
Cruickshank (1976)	×		×	×	×	×							×
Soar (1977)	×	×	×					×	×	×	—		
Rosenshine (1977)		× ×	×	×	×	×	× ×	×	×		×	×	
Gage (1978)		×			×						×	×	
Borich (1979)		×			×						×		

random may overlap considerably or very little. For example, four of the five randomly selected reviews included in Table II utilize the Brophy and Evertson (1974) and Stallings and Kaskowitz (1974) studies. On the other hand, several reviewers missed several of the relevant studies that were available to them, with or without explicit reasons. Exclusion of studies, in either case, leaves the review open to the possibility of bias in the selection of evidence (Heath & Nielson, 1974; Jackson, 1980; Rosenshine, 1970; Flanders, Note 1).

Rosenshine (Note 2), for example, has suggested that different reviewers have arrived at different conclusions because of the variations in their criteria for selecting studies, and Peterson (1979) has argued that conclusions drawn from recent reviews of process-product research are "simplistic" and that a "closer and more exhaustive search of the research literature is needed" (p. 46). Tables I and II support these criticisms of search and selection procedures and further suggest the need for explicit criteria to be included in future reviews.

An additional assessment of the review coverage can be obtained by comparing the yield of a more complete and explicit search and selection with the yields of a sample of 5 of the 19 reviews that treated positive reinforcement such as praise and feedback. Among the early reviewers in the decade, Rosenshine and Furst (1973) summarized the greatest number of studies among the five reviews: "Six experimental studies were found in which teachers were trained to increase their use of praise and other positive behaviors, as well as to decrease their use of criticism and other negative behaviors" (p. 158). In chronological order, Cruickshank (1976) discusses four studies of reinforcement; Rosenshine (1977), in a later review, discusses three; Bennett (1978), five of feedback; and Borich (1979), three of praise.

In contrast, by using systematic search and selection procedures, Lysakowski and Walberg (1981) found statistical data in 39 studies spanning a period of 20 years and containing a combined sample of 4,842 students in 202 classes in natural school settings. Eight of these studies were published before 1972, and 22 were published before 1976. This comparative assessment suggests reviewers of process-product research have failed to search diligently enough for primary studies or to state the reasons for excluding large parts of the research evidence.

Theoretical Constructs and Specific Variables

A preliminary analysis of the 35 variables or empirical indicators discussed in the 19 reviews suggested that a theoretical grouping of variables under rubrics or theoretical constructs would bring greater conceptual clarity to the analysis and synthesis of the reviews. The variables were found to fit reasonably well under four broad constructs: (1) Cognitive and Motivational Stimulation, (2) Student Engagement, (3) Reinforcement, and (4) Management and Climate. The conventional assumption implicit in the reviews is depicted in the one-way recycling of arrows on the left side of Figure 1: within the classroom environment, the reviewers generally assume that the causal flow or sequence is preponderantly from Stimulation through Engagement to Reinforcement and back to Stimulation. The possibilities of other causal flows such as episodic repetition of single constructs, sequence skipping, and reverse and third causes are implicitly excluded as alternative, causal hypotheses notwithstanding contrary evidence (Fiedler, 1975; Noble & Nolan, 1976) that cannot be completely ruled out by correlational studies.

The following working definitions of the constructs in Figure 1 and Table III were adopted:

(1) The construct, Cognitive Cues, refers to the type of instruction or stimuli the learner receives from the teacher. The teacher directs instruction or structures the lesson to enhance students' cognitive outcomes. This construct includes teachers' behaviors such as organization, academic focus, allocation of time, content coverage, sequencing of lessons, and assigning the appropriate difficulty of work. It also includes teacher behaviors such as frequency and appropriateness of questioning, type of questioning, instructional cues, and specificity and clarity of the lessons. Motivational Incentives are teacher behaviors that stimulate student learning through motivation such as teacher expectations, enthusiasm, and interest.

(2) Student Engagement is the apparent or observed time students are actively engaging or participating in, or attending to their lessons in response to teacher behaviors.

(3) Reinforcement deals with the way the teacher interacts with students to evaluate student learning outcomes. It refers to the effectiveness and extent of teacher praise, encouragement, criticism, use of student ideas, and feedback to students.

(4) The Management and Climate construct denotes the way teachers conduct the activities of the classroom and the atmosphere they create. It describes the control and climate established and monitored as well as the type of instruction (whole group or small group) the teacher utilizes. Management and climate are similar and bracketed together because they are supportive rather than direct influences on learning.

Within the four broad constructs, our conclusions regarding the 35 teaching variables were coded, if indicated, as positively, negatively, or inconclusively related to student achievement. In six reviews conclusions were qualified according to specific contextual or learner characteristics where the results were found as indicated in Table III. Except in verbose cases, the teaching variables are defined in the reviewers' verbatim terminology. Rosenshine's (1971a) variables, for example, were taken from the

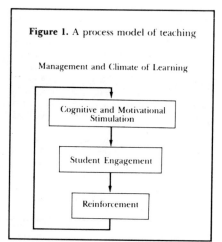

Figure 1. A process model of teaching

Management and Climate of Learning

Cognitive and Motivational Stimulation

Student Engagement

Reinforcement

TABLE III
Reviewers' Variables by Constructs

	Stimulation		Engagement	Reinforcement	Management
	Cognitive Cues	Motivational Incentives			
Bennett (1978)	Time allocation (+) Comprehension (0)		Active learning time (+)	Feedback (+)	
Berliner & Rosenshine (1977)	Goal setting (+) Time allocation (+) Academic focus (+) Questioning (+)			Feedback (+)	Monitoring (+) Atmosphere (+)
Bloom (1976)	Cues (+)		Participation (+)	Reinforcement (+) Feedback & Correctives (+)	
Borich (1979)	Questioning (+) Instructional materials (+) Control & structuring (+) Interaction (0) Student-initiated questions (+) Clarity (0)		Engagement (+)	Praise (+) Feedback (+)	Whole-class instruction (+) Flexibility (+) Teacher affect (+) Attention getting (+)
Brophy (1979)	Direct Instruction (+) Input, expectations, and pacing (+)	Input Expectations, and pacing (+)	Direct instruction (+)		Direct instruction (+)
Brophy & Evertson (1976)	Appropriate classroom work (+) Practice/feedback (+)	Attitude role definition (+)		Indirect teaching (−) Practice/feedback (+)	Classroom management (+)

Cruickshank (1976)	Variety of materials (+)	Time spent (+)	Motivational incentives (0); Diagnosis and evaluation (+)	Small group instruction (+)
Dunkin & Biddle (1974)	Climate and directness (0); Classroom system (0); Knowledge and intellect (0); Logic (0); Linguistic concepts (+); Sequencing (+)		Monitoring, interacting, and feedback (+); Climate and directness (0); Behavior modification (+)	Discipline and group management (+)
Gage (1978)	Appropriate work (+); Questioning (+)		Feedback (+)	System of rules (+); Monitoring (+); Organization and management (+)
Good (1978)	Direct instruction (+)			Classroom management (+)
Harris (1979)	Teacher expectations (+); Instructional time (+); Pace of instruction (+); Difficulty of material (+)	Attention (+); Academic engaged time (+)		Formality (+); Motivation and management (+); Attention to pupil needs (+)
Medley (1977)	Teacher use of time (+); Quality of instruction (+)	Teacher use of time (+)		Organizing for instruction (0); Environmental maintenance (+); Individual attention (+)

(Continued on next page)

TABLE III (Continued)

	Stimulation		Engagement	Reinforcement	Management
	Cognitive Cues	Motivational Incentives			
Rosenshine (1971a)	Frequency of questions (+) Types of questions asked (0) Structuring (+)			Nonverbal affect (0) Praise and encouragement (0) Use of pupil's ideas (0) Criticism (+) Indirect/direct ratio (0)	
Rosenshine (1971b)	Teacher cognitive behaviors (+/0) Flexibility and variability (+) Teacher-student interaction (0) Time (+/0)	Enthusiasm (+)		Teacher approval or disapproval (0)	Flexibility and variability (0)
Rosenshine (1977)	Time (+) Questions (+)		Student inattention (+)	Adult feedback (+/0) Student-initiated comments (−)	Work groupings (+) Management and control responses (0)
Rosenshine (1978)	Content coverage (+) Student attention or engagement (0) Academic focus (+) Verbal instruction (+)		Student attention or engagement (+)		Affective focus (+) Management (+)
Rosenshine & Furst (1973)	Clarity (+) Variability (+) Task-orientation (+)	Enthusiasm (+)		Criticism (+) Teacher indirectness (+)	

Soar (1977)	Student opportunity to learn (+) Use of structuring comments (+) Multiple levels of questioning (+)	Structuring behaviors (+)	Direction and control (+) Positive affect (+)
	Structuring activities (+) Low cognitive level (+)		
Stallings & Hentzell (1978)	Allocated time (+) Classroom processes (+)	Student engagement (+)	Classroom processes (+) Classroom management (+)

chapter titles in his book to characterize his review. In other reviews, such as Berliner and Rosenshine (1977) and Good (1979), section headings were used to specify the variables.

A problem of the process-product paradigm related to the definitions above is the ambiguity of constructs or variables. As Centra and Potter (1980) have pointed out, "a major problem with the research literature to date lies in the definition and measurement of teacher behavior" (p. 281). The concept of teacher structuring, for example, can mean several things: it can be interpreted as how teachers set the ground rules or manage their class, or it can refer to how teachers organize cognitive cues. Because such ambiguity was found for several of the variables in the reviews, in a few cases the reviewers' variables had to be placed under two or more constructs (e.g., Brophy's, 1979, description of the variable of "Direct Instruction" is so encompassing that it is coded under the constructs of Cognitive Cues, Student Engagement, and Management and Climate). Because the placement of some variables under constructs is arguable, one of us recoded five reviews picked at random from the 19 coded by the other author. The intercoder agreement is 97.7 percent. Such high agreement is attributable to the clarity of the reviews with respect to categorizing the association as positive, negative, or inconclusive.

Table III reveals several noteworthy patterns. First, the range of variables that are included under Cognitive Cues is greater than that of any other construct: 55 variables used by the reviewers are listed under this construct, while only five are listed under Motivation; 11 variables are listed under Student Engagement and 25 and 29 are listed, respectively, under Reinforcement and Management and Climate. Cognitive Cues, moreover, is the only construct that is addressed in all 19 reviews. Motivational Incentive is unmentioned in 14 reviews, despite the fact that the other five reviews conclude that it is positively associated with student learning. Student Engagement is considered in 10 reviews published since 1976. Reinforcement is covered in only 13 reviews and this may be attributable to the inconclusive results cited in earlier reviews. The Management and Climate construct is covered in 15 of the 19 reviews. After an

assessment of the coverage of the threats to methodological validity, the discussion quantitatively summarizes the conclusion of the reviews.

Methodological Validity Assessments

As noted in an earlier section, a number of sweeping statements about the quality of research on teaching have been made by reviewers in the mainstream as well as those outside the field. Some of these depreciate or derogate the methodological validity of research on the process-product paradigm; others make blanket assertions or dismiss aspects of research on the paradigm such as high-inference studies, those that do not examine aptitude-treatment interactions or ecological conditioning, and those that lack certain statistical or methodological features. Although the derogatory adjectives are unnecessary, such assertions may be acceptable as conclusions about research validity if specific, complete data are presented to support them within a systematic framework.

An obvious choice for such a framework is the systematic treatment of Campbell and Stanley (1963) in the first *Handbook of Research on Teaching*, which has exerted a major constructive influence not only on teaching research but throughout experimental and other observational research in the behavioral sciences. Various extensions of the Campbell-Stanley framework were made in the years soon after publication of this milestone chapter. These extensions, mostly published before 1970, enlarged the framework from internal and external validity to include statistical-conclusion and construct validity as well. Cook and Campbell (1979) collected, systematized, and illustrated 33 specific threats to observational validity under those four broad constructs (see Table IV).

One of us coded the extent to which each specific threat was represented in each of the 19 reviews; that is, whether the threat was merely mentioned, whether some illustrative studies reviewed were mentioned, and, most desirably, whether all studies in the review were categorized as to the degree that each threat was minimized so that the generalizability or robustness of the conclusions could be explicitly, preferably statis-

TABLE IV
Specific Indications of Four Validity Constructs

1. *Statistical conclusion validity:* Is study sensitive enough to permit reasonable statements about experiment?
    a. Low statistical power
    b. Violated assumptions of statistical tests
    c. Fishing and the error rate problem
    d. Reliability of measures (stability)
    e. Reliability of treatment implementation
    f. Random irrelevancies in experimental setting
    g. Random heterogeneity of responses
2. *Internal validity:* Is covariation causal?
    a. History
    b. Maturation
    c. Testing
    d. Instrumentation
    e. Statistical regression
    f. Selection
    g. Mortality
    h. Interactions with selection
    i. Ambiguity with selection
    j. Diffusion or imitation of treatments
    k. Compensatory equalization of treatments
    l. Compensatory rivalry by respondents receiving less desirable treatments
    m. Resentful demoralization of respondents receiving less desirable treatments
3. *Construct validity:* Is there a possibility of construing more than one construct?
    a. Inadequate preoperational explication of constructs
    b. Mono-operation bias
    c. Mono-method bias
    d. Hypothesis-guessing within experimental conditions
    e. Evaluation apprehension
    f. Experimenter expectancies
    g. Confounding constructs and levels of constructs
    h. Interactions of different treatments
    i. Interaction of testing and treatment
    j. Restricted generalizability across constructs
4. *External validity:* Can study be generalized to or across particular persons, settings, and times?
    a. Interaction of selection and treatment
    b. Interaction of setting and treatment
    c. Interaction of history and treatment

Note. Adapted from Cook & Campbell (1979)

tically, assessed (see Table V). One of us recoded five reviews picked at random from the 19 originally coded by the other author. The intercoder agreement is 97.9 percent. This high agreement is not as impressive as it first appears since 2,393 or 95.4 percent of the 2,508 possible categorizations (4 degrees of representation × 19 reviews × 33 threats) are cases of ignoring the specific threats to validity in the standard Cook-Campbell (1979) list. Redoing the coding according to the earlier Campbell-Stanley (1963) list of 12 threats to only internal and

external validity might roughly triple the rate of coverage in the corpus of reviews to about a 15 percent rate of mere mentioning of the threats, illustrating them with a few studies, or, rarely, comprehensively categorizing all studies reviewed.

Perhaps because of the long-standing emphasis on individual differences in educational psychology, external validity concerns are relatively well represented in the reviews (Table V). Social class, sex, and grade-level conditioning of teaching effects are often mentioned if not coded in the

TABLE V
Thirty-three Threats to Methodological Validity in 19 Reviews

	Types of Validation Considered			
	Statistical Conclusion	Internal	Construct	External
Bennett (1978)				ABC
Berliner & Rosenshine (1977)	BD	K	A	B
Bloom (1976)	A	di		ABC
Borich (1979)		f		ABC
Brophy (1979)	abdef		befG	ABC
Brophy & Evertson (1976)	def	dijk	af	ABC
Cruickshank (1976)				ABC
Dunkin & Biddle (1974)	ad	d	ag	abc
Gage (1978)	ab	i		
Good (1979)	abcde		a	abc
Harris (1979)				ABC
Medley (1977)	Abcde			ABC
Rosenshine (1971a)	ABD	i	ab	ABC
Rosenshine (1971b)	AB	D	g	ABC
Rosenshine (1977)				ABC
Rosenshine (1978)	d			ABC
Rosenshine & Furst (1973)	dg		Abc	ABC
Soar (1977)				ABC
Stallings & Hentzell (1978)	CDF	D		ABC

Note: Lower case letters indicate that the review mentions the threat coded in Table IV; upper case letters indicate that specific studies are mentioned with respect to the threat; italic upper-case letters indicate that all studies are categorized with respect to the threat.

reviews. Only five reviews, however, represent attempts to code all studies reviewed for external validity (Bloom, 1976; Borich, 1979; Medley, 1977; Rosenshine, 1971a, 1971b); but none of them used statistics such as simple *t* tests or Chi squares to assess the differential effects of teaching variables on various classifications of teachers, students, subjects, and settings. Thus, claims for differential effects of teaching on subclasses of students (aptitude-treatment interactions) or contexts remain appeals to authority rather than empirically supported generalizations.

Statistical-conclusion, internal, and construct validity are still less completely covered. Perhaps the most important example is that only three reviews mentioned point *i* under internal validity; that is, ambiguity about the direction of causal influence—in this case, that teaching variables cause student learning. It is well known that causality cannot be imputed from correlations, even partial correlations, with IQ or pretests sta-

tistically controlled (Campbell & Stanley, 1963). Because bidirectionality of teacher and student influence has been demonstrated experimentally and observationally (see Fiedler, 1975; Klein, 1971; Noble & Nolan, 1976, and the references in these papers), it is especially important to analyze the consistency of the results across studies employing simple correlational techniques and the more defensible, if more difficult to execute, experiments or multiple-regression studies that better control for student ability and motivation, amount of instruction, content coverage, home environment and other causally implicated variables. It is unfortunate that the reviews have not considered the specific threats to validity on a comprehensive, case-by-case basis.

The Conclusions of the Reviews

Given these deficits and caveats, what can be concluded about the reviews of the paradigm? First, the reviews reveal several statistically consistent findings. A summary of the conclusions for specific variables in Table III is presented in Table VI, which lists the overall findings of the 19 reviews under the four theoretical constructs. Following Table III, the results are represented as positive, negative, or inconclusive. Each of the reviewers' variables under each construct is averaged where possible to arrive at the overall results shown in the last two rows. For example, because two of the three variables in Rosenshine's (1971a) review under the construct of Cognitive Cues were positively related to students' learning, his review was coded as positive for Cognitive Cues. Similarly, because three out of the five variables under Reinforcement were positive, this review was also coded as positive for Reinforcement. Under Cognitive Cues in the Rosenshine (1971b) review, one

can see an even balance of positive and inconclusive findings. Therefore, this review was coded as half positive, and these results can be noted in the overall summary at the bottom of the table.

Table VI shows several consistent patterns. Cognitive Cues is the only construct that has been covered in all 19 reviews; of these, 17 concluded that they are positively related to student learning. The five reviews that covered the construct of Motivational Incentives all concluded that it is positively related to student learning. Ten of the 15 reviews of Student Engagement conclude that it is positively related to learning, and 9.5 of the 13 reviews covering Reinforcement conclude that it is positively related to learning. The Management and Climate construct is a focus in 15 reviews,

TABLE VI
Results Across Reviews

	Stimulation		Engagement	Reinforcement	Management
	Cognitive Cues	Motivational Incentives			
Bennett (1978)	+/0		+	+	
Berliner & Rosenshine (1977)	+			+	+
Bloom (1976)	+		+	+	
Borich (1979)	+		+	+	+
Brophy (1979)	+	+	+		+
Brophy & Evertson (1976)	+	+		0	+
Cruickshank (1976)	+		+	+	+
Dunkin & Biddle (1974)	0			+/0	+
Gage (1978)	+			+	+
Good (1979)	+				+
Harris (1979)	+	+	+		+
Medley (1977)	+		+		+
Rosenshine (1971a)	+			+	
Rosenshine (1971b)	+/0	+		0	0
Rosenshine (1977)	+			0	+/0
Rosenshine (1978)	+		+		+
Rosenshine & Furst (1973)	+	+		+	
Soar (1977)	+			+	+
Stallings & Hentzell (1978)	+		+		+
All Reviews					
Positive	17	5	10	9.5	13.5
Inconclusive	2	0	0	3.5	1.5
Significance Level	.01	.10	.01	.10	.01
Reviews without Rosenshine					
Positive	12.5	3	9	6.5	12
Inconclusive	1.5	0	0	1.5	0
Significance Level	.05	NS	.01	NS	.01

and 13.5 concluded that teachers' management behaviors and climate are positively related to student learning.

The binomial-sign probabilities of these results, assuming a 50-50 split in the population (Dixon & Massey, 1957, p. 417), are all significant at conventional levels or beyond as shown in the last several rows of Table VI. Thus the reviewers' conclusions are statistically consistent with one another in concluding that the greater use of each of the constructs is associated with greater levels of student learning. The reviews, however, are based on overlapping fractions of the total universe of primary studies; although the reviewers rarely discuss past reviews, they may have been influenced by them; and the reviews cannot be considered independent pieces of evidence. In addition, Rosenshine wrote 6 of the 19 reviews, all of which are included in the tables so as not to subjectively exclude parts of the corpus of evidence. Excluding Rosenshine's reviews from the statistical assessment, however, does not materially change the substance or consistency of the conclusions as also shown in Table VI, but reduces the number of cases for Motivational Incentives and Reinforcement to the point of nonsignificance.

Conclusion

In view of the problems of the reviews documented above, it is possible to take a grim view of the research on the process-product paradigm. By explicit standards the reviews may be done worse than the primary studies. A more positive and probably more scientific view is that, notwithstanding the faults of the primary research and the further obfuscation of the reviews, the results seem to be strong and robust enough to emerge with a fair amount of consistency that certainly deserves attempts to replicate.

A better guide for educational policy and practice than the past reviews are more scientifically designed assessments of the process-product research literature. Largely following Jackson's (1980) recommendations, for example, Lysakowski and Walberg's (1981) quantitative synthesis of 39 classroom studies show large, robust effects of one construct—reinforcement—on learning: the mean of experimentally praised or otherwise reinforced students lies at the 88th percentile of control group learning-outcome distribution. Contrary to previous opinion and reviews, the strong effects of instructional reinforcement appear constant across grades (kindergarten through college), socioeconomic levels, race, public and private schools, and methodological rigor of the research including experiments and correlational studies (although tangible reinforcements may be somewhat more effective than other ones; and girls and students in special schools and classes may benefit slightly more from reinforcement than other students).

Additional syntheses that search systematically for all the evidence on other teaching constructs, that code the studies explicitly for their chief substantive and methodological features, and that statistically weigh the evidence are also likely to show educationally and statistically significant effects of teaching processes. Such elusive phenomena as aptitude-treatment interactions, teacher-student matching, and ecological conditioning of effects, if they exist and can be replicated, are much more likely to be detected by these more systematic approaches than by the traditional narrative review.

Reviews of research on the process-product paradigm have a great number of serious flaws in search and selection procedures, validity assessments, and summarization of empirical results. It appears, nonetheless, that the magnitude of results in the primary studies are sufficient to have produced a substantial body of reasonably consistent, hard-won knowledge about the associations of teaching processes and student learning. This knowledge can be made much more scientifically and educationally creditable by more thorough, critical, and quantitative assessment in future reviews.

Reference Notes

1. Flanders, N. A. *Knowledge about teacher effectiveness.* Paper presented at the annual meeting of the American Educational Research Association, New Orleans, 1973.
2. Rosenshine, B. *Reviewing research: Different questions, different answers.* Unpublished manuscript, University of Illinois, 1978.

References

BARR, R., & DREEBEN, R. Instruction in classrooms. In L. S. Shulman (Ed.), *Review of research in education* (Vol. 5). Itasca, Ill.: F. E. Peacock, 1977.

BENNETT, N. Recent research on teaching: A dream, a belief, and a model. *British Journal of Educational Psychology*, 1978, *48*, 127–147.

BERLINER, D. C. Impediments to the study of teacher effectiveness. *Journal of Teacher Education*, 1976, *27*, 5–13.

BERLINER, D. C. Studying instruction in the elementary school. In R. Dreeben & J. A. Thomas (Eds.), *The analysis of educational productivity Volume I: Issues in microanalysis*. Cambridge, Mass: Ballinger, 1980.

BERLINER, D. C., & ROSENSHINE, B. The acquisition of knowledge in the classroom. In R. C. Anderson, R. J. Spiro, & W. E. Montague (Eds.), *Schooling and the acquisition of knowledge*. Hillsdale, N.J.: Lawrence Erlbaum, 1977.

BLOOM, B. S. *Human characteristics and school learning*. New York: McGraw-Hill, 1976.

BORICH, G. D. Implications for developing teacher competencies from process-product research. *Journal of Teacher Education*, 1979, *30*(1), 77–86.

BROPHY, J. E. Teacher behavior and its effects. *Journal of Education Psychology*, 1979, *71*, 733–750.

BROPHY, J. E., & EVERTSON, C. M. *Process-product correlations in the Texas Teacher Effectiveness Study: Final report* (Research Report No. 74–4). Austin, Tx.: Research and Development Center for Teacher Education, University of Texas, 1974.

BROPHY, J. E., & EVERTSON, C. M. *Learning from teaching: A developmental perspective*. Boston: Allyn & Bacon, 1976.

BROUDY, H. S. Historical exemplars of teaching method. In N. L. Gage (Ed.), *Handbook of research on teaching*. Chicago: Rand McNally, 1963.

CAMPBELL, D. T., & STANLEY, J. C. Experimental and quasi-experimental designs for research on teaching. In N. L. Gage (Ed.), *Handbook of research on teaching*. Chicago: Rand McNally, 1963.

CENTRA, J. A., & POTTER, D. A. School and teacher effects: An interrational model. *Review of educational research*, 1980, *50*, 273–291.

COOK, T. D., & CAMPBELL, D. T. *Quasi-experimentation*. Chicago: Rand McNally, 1979.

CRUICKSHANK, D. R. Synthesis of selected recent research on teacher effects. *Journal of Teacher Education*, 1976, *27*(2), 57–60.

DIXON, W. J., & MASSEY, F. J. *Introduction to statistical analysis*. New York: McGraw-Hill, 1957.

DOMAS, S. J., & TIEDEMAN, D. V. Teacher competence: An annotated bibliography. *Journal of Experimental Education*, 1950, *19*, 101–218.

DOYLE, W. Paradigms for research on teacher effectiveness. In L. Shulman (Ed.), *Review of research in education* (Vol. 5). Itasca, Ill.: F. E. Peacock, 1977.

DUNKIN, M., & BIDDLE, B. *The study of teaching*. New York: Holt, Rinehart & Winston, 1974.

FENSTERMACHER, G. A philosophical consideration of recent research on teacher effectiveness. In L. Shulman (Ed.), *Review of research in education* (Vol. 6). Itasca, Ill.: F. E. Peacock, 1978.

FIEDLER, M. L. Bidirectionality of influence in classroom interaction. *Journal of Educational Psychology*, 1975, *67*, 735–744.

FORMAN, D. C., & CHAPMAN, D. W. Research on teach-

ing: Why the lack of practical results. *Educational Technology*, 1979, *19*(1), 37–40.

GAGE, N. L. (Ed.), *Handbook of research on teaching*. Chicago: Rand McNally, 1963.

GAGE, N. L. *Teacher effectiveness & teacher education*. Palo Alto, Calif.: Pacific, 1972.

GAGE, N. L. A factorially designed experiment on teacher structuring, soliciting, and reacting. *Journal of Teacher Education*, 1976, *27*(1), 35–38.

GAGE, N. L. *The scientific basis of the art of teaching*. New York: Teachers College, 1978.

GAGE, N. L. & BERLINER, D. C. *Educational psychology*. Chicago: Rand McNally, 1975.

GALL, M. D., WARD, B. A., BERLINER, D. C., CAHEN, L. S., CROWN, K. A., ELASHOFF, J. D., STANTON, G. C., & WINNE, H. *The effects of teacher use of questioning techniques on student achievement and attitude*. San Francisco: Far West Laboratory for Educational Research and Development, 1975.

GLASS, G. V, COULTER, D., HARTLEY, S., HEAROLD, S., KAHL, S., KALK, J., & SHERRETZ, L. *Teacher "indirectness" and pupil achievement: An integration of findings*. Boulder, Colo.: Laboratory of Educational Research, University of Colorado, 1977.

GOOD, T. L. Teacher effectiveness in the elementary school. *Journal of Teacher Education*, 1979, *30*(2), 52–64.

GOOD, T. L., & BROPHY, J. *Educational psychology: A realistic approach*. New York: Holt, Rinehart, & Winston, 1977.

GOOD, T. & GROUWS, D. *Process-product relationships in fourth grade mathematics classrooms*. Final Report of National Institute of Education (Grant NEG-00-3-0123). Columbia: University of Missouri, 1975.

HARRIS, A. J. The effective teacher of reading, revisited. *The Reading Teacher*, 1979, *33*(2), 135–140.

HEATH, R. W., & NIELSON, M. A. The research basis for performance-based-teacher education. *Review of Educational Research*, 1974, *44*, 463–483.

JACKSON, G. B. Models for integrative reviews. *Review of Educational Research*, 1980, *50*, 438–460.

JOYCE, B. R. A problem of categories: Classifying approaches to teaching. *Journal of Education*, 1978, *160*, 67–95.

KLEIN, S. S. Student influence on teacher behavior. *American Educational Research Journal*, 1971, *8*, 403–421.

LIGHT, R. J., & SMITH, P. V. Accumulating evidence: Procedures for resolving contradictions among different research studies. *Harvard Educational Review*, 1971, *4*, 429–471.

LYSAKOWSKI, R. S., & WALBERG, H. J. Classroom reinforcement and learning: A quantitative synthesis. *Journal of Educational Research*, 1981, *75*, 69–77.

McDONALD, F. J. *Beginning Teacher Evaluation Study: Phase II, 1973–74. Executive Summary Report*. Princeton, N.J.: Educational Testing Service, 1976.

McDONALD, F. J., & ELIAS, P. *The effects of teaching performance on pupil learning. Beginning Teacher Evaluation Study: Phase II Final Report, Vol. I*. Princeton, N.J.: Educational Testing Service, 1976.

MEDLEY, D. *Teacher competence and teacher effectiveness*. Washington, D.C.: American Association of Colleges for Teacher Effectiveness, 1977.

NOBLE, C. G., & NOLAN, J. D. Effect of student verbal behavior on classroom teacher behavior. *Journal of Educational Psychology*, 1976, *68*, 342–346.

PETERSON, P. L. Direct instruction reconsidered. In P.

L. Peterson & H. J. Walberg (Eds.), *Research on teaching: Concepts, findings, and implications*, Berkeley, Calif.: McCutchan, 1979.

POPKEWITZ, T. S., TABACHNICK, B. R., & ZEICHNER, J. M. Dulling the senses: Research in teacher education. *Journal of Teacher Education*, 1979, *30*, 52–60.

ROSENSHINE, B. Interaction analysis: A tardy comment. *Phi Delta Kappan*, 1970, *8*, 445–446.

ROSENSHINE, B. Teaching behaviors related to pupil achievement: A review of research. In I. Westbury & A. A. Bellack (Eds.), *Research into classroom processes: Recent developments and next steps*. New York: Teachers College, 1971. (a)

ROSENSHINE, B. *Teaching behaviors and student achievement*. Slough: NFER Publishing Co., 1971. (b)

ROSENSHINE, B. Review of teaching variables and student learning. In G. D. Borich (Ed.), *The appraisal of teaching: Concepts and process*. Reading, Mass.: Addison-Wesley, 1977.

ROSENSHINE, B. Academic engaged time, content covered, and direct instruction. *Journal of Education*, 1978, *160*, 38–66.

ROSENSHINE, B. Content, time and direct instruction. In P. Peterson & H. Walberg (Eds.), *Research on teaching: Concepts, findings and implications*. Berkeley, Calif.: McCutchan, 1979.

ROSENSHINE, B., & FURST, N. The use of direct observation to study teaching. In R. Travers (Ed.), *The second handbook of research on teaching*. Rand McNally, 1973.

SHAVELSON, R., & DEMPSEY, N. Generalizability of measures of teaching behavior. *Review of Educational Research*, 1976, *46*, 553–611.

SOAR, R. S. *An integrative approach to classroom learning* (Final Report, Public Health Service Grant No. 5-R11-MH 01096 and National Institute of Mental Health Grant No. 7-R11-MH0245). Philadelphia: Temple University, 1966.

SOAR, R. S. *Follow Through classroom process measurement and pupil growth (1970–71) Final Report*. Gainesville,

Fla.: Institute for the Development of Human Development of Human Resources, University of Florida, 1973.

SOAR, R. S. An integration of findings from four studies of teacher effectiveness. In G. D. Borich (Ed.), *The appraisal of teaching: Concepts and process*. Reading, Mass: Addison-Wesley, 1977.

SOAR, R. S., & SOAR, R. M. An empirical analysis of selected Follow Through Programs: An example of a process approach to evaluation. In I. J. Gordon (Ed.), *Early childhood education*. Chicago: National Society for the Study of Education, 1972.

SOAR, R. S., & SOAR, R. M. Classroom behavior, pupil characteristics, and pupil growth for the school year and for the summer. *JSAS Catalog of Selected Documents in Psychology* 5 (1975): 200. Gainesville, Fla.: Institute for the Development of Human Resources, University of Florida, 1973 (Ms. No. 873).

STALLINGS, J., & HENTZELL, S. *Effective teaching and learning in urban schools*. Paper presented at the National Conference on Urban Education, St. Louis, Missouri, July 1978.

STALLINGS, J., & KASKOWITZ, D. *Follow Through classroom observation evaluation 1972–73*. Menlo Park, Calif.: Stanford Research Institute, 1974.

TIKUNOFF, W. J., BERLINER, D., & RIST, R. *An ethnographic study of forty classrooms*. (Technical Report No. 75-10-5) San Francisco: Far West Laboratory for Educational Research and Development, 1975.

TRAVERS, R. M. W. (Ed.). *Second handbook of research on teaching*. Chicago: Rand McNally, 1973.

WARD, B. A. & TIKUNOFF, W. J. *An interactive model of research and development*. San Francisco: Far West Regional Laboratory for Educational Research and Development, 1975.

WATSON, J. B. Psychology as the behaviorist views it. *Psychological Review*, 1919, *20*, 158–177.

WINNE, P. H., & MARX, R. W. Reconceptualizing research on teaching. *Journal of Educational Psychology*, 1977, *69*, 668–678.

34

The Relation Between Socioeconomic Status and Academic Achievement

Karl R. White

Although it is widely believed that socioeconomic status (SES) is strongly correlated with measures of academic achievement, weak and moderate correlations are frequently reported. Using meta-analysis techniques, almost 200 studies that considered the relation between SES and academic achievement were examined. Results indicated that as SES is typically defined (income, education, and/or occupation of household heads) and typically used (individuals as the unit of analysis), SES is only weakly correlated ($r = .22$) with academic achievement. With aggregated units of analysis, typically obtained correlations between SES and academic achievement jump to .73. Family characteristics, such as home atmosphere, sometimes incorrectly referred to as SES, are substantially correlated with academic achievement when individuals are the unit of analysis ($r = .55$). Factors such as grade level at which the measurement was taken, type of academic achievement measure, type of SES measure, and the year in which the data were collected are significantly correlated statistically with the magnitude of the correlation between academic achievement and SES. Variables considered in the meta-analysis accounted for 75% of the variance in observed correlation coefficients in the studies examined.

In summarizing the results of their now famous Equality of Educational Opportunity Survey (Coleman et al., 1966), Coleman and his associates concluded:

Taking all of these results together, one implication stands above all: that schools bring little influence to bear on a child's achievement that is independent of his background and general social context; and that this very lack of an independent effect means that the inequalities imposed on children by their home, neighborhood, and peer environment are carried along to become the inequalities with which they confront adult life at the end of school. (p. 325)

For many educators, the Coleman report (1966) confirmed what they thought they had known for years: that a strong relation exists between all kinds of academic achievement variables and what has come to be known as socioeconomic status (SES). Indeed, the existence and strength of this relation is so widely accepted that it is often cited as a self-evident fact. Statements such as the following are frequently made in

Requests for reprints should be sent to Karl R. White, Exceptional Child Center, UMC 68, Utah State University, Logan, Utah 84322.

scholarly writings with no further reference or supporting evidence.

The family characteristic that is the most powerful predictor of school performance is socioeconomic status (SES): the higher the SES of the student's family, the higher his academic achievement. This relationship has been documented in countless studies and seems to hold no matter what measure of status is used (occupation of principal breadwinner, family income, parents' education, or some combination of these). (Boocock, 1972, p. 32)

To categorize youth according to the social class position of their parents is to order them on the extent of their participation and degree of success in the American Educational System. This has been so consistently confirmed by research that it can now be regarded as an empirical law. . . . SES predicts grades, achievement and intelligence test scores, retentions at grade level, course failures, truancy, suspensions from school, high school dropouts, plans for college attendance, and total amount of formal schooling. (Charters, 1963, pp. 739, 740)

The positive association between school completion, family socioeconomic status, and measured ability is well known. (Welch, 1974, p. 32)

In light of the belief that socioeconomic status (SES) and various measures of academic achievement are strongly correlated, it is not surprising that some measure of SES is frequently used by behavioral scientists in

From Karl R. White, "The Relation Between Socioeconomic Status and Academic Achievement," 91 (3) *Psychological Bulletin* 461-481 (May 1982). Copyright 1982 by the American Psychological Association. Reprinted by permission of the publisher and author.

conducting research. After stating that the relation between SES and "almost any type of school behavior" was so well documented that it "had become axiomatic to social scientists," St. John (1970) concluded:

So powerful is the apparent effect of social class, that the influence of other background and school factors can be detected only if socioeconomic status (SES) is first neutralized through matching or statistical control. Accurate measurement of SES, therefore, is crucial to any social research in schools. (p. 255)

The most frequent applications of some measure of SES in conducting educational research include the following:
1. As a concomitant variable in an analysis of covariance, SES can be used in quasi-experimental studies to control for bias by statistically adjusting for pretreatment differences.
2. A measure of SES can be used to increase the precision of an experiment by using it as a stratifying variable or a covariate.
3. An SES variable can be used to investigate the presence of interaction effects (e.g., Does Method A work better with high-SES students, whereas Method B is more effective with low-SES students?).
4. As a descriptive variable, SES can be used to define the populations that were included in the research. Such information can be important for replicating findings or generalizing the results of a study.
5. A measure of SES can be used as a predictor variable (e.g., in making admissions decisions where only a limited number of resources are available, it might be important to know which students are most likely to be successful).
6. In investigating and trying to establish the validity of causal models, measures of SES can be included as one of the causal agents of various educational outcomes.

In reviewing the literature, it is easy to find examples of studies in which a measure of SES has been used in one of these applications. In spite of the frequency of use and the widespread acceptance of SES as an appropriate tool in educational research, the utility of SES for the purposes described above depends on the validity of that particular measure of SES and/or the strength of the relation between SES and the educational variable of interest. A careful re-

view of the available literature, however, reveals some disturbing and confusing facts about the relation between SES and academic achievement.[1]

First of all, even though "everybody knows" what is meant by SES, a wide variety of variables are used as indicators of SES. Standard, widely accepted definitions of SES are difficult to find. Chapin (1928) defined socioeconomic status as

the position that an individual or family occupies with reference to the prevailing average of standards of cultural possessions, effective income, material possessions, and participation in group activity in the community. (p. 99)

The Michigan State Department of Education (1971), in conducting their statewide assessment, defined SES similarly:

Student socioeconomic status is often thought to be a function of three major factors: 1) family income; 2) parents' educational level; and 3) parents' occupation. (p. 5)

Probably the best known, but by no means the most frequently used, measures of SES are the *Index of Status Characteristics* (Warner, Meeker, & Eells, 1949) and Hollingshead's *Two-Factor Index of Social Position* (Hollingshead & Redlich, 1958). The *Index of Status Characteristics* uses information about the family's (a) occupation of principal breadwinner, (b) source of income, (c) quality of housing, and (d) status of dwelling area to arrive at a score that is converted to one of five social classes. Hollingshead's scale uses indices of occupation and educational attainment to categorize families into one of five social classes.

Reading the literature leaves one impressed, and concerned, by the range of variables used as measures of SES. Traditional indicators of occupation, education, and income are frequently represented. Nevertheless, frequent references are found to such factors as size of family, educational aspirations, ethnicity, mobility, presence of read-

---

[1] Throughout the remainder of this article the term *academic achievement* will be used to refer to a broad range of educational outcome variables including scores on standardized achievement tests of various subject areas, class rank, grades, and measures of IQ. Where a specific measure of academic achievement is intended, it will be clearly identified.

ing materials in the home, and amount of travel, as well as school level variables such as teachers' salary, pupil/teacher ratio, per capita expense, and staff turnover. The implications of using such a variety of variables as indicators of SES will be discussed later in more detail. The caution of Christopher Jencks and his colleagues (Jencks et al., 1972), however, is a good reminder that things are not always what they are named.

The term "family background" can itself be somewhat misleading since differences between families derive not just from differences in home environment but from differences between neighborhoods, regions, schools, and all other experiences that are the same for children in the same family. . . . Social scientists often use the terms "family background," "social class," and "economic status" almost interchangeably. We think this is a mistake. . . . The way a family brings up its children is obviously influenced by its economic position. The extent of such influence is, however, a problem for investigation, not a matter of definition. (pp. 77–78)

The second major concern raised by reading the literature regards the strength of the relation between SES and academic achievement. It is not at all difficult to find studies that support the notion that there is a strong relation between SES and measures of academic achievement. Klein (1971) reported data in which the estimated[2] correlation between SES and science achievement for elementary school students was .802. Levine, Stephenson, and Mares (1973) found a correlation of .865 between composite standardized achievement test scores and socioeconomic status among big city urban schools. Using Warner et al.'s (1949) *Index of Status Characteristics*, Baker, Shutz, and Hinze (1961) reported a correlation of .680 with group IQ scores as measured by the California Test of Mental Maturity. Dunnell (1971) found a correlation of .755 between SES and Stanford Achievement Test scores among suburban elementary school students, and Thomas (1962), using Project Talent data for 206 secondary schools, determined that a correlation of .852 existed between reading comprehension and SES.

It is also relatively easy to find moderate-to-very-weak relations reported between SES and academic-achievement variables. Lambert (1970) reported a correlation of .434 between SES and scores on the Stanford Achievement Paragraph Reading Test for.

300 first graders. Knief and Stroud (1959) found that SES correlated .340 with the composite score on the Iowa Test for Basic Skills for 344 fourth-grade students. Fetters (1975) reported data from the National Longitudinal Study of the class of 1972 in which SES correlated .263 with reading achievement and .284 with math achievement. The Health Services and Mental Health Administration (1971) reported a study of over 7,000 fourth graders in which SES correlated .480 with group IQ scores. Hennessy (Note 1) found a correlation of .136 between SES and a composite factor of verbal achievement summarized from the Comparative Guidance and Placement Program test battery, and Wright and Bean (1974) found that SES correlated .124, .089, and .072 with the verbal and quantitative scores on the Stanford Achievement Test and Grade Point Average, respectively.

A fairly extensive review of the literature that considers the relation between SES and academic achievement will leave most readers confused. Frequently obtained correlations between SES and various measures of academic achievement range from .100 to .800. Although a number of reviews have been completed (Bryant, Glazer, Hansen, & Kirsch, 1974; Cuff, 1933; Duncan, Featherman, & Duncan, 1972; Findley & Bryan, 1970; Havighurst, 1961; Lavin, 1965; Loevinger, 1940; Neff, 1938), none provides an explanation of why so much variation in the magnitude of the correlation between SES and academic achievement exists in the published literature or what is the most reasonable estimate of the true or expected correlation between SES and academic achievement. The available reviews cite the results of from 10 to 20 studies and then discuss issues such as the pros and cons of various methods for collecting SES information, the theoretical causal relation be-

---

[2] As discussed in more detail later, many studies that have considered the relation between SES and academic achievement have not reported the results as correlation coefficients but have reported analysis of variance results, *t* tests, or nonparametric statistics. In many cases, it is possible to transform these results back into an estimate of the correlation coefficient. Techniques for accomplishing this are discussed fully in the procedures section.

tween SES and other variables, the relation between SES and such factors as ethnicity and intelligence, or the inequities that result from an unequal distribution of SES characteristics among the general population. The reader is usually left with the evidence from a relatively small number of nonrepresentative studies or with sweeping generalizations such as those cited at the beginning of this article as a basis from which to form a conclusion about the strength of the relation between SES and academic achievement.

The effectiveness of using a measure of SES for virtually all of the research applications for which it is typically used depends largely on the strength of the relation between SES and academic achievement. Therefore, the purpose of this study was to conduct a thorough review of the literature that considers the relation between SES and academic achievement in order to (a) establish the strength of the relation that can be expected between typically used measures of SES and academic achievement, (b) determine what factors contribute to the large amount of variance in the strength of previously reported SES/achievement correlations, and (c) make recommendations about the most appropriate way of using measures of SES in future research applications.

Procedures

In order to determine the magnitude of the relation between SES and academic achievement, and to investigate the factors that contribute to the variance in previously reported correlations between these two variables, meta-analysis techniques for integrating research findings originally proposed by Glass (1976) were used. Briefly summarized, meta-analysis requires the reviewer to locate either all studies—or a sufficiently large representative sample of studies—on a given topic, express the results of each study in a common metric, and then quantify or code the various characteristics of each study that may have affected its results. Common descriptive statistics (e.g., mean, median, standard deviation, and standard error of measurement) and relational statistics (e.g., correlation, cross-tabulations, multiple re-

gression, and analysis of variance) are used to study the association of these characteristics across all studies with variations in study outcomes. Because the results of all studies are expressed in a common metric, typically obtained results of studies with given characteristics can also be estimated.

Identifying a Sample

A great deal of the research that has used measures of SES has done so in a secondary or tertiary role and, as a result, is not cited in the usual indexes, computer reference banks, or bibliographies as dealing with SES. For example, the results of an analysis of covariance (with SES as a covariate) in which two reading curricula are compared for differences in reading comprehension would probably not be identified in most hand, computerized, or branching bibliography literature searches. Consequently, many of the studies where SES was not one of the primary variables of interest were probably not included in this analysis. The most probable effect of this sampling bias is that the studies included in the sample may have resulted in slightly higher estimates of the magnitude of the correlation between SES and academic achievement because of the more careful and extensive measurement of the SES variable when it is a primary, rather than secondary, focus of the study.

Studies to be included in this analysis were identified using the *Education Index*, the *Current Index to Journals in Education*, ERIC documents (via a computerized search), *Dissertation Abstracts International*, and the bibliographies of studies already obtained. In all, 248 studies were identified for possible inclusion in the meta-analysis. The content of 63 of these studies was not appropriate for the topic being investigated. Of the remaining 185 articles, 42 dealt only with philosophical issues or instrument development, and 42 did not report correlation coefficients or sufficient information needed to calculate a satisfactory estimate of the correlation coefficient. Consequently, 101 studies were actually included in conducting the meta-analysis. (References to those studies included in the meta-analysis and those studies that were examined but that could not be used are listed in the Appendix.)

Determining the Magnitude of the Correlation Coefficient

In most cases (71 out of the 101 studies) correlation coefficients were reported in the article. When no correlation coefficient was reported, every effort was made to include as many studies as possible in the meta-analysis. In studies that reported only t ratios, a point biserial correlation coefficient (r_{pbi}) was obtained by rearranging Equation 1 (see Glass & Stanley, 1970, p. 318):

$$t^2 = r_{pbi}^2 \frac{N - 2}{1 - r^2}. \tag{1}$$

When the results of an analysis of variance were reported without the corresponding correlation coefficient, the intraclass correlation coefficient η was obtained by Equation 2 (see Hays, 1973, pp. 683–684):

$$\eta = \sqrt{\frac{SS_b}{SS_T}}. \tag{2}$$

Because the Pearson product-moment correlation (r) is a measure of linear relationship, and η estimates curvilinear as well as linear relationship, η would tend to overestimate r in those cases where the relationship is not linear. The decision to use η as an estimate of r is consistent with the posture throughout the study to tend toward overestimation rather than underestimation in those cases where estimation is necessary.

Where an F ratio but no analysis of variance table was reported, sums of squares (SS) could often be reconstructed and used in Equation 2. In a few instances, it was necessary to reconstruct the actual F ratio from cell means and standard deviations.

When results were reported in a 2×2 contingency table, a tetrachoric correlation (r_{tet}) was estimated using methods developed by Jenkins (1955). In four instances where the original contingency table was larger than a 2×2, r was estimated by collapsing the larger table into a 2×2 table for all possible combinations, computing r_{tet} for each one, and taking the average as the final estimate of r.

Variables Coded for Each Study

Whether a meta-analysis is successful in explaining and summarizing the results of previous research depends largely on whether the proper variables are coded for each study. For example, a hypothetical explanation as to why so much variance exists in the magnitude of the correlation between SES and academic achievement might be that for very young children the correlation is very strong, but for older students the relation disappears. By coding the age of the students used in each study and examining the correlation between age of students in the study and magnitude of the SES/achievement correlation, one can determine the amount of the variance in previous research results that is accounted for by the age factor. If, however, age is not coded for most studies, the variance that is attributable to the age factor will remain unexplained.

There is no fail-safe technique for making sure that all of the proper variables are included in a meta-analysis. The selection of the variables to be included in this study was based on an extensive review of the literature, a pilot test of the coding instrument, and discussion with colleagues. The following variables were included:
1. The *unit of analysis* used in computing the correlation coefficient was coded as aggregated, confounded, or student. When an aggregated unit (such as school or district) was used, both the SES measure and the achievement measure were averages for the aggregated unit, and the correlation was computed between these average scores. When the unit of analysis was confounded, SES was measured at an aggregated level, and achievement was measured at the student level or vice versa. For instance, all students in the same school might be given the same SES rating but could have individual achievement scores. The student was identified as the unit of analysis when both SES and achievement were measured separately for each student.
2. *Type of achievement* measure was broken

down into verbal, math, science, composite achievement, IQ, and other.

3. *Grade level* of the students used in the study. When a correlation was reported for combined grades, for instance grades 4 through 8, the mean grade level was used.

4. *SES reporting error* was coded from 1 (little or no inaccuracy) to 4 (substantial inaccuracy) as an estimate of the potential inaccuracy of the information used as a measure of SES. For example, if education of parents was used as a measure of SES, it was coded 1 if parents were interviewed, 2 if students reported it, 3 if teachers estimated it, and 4 if someone in the central office estimated how various schools differed on this variable.

5. *Achievement range restriction* was coded from 1 (no restriction) to 4 (substantial restriction). An example of substantial restriction would be when the sample consisted only of children with an IQ of 130 or more.

6. *SES range restriction* was coded from 1 (no restriction) to 4 (substantial restriction). An example of substantial restriction would be when the sample consisted entirely of inner-city, low-income students.

7. *Percent ethnic minority* was the percentage of students in the sample from a racial or an ethnic minority (i.e., black, Chicano, Oriental, and American Indian). This variable was given or could be estimated in only about two-thirds of the studies.

8. *Year of study* was approximated by the year of publication.

9. *Number of items in the SES instrument.*

10. *Number of students* on which the correlation coefficient was based.

11. *Type of publication* where the information was reported was categorized by books, journals, and unpublished materials. The unpublished category consisted of dissertations, theses, and reports (such as project reports in government contracts).

12. *Sample* was coded 1 for samples that were taken from a small geographic region and 2 for nationally representative samples. Almost all studies were done in the United States. A few studies done in Canada and England were also included.

13. *Type of SES measure.* The factors in the following list were rated for each SES measure. Ratings were on a continuum from 0 (not represented in the instrument) to 3 (major representation in the instrument).

- income of family
- education of parents
- occupation of head of house
- home atmosphere (e.g., parents' attitude toward education, parents' aspirations for their children, cultural and intellectual activities of the family)
- dwelling value
- school resources
- subjective judgment
- other (e.g., number of siblings, ethnicity, and mobility of family)

14. *Number of SES groups* indicated how the SES variable was divided. For instance, students might be divided into two groups, low and high; or three groups, low, middle, and high. Where the SES rating was a continuous variable, a value of 9 was assigned.

15. *Internal validity of the study.* This was coded from 1 (high internal validity) to 3 (low internal validity). Examples of factors that contributed to a low internal validity are (a) using ethnicity as a measure of SES, (b) only taking the two extreme groups to compute the correlation, and (c) estimating the correlation coefficient from multiple t tests.

Results of the Meta-Analysis

In total, 101 studies yielding 636 correlation coefficients were included in the meta-analysis. Two of the primary objectives of the meta-analysis were (a) to establish the strength of the relation that can be expected between typically used measures of SES and academic achievement and (b) to determine how much of the variance in the magnitude of previously reported correlations between SES and academic achievement can be accounted for by systematic differences among the studies.

By summarizing the results across all studies as well as partitioning the results of the different coding categories, we learn much about the relation between SES and academic achievement. Collapsing across all coding variables reveals that the correlation coefficients for all studies form a somewhat skewed frequency distribution with a mean of .351, a median of .251, and a standard deviation of .225. These results, shown in Figure 1, indicate that for this sample of 101 studies the best estimate of the correlation between SES and academic achievement is only .251 (the median value of the distribution).

This information indicates that the relation between SES and academic achievement is probably much weaker than many people have assumed. Further information is necessary if we are to be confident of that conclusion and to understand what factors influence the magnitude of the correlation coefficient. Data from the next level of analysis are presented in Table 1. These data indicate that the magnitude of the correlation is significantly related to a number of variables. Most dramatic are the differences in the magnitude of the correlation between SES and academic achievement when different units of analysis are used to compute the correlation. The differences between using students and aggregated units of analysis are graphically shown in Figures 2 and 3.

The effect of using aggregated units of analysis in computing correlation coefficients has been known among statisticians for some time (Knapp, 1977; Robinson, 1950). Yet it is a fact that is frequently overlooked by most people in interpreting the results of research. Almost always, correlations computed from aggregated data will be much higher than correlations computed using individuals as the unit of analysis (see Robinson, 1950, for the supporting mathematical derivations). As the data in Figures 2 and 3 graphically illustrate, the unit of

Table 1

Magnitude of the Mean Correlation Between SES and Achievement As Different Study Characteristics Are Accounted For

Category	Unpartialed correlations			Correlations partialed on IQ		
	M	SD	N	M	SD	N
All correlations	.315	.225	620	.188	.159	16
Unit of analysis						
Aggregated	.680	.184	93			
Confounded	.338	.162	39			
Student	.245	.160	489	.152	.107	14
Type of publication						
Books	.508	.277	88			
Journals	.343	.204	219	.178	.169	14
Unpublished	.292	.184	313			
Validity						
Valid	.296	.220	489	.157	.105	14
Fairly valid	.357	.218	107			
Invalid	.486	.251	28			

Note. Categories where *n* < 5 have been omitted from the table.

analysis chosen by a researcher will have a dramatic effect on whether SES is likely to be a very useful tool for most research applications.

Also evident in Table 1 is the sizable decline in the magnitude of the mean correlation coefficient going from studies published in books (*r* = .508), to those published in journals (.343), to those from unpublished material (.242). This evidence lends some support to the common claim that the more prestigious outlets are more likely to publish

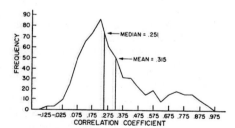

Figure 1. Frequency distribution of SES/achievement correlation coefficients for all studies (*N* = 620).

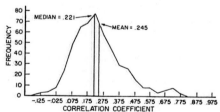

Figure 2. Frequency distribution of SES/achievement correlation coefficients for studies using the student as the unit of analysis (*N* = 489).

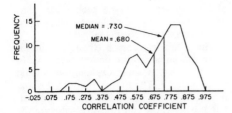

Figure 3. Frequency distribution of SES/achievement correlation coefficients for studies using aggregated units of analysis (N = 93).

statistically significant results, whereas a number of statistically insignificant but possibly valid findings go unpublished and consequently often unreported.

The results reported in Table 1 are consistent with the results reported in Table 2 when the confounding effect due to different units of analysis is eliminated.

In Table 3, the correlations between various study characteristics and the magnitude of the SES/achievement correlation are shown. These are reported at two levels: first, using only those coefficients that were obtained using the student as the unit of analysis, and second, using all 620 coefficients.

Some of the correlations in Table 3 are predictable from classical psychometric theory. When either or both of the achievement or SES measures are restricted in range, the mean correlation between the two is weak-

ened. As reporting error in SES increases (connoting a drop in instrument reliability), the correlation between SES and achievement is attenuated and consequently reduced. As the number of items in the SES measure increases, indicating increased reliability due to a more adequate sampling of the SES construct, the magnitude of the correlation increases.

In addition to confirming these expected results, other interesting information is revealed by the correlation coefficients in Table 3. The correlation with year of study, particularly when the student is the unit of analysis, indicates that a slight trend exists for more recent studies to find lower correlations. Two explanations can be offered. It is possible that first, the increased availability to people of all SES levels of such things as television, movies, community groups and organizations, and preschool, and second, the efforts of compensatory education have had a positive effect in reducing the strength of the relation that does exist between SES and academic achievement.

When students were used as the unit of analysis, the correlation suggests that the

Table 2
Magnitude of the Mean Correlation for Levels of Type of Publication and Validity of Study When the Student is the Unit of Analysis

Category	SES/achievement correlation	N
All correlations	.244	489
Type of publication		
Books	.312	165
Journals	.253	38
Unpublished	.204	286
Validity		
Valid	.234	414
Fairly valid	.296	71
Invalid	.462	4

Table 3
Correlations Between Study Characteristics and the Magnitude of SES/Achievement Correlation Coefficients

Study characteristic	Studies using student as the unit of analysis (N = 489)	All studies (N = 620)
Grade level	−.243	−.079
Reporting error in SES[a]	−.266	−.345
Range restriction in achievement[a]	−.127	−.132
Range restriction in SES[a]	−.130	−.071
% ethnic minority	−.301	−.317
Year of study	−.131	−.012
Number of items in SES measure	.308	−.287
N of study	−.144	−.174
Sample[b]	−.232	−.225
Number of SES groups	.013	.127
Study's internal validity[c]	.178	.187

[a] Range from 1 (low) to 4 (high). [b] Coded 1 (local) and 2 (national). [c] Range from 1 (high) to 3 (low).

Table 4

Correlations Between Grade Level and the Magnitude of the Correlation Between SES and Achievement Using Only Coleman's (Coleman et al., 1966) Data

Grade	Verbal achievement	Math achievement	Both math and verbal achievement
1	.212	.217	.214
6	.207	.209	.208
9	.176	.161	.168[a]
12	.175	.131	.153[a]

Note. Although Coleman collected data for grade 3, correlations for grade 3 are not reported because a different measure of SES was used. For each correlation, N = 20 unless otherwise noted.
[a] N = 40.

relation between SES and achievement drops off as students become older. A further test of this hypothesis is to examine the relation between grade level and size of the SES/ achievement correlation for just the data from the *Equality of Educational Opportunity Survey* (Coleman et al., 1966). The results, reported in Table 4, are illuminating because Coleman looked at four different grade levels using the same SES measures, the same kinds of achievement measures,

and the same analytical techniques, thus eliminating many possible sources of error in the correlation coefficient.

The trend in Table 4, though slight, is clear and enhances the findings reported in Table 3. Two possible explanations should be considered. The first is that schools and other socializing agents are providing equalizing experiences and thus are reducing the relation between SES and achievement as students grow older. The second is that a disproportionate number of lower achieving students drop out of school in the higher grades, thus reducing the variance in achievement and correspondingly the magnitude of the correlation. This second explanation is not entirely sufficient, however, insofar as one would not expect dropouts to occur frequently until at least grade 9 when students reach the age when in most states they are no longer required to attend school. It seems plausible that parts of both hypotheses, and possibly others, are influencing the results.

At the next finer level of analysis, the average correlation between SES and various types of achievement measures was examined as reported in Table 5. As can be seen, the number of available correlations begins

Table 5

Average Correlations Between SES and Achievement for Different Kinds of Achievement Measures

Category	Verbal		Math		Composite achievement		GPA all subjects		IQ	
	M	N	M	N	M	N	M	N	M	N
All correlations	.307	225	.246	143	.369	66	.256	47	.403	102
					Unit of analysis					
Aggregated	.676	35	.697	14	.636	15			.731	18
Confounded	.294	16							.337	10
Student	.234	174	.197	128	.270	46	.236	41	.333	74
					Type of publication					
Books	.447	40			.616	10			.592	19
Journals	.354	49	.382	18	.293	42	.235	30	.387	63
Unpublished	.248	136	.210	117	.420	14	.292	17	.273	20
					Validity					
Valid	.288	174	.194	128			.252	43	.419	81
Fairly valid	.368	42	.290	10	.297	48			.306	17
Invalid					.523	11				

Note. GPA = grade point average. Categories where n < 10 have been omitted from the table.

Table 6
Magnitude of the Mean Correlation Between SES and Achievement for Different Kinds of SES Measures

	Unit of analysis			
	Student		Aggregated	
SES measure	M	N	M	N
Income only	.315	19	.767	18
Education only	.185	116	.686	8
Occupation only	.201	65	.586	9
Home atmosphere only	.577	21		
School resources only			.619	28
Income and education	.230	36		
Income and occupation	.332	15		
Education and occupation	.325	20		
Income, education, and occupation	.318	27	.544	8
Income, education, and occupation plus something else major[a]	.365	22	.789	12

[a] This was a measure of home atmosphere, school resources, or some non-SES indicator such as ethnicity.

to be a problem and prevents definitive conclusions in some instances. Values that were based on fewer than 10 correlations have been deleted from the table.

With a few minor exceptions, probably attributable to small sample size, the results in Table 5 support the interpretations of the data in Table 1. In addition, information is provided about the size of the correlation for different types of achievement measures. The most meaningful category to examine is where the student was used as the unit of analysis and all other variables were collapsed. Values for grade point average (which admittedly may have problems with instrumentation) were somewhat lower (.256) than for composite achievement (.369), and the value for IQ (.403) was noticeably higher than any of the others.

The next step in the meta-analysis was to examine the magnitude of the correlation between SES and achievement as a function of the type of SES measure. Studies were divided into eight categories representing the kind of indicators that had been used for SES. The mean magnitude of the correlation is shown in Table 6 for studies that used an aggregated and those that used a student

unit of analysis (confounded units of analysis are not reported because of small sample sizes). Again, the low number of correlation coefficients included in some categories makes some of these results a bit tenuous.

Among the traditional measures of SES (income, education, and occupation), income is the highest single correlate of academic achievement. It is also evident that measures of SES that combine two or more indicators are more highly correlated with academic achievement than any single indicator. More striking, however, is the fact that measures of home atmosphere correlated much higher with academic achievement than did any single or combined group of the traditional indicators of SES. Recalling the comments by Jencks et al. (1972) cited earlier, there are many differences among families that can potentially affect the academic achievement of the children in addition to differences in education, occupational level, and income of the parents. It is not at all implausible that some low-SES parents (defined in terms of income, education, and/or occupational level) are very good at creating a home atmosphere that fosters learning (e.g., read to their children, help them with their homework, encourage them to go to college, and take them to the library and to cultural events), whereas other low-SES parents are not.

Nevertheless, even though measures of home atmosphere in this analysis account for from 4 to 11 times as much of the variation in academic achievement as do traditional measures of SES, a complete interpretation of the contribution of home atmosphere to students' academic achievement is fraught with problems of third variables and directionality. For instance, is the high correlation between home atmosphere and achievement because children do better in school if their parents help them with their homework and encourage them to go to college, or is it because parents start helping their children and taking an interest in their education because of the child's previous success in school? In other words, does home atmosphere cause the child's academic success, or does a child's academic success create a certain kind of home atmosphere? A definitive answer to this question was beyond the scope of this review, but it is a question that deserves further research.

Moreover, these results raise the question of whether SES, as it traditionally has been defined, is the most appropriate variable for most of the applications for which it has been used. If not, serious questions are raised about the conclusions that have resulted from the use of SES in the past research applications. Even though family background does have a strong relationship with achievement, it may be *how* parents rear their children (i.e., do they read to their children, take them to the library, encourage them in school, or help them with their homework?) and not the parents' occupation, income, or education that really makes the difference. Because income, education, and occupation do correlate with home atmosphere variables to some extent, a correlation (albeit, a fairly weak one) may exist between SES (income, education, and occupation) and achievement when the real variable of interest may be home atmosphere.

Unfortunately, the question cannot really be answered from data reported in Table 6. As mentioned, problems of directionality and third variables exist in trying to establish causality in addition to questions about the appropriate techniques for measuring home atmosphere. To date, only a few studies have been completed, but the results of these studies, as summarized in Table 6, suggest plausible and important hypotheses in need of additional refinement and testing.

The final step in the meta-analysis was to determine what percent of the variation in the magnitude of the correlation between SES and academic achievement could be accounted for by the characteristics of the studies. The coding variables of each study were used as predictors in a multiple regression equation to predict the magnitude of the correlation coefficient. The results are shown in Table 7 for four different multiple regression equations.

As can be seen, almost 75% of the variance in *r*s can be accounted for by the characteristics coded for each study. Well over half of the variation in *r*s is accounted for by characteristics that are completely under the control of the researcher, and more than one-quarter of the variance can be explained by the type of SES measure that is used.

Two other problems that have contributed to the difficulty of interpreting the strength of the relation between SES and academic achievement were discovered in conducting the meta-analysis. The first is the way in which results of studies are reported. Of 143 studies that examined the relation between SES and academic achievement, which were originally identified for inclusion in the meta-analysis, only about one-half reported the relation as a correlation coefficient. A summary of how results were reported is shown in Table 8.

When the results of studies that examine the relation between SES and academic achievement are reported as correlation coefficients, it is a simple matter to interpret the strength of the relation and to compare the results with those of other studies. Of course, there is nothing inherently wrong with reporting statistically significant main effects, means, or nonparametric statistics, but such statistics are less informative and for some audiences can be misleading about the strength of the relation between SES and academic achievement. When *N*s are fairly large, a factor need only be minimally related to the dependent variable to show highly significant statistical analysis of variance main effects. For instance, if 500 students were divided into high- and low-SES categories, there would be a statistically significant difference between the levels of SES at the $\alpha = .05$ level if SES were correlated with the dependent variable (e.g., achievement test scores) at $r = .10$. This would mean that only 1% of the total variance in achievement scores could be predicted from knowing the SES of the students, and 99% would remain unexplained. Similar but even more serious problems in interpreting the strength of the relation results when nonparametric statistics are used or when results are only visually inspected without the aid of statistical techniques.

The second problem, which was alluded to earlier, concerns the wide range of very different variables that are used as indicators of SES. In the absence of a widely accepted and precise definition of SES, this is not a surprising phenomenon. Nonetheless, the

Table 7
Amount of Variance in the Magnitude of the SES/Achievement Correlation that Can Be Predicted by Study Characteristics

Description of variables included	Study characteristics																Magnitude of r		
	Unit of analysis	Type of ACH meas.	Grade level	SES rept. error	ACH restriction	SES restriction	Ethnicity	Yr. of study	No. of SES items	N of study	Type of pub.	Sample type	Type of SES meas.	No. of SES groups	Validity of study	Multiple r	r^2	Corrected r^2
All study characteristics	•	•	•	•	•	•	•	•	•	•	•	•	•	•	•	.875	.765	.745
Characteristics under the researcher's control		•	•	•	•	•			•	•			•	•		.799	.638	.623
Characteristics under the researcher's control except unit of analysis		•	•	•	•	•			•				•	•		.603	.364	.334
Type of SES measure													•			.554	.307	.294

Note. ACH = achievement. Meas. = measure. Rept. = reporting. Pub. = publication. * indicates inclusion of that variable in the multiple regression formula.

Table 8

How Results of Relations Between SES and Achievement Were Reported in 143 Studies

Method of reporting	Frequency
Reported differences between groups using t or F statistics	37
Visually inspected results and concluded that differences existed	27
Reported chi-squared or non-parametric statistics	8
Reported correlational coefficients	71
Total	143

almost indiscriminate inclusion of whatever pleases a particular researcher as a measure of SES seriously weakens its validity as a research tool. In the 143 studies identified for inclusion in this meta-analysis, over 70 different variables were used (either alone or in some combination) as indicators of SES. Table 9 combines these variables into 43 categories and reports the number of studies in which each was used.

Conclusions and Recommendations

At the beginning of this article, six different situations were identified in which measures of SES were frequently used in educational research in conjunction with measures of academic achievement. Briefly reviewed, these situations include using a measure of SES as:
1. a concomitant variable in adjusting for bias or pretreatment differences among groups,
2. a covariate or stratifying variable to increase the precision of an experiment,
3. a stratifying variable to investigate the effect of interactions with other independent variables,
4. a descriptive variable to assist other researchers to replicate findings or generalize results,
5. a predictor variable, and
6. a causal agent.

The utility and wisdom of using SES in conjunction with academic achievement depends largely on the validity of the particular measure of SES and/or the strength of the relation between that measure of SES and academic achievement. By conducting a

Table 9

Variables Used as Indicators of SES and Their Frequency of Use

Variable	Frequency
Traditional SES	
Occupation of parents	88
Education of parents	57
Income of family	47
Dwelling quality	39
Possessions in the home	17
Frequency of dental work	6
Recipients of welfare	4
Have servants	7
Travel	2
Home atmosphere	
Academic guidance in the home	4
Work habits and democracy in the home	5
Family's attitude toward education	9
Quality of language in the home	6
Achievement motivation of child	2
Church attendance	2
Reading materials in the home	14
Family stability	10
Aspirations of parents for child	11
Amount of cultural activities in which family participates	15
Conversation in the home	4
School resources	
Age of building	2
Salary of teachers	4
Experience of teachers	2
Size and type of community	3
Size of district	2
Average absenteeism	1
Number of books in library	2
Presence of guidance program	1
Pupil/teacher ratio	2
Percent of teachers with MAs	4
State valuation per pupil	2
Instructional expense per pupil	6
Amount of federal funds received by school	2
Staff turnover	3
Presence of college prep program	2
Percent of last year's students who went to college	1
Miscellaneous	
Number of siblings	10
Pure judgment with no objective criterion	18
Population density	4
Ethnicity	4
Mobility	4
Country of parents' birth	2
Not reported	6

meta-analysis of the previously completed research in which the relation between SES and academic achievement could be examined, this study sought to:
1. establish the strength of the relation that can be expected between typically used measures of SES and academic achievement,
2. determine what factors contribute to the large amount of variance in the strength of previously reported SES/achievement correlations, and
3. make recommendations about the most appropriate way of using measures of SES in future research applications.

These objectives having been accomplished, the results of the meta-analysis are enlightening and provocative. The analysis is enlightening because it provides significant new information about the strength of the relation between SES and academic achievement as well as explains much of the cause for such large amounts of variance in the previous finding. In addition to organizing and making sense of previous research findings, the results of the analysis are provocative because a number of hypotheses are suggested that need to be confirmed or eliminated by future research.

The Strength of the Relation Between SES and Academic Achievement

Based on the data presented in these analyses, it can be concluded that as it is most frequently used (with the student as the unit of analysis) and traditionally defined (using one or more indicators of parents' income, educational attainment, or occupational level), SES is positively but only weakly correlated with measures of academic achievement. In such situations, measures of SES can be expected to account for less than 5% of the variance in students' academic achievement. Correlations of that magnitude seriously restrict the utility of SES in most of the research applications identified above.

The widespread, but apparently false, conclusion among many educators that a strong relation between SES and academic achievement "has been documented in countless studies" (Boocock, 1972, p. 32) is also at least partially explained from the results of the meta-analysis. First of all, in those cases where an aggregated unit of analysis is appropriate for the questions in which the researcher is interested, SES and academic achievement do appear to be strongly correlated. It must be remembered, however, that the strength of this relationship cannot and should not be generalized to situations where the student is the unit of analysis. When the student is the unit of analysis, SES and academic achievement are only weakly correlated.

Second, the way in which SES is defined is of critical importance in determining the strength of the relation between SES and academic achievement. As pointed out by the results of the meta-analysis, some of the measures that are used as indicators of SES, or that other researchers might consider a measure of SES (e.g., measures of home atmosphere), are much more strongly related to academic achievement than are traditional indicators of SES.

Finally, the way in which results of studies are frequently reported is probably in part responsible for creating the impression that SES and academic achievement are strongly correlated. Statistically significant findings in studies that use an SES factor in computing an analysis of variance, t test, or chi-squared analysis, have probably misled many researchers about the strength of the relation between SES and academic achievement.

Explaining the Variation in Previous Findings

As noted earlier, one of the most confusing things about reviewing the literature that examines the relation between SES and academic achievement is the wide range in the strength of this relation. Frequently reported correlations range from .100 to .800. From the results of the meta-analysis, it is clear that the unit of analysis used in computing the correlation coefficient and the definition of SES are important variables in explaining this large amount of variation. Many of the other variables (e.g., grade level, year of study, and type of achievement measure) included in the meta-analysis were also significant contributors to the explanation of variation in previous results. Almost 75% of the variation in previously reported correlations between SES and academic achievement was explained by the factors coded for each study. The importance of this finding is not only the large amount of variance that can be explained but also the fact that many of the most significant variables that influence the strength of the correlation are directly under the researcher's control.

Using Measures of SES as a Research Tool

The results of the meta-analysis indicate clearly that when the student is the unit of analysis and traditional measures of SES are used, there is very little utility in using a measure of SES as a covariate, stratifying variable, predictor, descriptive variable, or causal agent in studies dealing with academic achievement. The ineffectiveness of SES in these applications is due to the weak correlation between SES and academic achievement.

When schools or other aggregated groups are the appropriate unit of analysis (i.e., the unit about which conclusions will be drawn and to which results will be generalized), traditional measures of SES are usually correlated strongly enough with academic achievement measures to be useful as a covariate, predictor, or stratifying variable. In such situations the researcher should be particularly careful to specify that grouped data were used and that the magnitude of obtained correlations is much higher than would normally be expected when individuals are the unit of analysis.

The validity of using measures of SES based on aggregated units of analysis in building causal models of student achievement, such as would be done with path analysis, is less clear because the causal effect of SES is more relevant to individuals than to groups. Consequently, in building causal models, it is probably more appropriate to utilize data that have used the student as the unit of analysis.

The final recommendation for using SES as a research tool in conjunction with measures of academic achievement concerns the definition of SES. From reviewing the research, it appears that SES has become a convenient label to attach to a variety of different combinations of variables. A significant amount of confusion could be avoided if a distinct, widely accepted definition of SES existed. In the absence of such a definition, researchers would be well advised to avoid using the term *SES* as much as possible. Alternative labels such as family income, occupation of the head of the home, school resources, expenditure per pupil, or home atmosphere, with a precise definition of how the variable was measured, would do much to clarify the results of future research.

Suggestions for Future Research

Integrating and summarizing the results of previously completed research on a given topic often focuses attention on additional questions in need of research as well as provides answers to the study's original objectives. The results of this study suggest a number of tentative hypotheses that need to be tested by further research. For example, what is the causal relation, if any, between home atmosphere and achievement? Have publishing policies of journals (either implicit or explicit) overemphasized the importance of statistical significance? To what can the decline in the SES/achievement correlation from lower to higher grades or over time be attributed? The results of the meta-analysis offer some information about each of these questions, but more research is needed before confident conclusions can be drawn.

The results of the meta-analysis also allow confident conclusions about a number of important points. First, the expected strength of the relation between traditional measures of SES and academic achievement when individuals are the unit of analysis is much weaker than has frequently been assumed. The relation is so weak as to make traditional measures of SES of limited use as a research tool in conjunction with academic achievement. Finally, most of the variance in previously reported research can be accounted for by the systematic difference in study characteristics. This information does much to clarify our understanding and should prove useful in guiding future research and educational practice concerning the relation between SES and academic achievement.

Reference Note

1. Hennessy, J. J. *The relations between socioeconomic status and mental abilities in a late adolescent group.* Paper presented at the meeting of the American Educational Research Association, San Francisco, April 1976.

References

Baker, R. L., Shutz, R. E., & Hinze, R. H. The influence of mental ability on achievement when socioeconomic status is controlled. *Journal of Experimental Education,* 1961, *30,* 155-158.

Boocock, S. S. *An introduction to the sociology of learning.* Boston: Houghton-Mifflin, 1972.

Bryant, E. C., Glazer, E., Hansen, M. A., & Kirsch, A. *Associations between educational outcomes and background variables.* Denver, Colo.: National Assessment of Educational Progress, 1974.

Chapin, F. S. A quantitative scale for rating the home and social environment of middle-class families in an urban community: A first approximation to the measurement of socioeconomic status. *Journal of Educational Psychology,* 1928, *19,* 99-111.

Charters, W. W., Jr. The social background of teaching. In N. L. Gage (Ed.), *Handbook of research on teaching* (Ch. 14). Chicago: Rand McNally, 1963.

Coleman, J. S. et al. *Equality of educational opportunity survey* (A publication of the National Center for Educational Statistics). Washington, D.C.: U.S. Government Printing Office, 1966.

Cuff, N. B. Relationship of socioeconomic status to intelligence and achievement. *Peabody Journal of Education,* 1933, *11,* 106-110.

Duncan, O. T., Featherman, D. L., & Duncan, B. *Socioeconomic background and achievement.* New York: Seminar Press, 1972.

Dunnell, J. P. *Input and output analysis of suburban elementary school districts.* Paper presented at the meeting of the American Educational Research Association, New York, February 1971. (ERIC Document Reproduction Service No. ED 047 366)

Fetters, W. B. *National longitudinal study of the high school class of 1972: Student questionnaires and test results by sex, high school program, ethnic category, and father's education* (No. HE 19.308:L86). Washington, D.C.: U.S. Government Printing Office, 1975.

Findley, W. G., & Bryan, M. M. *Ability grouping: 1970—II. The impact of ability grouping on school achievement, affective development, ethnic separation and socioeconomic separation.* Athens: Center for Educational Improvement, University of Georgia, 1970. (ERIC Document Reproduction Service No. ED 048 382)

Glass, G. V. Primary, secondary, and meta-analysis of research. *Educational Researcher,* 1976, *5*(10), 3-8.

Glass, G. V., & Stanley, J. C. *Statistical methods in education and psychology.* Englewood Cliffs, N.J.: Prentice-Hall, 1970.

Havighurst, R. J. Social class influences on American education. In N. Henry (Ed.), *Social forces influencing American education* (The 60th yearbook of the National Society for the Study of Education, Pt. 1). Bloomington, Ill.: Public School Publishing, 1961.

Hays, W. L. *Statistics for the social sciences* (2nd ed.). New York: Holt, Rinehart & Winston, 1973.

Health Services and Mental Health Administration (Department of Health, Education and Welfare). *School achievement of children by demographic and socioeconomic factors, United States.* Rockville, Md.: Division of Emergency Health Services, 1971. (ERIC Document Reproduction Service No. ED 065 799)

Hollingshead, A. d. B., & Redlich, F. C. *Social class and mental illness.* New York: Wiley, 1958.

Jencks, C. et al. *Inequality: A reassessment of the effect of family and schooling in America.* New York: Harper & Row, 1972.

Jenkins, W. L. An improved method for tetrachoric *r.* *Psychometrika,* 1955, *20,* 253-258.

Klein, C. A. Differences in science concepts held by children from three social-economic levels. *School Science and Mathematics,* 1971, *71,* 550-558.

Knapp, T. R. The unit of analysis problem in applications of simple correlational analysis to educational research. *Journal of Educational Statistics,* 1977, *2,* 171-186.

Knief, L. M., & Stroud, J. B. Intercorrelations among various intelligence, achievement and social class scores. *Journal of Educational Psychology,* 1959, *50,* 117-120.

Lambert, N. M. Paired associate learning, social status and tests of logical concrete behavior as univariate and multivariate predictions of first grade reading achievement. *American Educational Research Journal,* 1970, *1,* 511-528.

Lavin, D. E. *The prediction of academic performance.* New York: Russell Sage Foundation. 1965.

Levine, D. U., Stephenson, R. S., & Mares, K. R. *An exploration of the use of socioeconomic census data to predict achievement and evaluate the effects of concentrated urban poverty among elementary schools in a big city.* Washington, D.C.: National Center for Educational Research and Development (DHEW/OE), 1973. (ERIC Document Reproduction Service No. ED 082 384)

Loevinger, J. Intelligence as related to socioeconomic factors. In G. M. Whipple (Ed.), *Intelligence: Its nature and nurture* (The 39th yearbook of the National Society for the Study of Education, Pt. 1). Bloomington, Ill.: Public School Publishing, 1940.

Michigan State Department of Education. *Distribution of educational performance and related factors in Michigan: A supplement.* Lansing: Author, 1971. (ERIC Document Reproduction Service No. ED 059 254)

Neff, W. S. Socioeconomic status and intelligence. *Psychological Bulletin,* 1938, *35,* 727-757.

Robinson, W. S. Ecological correlations and the behavior of individuals. *American Sociological Review,* 1950, *15,* 351-357.

St. John, N. The validity of children's reports of their

parents' educational level: A methodological note. *Sociology of Education*, 1970, *43*, 255-269.

Thomas, J. A. Efficiency in education: An empirical study. *Administrator's Notebook*, 1962, *11*, 1-4.

Warner, W. L., Meeker, M., & Eells, K. E. *Social class in America.* Chicago: Science Research Associates, 1949.

Welch, F. Relationships between income and schooling. In F. N. Kerlinger (Ed.), *Review of research in education.* Ithaca, N.Y.: Peacock, 1974.

Wright, R. J., & Bean, A. G. The influence of socioeconomic status on the predictability of college performance. *Journal of Educational Measurement,* 1974, *11*, 277-284.

Appendix

A. Studies Examined and Used in the Meta-Analysis

Aftanas, M. S., Robinson, M., Bell, A., & Schwartz, L. *A study of the psychological and social factors related to preschool prediction of reading retardation.* Paper presented at the National Convention of the Canadian Psychological Association, Winnipeg, May 1970. (ERIC Document Reproduction Service No. ED 041 976)

Anderson, R. F. Relation of Lorge-Thorndike Intelligence Test scores of public school pupils to the socioeconomic status of their parents. *Journal of Experimental Education*, 1962, *31*, 73-76.

Armos, D. J. School and family effects of black and white achievement: A re-examination of the USOE data. In F. Mosteller & D. P. Moynihan (Eds.), *On equality of educational opportunity.* New York: Random House, 1972.

Bachman, J. G. *Youth in transition: The impact of family background and intelligence on tenth grade boys* (Vol. 2). Ann Arbor: Survey Research Center, Institute for Social Research, University of Michigan, 1970.

Baker, R. L., Shutz, R. E., & Hinze, R. H. The influence of mental ability on achievement when socioeconomic status is controlled. *Journal of Experimental Education*, 1961, *30*, 155-158.

Bhushan, V. Comparison of IQ and socioeconomic index in predicting grade point average. *Education*, 1969, *90*, 167-169.

Brunt, H. N. Relationship between social studies, interests and educational achievement among children in primary school. *British Journal of Educational Psychology*, 1964, *34*, 327-329.

Burkhead, J., Fox, T. G., & Holland, J. W. *Input and output in large city high schools.* Syracuse, N.Y.: Syracuse University Press, 1967.

Burks, B. S. The relative influence of nature and nurture upon mental development: A comparative study of foster parent–foster child resemblance and true parent–true child resemblance. In G. M. Whipple (Ed.), *Nature and nurture: Their influence on intelligence* (The 27th yearbook of the National Society for the Study of Education, Pt. 1). Bloomington, Ill.: Public School Publishing, 1928.

Byrns, R., & Henmon, V. A. C. Parental occupation and mental ability. *Journal of Educational Psychology*, 1936, *27*, 284-291.

California State Department of Education. *California state testing program 1970-71: Profiles of school district performance. Technical supplement.* Sacramento, Calif.: Office of Program Evaluation, 1973.

(ERIC Document Reproduction Service No. ED 092 575)

Callaway, B. et al. Relationship between reading and language achievement and certain sociological and adjustment factors. *Reading Improvement*, 1974, *11*, 19-26.

Carter-Saltzman, L., Scarr-Salapatek, S., & Barker, W. B. Do these co-twins really live together? An assessment of the validity of the home index as a measure of family socioeconomic status. *Educational and Psychological Measurement*, 1975, *35*, 427-435.

Cattell, R. B. Some further relations between intelligence, fertility and socioeconomic factors. *Eugenics Review*, 1937, *29*, 171-179.

Channey, M. R. The relation of the home factor to achievement and intelligence test scores. *Journal of Educational Research*, 1929, *20*, 88-90.

Chapman, J. C., & Wiggins, D. M. Relation of family size to intelligence of offspring and socioeconomic status of family. *Pedagogical Seminary and Journal of Genetic Psychology*, 1925, *32*, 414-421.

Cobb, J. A. *Survival skills and first grade academic achievement* (Report No. 1). Eugene, Ore.: Center for Research and Demonstration in the Early Education of Handicapped Children, Oregon University, December 1970. (ERIC Document Reproduction Service No. ED 050 807)

Coleman, J. S. et al. *Equality of educational opportunity survey.* Washington, D.C.: National Center for Educational Statistics, 1966.

Coleman, W., & Ward, A. W. Comparison of Davis-Eells and Kuhlmann-Finch scores of children from high and low socioeconomic status. *Journal of Educational Psychology*, 1955, *46*, 465-469.

Comber, L. C., & Keeves, J. P. *Science education in nineteen countries: An empirical study.* New York: Wiley, 1973.

Crawford, P., & Eason, G. *School achievement: A preliminary look at the effects of the home.* Toronto, Ontario: Toronto Board of Education, Research Department, 1970. (ERIC Document Reproduction Service No. ED 047 777)

Cuff, N. B. Relationship of socioeconomic status to intelligence and achievement. *Peabody Journal of Education*, 1933, *11*, 106-110.

Curry, R. L. Effect of socioeconomic status on the scholastic achievement of sixth grade children. *British Journal of Educational Psychology*, 1962, *32*, 46-49.

Dave, R. H. *The identification and measurement of environmental process variables that are related to educational achievement.* Unpublished doctoral dissertation, University of Chicago, 1964.

Dunnell, J. P. *Input and output analysis of suburban elementary school districts.* Paper presented at the meeting of the American Educational Research Association, New York, February 1971. (ERIC Document Reproduction Service No. ED 047 366)

Ellison, R. L., James, L. R., Fox, D. G., & Taylor, C. W. *The identification of talent among Negro and white students from biographical data.* Washington, D.C.: National Center for Education Research and Development (DHEW/CE), 1970. (ERIC Document Reproduction Service No. ED 047 011)

Epstein, E. H. Social class, ethnicity and academic achievement: A cross-cultural approach. *Journal of Negro Education,* 1972, *41,* 202–215.

Estes, B. W. Influence of socioeconomic status on Wechsler Intelligence Scale for Children: An explanatory study. *Journal of Consulting Psychology,* 1953, *17,* 58–62.

Estes, B. W. Influence of socioeconomic status on Wechsler Intelligence Scale for Children: Addendum. *Journal of Consulting Psychology,* 1955, *19,* 225–226.

Evans, F. B. *A study of sociocultural characteristics of Mexican American and Anglo junior high school students and the relation of the characteristics to achievement.* Unpublished doctoral dissertation, New Mexico State University, 1969.

Felice, L. G. *Mexican-American self-concept and educational achievement: The effects of ethnic isolation and socioeconomic deprivation.* Paper presented at the meeting of the American Educational Research Association, New Orleans, February–March 1973. (ERIC Document Reproduction Service No. ED 075 126)

Fetters, W. B. *National longitudinal study of the high school class of 1972: Student questionnaires and test results by sex, high school program, ethnic category, and father's education* (No. HE 19.308:L86). Washington, D.C.: U.S. Government Printing Office, 1975.

Flanagan, J. C., & Cooley, W. W. *Project talent one year follow-up studies* (Cooperative Research Project No. 2333). Pittsburgh, Penn.: School of Education, University of Pittsburgh, 1966.

Flemming, C. M. Socioeconomic level and test performance. *British Journal of Educational Psychology,* 1943, *13,* 74–82.

Foster, L., & Nixon, M. Language, socioeconomic status and the school: An exploratory study. *Alberta Journal of Educational Research,* 1973, *19,* 87–194.

Freeman, F. N., Holzinger, K. J., & Mitchell, B. C. The influence of environment on the intelligence, school achievement and conduct of foster children. In G. M. Whipple (Ed.), *Nature and nurture: Their influence on intelligence* (The 27th yearbook of the National Society for the Study of Education, Pt. 1). Bloomington, Ill.: Public School Publishing, 1928.

Friedhoff, W. H. *Relationships among various measures of socioeconomic status, social class identification, intelligence and school achievement.* Unpublished doctoral dissertation, State University of Iowa, 1955.

Garms, W. I., & Smith, M. C. Educational need and its application to state school finance. *Journal of Human Resources,* 1970, *5,* 304–317.

Garrison, K. C. The relative influence of intelligence and sociocultural status upon the information possessed by first grade children. *Journal of Social Psychology,* 1932, *3,* 362–367.

Gibboney, R. A. Socioeconomic status and achievement in social studies. *Elementary School Journal,* 1959, *59,* 340–346.

Gough, H. G. Relationship of socioeconomic status to personality inventory and achievement test scores. *Journal of Educational Psychology,* 1949, *37,* 527–540.

Guthrie, J. T. Relationships of teaching method, socioeconomic status, and intelligence in concept formation. *Journal of Educational Psychology,* 1971, *62,* 345–351.

Guynn, K. P. *Effects of ethnicity and socioeconomic status on learning achievement of ninth and eleventh grade students.* Education specialist thesis, New Mexico State University, 1974. (ERIC Document Reproduction Service No. ED 088 655)

Harms, C. R. *The relationship between intelligence, physical growth, socioeconomic status, social acceptance and academic achievement in the elementary school* (Doctoral dissertation, Arizona State University, 1961). *Dissertation Abstracts International,* 1961, *22,* 2631. (University Microfilms No. 61-05368)

Hauser, R. M. *Socioeconomic background and educational performance* (Arnold M. & Caroline Rose Monograph Series). Washington, D.C.: American Sociological Association, 1971.

Havighurst, R. J., & Janke, L. L. Relations between ability and social status in a midwestern community: Ten-year-old children. *Journal of Educational Psychology,* 1944, *35,* 357–368.

Health Services and Mental Health Administration (Department of Health, Education and Welfare). *School achievement of children by demographic and socioeconomic factors, United States.* Rockville, Md.: Division of Emergency Health Services, 1971. (ERIC Document Reproduction Service No. ED 065 799)

Heimann, R. A., & Schenk, Q. F. Relations of social class and sex differences to high school achievement. *School Review,* 1954, *62*(4), 213–221.

Hennessy, J. J. *The relations between socioeconomic status and mental abilities in a late adolescent group.* Paper presented at the meeting of the American Educational Research Association, San Francisco, April 1976.

Herr, A., & Tobias, S. Achievement via programmed instruction and socioeconomic status. *Psychology in the Schools,* 1970, *1,* 53–56.

Hidreth, G. Occupational status and intelligence. *Personnel Journal,* 1935, *13,* 153–157.

Hill, E. H., & Giammatteo, M. C. Socioeconomic status and its relationship to school achievement in the elementary school. *Elementary English,* 1963, *40,* 265–270.

Hopkins, K. D. et al. *A technical report on the Colorado needs assessment program.* Boulder, Colo.: Laboratory of Educational Research, University of Colorado, 1977.

Howard, M. J., Hoops, H. R., & McKinnon, A. J. Language abilities of children with differing socioeconomic backgrounds. *Journal of Learning Disabilities,* 1970, *3,* 328–335.

Ikeda, K. *The association of racial status, socio economic status and measured ability upon academic performance in a liberal arts college.* Paper presented at the meeting of the Ohio Valley Sociological Society, Cleveland, April 1971.

James, A. N., & Pafford, W. N. Relationship between academic achievement in science and father's occupation. *Science Education,* 1973, *57,* 37–41.

Katzmann, T. M. Distribution and production in a big city elementary school system. *Yale Economic Essays,* 1968, *8,* 201–256.

Kerckhoff, A. C. *Antecedents of academic performance and educational attainment* (Final report, Project B-226). Chicago: Spencer Foundation, 1975.

Kiesling, H. J. Measuring a local government service: A study of school districts in New York State. *Review of Economics and Statistics,* 1967, *49,* 356–367.

Klein, C. A. Differences in science concepts held by children from three social-economic levels. *School Science and Mathematics,* 1971, *71,* 550–558.

Knief, L. M., & Stroud, J. B. Intercorrelations among various intelligence, achievement and social class scores. *Journal of Educational Psychology,* 1959, *50,* 117–120.

Kornhauser, A. W. The economic standing of parents and the intelligence of their children. *Journal of Educational Psychology,* 1918, *9,* 159–164.

Krus, P. H., & Rubin, R. A. *Use of family history data to predict educational functioning from ages five through seven.* Paper presented at the meeting of the American Educational Research Association, Chicago, April 1974. (ERIC Document Reproduction Service No. ED 090 274)

Kunz, J., & Meyer, J. E. Comparison of economically disadvantaged and economically advantaged kindergarten children. *Journal of Educational Research,* 1969, *62,* 302–305.

LaCivita, A. F., Kean, J. M., & Yamamoto, K. Socioeconomic status of children and acquisition of grammar. *Journal of Educational Research,* 1966, *60,* 71–74.

Lambert, N. M. Paired associate learning, social status and tests of logical concrete behavior as univariate and multivariate predictions of first grade reading achievement. *American Educational Research Journal,* 1970, *1,* 511–528.

Levine, D. U., Stephenson, R. S., & Mares, K. R. *An exploration of the use of socioeconomic census data to predict achievement and evaluate the effects of concentrated urban poverty among elementary schools in a big city.* Washington, D.C.: National Center for Educational Research and Development (DHEW/OE), 1973. (ERIC Document Reproduction Service No. ED 082 384)

Lloyd, D. N. *Reading achievement and its relationship to academic performance: Pt. III. Relationships of family background and third grade performance to sixth grade reading achievement* (Laboratory Paper #29). Rockville, Md.: National Institute of Mental Health, 1972. (ERIC Document Reproduction Service No. ED 064 704)

Lowe, W. E. *A study of the relationship between the socioeconomic status and the reading performance of Negro students enrolled in the public schools of Carolina County, Virginia.* Unpublished doctoral dissertation, George Washington University, 1969.

Marjoribanks, K. Environmental correlates of diverse mental abilities. *Journal of Experimental Education,* 1971, *39,* 64–68.

Marjoribanks, K. Environment, social class, and mental abilities. *Journal of Educational Psychology,* 1972, *63,* 103–109.

Mayeske, G. W. et al. *A study of our nation's schools: A working paper.* Washington, D.C.: U.S. Department of Health, Education and Welfare, Office of Education, 1969. (ERIC Document Reproduction Service No. ED 036 477)

Means, G. H., Means, R. S., Osborne, J. L., & Elsome, B. F. Task persistence as a function of verbal reinforcement and socioeconomic status. *California Journal of Educational Research,* 1973, *24,* 5–11.

Mensing, P. M., & Traxler, A. J. Social class differences in free recall of categorized and uncategorized lists in black children. *Journal of Educational Psychology,* 1973, *65,* 378–382.

Miller, G. W. Factors in school achievement and social class. *Journal of Educational Psychology,* 1970, *61,* 260–269.

Miller, W. H. Examination of children's daily schedules in three social classes and their relation to first grade reading achievement. *California Journal of Educational Research,* 1970, *21,* 100–110.

Milner, E. A study of the relationship between reading readiness in grade one school children and patterns of parent–child interaction. *Child Development,* 1951, *22,* 95–112.

Miner, B. Sociological background variables affecting school achievement. *Journal of Educational Research,* 1968, *61.* 372–381.

Montague, D. O. Arithmetic concepts of kindergarten children in contrasting socioeconomic areas. *Elementary School Journal,* 1964, *64,* 393–397.

Noll, V. H. Relationship of scores on Davis-Eells Games to socioeconomic status, intelligence test results and school achievement. *Educational and Psychological Measurement,* 1960, *20,* 119–129.

Ornstein, J. *Some findings of sociolinguistic research on Mexican-American college age bilinguals.* Paper prepared for Society for Applied Anthropology, Tucson, April 1973. (ERIC Document Reproduction Service No. ED 080 253)

Pattison, S. J., & Fielder, W. R. Social class and number concepts among young children. *California Journal of Educational Research,* 1969, *20,* 75–84.

Purves, A. C. *Literature education in ten countries: International studies in education.* Stockholm, Sweden: Almquist & Wiksell, 1973.

Raymond, R. Determinants of the quality of primary and secondary public education in West Virginia. *Journal of Human Resources,* 1968, *3,* 450–470.

Reid, W. R., & Schoer, L. A. Reading achievement,

social class and subtest pattern on the WISC. *Journal of Educational Research*, 1966, *59*, 469–472.

Robinson, M. L., & Meenes, M. Relationship between test intelligence of third grade Negro children and the occupation of their parents. *Journal of Negro Education*, 1947, *16*, 136–141.

Rodgers, D., Slade, K., & Coney, R. Oval language, reading ability and socioeconomic background in three grade one classes. *Alberta Journal of Educational Research*, 1974, *20*, 316–326.

Sewell, W. H., Haller, A. D., & Ohlendorf, G. W. The educational and early occupational status attainment process: Replication and revision. *American Sociological Review*, 1970, *35*, 1014–1027.

Shaw, D. C. The relation of socioeconomic status to educational achievement in grades four to eight. *Journal of Educational Research*, 1943, *37*, 197–201.

Smith, M. S. Equality of educational opporunity: The basic findings reconsidered. In F. Mosteller & D. P. Moynihan (Eds.), *On equality of educational opportunity*. New York: Random House, 1972.

Stanfiel, J. D. Socioeconomic status as related to aptitude, attrition, and achievement of college students. *Sociology of Education*, 1973, *46*, 480–488.

Thomas, J. A. Efficiency in education: An empirical study. *Administrator's Notebook*, 1962, *11*, 1–4.

Thorndike, R. L. *Reading comprehension in fifteen countries: International studies in education*. New York: Wiley, 1973.

Valenzuela, A. M. *The relationship between self-concept, intelligence, socioeconomic status and school achievement among Spanish-American children in*

Omaha. Education specialist thesis, University of Nebraska, 1971. (ERIC Document Reproduction Service No. ED 056 785)

White, K. R. *Data calculated from 1971 Colorado state assessment pilot results*. Unpublished manuscript, Laboratory of Educational Research, University of Colorado at Boulder, 1974.

White, K. R. *The relationship between short self-report measure of socioeconomic status and academic achievement*. Unpublished master's thesis, School of Education, University of Colorado, 1976.

Whiteman, M., & Deutsch, M. Social disadvantages as related to intelligence and language development. In I. S. Deutsch & A. Jensen (Eds.), *Social class, race and psychological development*. New York: Holt, Rinehart & Winston, 1968.

Winch, W. H. Christian and Jewish children in East-End elementary schools: Some comparative mental characteristics in relation to race and social class. *British Journal of Psychology*, 1930, *20*, 261–273.

Wolf, R. M. *The identification and measurement of environmental process variable related to intelligence*. Unpublished doctoral dissertation, University of Chicago, 1964.

Worley, S. E., & Story, W. E. Socioeconomic status and language facility of beginning first graders. *The Reading Teacher*, 1967, *20*, 400–403.

Wright, R. J., & Bean, A. G. The influence of socioeconomic status on the predictability of college performance. *Journal of Educational Measurement*, 1974, *11*, 277–284.

B. Studies Examined But Not Used in the Meta-Analysis

Asbury, C. A. Sociological factors related to discrepant achievement of white and black first graders. *Journal of Experimental Education*, 1973, *42*, 6–10.

Bell, A. E., & Aftanas, M. S. *A study of intellectual and socioeconomic factors related to rote learning, reasoning and academic achievement*. Paper presented at the meeting of the Canadian Psychological Association, Winnipeg, May 1970. (ERIC Document Reproduction Service No. ED 041 967)

Brown, E. K. *Underachievement—A case of inefficient cognitive processing*. Paper presented at the meeting of the American Educational Research Association, New York, February 1971. (ERIC Document Reproduction Service No. ED 048 419)

Brunner, E. de S. Educational attainment and economic status. *Teachers College Record*, 1948, *49*, 242–249.

Callaway, B. Pupil and family characteristics related to reading achievement. *Education*, 1972, *92*(3), 71–76.

Choppin, B. Social class and educational achievement. *Educational Research*, 1968, *10*, 213–217.

Chopra, S. L. Parental occupation and academic achievement of high school students in India. *Journal of Educational Research*, 1973, *60*, 359–362.

Coleman, A. B. Why the differences in achievement between children in different social classes? *Peabody Journal of Education*, 1968, *46*, 66–70.

Coleman, H. A. Relationship of socioeconomic status

to the performance of junior high students. *Journal of Experimental Education*, 1940, *9*, 61–63.

Collins, J. H., & Douglass, H. R. The socioeconomic status of the home as a factor in success in the junior high schools. *Elementary School Journal*, 1937, *38*, 107–113.

Courtis, S. A. The influence of certain social factors upon scores on the Stanford Achievement Tests. *Journal of Educational Research*, 1926, *13*, 311–329.

Donovan, D., Heyser, R., Kearney, P., & Olsen, J. *Distribution of educational performance and related factors in Michigan: The sixth report of the 1970–71 Michigan educational assessment program*. Lansing: Michigan State Department of Education, 1972. (ERIC Document Reproduction Service No. ED 072 088)

Flaugher, R. L. *Patterns of test performance by high school students of four ethnic identities* (Project Access Research Report No. 2). Princeton, N.J.: Educational Testing Service, 1971. (ERIC Document Reproduction Service No. ED 055 102)

Gilbert, C. D., & Mortenson, W. P. Problem solving behavior of first grade children from differing socioeconomic backgrounds. *School Science and Mathematics*, 1973, *13*, 398–403.

Greenberg, S., & Formanek, R. Social class differences in spontaneous verbal literature. *Child Study Journal*, 1974, *4*(3), 145–154.

Haggerty, M. E., & Nash, H. B. Mental capacity of children and paternal occupation. *Journal of Educational Psychology*, 1924, *15*, 559–572.

Hanson, E., & Robinson, H. A. Reading readiness and achievement of primary grade children of different socioeconomic strata. *The Reading Teacher*, 1967, *21*, 52–56.

Haught, B. F. The relationship of intelligence of college freshmen to parental occupation. *Psychological Monographs*, 1938, *50*(5, Whole No. 225).

Hawkes, T. H., & Furst, N. F. Race, socioeconomic situation, achievement, IQ, and teacher ratings of students' behavior as factors relating to anxiety in upper elementary school children. *Sociology of Education*, 1971, *44*, 333–350.

Holley, C. E. The relationship between persistence in school and home conditions. In G. M. Whipple (Ed.), *The 15th yearbook of the National Society for the Study of Education* (Pt. 2). Bloomington, Ill.: Public School Publishing, 1916.

Jantz, R. K. Effects of sex, race, IQ and SES on the reading scores of sixth graders for both levels and gains in performance. *Psychology in the Schools*, 1974, *11*, 90–94.

Jensen, A. R. Interaction of Level I and Level II abilities with race and socioeconomic status: *Journal of Educational Psychology*, 1974, *66*, 99–111.

Jones, D. C., & Carr Saunders, A. M. The relation between intelligence and social status among orphan children. *British Journal of Psychology*, 1927, *17*, 343–364.

Keough, J. J. Relationship of socioeconomic factors and achievement in arithmetic. *The Arithmetic Teacher*, 1960, *7*, 231–237.

Kniveton, B. H., & Pike, C. L. R. Social class, intelligence and the development of children's play interests. *Journal of Child Psychology*, 1972, *13*, 167–181.

Lavin, D. E. *The prediction of academic performance*. New York: Russell Sage Foundation, 1965.

Linton, T. H. *A study of the relationship of global self-concept, academic self-concept and academic achievement among Anglo and Mexican-American sixth grade students*. Paper presented at the meeting of the American Educational Research Association, Chicago, April 1972. (ERIC Document Reproduction Service No. ED 063 053)

Michigan State Department of Education. *Distribution of educational performance and related factors in Michigan* (Assessment Report No. 5). Lansing: Author, 1970. (ERIC Document Reproduction Service No. ED 046 988) (a)

Michigan State Department of Education. *Levels of educational performance and related factors in Michigan* (Assessment Report No. 4). Lansing: Author, 1970. (ERIC Document Reproduction Service No. ED 046 987) (b)

Michigan State Department of Education. *Distribution of educational performance and related factors in Michigan: A supplement*. Lansing: Author, 1971. (ERIC Document Reproduction Service No. ED 059 254)

Mortenson, W. P. Selected pre-reading tasks, socioeconomic status, and sex, visual and auditory discrimination. *The Reading Teacher*, 1968, *22*, 45–49.

Neighbors, O. J. Retardation in the schools and some of the causes. *Elementary School Teacher*, 1910–11, *11*, 119–135.

Osborn, R. C. How is intellectual performance related to social and economic background. *Journal of Educational Psychology*, 1943, *34*, 215–228. (ERIC Document Reproduction Service No. ED 080 253)

Peck, R. F. *A gross-national comparison of sex and socioeconomic differences in aptitude and achievement*. Paper presented at the meeting of the American Educational Research Association, New York, February 1971. (ERIC Document Reproduction Service No. ED 049 315)

Rose, A. W., & Rose, H. C. Intelligence, sibling position and sociocultural background as factors in arithmetic performance. *The Arithmetic Teacher*, 1961, *8*, 50–56.

Ruddell, R. B., & Graves, B. W. Socio-ethnic status and language achievement of first grade children. *Elementary English*, 1968, *45*, 635–642.

Ryker, M. J., Rogers, E. C., & Beaujard, S. P. Six selected factors influencing educational achievement of children from broken homes. *Education*, 1971, *91*, 200–211.

Schneider, J. M., & Brookover, W. E. *Academic environments and elementary school achievement*. Paper presented at the meeting of the American Educational Research Association, Chicago, April 1974. (ERIC Document Reproduction Service No. ED 091 858)

Sukhendra, L. C. Cultural deprivation and academic achievement. *Journal of Educational Research*, 1969, *62*, 435–438.

Telegdy, G. A. The relationship between socioeconomic status and school readiness. *Psychology in the Schools*, 1974, *11*(3), 351–356.

Templin, M. C. Relation of speech and language development to intelligence and socioeconomic status. *Volta Review*, 1958, *60*, 331–334.

Williams, M. M. *Race, poverty and educational achievement in an urban environment*. Paper presented at the American Psychological Association Annual Convention, Honolulu, September 1972. (ERIC Document Reproduction Service No. ED 070 797)

35

A Meta-Analysis of Pretest Sensitization
Effects in Experimental Design

Victor L. Willson and Richard R. Putnam

A meta-analysis of outcomes from 32 studies investigating pretest effects was conducted. All outcomes were computed as standardized differences between pretested and nonpretested groups. Eleven other variables were coded for each outcome. Initial descriptive statistics were indicative of differences between randomized and nonrandomized studies, so all further analyses were based on randomized group outcomes (n = 134). For all outcomes the average effect size was +.22, indicating the general elevating effect of pretest on posttest. Cognitive outcomes were raised .43, attitude outcomes .29, personality .48, and others about .00 standard deviations. Sixty-four percent of all effects were positive, and 81 percent of the cognitive effects were positive. Duration of time between pre- and posttesting was related to effect size, with effect size generally being small for durations less than a day or over 1 month. Year of publication, sample size, presence of experimental treatment, and sameness or difference of pretest and posttest were not significantly related to effect size. Researchers must continue to include pretest as a design variable when it is present, and to estimate its effect.

The pretest is a common condition of experimental and nonexperimental research. Campbell and Stanley (1966) discussed it in their landmark review of experimental design considerations. Bracht and Glass (1968) and Welch and Walberg (1970) have presented more recent reviews of the effect of pretesting on posttest scores. Jaeger (1975) has advocated the use of pretests for many evaluation and research applications. The independent experimental contribution of pretests to dependent variables is unknown. Welch and Walberg's (1970) summary listed previous results in the usual review format of significance or nonsignificance. They concluded that the long-term cognitive effects are small or nil, while there may be short-term effects. These effects, they suggested, are greater for attitude tests than for cognitive tests.

From Victor L. Willson and Richard R. Putnam, "A Meta-Analysis of Pretest Sensitization Effects in Experimental Design," 19(2) *American Educational Research Journal* 249-258 (Summer 1982). Copyright 1982, American Educational Research Association, Washington, D.C. Reprinted by permission.

The recent work of Glass (1976) and his colleagues and students in statistical review of research, termed meta-analysis, allows a systematic analysis of the pretest experimental effect. Instead of relying on binary decisions about significance, the pretest effect is examined as a standardized difference between pretested and nonpretested groups. This study estimates the pretest effect utilizing meta-analytic techniques and investigates moderator variables associated with the potential pretest effect.

PROCEDURES

Literature Search

The meta-analysis techniques for integrating existing research findings as proposed by Glass (1976) were used to explore pretest sensitization and to determine the nature of its effect. Briefly summarized, this approach requires that either all studies or a sufficiently large sample on a given topic be located. Each study is treated as an individual unit of analysis with multiple dependent variables and/or multiple comparison groups considered as separate samples.

The method used in compiling the literature for examination was twofold. The Automated Information-Retrieval Service (AIRS) at Texas A&M was employed to retrieve relevant information from the Educational Resources Information Center (ERIC), Psychological Abstracts, and the Social Science Citation Index. Also, references cited in the Welch and Walberg (1970) article were reviewed and a branching technique was used in an effort to locate all possible literature of interest to the present study. The studies cited by Welch and Walberg, as well as their own results are included here.

When the task of locating the material for study was completed, the research reports were screened for appropriateness of content, and articles focusing on outcomes other than human educational and psychological phenomena were omitted (e.g. animal studies, social interaction studies, neonatal responses studies). Also, studies in which all groups were pretested were omitted. A total of 33 studies was located, including 4 dissertations which had recoverable data or for which data were obtained from the authors through correspondence.

Variables Coded

The variables extracted from each study in the literature search were year of publication, subjects' grade in school or age, sex of subjects (all males, all females, or mixed), duration of time between pretest and posttest, citation (or not) of test reliability, sample size, randomization or nonrandomization in selection of subjects, random or nonrandom assignment of subjects to groups, presence or absence of relevant treatment between pretest and posttest, category of dependent variable, similarity or dissimilarity of pretest and posttest, and effect size of pretest on posttest. The variables were chosen on the basis of theoretical relevance to the pretest effect, interest for experimental design, and utility in previous meta-analysis. For example, year of publication has been shown by Smith and Glass (1977) and Glass, Smith, and Barton (Note 1) to be related to effect size in several areas of research. Smith and Glass (1977) showed a similar effect for duration of treatment of psychotherapy outcomes. They also compared randomized with nonrandomized experiments, demonstrating no difference in psychotherapy outcome effect sizes.

Dependent variables in each study were first coded by name of test or scale, but it soon became apparent that a larger categorization was needed. Most outcomes were easily categorized as cognitive (achievement test score) or attitudinal. While five other categories were ultimately distinguishable (physical performance, rating of performance, projective score, personality scales, and choice preference), the number of outcomes for these was found to be small compared with those of the first two categories.

Duration of time between pre- and posttesting was categorized ex post facto into four categories: (1) hours, with duration of 2 hours or less; (2) days, with duration less than or equal to 7; (3) weeks, with duration less than 13; and (4) months, with duration between 1 and 9. No studies researched in this paper investigated pretest effects for duration greater than 9 months.

Effect sizes were computed from summary statistics reported by authors. Group means were required in order to include a study except when t-statistics, F-statistics with one degree of freedom, or point biserial correlations were reported (see Glass, 1978, for procedures designed to equate statistics to effects). Each experimental design was reduced to one or more of the following forms (see Campbell & Stanley, 1966):

$$
\begin{array}{llll}
\text{I.} & \text{R} \quad \text{O} \quad \text{XO} & \text{II.} & \text{R} \quad \text{O} \quad \text{O} \\
& \text{R} \quad\quad \text{XO} & & \text{R} \quad\quad \text{O} \\
\text{III.} & \quad\; \text{O} \quad \text{XO} & \text{IV.} & \quad\;\; \text{O} \quad \text{O} \\
& \quad\quad \text{XO} & & \quad\quad \text{O}
\end{array}
$$

Thus, if no comparison of group means conformed to types I–IV, the study was ignored. For each form I–IV the effect size was defined as:

$$
\text{Effect size} = \frac{\bar{X} \text{ pretested} - \bar{X} \text{ not pretested}}{s_{\text{not pretested group}}} \tag{1}
$$

When the standard deviation of the not-pretested group was unavailable and not recoverable, a pooled variance statistic was used. If mean square error in a study was available, its square root served as standard deviation. If a t-statistic or F-statistic was reported, the following transformation allowed estimation of the effect size (Glass, 1978):

$$
\text{Effect} = t(1/n_1 + 1/n_2)^{\frac{1}{2}}, \quad t = \sqrt{F}, \tag{2}
$$

where n_1, n_2 = sample sizes for the two groups. It is possible that some bias results in such cases if the pretest affects variance of posttest scores. A test of this hypothesis was made by forming an F-ratio of pretested group variance divided by unpretested group variance for 23 identifiable cases. Two of the 23 (8.7%) were significant at $p = .05$, indicating no variance bias. In some designs it was possible to estimate mean square error from the means of two or more control groups, none of which was pretested (all were required to be of the same form for estimation). For these groups mean square between was computed and the square root taken to be an estimate of group variability in the absence of pretest effect. The expected value of this mean is the population variance of error. The effect was then computed using equation (2). Irrelevant crossing variables were eliminated in factorial designs by averaging across them to obtain marginal means appropriate to forms I to IV.

In some designs several effects were computable utilizing different groups. This was commonly the result of several different treatments being administered. Each possible effect was coded in these designs. When several dependent variables were examined in a study a separate effect was computed for each dependent variable. This resulted in a few studies yielding a large number of effects. The number of effects per study varied from 1 to 23. In some studies dependent variables were all of one category (e.g., attitude) while in others dependent variables represented two or three categories of outcome.

The *sign* of the effect size is of great importance to interpretation of results. For cognitive outcomes a positive effect implies a higher test score for the pretested group. For attitude outcomes positive effect was defined as a more favorable attitude toward the subject. Sign of the effects was reversed to fit this definition. For behaviors and personality measures the positive direction reflected the experimental aim of the study; for example, avoidance behaviors should decrease in a systematic desensitization to fear of snakes. Thus, fewer avoidance behaviors was a positive outcome in this case. In a science curriculum study one dependent variable was the number of high school student activities related to science. An increase in this number was taken as a positive outcome.

Data Analysis

The first analysis was the extraction of descriptive statistics. Of special importance are the distributions of effects for randomized and nonrandomized studies. If the distributions are statistically indistinguishable then they may be pooled for subsequent analyses, as Smith and Glass (1977) did for psychotherapy outcomes. If different, the nonrandomized effects are presumed to have an unknown bias and are not investigated further. This bias might be due to selection.

The next analysis was examination of the relationship of each coded variable to effect size. Correlation, multiple regression, and analysis of variance all were applied, depending on the nominal or interval character of the variables.

RESULTS

Thirty-two separate studies were analyzed with the pretest effect as a primary focus. From these studies 164 separate effects were extracted and coded with the other independent variables. Summary statistics for these effects are given in Table I, along with summary statistics for subsets of the studies based on randomized or nonrandomized assignments to pretest conditions. The randomized effects have a different mean ($t = 1.72$, $df = 75.6$; $p < .09$, Satterthwaite's approximation using unequal variances) and different variance ($F = 3.12$, $df = 133, 29$; $p < .01$) from the nonrandomized effects. Consequently, it is concluded that nonrandomized study effects are biased systematically and are excluded from further analysis.

Summary statistics for randomized study effects are given in Table II. Effects of subjects who received a treatment (Form I) had a mean of .13, not significantly different from untreated subject effects, mean .39. Both distributions are skewed positively.

The time between pretest and posttest as measured in hours, days, weeks, and months is related to effect size ($F = 3.73$, $df = 126$). The pattern of means suggests small effects for delays of less than 1 day or over 1 month with larger effects for several days to 2 weeks. There are many gaps in the intervals observed in the studies. Most short delays observed were of a duration less than 1 hour. All studies with delays longer than a few hours and less than a week utilized 2- or 3-day durations. Other studies used delays of 7, 10, 11, and 12 days, while longer term studies used 2 weeks, 35 days, 45 days, 10 weeks, 91 days, and 9 months. A systematic investigation of delay time between pretest and posttest would help to clarify the nonlinear relationship apparent from these data.

Category of outcome yields some slightly surprising results. Cognitive effects under pretest conditions are almost a half standard deviation above

TABLE I
Summary Statistics for Pretest Effect Size Distribution

	N	Mean	SD	Percentage Positive Outcomes	Max.	P_{90}	P_{50}	P_{10}	Min.
All Studies	164	.17	1.04	57	4.46	1.15	.09	−.64	−3.25
Nonrandomized Studies	30	−.04	.63	53	1.15	.44	.04	−.61	−2.35
Randomized Studies	134	.22	1.11	63	4.64	1.31	.06	−.68	−3.25

TABLE II

Summary Statistics of Randomized Study Effects for Selected Independent Variables

	N	Mean	SD	Percentage Positive Outcome	Max.	P_{90}	P_{50}	P_{10}	Min.
Treated Groups	89	.13	1.11		4.16	1.16	.04	−.89	−3.25
Untreated Groups	45	.39	1.09		4.46	1.54	.19	−.49	−1.63

$t = 1.33$ $df = 132$

	N	Mean	Omnibus F-Statistic	Mean Square Error	Duncan's Multiple Range
Duration			3.37*	1.13	
Hours	38	.14			M H D W
Days	38	.44*			
Weeks	15	.81*			
Months	39	−.15			
Outcome Category			1.43	1.20	
Cognitive	32	.43			
Attitude	62	.29			
Physical Performance	6	−.13			
Ratings of Performance	7	.12			
Projective	8	.48			
Preference	8	−.08			
Personality	11	−.55*			
Pretest-Posttest			.415	1.20	
Same	99	.25			PS C 4 9 11 HS AD
Different	35	.11			
Grade/Age of Subjects			6.33*	.987	
Adult	18	−.40*			
College	88	.29*			
High School	4	.18			
Grade 11	12	.04			
Grade 9	8	.12			
Grade 4	2	.10			
Preschool	2	4.06			
Correlation with Effect			N	R	
Year of Publication			134	−.12	
Sample Size			134	−.06	
Reliability of Outcome Reported? (1 = yes, 0 = no)			112	−.09	
Random Selection of Subjects from Population? (1 = yes, 0 = no)			134	−.05	

* $p < .05$.

nonpretested groups, and 81 percent of the effects are positive. For attitude outcomes the effect mean is about .29 with 62 percent of the effects positive. This is a reversal of the conclusion of Bracht and Glass (1968) and Welch and Walberg (1970). Closer examination of the cognitive outcomes provides some useful results, given in Table III. No clear conclusions about delay between pretest and posttest are possible, given the large effects that occurred for duration of 1 week's order of magnitude, since it is based on only two effects in a study concerning preschool children. Pretest effect appears to be larger for untreated groups than for treated groups.

For attitude outcomes many results for cognitive outcomes are reversed. Pretest effect appears larger for delays on the order of a few days to 2 weeks. Pretest effect is greater on different content posttests, and there is little difference in effect size between treated and untreated groups.

Personality measure outcomes had a large negative pretest effect ($-.55$). The meaning of this effect must be considered in terms of these measures. A negative effect was typically associated with change toward an undesirable psychological state (e.g., neurotic condition, hysteria). These negative effects tend to mask the generally positive effects from most other measures.

Sex effects were not estimable since the overwhelming majority of studies (all but two) had mixed sex groups. Grade or age level of subjects is

TABLE III

Summary Statistics of Randomized Study Effects for Cognitive and Attitude Outcomes

	Cognitive Outcomes			Attitude Outcomes		
	N	Mean	F	N	Mean	F
Duration			54.60*			1.00
Hours	16	.28		13	−.05	
Days	2	.17		30	.51	
Weeks	2	4.06*		13	.31	
Months	12	.06		6	−.13	
Pretest—Posttest			.63			2.63
Same	25	.51		45	.14	
Different	5	.81		17	.68	
Treatment						.004
Treated Group	26	.34		34	.30	
Untreated Group	6	.81		28	.28	
Grade/Age of Subjects			30.31*			.81
Adult	2	.01		2	−.35	
College	13	.30		56	.34	
High School	4	.18		—	—	
Grade 11	6	.10		4	−.02	
Grade 9	8	.12		—	—	
Grade 4	2	.14		—	—	
Preschool	2	4.06*		—	—	

* $p < .05$.

significantly related to effect ($F = 6.33$, $df = 6,127$; $p < .05$) but the significance is due to two cognitive outcomes observed with preschool children and the adult effects that have a number of personality test effects. Duncan's range tests indicate homogeneity among school and college students.

Year of publication, sample size, and design characteristics (report of reliability, random selection of subjects from population) were nonsignificantly correlated with effect size. No multiple regressions were statistically or practically (R-square over .05) significant.

DISCUSSION

The results of this meta-analysis of pretest sensitization effects provide two conclusions which have implications for educational, psychological, and sociological research. The first is that there is a general pretest effect which cannot be safely ignored. Nonrandomized studies with pretests must be viewed with additional suspicion, since the results of the data analysis reported here indicate a systematic bias due to pretest in these studies. Selection of subjects is the likely internal validity threat.

The second conclusion about pretest effects is that they do not appear to be uniform across psychological domains. The differences in effects under treatment conditions for cognitive and affective outcomes can be explained by reactive interference of treatments in cognitive situations. Treatments seem not to effect affective outcomes similarly.

The interesting reversal of effects under similar or dissimilar pretest to posttest conditions for cognitive and affective outcomes might be explained as follows. Cognitive gains will be largest with memory and practice effects when pretest and posttest are the same. Gains might still be made with dissimilar tests due to familiarity with testing procedure. For affective outcomes there may be halo effects in which everyone feels better on second attitude testing combined with regression when the pretest is dissimilar to the posttest. This presumes groups were extreme with respect to norms for pretest. In at least four studies involving affective outcomes, subjects were selected for some extreme condition.

A subset of the pretest sensitization literature has been concerned with the interaction of pretest condition and treatment. Globally this hypothesized interaction does not appear to be large, if it exists at all, since the effect size for treated and untreated groups are so similar.

The studies reported here are not sufficiently exhaustive to provide definitive statements about conditions for variation of pretest sensitization, but promising areas of investigation are change in cognitive effects over grade and age levels, transfer of pretest effect to different posttests, and change in effect over delay time between pretest and posttest from hours to months.

REFERENCE NOTE

1. GLASS, G. V, SMITH, M. L., & BARTON, M. A. Methods of integrative analysis (Report on Grant #NIE-G-78-0148). Boulder: University of Colorado, Laboratory of Educational Research, August 1979.

REFERENCES

Listed below are references as well as bibliographic items that were used in the data analysis and may be of interest to the reader.

ANDERSON, E. J. The effects of combined learning cues on teacher learning outcomes. *Journal of Research in Science Teaching*, 1978, *15*, 221–226.

BRACHT, G. H., & GLASS, G. V. The external validity of experiments. *American Educational Research Journal*, 1968, *5*, 437–474.

CAMPBELL, D. T., & STANLEY, J. C. *Experimental and quasi-experimental designs for research.* Chicago: Rand-McNally, 1966.

COWAN, G., & KOMORITA, S. S. The effects of forewarning and pretesting on attitude change. *Educational and Psychological Measurement*, 1971, *31*, 431–439.

ENTWISLE, D. R. Interactive effects of pretesting. *Educational and Psychological Measurement*, 1961, *21*, 607–620.

GASKELL, G. D., THOMAS, E. A. C., & FARR, R. M. Effects of pretesting on measures of individual risk preference. *Journal of Personality and Social Psychology*, 1973, *25*, 192–298.

GLASS, G. V. Primary, secondary, and meta-analysis of research. *Educational Research*, 1976, *5*(10), 3–8.

GLASS, G. V. Integrating findings: the meta-analysis of research. *Review of Research in Education*, 1978, *6*, 351–379.

GREITZER, G., & JEFFREY, W. E. Negative effects of pretest in training conservation of length. *Developmental Psychology*, 1973, *9*, 435.

HARTLEY, J. The effect of pretesting on posttest performance. *Instructional Science*, 1973, *2*, 193–214.

HUNT, R. G., & LICHTMAN, C. M. Pretest influences in evaluating organizational effects of a supervisory counseling training program. *Journal of Applied Behavioral Science*, 1972, *8*, 503–507.

ISRAEL, A. C., BECKER, R. E., & NEILANS, T. H. Contribution of pretesting to several measures of semantic desensitization effectiveness. *Journal of Consulting and Clinical Psychology*, 1977, *45*, 1197–1198.

JAEGER, R. M. Some new developments and discoveries for evaluative analysis. *CEDR Quarterly*, 1975, *9*(3), 3–7.

JONES, J. M. Reactive effects of pretesting and test length in attitude research. *Psychological Reports*, 1973, *33*, 107–114.

KAZDIN, A. E. Effect of suggestion and pretesting on avoidance reduction in fearful subjects. *Journal of Behavior Therapy and Experimental Psychiatry*, 1973, *4*, 213–221.

KROEKER, L. L. Pretesting as a confounding variable in evaluating an encounter group. *Journal of Counseling Psychology*, 1974, *21*, 548–552.

LANA, R. E. A further investigation of the pretest treatment effect. *Journal of Applied Psychology*, 1959, *43*, 421–422.

LANA, R. E. Pretest treatment interaction effects in attitudinal studies. *Psychological Bulletin*, 1959, *56*, 293–300.

LANA, R. E. The influence of the pretest on order effects on persuasive communications. *Journal of Abnormal and Social Psychology*, 1964, *69*(3), 337–341.

LANA, R. E. Inhibitory effects of a pretest on opinion change. *Educational and Psychological Measurement*, 1966, *26*(1), 139–150.

LANA, R. E., & KING, D. J. Learning factors as determiners of pretest sensitization. *Journal of Applied Psychology*, 1960, *44*, 189–191.

LANA, R. E., & MENAPACE, R. H. Subject commitment and demand characteristics in attitude change. *Journal of Personality and Social Psychology*, 1971, *20*, 136–140.

McCAULEY, C., TEGER, A. I., & KOGAN, N. Effect of the pretest in the risky shift paradigm. *Journal of Personality and Social Psychology*, 1971, *20*, 379–381.

NOSANCHUK, T. A., & HARE, R. D. Word recognition threshold as a function of pretest sensitization. *Psychonomic Science*, 1966, *6*, 51–52.

PAULING, F. J., & LANA, R. E. The effects of pretest commitment and information upon opinion change. *Educational and Psychological Measurement*, 1969, *29*, 653–663.

ROSNOW, R. L., HOLPER, H. M., & GITTER, A. G. More on reactive effects of pretesting in attitude research: Demand characteristics or subject commitment? *Educational and Psychological Measurement*, 1973, *33*, 7–17.

ROSNOW, R. L., & SULS, J. M. Reactive effects of pretesting in attitude research. *Journal of Personality and Social Psychology*, 1970, *15*, 338–343.

SHEARN, D. F., & RANDOLPH, D. L. Effects of reality therapy methods applied in the classroom. *Psychology in the Schools*, 1978, *15*, 79–82.

SMITH, M. L., & GLASS, G. V. Meta-analysis of psychotherapy outcome studies. *American Psychologist*, 1977, *32*, 752–760.

SOLOMON, R. L. An extension of control group design. *Psychological Bulletin*, 1949, *46*, 137–150.

SPANOS, N. P., McPEAKE, J. D., & CARTER, W. Effects of pretesting on response to a visual hallucination suggestion in hypnotic subjects. *Journal of Personality and Social Psychology*, 1973, *28*, 293–297.

WELCH, W. W., & WALBERG, H. J. Pretest and sensitization effects in curriculum evaluation. *American Educational Research Journal*, 1970, *7*, 605–614.

AUTHORS

VICTOR L. WILLSON, Associate Professor of Educational Psychology, Department of Educational Psychology, Texas A&M University, College Station, TX 77843. *Specializations:* Research methodology, measurement.

RICHARD R. PUTNAM, Lecturer, Department of Educational Psychology, Texas A&M University, College Station, TX 77843. *Specializations:* Learning, development, administration of student services.

36

Methodologically Based Discrepancies in Compensatory Education Evaluation

William M.K. Trochim

Meta-analysis of several hundred evaluations of Title I compensatory education programs shows that two distinct research designs consistently yield different results. The norm-referenced model portrays programs as positively effective while the regression-discontinuity design shows them to be ineffective or even slightly harmful. Three potential biasing factors are discussed for each design—residual regression artifacts; attrition and time-of-testing problems in the norm-referenced design; and assignment, measurement, and data preparation problems in the regression-discontinuity design. In lieu of more definitive research the tentative conclusion is that in practice the norm-referenced design over-estimates the program effect while the regression-discontinuity design underestimates it.

$\mathcal{T}$he complex nature of social phenomena and the inherent limitations of available research methodologies suggest that definitive conclusions about the effectiveness of social programs can best be approached through multiple replications of evaluative studies. However, even when multiple replications exist, discrepancies in their results can act to prevent generalizations across studies. This article discusses a conflict in the results obtained from a large number of individual evaluations which appears to be best explained by methodological factors. The conflict arises in compensatory education evaluation and, specifically, in the evaluation of programs funded under Title I

AUTHOR'S NOTE: *This work was supported by NIE Grant G-81-0086 (William Trochim, Principal Investigator), NSF Grant DAR 7820374 (Robert Boruch, Principal Investigator), NIE Grant G-79-0128 (Robert Boruch, Principal Investigator), and NSF Grant BNS 792-5571 (Donald T. Campbell, Principal Investigator).*

From William M.K. Trochim, "Methodologically Based Discrepancies in Compensatory Education Evaluation" 6 (3) *Evaluation Review* 443-480 (August 1982). Copyright 1982, Sage Publications, Inc.

of the Elementary and Secondary Education Act of 1965. When individual estimates of program effect are averaged by research design across studies of similar Title I compensatory education programs, the results for one commonly used research design portray the programs as positively effective while the results obtained using another design show the programs to have a zero or slightly negative effect.

This pattern of results raises several important issues. Perhaps most obvious is the question of why the discrepancy occurs at all. Certainly the results cast doubts on any notion that the two research methods in question can be considered "equivalent" or can be expected to yield "equivalent" results. Assuming that the programs studied are fairly similar, it seems reasonable that there might be definable methodological factors associated with the use of each design which help explain why they yield different results.

The identification of design-related bias is a meta-evaluative issue worthy of consideration. Ideally, it would be best to vary designs and uses of the designs systematically across studies so that design components which lead to discrepancies in results could be more definitively identified. This has not been done in this context, however, and given typical financial and temporal restraints, is not likely to be practically feasible in many other settings. A more reasonable approach to this meta-analysis problem involves the post hoc examination of studies in the hopes of identifying major design factors related to conflicting results. In addition to this meta-evaluative problem are issues involving the interaction of substantive and methodological theory. One such issue concerns which of the two designs, if either, should be given more importance in the interpretation of the effectiveness of the programs in question. Another problem arises because design-related bias can act as a source of conflict between the policy-making and evaluation communities. Certainly the credibility of evaluation to some extent rests on the ability of evaluators and methodologists to isolate design factors which lead to conflicting results.

This article discusses several of the most important likely methodological reasons for the discrepancy in results observed in this research context. Some of these explanations are related to general characteristics of the designs themselves while others are more germane to the use of the designs within the specific context of compensatory education. The remainder of this article involves a brief description of the research context and the designs involved, the presentation of evidence for the discrepancy in the results, and a discussion of several of the more plausible potential explanations for this discrepancy.

THE RESEARCH CONTEXT: TITLE I OF ESEA

The results discussed here are set in the context of the largest single federal compensatory education program—Title I of the Elementary and Secondary Education Act (ESEA) of 1965. In 1979, over $5.5 billion was authorized by Congress for implementation of Title I requirements, and nearly $3.4 billion was appropriated. Approximately 9 million low-income children were served and between 5 and 6 million of these were of elementary school age. Nearly 87% of all public school districts in the United States received Title I funds (National Center for Education Statistics [NCES], 1979) which support between 3 and 4% of all national elementary and secondary education expenses (U.S. Office of Education, 1979). Title I programs are usually (but not necessarily) confined to basic skill areas such as mathematics, reading, and language arts.

Title I is the first major social legislation which specifically required routine evaluation of its programs. The evaluation system which was constructed is characterized by a common measurement metric and by three alternative research designs, one of which a school district may choose for evaluation purposes. The metric, termed the Normal Curve Equivalent (NCE) Score is a standard score with a mean of 50 and a standard deviation of 21.06. District-level estimates of program effect which are generated by the chosen design are reported on this scale to enable aggregation of gains at the state and national level.

The three research designs have been termed Model A: the Norm-Referenced Model; Model B: the Control Group Model; and Model C: the Special Regression Model. A recent national survey of school districts (NCES, 1979) estimates that of the school districts which responded, 87% had Title I programs in the 1978-1979 school year and 63% had used a definable research model. Of those which had used a model, 86% used Model A, about 2% used Model B, about 2% used Model C, and 10% made use of an alternative or locally developed model. In a less formal attempt to contact users of Model B and C, however, Trochim (1980) found approximately 40 school districts using Model C and fewer than five which used Model B. Because so few instances of Model B could be located, this research is concerned only with a comparison of results for Models A and C.[1] For purposes of exposition, Model A is termed here the NR (Norm-Referenced) Design while Model C is labelled the RD (Regression-Discontinuity) Design because this latter nomenclature is more widely recognized outside of Title I compensatory education than the "Special Regression" label. These two designs can be described briefly as follows:

The Norm-Referenced (NR) Design. Under this design students are administered a test which is used for assignment to the Title I program. Assignment might be made on the basis of some cutoff score on this test, with all students scoring below a certain selected value being assigned to the program, or test scores may be used in an advisory way with qualitative judgements as the deciding factors. For example, Tallmadge (1978) states: "If selection test results conflict with teacher opinions, then these opinions may be used to change the assignment of individual children[p. 6]." Once program students have been selected they are given a pretest, and after the program are given a posttest. The analysis involves computing the mean pretest and posttest scale scores for the program students who took both tests, converting these to the equivalent national norming group percentiles using tables supplied by the test producer, and finally, converting these percentiles into average NCE scores. The estimate of program effect is simply the difference between the posttest and pretest average NCE values for the program students. The crucial assumption in this design is that in the absence of any program the average percentile rank of the group (and hence, the average NCE value) would be the same on the pretest and the posttest. That is, in the null case the program group should on both tests maintain the same relative position within the population of the norming sample. In effect, the implied or pseudo-comparison group is a hypothetical subgroup of the norming population which achieved the same average pretest percentile score as the program group. Gains in average percentile rank or average NCE score theoretically reflect gains of the program students relative to this pseudo-comparison group.

The Regression-Discontinuity (RD) Design. With this design students are assigned to program or comparison groups by means of a cutoff score on the pretest. For example, all students scoring below the 30th percentile on an achievement pretest might be assigned to the Title I program while all others would act as the comparison group. After the program, students in both groups are administered a posttest. Although the design is usually termed the "Special Regression Model" within Title I circles, it is in essence the regression-discontinuity design as described in Cook and Campbell (1979) and Campbell and Stanley (1966). Hypothetical data from such a design are illustrated in Figure 1. Each point on the figure represents a single pretest and posttest score for an individual student. Program group student scores are indicated by an "X" while comparison group student scores are indicated with an "0". The cutoff value in this simulated data is a pretest score of 0. Figure 2 indicates the regression lines for these data. The dashed line in the figure is the extension of the comparison group regresion line into the program group pretest range. This dashed line represents the program group posttest performance which would be expected if the program had no effect. In this example the actual

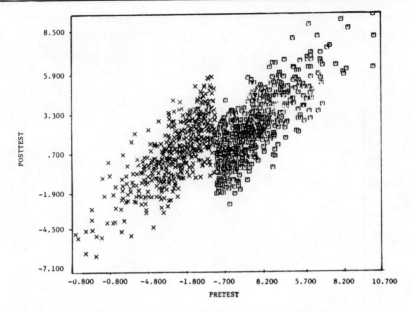

Figure 1: Hypothetical Data for Regression-Discontinuity in Compensatory
         Education

program group regression line is displaced above this projection for any pretest
value. One might conclude that on the average the program resulted in an increase
in posttest performance over what would be expected normally. In Title I
evaluation the statistical analysis of data from the RD design involves computing
separate linear regression lines for the program and comparison groups and
estimating the difference between the projection of the comparison group line and
the program group line at both the cuttoff value and the program gropu pretest
mean.

These two designs represent distinct methodological traditions in
applied social research. NR-type designs have been used or implied in
much of the educational research which relies on normative information
from standardized tests for an estimate of the growth which would be
expected in the absence of special training (Tallmadge, 1980). The RD
design represents a tradition in quasi-experimental pretest-posttest
control group designs as illustrated in the work of Campbell and Stanley
(1966) and Cook and Campbell (1979). Conflicts in the results yielded by
these two designs within the context of compensatory education are

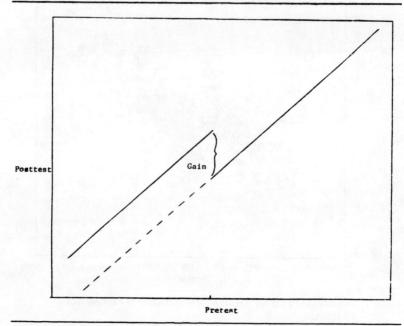

Figure 2: Regression Lines for Hypothetical Regression-Discontinuity Data in
Figure 1

therefore likely to have implications for instances of these two traditions
in other applied social research arenas.

THE PATTERN OF RESULTS

Three major sources of information provide evidence for a discrepancy in the average gains obtained when using the NR and RD
designs—interviews of Title I evaluators at the local and regional levels,
review of relevant Title I literature, and the distributions of gain
estimates obtained from Title I programs.

Trochim (1980) reports the results of interviews conducted with at
least one representative of each of the ten Title I regional Technical
Assistance Centers (TAC) and many local Title I evaluators. Interview-
ees who were aware of instances of both designs indicated virtually
unanimously that the designs appeared to yield different results on the

average. It was also generally agreed that the average results from the NR design tended to be higher than those from the RD design. Furthermore, persons who were most familiar with the results from many evaluations corroborated the notion that in general the NR design yielded positive gains while the RD design yielded gains which were near zero or even negative.

This discrepancy has been acknowledged in the Title I literature. Hardy (1978) and Echternacht (1978, 1980) cite results obtained in Florida where sufficient instances of both designs permitted the determination of a pattern of results. Others who have attempted to compare the two designs directly on the same program (Murray, 1978; House, 1979; Long et al., 1979) obtained results which are not inconsistent with the general pattern cited here, although these studies are based on too few instances to permit confident generalizations.

The most convincing evidence for the pattern of gains for the two designs comes from the State of Florida, largely because there are sufficient instances of the application of both designs to permit meaningful comparisons. All estimates of program effect in Florida for the NR design for the 1978-1979 school year (n = 614) and all estimates for the RD design for the 1977-1978 and the 1978-1979 school years (n = 273) have been obtained. The average gains were 6.595 NCE units (SE= .302) for the NR design, –.799 NCE units (SE= .398) for the RD estimate at the program group pretest mean and –2.371 NCE units (SE= .377) for the RD estimate at the cutoff. The distributions of gains for these three estimates are depicted in Figure 3. Clearly, the evidence indicates that on the average the NR design yields significantly positive estimates, while the RD design appears to yield a zero or perhaps slightly negative gain.

Other studies of compensatory education provide little guidance concerning which of these two designs yields estimates which are closer to the truth. On the basis of what is known about the effects of compensatory education in general, it is difficult to say what the "expected" gain might be. Many previous studies have been criticized on methodological, measurement, or analytic grounds (Wick, 1978; Campbell and Erlebacher, 1970; Campbell and Boruch, 1975). Even granting that biases in analysis have been against finding effects, programs of this nature have not been found to be conspicuously effective when more appropriate modes of analysis have been used (Magidson, 1977; Bentler and Woodward, 1978). In spite of this, significantly harmful effects have so far primarily been explainable as mistaken methodology. Thus, in order to determine the likely source of the discrepancy in results

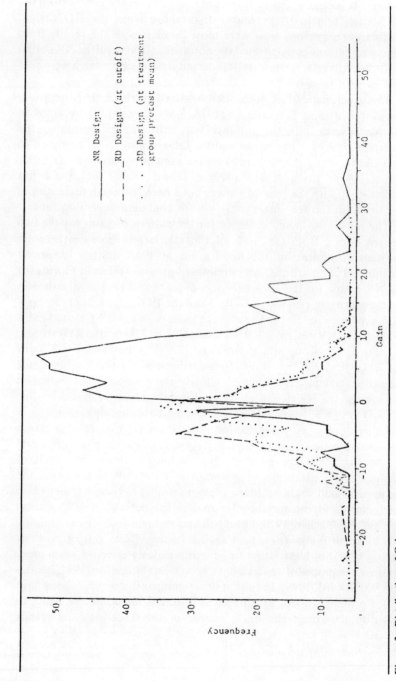

Figure 3: Distribution of Gains

reported here it is necessary to examine the designs in question within the context of Title I evaluation.

SOME LIKELY SOURCES OF
THE DISCREPANCY IN RESULTS

It is possible, although hardly plausible, that both designs could be yielding accurate estimates of effect even though they disagree. For example, it may be that since the NR design tends to require less cost and effort than the RD design, districts which use it have more time, money, or energy to devote to programmatic efforts. The discrepancy in gains might then be attributable to differential implementation of the programs rather than to the designs themselves. However, explanations of this type are not likely and it is reasonable to hypothesize that one or both of the designs yields biased estimates of effect.

It is useful to begin an investigation of bias by considering how the methodological community views the strengths and weaknesses of each of the designs. Judgements about the relative strengths of research designs are often made in the methodological literature and, in general, the RD design is usually depicted as "theoretically" stronger than the NR model (Tallmadge and Wood, 1978; Murray et al., 1979; Echternacht, 1979). Typical of such distinctions is a statement by Linn (1979) where "Model A" is the NR design and "Model C" is RD:

> If viewed as research designs, the three RMC models are ranked easily in terms of their relative internal validity. In its idealized form Model B is a classic experimental design and ranks highest in terms of internal validity. Model A ranks third, with Model C somewhere in between. This ranking agrees with the stated order of preference provided by developers of the models [p. 25].

The quality of the NR design has been questioned in several key areas (Hansen, 1978)—the appropriateness of using the norming sample for comparison, especially when many norm students also receive compensatory education; the viability of the equipercentile (or, more properly, equi-NCE) assumption which holds that in the null case the program group pre- and post-average NCEs should be equal; the use of out-of-level testing; and, the testing of students at different times during the academic year than the norm group was tested.

While the RD design is generally perceived as methodologically stronger than NR, it is also usually seen as more difficult to implement.

This is at least in part due to the requirement of strict adherence to the cutoff value in assignment, to the need to compile data for both program and comparison students, and to the relatively more complex statistical analysis which must be conducted.

The remainder of this article addresses three potential biasing factors for each of the designs. These are by no means the only such factors nor are they necessarily the most important ones. Each of these factors is considered likely to be present within Title I evaluation contexts although it is dificult to estimate the degree and, in some instances, the direction of bias which might be expected. Three problems relevant to the NR design will be discussed first, followed by consideration of three major problems with the RD design.

THREE POTENTIALLY BIASING FACTORS
IN THE NR DESIGN

RESIDUAL REGRESSION ARTIFACTS IN THE NR DESIGN

A distinguishing characteristic of the NR design is the requirement of a selection measure which is separate from the pretest. This was included in an attempt to avoid the commonly recognized phenomenon of regression to the mean. Before examining whether the separate selection measure in fact eliminates the regression phenomenon, it is useful to review briefly the traditional presentation of the regression artifact.

It is well known that when a group is selected from one end of a distribution of scores their mean on any other measure will appear to "regress" toward the overall mean of this other distribution. If the selection measure is a pretest and the other measure a posttest, students will appear on the average to change even in the absence of a program. The amount of regression to the mean which occurs between any two measures, x and y, can be specified. A group may be chosen from the lower end of the distribution of variable x as shown in Figure 4. When the standard deviations of the two distributions are equal (e.g., they are in standard score form) the correlation between the two measures is a direct reflection of the amount of regression to the mean. In fact, the symbol for the correlation, r, was originally used to signify regression in this sense. Specifically, $100(1-r_{xy})$ gives the percentage of regression to the mean for standardized variables. As illustrated in Figure 4, if there is a perfect correlation between x and y there is no regression to the mean

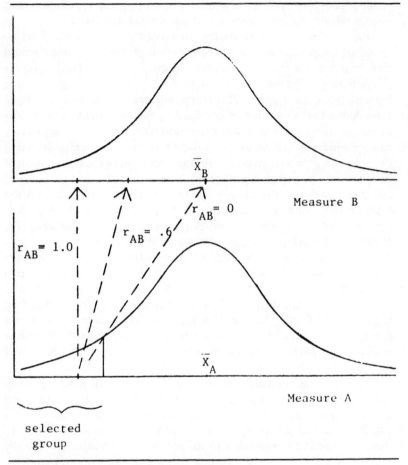

Figure 4: Regression Artifact with Two Variables

(i.e., $100(1-1) = 0\%$ regression). Conversely, if there is no correlation (i.e., $r_{ry} = 0$) there is maximum regression to the mean (i.e., $100(1-0)= 100\%$ regression). If $r_{xy} = .6$ the mean of the selected group on y will be 40% closer to the overall mean of y than their mean on x is to the overall x mean (i.e., $100(1-.6)= 40\%$ regression). If x is a pretest and y a posttest, except when they are perfectly correlated, the typical compensatory education program group will appear to have improved even in the absence of any program simply because of the regression artifact which results from the less than perfect pretest-posttest correlation and selection from the lower extreme of the pretest distribution.

The NR design was constructed to avoid the regression artifact by including a separate selection test. It was thought that assignment would then be independent of the potential regression artifact. The fact is that this separate selection measure is likely to remove only part of the regression to the mean.[2] The regression artifact argument can be extended to the NR design by considering an assignment variable, z, a pretest, x, and a posttest, y, all in standard score form and hence having equal standard deviation units. In this example, the assumption is that the program group is selected from the lower end of the distribution of variable z as is commonly done in Title I (i.e., if z is a measure of achievement those "most needy" would be chosen). If the correlation between the assignment measure and the pretest is $r_{zx} = .8$, (Figure 5) there would be regression to the mean from z to x of 20%. Further, if the correlation between the assignment measure and the posttest, y, is $r_{zy} = .5$, regression to the mean from z to y equalling 50% of the distance toward the overall mean of y would exist. By subtracting these two regression artifacts the amount of regression between the pretest and posttest, in this case 30%, is obtained. This is termed here the "residual regression artifact." The use of a separate selection measure in this example has reduced but not removed the regression artifact and one would again find that students improve from pretest to posttest even if no program is ever given.

The size of the residual regression artifact in the NR design depends entirely on two correlations, r_{zx} and r_{zy} where these are correlations between standardized variables. If $r_{zx} > r_{zy}$ some regression to the mean will be unaccounted for by the separate selection measure. If $r_{zx} = r_{zy}$ there is no residual regression to the mean. If $r_{zx} < r_{zy}$ there is actually regression away from the posttest mean and the program students appear to lose ground from pretest to posttest. In order to judge whether a separate selection measure removes the regression artifact one needs to determine which of the three patterns of correlations, if any, is typically obtained.

In general, it is reasonable to assume that correlations are higher the closer in time two measurements are taken. Thus, over time, repeated measures of the same variable tend to show progressively smaller correlations with the first measurement. The size of the correlations r_{zx} and r_{zy} therefore depends on two factors—the time between the measurement of x, y, and z and the rate at which the correlations erode over time. Figure 6 shows a hypothetical erosion pattern and two measurement scenarios. In the first case (left side of Figure 6) the pretest

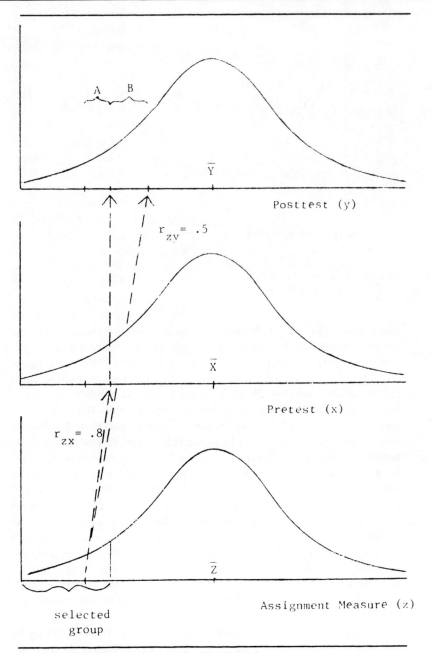

Figure 5: "Residual Regression Artifact" in Model A

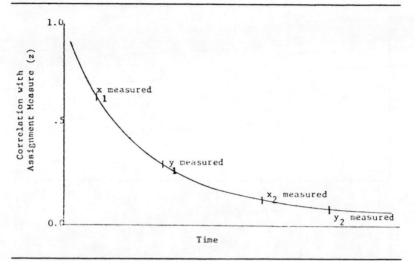

Figure 6: Hypothetical Correlation Erosion Pattern in Relation to Time of Pretest (x) and Posttest (y) Measurement

and posttest (x_1 and y_1) are measured while their correlations with the assignment variable are eroding at a rapid rate. In the second case (right side of the graph) both measures (x_2 and y_2) are taken after the greatest erosion has occurred. In both scenarios the same time elapses between the pretest and posttest. While a residual regression artifact occurs in both cases, it is much smaller in the second case than the first.

Theoretically, if one knows the correlations r_{zx} and r_{zy} in the absence of a program effect, it should be possible to adjust estimates of gain to account for the residual regression artifact. However, corrections of this type are hazardous for two reasons. First, they require knowledge of the temporal erosion pattern and this is likely to vary for different traits, and even perhaps for different tests of the same attribute (e.g., different levels or forms of achievement tests). Second, even if the overall rate of erosion is reasonably known, accurate estimates of the correlations in the absence of a program effect are necessary. This would necessitate use of some type of comparison group or, for the NR design, use of published correlations over time. In either case, the quality of such corrections would be doubtful and only serve to increase the assumptive character of the design.

The degree to which the discrepancy in results reported earlier may be due to the residual regression artifact is difficult to estimate for the same

TABLE 1
Average NCE Gain for Projects Grouped by Pretest Mean NCE

Pretest Mean NCE[a]	N	NCE Gain
0-5	7	18.30
5-10	10	10.67
10-15	13	15.29
15-20	37	9.46
20-25	116	8.23
25-30	161	6.40
30-35	126	5.57
35-40	80	5.05
40-45	40	4.00
45-50	18	3.58

a. Projects with Pretest mean NCEs which fell on interval boundaries were assigned to the lower value interval. For example, the first interval is actually 0-4.999 . . . but was rounded for clarity of presentation.

reason that it is hard to devise corrections for the residual regression bias. However, it is possible to get some empirical confirmation that a bias is occurring by examining the pattern of results obtained for the NR design in Florida. This can be done by classifying the studies into NCE intervals on the basis of group pretest means. If a residual regression artifact is operating, gains for groups who scored low on the pretest should be greater on the average than gains of the higher pretest scoring groups. Table 1 shows average gain for projects which are grouped into ten intervals of five NCE units each, covering a range of 0 to 50 NCEs. Six projects were excluded from the table (therefore, n = 608) because their average pretest score exceeded the mean of 50 NCE units. Clearly, the results do nothing to repudiate the hypothesis that a positive bias due to a residual regression artifact occurs with the NR design. Although a similar pattern would be expected if there were an interaction effect between the program and the pretest, this is considered a less plausible explanation than the residual regression artifact one.

ATTRITION BIAS IN THE NR DESIGN

Although the NR design requires that a selection measure be administered to all potential participants, only program students are given the pretest and posttest. The required analysis for estimating gain is based on the pretest and posttest averages for only those students who took both tests. Two attrition-related problems tend to arise when dropouts are nonrandom. First, if only matched cases are used (as required) one can at least expect the positive bias due to the residual regression artifact for the matched (i.e., nonattrited) students. This may be greater or less than the bias expected for the entire original sample depending on whether attrition is disproportionately greater for higher- or lower-scoring program students. In addition, attrition of this sort obviously calls into question the use of the norming sample as a comparison standard.

The second attrition-related problem occurs if the requirement that only matched cases be analyzed is violated. This will be termed the unmatched attrition case. Here, if a program student takes one test and not the other, the available test score is still included in the group averages. While this is a clear violation of the Title I requirements, there is some reason to believe that the difficulty of matching pretest and posttest scores (Trochim, 1980) leads school districts into this practice.

The major purpose of this discussion is to determine the likely effects of unmatched attrition on estimates of gain, and ultimately, the discrepancy in results. The effects of such attrition between the pretest and the posttest will be considered first. Subsequently, the combined effects of attrition between the selection measure and pretest and the pretest and posttest will be discussed.

The typical Title I program group is composed of students whose pretest scores will in most cases be below the population average of 50 NCE units. If unmatched attrition is proportionately greater among students who score below the prestest mean of the program group, a positive bias will result. This is due to two factors. First, the remaining group will consist of the higher-scoring program students. In the absence of any program an apparent gain will occur from the observed pretest mean (which includes attrition cases) to the observed postest mean. Second, in addition to this gain there will also tend to be a positive regression artifact bias from the remaining students' pretest mean to their posttest mean. Thus, the positive regression artifact will augment the positive bias due to the high-scoring remaining group.

The direction of bias is not easily specified when there is proportionately greater unmatched attrition from the high-pretest-scoring program students. The remaining group would have a lower pretest average, indicating a potential negative bias. However, a positive regression artifact bias is also expected for this group. Thus, when attrition occurs primarily among high pretest program students, a positive regression artifact bias competes with a likely negative bias resulting from the low scoring remaining group.

Consider a hypothetical example of how a positive bias can result when attrition occurs among the higher pretest scorers. It is assumed that the entire program group had a pretest mean of 20 NCEs and that after attrition of the higher scorers the remaining group would have a pretest mean of 15 NCEs. The observed pretest mean is therefore 20 NCEs but the expected posttest mean in the absence of the regression artifact would be 15 NCEs for an apparent negative bias of –5 NCEs. However, if in this example the standardized r_{xy} = .8 there would be a positive regression to the population posttest mean of 20% (i.e., $100(1-.8) = 20\%$ of the distance between the expected posttest mean of 15 NCEs and the population mean of 50 NCEs. Thus, there would be a positive regression artifact bias of 7 NCE units, that is, $.2(50-15) = 7$, and there would be an *overall positive bias* of 2 NCE units.

Several conclusions are reasonable at this point. First, if unmatched attrition occurs primarily in the lower pretest scorers there will be a positive bias. Second, slightly greater rates of attrition among higher pretest scorers are also likely to result in a positive bias (although this would be less than for attrition of lower scorers). Finally, the attrition bias will be negative in direction only when there is a disproportionately great enough attrition rate among higher scorers so that the resulting loss due to lower-scoring retainees exceeds their gain due to regression to the mean.

Because attrition rates for various pretest levels are not routinely reported in the Title I literature it is difficult to say what pattern of attrition is most common. With no knowledge of the distribution of attrition rates it is reasonable to conclude that attrition between the pretest and posttest will in general be more likely to result in a positive bias. One can, however, obtain a rough idea of the likely attrition pattern by examining the major sources of attrition. Kaskowitz and Friendly (1980) report several likely sources:

—students entering and leaving a school or district;

—students entering and leaving a project;

—students being held back or double promoted in grade progression;

—absence on test dates;

—invalid test administration;

—loss of data in processing and editing;

—deliberate omission of data.

For most of these factors it is plausible to argue that attrition would be more likely to occur at a greater rate among the lower-scoring students because these students would be more likely to miscode answer sheets, have greater absenteeism, be held back a grade, be discouraged and leave the program, and so on. If this assessment is correct, greater confidence can be placed in the likelihood of a positive bias due to unmatched attrition.

The more realistic case of attrition between both the selection and pretest and the pretest and posttest is more complex but leads to similar conclusions. Attrition bias may either inflate the pretest program group average or, less often, result in a lower pretest mean for the reasons discussed above. Because lower or higher pretest means will result in different amounts of residual regression artifact bias, attrition between the selection measure and pretest may affect the amount of bias resulting from attrition between the pretest and posttest. However, even in this three-variable case, the direction of bias will still be positive except when there is enough attrition among higher scorers to enable the negative bias of the low-scoring remaining group to exceed the residual regression artifact bias. On this basis it is reasonable to conclude that the discrepancy in results yielded by the NR and RD designs may in part be attributable to a positive unmatched attrition bias in the NR design.

TIME-OF-TESTING BIAS IN THE NR DESIGN

The NR design relies on a comparison between the program group and what has been termed here a pseudo-comparison group which is a hypothetical subsample of the norming group which is similar to the program students. It is important, therefore, to examine how test norms are developed in order to determine the reasonableness of such a comparison.

Typically, test publishers developed norms for a test on the basis of an annual test administration. Thus, samples of students might be tested in the fall of one year and the fall of the next or in the spring of one year and the spring of the next. In the typical NR design scenario, the selection test consists of an annual district-wide achievement test in the spring; the pretest is based on fall administration of the test to the program students and the posttest is comprised of the annual test given in the following spring (which then becomes the selection test for the subsequent year). If a test were normed on the basis of annual test samples, either the pretest or posttest in the NR design would have to be compared with interpolated norms. Thus, if the test had been normed based on fall-to-fall testing the spring norm would be an interpolation, while if the test had been normed spring-to-spring the fall norm would be an interpolation. As Linn (1979) explains:

> Normatively derived scores for other testing dates were usually obtained by linear interpolation with the three summer months treated as a single month. That is, it was assumed that growth was linear for the nine month school year and that one additional month's gain was made during the summer.

Thus, when the test was normed based on annual administrations, either the obtained pretest or posttest in the NR design is typically compared with an interpolated norm. Specifically, the question is whether the difference between an obtained and interpolated norm is the same as the difference which would be found if an actual testing were substituted for the latter.

Several attempts have been made to answer this question using data based on fall and spring norm testings. The results of these studies must be interpreted cautiously because they are often based, at least in part, on cross-sectional rather than longitudinal data. However, the general pattern of results indicates that larger gains occur between fall and spring testings (Beck, 1975; David and Pelavin, 1977; Linn, 1979), than between spring and fall testings. This is typically attributed to a lower rate of growth over the summer months.

A hypothetical graph of changes across testing times which is similar to those reported in the literature (Linn, 1979) is depicted in Figure 7. Such a pattern might be obtained if the same group of norm students were measured in the fall and spring for two successive years assuming that there are no clear floor or ceiling effects at any testing. It is important to recognize that the solid line depicts the growth pattern expected in norm scores even with the typical "summer growth" correction. The dashed lines between the two fall tests and two spring tests indicate hypothetical linear interpolations which might be used to obtain estimates of norm group performance for points in time between the norm testing administrations. In general, the figure shows that when the test has been normed with fall-to-fall tests the spring norm will be underestimated while with spring-to-spring norming the fall norm will be overestimated.

Assuming that this pattern is accurate, it is relatively easy to determine the bias which may result from using tests which are normed on the basis of such annual testings. If the test which is used in a

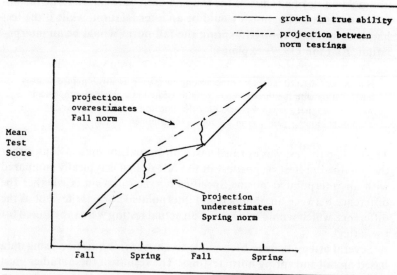

Figure 7: Time of Testing Bias

particular NR design was normed with fall-to-fall testings, the spring norm will be an underestimate of the true norm value. In the absence of a program effect, the program group will appear to improve from fall to spring simply because the norm posttest value is underestimated. Similarly, if the test which is used was normed using spring-to-spring testings, the fall norm will be an overestimate of the true norm value. Thus, in the absence of any program effect, the Title I program group would appear to be lower than the estimated pretest norm and therefore would show pretest-posttest improvement relative to the norm sample simply because the pretest norm is an overestimate. In this hypothetical scenario it is clear that whenever the test which is used was normed on the basis of annual testings the estimate of program effect is likely to be positively biased.

In practice, the situation is likely to be more complex. Tests may not be administered near the norm or interpolated norm testing dates and it may be necessary for a school district to attempt to construct local interpolations or extrapolations appropriate to local test administration times. In addition, in order to avoid floor and ceiling effects it is sometimes necessary to use different levels of a test for pretest and posttest. In this case, norms are dependent on the standardized scales developed by the test producers to "vertically equate" scores from different levels of a test. In any event, it is clear that the use of normative test data in the NR design relies on assumptions about change in the norming sample. In many cases these assumptions are unverified or, as in this case, actually suspect.

To some extent this time-of-testing problem can be reduced if tests are normed on the basis of fall-to-spring-to-fall longitudinal norm samples. There is some indication that test producers appreciate this fact and have modified or are considering modifying their norming procedures. Nevertheless, this is a relatively recent trend and it is a fair assumption that the majority of the 614 NR design projects which are aggregated in this article relied on tests which were normed on the basis of annual testings. Because of this, it is reasonable to conclude that the discrepancy in the results generated using the NR and RD designs can be attributed, at least in part, to a positive bias which results from time-of-testing problems in the NR design.

THREE POTENTIALLY BIASING FACTORS
IN THE RD DESIGN

The RD design is based on the assumption that the true pretest-posttest relationship is known or can be estimated from the data at hand. Typically, a regression model is fit to the data which describes this relationship. Estimates of program effect are based on this model and thus, factors which lead to biased effect estimates must impinge upon the regression-modeling process in some way. Because of this, it is important to examine briefly the major issues in the statistical analysis of the RD design before turning to an elaboration of several likely biasing factors and the way in which they affect the analysis.

A general polynomial regression model which is often appropriate for data from the RD design is given in Trochim (1980):[3]

$$y_i = \beta_0 + \beta_1 x_i^* + \beta_2 z_i^* + \beta_3 x_i^* z_i + \ldots$$

$$\beta_{n-1} x_i^{*s} + \beta_n x_i^{*s} z_i + e_i$$

where:

x_i^* = preprogram measure for individual i minus the value of the cut-off, x_0 (i.e., $x_i^* = x_i - x_0$)

y_i = postprogram measure for individual i

z_i = assignment variable

β_0 = parameter for control group at cutoff (i.e., intercept)

β_1 = linear slope parameter

β_2 = parameter for treatment effect estimate

β_n = parameter for the sth polynomial in x*, or for interaction terms if paired with z

e_i = normally and independently distributed random error

The major hypothesis of interest is

$$H_0: \quad \beta_2 = 0$$

tested against the alternative

$$H_1: \quad \beta_2 \neq 0$$

Several important assumptions of this general model must be recognized. First, it is only appropriate if the assignment strategy is correctly implemented, that is, there is no misassignment relative to the pretest cutoff score. Second, it is assumed that the true pretest-posttest relationship can be adequately described as a polynomial in x. If the true model is instead logarithmic, exponential, or some other function, this model is misspecified and estmates of program effect may be biased. Even in these cases it may sometimes be possible to transform the data so that a polynomial model is appropriate. For example, if the true pre-post relationship is logarithmic, one can use the logarithm of y instead of y in the model. Third, the model allows for changes (or interaction terms) in slope or function between the program and comparison groups. Thus, one can fit the same linear, quadratic, and cubic functions across both groups as well as separate ones within each group. Fourth, the program effect is estimated only at the pretest cutoff point. This is accomplished by subtracting the cutoff value, x_0, from each pretest score, thus setting the cutoff equal to the intercept (i.e., $x_0 = 0$). This differs from the typical Title I analysis where estimates are calculated at both the cutoff value and the program group pretest mean (Tallmadge and Horst, 1976; Tallmadge, 1976).

This restiction is included because of the inherent instability of extrapolations of regression lines. Estimates of effect at the cutoff point involve no extrapolation whereas estimates at the program group pretest mean require extrapolation of the comparison group model into the region of the program group scores. The general model could, however, be easily modified to estimate program effect at the program group pretest mean by subtracting this mean instead of the cutoff from each pretest test score.

It is important to recognize that the recommended Title I analysis is simply one possible subset of the more general model offered here. Specifically, the Title I model fits straight lines to each group and allows these lines to have different slopes. In the notation of the general model, the Title I analysis is

$$y_i = \beta_0 + \beta_1 x_i^* + \beta_2 z_i + \beta_3 x_i^* z_i + e_i$$

where x_i is the pretest score for individual i with the cutoff value subtracted when estimates are at the cutoff or the program group pretest mean subtracted when estimates are made at that point.

Ideally, one wishes to select that subset of variables from the general model described above which best describes the true pretest-posttest relationship. A number of standard procedures are available for such model specification (Hocking, 1976). The final model which is selected may be under-, over-, or exactly-specified. A model is exactly-specified when it includes only the variables which are in the true model. It is overspecified if it includes all variables in the true model as well as additional extraneous terms. It is underspecified if it does not include all variables in the true model (even if additional extraneous terms are included). Trochim (1980) has demonstrated that estimates of effect are biased if the model is underspecified. Both exact and overspecification result in unbiased estimates although precision is lost with overspecification.

This brief discussion of the statistical analysis of the RD design is included here to illustrate the restrictive assumptions of the Title I analytic strategy. All three of the problems discussed below tend to lead to nonlinear pretest-posttest distributions regardless of the true model which would have occurred if the problems had been absent. Thus, the Title I analysis, which assumes a linear true model, will tend to be underspecified and to yield biased estimates in the situations described below. In most cases it will be shown that the bias is negative in direction and that the problems could therefore be contributing to the discrepancy in gains between the NR and RD designs.

MISASSIGNMENT BIAS IN THE RD DESIGN

Most school districts which use the RD design employ some procedure which makes it possible to challenge the assignment of a student by the cutoff criterion. Usually a challenge is initiated by a teacher although the source may at times be a parent or school principal. A greater proportion of students tend to be challenged into the program group than out of it. In some cases the teacher's judgment is considered sufficient evidence to warrant a change of group status, but more often the student is retested and a cutoff score on the retest is used as the criterion. Challenges can be motivated by an honest belief in the fallibility of the test instrument, by political factors or favoritism, by a reluctance to deny potentially useful training to "borderline" students, and for a number of other reasons. Trochim (1980) points out that the practice of challenging assignment is widespread, that there is often no limit put on the number of times a student may be retested, and that challenges sometimes go unreported.

The central question here is whether misassignment relative to the cutoff score might be related to the pattern of gains described above. It is useful to construct a hypothetical example to help clarify what might occur. In this example it is assumed that all of the challenges in a district are those which shift students into the program. If the challenges are reasonable, these might be students who parents, teachers, or administrators feel scored artificially high on the pretest—their true ability should have placed them in the program group. Furthermore, one might expect that these lower-ability students would on the average perform more poorly on the posttest than others who received the same pretest scores. An extreme version of this hypothetical group is indicated by the darkened portion of the graph in Figure 8. It is important to recognize that the graph portrays the original bivariate distribution and would be the same whether the challenge is based on teacher judgments or retest scores.

There are a number of potential strategies for analyzing data when challenges have been allowed. One could, for example, act as though the challenges were never made. In fact, if the challenges go unreported the evaluator cannot be aware of them and will simply analyze the

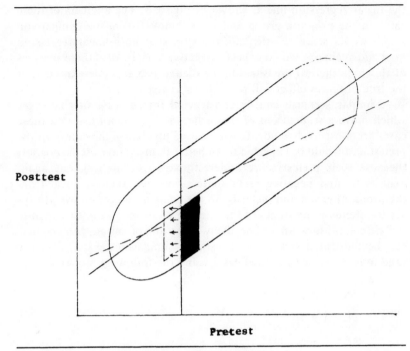

Figure 8: The Effect of Challenges on Within-Group Slopes

data using the assignment indicated by the pretest cutoff score. For the null case depicted in Figure 8 no bias would be expected. However, if the program is effective the challenged cases should evidence this effect. If the analysis assumes that these students are in the comparison group, that group's posttest scores would be increased near the cutoff point and the slope of the comparison group linear regression line would be attenuated somewhat resulting in an underestimate of the program effect. If the challenges are reported, one might be tempted to analyze the data on the basis of actual assignment (i.e., as challenged). Here, in both the null and effect cases the slope of the program group linear regression line would be attenuated somewhat (due to inclusion of the low posttest scoring challenge students) and a negative pseudo-effect would be expected. Another strategy would be to exclude the challenge cases in the analysis using their retest scores in place of the pretest. This would have the effect of increasing the number of the cases immediately below the cutoff value which also tend to fall below the linear regression line as shown in Figure 8. The addition of these cases in the program group and their removal from the comparison group would serve to attenuate the slopes of both linear regression lines and again one would expect a negative bias. In all of these analyses of this hypothetical "reasonable" challenge scenario one expects that the true program effect will be underestimated.

A similar scenario can be constructed for the case of challenges which move a student out of the program. If it is assumed that these cases are most likely students who scored just below the cutoff on the pretest and would be expected to do better than average on the posttest (because their pretest score underestimates true ability), one again expects to find negative pseudo-effects because their removal from the program group and inclusion in the comparison group will always act to attenuate the slopes of the linear regression lines in each group.

These intuitions about the likely direction of misassignment bias can be illustrated through some simple simulations. First, data are randomly generated for 1000 cases using the following models:[4]

$$x = T + e_x$$
$$TE = T + e_{TE}$$
$$RE = T + e_{RE}$$

where T is true ability, all e's are independent random error, x is the pretest, TE is the teacher rating of student ability, and RE is the score obtained for students who are retested. Thus it is assumed that the pretest, retest, and teacher rating are all imperfect but fairly reliable measures of true ability (e.g., achievement in reading or math). Second, assignment to program or comparison groups is constructed for three cases:

Sharp assignment:

$z0 = 1$ if $x \leqslant 0$
$\quad = 0$ otherwise

Teacher challenges:

$z1 = 1$ if $x \leqslant 0$ or $(x > 0$ and $TE \leqslant 0)$
$\quad = 0$ otherwise

Retest challenges:

$$z2 = 1 \text{ if } x \leqslant 0 \text{ or } (x > 0 \text{ and } (TE \leqslant 0 \text{ and } RE \leqslant 0))$$
$$= 0 \text{ otherwise}$$

The cutoff score of zero is arbitrary. The case of sharp assignment is included as a no-bias comparison. The program group consists of the lower pretest scorers and challenges are only in the direction of into the program. It is assumed that retests are given (i.e., can be a factor in assignment) only if a teacher recommends it (i.e., the teacher first judges that the student was misassigned). Thus, the retest challenge procedure is more restrictive in these simulations than the teacher challenge procedure. Third, posttest scores can be calculated under the general model:

$$y = T + gz + e_y$$

where y is the posttest, g is the program effect (either 0 or 3 units), and z is the dummy assignment variable (either z0, z1, or z2). Thus, the posttest is also a fallible measure of ability and is linearly related to the pretest through the common true score, T. Finally, the following analyses are applied to the simulated data:

(1) No challenges, analysis using actual assignment. This case is included as a no-bias comparison case.
(2) Teacher challenges, analysis using actual assignment. This analysis would only be feasible if teachers report the challenges and the actual challenged assignment variable (z1) is used.
(3) Teacher challenges, analysis using pretest assignment. Here it is assumed that the analyst is not aware of the challenges and that the original pretest assignment variable (z0) is used.
(4) Retest challenges, analysis using actual assignment. Again, this analysis is only feasible if the challenges are known to the analyst and the actual assignment variable (z2) is used.
(5) Retest challenges, analysis using pretest assignment. Again, it is assumed the analyst is unaware of the challenges and that the pretest assignment variable (z0) is used.
(6) Retest challenge, analysis using retest scores of challenged cases. Here the retest scores are substituted for the pretest scores of challenged cases.
(7) Teacher challenge, challenged cases excluded.
(8) Retest challenge, challenged cases excluded.

Each analysis is conducted using the following two-step procedure:

Step 1: $y = \beta_0 + \beta_1 x + \beta_2 z + e$

Step 2: $y = \beta_0 + \beta_1 x + \beta_2 z + \beta_3 xz + e$

The first step fits a straight line with the same slope in the program and comparison groups while the second step allows the slope to differ between groups. Thus, step 1 represents the true simulated pretest-posttest relationship (in the absence of challenges) while step 2 is equivalent to the recommended Title I analytic approach. A total of twenty simulation runs were conducted for each combination of analysis (i.e., analyses 1 to 8) and gain (i.e., 0 or 3).

The average estimates of program effect (β_2) and standard errors across twenty runs are given for both steps in Table 2. Of course, when there is no effect one expects that use of the pretest assignment variable (z0) in the analysis will yield a zero effect estimate whether there were challenges or not. This is corroborated in Table 2 by the fact that estimates of effect under analyses 1, 3, and 5 are the same in the null case. With this exception in mind, it is clear that all analyses involving challenges tend to result in biased estimates of effect and in every case the bias is negative (i.e., the program effect is underestimated). Confidence intervals can be constructed using the standard errors provided. In every case, the upper limit of the .95 confidence interval falls below zero (i.e., $\beta_2 + 2SE(\beta_2) < 0$). Not surprisingly, teacher challenges tend to result in a greater bias than retest challenges in part because in these simulations the latter is more restrictive and results in fewer numbers of challenged cases. Results appear to be least biased when retest scores are substituted for the pretest scores of challenged cases. In practice, the results for this analysis may be more biased due to problems of equating the scales of pretests with retests given at a different time. In general, knowledge of challenges and use of actual assignment in the analysis yields less bias than use of the original pretest assignment.

These simulations are only intended to be illustrative. Certainly it might be useful to add more runs, include curvilinear pre-post relationships, systematically manipulate the true score and error variances, include other possible analyses and challenge scenarios, and so on. Nevertheless, these simulations do illustrate that even under relatively "ideal" conditions (e.g., normally distributed variables, unidirectional challenges, linear pre-post relationships, fairly reliable measurement), misassignment in the compensatory education case tends to lead to

TABLE 2

Estimates of Gain (β_2) and Standard Errors for Simulations of Several Challenge Procedures

Analysis	True Gain (g) = 0				True Gain (g) = 0			
	Step 1		Step 2		Step 1		Step 2	
	β_2	σ_{β_2}	β_2	σ_{β_2}	β_2	σ_{β_2}	β_2	σ_{β_2}
1. No challenges	.003	.030	.002	.030	3.031	.031	3.031	.032
2. Teacher challenge, analysis using actual assignment	-.500	.027	-.495	.030	2.511	.035	2.519	.036
3. Teacher challenge, analysis using pretest assignment	.003	.030	.002	.030	2.154	.042	2.163	.041
4. Retest challenge, analysis using actual assignment	-.375	.030	-.368	.032	2.622	.040	2.630	.040
5. Retest challenge, analysis using pretest assignment	.003	.030	.002	.030	2.551	.037	2.556	.037
6. Retest challenge, analysis using retest scores	-.127	.031	-.139	.032	2.881	.037	2.871	.037
7. Teacher challenge, challenge cases excluded	-.258	.031	-.278	.032	2.762	.038	2.744	.038
8. Retest challenge, challenge cases excluded	-.172	.031	-.179	.032	2.837	.037	2.831	.037

underestimates of the program effect using the RD design. Because of this, the misassignment problem must be considered a plausible explanation for at least part of the discrepancy in the results yielded by the NR and RD designs.

MEASUREMENT-RELATED BIAS
IN THE RD DESIGN

Two separate measurement issues are discussed here, both of which are likely to have an effect on the pattern of gains obtained with the RD design. The first problem concerns the potential for floor and ceiling effects in the measures. These would result, respectively, from a test which is either too hard or too easy for the group in question. For example, if the test is too difficult, a number of students will receive the lowest possible scores. Their scores will not be indicative of their true ability because the test does not measure that low. Floor or ceiling effects on the pretest would tend to result in a more positive pre-post slope in the vicinity of the floor or ceiling. Conversely, such effects on the posttest would tend to attenuate the slope in the vicinity of the floor or ceiling. The situation becomes especially complicated when considering that it is possible to have a floor or ceiling effect or both on either the pretest or posttest or both.

The second measurement issue of relevance is related to the chance level of the test. The concept of chance level can best be understood through a simple example. A hypothetical multiple choice test has 100 items, each having four possible answers. If a respondent guesses on all 100 items one would expect by random chance alone that the average test score would be 25. Thus any student scoring in the vicinity of or lower than a score of 25 could have been guessing throughout the exam. If a student guesses on the pretest and either does or does not guess on the posttest there should be no statistical relationship, or correlation, between the two tests. Assuming that a portion of the students are guessing, cases with pretest scores near the chance level are likely to exhibit a lower pre-post correlation, and consequently a lower pre-post slope, than cases having higher pretest scores.

The direction of bias which would result from either of these two measurement problems depends in general on both the nature of the problem and the placement of the cutoff. For example, if there is a chance level or posttest floor effect, the pretest-posttest relationship might be best described by a line like the one shown in Figure 9. With a high pretest cutoff value the figure demonstrates that estimates of

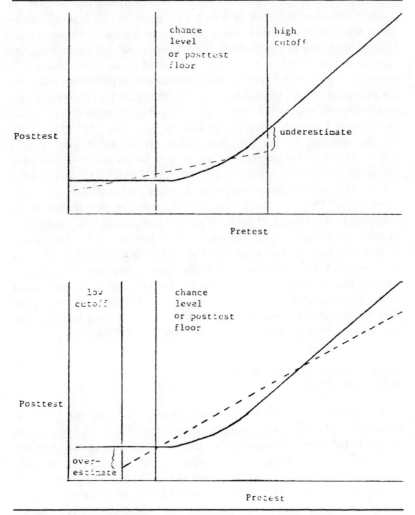

Figure 9: Effects of Cutoff Placement and Chance Levels or Floor Effects on Estimates of Effect

gain would be negatively biased. Conversely, with a low cutoff, estimates would tend to be positively biased.

It is possible to get some indication of the likely direction of bias in practice by examining gains in relation to typical cutoff percentiles.

The median cutoff percentile for the 273 RD designs from the State of Florida described earlier is 28.6 with a range of 7 to 50. It is difficult to know whether this median value tends to be above or below typical chance level values or posttest floor ranges without examining the specific chance levels for the tests that were used. Nevertheless it is possible to get a rough idea of the effect of cutoff placement alone on the estimates of gain by looking at the average gain for all projects with cutoffs above and below the median cutoff percentile. When cutoff values were below the median the average gain was .2563 (SE = .720) for the estimate at the program group pretest mean and −2.3127 (SE = .737) for the estimate at the cutoff. When cutoff values were above the median, the average gain was −1.6527 (SE = .412) and −2.4181 (SE = .334) for estimates at the program group pretest mean and cutoff, respectively. Thus, for both estimates the average gain tended to be lower the higher the cutoff value. While these results must be interpreted cautiously (at least in part because of poor reporting of or adherence to cutoffs), they do not repudiate the notion that higher cutoffs may be associated with negative bias while lower ones may be linked to positive bias. In any event, the potential for bias due to the placement of the cutoff relative to the chance level of the test or floor and ceiling effects must also be considered a plausible contributing factor to the discrepancy between the results of the NR and RD design.

DATA PREPARATION PROBLEMS
IN THE RD DESIGN

A large number of exclusions are routinely made in Title I evaluations in the process of preparing the data for statistical analysis. Cases are excluded from the analysis for lack of a pre-post match, because the student was "challenged" or misassigned, because the student moved either within the district or out of the district, and so on. Some exclusions are likely to have a consistent effect on estimates of gain and must be considered plausible sources of the discrepancy in gains.

This can be illustrated with the commonly made exclusion of grade repeaters, that is, those students who are held back a grade from one year to the next. It is certainly reasonable to expect that most of the students who repeat a grade are low achievement-test scorers who are eligible for Title I service. If there are a fair number of repeaters and if these cases are routinely excluded from the data analysis it is likely that the program group regression line, and subsequently the estimate

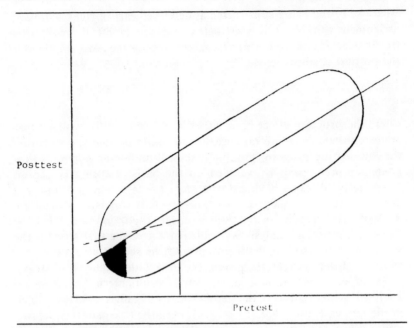

Figure 10:   Effect of Excluding Title I Repeaters

of gain, will be distorted. Furthermore, it is not unlikely that these students come from even the lower portion of the Title I program group distribution and that they have more than the average share of disciplinary problems, learning disabilities, and so on. It is possible to conceive of circumstances in which excluding such students actually makes the Title I program look worse. A polar case is illustrated in Figure 10. It is assumed that the "hard-core" repeaters are low in true ability and, therefore, score low on both the pretest and posttest. Hypothetically, the majority of these cases should fall in the region indicated by the blackened portion of the figure. If such students are excluded, the slope of the program group regression line would be attenuated and an apparent negative gain would result. A similar scenario can be constructed for the exclusion of students who move either within or across districts.

The effects of excluding grade repeaters can also be illustrated through simulations. Here, a pretest is constructed using the model

$$x = T + e_x$$

where x, T, and e_x are constructed as described earlier. Next, a dummy assignment variable, z, is constructed. Again, a cutoff of zero is arbitrarily selected and the low pretest scorers receive the program. Finally, the posttest is constructed

$$y = T + gz + e_y$$

where the program effect (g) is either 0 or 3 units. It is assumed that grade repeaters on the average are the lowest in true ability, even within the low-scoring program group. In these simulations a hypothetical grade repeater group is excluded on the basis of their true scores. Specifically, all cases having a true score (T) less than -4.5 units are excluded from the analysis. As in the previous simulations there are n = 1000 cases in each run and twenty runs for each condition. The same two-step regression analysis is conducted where the first step fits the same linear function in both groups and the second step allows the slopes to differ between the groups (i.e., the Title I analytic strategy).

In the no exclusion case, as expected, results are unbiased for all analyses. With exclusions, the step 1 estimate of gain is -.093 (SE = .026) in the null case and 2.968 (SE = .036) when the true gain is equal to 3 units. When low true scorers are excluded from the step 2 (Title I) analysis, the estimate of gain is -.163 (SE = .025) in the null case and 2.90 (SE = .039) when true gain is 3 units. Obviously these simulations can only be considered illustrative. Nevertheless they do support the ideas that even under fairly optimal conditions (e.g., fairly reliable measures, normally distributed variables, linear pre-post relationships, less than 8% exclusions) the exclusion of grade repeaters can lead to biased estimates of program effect and that the bias is likely to be an underestimate of the true effect.

Another data preparation problem which can lead to bias is the occurrence of data coding errors. For example, matching of individual pretest and posttest scores is usually made using the name or ID number for the student. Both are subject to miscoding. In addition, because matching is typically done by computer it is usually essential that the coding of the name be identical on both tests. Mismatching can occur if the "long" name is coded on one test and the "short" name on the other (CATHERINE versus CATHY), if the middle initial is on one and not the other, because the middle initial is placed in the first name field, because of extension of the first name into the middle field (VINCEN E versus VINCEN T), because of abbreviated first names

(ROBT versus ROBERT), if the name is changed between testings (CLAY versus ALI), and for a variety of other reasons.

Problems of data preparation tend to result in bias if the characteristic on which a data exclusion is based is nonrandomly distributed across pretest scores. For example, if there is reason to believe that program students move or repeat grades more frequently or are more likely to make coding errors, exclusion of these student's test scores is more likely to distort the true function and bias estimates of effect. For reasons similar to the grade repeater case it may be reasonable to expect that the bias would be negative in direction. Thus, data preparation problems must be considered potential contributing factors to the discrepancy in the results of the NR and RD designs.

DISCUSSION

The discrepancy in results discussed here has implications for far more than just the arena of compensatory education evaluation. To the credit of the Title I evaluation system, the problem is noticeable primarily because there are a sufficient number of replications of each design to enable a comparison to be made. Certainly those who are engaged in the recently emerging area of meta-evaluation need to be cognizant of the potential for methodologically based meta-analytic factors. Analyses of multiple replications of evaluative studies should incorporate tests of differences between methodologies and, where discrepancies are detected, attempt to determine their causal factors.

Much of the previous discussion has to be classified as speculative in nature largely because many of the potential causal factors for the discrepancy are related to problems in implementing the research such as measurement difficulties, attrition, ill-advised data exclusions, time of testing problems, and the like. Data on the frequency and extent of such difficulties is not routinely collected in evaluation research studies. The obvious implication is that, wherever possible, it ought to be.

At this point, definitive conclusions about the effects of Title I compensatory education on achievement are not forthcoming. The more optimistic portrayal yielded by the NR design suggests a modest positive effect in the vicinity of 7 NCE units. However, the discussion presented earlier suggests that this design is likely to yield positively biased estimates of effect. On the other hand, the RD design, usually considered the methodologically stronger of the two, portrays the programs as ineffective or even slightly harmful, although the implication of the previous discussion is that this design in practice tends to yield results which underestimate the true effect. The conclusions may, of course, be dependent on a fortuitous selection of potential biasing factors. There are undoubtedly other factors involved in the discrepancy but it is not clear whether they would be prominent enough to change the patterns of bias expected on the basis of the factors presented here. It appears that the best estimate of the effect of Title I compensatory training lies somewhere between those yielded by the NR and RD designs. However, it seems prudent to withhold final judgment on the matter until more definitive information on the quality of the designs can be acquired and analyzed.

NOTES

1. The third design (Model B) is either a pretest-posttest true experiment or a nonequivalent group design depending on whether assignment to group is random or not.

2. The argument presented here is based on the Glass memo reported in Echternacht (1978).

3. See Trochim (1980) for a more detailed discussion of the statistical analysis of the RD design.

4. Subscripts indicating individual cases are omitted from the models for the sake of clarity.

REFERENCES

BECK, M. D. (1975) "Development of empirical 'growth expectancies' for the Metropolitan Achievement Tests." Presented at the annual meeting of the National Council on Measurement in Education, Washington, D.C.

BENTLER, P. M. and J. A. WOODWARD (1978) "A Head Start reevaluation: positive effects are not yet demonstrable." Evaluation Q. 2: 493-510.

CAMPBELL, D. T. and R. F. BORUCH (1975) "Making the case for randomized assignment to treatments by considering the alternatives: six ways in which quasi-experimental evaluations in compensatory education tend to underestimate effects," in C. A. Bennett and A. A. Lumsdaine (eds.) Evaluation and Experiment. New York: Academic Press.

CAMPBELL, D. T. and A. ERLEBACHER (1970) "How regression artifacts in quasi-experimental evaluations can mistakenly make compensatory education look harmful," in J. Hellmuth (ed.) Compensatory Education: A National Debate. New York: Brunner/Mazel.

CAMPBELL, D. T. and J. C. STANLEY (1966) Experimental and Quasi-Experimental Designs for Research. Chicago: Rand McNally.

COOK, T. D. and CAMPBELL, D. T. (1979) Quasi-Experimentation: Design and Analysis Issues for Field Settings. Chicago: Rand McNally.

DAVID, J. L. and S. H. PELAVIN (1977) "Research on the effectiveness of compensatory education programs: reanalysis of data." SRI Project Report URU-4425. Menlo Park, CA: SRI International.

ECHTERNACHT, G. (1980) "Model C is feasible for Title I evaluation." Presented at the annual meeting of the American Educational Research Association, Boston.

——— (1979) "The comparability of different methodologies for ESEA Title I Evaluation." Presented at the annual meeting of the American Psychological Association, New York.

——— (1978) A Summary of the Special Meeting on Model C Held in Atlanta in January 1978. Princeton, NJ: Educational Testing Service. (unpublished)

HANSEN, J. B. (1978) Report of the Committee to Examine Issues Related to the Use of the Norm Referenced Model for Title I Evaluation. Portland, OR: Northwest Regional Educational Laboratory.

HARDY, R. (1978) "Comparison of Model A and Model C in Florida." Atlanta: Educational Testing Service. (Memo)

HOCKING, R. R. (1976) "The analysis and selection of variables in linear regression." Biometrics 32 (March): 1-49.

HOUSE, G. D. (1979) "A comparison of Title I achievement results obtained under USOE Models A1, C1 and a mixed model." Presented at the annual meeting of the American Educational Research Association, San Francisco.

KASKOWITZ, D. H. and L. D. FRIENDLY (1980) "The effect of attrition on the Title I evaluation and reporting system." Presented at the annual meeting of the American Educational Research Association, Boston.

LINN, R. L. (1979) "Measurement of change." Presented at the second annual Johns Hopkins University National Symposium on Educational Research, Washington, D.C.

LONG, J., HORWITZ, S., and A. PELLEGRINI (1979) "An empirical investigation of the ESEA Title I Evaluation system's no-treatment expectation for the special regression model." Presented at the annual meeting of the American Educational Research Association, San Francisco.

MAGIDSON, J. (1977) "Towards a causal model approach for adjusting for pre-existing differences in the non-equivalent control group situation: a general alternative to ANCOVA." Evaluation Q. 1: 399-420.

MURRAY, M. (1978) "Models A and C: theoretical and practical concerns." Presented at the Florida Educational Research Association Convention, Daytona Beach, Florida.

MURRAY, S., J. ARTER, and B. FADDIS (1979) "Title I technical issues as threats to internal validity of experimental and quasi-experimental designs." Presented at the annual meeting of the American Educational Research Association, San Francisco.

NCES [National Center for Education Statistics] (1979) "Quick Survey on Title I Evaluation Models." Washington, D.C.

TALLMADGE, G. K. (1980) "An empirical assessment of norm-referenced evaluation methodology." Mountain View, CA: RMC Research Corporation. (unpublished)

——— (1978) Selecting Students for Title I Projects. Mountain View, CA: RMC Research Corp.

——— (1976) "Cautions to evaluators," in M. J. Wargo and D. R. Green (eds.) Achievement Testing of Disadvantaged and Minority Students for Educational Program Evaluation. New York: McGraw-Hill.

——— and D. P. HORST (1976) "A procedural guide for validating achievement gains in educational projects." Monographs on Evaluation in Education, No. 2. Washington, DC: U.S. Department of Health, Education and Welfare.

TALLMADGE, G. K. and C. T. WOOD (1978) User's Guide: ESEA Title I Evaluation and Reporting System. Mountain View, CA: RMC Research Corporation.

TROCHIM, W. (1980) "The regression-discontinuity design in Title I evaluation: implementation, analysis and variations." Ph.D. dissertation, Northwestern University.

U.S. Office of Education (1979) ESEA Title I Annual Report. Washington, DC.

WICK, J. W. (1978) Title I Elementary and Secondary Education Act: Formation, Function and Purposes, 1965-1978. Chicago, IL: City of Chicago, Department of Education. (unpublished)

William M.K. Trochim is Assistant Professor of Human Service Studies at Cornell University. His research interests are primarily in the area of evaluation methodology, especially quasi-experimental design and analysis, and the study of research implementation.

Evaluation Studies Review Annual

VOLUME 1

edited by GENE V GLASS

"A broad ranging and methodologically eclectic anthology. . . . Sections dealing with crime and justice, welfare and social services, and mental and public health are superbly done. . . . This is a book that should be found in the reference section of all university libraries."

—Perspective

ABRIDGED CONTENTS: Part I. Theory and Methods of Evaluation / Part II. Studies in Education / Part III. Studies in Mental Health and Public Health Services / Part IV. Studies in Welfare and Social Services / Part V. Studies in Crime and Justice

Prominent Contributors to Volume 1 include: Robert F. Boruch, James A. Ciarlo, James S. Coleman, Robert H. Haveman, Ernest R. House, H. Laurence Ross, and Michael Scriven.

1976   672 pages   ISBN 0-8039-0704-4 hardcover

VOLUME 2

edited by MARCIA GUTTENTAG with Shalom Saar

Articles illuminate major areas of concern to evaluators: integration—rather than production —of data; validity of data integrations; and the relevance of evaluation to policy formulation.

ABRIDGED CONTENTS: Part I. Thinking About Evaluation / Part II. Evaluation Methodology and Data Integration / Part III. Evaluation into Policy / Part IV. Evaluation in Education / Part V. Studies in Crime and Justice / Part VI. Studies in Human Services: Health and Labor

Prominent Contributors to Volume 2 include: Richard A. Berk, Robert F. Boruch, Donald T. Campbell, Nathan Caplan, James A. Ciarlo, James S. Coleman, Lois-ellin Datta, Howard R. Davis, Howard E. Freeman, Marcia Guttentag, Malcolm W. Klein, Richard J. Light, Laurence E. Lynn, Jr., Stuart S. Nagel, Peter H. Rossi, and Richard D. Schwartz.

1977   736 pages   ISBN 0-8039-0724-9 hardcover

VOLUME 3

"This volume meets the need for a compendium of recent research. . . . The articles were carefully selected, and the introductions to each section are well-written, brief summaries of the articles. The selections themselves are a good reflection of the present state of evaluation research."   *—Contemporary Sociology*

ABRIDGED CONTENTS: Part I. The Policy and Political Context of Evaluation / Part II. Methodology / Part III. Health / Part IV. Income Maintenance / Part V. Criminal Justice / Part VI. Education / Part VII. Mental Health / Part VIII. Evaluations in the "Public Interest"

Prominent Contributors to Volume 3 include: Richard A. Berk, H.J. Eysenck, Gene V Glass, Ernest R. House, Henry M. Levin, Laurence E. Lynn, Jr., Nathan Maccoby, Michael Q. Patton, Frederick Mosteller, Peter H. Rossi, Aaron Wildavsky, and Walter Williams.

1978   784 pages   ISBN 0-8039-1075-4 hardcover

VOLUME 4

edited by LEE SECHREST and Associates

"[Emphasizes] the methodological and technical state of the art. . . . Readable and incisive articles . . . cover the full range of current concerns with evaluation methods. . . . Should be . . . [a book] that finds its way to the shelves of active evaluation researchers. Evaluation research has become a diverse enterprise, and the volume adequately and smartly deals with this diversity."

ABRIDGED CONTENTS: Part I. The Theory and Philosophy of Evaluation / Part II. Alternative Methodologies and Strategies / Part III. Technology of Evaluation / Part IV. Evaluation Studies / Part V. Unanticipated Findings / Part VI. Utilization

Prominent Contributors to Volume 4 include: Scarvia B. Anderson, Alfred Blumstein, Robert F. Boruch, Thomas D. Cook, Richard J. Light, Richard McCleary, Daniel Patrick Moynihan, Peter H. Rossi, and Paul M. Wortman.

1979   768 pages   ISBN 0-8039-1329-X hardcover